William Stringfellow in Anglo-American Perspective

Edited by

ANTHONY DANCER
Associate Vicar and Cathedral Missioner,
Christchurch Cathedral, Nelson, New Zealand

ASHGATE

Published by
Ashgate Publishing Limited
Gower House
Croft Road
Aldershot
Hampshire GU11 3HR
England

Ashgate Publishing Company
Suite 420
101 Cherry Street
Burlington, VT 05401-4405
USA

Ashgate website: http://www.ashgate.com

British Library Cataloguing in Publication Data
William Stringfellow in Anglo-American perspective
   1. Stringfellow, William
   I. Dancer, Anthony, 1967-
   230'.044'.092

Library of Congress Cataloging-in-Publication Data
William Stringfellow in Anglo-American perspective / [edited by] Anthony Dancer.
   p. cm.
 Includes bibliographical references and index.
 ISBN 0-7546-1643-6 (alk. paper)
 1. Stringfellow, William. I. Dancer, Anthony, 1967-

BX4827.S7954W55 2005
230'.044'092—dc22

2004025368

ISBN 0 7546 1643 6

Printed and bound in Great Britain by MPG Books Ltd, Bodmin, Cornwall

WILLIAM STRINGFELLOW IN ANGLO-AMERICAN PERSPECTIVE

William Stringfellow (1928–1985) was a unique figure in theology and law. One of the few American theologians of whom Karl Barth and Jacques Ellul spoke and related to with affirmation and affection, Stringfellow did theology 'underground', in the shadows, amongst the marginalised, with the disaffected. Consequently, whilst highly regarded by many acclaimed theologians of his day, he has remained on the margins of the theological academy.

As one of freedom's greatest allies, and death's fiercest adversaries, Stringfellow espoused a theology of Christian practice. This book examines Stringfellow's unusual theology, and the man behind it, and assesses the significance of his thought for contemporary theology, mission and the political character of practical theology and the Christian life. Part I gathers writings of Stringfellow to offer a unique opportunity to encounter his work first hand, bridging the chasm between academic reflection and grass-roots theological practice with which Stringfellow was concerned. Part II presents contributions from leading theologians, pastoral practitioners, educators and lawyers and offers a unique exploration of contemporary anglo-american theology.

Anthony Dancer is Associate Vicar and Cathedral Missioner at Christchurch Cathedral, Nelson, New Zealand.

For Billy and Annie

Contents

PART II   Reflections

List of Contributors

Simon Barrow is Executive Secretary of the ecumenical Churches' Commission on Mission (CCOM) of Churches Together in Britain and Ireland (CTBI). He is Policy Advisor for Ekklesia, a theological think-tank on the web. He was formerly Assistant General Secretary of CTBI, and has published widely in the area of mission and society.

Mark Chapman is Vice Principal of the Ripon College Cuddesdon, Oxford. He has written extensively on the history of theology in the 19th and 20th centuries, and is particularly interested in the area of social theology.

Anthony Dancer is currently working at Nelson Cathedral in New Zealand, developing initiatives in mission, reconciliation and theological education. His doctoral research examined the life and work of William Stringfellow.

Andrew Goddard teaches Christian Ethics at Wycliffe Hall, Oxford, and is Editor of *Anvil*. He is on the Board of Directors of the International Jacques Ellul Society. As well as his work on Ellul, he has written in the area of sexual and political ethics.

Ken Leech is an Anglican priest who has worked in the East End of London for over 40 years. He first encountered Stringfellow when visiting the churches in East Harlem in 1970.

Andrew McThenia Jr. is James P. Morefield Professor of Law, Emeritus, at Washington & Lee University. He has written extensively on law and theology, and especially the work of William Stringfellow. He and Bill Wylie-Kellermann are working on Stringfellow's biography.

Mark Thiessen Nation was for some years the director of the London Mennonite Centre, and is now Associate Professor of Theology at Eastern Mennonite University, Virginia. He is author of many articles and books on the work of John Howard Yoder, on whom he also did his doctoral research.

Christopher Rowland is Dean Ireland's Professor of Exegesis of Holy Scripture at the University of Oxford and is interested in apocalyptic, Liberation Theology, William Blake and the radical traditions in Christian history.

Rowan Williams is Archbishop of Canterbury and a much respected theologian. He is interested in spirituality and public engagement, and has taught and written a great deal in both areas, as well as two books of poetry.

Bill Wylie-Kellermann is a program director for the Seminary Consortium for Urban Pastoral Education (SCUPE) in Chicago. He is also on the steering committee of *Word and World: A People's School*, and has written extensively on the principalities and powers, and William Stringfellow. He and Andrew McThenia are working on Stringfellow's biography.

Foreword

Tim Dakin

There is nothing half-hearted about Stringfellow. Thus his theology is not backed up with footnotes, but by the story of a lifetime of engagement with the culture and church of his day. So where he lived (in East Harlem), the work he did as a lawyer (defending cases of the underprivileged), the local Christian community to which he belonged, and his wider church commitments all show us *his* kind of theology – a practical theology for mission.

Stringfellow is still important for a number of reasons. One reason is because he adopts a missionary approach to his own culture. He sees that his American culture is only nominally Christian. In fact Stringfellow thinks his culture needs challenging because it has been taken over by principalities and powers that are not of Christ. Today we know Western culture is in crisis and the Christian community has a responsibility to make this known and to offer an alternative. The crisis is deeper than the variety of ways Christ and culture can be related (as in H.R. Neibhur's classic book, *Christ and Culture*); it is about how Christians are called to generate a culture of values by maintaining a Biblical witness.

Stringfellow expressed this passionate concern by his use of images like 'exile' and 'alien'. Christians need to recognize that they are in exile and are aliens in their own culture. This disturbing viewpoint is not only even more true for us today (with the worldwide dominance by Western economies and cultures *and yet* the decline of the Western church), but it also points to a profound and fundamental understanding of Christian existence, one that has its roots in books like 1 Peter. In 1 Peter one of the images of the Christian community is that of resident aliens. Christians are called to live as resident aliens, recognizing that this identity is not just a temporary dislocation but is inextricably linked to following Christ.

Christ "the True Witness" (as Barth called him) took on 'the powers' of his day by being faithful to the values of the Kingdom of God. Thus Jesus' living witness was supremely expressed in his suffering and death; which became a liberating triumph for us all through Jesus' resurrection. In taking on the powers, Jesus showed how the Kingdom of God is beyond borders and ethnic boundaries. The Jesus who is "both native and stranger in every context" (a Rowan Williams' phrase) releases us from the territorial powers, but also enables us to celebrate the reconciliation of difference in diversity. This celebration of life in its diversity can be found in Stringfellow's positive images of the church as circus and carnival. The dark shadow over the worldwide Church today is what to do when diversity becomes irresolvable difference because of value-based disagreements. Stringfellow's personal life and his professional support for 'divergent' bishops prefigure some of our contemporary struggles. So through Stringfellow's passionate and prophetic life we are invited to grapple with difficult questions in which we need not hide either our vulnerability nor yet our own passions and commitments to gospel of the Lord Jesus Christ.

Stringfellow appeals to a wide range of readers. I first came across him when reading Karl Barth who mentions him in the Foreword of the American edition of his lectures on *Evangelical Theology* (T&T Clark, 1963/1975). Barth thought highly of Stringfellow and recommended that people should listen to him. My appetite was further whetted by Peter Eaton's appreciation of Stringfellow's theology and life in a collection of essays, dedicated to Stringfellow and appropriately entitled *The Trial of Faith* (Churchman, 1988), which are very different in range and character to Barth's theology. Yet I was spurred on to really engage with Stringfellow by a chance meeting with Andrew McThenia when I was on a short study trip to General Theological Seminary, New York. It was Andrew's personal reflections on Stringfellow that brought alive the man in the books. It is the man in the books that this volume is all about, i.e. "theology in the life of Bill".

I hope that others will, in their own way, 'discover' William Stringfellow. I became interested in him because he offered one way of doing practical mission theology. His theology was charged by the concerns of his day with which he engaged passionately and practically from that disturbing perspective of the apocalyptic writings of the Bible.

Through this book Anthony Dancer enables a new generation to discover Stringfellow. It is an opportunity to do what Barth recommended, to *listen* to Stringfellow, and to do so in the company of others whose reflections provide a *conversation* that brings out the best and also acknowledges the fragilities of Stringfellow's own kind of practical mission theology.

Tim Dakin
General Secretary CMS

Introduction

Anthony Dancer

I've said to Bill uneasily:
dreams in that house are like a hot pot
constantly stirred, fumes intense, voices
grandiloquent. What gives?
Bill paused between beats, like the sea.
Like the sea, he's no explainer, but pure depth.
He's not on earth to unravel dreams –
to precipitate them rather, like a slowly turned
vintage vat. Drink then, and dream on.

Daniel Berrigan

I never met William Stringfellow in person, but his life and work changed my own; one cannot read Stringfellow and remain unmoved. It would appear that in various ways, he has had a similar affect upon the contributors to this book.

William Stringfellow (1928-1985) was one of the twentieth century's more enigmatic and elusive theologians; a precipitator of dreams, for sure. To some, his writings can seem a little unusual or foreign, and to some it would be fair to say that his life and his writings can appear something of an enigma.[1] Little on him has been published, and his writings are fairly inaccessible, with little of his writing remaining in print.[2] It is true that his writings sometimes can appear a little obscure; at first glance, any struggle might appear to be easily attributable to the seemingly alien polemic, rather than any apparent theological complexity in his language. It is precisely this rich polemic that makes him so distinct, and so engaging, and to miss that would be a sad oversight indeed. The writings in this book help and encourage us to become familiar with the foreign.

Ironically, Stringfellow's writings represent one of the finest examples of Christian polemical discourse written *as* an alien and a foreigner in the twentieth century; he was a Christian living amidst 'the fall' and, in so many ways, amidst the marginalized. He echoed the biblical tradition of the prophets by calling the nation and the church to account and proclaiming the gospel of Jesus Christ. Although he died young the historical tradition in which he stood is continued by

---

[1]   Although in progress, to date no biography has been written on Stringfellow.

[2]   In the last few years, WIPF & Stock (www.wipfandstock.com) have republished a number of Stringfellow's books, with more hopefully in the pipeline. Bill Wylie-Kellermann's excellent anthology, sadly no longer in print, has become the primary way in which many have engaged Stringfellow's work in recent years (Wylie-Kellermann, 1994).

many faithful Christian communities and individuals: all those who speak and live as aliens in a strange land.

Stringfellow's life echoes his theology, and his theology echoes his life. The relationship between the two would seem symbiotic. For Stringfellow, life and theology were as one; his writing, thinking, and actions all reflect this, for deeply and practically imbedded in his life and work is a theology of Word and Spirit (a christological pneumatology). Stringfellow's theology was at once narrative, biographical, and biblical. Yet his methodological and practical conviction that biography is theology, and the life of faith in the world to which this conviction gave rise, resulted in the theological establishment largely ignoring him during his lifetime. Conversely, this book reflects the ever-growing interest in his life and work that has emerged in more recent years, and as such is a unique conversation with this elusive and seemingly obscure figure. So, as Stringfellow himself was so fond of doing, let us start with a story that further illuminates this man's life-work.

Karl Barth visited America just once in his life, and when he did so he made a point to meet William Stringfellow,[3] intrigued as he was by this bright and fairly noisy young American. At Chicago during an evening of questions and answers, amidst well known and highly regarded theologians of the academy, during his address Barth indicated Stringfellow and declared to the gathered assembly that America should "listen to *this* man". It is an oft quoted incident, and for obvious reason. It was not every day that Barth commended someone, and there were many gathered academics no doubt hoping for his commendation. Therefore, to single Stringfellow, a lawyer and lay theologian out at the expense of others in the panel (which included the likes of Hans Frei), was to make some sort of European declaration of discernment about Stringfellow. It is this declaration that lies behind the Anglo-American character of this book; for as Barth reminds us, Stringfellow is someone to whom we should listen, and with whom we should engage.

Yet when I look at their exchanges and listen to the recordings,[4] I am also aware of Barth's closing remarks, and wonder about their significance for interpreting his earlier exultation of Stringfellow. Recognizing the fundamental character of the nation he addresses, Barth concluded his address by saying: "If I were an American I would elaborate a theology of freedom". Clearly Barth was not an American, and he had foresworn not to speak directly about the American scene. However, Stringfellow *was* an American, and in his life and work he explicated a theology whose freedom was grounded not in the (democratic) nation, but in the Gospel. He was also speaking, often critically, from outside the academy, located in the margins. I believe this is what appealed to Barth. Stringfellow was one of freedom's greatest allies, and death's fiercest adversaries.

---

[3]   As well as a colloquium at Chicago Divinity School in which Stringfellow participated as a member of the panel of America's 'young theologians' – the new generation for theology – Barth and Stringfellow spent time together in New York, Stringfellow's home at the time.

[4]   It is important to do both, owing to Chicago Divinity School's editing of the transcripts and the resulting obliteration of both the tone and substance of significant portions of what was said.

Through his life and work he espoused a theology of Christian practice: a radical spirituality of the missional life of the church in the world.

Although an American, the prophetic voice of Stringfellow was significantly influenced by continental politics, culture and theology, most especially through a post-war period of study at the London School of Economics (1947-1949), time stationed in Germany as a supply clerk with the American army (1950-1953), and extensive work and travels with the World Student Christian Federation and SCM. Through these travels he encountered the Confessing Church, the ecumenical movement and the ruins and resilience that characterized some of the context and culture emerging in the wake of the Second World War. It made a lasting impression upon him, and provided him with a critical distance upon the context of his life-work in America.

The chapters of this book resonate with the Anglo-American influences and contexts of his own life-work, and offer both appreciation of, and critical perspective upon it. Many of them began life as part of a conference I organized in Oxford during 1997. Of course, as well as being geographically diverse, the contributors come from a variety of backgrounds: academic and non-academic, lay and ordained, from 'professions' of academy, church, law, activism, education, mission, and they reflect a range of ecclesiological and theological traditions and denominations. The evident diversity of the contributors is a reflection of the broad and eclectic focus of Stringfellow's life and work, which spanned the borders of nation, church, theology and academy. Within their diversity, they are united by a biblical concern for the margins.

There is, however, one glaring and obvious exception to this diversity: the authors are all male. This was in no way a conscious decision. Although female theologians were invited to contribute in order to provide a conversational balance and perspective, sadly none felt able to do so. I hope that in future conversations we may hear this missing voice.

This book is not a hagiography. It is a conversation reflecting the wide variety of interests, traditions and contexts out of which the various contributors operate. It will become clear that in various ways the contributors display quite diverging opinions about some aspects of Stringfellow's life-work, and those are often the most productive conversations one can have.

Stringfellow's life-work can be understood as an embodiment of a conversation: a conversation between the Word and the world, or to think of it another way, the conversation between the freedom of God and the freedom of humanity, which he inhabited. Inhabiting it was an awkward thing, for as Stanley Hauerwas and Jeff Powell have identified (Hauerwas and Powell, 1995), he didn't fit as a theologian or a lawyer (arguably, Stringfellow's two greatest preoccupations). That's a tough place to live your life – on the edge and in the margins. Yet in some ways he positively relished the angular and the awkward. Not simply out of some perverse human desire (although there was probably some of that going on at one level or another), but out of commitment to living an authentic and faithful life authored and shaped by the Word of God in the world, and a desire to encourage others to see and do likewise. It was the *angularity* or *asymmetry* of faithful living. This will, I suspect, become clear as one reads both

Stringfellow's own writing, and that of the contributors.[5] As with anyone, if we want to come to a greater appreciation of Stringfellow's life-work we need to get to know him a little, and to do that we need to spend time with him and his writings.

To this end, this book has two parts. The first is intended as a resource of primary material, and consists of a selection of Stringfellow's writings. They provide a first hand insight into both his thinking and the character of his writing, and I hope provide a fruitful resource for your own theological reflection. I have taken the opportunity to amend the gender exclusive language he used in some of his earlier work. In the second revision of *Instead of Death* Stringfellow made similar amendments to his own writing, and I have been mindful of these. I believe the result allows his work to speak afresh unencumbered by that particular principality.

The writings of part one also provide a context for the second part of this volume, which offers critical reflections upon, and engagements with, Stringfellow's life and work from Anglo-American perspectives. The conversation engages varied significant aspects of his life-work, and reflects about the relationship of his life-work to that of others. Generally, the conversation is concerned with helping us to better understand what it means to be a Christian and to be and do church on the one hand, and how one engages the Bible and the world on the other. Although each part can stand independently of the other, together they are designed to enable the reader to enter the conversation as much as is practicably possible, and perhaps continue it elsewhere.

I have resisted the customary practice of providing a synopsis of each chapter. Personally, I often find the rehearsal of the contributor's arguments in an introduction, and the unavoidable and often unintentional interpretation that is put on them as a result, to be more of a hindrance than a help. Stringfellow was always concerned about the use of labels and the way they tend to constrain rather than liberate. These days, that doesn't make him all that unique; it seems to be a common refrain, and one that advertisers and various multi-national companies thrive on in their advertising campaigns, fostering 'free' expression of pseudo-individuality. Yet when Stringfellow said it he wasn't concerned about preserving his own distinctiveness, his own ego, or maintaining his own peculiarity amidst a culture of similarity or sameness for his own egocentric purposes. He concern was for inhabiting the peculiarity and particularity of the Gospel. He maintained that theological and ethical preconceptions and pre-judgements were signs of people's inability to listen, and thus their inability to be faithful to the Gospel. It is a theological, hermeneutical and of course political truth that we could do well to hear today. Therefore, I hope you experience my omission as a liberating experience; after all, there is a point in time when we simply need to let the text speak. Stringfellow's ability to write and live in a way which reflected how the unity of the Gospel embraced the diversity of peoples and their contexts in radical

---

[5]   For those who are interested in discovering more about Stringfellow, I would urge you to read McThenia (1995), Wylie-Kellermann (1994), Slocum (1997) and my own examination of his life and work, Dancer (2001).

truth and love is a mark of its importance for contemporary theological discourse. I hope it is one echoed here. Each chapter will surely tell its own story, reflecting the author's varied interests, passions, concerns, background, context, and (if we are honest) prejudices and predilections.

It is perhaps worth noting too that Stringfellow also stressed that *in*consistency, rather than consistency, was a central feature of the Gospel, and what it meant to be a biblical person. Certainly he wasn't just playing with words here, nor covering up for various apparent inconsistencies in his own theology. Put otherwise, this emphasis upon *in*consistency echoes an overarching commitment to the logic of the gospel; the work of Word and Spirit at play in the world. Given that the academy and the church have so often emphasized the antithesis, this is doubtless something that we, alongside the contributors to this volume, will wrestle with.

Finally, it is with immense gratitude that I acknowledge Sarah Lloyd at Ashgate Publishing: she alone had the vision and enthusiasm to commit to publishing this book, and so allow us to have opportunity to engage in this conversation. She has displayed the greatest of patience. I am in her debt. Thank you also to Scott Kennedy of the Stringfellow Trust, Eschaton Foundation, in granting permission to reprint from Stringfellow's written works. Here is also the place I wish to record my thanks to Ian Beattie for his diligence in proof reading the manuscript. The mistakes that remain are mine. I also want to acknowledge my gratitude to the patience of the authors who contributed to this book. With the changes and chances of life, my work as editor has taken far longer than I had envisaged, and certainly longer than I would have liked. In life, as in fiction, the place you end seldom looks like what you imagined when you set out. It is certainly the case with this project; so I would like to thank all those with whom I have had the privilege to travel thus far, and most especially, Bill Stringfellow.

"Drink then, and dream on."

PART I

Writings

Chapter 1

On Reading Stringfellow

Anthony Dancer

Anyone who writes about the book of Revelation as a book of ethics, as Stringfellow did, is going to present the reader with one or two challenges. Writing in a tradition proximate to the biblical prophets, and embracing the language of apocalyptic, the apparent obscurity or angularity of some of Stringfellow's language might seem odd to our ears. That is as it was intended. This chapter offers some reflections on Stringfellow's life-work that introduce the 'shape' of his writing. These reflections represent some strands of my own thinking, which have converged around my consideration of Stringfellow over the years.

There is an abiding *intratextuality* to Stringfellow's own understanding of, and approach to scripture, whereby the world of the bible (scripture) absorbs the work-a-day world we inhabit. In essence, Stringfellow "asserts the hermeneutical priority of scripture over its interpreter" (Wood, 1987:17). This is seen most concisely in the preface to *Ethic for Christians and Other Aliens in a Strange Land* when he asserts his aim is to "treat the nation within the tradition of biblical politics – to understand America biblically – *not* the other way around, *not*...to construe the Bible Americanly" (Stringfellow, 1973:13). It would appear that he practised at the grassroots location of the self-reflective theological activist (what we might term a *practical theologian*) what was later pursued at a methodological level of the academic.[1]

Stringfellow's life-work[2] was both eclectic and diverse in its gaze. Yet such diversity was unified by his simple and faithful desire to proclaim the Word of God in the fullness of its missio-political contexts. The predominantly narrative and polemical style of his writing lends itself to this. However, although his writings have a feeling of immediacy about them, a "theology in a hurry" as Kenneth Leech has remarked, they are not isolated or separate from each other, but rather are unified aspects of a commitment to a bigger picture. Stringfellow's commitment throughout his adult life was to politics on the one hand and the Christian faith on

---

[1]   George Lindbeck and Hans Frei are perhaps the two theologians most widely associated with the hermeneutics of intratextuality, see Lindbeck (1984) and Frei (1974, 1975, 1992, 1993). Frei and Stringfellow were loosely associated via a few projects in the 1950s and later, relating to discussions regarding the church and the university, and the Barth panel of young theologians in 1962.

[2]   This phrase is used to convey the indissoluble interdependence between both Stringfellow's life and work.

the other; politics and faith were the 'twin pillars' of his life and work. Consequently his personal and social context (the private and political life) occupied a prominent place in his theological landscape. It would be fair to say the diversity of Stringfellow's life-work was born of context, and its unity born by virtue of God's presence in the world as Word and Spirit (Spirit-Christology).

Yet there is a need to come to Stringfellow's life-work with an air of naïveté; the narrative needs to be engaged on its own terms. This is not by any means an uncritical all-accepting engagement, for the terms of the narrative are themselves critical; however it does require that we first and foremost let the text speak to us and absorb us into its world (which is itself the conjunction of Stringfellow's socio-political world and the biblical world). It is only then that the full, persuasive and transformative power of his writing will be most fully experienced. The rest of this chapter explicates a rationale for this need for naïveté, offering reflections and a framework within which to engage Stringfellow more on his own terms, and less on ours; a listening which is surely the duty of any task which desires to call itself theology.

Perspectives

Ingolf Dalferth puts forward a very distinctive view of theology and the Christian life. When read alongside Stringfellow it offers a framework for understanding Stringfellow's life-work that is both helpful and illuminating; and so it is to Dalferth and Stringfellow we now turn our attention. We begin with the issue of perspectives.

In Stringfellow's theology there is a union of life and work, acting and writing; theology was no mere abstraction for him, but was wrapped up intrinsically in the diverse business of life. His eclectic and diverse gaze, and his fundamental commitment to Word and world, makes the issue of perspectives a prominent and practical one for us as we consider his life-work. If we are to proceed meaningfully we need to take seriously the fact that all attempts to resolve the issue of perspectives are themselves perspectival, not universal. Ultimately, as Dalferth explains, there can be

> no single solution to the problem of perspectives. Perspectives are views of the world from different places, partial perspectives views of some things, and universal perspectives views of everything, including themselves, from a given place. (Dalferth, 1988:127)

Bertrand Russell identifies a perspective as "the view of the world from a given place" (Russell, 1921:101).[3] In the light of Russell and Dalferth, Stringfellow's commitment to unravelling the Christian life of witness would appear to tell the story of a life spent devoted to the explication and elucidation of faith and the

---

[3]   It is worth noting that 'place' is here not limited to the geographic, but encompasses social, economic, political, epistemological locations, for example.

negotiation of perspectives (mutually informative perspectives of faith and culture, for example). His was a life given over to the politics of mission and ministry; to the process of conversion and faithful living from a 'given place'. It was a life, in short, given over to the work of God, a life seeking to be interpreted and made sense of.

Stringfellow's commitments to both the authority of the Bible and to his context were absolutely central in this process of sense-making. Here we perceive something of the tension that sits behind the perception of him 'not fitting'; namely, a foundational and radical commitment to the Bible on the one hand (faith), without being a 'conservative' or a 'fundamentalist', accompanied by an equally foundational commitment to context on the other (culture), without being a 'liberal' or 'unbiblical'. Word and the world are symbiotic in their foundational role of informing and forming his life-work.

All this makes Stringfellow vulnerable to a number of potential criticisms. For instance, he is vulnerable of being found to be 'unbiblical', 'inconsistent', or failing to engage culture in the terms culture can easily understand (especially a culture whose systems and structures are influenced by enlightenment and post-enlightenment thinking). However, for him it was a self-declared vulnerability to the Word and the world; a vulnerability to God's being and action in the world, and to the fact and practice of our own humanity which directly confronts the relationship between faith and culture – two of the most obvious perspectives with which Stringfellow had to deal. Rather than conflate one with another, or fix the identity of the referent from either one perspective or the other (faith or culture), Stringfellow devotes his energies to articulating harmony between perspectives which takes seriously the activity of God in culture, as both Word and Spirit. I find this enormously hopeful.

These perspectives of faith and culture have been theology's constant companions, and their resolution or harmony a seemingly constant aim. How these perspectives are harmonized, in order that we can take seriously both our faith and our context while avoiding an epistemological watering down or self-defeating compromise, has been a central theological concern for many over the years. Some have sought a resolution through a 'neutral' common topic, others prefer to seek it through affirming difference and continued conversation, while still others assert the primacy of their own perspective for considering the world at the expense of all other perspectives. However, owing to the perspectival nature of knowledge, all attempted solutions meet with a variety of problems. It is for that reason that Dalferth has suggested we seek not so much resolution, but *harmony*. I find this a very helpful insight as we consider Stringfellow's life-work.

Dalferth identifies the process of finding harmony between perspectives as not a matter of finding fixed referents. This means that the truth and meaning of a given perspective is bound up in its relationship with other perspectives and has a necessary relational dynamic. For example, the meaning of resurrection is not determined over against the culture in which it is proclaimed and celebrated, nor, necessarily, is its truth simply culturally determined by its contemporary context. Dalferth suggests that signs and their signification and communication are central to any resolution of perspectives, and enable translatability between perspectives using a "common semiotic repertoire" (Dalferth, 1988:148). Translatability between perspectives is a permanent cultural process of "assimilation by interpretation" (Lindbeck, 1984:138), and requires mutual understanding.

> Securing it is not a matter of discovering the true nature of reality. It is a matter of creatively designing semiotic means to be used and interpreted in either perspective. In short, semiotic creativity, not the discovery of truth, is the key to translatability; and translatability, not identity, is what we need to harmonize our perspectives. (Dalferth, 1988:148)

Stringfellow would not have chosen to articulate his activities in the same language Dalferth uses. Nevertheless, he would appear to reflect the pursuit of harmony between perspectives through using semiotic creativity along the lines that Dalferth describes.

So, according to Dalferth, translatability, rather than ever-stronger assertion of any single perspective, is the key to harmonizing perspectives, and semiotic creativity is the key to translatability. We can put this in another, more overtly, missiological way by saying that the creative discernment and deployment of (Christian) signs and symbols in the public realm is the key to translatability between the Christian perspective and other perspectives upon reality. Deploying and interpreting signs is given central importance by Stringfellow, who affirms the gift of discernment, of signs and spirits, as a "basic genius of the biblical life style" (Stringfellow, 1973:138) of living humanly, in resistance to the power of death, amidst the fall. Discernment then, is the apocalyptic practice of reading signs (and symbols) through which one stands in hopeful resistance to the power of death.[4] It embodies the practice of semiotic creativity in the ordinary world as the Christian sees and hears God's life-giving activity for creation in that world, and "exposes and rebukes idolatry" (Stringfellow, 1973:139). Essentially, it is the basic form of Christian witness in the world.

It is significant, therefore, that even a cursory look at Stringfellow's life-work will reveal abundant use of precisely such signs and symbols – some of the more distinctive are 'Babylon' and 'Jerusalem', the 'power of death', and the principalities and powers.[5] Their meaning is culturally shaped through a radical

---

[4]   Apocalyptic in this sense is synonymous with revelation, and refers to the breaking in of the unknown into the known, of reality being made known (Rowland, 1988:70-75).

[5]   In fact, it was through the people of East Harlem, and his exposure to the Word and his context that he gradually learnt what those indigenous to Harlem knew already: "namely, that the power and purpose of death are incarnated in institutions and structures, procedures and regimes – Consolidated Edison or the Department of Welfare, the Mafia or the police, the Housing Authority or the social work bureaucracy, the hospital system or the banks, liberal philanthropy or corporate real estate speculation. In the wisdom of the people of the East Harlem neighbourhood, such principalities are identified as demonic powers because of the relentless and ruthless dehumanization which they cause" (Stringfellow, 1976a:5).

translatability between Christian and other perspectives, yet at the same time there is a sense in which they absorb the world, and so make sense of the world.

This takes place because the meaning of the symbol cannot be contained wholly within the meaning of the world's language – it has a 'surplus' of meaning, and with it a transcendent or eschatological quality. However, there is an equally apparent sense in which the biblical signs and symbols only make sense, or acquire meaning, through the socio-political perspectives of context (other perspectives). Reference, meaning, and translatability in other words don't happen in a vacuum.

Dalferth suggests that semiotic creativity is the key to translatability between internal (e.g. faith) and external (e.g. culture) perspectives upon faith. Stringfellow's own semiotic creativity was in no short supply, and its source was predominantly biblical, for his self-confessed purpose was to address the biblical illiteracy in the United States amongst conservatives and liberals alike. This semiotic creativity functions as the key to *Christian witness*[6] – Christian life in the world as a sign of the presence and action of the Risen Lord. Such signs and symbols do not exist in and of themselves, but are interpretative in their nature, seeking to make and be made sense of; they form part of what makes sense of us and our world.

Dalferth's process of semiotic creativity offers us an important way of viewing Stringfellow's life-work, and the process of revelation itself. It sheds light on the process of God's speaking to us, and the translatability of those perspectives between God and us, through both ongoing revelation and incarnation.

Perhaps the many diverse descriptions of Stringfellow's life-work as lawyer, theologian, advocate, friend, connoisseur of the circus, etc. might also best be understood in semiotic terms. If so then their misconstrual as simple truth (universalizing depictions orientated towards identity) rather than signs or symbols (signifiers orientated towards translatability *between* the descriptions), perhaps indicates failure to perceive Stringfellow's life-work as *faithful witness to the truth*, and consequently misses the dynamic and dynamic semiotic reality of his life-work in particular, and the Christian life in general, along with its semiotic 'force' or persuasiveness.[7]

---

[6]   Such semiotic creativity might conceivably include Christian action in the world as a sign of the reality and presence of the Risen Lord, and restored creation.

[7]   This semiotic force is most clearly apparent in the way Stringfellow radicalizes signs apparent in culture by witnessing through his theology to the way they are ultimately transfigured through the resurrection of Jesus Christ. In that sense, Stringfellow tells the 'truth' about the symbols (what he refers to in some instances as the principalities and powers) present in culture, such as the government, Marilyn Monroe, General Electric, etc. He also subjectifies the object of the signs (the signified): the problem with attempts to overcome the 'other' is that they objectify the other along with the subject of faith (Jesus Christ as transcendent). In Stringfellow, the object (transcendent) is engaged as subject (immanent) through a form of incarnational theology of Word and Spirit. Perichoresis (mutual coinherence) is central to this life, and the way in which semiotic force operates in Stringfellow.

It is also significant that the semiotic creativity of which Dalferth speaks is a characteristic feature of the ongoing process of conversion, or the lifelong process of 'putting on our new self' in movement towards the fullness of Christ. This process is an experience in which, as Christians, we are all engaged, and it takes on the narrative form we know as biography.

Biography as Theology

Biography is the unfolding story of our encounter with the world and the risen Lord's subsequent encounter with us over the course of our life. Put another way it is the story of inhabiting restored creation, the unfolding perichoretic (Loder and Neidhardt, 1992:287-306) self-discovery of our restored selves, and the inhabitation of that self. It is the story of conversion, of *reality being made known*, and of our self-consciously inhabiting our identity. It is therefore apocalyptic and eschatological in character,[8] and is wrapped up in the process of semiotic creativity, for biography is the story of our reading, discernment, and interpretation of the signs (and our response to them). As Stringfellow writes:

> Discerning signs has to do with comprehending the remarkable in common happenings, with perceiving the saga of salvation within the era of the Fall. It has to do with the ability to interpret ordinary events in both apocalyptic and eschatological connotations, to see portents of death where others find progress or success but, simultaneously, to behold tokens of the reality of the Resurrection or hope where others are consigned to confusion or despair. Discerning signs does not seek spectacular proofs or await the miraculous, but, rather, it means sensitivity to the Word of God indwelling in all Creation and transfiguring common history, while remaining radically realistic about death's vitality in all that happens...In the face of death, live humanly. In the middle of chaos, celebrate the Word. Amidst babel...speak the truth. (Stringfellow, 1973:138-39, 142)

Both the content and form of Stringfellow's words express the creative characteristics already described. This apocalyptic and eschatological character of biography and our identity is the process of God's self revelation to us (of God's self and our self) and the working out of our salvation. Stringfellow refers to this as 'vocation', and Dalferth as 'orientation'. This process is trinitarian, for as Dalferth identifies:

> Theological explication of faith is bound to become an explication of the eschatological reality of Christ...for theology to be possible Christ must have risen...By insisting on the intrinsic reference of all Christian talk of God to the eschatological reality of God's self-communicating presence in Jesus Christ and through the Spirit, the doctrine of the Trinity has not a descriptive but a regulative function. It permanently reminds us that

---

[8]   For an excellent discussion of the nature of apocalyptic, especially with regard to apocalyptic equating to reality being unmasked or made known, see Rowland (Rowland, 1988:70-75).

there is a fundamental difference between God and our conceptions of God; that God has disclosed himself in Jesus Christ as love so that there, and there alone, comprehensibility prevails over incomprehensibility; that without God's self-presentation and self-communication in Christ and through the Spirit we cannot re-orient our lives in the light of his love. (Dalferth, 1988:170)

The semiotic creativity which so pervades Stringfellow's life-work functions to consistently remind us of God's self-presentation in pursuit of harmony between perspectives, or what we might otherwise call *peace*.[9] It achieves this by also dealing with the 'problem' eschatologically. As such it is a theology, despite its critical tones, which is fundamentally grounded in grace and hope: the grace of God's dealings with us, and the hope which sustains us in our faith.

The role the Bible takes in his life-work bears witness to this, for in a sense it functions as a kind of perfect, full or complete biography. His interpretation of this perfect biography is governed by an ethic of *repetition* by the believer, whereby we take on board the "eschatological assumption of our mundane reality into the reality of the risen Christ" (Dalferth, 1988:126).

Stringfellow was explicit about his commitment not only to biography, but also to understanding biography as theology. Biography unifies his life and work, and his commitment to biography directly affects the way in which he uses scripture.[10] For him,

> *any* biography and *every* biography, is inherently theological in the sense that it contains already – literally by virtue of the Incarnation – the news of the gospel whether or not anyone discerns that. *We* are each one of us parables. . . What I am discussing is how the living Word of God is implicated in the actual life of this world. (Stringfellow, 1982b:20)

Understanding theology as biography renders experience as a significant (if not *the* significant) resource for theology. Stringfellow identifies this experience as the Word encountering us in the world, rather than purely our experience of the world or of God in isolation from each another; the experiential initiative rests with the Trinity, and this, he says, is essentially the doctrine of revelation. For Stringfellow "every biography is significant for the knowledge it yields of the Word of God incarnate in common life, whether or not the subject of the biography is aware of that significance of his or her own story" (Stringfellow, 1982b:21). The event and process of being aware of *this* significance of one's biography is what Stringfellow

---

[9]   Perhaps the harmony between perspectives which we have been discussing is another way of talking about peace. Understanding it as peace helps us not only reflect upon the nature of peace itself, but also would provide an interesting point of departure for discussions given the popular grassroots peace movement which emerged out of the context of the 1960s and 1970s – the period in which so much of Stringfellow's life-work was itself developed.

[10]   Narrative and biography are subjects of significant theological discussion. See, for example: Crites (1971), Frei (1993), Stroup (1981), Sykes (1985), Green (1987), McClendon (1974).

understands as *vocation*. Vocation is the conscious embodiment of one's biography in both history and hope.

Not surprisingly therefore, much of Stringfellow's writing is itself biographical, either explicitly (see his three autobiographical volumes)[11] or implicitly (in his social engagement with his political and social context); and his language is replete with semiotic creativity. This creativity allows one to traverse the diverse perspectives and particulars of life and its contexts, through the assimilation and inhabitation of life-giving symbols; a process synonymous with *discipleship*. The key to this unfolding self-understanding (vocation) of one's restored identity (resurrection), and the subsequent witness to the reality from which it came, is translatability. It is translatability between perspectives which enables understanding. But of what kind of knowledge is such understanding constituted? Here we remain with the significance of *vocation* in Stringfellow's theology, for his theology could fairly be described as a vocational (or practical) theology.

Vocation as theology is a theology of revelation. By its very nature it is orientational theology. As revelation, it orientates us in relation to interpreting and living the Christian life in the world, and it orientates us in relation to the Word's encounter with us and our encounter of the Word, through which process we hear and inhabit our identity. Theology so conceived is a practical discipline, and again, Dalferth illuminates this:

> Theology is not a theoretical discipline concerned with explanation, but a practical discipline of orientation. Orientation, however, is a complex process, more complex than describing or explaining something. It involves reliably ordering for ourselves the world in which we live, and positioning ourselves within this order, and so marking the perspective and horizon, within which and from which we may perceive our world and ourselves, in which we are to live and act, if we want to live in a way that is beneficial and does not harm or damage life or its possibilities...[Theology does] not add a further aspect to the picture of the reality and possibility of the world painted by the sciences and philosophy, rather it alters the entire frame of the discussion. (Dalferth, 1999:125-26)

It is worthwhile considering what Dalferth is saying in relation to the wider theological enterprise, for according to him theological knowledge is quite distinct from other forms of knowledge and should not be confused with them. Theological knowledge is essentially anthropological in character; it is knowledge of who we are or could be in Christ, and tells us what it means to live as humans together. It is knowledge *from* a given perspective, *for* living the Christian life in the world. There are many who would prefer to see theology as description. However, theology as description does not adequately account for the action that theological knowledge implies; it is all together too passive. Theological knowledge is knowledge which cannot be purely descriptive, for "it involves normative decisions about how we want to and ought to live as humans. This in turn relies on an understanding of our humanness, which, according to the insight of theology, is

---

[11]   See Stringfellow (1964c, 1970c, 1982b).

under-determined when we fail to orient ourselves and our relationship to others in relation to the Creator of all" (Dalferth, 1999:126).

There are two points of note here. First, faith is not knowledge about God, but the action of God revealing himself to us in our encounter with God. Practical theology is the knowledge of faith, and the knowledge of faith is God revealing God's self to us: it is trinitarian in form, functioning in a demonstrative way, as opposed to descriptive or reflective. Secondly, the role of science (which concentrates on description, analysis, and explanation of reality) and philosophy (nurture, cultivate and improve competence in perceiving the possible in the actual, i.e. questions of possibility) are quite distinct from the role of theology, which uses the language of "eschatological indicative" (Dalferth, 1999:127). Dalferth continues:

> [Theology] does not therefore deal with an additional aspect of reality and possibility, but sets all reality and possibility together in a different perspective and horizon in which they are determined in relation to God. (Dalferth, 1999:127)

The discussion thus far has focused quite extensively on Dalferth, because from a methodological perspective his words echo and embellish Stringfellow's: "Theology isn't just theory, it's confession" (Stringfellow, c.1959-1960:2). For Stringfellow, theology is confession of a perspective through which all reality is 'absorbed' and determined in relation to God, and the living of this theological-life is the Christian life or *vocation*.

Stringfellow's was a life lived in faith, in diverse and ad-hoc ways. Embracing his life and work was a Spirit-Christology that provided ad-hoc harmony between the perspectives. This Spirit-Christology was at the centre of a life committed to exploring what he called *vocation* (what we might more commonly describe as the process of conversion or journey towards authenticity), in its personal and public dimensions. Yet the ad-hoc harmony his Spirit-Christology provides must surely be understood more as a unifying principle, rather than a single-solution.

As I draw these preliminary comments and thoughts to a close, it is my hope that they offer useful signposts as we approach Stringfellow's life-work and the ensuing conversation, and begin to make our own pathway of discernment and clarity through it. Dalferth's notion of theology as a practical discipline of orientation brings with it a new framework and method for examining and interpreting Stringfellow, and understanding the various eclectic perspectives both within and upon his own life-work. Additionally, the biographical nature of theology helps us to see the way anthropology, christologically and pneumatologically determined, is at the very heart of Stringfellow's theological enterprise; it is the story of inhabiting restored creation. Whilst the discussion has perhaps been of a methodological nature, I hope that we do not get subverted from the very practical theological task of the Christian life with which Stringfellow challenges us. It is perhaps useful as a tool of interpretation and understanding – but let's not mistakenly think that such is the primary discourse of theology and the Christian life.

The result affirms Stringfellow as primarily and essentially a *practical theologian* (distinct from a pastoral theologian), concerned with the radical explication and exploration of the Christian life as ministry and mission in the world and in the church. His attentions are concerned, in other words, with the lifelong process of prophetic, radical discipleship that is the Christian life; and Stringfellow beckons us to follow along that path.

Finally, to summarize our discussion of Dalferth and Stringfellow: semiotic creativity is a feature of the ongoing process of conversion and is bound up in the discipleship of the Christian life. The unfolding story of discipleship is called biography (vocation), and can be described as the ongoing (dynamic) story of encounter and reflection in eschatological and trinitarian perspective. Vocation is essentially the learning, enacting and inhabiting of this semiotic creativity, or put otherwise, it is the process of integration, interpretation and transfiguration of signs and symbols in the Word and through the Spirit, in an attempt to orientate oneself most humanly in relation to the world. Biography is theology, and theological knowledge is orientational knowledge. Orientational knowledge is discerned not in abstract but *in* and *for* praxis. It therefore necessitates at least two discussions concerning the character of the Christian life, namely ministry and mission, for these are the focus of orientational knowledge. Practical theology is an act of obedience to the call of the Risen Lord; as a practitioner (an obedient servant) Stringfellow calls us and the world to obedience through ministry and mission. Thus his life is a witness to his theology, his theology is a ministry to us, and both are a witness to the Risen Lord. Orientation, and what it comprises, can therefore be understood also as an account of the doctrine of revelation, embracing in its trinitarian form, creation, justification, and sanctification, and the mode of life through which we live. This is the trinitarian life in eschatological perspective.

Living Biblically

William Stringfellow, *Journal of Religious Thought*,
Vol. 37, 1980, pp.59-62

The truth is, I spend most of my life now with the Bible, reading or, more precisely, listening. My mundane involvements, ostensibly distinguished from this vocation – practicing some law, attention to the news of the moment, lecturing about the country, free-lance pastoral counseling, writing, activity in church politics, maintaining my medical regime, doing chores around the Block Island premises – more and more readily become incorporated into this main preoccupation so that I cannot really separate the one from the other any longer. This merging of more or less everything into a biblical scheme of living happens to me, I think, because the data of the Bible, and that of anyone's existence in common history is the same and the vitality of the Word of God in both the Bible and common history is characteristically similar. So one comes, after awhile, to live in a continuing biblical context and (in that event one) is spared both an artificial compartmentalization of one's person and a false pietism in living.

The biblical adventure continues, I expect, forever and ever: always familiar and always new, at once complete yet inexhaustible, provocative and surprising, gratuitous and liberating. Insofar as I am a beneficiary of the biblical witness (in the period between writing *Instead of Death* and now) the significant change that I am able to identify, so far as my own thinking is concerned, has to do with the abolition of false dichotomies, as between the personal and the political or as between the private and the public. What verified this for me, in an outstanding sense (since writing *Instead of Death)*, was the illness which placed my life in crisis in the period from 1967 through 1969. A chronicle of that experience is related in *A Second Birthday.* In the radical endangerment of the illness, protracted as it was, I could recognize that the death which so persistently threatened me, the death so aggressive in my body, the death signified in unremitting pain, the death which took the appearance of sickness – that death was familiar to me. I had elsewhere encountered that same death. (Actually, I had encountered that same death everywhere.) The previous decisive exposure, of which I had total recall during the illness, had been a decade or so before while working as a lawyer in East Harlem. There I contended in daily practice with the routine of cases and causes in the urban ghetto with death institutionalized in authorities and agencies and bureaucracies and multifarious principalities and powers. I had slowly learned from that involvement something that folk indigenous to the ghetto commonly discern, namely, that the power and purpose of death is incarnated in institutions and structures, procedures and regimes – such as Consolidated Edison or the Department of Welfare, the Mafia or the police, the Housing Authority or the social work bureaucracy, the hospital system or the banks, liberal philanthropy or the corporate real estate speculators. In the wisdom of the people of the East Harlem neighborhood, such principalities are readily, spontaneously, and truly identified as demonic powers by the relentless, ruthless dehumanization which they wreek and work.

In my years in East Harlem, I became so enlightened about institutional death that death no longer was an abstraction and was no longer narrowed to merely funereal connotations. I had begun, then and there, to comprehend death theologically as a militant moral reality. Hence, the grandiose terms in which the Bible denominates the power of death began to have a concrete significance for me. When, subsequently, death visited me in (apparently) a most private and personalized manner, in the debilitations of prolonged illness and in the aggressions of pain, I was able to see that this represented the same power – the same death – that I had seen before, in quite another guise, vested in the principalities active on the East Harlem scene. Divergent, or even unconnected, as the two situations seemed to be – the one so public and political, the other so private and personal – there was an extraordinary and awful coherence in each situation in the vitality and intent of death. And, thus, the asserted or assumed dichotomy between the public and the personal appearances of death is very superficial, or, it is a deception abetting the thrall of death over human beings.

In later reflection, I would press the point further. I confess that the experience of exposure to death and of coping with death in the ghetto of East Harlem became critical to such capacity as I received to endure and survive – more exactly, to transcend – profound illness.

The virtual abolition of distinction between the private and the political realms resolves a secret of the gospel which bothers and bemuses a great many people of the church, though they may seldom be articulate about it. Most churchfolk in American Christendom, especially those of a white bourgeois rearing, have, for generations, in both Sunday School and sanctuary, been furnished an impression of Jesus as a person who went briefly about teaching love and doing good: gentle Jesus, pure Jesus, meek Jesus, pastoral Jesus, honest Jesus, fragrant Jesus, passive Jesus, peaceful Jesus, healing Jesus, celibate Jesus, clean Jesus, virtuous Jesus, innocuous Jesus. Oddly enough, this image of Jesus stands in blatant discrepancy to biblical accounts of the ministry of Jesus familiar to everyone. Jesus is known to have been controversial in relation to his family and in synagogue appearances, to have suffered poignantly, to have known complete rejection of intimates no less than enemies, and to have been greeted more often with apprehension than acclaim. More particularly, this notion of an innocuous Jesus contradicts the notorious and turbulent events now marked as Holy Week in which the historical Jesus is pursued as a political criminal by the authorities, put to trial and condemned, mocked and publicly humiliated, executed in the manner customarily reserved for insurrectionists, and, all the while, beheld by his followers with hysteria and consternation. While the traditional churches have invested so much in the innocuous image of Jesus, they have not been able to suppress and remove from common knowledge the public clamor of Holy Week. This has placed churchpeople in the predicament of having two simultaneous conflicting views of

Jesus with little help available as to whether the two are reconcilable and, if not, as to which is to be believed. I think most just linger in the quandary.

I recall, as a younger person, how uneasy I used to feel in church when Lent, especially Holy Week, would happen and when, suddenly, it seemed, all that we have been told during the other church seasons about Jesus would be refuted in the recital of gospel accounts. There were those obvious questions which were never raised. Why, if Jesus was so private, so kind, so good, was he treated like a public criminal? Why would the State take any notice of him, much less crucify him? I became aware that others felt this discrepancy, too, and that some met it by steadfastly concentrating on the idea of an innocuous Jesus since that convenienced their way of life and helped to overlook the contrary evidence of Holy Week and the disquiet it occasioned. Some others opted the other way. They "ideologized" Jesus, rendering him a mere political agitator. I found both of these attempts deeply unsatisfactory, both being narrow and acculturated versions of Jesus, the one pietistic, the other political.

And if the church failed to deal with this remarkable discrepancy, one still might have recourse to the New Testament to ascertain whether the contrasting images of Jesus had basis and, then, to comprehend the issues posed in Holy Week. The secret has to do, I learned in the Bible, with the political significance of the works, discrete though they be, attributed in the gospels to Jesus, and, similarly, the political implication of his sayings. Both are cryptic. Characteristically Jesus tells a parable, ending the recital with the remark "those who have ears, let them hear." Or, characteristically, he heals someone in some way afflicted in mind or body and then cautions the one healed and those who may have witnessed the happening not to publicize it. It is only when his parables or his works become notorious that the authorities move against Jesus (the particular precipitant episode being the raising of Lazarus). Why do the rulers of the world regard Jesus so apprehensively: Why is he an offence – and a threat – to their regime? The answer that emerges in the biblical accounts is that in teaching and in healing Jesus bespeaks and demonstrates an authority and capability over the power of death, and it is that very same power of death in the world which supplies the only moral sanction for the state, or its adjacent ruling principalities. Thus Jesus preached and verified a freedom from captivation in death which threatens in the most rudimentary way the politics of this age. The rulers perceive this to be their undoing, once they have learned of Jesus and of what he has said and done. Thus, the very events which have been most private or most discrete in Jesus's ministry take on the most momentous political meaning, and if, in the days of Holy Week the truth of the confrontation becomes public, it will be seen that it has been premonitive throughout the life of Jesus – from Herod's attempt to murder the child through the temptations to submit to the power of death in the wilderness – portrayed in explicit political terms.

It is the coherence of the power of death multifariously at work in the world which explains why the public authorities cannot overlook the ministry of Jesus when it becomes apparent to them that he possesses authority and exercises capability over the power of death, as exemplified in his preaching and healing. In the midst of the consummate public confrontation between the political principalities and Jesus during Holy Week, on Maundy Thursday, Jesus promises that his disciples will receive and share through his triumph over the power of death in that same authority and capability over death in this world. And so it is that his promise is fulfilled at Pentecost, and thereafter, whenever that authority is shown, wherever that capacity is verified, insofar as the Christians live faithfully in the knowledge of the power of the resurrection, freed from captivation or intimidation by the power of death they have already known through the hostility and harassment of the ruling principalities similar to that which Jesus knew.

Interpreting the Bible

William Stringfellow, *Count it All Joy*, pp.15-20

Listening to the Word of God

I beg you not to be misled by my affirmation of the availability and centrality of the Word of God in the Bible, nor by my deploration of the diffidence toward the Bible in American Protestant preaching, liturgies, and teaching. As to the latter, I know that there are, here and there, notable exceptions to the allegations made; that there are such exceptions only sharpens the indictment. As to the former, let it be said bluntly that my esteem for the Word of God in the Bible does not mean that I am a Biblical literalist or a fundamentalist of any sort. Paradoxically, the trouble with fundamentalists, as I try to listen to them, is their shocking failure to regard and use the Bible conscientiously enough. If they honored the Bible more highly they would appreciate that the Word of God will endure demythologizing, that the Word cannot be threatened by anything whatever given to people to discover and know through any science or discipline of the world, or hindered by textual criticism, or hampered by linguistic analysis, or harmed by vernacular translations. All these are welcome to Christians as enhancements of the knowledge of the fullness of the Word of God and of the grandeur of human access to the Word. More than that, if the fundamentalists actually took the Bible seriously they would inevitably love the world more readily, instead of fearing the world, because the Word of God is free and active in this world and Christians can only comprehend the Word out of their involvement in this world, as the Bible so redundantly testifies.

I am no Biblical scholar; I have neither competence nor temperament to be one. The ordinary Christian, lay or clergy, does not need to be a scholar to have recourse to the Bible and, indeed, to live within the Word of God in the Bible in this world. What the ordinary Christian is called to do is to open the Bible and listen to the Word.

Listening is a rare happening among human beings. You cannot listen to the word another is speaking if you are preoccupied with your appearance or impressing the other, or if you are trying to decide what you are going to say when the other stops talking, or if you are debating about whether the word being spoken is true or relevant or agreeable. Such matters may have their place, but only after listening to the word as the word is being uttered. Listening, in other words, is a primitive act of love, in which a person gives oneself to another's word, making oneself accessible and vulnerable to that word.

It is very much like that when anyone comes to the Bible. They must first of all listen to the Word which the Bible speaks, putting aside, for the time being, such other issues as whether the Word is credible or congenial or consistent or significant. By all means, if you will, raise these questions, but, first, listen to the Word.

Let the Bible be treated, too, with at least the respect you accord a letter from a person. If you receive a letter and care to know the word of the letter you would not open it, read a paragraph or two and then abandon it for two or three months, pick it up again to read a few more sentences on another page, leave it aside once more and later return to it again. No. If you care about the word of the letter, you would open it and listen to it attentively as a whole. After that, you might go back to this or that part of it to ponder or dispute, but first you would read it in its own context, asking only, What is being said? What is the word? The Bible deserves that much regard. And, if one cares to discern the Word of God in the Bible, then one must listen to the Bible in the Bible's own context and not deal with the Bible in a random, perfunctory, smattering fashion.

Some will think this a naive approach to the Word of God in the Bible. I suppose it is just that. It is one which simply affirms that the Word of God has content, integrity and life which belongs to God Himself and that this can be received and comprehended by ordinary human beings. It is a view that regards the Bible more as a newspaper than as a systematic body of theological doctrine or as religious instruction or as moral law or, for that matter, as mere esoteric mythology. The Bible reports the news of the Word of God manifest and militant in the events of this history in a way that is accessible, lucid and edifying for the common reader. The Word of God is for people, and through the Bible that Word is addressed to people where they are, just as they are, in this world.

Such naïveté toward the Word of God does not repudiate or threaten other ways in which the Bible may be esteemed and used – as theology, mythology, poetry, literature, symbol, prophecy, ethics, or chronicle. But it does insist that anyone may listen to the Word in the Bible innocent of any special skill or learning. And it does mean that all other uses of the Bible are subject to the discipline of God's own living Word as such and not the other way around, when people impose their own opinions, prides, methods and interpretations upon the Bible as if to test the Word of God by human words. God speaks for Himself in this world, no one speaks in His stead; though, by God's grace, a person may hear God's Word and become a witness to it.

Interpreting the Bible

In the churches and outside the churches it is quite popular in the present day (though also, as the Letter to the Colossians indicates, in earlier times) to suggest that the content of the Word of God in the Bible is a matter of such indifference to God that it is only a question of human interpretations and insights. The unavoidable corollary is that one person's view is as apt as another's, which is, of course, a way of denying the integrity of the Word of God and, as the 'death of God' vogue illustrates, ends in a denial of the existence of God.

A similar issue arises in the relationships of persons. This introduction is, for example, being written during a visit to Australia, during which I have met a great variety of people in a diversity of situations. In another two weeks, if the world lasts that much longer, and if I live, I will be back at work in New York encountering clients and colleagues there. If, somehow, all of those with whom I have been in this time, gathered together in the same room, they would each be able to speak of the one whom each has met in terms of the specific and various circumstances of each meeting. If I have integrity as a person, it will be discernible, as each one speaks of having somewhere and somehow met me, that each and every one testifies to having met the same person despite the diversity of conditions and locations of these happenings. Though the testimony of these many witnesses vary in many ways, it will nonetheless be evident that it is one person of whom they speak, who has been made known to them in different places and manifold circumstances. On the other hand, if, as a person, I have no integrity, if I am instead playing roles in these varying situations, if my own existence is a pretence and has no independence from the impressions or opinions of those whom I meet here and there, then it is as if I exist only in the interpretations of others; then it is as if I do not really exist at all.

The problem of the interpretations that people make of the Bible is similar. The Bible is a wondrously diversified testament of the Word of God disclosed to humanity in an array of events in which it is discernible that it is the same One of whom all these witnesses speak. God is and God possesses an existence and integrity of His own quite free from those who witness to Him or those who feign to do so. The versatility of God's witness to Himself in the Bible and continually in the world must not be used against God to try to prove that His Word is no more than what people interpret it to be. Rather this versatility of witness should provoke people to marvel at God's freedom and elusiveness from being captured by the intelligence, pietism, imagination or merit of humankind.

In other words, let all religious people beware. Their earnest longing for God is predicated on the reservation on their part that it is necessary for them to do something to find God. The Word of God in the Bible, however, is that God does not await human initiative of any sort but seeks and finds people where they are, wherever it be. No one can approach the Bible with any expectation of there discerning the integrity of the Word of God in such radical versatility if the mind is still obstructed or the heart is still hardened by the notion that it is one's task to locate or define God.

So, if I know who I am as a person and if I care to be known to another, it is a matter of my discretion that I make myself known to another. There is nothing that another can do about it, except to welcome or reject the gift, but neither of these affects my existence as such or the tender of knowledge of myself to the other. Similarly, insofar as God cares to be known of humankind, it is alone for Him to make Himself known, which, according to the manifold witness of the Bible, is exactly what He has done in this world.

To know the Word of God in the Bible, people must come to the Bible with a certain naïveté, confessing that if God exists at all, He lives independently, though not in isolation, from human intelligence, longing, emotion, insight or interpretations, even those which divine the truth. They must be open to God's initiative. They must be bereft of all preconceptions. They must surrender all their own initiative. They must forego anything that would demean God to dependence upon his thoughts, words, entreaties, deeds or moods. They must take the appalling risk – by giving up all hypotheses, speculations, ideas and deductions about God – that God is not and that there is only death. When one is so naked, so helpless, so transparent, when one so utterly cease to try to justify oneself or anyone or anything else, one first become vulnerable to the Word of God, which overcomes oblivion, heals deafness, restores sight and saves people from manipulation, arrogance and folly in confronting the Word of God in the Bible. When one becomes that mature as a human being one is freed to listen and at last to welcome the Word in the Bible, and one is enlightened to discern the same Word of God at work now in the world, in (of all places!) one's own existence as well as in (thank God!) all other life. Thus is established a rhythm in the Christian's life encompassing intimacy with the Word of God in the Bible and involvement with the same Word active in the world.

Biblical Politics

William Stringfellow, *Ethic for Christians*, pp.14-15

This book is necessarily at once theological and political for the good reason that the theology of the Bible concerns politics in its most rudimentary meaning and in its most auspicious connotations.

The biblical topic is politics. The Bible is about the politics of fallen creation and the politics of redemption; the politics of the nations, institutions, ideologies, and causes of this world and the politics of the Kingdom of God; the politics of Babylon and the politics of Jerusalem; the politics of the Antichrist and the politics of Jesus Christ; the politics of the demonic powers and principalities and the politics of the timely judgment of God as sovereign; the politics of death and the politics of life; apocalyptic politics and eschatological politics.

Throughout the diversity of the biblical saga as history and as literature, the priority of politics remains prominent. The Bible expounds with extraordinary versatility, now one way and then another, and another, the singular issue of salvation – which is to say, the preemptive *political* issue. It bespeaks the reality of human life consummated in society within time in this world, now and here, as the promise of renewal and fulfillment vouchsafed for all humans and for every nation – for the whole of Creation – throughout time.

Despite the habitual malpractice of translating biblical politics as the American story, there is also the odd and contradictory custom among many Americans to denounce the truth that the Bible is political. Frequently, if incongruously, these two convictions are held concurrently by the same person, or by the same sect or church or social faction. American experience as a nation – as well as biblical scholarship – discredits any attempted Americanization of biblical politics and confounds the notion that the Bible is apolitical. What is surprising is that the latter belief persists even though so many of the biblical symbols are explicitly political – *dominion, emancipation, authority, judgment, kingdom, reconciliation* among them – and even though the most familiar biblical events are notoriously political – including the drama of Israel the holy nation, the Kingdom parables in Christ's teaching, the condemnation of Christ as King of the Jews by the imperial authorities, the persecutions of the Apostolic congregations, the controversies between Christians and zealots, the propagation of the Book of Revelation.

Well, I do not amplify the matter here, apart from noticing that the view that the Bible is politically neuter or innocuous – coupled, as it may be, ironically, with an American misuse of biblical politics – maintains wide currency in this nation. And this view sorely inhibits a biblical comprehension of America as a nation.

The Liturgy as a Political Event

William Stringfellow, *Dissenter in a Great Society*, pp.150-64

Our gratitude for the contemporary friendly disposition among the multiplicity of people who call themselves Christians and among the several churches should tempt none to minimize either the profundity or the pathology of the estrangement to which all people who are baptized are heirs. These experiences of renewed contact, genuine humility, and mutual respect should not quiet the conscience of Christians but, rather, provoke greater awareness of continuing divisions.

At no point in the witness of the Church to the world is its integrity as a reconciled society more radical and more cogent than in the liturgy, the precedent and consummation of that service which the Church of Christ and the members of this Body render to the world. Of course, there are many Protestants who regard the liturgy as peripheral to the Christian life. Some even boast that *they* have no liturgical life, but this is a betrayal of ignorance, since liturgy means nothing more than style of life. In the broadest sense, all of life is liturgical. The conventions and ceremonies of courtship are a liturgy, articulating and dramatizing the love between a man and a woman. Or, to take a less attractive example – Joe Valachi, in the Senate hearing in which the chief witness expounded at great length upon the peculiar actions and symbols and rituals which constitute the extraordinarily sophisticated liturgical fabric of the Cosa Nostra.[1]

As for the Church, all forms of its corporate life – from the Quakers sitting in silence in a circle, to the exuberance and patience of a Negro congregation, and the majesty and richness of the venerable Orthodox service – are liturgical. The only serious question is whether or not a given liturgical practice has integrity in the Gospel. There are both laypeople and clergy who regard liturgy as an essentially religious exercise – separate, disjoined, self-contained, unrelated – confined to the sanctuary and having nothing to do with this world. Some even regard liturgy superstitiously, as something having an intrinsic efficacy, as a means of procuring indulgences, as if God were so absurd – and so ungodly – as to be appeased by the redundant incantations of people.

There is, however, nothing so spooky or lucky about the liturgy, and nothing magical or mechanistic about its performance. The liturgy of the Gospel is, on the contrary, a dramatic form of the ethical witness of Christians in this world. In this sense, though there may be much variety in different times and cultures in regard

---

[1] Editor's note: Valachi was a Mafia member who, faced with spending many years in prison, violated the organization's code of silence and turned informer, making public many of the inner-workings of the Mafia (La Cosa Nostra) in New York.

to language, music, action, and movement, the liturgy is always characterized by certain definitive marks:

1) *Scriptural Integrity* – The liturgy of the Gospel is the theatricalization of the biblical saga of God's action in this world, thus relating the ubiquity of the Word of God in history to the consummation of the Word of God in Jesus Christ. A biblically authentic and historically relevant liturgy is always the celebration of the death and Resurrection of the Lord; the most decisive event in all history is remembered and memorialized in a context in which God's every action in this world since creation is recalled and rehearsed, and the hope of the world for the final reconciliation is recited and represented in the liturgical portrait.

The scriptural integrity of the liturgy requires that the laity not be spectators but participants – not as a matter of piety, not merely for their own sake but because they gather, as a congregation, as delegates and, indeed, advocates of the world.

That is why the traditional Protestant "preaching service" – even when the preaching is an exposition of the Word of God, and not some religious diatribe – is an impoverished and inadequate liturgy for the Church; by the same token, that is why the Mass recited in the absence of a congregation, or celebrated in a language not familiar to the people, is a compromise of the scriptural integrity of the liturgy.

2) *The Historicity of the Liturgy* – The liturgy of the Gospel is both a transcendent event and a present event. It shatters the categories of time and space and location because it both recalls and dramatizes the estate of Creation in the Word of God, and beseeches and foretells the end of this history. As a transcendent event, the liturgy recollects *all* that has already happened in this world from the beginning of time, and prophesies *all* that is to come until the end of time.

But the liturgy is also a contemporary event, involving these particular persons gathered in this specific place in this peculiar way. The reconciliation celebrated in the liturgy is not only a reconciliation remembered from Creation or expected eschatologically but also in actual event the reconciliation here and now of those gathered as a congregation and society within and among themselves, and between each and all of them and the rest of the world.

That is precisely why the confessions and the intercessions of the people of the congregation within the context of the liturgy are so indispensable to its integrity. *This* is the time and *this* is the place and *this* is the way, in a most immediate sense, in which the whole, manifold, existential involvement of the members of Christ's Body in the everyday life of the world – both all that seems good and which we are tempted to honor or praise, and all that seems evil and which we are fond of rationalizing or denying – is offered and consecrated for the discretion of Christ Himself, the Redeemer of all people and all things.

Thus the liturgy is the normative and conclusive ethical commitment of the Christian people to the world. The liturgy is the epitome of the service which the Christian renders the world. All authentic witness in the name of Christ, exemplifying in the world the virtue of Christ, which Christians undertake in their dispersion in the practical life of the world, is portrayed in the liturgy celebrated in the gathered congregation.

3) *The Sacramental Authenticity of the Liturgy* – It is both this transcendence of time in time and the scriptural integrity of the liturgy of the Gospel which

constitutes the sacramental essence of the liturgy. The actual, visible, present event retains all its own originality and contemporary significance as a particular reconciled community, and at the same time is transfigured to embody to the world the cosmic enormity of the reconciling accomplishment of Jesus Christ.

Thus the liturgy as sacrament is inherently different from religious ritualism, in which the propriety of the ritual practice itself is all that matters. (Such may be sufficient for initiation or elevation in the Masons or the Knights of Columbus, but ritualistic piety is radically inappropriate to the Eucharist.) Notice, too, that the liturgy as sacrament appropriates as its ingredient symbols, among others, the ordinary things of the common existence of the world – bread, wine, water, money, cloth, color, music, words, or whatever else is readily at hand. Sacramentally, we have in the liturgy a meal which is basically a real meal and which nourishes those who partake of it as a meal. At the same time, this meal portrays for the rest of the world an image of the Last Supper, of which Christ Himself was Host, and is also a foretaste of the eschatological banquet in which Christ is finally recognized as the Host of all people.

The liturgy, therefore, wherever it has substance in the Gospel, is a living, political event. The very example of salvation, it is the festival of life which foretells the fulfillment and maturity of all of life for all of time in *this* time. The liturgy *is* social action because it is the characteristic style of life for human beings in this world.

The Political Authority of Baptism

A particular confusion has arisen in the American churches, especially in this last decade, because of the clergy's involvement in direct social action. Although several Roman Catholic priests have lately been disciplined for speaking out on specific issues, this is a confusion which particularly afflicts Protestants, because they have far less certainty about the office of the clergy in relation to the ministry of the laity dispersed in the world.

What must never be lost sight of in the relations of clergy and laity is Baptism. All baptized people, whatever their work or rank, location or function, charismatic gifts or personal talents, share in the one ministry of the Body of Christ for the world *in* the world. Indeed, according to I Corinthians, every baptized person is beneficiary of the charismatic gift of faith. Baptism bestows the power to live in Christ as a servant of the world.

This gift and office of service to the world is vouchsafed for all baptized people, and is not superseded or minimized by ordination. Clergy remain, in a sense, lay people, and retain the same authority and responsibility as all other laypeople. Ordination gives them the office of priest and charges them with the functions of that office to serve the laity in the administration of the sacraments, the preaching of the Word of God in the congregation, and the nurture of the members of the congregation, both as individuals and as a body.

It is, of course, often the practice to commission clergy to perform other services in addition to those for which they are ordained, particularly in relation to the maintenance of the institution of the Church or the administration of a parish. These tasks are not essentially related to the peculiar work of the priesthood, though they may be essential to, or convenient for, the existence of the Church or of a particular parish. These are functions that a layperson, however, might undertake, which means that priests, even in this parish, are sometimes engaged in work as laypeople.

Ordination does not remove the clergy from the world, though that which characterizes their specific office in ordination is an esoteric and internal servanthood within the Church. Thus, clergy who become publicly involved in antiwar protests or in support of 'my country, right or wrong', in the civil rights demonstrations and school boycotts, or as Kloods (chaplains) for the Ku Klux Klan and apologists for racism, or in public issues of any sort, do so as laity. There is nothing specific or peculiar pertaining to the functions for which they are ordained that authorizes such involvement. As with any Christian, what authorizes their political involvement is Baptism; what informs and disciplines their commitment must not be any personal whim or prejudice or any allegiance to worldly interests or factions but what it means to be a baptized person.

All Christians act politically and socially under the peril of dishonoring – and even, at times, disowning – the estate of reconciliation with all people vouchsafed to them in Baptism. Indeed, this fact is the Christian's only recourse against making political decisions according to the discriminations of others.

For anyone who is baptized, the world as it is, is precious. It is the recipient of love because God made it; as the Apostle James reminds us. His Word is to be beheld in all things and in all people. Christians are called to enjoy God's presence in the world for the sake of those in the world who cannot yet do so. While involved in this world, the Christian is characteristically, profoundly, and constantly immersed in the Bible, because it is the testimonial evidence of God's care for, and activity in, this world. From the Bible, we discern the manner of God's presence and vitality in the world's common life. Christians see the ministry of Jesus Christ as the example of what it is to be reconciled within one's self, with all people and all things in the mercy and judgment of God.

The Marks of Christian Involvement

In welcoming the Word of God in the world – and hence, in participating in the controversy and conflict of society – perhaps the first thing for both clergy and laity to keep in mind is that in this world there is no such thing as neutrality about any public issue. To be sure, some societies permit a greater freedom of involvement in public dialogue to their citizens and their institutions than do others, but in no society, least of all one which professes to be a political democracy, is abstinence from public controversy an alternative, or neutrality in public affairs an option. Every citizen and every institution is involved in one way or another, either by intention or by default.

Those who suppose they can withdraw only deceive themselves, because deliberate abstinence or asserted neutrality are themselves forms of involvement in politics.

It is possible to conceive of circumstances where these forms of involvement may be intentional and rationalized, but let no citizen or institution, including the Church, be so naive as to consider that these are anything else than particular ways of being involved in politics and social issues.

To take the most obvious example: In American society, citizens who do not cast their vote give the weight of their vote to the candidate who happens to win the election. Their abstinence, or neutrality, amounts to support for the winner, since their vote, if cast, might have defeated the candidate who won. The issue, in such circumstances, is not really either abstention or neutrality but the uncritical and undiscriminating use of suffrage. Such citizens allows others to determine by their votes the political consequences of their default. It is surely a form of involvement, but it seems generally a stupid way to be involved, except where there is no significant distinction between candidates – a circumstance which has often confronted Negro voters.

Much the same applies to the great institutional powers within a society. One has only to recall what happened in Germany in the thirties to see that what contributed more than perhaps anything else to the usurpation of political democracy and the rise of totalitarianism was the silence and default of Church and university. The Church and the university as institutions, as well as multitudes (though not all) church members and intellectuals, became accomplices of Hitler's rise to power by their blindness to political realities, by their preoccupation with academic theology, by their reluctance to speak out, by their refusal to protest.

There were, of course, the paramilitary groups, the radical anti-Semites, the political fanatics actively seeking to establish Nazism in power, but they were mightily and, in retrospect it seems, indispensably supported by withdrawal, neutrality, silence, and default by Christian people and by the intelligentsia, save for those few who did speak out and were either banished from the nation or imprisoned or condemned to die.

In politics, and most plainly in the politics of democracy, every citizen and every institution is involved, whether they want to be or not. Since this is so, the one virtually certain way to be conformed to the world, as no Christian should, the way to be defiled in one's involvement, is in futilely practicing abstinence and supposing that one is thereby not involved.

The proximate and provisional nature of secular political movements and social issues in no way counsels Christians to be apathetic about such matters. Let it be as plain as it can be: although a deliberate abstinence may on occasion be rationalized, abstinence which is inadvertent or the fruit of apathy or complacent default or feigned non-involvement is, theologically speaking, a form of nihilism, an affirmation of death as the ultimate reality in human existence.

For the Christian the necessity, and indeed inevitability, of involvement goes deeper than all this: the most elementary characterization of the Gospel of Jesus Christ is the Incarnation. The Incarnation is not a theological abstraction – though it is often presented that way in catechism. It is not some quaint or spooky figure of speech. It is not even a difficult mystery; on the contrary, the Incarnation means that God Himself, in Christ, has shattered for us the very mystery of His being and purpose and activity in this world. The Incarnation means that God's passion for the world's actual life – including its politics, along with all else – is such that He enters and acts in this world for himself. Apart from the Incarnation there is no meaning in the Christmas message that God is with us, nor in the Easter assurance that God acts in this world for the benefit of all people, nor in the Pentecost evidence that God inaugurates the true society which is the Church.

In other words, the Church and Christians are not simply involved in politics because of the nature of politics as such – by which all are involved and abstinence is a fiction – but because they honor and celebrate God's own presence and action in this world, because they know that the world – in all its strife and confusion, brokenness and travail – is the scene of God's work and the subject of God's love.

According to the Gospel, God is not confined to the sanctuaries of the Church. He is not enshrined in any altar. The reason Christians gather now and then in their sanctuaries is not because God is there but rather to celebrate and proclaim God's presence and action outside the sanctuaries in the common life of the world. Worship which has integrity in the Gospel is always an intercession by God's people for the cares and needs of the world, and always a thanksgiving – a eucharist – for God's love for the world. Worship at the altar is thus authenticated by the constant involvement of the people of the Church in the world's life and by the public witness of the Church in the world.

It is sometimes asserted that the Church should concern itself only occasionally in public affairs, where society is confronted with a "moral" issue. The problem with that view is that it oversimplifies the moral conflict in the world. There is no issue in society which is not a moral issue in both the transient human sense and also as one which God judges. In a fallen world, all people live at each other's expense, and every decision and action, even those which seem trivial or only private or unambiguous, is consequentially related to the lives of all people.

What you or I decide and do affects all other people, and every decision or action or omission is thus not only a moral but a theological issue, a sacrament of one's responsibility for and love for one's self and others, or else a sign of one's disregard for and alienation from one's self and others. Indeed, on the Last Day, though not before, God's own judgment of every act, word, and deed of every person will expose the true moral disposition of each in relationship to all. Meanwhile, each of us must make our own decisions, knowing that each decision is a moral decision with consequences for all other people, but not knowing what many of those consequences are or will be until we are judged by God's mercy. Meanwhile, all Christians, remembering their Baptism, must take their stand in the practical affairs of this world in fear and trembling.

But if there is no option of withdrawal, if silence is a form of involvement, if default abets the winning side, if all are in fact involved, how shall Christians and how shall the Church be responsible in their political involvement? How shall they be involved and yet remain unstained by the world?

Surely the answer to that is: in the very manner of Christ's own ministry in this world.

There is no convenient set of rules, no simple blueprint, no simplistic ethics of decision for the Christian. The Christian witness in society does not consist of praising and practicing the "Golden Rule," which, after all, is a secular ethic of self-interest that demeans the essence of the Gospel. But there are at least some clues about the style of witness characteristic of the Christian life in the world, both for the Church as such and for the individual member of the Church.

1) *Realism:* Christians are those who take history very seriously. They regard the actual day-to-day existence of the world realistically, as a way of acknowledging and honoring God's own presence and action in the real world in which people live and fight and love and vote and work and die. And Christians know, more sensitively and sensibly than other people, that this world is a fallen world, not an evil world but the place in which death is militant and aggressive and at work in all things. Christians know that in this world in which, apart from God's work in all things, death is the only meaning, all relationships have been broken and all people suffer estrangement from one another and alienation from themselves. Of all people, Christians are the most blunt and relentless realists; free to face the world as it is without flinching, without shock, without fear, without surprise, without embarrassment, without sentimentality, without guile or disguise. They are free to live in the world as it is.

2) *Inconsistency:* Christians, in their fidelity to the Gospel in their witness in this world, will appear inconsistent to others in public views and positions. They cannot be put into a neat pigeonhole, their stance and conduct are never easily predictable. Christians are nonideological persons in politics, and there is no other label appropriate for them than Christian. They know that no institution, no ideology, no nation, no form of government, no society, can heal the brokenness or prevail against the power of death. And though Christians act in this world and in particular circumstances in a society for this or that cause, though Christians take their stand and speak out specifically, they do so not as the servant of some race or class or political system or ideology but as an expression of their freedom from just such idols.

3) *Radicalism:* That means, of course, that the posture of Christians is inherently and consistently radical. (I do not use the word in any of its conventional economic or political connotations.) Christians are perpetually in the position of complaining about the status quo, whatever it happens to be. Their insight and experience of reconciliation in Christ are such that no estate in secular society can possibly correspond to, or much approximate, the true society of which they are citizens in Christ.

They are – everywhere, in every society – aliens. They are always, in any society, in protest. Even when a cause which they have themselves supported prevails, they will not be content but will be the first to complain against the "new" status quo.

To recall an example given earlier, many Christians at the present time in the United States are deeply and actively involved in the struggle to achieve integration in American public life. The Christian in that struggle, however, will characteristically be the first to recognize that integration of American society, as much as it is absolutely essential to the survival of this nation, is in no way to be confused with or identified with the Kingdom of God. Integration, from a Christian point of view, must be counted as a modest, conservative, attainable, and necessary social and political objective in this nation at this time. It is by no means the measure of reconciliation among people in this world.

4) *Intercession:* Christians are concerned, politically, for all people in all the diversity of problems and issues of public life. Characteristically, the sign of the inclusiveness and extremity of Christian concern is represented and embodied in their specific care for those who, in a given time in society, are the least in that society, for those whom all the rest have ignored or forgotten or cast out or otherwise have abandoned to death.

The venerable ministry of Christians for the poor since the very days of the New Testament, for instance, is not simply compassion for their endurance of unemployment or hunger or cold or sickness or rejection by society, but is also, at the same time, a way of caring for all others in society who are not poor or who have some security from the assaults of poverty. Christians know that their passion for the world, their involvement in society, their stand in politics, their witness in the present age, encompass even their own enemy, even those whom they oppose in some specific controversy, even those who would deny the freedom of their witness, even those who hate them, and especially those who are threatened by their witness.

The Christian political witness, for the individual Christian and for the body of the Church, means demonstrating in and to the world what the true society is by the living example of the society of the Church.

The Christian political witness is affirming and loving the essential humanity of all in Christ in the midst of our abdication of human life and despite the whole array of death's assaults against human life.

The Christian political witness is the audacity to trust that God's love for this world's existence is redeeming, so Christians are human beings free to live in this world by grace in all practical matters and decisions.

That is why the Church of Christ is the only society in this world worthily named great.

The Freedom of the Christian Life

William Stringfellow, *A Private and Public Faith*, pp.68-73

The presence of God's Word in common life and the gift of discernment of that Word in the world mean a very radical freedom for Christians, and for the Church, in the world, and in the service of the world. There is no place in which that freedom may not be exercised, for there is no place in which the Word of God is absent. There is no time in which that freedom is restricted since the One the world awaits has already come.

The freedom of the Christian life and the service to the world accomplished when that freedom is exercised is not to be confused with conventional charity – with 'doing good', with helping other people in the ordinary meaning of those words, with good works. In East Harlem, and elsewhere, I have seen a lot of conventional charity. East Harlem is virtually invested with social workers and voluntary and governmental agencies of all sorts, all heartily engaged in helping the people of the neighborhood with the rearing of children, the maintenance of marriages, the finding of jobs, the curbing of delinquency, the rehabilitation of addicts, the procurement of housing, the protection of tenants, and all the rest. Now I do not deprecate any of this, but it must be distinguished from the witness and service of Christians.

For one thing, the great peril in the notion that we may intentionally do, and know that we are doing, good for another person is that it preempts the office of God in judging the actions and decisions of people. Those who claim for their action toward another person that their action is good are in the arrogant position of asserting that they know already how God will judge their act or decision.

Beyond that, however, is the further peril of tyrannizing the one of whom it is said that he/she is being helped. The danger is that in the reason for doing what is thought or said to be good to another the one who has acted intends and feels to be justified. So the real issue, in such action, is not the other's welfare, but your own; not their nurture, but your justification. Notice, too, how often the standard of help – rehabilitation, as it is usually called – is not just made up of the common morality of middle class society, but specifically in how far the client or patient or case imitates and becomes like the case worker or probation person or professional – that is, in how far the one who is being helped becomes like the one who is helping. This is a temptation present in any situation where some form of conventional charity is undertaken where there is a direct contact between persons, as distinguished from conventional charity – social work, counseling, medical care, and the like – organized on an impersonal and bureaucratic basis. And while I am sympathetic with criticisms of the latter, for their depersonalizing impact upon those who receive services, the former instance may in fact involve a more terrible tyranny of one person over another. I think a lot of people are murdered in the name of the good which is done to them.

Christians would, characteristically, be sensitive to these temptations in conventional charity since they have no longer any reason to be anxious about their own moral justification. They know that God judges as He will and that a person's justification consists not in the good that they intend or do, but in the mercy and grace of God. And Christians are concerned not so much with conventional charity, with coping with human problems or social issues according to the tradition of society, as with the representation in the life of society, with all its human problems and social issues, of the intercession of Christ for the whole of life and for every fragment of life.

One of the earliest clients that I had in East Harlem was a boy whom I will call Ramon. He came to me one night and said: "You're a lawyer – tell me what to do. The police are looking for me and I want to go into the Marines and I want to know what will happen if I do that or what will happen if I turn myself in to the police." He wanted to clear up the present chapter in his life before going on to a new life and wondered what he should do about the fact that the police wanted him for questioning. In investigating the matter, I discovered that the police were interested in questioning him about an incident that had taken place in the neighborhood some eighteen months prior to the time he came to me.

One night in the early summer, he and some of the other boys from his gang had been loitering on the street and a girl had come by whom some of the boys, although not my client, had taken up on the roof of a nearby tenement and there each of them committed what is legally called statutory rape, since the girl was legally not of the age of consent, but what is colloquially called in East Harlem a 'line-up'. Initially there were four boys involved. During the incident one of the boys came down and told Ramon that the girl wanted him to come to the roof, which he did, and he then also had intercourse with her. This was still, of course, statutory rape in Ramon's case, because of the girl's age, though she apparently had specifically consented to and, indeed, solicited him. Cases of this sort are not too frequently subject to police investigation or criminal prosecution unless some complaint is made or the matter somehow otherwise reaches the attention of the authorities. In this instance, the girl was hospitalized in the next few days, the hospital reported the matter, and so there was an investigation by the police. In due course the four boys involved in the original incident were picked up, but not Ramon. None of the boys arrested disclosed Ramon's name or whereabouts. Eventually the other boys were charged, tried, convicted, and imprisoned. Ramon knew that he was wanted by the police and was shrewd enough to move from his parent's tenement to a relative's home in an adjacent precinct. And there he had remained ever since without being apprehended.

It seemed likely that Ramon could remain there indefinitely without great jeopardy of being arrested, although there would always be some risk of that. It also seemed clear that if Ramon were picked up or if he surrendered to the police, he would, like his friends, be tried and convicted and imprisoned.

While I was investigating the matter and wondering what counsel to give to Ramon, I was visited by two people from the neighborhood interested in Ramon and in this case. One visitor was a seminarian who, as part of his field work assignment, was working with the gang to which Ramon belonged, coaching them in basketball. When the seminarian came to me he said "I heard that Ramon has talked with you about giving himself up to the police. That's the first time this kid has shown any sense of responsibility about what happened with that girl or about much of anything else." This, incidentally, was not the case, because within his society, within his gang, Ramon had a very great sense of responsibility, even though he may not have had much toward society outside his gang, toward society hostile to his society. Anyway, the seminarian thought of Ramon as irresponsible and welcomed his consideration of surrendering to the police as a sign of responsibility. But the seminarian raised another consideration: he proposed that he and I, as Christians, should so counsel with Ramon that there would be precipitated, out of his anxiety about whether to give himself up, a personal crisis, a repentance for what he had done, and, hopefully, a traumatic conversion. Then, figured the seminarian, after Ramon becomes a Christian, after his conversion, he will himself know what he should do about the police.

It all seemed very manipulative and a bit morbid, as I recall, but the seminarian had, nevertheless, raised a serious issue, that is, the primary concern for the evangelization of all people, including Ramon.

The second visitor was a minister from one of the neighborhood churches. He said that he had also heard of Ramon's visit to me and that I should know that "Ramon is a menace". The boy had gotten away with rape and, the minister alleged, though he had no legal proof, Ramon had also been involved in other 'line-ups' from time to time that had never been investigated by the police, and had also been implicated in a robbery about which no police action had been taken. Ramon was increasingly lionized by his friends because of his skill or success in getting away with all this, according to the minister, and was therefore a bad influence on other boys. "For the good of society, for the good of the neighborhood," the minister proposed, "we should get him to turn himself in." And though, as a lawyer, I thought the minister less informed or concerned than he might have been, about the necessity to protect an accused person until his guilt is legally established, I acknowledge that he raised a significant issue, and one for which Christians have always had great concern, namely, the welfare and safety and order of society as a whole.

In spite of the issues raised by the seminarian and by the minister, I decided that my own advice to Ramon would be to join the Marines. Admittedly, there is perhaps not much choice between staying in East Harlem and risking arrest or some further trouble, or surrendering to the police and going to jail, or joining the Marines, but perhaps, if Ramon went into the military service he might learn something useful for later employment – a trade skill, or the improvement of his English, or the like – possibilities which were not in prospect either in remaining in East Harlem or in going to jail. Maybe there was a little better chance for his life if he took this course; both prison and East Harlem seemed to offer only more trouble for Ramon. And this was something he wanted himself to do, if he could.

Legally there was no impediment to his joining the Marines. He was wanted for questioning, but he had not been charged, indicted, convicted of any crime.

Ramon was legally still innocent of any crime. When he joined the Marines he would have to sign a form under oath that he had not been indicted or convicted, and he could do this.

Ramon's self-interest seemed to be in entering the service. The story of Ramon portrays something of the style of the Christian life and witness in the world. It points, for instance, to the fact that there is never an abstract, single 'Christian answer' to an issue to which all Christians are bound to adhere or conform. On the contrary, the positions taken by the three Christians on the scene, implicated in one way or another in the actual case, the seminarian and the minister and myself, are all responsible Christian positions. Christians care that every person be evangelized, as the seminarian represented. Christians care for all of society, as the minister represented. Christians care for people in a radically individual sense and are free to advocate the cause of one, as in this case of Ramon, as over against everyone and everything else in the world.

The image of Christian action in the world is that of the people of God living in dispersion in the world and in any corner of the world, finding trustworthy God's promise that He cares for all people and for each person. Moreover, Christians are free in their dispersion to intercede for the cause of anyone – even one who is said by others to be unworthy – and thereby to represent in the world the intercession of Christ for everyone – even though none be worthy. The image of Christian witness in the world is that of a people who have so completely divested themselves of their own individual self-interest that they may intercede – stand in the place of, represent, advocate – the cause of another, any other at all. And then, now and again, the people return from their extraordinarily versatile involvement in the life of the world, to gather as the Church to represent, before God, the world out of which they have come, in all its concreteness and conflict and change, and to celebrate as the Church the presence of the Word of God as they have known it in the world.

The Church's Need of the World

If the life of the Church, either of the members dispersed in the world or of the gathered worshipping community, is to be an exercise of the power to discern the presence of the Word of God in common life and is to be a radically free and versatile involvement in the turmoil and travail of the world's everyday existence; if the life of the Church is to be intercessory; and if the Church is to be the servant of the world in the name and in the style of Christ, then Christians must live in the world – and not for their own sake, and not for the sake of the Church, much less for the sake of any of the churches, not even for God's sake, but for the sake of the world. That is to say, the Christian must live in this world, where Christ lives: the Christian must live in this world *in* Christ.

Yet what Christians are faced with are churches, at least in Protestantism, which at every echelon of their existence – Sunday school, youth fellowships, vestries and sessions, agencies, councils, denominations, congregations and parishes, women's work, rummage sales, bingo games and coffee hours, sermons, seminaries, boy scouts, choirs and dial-a-prayers, bastard architecture, segregated premises, effete or effeminate images of Jesus, grossly inflated bureaucracies and all the rest – churches which are to a great extent separated from the world, afraid of the world, which feel unprepared, insecure, and inadequate for the mission of the Church in the world, and for whom the jargons of theological discussion or the examples of the clergy or the formalities of the practice of religion are no assurance or adequacy. These churches more and more retreat into themselves. They become so inverted, so caught up in internal maintenance and procedure, so entrapped in preserving and proliferating a cumbersome, costly, self-serving, officious, indulgent, soft ecclesiastical apparatus that it becomes easy to think that they don't have to care about the world any more since they are so much consumed in caring for themselves.

Nevertheless, it is when and where the churches are most estranged from and least involved in the common life of the world that the churches are the most worldly, and most resemble the worldly principalities and powers. The separation of the churches from the world, the superstition that the Word of God is or can be isolated from ordinary, everyday life, the preoccupations of the churches with conserving their own existence rather than serving the world – all these are the substance of estrangement from Christ. Where the churches do not care for the world, they do not really care for Christ.

I know a clergyman who was recently coerced into leaving his work in New York City because his ecclesiastical superiors informed him that his ministry was becoming 'too specialized'. He cared for the world and he spent his time in the world. The only time you could find him on the church premises was when he was presiding at worship. The rest of the time he could be found in the street, or in a home, or in a bar, or in the neighborhood political club, or at the precinct police station, or in a candy store, or in some other place where people are. But he was told that he spent too much time with people, especially with some who were junkies or prostitutes or colored or poor or otherwise 'undesirable'. What happened to him is a measure of how deeply estranged the churches are from the world – and from Christ. What happened to him is a sign of how embarrassing the Gospel has become to the churches.

Christians must enter the common life of the world fully and unequivocally in order to know the Word of God, in order to witness to the Word of God in the world, in order to worship God at all. The several churches, now becoming so audible about their concern for the reunion of the Church, must become and be deeply and passionately immersed in service to the world if the unity of the Body of Christ is to be recovered and restored. For the sake of Christian unity, the churches need the world because the Word of God is present in the world anyway and already. And Christians individually and the churches severally can be, should be, immersed in the world's life to the extremity of giving up their own present lives for the world's sake. For the "ecumenical movement" this is of enormous practical significance: in giving up their present lives for the world, Christians will learn of unity. They will discover how to give up their lives for each other and for a better life, for a new life, for a renewed life together.

The Fear of God

Him we proclaim, warning everyone and teaching everyone in all wisdom, that we may present every man mature in Christ.

Colossians 1:28

The ministry of the Church as the Body of Christ in the world is the same as the ministry of Christ. The ministry of Christ is the ministry of a servant in the world and for the world – a servant of the world in the name of God.

Perhaps it is helpful to notice a few things about the ministry of Christ. One is that the ministry of Christ is a ministry of great extravagance – of a reckless, scandalous expenditure of His life for the sake of the world's life. Christ gives away His life. The world finds new life in His life and in His gift of His life to the world. His is not a very prudential life, not a very conservative life, not a very cautious life, not – by ordinary standards – a very successful life.

He shunned no one, not even adulterers, not even tax collectors, not even neurotics and psychotics, not even those tempted to suicide, not even alcoholics, not even poor people, not even beggars, not even lepers, not even those who ridiculed Him, not even those who betrayed Him, not even His own enemies. He shunned no one.

The words that tell of the ministry of Christ are words of sorrow, poverty, rejection, radical unpopularity. They are words of agony.

It seems ridiculous to apply such words to the ministry of churches nowadays. Yet where these words cannot be truthfully applied to the ministry of the churches today they must then be spoken against the churches to show how far the churches are from being the Body of Christ engaged in the ministry of Christ in the world.

The Church exists as the company of participants in God's witness to Himself in the world. The Church exists for the sake of the world into which God enters and in which He acts and for which He expends His own life. Those who are participants in the Church, those who are incorporated into this Body, those who are baptized into this company have not only the personal freedom to expend their own life without guile or calculation or fear of death – or any more minor prudence – but also, characteristically, they are indifferent to whether or not the churches maintain an amiable reputation in society, or whether or not the churches have much wealth and a sound investment program, or whether or not the churches, or the ecclesiastical authorities, have much political influence. On the contrary, Christians are suspicious of respectability and moderation and success and popularity. And this is so because the genius of the Christian life, both for a person and for the company of Christians, is the freedom constantly to be engaged in giving up its own life in order to give the world new life. All the questions of status and power and reputation, and all defensive, conservative and self-serving questions about preserving the institutional existence of the churches are matters of some indifference except insofar as they impede the ministry of the Body of Christ, entice people into false religion and a wrong understanding of what the Christian society is, and lure them into misleading notions of what the Christian life is all about.

How much or how often the churches are engaged in serving themselves instead of the world, that is, how far they have withdrawn from the ministry of the Body of Christ, are matters of practical consequence. For example, I had one day to fly to Boston to visit the Harvard Business School to give a lecture. I was late (some friends would say, as usual) in leaving my apartment to get out to the airport. Just as I was about to go, the telephone rang. I had not the will power not to answer it, in spite of my rush. It was a clergyman who was calling. "I have a woman in my office," he told me, "who is going to be evicted in the morning. Tell me what to do for her." I asked him a few questions and, as it turned out, the grounds for the eviction were the non-payment of the rent. The woman apparently had no money to pay her rent. She had, or asserted that she had, certain complaints against the landlord, but the complaints that she had were not sufficient, assuming that they could be legally established, to justify non-payment of the rent. They were no defense to the eviction, and if she wished to pursue them it would have to be done in a separate action against the landlord, apart from the eviction proceeding. By this time I was even more anxious about catching the airplane and said to the minister, "Well, sell one of your tapestries and pay the rent," and hung up and caught the plane. On the plane I thought the telephone conversation over and thought that perhaps I had been rude and too abrupt in answering the minister that way and I considered calling him back after landing to apologize. But by the time the plane landed at Logan Airport I had rejected that idea. My answer had not been rude or irresponsible. On the contrary, exactly what he and the people of his congregation, which does have several beautiful and valuable tapestries, must be free to do is to sell their tapestries to pay the rent – to pay somebody else's rent – to pay anybody's rent who can't pay their own rent. If they have that freedom, then, but only then, does the tapestry have religious significance; only then does the tapestry enrich and contribute to and express and represent the concern and care which Christians have in the name of God for the ordinary life of the world. The tapestry hanging in a church becomes and is a wholesome and holy thing, an appropriate and decent part of the scene of worship, only if the congregation which has the tapestry is free to take it down and sell it in order to feed the hungry or care for the sick or pay the rent or in any other way serve the world. The tapestry is an authentically Christian symbol only when it represents the freedom in Christ to give up any aspect of the inherited and present life of the institutional church, including, but not limited to, possessions, for the sake of the world.

The churches in America have many possessions, tapestries and otherwise, which they can have and hold with integrity in any Christian sense only insofar as they are free to give them up for the world as a witness to the ministry of Christ, as a sign of dying in Christ, as an honoring of the Word of God.

Ironically, this sort of freedom from possessions and property, but just as much, also, from considerations of reputation and status and political power and the like, is by no means an issue just for the churches in the affluent sectors of American society. It is a very serious issue as well for churches in the slums, in the inner city. There the churches, for the most part, have supposed that the inner city must become much more like the outer city before the Gospel can be heard. They have thought that mission follows charity. They have favored social reform and causes and crusades and postponed mission. I am all for changing the face of East Harlem and similar neighborhoods, but the mission of the Church depends not upon social reformation in these neighborhoods, as desperately as that is needed, but upon the presence of the Word of God in the society of the poor as it is right now. If the mere Gospel is not a whole salvation for the most afflicted person, it is no comfort to others in less affliction. Mission does not follow charity. Faith does not follow works either for donor or recipient; on the contrary, mission is itself the only charity which Christians have to offer the poor, the only work which Christian have to do.

The premise of most urban church work, it seems, is that in order for the Church to minister among the poor, the Church has to be rich, that is, to have specially trained personnel, huge budgets, many facilities, rummage to distribute, and a whole battery of social services. Rather, the opposite is the case. The Church must be free to be poor in order to minister among the poor. The Church must trust the Gospel enough to come among the poor with nothing to offer the poor except the Gospel, except the power to discern and the courage to expose the Gospel as it is already mediated in the life of the poor.

When the Church has the freedom itself to be poor among the poor, it will know how to use what riches it has. When the Church has that freedom, it will know also how to minister among the rich and powerful. When the Church has that freedom, it will be a missionary people again in all the world. When the Church has the freedom to go out into the world with merely the Gospel to offer the world, then it will know how to use whatever else it has – money and talent and buildings and tapestries and power in politics – as sacraments of its gift of its own life to the world, as tokens of the ministry of Christ.

Loneliness, Dread and Holiness

William Stringfellow, *Christian Century*, Vol 79 Oct 1962, pp.1220-22

Three times I besought the Lord about this, that it should leave me; but he said to me, 'My grace is sufficient for you, for my power is made perfect in weakness.

2 Corinthians 12:8-9a

Loneliness is as intimate and as common to humans as death. Loneliness is a person's specific apprehension of their own death in relation to the impending death of all people and all things. Loneliness is the experience in which a person's fear of their own personal death coincides with their fright at the death of everyone and everything else. Loneliness is not a unique nor an isolated experience; on the contrary, it is the ordinary but overwhelming anxiety that all relationships are lost. Loneliness does not deny or negate the existence of lives other than the life of the lonely one, but it so vividly anticipates the death of such other lives that they are no sustenance or comfort to the life and being of the one who suffers loneliness.

Loneliness is the most caustic, drastic and fundamental repudiation of God, the most elementary expression of original sin. There is no one who does not know loneliness. Yet there is no one who is alone.

Loneliness does not respect persons, but afflicts all – men and women, those of status and the derelicts, the adolescents and the old people, the single and the married, the learned and the illiterate – and, one might add, the clergy and the laity. It is an ordinary affliction, though perhaps more noticed and more readily admitted among some than others – among those, for instance, whose loneliness becomes so desperate as to be pathological, among those forgotten by society in prisons or hospitals or on skid rows, among both older and younger single folk.

Loneliness is, or seems to be, more evident in the city, since the largest group of people now migrating to the city are no longer distinguished by nationality or race but by the fact that they are single. These migrants are mainly young people – students or recent graduates, artists and professionals, white-collar workers of all sorts – coming to the city to work and live and look for each other. Along with older men and women – the widowed and the retired – they make single people a substantial part of the urban scene.

That the proportion of single people is larger in the city than elsewhere does not prove that loneliness is more prevalent there. But it is perhaps more apparent in the city; and the fictions which attach to the escape from loneliness are perchance pursued more publicly and more frantically. The very size of the city and the versatility of its life promise some therapy for loneliness and some distraction from it.

This matter is too profoundly subjective for me to pretend to be very analytical about it. But some of the fictions associated with loneliness can be identified, though they cannot be sharply distinguished one from another and are often simultaneously significant in the same person's loneliness.

There is, first, the fiction that loneliness is contingent upon time, that it essentially means unfilled or unused time, that it is a vacuum in which one exists between periods of occupation in work or play or in the absence of companions. Loneliness, here, is the experience of void. The void may be mere boredom, that is, activity for the sake of using up surplus time because of a shortage of work or play or companionship. Many just work. They leave their jobs only to sleep alone or eat alone; they try to remain so occupied and so preoccupied in work that the empty time is filled.

The exploitation of boredom in the city, the supply of things to do and places to go in order just to spend leftover time, is organized commercially in an elaborate fashion. Dance studios, health salons, clubs engaged in acquainting people with each other, private panics to which invitations can be purchased – these and many more traffic in boredom, profit from promising that time will be consumed for those who pay the price.

Meanwhile, on every corner is a bar – not the elegant places which cater to the transient lonely, but the little neighborhood taverns in which, night after night, sit side by side on rows of stools the very same people who live side by side in the same block or building, exchanging boredom for oblivion.

If one will, one can patronize more esoteric establishments with special resources – prostitutes or homosexuals or whatever one wants – and there relieve loneliness in lust. These are establishments often populated by those who realize that loneliness is more than the burden of time and who are beguiled by another fiction: that loneliness can be conquered by erotic infatuation. Here are folk, whether men or women, whether looking for the same or the other sex, for whom seduction becomes a way of life, who insist on the importance of what meets the eye – physique, clothes, the appearance of youth. Here are the lonely whose search for a partner is so dangerous, so stimulating and so exhausting that the search itself provides an apparent escape from loneliness. But when a partner is found for an hour or a night or a transient affair, the search immediately resumes, becomes compulsive. And while erotic companionship seems more appealing – and more human – than resignation to boredom, while touching another may be more intimate and more honest than watching another, none may really find their own identity in another, least of all in the body of another.

Perhaps this is the most absurd fiction of them all: the notion that is present, primitively, in erotic partnerships but also very often in other relationships – between parents and children, in friendship, in marriage – that one's own identity must be sought and can be found in another person. This is, of course, an idea of venerable origin – the Greeks thought that man and woman are two halves in pursuit of a whole person to be found in their joining. Today it is popularized, for example, in the ridiculous idealism of much instruction about 'Christian marriage', or in the disguised erotica published, say, in the *Ladies Home Journal*.

To hold that one takes one's identity from the person of another is to equate love with possession. In any such liaison fits of jealousy are appropriate and inevitable, for each time the other's attention or affection is drawn to somebody else, the one whose identity is taken from that other's life is damaged. At worst the fiction that one's identity is to be found in another is cannibalistic, a devouring of another; at best it is a possessive, if romantic, manipulation by one of another in the name of love.

None of these fictions significantly addresses the experience of loneliness, none is more than an illusory comfort for the lonely. Separately or together they are omens of the very reality of which loneliness is the foretaste: *death*. How could any of them then have power to answer loneliness? How could any do other to dramatize loneliness all the more? Is there any answer to loneliness?

Will you look for release in your work? It can fill the time but not the void. Work is the estrangement of people from the rest of creation. Work means the bondage of people to the rest of creation, a sign of death, as great a burden to a person as the isolation of people from each other which is time.

Will you turn then to leisure? Fool, leisure is merely a euphemism for work, embodying the same animosity between humanity and the rest of creation. Leisure – nonwork in any of its other varieties, for that matter – is as much an anticipation of death as work.

Perhaps another drink will help. Maybe a drink will induce you to forget that this loneliness is not the absence of others, but your presence among others where your presence is treated as absence. Perhaps another drink will help you forget that you are regarded as if you are dead. Perhaps another drink will let you forget you are forgotten.

Get some sex. If you find some, perchance you will find yourself too; if you find some, at least you will not be alone, though you will still be lonely. And if, after a while, you have no luck in finding either sex or yourself, your fatigue in the search will overcome both your desire and your need, and then at least you will be able to sleep alone again long enough to wake refreshed enough to resume the search. Live in the consolation of looking for what you need where it surely cannot be found and you will always harbor, if nothing else, a little hope. That is the way to die.

See a psychiatrist. You cannot cope with loneliness alone. Maybe, if you search yourself and your biography with a doctor's patience, you can find something or someone to blame yourself on. Anyway, you can explain your anxieties to such, even if they cannot absolve you of any guilt. Perhaps they can help you to abide your own death, even though they cannot save you from it.

Maybe you will find a lover. Any face that passes on the street might be your lover. Do you wonder how you look to those who pass? Do they wonder the same of you? Dare you speak or make any gesture? If you do, they may turn away. They may murder you when all you want is their love. No, loneliness is more familiar than annihilation, and thus seems more secure. Better stay where you are.

Try marriage. It is the more sensible course. You ought to be able to make a go of it. Lots of people have done so. No more returning to an empty room; there will be another to share the emptiness. And there may be more to share than emptiness.

Your better half may be the part of you that's missing. You may discover who you are in your mate or, failing that, in your offspring. And that would after all be better than dying as you are, alone.

Be more positive! Now, there's a thought. Defeat your loneliness by affirming that it does not exist. Hypnotize yourself. Make believe, as children do, and it will seem for a little while just as you pretend it is – until the rueful day when you realize that things are not as bad as they seem only because in fact they seem as bad as they are.

End it now. This living is not life; it is death. Why not salute the fact and dramatize it? Wherever you turn you see the face of death: all these disguises do not hide *that* face. All these temptations are emissaries of death. The presence of death is everywhere, the power of death is awful. Why not find out how great death is? End it all now. If death is so great, then this foretaste of death, this loneliness, will be ended in death. Then you won't be lonely anymore. Then you won't *be*.

Poor you! Pity yourself: everybody else does. Loathe the fact that you cannot remember who you are and so no one else can recognize you. Hate (hate is what pity is) the fact that you are someone other than the one you wish to be, someone other than the one you imagine would earn the love of others. You idiot! Love cannot be earned. No one deserves a gift, else where's the act of giving? Love is volunteered, and if you do not know that you are loved it is not you who are rejected, it is you who are repudiating the one who loves you. Pity yourself for that.

Pray. It is a last resort, I know. Still, nothing else dispels this gruesome desolation. But how do you do it? That's just the trouble, friend. Prayer is nothing you do; prayer is someone you are. Prayer is not about doing, but about being. Prayer is about being alone in God's presence. Prayer is being *so* alone that God is the only witness to your existence. The secret of prayer is God affirming your life. That, that alone, is incompatible with loneliness. If you pray, you cannot be lonely. Prayer *is* the last resort.

There is no one who does not know loneliness: even Jesus Christ. He did not succumb to loneliness because there is no one who is alone.

On the face of the Gospel narrative is the lonely Christ. Nobody greeted, nobody honored, nobody understood, nobody loved him, nobody celebrated his vocation. Nobody loved him for being the One he is. In his birth he was sought as an earthly ruler. He suffered the rebuke of Mary and Joseph when as a child he was found in the temple in discourse with the teachers. John the Baptist was bewildered and protested when Jesus submitted to baptism. It was rejection of Jesus when his relatives called on him to name them in preference to the crowd. He healed the sick, but both sick and well mistook his power. When he spoke in the temple he was not heard. The same temptations that visited him in the wilderness returned to taunt him in the political triumph of Palm Sunday, but his disciples were – as many are to this day – perplexed that he withstood such attractive temptations. Israel, which had boasted in her waiting for his coming, found him subversive when he came. Rome was an accomplice in his condemnation. At Gethsemane, while he was alone in prayer, his friends slept and his enemies plotted to destroy him. Judas betrayed him, Peter denied him, the others fled. A thief ridiculed him on the cross. The people had shouted for his death. Unwelcome, misunderstood, despised, rejected, unloved and misloved, condemned, betrayed, deserted, helpless, he was delivered to death as if he were alone.

In surrender to death, in hell, in that event in which the presence and power of death is most notorious, undisguised, militant, and pervasive, the reality and grace of God triumph. Christ descended into hell: Christ is risen from death.

In the submission of Christ to death, the power of death is dissipated. In the subjection of Christ to death, the dread is taken out of loneliness. Christ suffered loneliness without despair. And in the radical loneliness of Christ is the assurance that no one is alone.

In the event in which an individual is alone with personal death – when all others and all things are absent and gone – God's initiative affirms that very one's creation, and that person is given life anew. In the moment and place where God is least expected – in the barrenness and emptiness of death – God is imminent. It is in this event that one discovers that it is death which is alone, not oneself.

There is no one who does not know loneliness: even Jesus Christ; but Christ himself has shown that there is no one who is alone.

You are not alone. Do not be so proud any more of your loneliness; it is only the shadow of your death, and your death, your loneliness, is like the death of every other human. But your death is overpowered in the patience of God's love for you. Your fear that you are not loved does not negate the gift which God's love is. Your loneliness does not avoid God's love it only repudiates his love for you. You cannot leave God's presence. You are not alone.

Now you are free. You are free from the idol your own death becomes in loneliness. You are free from all the frantic escapes, free from trying to purchase love, free from anonymity. You are free now from searching because you have been found. You are free: your life found in the life of God. You are not alone.

Now you can love. Love yourself. That is the root of all other loves. Love yourself: that means your final acceptance of and active participation in God's love of you. Love yourself. If you love yourself you will become and be one who can love another. Love yourself and then your love of others will be neither suicidal nor destructive, neither jealous nor possessive; then your love of yourself will enable, enbody, enrich and elucidate your love of others, and your other loves will do the same to your self-love. And when you love others, tell them so, celebrate your love not only by words but by your life toward them and the whole world. Your specific love of another is verified and supported in your love of all others and of all things, even those which seem to be unlovable, unworthy to be loved. Let that be the manner of your witness to the One who persists in loving everyone though none is worthy, not even one. You are not alone.

Don't be afraid. There is no more to fear. Do not fear rejection. If you fear rejection by another you do not love that other; you are only being anxious for their love of you. Those who are free do not seek the love of others. They do not fear that their love will be rejected, for rejection – as we know from the night in which Christ was betrayed – does not destroy love and does not destroy the one who loves. Don't be afraid; you are not alone.

Now you are whole. Your work and the time you spend not working both become sacraments of the solidarity between yourself and the rest of creation, sacraments of the reconciliation wrought for you by Christ. Now work and leisure become virtually indistinguishable from worship – that is, from the enjoyment of God's love not just for you but for all, including those who do not yet enjoy God's love for themselves or for anyone or anything else. The enjoyment of God in this way is, of course, the estate of holiness. Holiness does not mean that you are any better than anyone else. Holiness is not about goodness; holiness is not common pietism. Holiness is not about pleasing God, even less about appeasing God. Holiness is about enjoying God. Holiness is the integrity of greeting, confessing, honoring and trusting God's presence in all events and in any event, no matter what, no matter when, no matter where.

Therefore, rejoice. Reckon your weakness as praise of God's power, endure suffering in joy, risk your life on the veracity of Christ, count your loneliness a means of grace.

A Sacramental Ethic

William Stringfellow, *An Ethic for Christians*, pp.53-64

Babylon!
Jerusalem!!
Apocalypse!!!
Eschaton!!!!

How do these names, these events, have practical consequence for the United States of America – or for any other principality – in the decade of the seventies? Daily the American nation is sorely beset by crises of fatal potential for both human life and institutional existence. And if that, indeed, suggests basic Babylonian similarities and invites apocalyptic descriptions, where in America is Jerusalem discerned? How can the eschatological hope be affirmed? What does hope mean ethically? Or politically?

On obvious, ominous, urgent fronts, society in America is right now desperately beleaguered by war and the entrenched commerce of war, by ecological corruption and the population problem, by profound racism and urban chaos, by technology and unemployability, by inflation and taxation. And all of these issues are compounded by unaccountability, secrecy, and practiced deception in government, by manifold threats to established authority and intimidating official abuse of the rule of law, by vested intransigence to significant change and primary recourse to violence by agents of conformity and advocates of repression as well as some few professed revolutionaries. If a person looks to Revelation – especially its Babylon passages – as a political as much as theological tract at the time and in the circumstances in which it was uttered, is that of any help now, in this American situation? If, as is urged here, the biblical Babylon represents the essential estate of all nations and powers, verified empirically in the moral condition of any nation at any time in history, and if the biblical Jerusalem refers to Christ's Church in her vocation as the holy nation, standing apart from but ministering to the secular powers, how is that edifying to a Christian (or anyone else) who is today an American citizen? How must that concern us in decisions and conduct affecting allegiance to the nation, the claims of civil obedience, assent to prevalent social purposes, response to the pressures for conformity, participation in the rituals of national vanity, rendering honor to incumbent political authority, the prospects for reform or other change, the efficacy of protest, the tactics of resistance? Again, how does the biblical juxtaposition of Babylon and Jerusalem set a precedent for and inform the life-style and witness of the Church of Christ in America now? What do the ethics of biblical politics have to do concretely with the politics of the principalities and powers in America now?

To all such queries, biblical politics *categorically* furnish no answers.

The ethics of biblical politics offer no basis for divining specific, unambiguous, narrow, or ordained solutions for any social issue. Biblical theology does not deduce 'the will of God' for political involvement or social action. The Bible – if it is esteemed for its own genius – does not yield 'right' or 'good' or 'true' or 'ultimate' answers. The Bible does not do that in seemingly private or personal matters; even less can it be said to do so in politics or institutional life.

This is not to say that biblical people, living on the contemporary scene in America or anywhere else, are thus consigned to holy ambivalence, well-intentioned indecision, or benign negligence in social crisis or public controversy. This does not counsel, comfort, or condone apathy, default, withdrawal, or any type of quietism (which, appearances to the contrary, are forms of political commitment, not options of abstention from politics). This does declare that the biblical witness affords no simplistic moral theology, no pietistic version of social ethics. Folk who yearn for the supposed reassurance of that kind of ethics can resort to the nation's civil religion or one of its legion equivalents; they will find no support or encouragement in the Bible.

The impotence of any scheme of ethics boasting answers of ultimate connotation or asserting the will of God is that time and history are not truly respected as the context of decision-making. Instead they are treated in an abstract, fragmented, selective, or otherwise, arbitrary version hung together at most under some illusory rubric of 'progress', or 'effectiveness', or 'success'. From a biblical vantage point as much as from an empirical outlook, this means a drastic incapacity to cope with history as the saga in which death as a moral power claims sovereignty over human beings and nations and all creatures. It means a failure to recognize time as the epoch of death's worldly reign, a misapprehension of the ubiquity of fallenness throughout the whole of Creation, and, in turn, a blindness to imminent and recurrent redemptive signs in the everyday life of this world.

Meanwhile, biblically speaking, the singular, straightforward issue of ethics – and the elementary topic of politics – is *how to live humanly during the Fall*. Any viable ethic – which is to say, any ethics worthy of human attention and practice, any ethics which manifest and verify hope – is both individual and social. It must deal with human decision and action in relation to the other creatures, notably the principalities and powers in the very midst of the conflict, distortion, alienation, disorientation, chaos, decadence of the Fall.

The ethics typically concocted from religion or ideology or philosophy, including the Christianized, if unbiblical, editions of the same, do not meet this necessity. In fact, they repudiate time and common history as the sphere of ethical concern and political action in multifarious ways. They may focus upon asserted prospects beyond history, outside of familiar time (like promises of afterlife or visions of a hypothetical ideal society). They may deny the moral significance of time as the era of the Fall and diminish history as the story of the Fall (as where imperial myths or doctrines of progress prevail). They may become literally reactionary by reverting to nostalgia (as when the past, in either fictional or factual variation, is posited as social model or goal), or they may suffer no eschatological insight (being oblivious to the possibility of human transcendence of time within history) and remain, hence, radically irrelevant to immediate mundane issues.

Biblical ethics do not pretend the social or political will of God; biblical politics do not implement 'right' or 'ultimate' answers. In this world, the judgment of God remains God's own secret. No creature is privy to it, and the task of social ethics is not to second guess the judgment of God.

It is the inherent and redundant frustration of any pietistic social ethics that the ethical question is presented as a conundrum about the judgment of God in given circumstances. Human beings attempting to cope with *that* ethical question are certain to be dehumanized. The Bible does not pose any such riddles nor aspire to any such answers; instead, in biblical context, such queries are transposed, converted, rendered new. In the Bible, the ethical issue becomes simply: *how can a person act humanly now?* Be cautioned once more that by putting the ethical question so starkly, no pretext is furnished for reading it as a private or individualistic query. Indeed, the use of the adverb *humanly* renders the question political; there is, in the biblical witness, no way to act humanly in isolation from the whole of humanity, no possibility for a person to act humanly without becoming implicated with all other human beings.

Let me state the same concern somewhat differently, in the context of biblical politics. Here the ethical question juxtaposes the witness of the holy nation – Jerusalem – to the other principalities, institutions and the other nations – as to which Babylon is a parable. It asks: how *can the Church of Jesus Christ celebrate human life in society now?*

I hope this manner of expressing the basic Concern of social ethics, as posed biblically in contrast with various nonbiblical or pagan constructions, sufficiently emphasizes the vocational aspect of ethical decision and political action. The ethical wisdom of human beings cannot, and need not, imitate or preempt or displace the will of God, but is magnificently, unabashedly, and merely human. The ethical discernment of humans cannot anticipate and must not usurp the judgment of God, but is an existential event, an exercise of conscience – transient and fragile. To make such an affirmation and confession involves a radical reverence for the vocation of God and an equally radical acceptance of the vocation to be human. Moreover, it is the dignity of this ethical posture which frees human beings, in their decisions and tactics, to summon the powers and principalities, and similar creatures, to their vocation – the enhancement of human life in society (Gen. 1:20-31; cf. Mark 10:42-43).

Where is Jerusalem?

Confronting the powers with their creaturehood – admonishing the principalities about their vocation as creatures called to serve the social need of human beings – is a requisite for Jerusalem. Such action can perhaps be most readily perceived in circumstances where the Church of Christ can be affirmed as the exemplary society or holy nation living in the midst of, yet set apart from, the nations and assorted principalities of the world: where Jerusalem is living juxtaposed with Babylon.

Yet surveying the contemporary churchly scene in the United States, one is much tempted to forego mention of the Church. Indeed, I notice that this is substantially what both adherents of social gospel pietism and zealots of evangelicalism have done while opting for, as they each do in their own ways, a supposed redemption by osmosis. I sympathize with their vain exaggerations of the efficacy of individualistic change and commitment, decision, and action. The Church, actually functioning as the ecumenical community or holy institution, is so hard to find or identify. If one speaks of Babylon, there is little hindrance in locating Babylon; it is not so very difficult to discern the Babylonian character of nations or other principalities. But if one bespeaks Jerusalem, as the new or renewed society of mature humanity, where is this Jerusalem? The answer cannot be in some spiritualized, spooky, sentimental conception of Church. The biblical precedents in the Old Testament witness and in Pentecost are not of some nebulous, ethereal, idealistic, otherworldly, or disembodied Church but of a visible, historic community and institution. They signal a new nation incarnating and sacramentalizing human life in society freed from bondage to the power of death. Where, nowadays, in America, is there such a Jerusalem reality of the Church?

It requires more bravado than I can muster to respond to this question by identifying *any* of the churches or sects or denominations or ecclesiastical principalities of the American status quo with the Jerusalem aspect of the Church of Christ. In their practical existence, the familiar, inherited churchly institutions here bear little resemblance – even residually – to the Church as holy nation. In fact, some aboriginal American religions falsely impute the biblical vocation of the holy nation to America, in place of the Church of Christ. If Jerusalem and Babylon are each regarded as parables, it is the Babylon image which is most apt for the conventional American churches – along with many other comparable powers within the precincts of Babylon, like the Pentagon (to name a rival bureaucracy), or the Mafia (to mention a rival in wealth), or the Teamsters Union (as an ethical rival). With these and similar principalities, the churchly enterprises are much engaged in elaborate worship of death. They are vainglorious about reputation, status, prosperity, success; they are eager to conform, solicitous of patronage from the political regime, derisive of the biblical witness, accommodated to American culture. In fact, the American churchly institutions, for the most part, are not truly involved in apostasy – that is, in betraying the faith – or even in hypocrisy – that is, in practicing something other than what is preached. There can be no apostasy, if the faith has not been upheld; there can be no hypocrisy, if the gospel has not been preached.

The problem is more elementary and has to do with the specific cultural origins of so many of the American sects and denominations. It is not surprising to hear their propagation of the civic religion of the nation since their own traditions were generated in American culture, in Babylon, and not in Pentecost or in the subsequent biblical witness in history. So it is not that such "churches" have abandoned the gospel they once upheld and have become acculturated and conformed, but that they have been from their origins American cultural productions or Babylonian shrines.

I do not hereby dismiss categorically the whole of American Christendom. I do not suppose, either, that none of the churches on the American scene have memory of the biblical witness, because some do, notably the immigrant (as contrasted with the indigenous) churches. I do not conclude that no Christians can be found on churchly premises, including those which most blatantly are Babylonian, shrines. I am saying that if you look for the Jerusalem reality of Church among the established ecclesiastical and churchly bodies, what you will find is chaos. Yet in the very same places, as well as elsewhere, can also be identified and affirmed some congregations and paracongregations, some happenings, some celebrations, some communities, some human beings who do suffer and enjoy the Jerusalem vocation in the midst of the chaos. The bizarre estate of the American churches does not mean, after all, that the Holy Spirit, so militant at Pentecost, has never visited America. Whether secreted within the established churches or detached from them, there lives in America a confessing movement – dynamic and erratic, spontaneous and radical, audacious and immature, committed if not altogether coherent, ecumenically open and often experimental, visible here and there and now and then, but unsettled institutionally, most of all – enacting a fearful hope for human life in society.

A specific instance of the emerging confessing movement in America can be found in the jails and prisons. In many of these, communities of mutual help and social concern have come into being and, among some prisoners, an intercessory witness, which is virtually monastic in character. What is taking place within prisons is deeply rooted in and informed by Bible study. The same is true of aspects of the confessing movement evident among young Christians such as the 'Post-Americans'. The charismatic renewal, immature though it yet may be, must also be comprehended within the reality of a confessing movement, along with some of the house churches or similar gatherings.

I have some hesitation, I must admit candidly, in using any name or term – like 'confessing movement' – to refer to manifestations of the Jerusalem vocation of the Church. Naming any happening as Church tends to diminish the spontaneity and momentary character of the reality of the Jerusalem event in history. Or, to put the same concern differently, while Babylon represents the principality in bondage to death in time – and time is actually a form of *that* bondage – Jerusalem means the emancipation of human life in society from the rule of death and breaks through time, transcends time, anticipates within time the abolition of time. Thus the integrity or authenticity of the Jerusalem event in common history is always beheld as if it were a singular or momentary or unique happening. To be more concrete about it, if a congregation somewhere comes to life as Jerusalem at some hour, that carries no necessary implications for either the past or the future of that congregation. The Jerusalem occurrence is sufficient unto itself. There is – then and there – a transfiguration in which the momentary coincides with the eternal, the innocuous becomes momentous and the great is recognized as trivial, the end of history is revealed as the fulfillment of life here and now, and the whole of creation is beheld as sanctified.

So far as the human beings who are participants and witnesses in any manifestation of the Jerusalem reality of the Church are concerned, nothing similar may have happened before and nothing similar may happen again. But that does not detract from the event; it only emphasizes that the crux of the matter is the transcendence of time, rather than temporal continuity. This is why, obviously, I have earlier said that even though it becomes ludicrous to argue that the established churches in America represent Jerusalem, nevertheless – *here and there and now and then* – Jerusalem *is* apparent and militant on the scene of American Christendom. And, if it be any comfort, much the same thing must be said of the situation in earliest days of the Church, as the Book of the Acts of the Apostles verifies (Acts 15:1-21; cf. Gal. 1:6-17, 2:1-10).

However chary it may be necessary to be about the whereabouts of Jerusalem both within and without the churchly status quo, it is not possible to avoid the issue, as individualistic dropouts and assorted purists and pietists are tempted to do. There is no unilateral, private, insulated, lonely, or eccentric Christian life. There is only the Christian as the member of the whole body; the Christian vocation for every single Christian is inherently ecumenical; the exclusive context of biblical ethics is biblical politics; even when Christians act apparently alone they do so as surrogates for the Church; baptism signifies the public commitment of a person to humanity.

These are all expressions of the necessity of facing the question of how, concretely, the Jerusalem reality of the Church becomes manifest, from time to time and from place to place; these are various ways of affirming the corporateness of the Christian vocation and of emphasizing that ethical decisions and acts are essentially vocational – that is, they have to do with becoming and being human and not with guessing or imitating God's will. Of course, I include in this vocational designation of ethical conduct the exercise of conscience, though I am mindful that conscientious witness is very often misconstrued as the most private and, even, idiosyncratic insight. The stereotypical response to an act of conscience is an accusation of arrogance by which someone who has done nothing denounces the conscientious for claiming moral superiority. That may be an appropriate construction of the nature and operation of conscience so far as the world is concerned, but it is not the biblical comprehension of conscience. Biblically, the exercise of conscience is not at all individualistic but the implementation of a person's elemental responsibility to human life, both one's own humanity and that of all others, as the famous commandment mentions (Matt. 22:34-40). It is not only not idiosyncratic, but rather the opposite, since the conscientious stand does not separate from but instead identifies with the common interest of human life. And the act of conscience is not inherently arrogant, as the conformed or the lazy or the fearful assert, because it strives not to approximate divine judgment but to represent mature human will.

There is a kind of confusion which prompts the thought that conscience is eccentric and arrogant rather than political and, actually, very humble – an enactment of the dual commandment, in fact. The principal reason for it is the false presupposition which frequently modifies ethical opinion that it is a necessity to be consistent and that a decision made today must be able to be rationalized in terms of prior actions, just as what may be determined tomorrow is narrowed to what can be logically or abstractly reconciled with what has been said and done today.

This loyalty to consistency may be the way of the Greek mind, or of the American mentality, but it is alien to the biblical style. It may be apropos in philosophy, ideology, or, sometimes, religion, but it is not a feature of the gospel. It may contain morbid appeal for those professing Christianity who are nevertheless hung up in anxiety about their own justification, but consistency is no virtue for Christians. The ethical issue, whatever the particular existential circumstances, biblically speaking, concerns how to live, what to decide, how to act humanly in the midst of the Fall. That question occurs and recurs in every moment, and the response to it is always in each moment, imminent, and always breaking through the moment, transcendent. By dwelling upon the simultaneous imminence and transcendence of ethical decision, I do not gainsay experience or edification or maturation. In each of those senses, there is connection between the decisions and deeds of this day and the day before and the day to come (if it comes!!). But those relationships are not reduced to some blind adherence to consistency. Indeed, where such a rubric of consistency is imposed or assumed it is evidence of a drastic failure to take seriously the history of this world as the saga of the Fall and of a blindness to redemptive signs within that same saga. Where consistency prevails, the incarnational character of common history is ignored.

In biblical ethics, a Christian is implicated in merely but truly human decisions. These are unpredictable; extemporaneous; serious but not pretentious; conscientious but not presumptuous; dynamic and never immutable; historically serious and realistic and, hence, often inconsistent; momentary or imminent and yet transcendent, commonplace, and sacramental.

A Christian lives politically within time, on the scene of the Fall, as an alien in Babylon, in the midst of apocalyptic reality. Coincidentally, a biblical person lives politically, on the identical scene, as member and surrogate of Christ's Church, as a citizen of Jerusalem, the holy nation which is already and which is vouchsafed, during the eschatological event. In ethical decision and in political action, in this world, a Christian is always, as it were, saying *no* and *yes* simultaneously. A Christian says *no* to the power of death but in the same breath bespeaks the authority of life freed from bondage to death. A Christian exposes the reign of death in Babylon while affirming the aspiration for new life intuitive in all human beings and inherent in all principalities. A Christian confounds the wiles and stratagems of death by insistently, defiantly, resiliently living as no less and none other than a human being; a Christian enjoins the works of death by living in human fulfillment now. A Christian warns of the autonomy of God's judgment while rejoicing in the finality of God's mercy. A Christian suffers whatever death can do while celebrating the resurrection from death here and now.

One marvelous example of the biblical genius in discerning the ethical as the sacramental has, of course, been rendered at the outset of this book, in citing the jubilation of the heavenly chorus at Babylon's doom. The ethical question *what is to be done when the great city dies?* is answered in a sacramental way – *sing praise of the sovereignty of God over all nations*. In the event, the *no* which issues against death *is* at once the *yes* which celebrates life as a gift.

Christ and the Powers of Death

William Stringfellow, *Free in Obedience*, pp.49-59, 62-4, 70-73

Now in putting everything in subjection to man, he left nothing out of his control. As it is, we do not yet see everything in subjection to him. But we see Jesus, who for a little while was made lower than the angels, crowned with glory and honor because of the suffering of death, so that by the grace of God he might taste death for everyone.

Hebrews 2:8b-9

Christ defeats the temptations of worldly power with which death confronts him on Palm Sunday; in the days immediately following he is delivered to death by one of his disciples, condemned to death by the ruling authorities of the nations of Israel and Rome, and abandoned to death by the rest of his disciples.

Christ is neither delivered nor abandoned by his disciples into the hands of just some evil, envious, or frightened people: he is given over, and he surrenders, to Israel and Rome. And in the encounter of Christ with these powers there is exposed the relationship between Christ and all principalities and powers. The ecclesiastical and civil rulers who accuse, try, condemn, and execute Christ act not essentially for themselves as individuals, but as representatives – indeed, as servants – of the principalities. It is, of course, in the name of these powers that Christ is put on trial. He is accused of subverting and undermining the nation, of threatening the nation's existence, survival, and destiny.

That *this* is the accusation should, by the way, dispose of the legend, so popular in modern treatments of the trial of Christ both in Good Friday sermons and popular secular versions of the event, that Christ is innocent of any offense, and tried and condemned because of some corruption or failure or miscarriage of justice. Of the charge against him, Christ is guilty beyond any doubt.

In any case, the significant aspect of the trial is that it is not just an encounter between Christ and some individuals who were his enemies. The most decisive clash in all history is this one between Christ and the principalities and powers of this world, represented by and symbolized in Israel and Rome.

The understanding of principalities and powers is lost nowadays in the churches, though, I observe, not so much so outside the churches. About a year ago, for example, I was invited to lecture at the Business School of Harvard University; earlier on the same day, I also met informally with some students at the Divinity School. Since graduates of the Business School live their professional lives and work so obviously within the spheres of dominance of great corporate and commercial principalities, I decided to speak there about the meaning of the principalities. Although the Business School students were not especially theologically sophisticated, and certainly none had been theologically trained, they displayed an awareness, intelligence, and insight with respect to what principalities are and what are the issues between principalities and human beings. Yet, when the same matters had been discussed earlier with the divinity students, I found that most of them felt that such terms as 'principalities and powers', 'ruling authorities', 'demons', 'world rulers of the present darkness', 'angelic powers', and the like – terms so frequently used in the Bible – were archaic imagery having no reference to contemporary realities.

It appears, in other words, to be widely believed in the churches in the United States that the history of redemption is encompassed merely in the saga of relationships between God and human beings. What there is of contemporary Protestant moral theology typically ignores any attempt to account for, identify, explicate, and relate the self to the principalities, although empirically the principalities seem to have an aggressive, in fact possessive, ascendancy in American life. Because the biblical references to principalities and angelic powers are so prominent and because the powers themselves enjoy such dominance in everyday life, their meaning and significance cannot be left unexamined.

What are principalities and powers? What is their significance in the creation and in the Fall? What is their relationship to human sin? How are these powers related to the presence and power of death in history? What is the meaning of the confrontation between Christ and the principalities? Does a Christian have any freedom from their dominion? There can be no serious, realistic, or biblical comprehension of the witness of the church in the world unless such questions as these are raised and pondered.

What are Principalities?

There is nothing particularly mysterious, superstitious, or imaginary about principalities, despite the contemporary failure to discuss them theologically. The realities to which the biblical terms *principalities and powers* refer are quite familiar to modern society, though they may be called by different names. What the Bible calls *principalities and powers* are called in contemporary language *ideologies, institutions*, and *images*.

A principality, whatever its particular form and variety, is a living reality, distinguishable from human and other organic life. It is not made or instituted by human beings but, as with humans and all creation, made by God for God's own pleasure.

In the biblical understanding of creation, the principalities or angelic powers, together with all other forms of life, are given by God into human dominion and are means through which human beings rejoice in the gift of life by acknowledging and honoring God, who gives life to all and to the whole of creation. The dominion of humanity over the rest of creation, including the angelic powers, means the engagement of human beings in the worship of God as the true, realized, and fulfilled human life and, at the same time and as part of the same event, the commitment by them of all things within their dominion to the very same worship of God, to the very same actualization of true life for all things. All persons, all angels, and all things in creation have origination, integrity, and wholeness of life in the worship of God.

Just as people differ in their capacities in one sense or another, just as there are varieties in human life, so also there are varieties of principalities that can be distinguished one from another, though they all retain certain common characteristics. Let us consider various examples of principalities.

Principalities as Images

One kind of principality is designated by the word *image. An* obvious example of this sort is the image that comes to be associated with some celebrity and bears the same name as the celebrity. Thus, there was for a time the movie star named Marilyn Monroe. The person is now dead, but the image 'Marilyn Monroe' is by no means dead. Not only have certain memories either personal or public survived the death of this person, but the name survives; the name, in fact, attaches to a reality that was given new life when the person of that name died. The image called 'Marilyn Monroe' is not dead because there were two lives that claimed and used that name: one a principality, the other a person; only the latter died, the former is, if anything, livelier than ever.

All the talk of Marilyn Monroe as the great American 'sex goddess' or as 'the symbol of youth' is not just the prose of Hollywood journalists, whether they realize it or not. Marilyn Monroe, whoever she was as a person, was and is a genuine idol, an entity, bearing the same name and likeness as the person, with an existence, character, and power quite distinguishable from the person who bore the name.

An image is a very common variety of angelic power, though often of much less dignity and influence in the world than other kinds of principalities. In fact, every person is accompanied in life by an image; a person is often controlled or destroyed by that image, and invariably it survives the individual's life.

Once in a while the public image of a person becomes much more than just an idol, becomes a principality of such magnitude that the image is comparable to an institutional or ideological principality. Adolf Hitler, for instance, whoever was the person by that name, became and is to this day such a principality. And in terms of the relationship between Hitler the person and Hitler the principality, it may well be that long before his actual suicide the person named Hitler had been wholly obliterated by the principality named Hitler; that the person had, indeed, been possessed by a demon of that name; and that the devastation and massacre wrought in the name of Hitler was not the work of just some dark genius of the man, nor even of the man's insanity or gross criminality, but of the awesome demonic power that possessed him.

In any case, the form of principality identifiable as the public image bearing the name of a person exists independently of that person (though the person may be wholly dependent upon the principality). The form is distinguishable from the person, lies beyond control, and is in conflict with the person until the person surrenders life in one fashion or another to the principality. The principality requires not only recognition and adulation as an idol from movie fans or voters or the public, but also demands that the person of the same name give up his or her life as a person to the service and homage of the image. And when that surrender is made, the person in fact dies, though not yet physically. For at that point one is literally possessed by one's own image. The demand, then, made in the conflict between the principality and the personality is one in which the whole life of the person is surrendered to the principality and is given over to the worship of the image.

Principalities as Institutions

The institutional principalities also make claims upon human beings for idolatrous commitment in that the moral principle that governs any institution – a great corporation, a government agency, an ecclesiastical organization, a union, utility, or university – is its own survival. Everything else must finally be sacrificed to the cause of preserving the institution, and it is demanded of everyone who lives within its sphere of influence – officers, executives, employees, members, customers, and students – that they commit themselves to the service of that end, the survival of the institution.

This relentless demand of the institutional power is often presented in benign forms to a person under the guise that the bondage to the institution benefits the person in some way, but that does not make the demand any less dehumanizing. I recall, for example, the situation of a law school classmate of mine. When he was graduated he accepted a position with one of the great Wall Street law firms, an institutional power in its own right, though engaged in serving some of the great corporate principalities. During the summer, before he began work at the firm, he married. He did not consult or inform his superiors in the firm about his marriage prior to the event. Later, when he reported for work and the firm learned that he was now married, he was told that he should have consulted the employer before marrying, but, since he was married, it would be advisable for him and his wife to refrain from having any children for at least two or three years. Furthermore, for the sake of his advancement in the firm, he should and would want to devote all of his time both in the office and in his ostensibly personal life to the service of the firm, and children might interfere with this. In the end, the claim for service that an institution makes upon human beings is an invitation to surrender their lives in order that the institution be preserved and prosper. It is an invitation to bondage.

Principalities as Ideologies

Ideology is perhaps the most self-evident principality in the world at the present time. Communism, fascism, racism, nationalism: all these are principalities and powers. Humanism, capitalism, democracy, rationalism – though Americans think of these as benevolent powers – are also principalities and share all the essential characteristics of those ideologies to which America's enemies are committed.

Communism – or, more precisely Marxism as distinguished from Leninism, Stalinism, or post-Stalin Soviet communism – is a particularly lucid illustration of the nature of an ideological principality. Marxism asserts that it reveals and upholds the secret of history, that the destiny (literally, salvation) of all humanity and all nations is to be found and fulfilled in the ascendancy and dominion of Marxism in the world. It claims sovereignty over all history, and the moral significance of any person's life (or, for that matter, the existence of any institution or nation) is determined in relation to the power and prosperity of the Marxist ideology. This ideology therefore, requires of people, institutions, and nations an unequivocal and militant obeisance, a sacrifice of all other supposedly lesser causes and rights to the idol of Marxism.

Other totalitarian ideologies have, of course, represented the same sort of example of the principalities and powers that Marxism today represents. But do not suppose that the ideology of American society, though more diffuse and less systematic and theoretical than Marxism or the other totalitarian ideologies, is any different in its essential characteristics as a principality. Americans are now constantly, incessantly, and somewhat vehemently assailed with the word that the ultimate moral significance of their individual lives is embodied in and depends upon the mere survival of the American nation and its 'way of life'. There seems, to me at least, less and less of a public consensus about the content and style of that American way of life, just as there is an obviously increasingly intense controversy within the communist world as to what the Marxist way of life is and is to be. But that only means that the survival of the nation as such becomes the idol, the chief object of loyalty, service, and idolatry. Or, to put it a bit differently, the historic ideological realities in American history, those of capitalism and democracy, are now perhaps displaced by elementary nationalism. But in any case the preeminent factor in terms of which, it is claimed, human beings will find their own justification is in service to the nation, in the offering of all other things for the sake of national survival. Or, in the inaugural words of President Kennedy: "Ask not what your country can do for you; ask what you can do for your country."

It should be recognized that in describing the principalities and powers in terms of the realities that are nowadays called images, institutions, or ideologies, no attempt is intended to distinguish sharply the varieties of principalities. Frequently, one will have characteristics of the others. Although according to these descriptions the principality bearing Hitler's name would be called an image, this was, as has been pointed out, a principality that had the attributes of ideological and institutional principalities. For example, every nation is a principality, but it would be ridiculous to identify a nation as just an institutional power, although it is that clearly when one considers it in the sense of the governmental structures in a society. At the same time, the nation is associated with ideological powers and partakes of the nature of them – the American nation with the ideological elements of democracy and capitalism, the Soviet nation with the ideological forces called communism, some of the new nations of Africa and Asia with the ideologies of nationalism, and so on. Sometimes, too, the principality of the nation is, as it were, personified in the image of a ruler. Thus in France, De Gaulle *is*, as he himself seems fond of mentioning, France. And that is not only embodied in the constitutional institutions of the French nation but in the image of De Gaulle himself.

The Meaning of the Demonic

Like all people and all things, the angelic powers and principalities are fallen and are become demonic powers. *Demonic* does not mean evil; the word refers rather to death, to fallenness. An angelic power in its fallen estate is called a demonic power because it is a principality existing in the present age in a state of alienation from God, cut off from the life originating in His life, separated from its own true life, and, thus, being in a state of death. In the Fall, every human being, every principality, every thing exists in a condition of estrangement from its own life, as well as from the lives of all other human beings, powers, and things. In the Fall, the whole of creation is consigned to death.

The separation from life, the bondage to death, the alienation from God that the Fall designates is not simply to be accounted for by human sin. The Fall is not just the estate in which humans reject God and exalt themselves, as if they were like God. The term does not merely mean the pretensions of human pride. It is all that and something more. The Fall is also the awareness of human beings of their estrangement from God, themselves, each other, and all things, and their pathetic search for God or some substitute for God within and outside themselves and each other in the principalities and in the rest of creation. So human beings, in their fallenness, are found sometimes idolizing themselves, sometimes idolizing snakes, bugs, other creatures, or natural phenomena, or sometimes idolizing nation, ideology, race, or one of the other principalities.

The search is pathetic because it is futile. The principalities are themselves consigned to death just as much as the people who worship them. Thus, the idolatry of the demonic powers by humans turns out always to be a worship of death.

To put it another way, that dominion that human beings receive from God over the rest of creation (including their dominion over the principalities) is lost to them in the Fall and, as it were, reversed, so that now the principalities exercise dominion over human beings and claim in their own names and for themselves idolatrous worship from human beings. People do not create the principalities nor do they control them; on the contrary, people exist in this world in bondage to the principalities. No one escapes enduring the claims for allegiance and service of the principalities. For a person to live in the state of fallenness is to endure these very claims.

Whatever other distinctions may be made among the various principalities, remember that they are themselves fallen and demonic; the substance of the claim for idolatry that all principalities assert against human life is the same. Concretely, each principality boasts that people will find the meaning and fulfillment of human life in service to the principality and to that which abets its survival; a profound concern for self-survival is the governing morality of every principality. This comes first. To this all other interests must be sacrificed; from this all else, including an individual's life and work, takes its significance; by this is a person judged.

The principalities claim, in other words, sovereignty over human life and history. Therefore, they not only compete and conflict with one another for the possession and domination of the lives of human beings, but they also deny and denounce the sovereignty of God. But do not let the arrogance of the idols conceal this fact: when a principality claims moral pre-eminence in history or over a person's life, it represents an aspiration for salvation from death and a hope that service to the idol will give existence a meaning somehow transcending death.

Christ and the Principalities

Although the clash between Christ and the principalities in his trial and execution is the decisive and normative encounter, it is not at all the only occasion in the historic ministry of Christ when he is confronted by the principalities. The final showdown is again and again foreshadowed in Christ's life on earth.

The apprehension with which he is regarded by the worldly authorities during the Palm Sunday celebration and during Holy Week is first exposed in the consternation and rage with which Herod received the news of Christ's coming into the world. At the same time, remember that it is part of the authentic miracle of Christmas that those who gathered at the stable to adore him do so as representatives of the whole of creation, as emissaries of all humans and all creatures and all things. Those who come to worship and honor Christ in his birth include the magi who come as ambassadors of the principalities of the world. For a moment, as it were, in the Christmas event the sovereignty of Christ over all the world is revealed, and it is in that event that the world has a glimpse of the very restoration of creation from the Fall, a foretaste of the world become the Kingdom of God.

The lordship of Christ is disclosed in the adoration in the Christmas miracle, but the hysteria and hostility of Herod at Christ's coming into the world foreshadows the later encounters between Christ and the principalities. The time of Christ's temptation in the wilderness as a particularly significant episode has already been mentioned. But, in addition to that, Christ confronts the principalities when he stills the tempest, heals the sick, frees the demoniac, upsets the traditions of Israel by eating with sinners, or shows that he is Lord of the Sabbath. And, Christ's wilderness temptation is repeated in Palm Sunday. Yet that is not the last encounter between Christ and the principalities, for he goes to cleanse the temple, and Lazarus is raised from death. Then, betrayed and forsaken to death by his disciples, condemned to death by the rulers and crucified and buried, he descends into hell – into the event in which the presence and power of death is most militant, pervasive, ruthless, and undisguised.

In some of the episodes, as in the wilderness, the crucifixion, and the descent into hell, death openly confronts Christ; in others, Christ is visited by one or another of the principalities as emissaries of death. In all of these encounters, the principalities represent the awesome and manifold powers of death.

The victor in each specific encounter is Christ. That is important because it means that the power of Christ over death is not merely a transcendence of death as the terminal experience or as biological extinction. Thinking of the resurrection as having reference only to the crucifixion and entombment of Christ (the terminal event of his earthly life) underlies the wistful, vain, and false ideas about the immortality of the soul or life after death that so violate the gospel and corrupt the minds of many church people. Each specific confrontation between Christ and death and between Christ and one of the principalities as one of the powers of death foreshadows the resurrection, exposes and heralds the overwhelming authority over death that Christ has and holds from the beginning of time to the end of time. And the resurrection encompasses and represents all of these particular historic encounters in a single, consummate, and indeed cosmic disclosure of the triumph of Christ over death.

The resurrection is impregnated with all that has gone before; these encounters of Christ with death and its powers in history mean that his triumph over death there shown is offered for human beings and for the whole world. His victory is not for himself but for us. His power over death is effective not just at the terminal point of a person's life but throughout one's life, during *this* life in *this* world, right now. This power is effective in the times and places in the daily lives of human beings when they are so gravely and relentlessly assailed by the claims of principalities for an idolatry that, in spite of all disguises, really surrenders to death as the reigning presence in the world. His resurrection means the possibility of living in this life, in the very midst of death's works, safe and free from death.

But what of all of these notions and speculations about a life after dying, after the day of the undertaker? The Christian, the one living by the authority of and in the freedom of the resurrection, is saved from fond and wishful thinking about that. Christians have no anxiety about their disposition after their lives in this world: in fact, they know little or nothing about the matter; but they know all that they need to know, which is that the reality and truth of the resurrection has been in the present life so radically verified and realized that they are confident and joyful in leaving themselves in the judgment and mercy of God, in all things, for ever and ever.

Christ's resurrection is for human beings and for the whole of creation, including the principalities of this world. Through the encounters between Christ and the principalities and between Christ and death, the power of death is exhausted. The reign of death and, within that, the pretensions to sovereignty over history of the principalities, is brought to an end in Christ's resurrection. He bears the fullness of their hostility toward him; he submits to their condemnation; he accepts their committal of himself to death, and in his resurrection he ends their power and the power they represent. Yet the end of the claims of the principalities to sovereignty is also the way in which these very claims are fulfilled in Christ himself. The claim of a nation, ideology, or other principality to rule history, though phoney and futile, is at the same time an aspiration for salvation, a longing for the reality that does, indeed, rule history. In the same event in which the pretension of the principality is exposed and undone, how and in whom salvation is wrought is disclosed and demonstrated. In Christ the false lords of history, the principalities, are shown to be false; at the same time, in Christ the true Lord of history is made known. In Christ is both the end and fulfillment.

The Nationhood of the Church

William Stringfellow, *Conscience and Obedience*, pp.99-105

When and where the church participates in the biblical witness in history and is an advocate for any victim of political authority – or for a victim in any other sense of the power of death at work in the world – the church risks the suffering of the victim. That is enough to show the connection in the present age between the mission of the church and any persecution, ridicule or other hostility which the church endures. That is to say, in antagonistic circumstances, the church suffers as a surrogate for the world, bearing the burden of the victim and, for that matter, of the aggressor as well.

There is, unfortunately, a pathetic legacy of dissembling about this situation of the church. A familiar aspect of it is the romanticizing of the era of Roman persecution of the early church which, in effect, laments the closing of arena spectacles pitting lions against Christians as a way of excusing the corruption and floundering of the church ever since. The inference seems to be that the church should seek persecution in order to engender incentive to be stalwart in the gospel. Such sentiments are, of course, plainly refuted in the New Testament both by the accounts of the ministry of Jesus – there is no evidence that he sought crucifixion – and by the witness of the apostolic church – the indication is the apostles were very concerned to spare the church persecution (see the First Letter of Peter).

The church, anyway, needs no compulsion to gain persecution, in any circumstances at any time in this age, because the power of death, incarnate in the political principalities, as in other ways, is truly incorrigible. Death is the aggressor and though the apparitions and forms which the power of death assumes are variegated, that does not imply that death can be quantified. It is no longer the custom to cast Christians into dens of beasts, but that does not mean the persecution has ended. And, whatever else may be attributed to the impress of the Constantinian arrangement, its comity did not abate the hostility which the church, where it is exemplar and advocate of life, endures for the time being in this world.

In quite the same vein, too much is made of the witness of particular Christians so that it is regarded as exceptional (rather than exemplary) and so some few are installed as martyrs, as heroic figures, as super-Christians. An instance is found in the lore which has accrued to Dietrich Bonhoeffer. I do not hesitate at all to venture that Bonhoeffer would be deeply provoked by the way his witness has been construed as so unusual that it is unedifying to ordinary people of the church, so bold that it excuses inaction rather than inspiring it. Another case in point, within my direct knowledge, occurred when Daniel Berrigan, S.J., was seized by the federal police at my Block Island home while he was a fugitive felon, having resisted the criminal war policy of the incumbent regime in America. In covering the event, one of the Providence television stations interviewed John McLaughlin, who then was a Jesuit and a candidate for the United States Senate from Rhode Island, and who was later compensated for his defeat in that campaign by appointment to the White House staff where, in due course, he became the official Watergate casuist. In the television interview on August 11, 1970, McLaughlin was asked his reaction to the activities of his Jesuit brother. He rambled on for a while about how some work for change from within the system (e.g. McLaughlin as senatorial candidate) while others act outside the system (e.g. Berrigan as convicted war resistor). But, then, concluding, McLaughlin declared: "Of course, you must realize Dan is a poet!" He might have said "martyr" or "kook" or "prophet" or "lunatic" or "hero" or "fanatic" or "fool" – the intent was the same: to discharge Berrigan from the realm of common human beings and to dismiss Berrigan's witness by styling it exceptional.

The point is, of course, that there are no martyrs at all in the church because of the veracity of the sacrifice of the Word of God in Christ for the world. There is nothing to be added to Christ's sacrifice. No Christian in witness to Christ's sacrifice volunteers any sacrifice of his or her own. The whole idea of there being any martyrs for the gospel is an embellishment misleading the church and its members and furnishing pretext to simply cop-out.

This whole syndrome in the contemporary church sponsors the notion that, though there may be occasional poets, fools, or super-Christians, with the alleged ending of persecution, all that remains between the church and political authority are some few issues which may prompt intermittent incidents of individual civil disobedience. There are still some Quakers on the scene, plus scattered Anabaptists, but, in general, in the contemporary church, in America and places like America, the questions of obedience and conscience are usually deemed to affect individuals, not the church as an institution and society. And the decisions such persons make are thought to be idiosyncratic and, moreover, arrogant – that is, implicating a claim of superior insight into the will and judgment of God.

The term conscience is used only rarely in the New Testament, and not as such in the Old Testament. Apart from its use in association with obedience in Romans, where Paul makes no equation between conscience and the will of God, but, on the contrary, makes clear that conscience is subject to judgment, the most notable mention of conscience is in the First Epistle of Peter. That epistle expounds the meaning of baptism as the sacrament of the new and mature humanity of persons in Christ, of the new citizenship in Christ compared to the old citizenship under Caesar. Far from having eccentric denotations, conscience is an expression of the identification of baptized people with the whole of humanity.

Similarly, Romans:12 hinges the chapter's discourse on the life of the body of Christ in the world upon not being conformed to the world but being transformed by the renewal of the mind. In Christian faith, conscience does not mean a private, unilateral, self-serving, morally superior opinion held by an individual disconnected from the community, but it bespeaks the freedom to transcend self, to expend life, to share in suffering, to risk death for the sake of others and on behalf of the world which is integral to becoming a member of the corpus of the church.

Conscience, for Christians, rather than being solitary or eccentric, bespeaks the church's witness of advocacy.

Let it be said that when I name the church, I do not have in mind some idealized church, or some disembodied or uninstitutionalized church, or just an aggregate of individuals. I mean the church in history, the church constituted and precedented in history at Pentecost, the church which is an organic reality: visible as a community, institutionalized as a society. I refer to the church as a new household or to the church as congregation. Most concretely, I name the church as the holy nation.

The church which is the holy nation is not metaphorical, but it is the church called into being at Pentecost: the church which is the new Israel of God in the world; the church which is both progeny of the biblical tradition of Zion and pioneer of the kingdom of God; the church which is the exemplary nation juxtaposed to all the other nations; the church which as a principality and institution transcends the bondage to death in the midst of fallen creation; the church which presents and represents in its corporate life creation restored in celebration of the Word of God; the church in which the vocation of worship and advocacy signifies the renewed vocation of every creature; the church which anticipates the imminent and prompt redemption of all of life.

The church's calling as the holy nation has been profoundly distorted since Pentecost, and, manifestly, especially so under the aegis of the Constantinian detente with the rulers and regimes of the present age. Insofar as there was in the fourth century definite incentive to enter that comity in order to alleviate persecution, the purpose remains unaccomplished. If Christians have been spared the savagery of beasts or if the more notorious vulgarities of emperor worship have been abated, other forms of persecution have succeeded and the hostility of demonic principalities and powers toward the church has not diminished. By the twentieth century, the enmity of the power of death toward the church had come to be enacted in the grandiose idolatry of the destiny of British colonial imperialism, or in the brutal devastation of the church following upon the Soviet Revolution, or in the ruthless Nazi usurpation of the church in the name of 'Germanizing' or 'purifying' Christianity so as to have this accomplice in the pursuit and in the incineration of the Jews.

Meanwhile, in America, the pluralism of religions and the multiplicity of denominations have abetted the inception of civil religion, which has assorted versions, but the major thrust of which imputes a unique moral status to the nation, a divine endorsement for America, which, in its most radical composition, disappropriates the vocation of church as the holy nation.

Thus the church becomes confined, for the most part, to the sanctuary, and is assigned to either political silence or to banal acquiescence. Political authority in America has sanctioned this accommodation principally by the economic rewards it bestows upon the church. The tax privilege, for example, to which the church has acceded, has been a practically conclusive inhibition to the church's political intervention save where it consists of applause for the nation's cause. Furthermore, the tax preference or political subsidy the church has so long received has enabled, perhaps more than anything else, the accrual of enormous, if unseemly, wealth.

In the American comity, the church has gained so huge a propertied interest that its existence has become overwhelmingly committed to the management of property and the maintenance of the ecclesiastical fabric which that property affords. It is a sign certainly of the demonic in institutional life where the survival of the principality is the dominant morality. That mark is evident in very many professed churches in America. I cannot imagine any other way, at this point, to free the church to recover its vocation as the exemplary principality or holy nation, than by notorious acts of disavowal of this traffic with political authority. The church in America needs to divest property, not hoard it any longer and, as part of that I urge renunciation of the tax privilege so that the church could be freed to practice tax resistance. If that portends direct collision with political authority and involves such risks as official confiscation of church properties – which it does – then my only response is that it promises a way of consolidating losses.

The suppression of the comprehension of the church as the holy nation or as the priest among the nations, whether in America or elsewhere, causes, I think, the importance of the dispersion of the church to be minimized or even overlooked. Yet it is impossible to contemplate the nationhood of the church without retaining the sense of the eschatological imminence that has been previously discussed. The imminence is conveyed where the church lives in dispersion throughout the world, confronting every nation and tribe, tongue and culture as an embassy of the Kingdom. Such dispersion is, on one hand, incompatible with the Constantinian ethos, but, on the other, it verifies the truly ecumenical reality of the church in this world.

More than that, the dispersion inherent in the church's identity as the priest of nations and forerunner of the Kingdom is, I believe, temporal as much as spatial. The church is dispersed in space and thus indulges no dependency upon particular nations or regimes of nations but by its presence disrupts every nation and every regime. The church also remains dispersed in time, forbearing to become vested in a specific institutional mode indefinitely, or as if in perpetuity, but the event of the church constantly, repeatedly fractures time. That is to say, the church as institution or nation is, first of all, an event of the moment, gathered here or there, but that does not predetermine whether or how the church will appear again. The church is episodic in history; the church lives in imminence so that the church has no permanent locale or organization which predicates its authenticity as the church. This may seem a hectic doctrine of the church to the Constantinian mentality. It is. But it is so because it suggests the necessity of breaking away from Constantinian indoctrination in order to affirm the poise of the church awaiting the second advent of Jesus Christ.

Mythology of the Justified Nation

William Stringfellow *Politics of Spirituality*, pp.52-68

The American anxiety concerning justification is not a merely private matter but has manifold political ramifications. Perhaps the most notorious political consequence of this anxiety, expressed on a societal and cultural level in openly political terms, is the mythology (not to say fantasy) of America as the holy nation. The doctrine, which has diverse origins in the American experience as a nation, is that America is a nation with a unique destiny, bestowed upon it by God.

This has had particularly vehement lip service in the Presidency of Ronald Reagan: in many instances he has pronounced America the embodiment of good, while America's presumed enemies, especially the Soviet Union, embody objective evil. Reagan thereby goes significantly beyond conventional or simplistic patriotic rhetoric. He is talking about imagined ultimate/cosmic confrontations.

Yet what is thus alleged about America's character as a nation and about the historic destiny of the nation has a curiously familiar sound because it is, in fact, a bastard version of the biblical news about the election of Israel and then, in the New Testament, the vocation of the church as the exemplary nation or as the priest among the nations.

The appropriation of the biblical tradition concerning the holy nation for application to *any* secular regime, like the United States of America, is a profound affront at once to biblical faith and to the witness to the biblical events, as well as to the church of Christ. In an earlier time in the church's life, such an offense on the part of a ruler or incumbent official – like a president – might well have provoked the sanction of anathema. Do not suppose I am one bit facetious in considering that anathema should have been, in the present day, pronounced against President Reagan for his incessant trivialization of the Bible and its content. And he has no defense against anathema in a plea of sincerity. (There are, of course, many critics who label Reagan a hypocrite because he seldom darkens a church doorway. He used to say, when asked about his absences from church services, that his religion is too private a matter to warrant church attendance. That sounds sincere enough to me, though it clearly places Reagan outside the scope of biblical faith.) In any circumstance sincerity is no defense, and sincerity in denouncing and belittling the gospel only compounds the affront. Reagan's entire well-worn story about America the holy nation, America the divine favorite among the nations, America the chosen nation is the rhetoric of fantasy, not history; of delusion, not revelation; of gross vanity, not fidelity or virtue. It is utterly anomalous – an outrage – that Reagan should hear any applause for his rhetoric or receive any adherents to his mythology about America as the 'justified' nation, particularly from any constituency professing to be part of the church.

Understand, please, that I am not indulging here in a partisan comment. And I do not single out Reagan in a way that implies he is unique in his behavior and his pontifical remarks in regard to the nation's moral disposition and its ultimate destiny. There are now, and there have been for generations, Americans prominent in the political establishment, rulers and authorities of many partisan affiliations, in addition to ecclesiastical leaders and officials and hosts of preachers, who have mouthed various versions of this same fabrication about America being an especially favored among nations by God. The natural and diverse beauty of the continent is taken to be a sign of that divine preference, and the same idea is then translated into the grandiose dimensions of American technological prowess and military superpower, or into 'the American standard of living', or laissez-faire capitalism, or prosperity, or pre-eminence in science, and so on and on. The whole political discussion about maintaining America as 'Number 1' among the nations, which has, notably, developed since the frustration of American superpower in Korea and then, grotesquely, in Vietnam, and subsequently in Lebanon and in Latin America, is part of this pathetic syndrome. The basic impression is that God has *so* favored America that God has rewarded America – by making and keeping the nation as "Number 1" – in advance of the Judgment.

That is only one of the ways in which this fantasizing about the nation works havoc (mainly in the form of mockery and ridicule) with biblical faith. For any professed church folk to be privy to these shibboleths about the nation is scandalous; for the president or adjacent high authorities to indulge and propagate the same is dangerous; for this credo to become widely accepted among the general citizenry borders on some sort of mass hallucination.

So Reagan is mentioned here by name because he has been an incumbent president and, in that capacity, has brought himself into the matter and extended the topic to greater extremities of rhetoric and myth than ever before. But, in naming him, we must keep in mind that there are legions more, among the American people and among those who purport to rule this society. Most sad to say, in these same ranks are multitudes of church-related folk, some hapless, some guileful, articulating these same themes.

I wish this whole matter were innocuous, just an irritation occasioned by careless and excessive language, a mere distortion of some elements of America's past, an issue of 'civic religion', which, though intellectually corrupt and bankrupt in terms of spirituality, is unlikely to disrupt society in a practical manner. But this is not an innocuous cause; it is one both pernicious and perilous for society and one rapidly becoming a crisis.

I do not give much credence to conspiratorial interpretations of history, but I apprehend that the truth is that there are persons and organizations and financing resources seeking to transmute the mythology and rhetoric concerning America the holy nation into a political and ideological movement to 'convert' America into a so-called Christian nation. Some of these powers speak of restoring America as a 'Christian nation' – in blatant falsification of American history as well as remarkable distortion of what it means, in biblical perspective, to be Christian. The stridency of Mr. Reagan's exclamations concerning the nation's peculiar, divine-oriented destiny feeds the extraordinary goal which these certain principalities and persons intend to attain. Their determination already is sufficient to rationalize the purging (I use the term literally) of those who stand in their way, whether the latter be from the churches or the traditional political parties or the media or among incumbent officeholders or assorted non-Christian minorities. I conclude that such forces actually gather; they meet, they strategize, they launch pilot exercises, they recruit support, they get ready for their own style coup d'etat. Meanwhile, they manipulate Reagan and others who have power or influence temporarily, and they largely dominate and direct a vast, unfortunate, misled constituency – generally assembled as the 'Moral Majority' – who have become ripe for such exploitation because of their long experience of economic, cultural, and political rejection in America. They are enough disillusioned that they are no longer willing to abide waiting for recognition and for their share of *everything* until the Kingdom comes. They have always been impatient for *that,* and now the promise of *something* for them in 'the Christian nation' (if not in the Eschaton) is a promise they have nothing to lose in embracing. And, it must be acknowledged, those who are doing the exploiting of the hapless multitude are very skillful and ambitious hucksters indeed.

This cause of the so-called Christian nation has already accomplished notable successes politically, particularly in its vendettas against certain legislators, in its surveillance network, in locating and committing huge funding, and in its preliminary agenda of 'family' laws: its oppression – sometimes of hysterical scope – of homosexuals and its assault upon the First Amendment, its disruption of the free library system, its interference with school administrations and curriculum policies, and its efforts to legislate morality in the narrowest construction of that term. In 1984, Mr. Reagan, a presidential candidate for reelection (in manifest need of some public distraction from his failures in foreign policy, his dispatching of marines to their doom, the multifarious mundane corruptions of his highest-level appointees, and his callous rejection of the poor and dispossessed and aged and handicapped and ill and unemployed and unemployable), by pushing the snarled school prayer issue to the forefront, has given those seeking to found or restore 'a Christian nation' in America a large opportunity to pursue their aims under cover of the school prayer debate.

The school prayer controversy is one of those debilitating public disputes that is mostly sham and not substance, the sort of conflict which conceals other issues that seldom openly surface and thus are infrequently either honestly faced or appropriately settled. It is, therefore, a situation with many possibilities for distraction or diversion and with a multitude of opportunities for manipulation for covert purposes. The literal public debate in the school prayer issue has a strong resemblance to an exchange of cursings instead of an informed dialogue about policy alternatives. And the prayer controversy has been a virtually classic example of the substitution of a public relations campaign for deliberative policy-making. It is, in other words, not only the case that we have been diverted from Central America and what is happening there by indulgence in the public arguments about school prayer, but within the context of those arguments there has been little of a substantive character and very much sound and fury.

Consider the repeated one-liner, used by advocates of prayer in the schools, including Ronald Reagan, to the effect that the Supreme Court in its Constitutional bar to school prayer had "expelled God from school". This is patently absurd talk. Constitutionally irrelevant and, perhaps more significant, an open ridicule of God. It does not, in the first place, speak of the living God at all but of some notion or conception of 'God' – a puny one, at that – the location or other reference to which is dependent upon the actions of human beings, or of some humans and institutions. The Supreme Court, the school board, a teacher, or whoever is to determine, according to this profane remark, where 'God' is and, indeed, what (what, not who, is the correct term here) God is thought to be. I believe that such a comment, and the view of deity it conceals, may be offensive to many persons and communities, but whatever the circumstance with others, it is radically objectionable to biblical faith and to the community of the church of Christ. From a biblical point of view, there is nothing whatever that the Supreme Court or any school board or any principalities or any persons – including any President of the United States – can say or do that can determine the character or action of the Word of God in common history – and nothing, issuing from any such source, that can obviate, diminish, alter, modify, prejudice, detract from, or otherwise change the pervasive presence of the Word of God in this world. For Christians, when it is said the court decision has "expelled God from school", the speaker is both denouncing and denying the presence of the Word of God everywhere in this world or, what is also conceivable, the one speaking is supercilious and ignorant and simply does not know what he or she is talking about.

By the same token, the access of a human being, including students and teachers, to the Word of God is in no way curtailed or lessened or estopped or rendered any more difficult by the decision made by the Supreme Court. Nor has prayer been inhibited in any manner whatsoever. In fact, as one would expect, those who complain that 'God' has been lately expelled from school are for the most part incapable of enunciating in comprehensible language and syntax what is the reality of the relationship of prayer. One ends up with some plaintive exercises – nonprayers or antiprayers addressed to some nongod or antigod. Better that the children spend a few moments at the opening of the school day meditating on the meaning of the Constitutional amendments that comprise the Bill of Rights: Let them be spared the foolish indignity of making believe they are praying to a make-believe deity conjured up in a White House press handout.

The Necessity of Repentance

Biblical spirituality is not expressed in goals and agendas, regimens and attainments; it is not concerned in any degree with any effort to earn justification. Those who expend themselves in accordance with some scheme which bears a label of spirituality in order to try to prove or verify their moral worth are in reality attempting to second-guess how they are and will be judged in the Word of God at the ending of the history of the present age. That attempt can avail nothing whatever. The Judgment of the Word of God – both in its general character as the consummation of history and also in its particularity, whereby every thought, word, deed, and omission of every person and every principality from the commencement of time remain secret as the very Word of God until uttered. There is no foresight available to either institutions or humans which has the integrity to forecast the tenor of the Judgment as an event or the substance of the Judgment with respect to any creature or any decision or act of any creature. So far as human beings are concerned, such anxieties concerning justification or attempts to anticipate how the Word of God judges this or that exceed the actual capabilities of humans. Hence the very effort to second-guess the Judgment must be counted as a de-humanization of persons which is very radical and very fearsome. Part of the reality of what happens in such circumstances is, paradoxically, not a projection of the Judgment which is coming but a recapitulation of the primal issue between humankind and creation and the Word of God, which, in traditional biblical insight, occasions the fall and the consignment of the whole of creation to the power of death. That issue concerns a vanity which belittles God and the office of God. Repentance of that initiates biblical spirituality.

Are human beings, then, just hapless victims of the fall awaiting the secret Judgment of the Word of God at the end of the era? By no means. To affirm that humans (and principalities, for that matter) are incapable of acting to justify themselves as they are also incapacitated from sanctifying themselves simply means, on one hand, that the work of redemption in fallen creation is entirely and aptly the vocation of the Word of God in this world, and that the human and corporate recognition of that truth is essentially a matter of confession and repentance. The content or message of such confession and repentance is the radical acknowledgement of helplessness. As it has been put before, if you want to know what you can do to justify yourself, the biblical response is: You must give up trying to justify yourself and confess your utter helplessness in the face of the power of death. This repentance is the substance of biblical spirituality. *Utter* helplessness is what is involved, without any equivocation or qualification or deferral or caveat or double-talk. The repentance at issue is such that it apprehends the empirical risk of death or of abandonment; that is, the risk that there is no Word of God to identify you and give you your name. Without that gift of your name, you do not exist; you are dead or, as they say, as good as dead.

As it is for persons, so it is for the principalities and powers, the nations and institutions, the regimes, systems, authorities, bureaucracies, causes, organizations, ideologies, classes, and similar realms. It has, after all, been evident since the vocation of John the Baptist – and, in the Old Testament, since the witness of Isaiah – that repentance and the confession of the vitality of the Word of God are not merely personal or private matters but are notoriously public and blatantly political.

The problem of America as a nation, in biblical perspective, remains this elementary issue of repentance. The United States is, as all nations are, called in the Word of God to repentance. That, in truth, is what the church calls for, whether knowingly or not, every time the church prays *Thy Kingdom come.*

America needs to repent. Every episode in the common experience of America as a nation betells that need. If such be manifest in times of trauma and trouble – such as now – it is as much the need in triumphal or grandiose circumstances.

The nation needs to repent. If I put the matter so baldly, I hope no one will mistake my meaning for the rhetoric of those electronic celebrity preachers who sometimes use similar language to deplore the mundane lusts of the streets or the ordinary vices of people or to berate the Constitutional bar to prayer, so-called, in public schools while practicing quietism about the genocidal implications of the Pentagon's war commerce or extolling indifference toward the plight of the swelling urban underclasses.

Topically, repentance is *not* about forswearing wickedness as such; repentance concerns the confession of vanity. For America – for any nation at any time – *repentance means confessing blasphemy.*

Blasphemy occurs in the existence and conduct of a nation whenever there is such profound and sustained confusion as to the nation's character, place, capabilities, and destiny that the vocation of the Word of God is preempted or usurped. Thus the very presumption of the righteousness of the American cause as a nation *is* blasphemy.

Americans, for some time now, have been assured, again and again, that the United States will prevail in history because the American cause is righteous. Anyone who believes that has, to say the very least, learned nothing from the American adventurism in Vietnam. Then, a succession of presidents made similar pronouncements, but America suffered ignominious defeat nonetheless. And if in the last few years some sense of guilt about Vietnam has begun to surface, this has been, for the most part, a strange and perverted sentiment because it has attached not to the crimes of American intervention in Southeast Asia – to massacre, despoilment, and genocide – but to the event of American defeat. To feel guilty because America lost, rather than because of what America did, is another, if macabre, instance of false righteousness. That is only the more underscored when the unlawful invasion of Grenada is examined as an attempt to fantasize the victory for American superpower which was missed in Vietnam.

Furthermore, the confusion of a nation's destiny, and of a nation's capabilities, with the vocation of the Word of God in history – which is the *esse* of blasphemy – sponsors the delusion that America exercises domination over creation as well as history and that it can and should control events in the life of creation. Other nations, ancient and modern, as has been mentioned, suffer similar delusions, but if there ever has been a nation which should know better (that is, which should repent), it is America, if only because of the American experience as a nation and a society in these past few decades.

After all, it is only in the period since, say, Hiroshima, in which American power, rampant most conspicuously in the immense, redundant, overkill nuclear weapons arsenal, has been proven impotent, because if it is deployed, it portends self-destruction, and if it is not, it amounts to profligate, grotesque waste. In either instance, American nuclear arms are rendered practically ineffectual in dominating events, but they still mock the sovereignty of the Word of God in history.

Much the same must, of course, be said of the nation's society and culture, which has become, as I have earlier remarked, overdependent upon the consumption ethic, with its doctrines of indiscriminate growth, gross development, greedy exploitation of basic resources, uncritical and often stupid reliance upon technological capabilities and incredible naiveté about technological competence, and crude, relentless manipulation of human beings as consumers. Increasingly, now, people can glimpse that this is no progress, no enhancement of human life, but wanton plunder of creation itself. People begin to apprehend that the penultimate implementation of the American consumption ethic is, bluntly, self-consumption. In the process, it has become evident as well that the commerce engendered by the American consumption ethic, together with the commerce of weapons proliferation, relates consequentially to virtually every injustice of which human beings are victims in this nation and in much of the rest of the world.

And so I say the United States needs to repent; the nation needs to be freed of blasphemy. These are, admittedly, theological statements. Yet I think they are also truly practical statements. America will remain frustrated, literally demoralized, incapable of coping with its concrete problems as a nation and society until it knows that realism concerning the nation's vocation which only repentance can bring.

One hopes repentance will be forthcoming. If not, it *will* happen: in the good time of the Judgment of the Word of God.

Meanwhile, in this same context, persons repent and all persons are called to repentance. The confession and repentance of an individual does not take place, as some preachers and the like aver, in a great void, abstracted from the everyday existence of this world. The experience of each penitent is peculiar to that person, but that does not mean it is separated from the rest of created life.

This is the reason why the foisting of any stereotype of the experience upon people is coercive and false and, indeed, self-contradictory. It must be recognized, however, that this is quite what is involved where, for an example, a so-called born-again Christian stereotype is asserted. I can testify personally that I have been 'born again' – my account constitutes the book aptly titled A *Second Birthday* – *but* that appears to mean something substantively different from sudden, momentary trauma. I do not thus imply that the latter is invalid or necessarily incomplete or otherwise questionable, but I do question the composition of *any* stereotype of the experience and the insinuation that it is normative, much less mandatory.

What is implicated in confession and repentance, which inaugurates the practice of a biblical spirituality whatever the style or detail of what happens to a particular person, is the establishment or restoral by the Word of God of that person's identity in the Word of God in a way in which the query *Who am I?* merges with the question *Where is God?* The transaction comprehends, as has been said, the risk that there is no one or nothing to affirm a person's existence and identity. As I have put it before, the confession of utter helplessness, the repentance which is requisite and efficacious, always involves the empirical risk of death. At the very same time, this repentance foreshadows and anticipates the perfection of each person's and each principality's vocation in the Kingdom of God.

Justification and Hope

Since the disillusionment and defection of Judas, a recurrent issue for people of biblical faith has been the confusion between justification and justice. It is, in fact, out of contemporary manifestations of that very confusion, especially during the decade of the sixties, that many Christian activists (as the media style them) have become more curious about spirituality and have begun to explore the significance of biblical spirituality for political decisions and actions. The widespread posthumous interest in the witness and ministry of Thomas Merton is one significant sign of that, as I have said.

I do not venture to unravel the confusion regarding justification and justice in terms of its prolonged and agitated annals in Christendom. I speak of the matter only theologically, not historically and analytically. As I understand it, justice is the accomplishment of the Judgment of the Word of God in the consummation of this age and embodies all the specifications, all the particular details of the Judgment with respect to all things whatsoever. Justice, as it is articulate in the Judgment, is essentially an expression of the faithfulness of the Word of God to the creation of the Word of God.

There is no capability in human effort or in the enterprise of nations or other principalities to approximate the justice of the Judgment. The decisions and actions of persons and powers may, in a sense, aspire to or render tribute to the justice of the Judgment, but they cannot fabricate it or duplicate it or preempt it. And, as has been mentioned, when they suppose that they have in given circumstances imitated or second-guessed the Judgment and its justice, they are most in jeopardy so far as the integrity of their respective vocations is concerned. Persons and principalities can neither play God nor displace God without risking self-destruction. This does not denigrate at all the struggle for justice in merely human and institutional terms; in fact, it upholds that struggle even in recognizing how fragile, transient, and ambiguous it is – and dynamic – how open it is to amendment, how vulnerable to change.

Within the scene of this world, now, where the struggle for justice in merely human and institutional translations is happening, and in the midst of the turmoil that stirs, the Word of God, as a matter of God's own prerogative, freedom, and grace, offers the assurance of redemption, the promise of wholeness and integrity and communication, the message of hope in the Kingdom which is to come together with the Judgment of the Word of God and the justice which that Judgment works.

This justification is both credible and accessible, not because any person, or any society, is worthy but because the Word of God is extravagant or, if you will, because the *Word of God is godly*. *So* the grace of the Word of God transcends the injustice of the present age, agitates the resilience of those who struggle now to expose and rebuke injustice, informs those who resist the rulers of the prevailing darkness, and overflows in eagerness for the coming of One who is the Judge of this world and whose justice reigns forevermore. By virtue of justification, we are freed now to live in hope.

A Lawyer's Work

William Stringfellow *A Simplicity of Faith*, pp.125-33

If politics, from time to time, has spawned for me prosaic temptation to mistake career for vocation, being a lawyer has not bothered me in any comparable way. I was spared that before I even entered Harvard Law School because of my disposition of the substantive issue of career versus vocation while I was a graduate fellow at the London School of Economics and Political Science. As I have remarked heretofore, I had elected then to pursue *no* career. To put it theologically, I died to the idea of career and to the whole typical array of mundane calculations, grandiose goals and appropriate schemes to reach them. I renounced, simultaneously, the embellishments – like money, power, success – associated with careers in American culture, along with the ethics requisite to obtaining such condiments. I do not say this haughtily; this was an aspect of my conversion to the gospel so, in fact, I say it humbly.

In the time that intervened between London and Harvard (part of which I spent traveling extensively in Europe and in Asia – often at the behest of the World Student Christian Federation – and the remainder of which I served in the Second Armored Division – *Hell-on-Wheels*, was its watchword – assigned to the North Atlantic Treaty Organization forces) my renunciation of ambition in favor of vocation became resolute; I suppose some would think, eccentric. When I began law studies, I consider that I had few, if any, romantic illusions about becoming a lawyer and I most certainly did not indulge any fantasies that God had called me, by some specific instruction, to be an attorney, or for that matter, to be a member of any profession or any occupation. I had come to understand the meaning of vocation more simply and quite differently.

I believed then, as I do now, that I am called in the Word of God – as is *everyone* else – to the vocation of being human, nothing more and nothing less. I confessed then, as I do now, that to be a Christian means to be called to be an exemplary human being. And, to be a Christian *categorically* does not mean being religious. Indeed, all religious versions of the gospel are profanities. Within the scope of the calling to be merely, but truly, human, any work, including that of any profession, can be rendered a sacrament of that vocation. On the other hand, no profession, discipline or employment, as such, is a vocation.

Law students, along with those in medicine, engineering, architecture, the military, among others, are subjected to indoctrinations, the effort of such being to make the students conform quickly and thoroughly to that prevailing stereotype deemed most beneficial to the profession and to its survival as an institution, its influence in society, and its general prosperity. At the Harvard Law School, this process is heavy, intensive, and unrelenting, though I imagine that such indoctrinations are all the more so in pseudo-professional institutions, like those training insurance agents, stockbrokers, or realtors. Over and over again, while I was in the law school, I was astonished at how eagerly many of my peers surrendered to this regimen of professionalistic conditioning, often squelching their own most intelligent opinions or creative impulses in order to conform or to appear to be conforming.

Initiation into the legal profession, as it is played out at a place like the Harvard Law School, is, as one would expect, elaborately mythologized, asserts an aura of tradition, and retains a reputation for civility. All of these insinuate that this process is benign, though, both empirically and in principle, it is demonic. One notices that the medical establishment has gone much further than has the legal profession in indulging this sort of mythologizing, with the conspicuous collaboration of commercial television, and, before that, the movies. (After all, the mythological forerunner of *Marcus Welby* was *Dr. Christian.*) I think none of the other professions has countenanced such pretentious and gratuitous self-images as the medical profession has, but the same issue of mythologizing is associated with all the professions, and with most other occupations as well. There is radical discrepancy between myth and truth in internal indoctrinations focused on conforming practitioners and external publicity propagated about the various professions. I understand in hindsight that the vocational attitude I had formed in London, and later, the experience I had as law student, apprehended the legal profession specifically, and the professions, disciplines and occupations in general, in their status among the fallen principalities and powers engaged (regardless of apparently benign guises and pretenses) in coercing, stifling, captivating, intimidating, and otherwise victimizing human beings. The demand for conformity in a profession commonly signifies a threat of death.

In that connection, my commitment to vocation instead of career began, while I was still in the law school, to sponsor far-reaching implications for how I could spend the rest of my life. Anyway, I suffered the overkill ethos of the Harvard Law School – I think – with enough poise as a human being to quietly, patiently, vigilantly resist becoming conformed to this world.

The upshot of that resistance was that I emerged from the law school as someone virtually opposite of what a Harvard Law School graduate is projected by the prevailing system to be. I do say *that* proudly, and gladly.

Do not misunderstand me: I enjoyed the law school, but I did not take it with the literally dead earnestness of those of my peers who had great careers at stake. I respected the intellectual vigor of its environment, but I was appalled by the overwhelming subservience of legal education to the commercial powers and the principalities of property. I thought that a law school should devote at least as much attention in its curriculum to the rights and causes of people as it does to vested property interests of one kind or another. I also thought, while I was in law school, that *justice* is a suitable topic for consideration in practically every course or specialization. Alas, it was seldom mentioned, and the term itself evoked ridicule, as if justice were a subject beneath the sophistication of lawyers.

Since 1956, when I was graduated, I have been enabled to remain in touch with legal education in a more than perfunctory manner because I am often invited as a visiting lecturer in various law schools around the country. Thus I am aware that there have been some significant, if modest, curricular reforms in many law schools lately, including work in urban law, poverty law, consumer law, and some cross-disciplinary efforts between law and other graduate disciplines.

Be that as it may, when I went to the East Harlem ghetto directly upon finishing at the law school, and began to practice law there on my own, it was regarded by most of my peers as a curious venture, idiosyncratic and controversial. *My People is the Enemy* tells of that experience. That book had some impact in exposing the neglect of people, especially the dispossessed of the inner city regions, by the legal profession, in part attributable to the co-option of lawyers and legal education by commercial or similar principalities and powers. For instance, while Robert Kennedy was Attorney General of the United States, an emissary of Kennedy's came to me one day in New York City. He announced that the Attorney General had determined to convene a conference of lawyers from areas throughout the nation to examine issues of the law and the poor, and to consider how the legal profession might more responsibly serve the needs and interests of the poor in society. The Attorney General, my informant declared, had read *My People is the Enemy* and had been moved by it, and had dispatched him, he stated, "to pick your brain" about these matters in the hope that this would yield ideas for the conference which was contemplated. "I had better tell you first, however" my visitor confided, "that you will not be invited to speak to the conference – you're too radical" I found such candor appealing, and the interview commenced.

Robert Kennedy was, however, mistaken in an assessment that, as a lawyer, I am 'radical'. I do not think such labels – 'radical' 'liberal' 'conservative' 'reactionary' – edifying because they are so ambivalent in meaning, and I infrequently use them myself. But, if such classifications are invoked, in my opinion I could scarcely be counted as "radical" within the context of the legal tradition that has been inherited in America. My practice of law for a quarter of a century amply verifies this. I have been an advocate for the poor, for the urban underclass, for freedom riders and war resisters, for people deprived of elementary rights: children, women, blacks, Hispanics, native Americans, political prisoners, homosexuals, the elderly, the handicapped, clergy accused of heresy, women aspiring to priesthood. The consistent concerns of my practice have been the values of the constitutional system, due process of law, and the rule of law. What is radical about that? Perhaps these represent views of the law and society that could have been said to be radical in the thirteenth century, at the time the Magna Charta was ratified, but if they seem radical nowadays it is because so few lawyers care about them.

In East Harlem, on Block Island, in ecclesiastical courts as well as secular venues, as in the law school, I simply do not share in that feigned professional sophistication that sponsors and inculcates the indifference of lawyers to the constitutional priorities, particularly the Bill of Rights, or that rationalizes a preference for the *laissez faire* interests of commerce as opposed to the freedom, safety, and welfare of human beings, or that asserts a so-called sanctity of property that devalues and demeans human life.

Despite the notoriety that has been attached to the witness of civil disobedience, notably in the era of Martin Luther King, Jr., and then in the antiwar movement of the Sixties, there has been little threat to the rule of law in these protests. In fact, the major burden of them has been to act to redeem the constitutional system. The substantive danger to this society, so far as law is concerned, comes from the operation of lawless authority and the substitution of the power of coercion for the rule of law. For more than two decades now, the nation has suffered one outrageous spasm of official lawlessness after another. If this came into climactic focus in Watergate, in the aborted impeachment of President Nixon, and the nominal punishment of a handful of culprits in high places, that comes nowhere near exhausting the scandal of illegal, unconstitutional, and often criminal offenses accomplished by military, police, security, and intelligence officials within the federal regime, not to mention their counterparts in state and some local agencies. Reread the Kerner Commission findings. Recall the literally fantastic machinations of successive C.I.A. administrations, and then notice as well that the C.I.A. and the rest of the so-called intelligence complex still operates without presidential restraint, without parliamentary control, without any effectual accountability under the American constitutional system. Meanwhile, the F.B.I. is extolled by the incumbent President for its past flagrant infractions of constitutional limitations; and an immense and intricate scheme to rehabilitate its public image, following upon the most constitutionally obnoxious disclosures of official lawlessness under the auspices of J. Edgar Hoover, has been mounted, which involves the official procurement of crime. At the same time, the police power in most state and urban jurisdictions has been transmuted – partly under the patronage of the Pentagon – from a civilian to a paramilitary force in society, reflecting a contempt for constitutional safeguards and an overkill reliance upon violence. And all of this, and much, much more of the same, has been accompanied by the unrelenting barrage of propaganda on commercial television glorifying official violence as heroic, requisite, and efficient, even though it usurps constitutional rule.

Advocacy as a Pastoral Gift

When I first arrived in 1956 in East Harlem, I supposed that the rudimentary problem respecting the law was a failure to fully implement the existing American legal system among citizens who were economically dispossessed and who were victimized by racism. My supposition was, I soon enough discovered, mistaken. The issue, so far as the law was concerned, in the ghetto was the existence of another ruling system, distinct and apart from the constitutional and legal system pertaining elsewhere in the nation, based on coercion and the threat of coercion by those institutions and people who had commandeered the capabilities of coercion. It was a system of lawless authority, of official violence, a primitive substitution for the law. I wrote then that if such an extraordinary condition were allowed to continue and to fester, it would, sooner or later, infect and afflict the whole of this society. It has. There is a connection – direct and terrible and coherent – between the kind of regime to be found in the ghettoes in the Fifties and the way lawless authority and official violence dominate the life of most of this society today. And let no one pretend that a place like Block Island has been exempt from similar issues: until only some few years ago contempt for due process of law was the most conspicuous attribute of the town's administration.

If I hold lawyers especially responsible for the usurpation of constitutional rule in America because they, as a class and a profession, have been so lured and preoccupied with greed and apathy, I also ask myself, nearly every morning, whether my remaining an attorney condones – or appears to condone – the decadence against which I complain. Anthony [Towne] and I often talked of this relentless tension that I feel in being a lawyer. Without his care and wisdom – sometimes delivered somberly, sometimes in repartee – that tension, I am aware, heightens. I do not know, now, what the limits of my endurance in the circumstances are. I am certain, however, that stoicism can be of no relevance.

A critical dimension of this tension occasioned by being a biblical person who works as a lawyer is that the role of legal advocate at once coincides with and interferes with the pastoral calling to which I am disposed charismatically. In that calling, advocacy expresses the freedom in Christ to undertake the cause of another – including causes deemed 'hopeless' to intercede for the need of another – without evaluating it, but just because the need is apparent, to become vulnerable – even unto death – in the place of another. By contrast, advocacy in the law is contained within the bounds of the adversary system, with all its implications of competitiveness, aggression, facetious games, debate's craft, and winning *per se*. There have been circumstances in my experience when the advocacy of the Christian in the world coincides with the advocacy of the lawyer (as in the cases concerning the ordination of women), but there seem to be far more instances when the one interferes with the other (as in war resister cases). In part, here, of course, I am pleading within the legal profession for a more holistic approach to clients and cases than that afforded by the adversary system. Yet, more than that, I continue to be haunted with the ironic impression that I may have to renounce being a lawyer the better to be an advocate.

Poverty, Charity, and Mission:
East Harlem Protestant Parish

William Stringfellow, *My People is the Enemy*, pp.85-99

Meanwhile, there were other fronts which required attention besides the politics of the city and the practice of law in Harlem. I had come initially to Harlem as a member of the group ministry of the East Harlem Protestant Parish, out of concern for the mission of the Church to the poor and to those socially discriminated against in the city.

When I first moved to the neighborhood the parish was suffering from a terrific confusion as to the nature of the Church and the meaning and manner of the Church's task in a place such as Harlem. At the heart of these issues were some of the same matters which so divide the several churches outside of Harlem. They provoked deep divisions within the parish, particularly among the members of the group ministry, who, apart from myself and one other man, were clergymen.

Through its first years in the neighborhood the parish had become deeply conformed to the world. Conformity to the world is a temptation which assails the Church no less in the slums than in the suburbs. Conformity to the world exists whenever and wherever the Church regards its message and mission to be primarily determined by, or essentially dominated by, the ethos of secular life and the society which surrounds the Church.

The young ministers who had come out of Union Theological Seminary to found the East Harlem Protestant Parish were much tempted to such conformity. They had seen the Protestant churches abandon the inner city, both physically and psychologically, and were aroused by this attachment and conformity of Protestantism to middle-class American society. They would bring the ministry of Protestantism back into the inner city and work there among the poor and the dispossessed. In doing so they were confronted with how the ministry could be exercised in the midst of the long-festering, complex, and, to them – since they were white middle- and upper-class people – unfamiliar social problems that characterize urban slum society. To these problems they brought two things – a hostility toward the conventional churches outside the slums, which caused them to think they had little or nothing to learn from the life of the Church outside East Harlem, and a sincere passion for social change and revolution, even, in East Harlem. These two emotions joined to underscore the view that before the Gospel could be preached and received by the people of the slums, the way for the Word had to be prepared by improving the education of the people, renovating their housing, finding jobs for them, clearing the streets of garbage and debris, challenging the political status quo, alleviating the narcotics problem, and by social action of all sorts. When some of these issues had been resolved, when the lives of the people were less burdened with poverty, discrimination, illiteracy, and ignorance, then the time would come to preach the Gospel and then the people, no longer so preoccupied with their afflictions, would be able to hear and embrace the Gospel. One of the earlier parish documents declares that the parish "is a group ministry of twelve men and women working at the neighborhood level to help people face and work on their problems". Ironically, in spite of their rejection of middle-class Protestantism, the group ministry initially seems to have seen its task as making the East Harlem neighborhood more nearly middle class! Such a prejudgment is marred by the same sort of confusion that beset many missionaries who, in the early days of American foreign missions, went to Africa, Latin America, and the Far East, and who thought that before the people indigenous to those places could understand and receive the Word of God in Christ, they first had to be Westernized.

One of the paradoxes is that, unlike the people to whom the Western missionaries ventured, the American Negro is not foreign to the traditions, culture, class ethos, and social mores of American society. All these are his own inheritance. The American Negro, in other words, is an *American* – and has been such, for as long or longer than any other ethnic group in the United States. What they remember is American, not African. What they remember is, however, an American ethos, from which they have been deliberately excluded. What they remember is that they have been forcibly separated from those things which are as much their own as any other American's. What they remember are the very promises of the American Revolution – human dignity and equal treatment, fair representation and the opportunity to be politically free, the right to education and employment and a decent place to live and raise their children. No one has to instill these ideas and aspirations in American Negroes. They have inherited and remember them, despite three hundred years of slavery and segregation. They honor them by enduring their breach. They honor them more than most other Americans.

In any event, the preaching and service of the Gospel do not depend upon any special social change, ideationally or in any other way. The Gospel does not even depend upon the American way of life, either in its integrity or its breach.

I am as much in favor of social change in the urban ghettos as the next person, perhaps more (though I am by no means persuaded that the standard of social improvement should be that of the great American bourgeoisie), but the message and mission of the Church in the world *never* depend upon the specific physical, political, cultural, social, economic, or even psychological situations in which the Church, or the people of the Church as missionaries, find themselves. If the Gospel is so contingent as that, it is no universal Gospel. If the Gospel is so fragile that it may not be welcomed by anyone who, say, are hungry, unless they first be fed, then this is no Gospel with any saving power, this is no Word of God which has authority over the power of death. The Gospel, if it represents the power of God unto salvation, is a Word which is exactly addressed to persons in this world in their destitution and hunger and sickness and travail and captivity and perishing, in a way which may be heard and embraced by people in any of these, or in any other, afflictions.

That is, by the way, the original portrait and report of Christian witness in the world, in the days of the Acts of the Apostles.

The Church is much tempted by conformity to the world, by accommodating the message and mission to the particular society in which the Church happens to be, in the slums and in the suburbs, instead of honoring the integrity of the Gospel for all societies and for all sorts and conditions of people in all times and places. This temptation beguiled the group ministry of the East Harlem Protestant Parish. They plunged into all sorts of social work and social action – narcotics, politics, neighborhood improvement, education, housing, and the rest. They instituted therapy and counseling for addicts, engaged in voter registration, lobbied for new playgrounds, organized P.T.A.s, complained about slum landlords, and, generally, made themselves a nuisance to those in power in the neighborhood. It was, in many ways, an admirable, if idealistic, and, in Christian terms, naive effort. But they neglected and postponed the proclamation and celebration of the Gospel in East Harlem. In the congregations of the parish, the Bible was closed; in the group ministry there was even scorn for the Bible as a means through which the Word of God is communicated in contemporary society. The liturgical life of the congregations grew erratic and fortuitous, depending upon the personality and whim, even, of the minister presiding at the time. There was no concord or confession of the faith among either the group ministry or the lay people; there was a radical substitution of conventional charity for the mission of the Church. The parish – and especially the group ministry – was becoming dependent, in its *raison d'être,* upon its 'good works', rather than upon the Gospel, as such, for its justification.

In such circumstances, the hostility of the group ministry toward the Church outside East Harlem, and, indeed, toward other churches within East Harlem unaffiliated with the parish – such as the Chambers Memorial Baptist Church or St. Edward the Martyr or The Church of the Good Neighbor or the Roman Catholic Churches thereabouts – became more arrogant and proud. Not long after I had come to East Harlem, one of the clergy in the group ministry blandly explained that the Church outside East Harlem was dead and that the East Harlem Protestant Parish represented the "New Jerusalem" – to quote his exact words – of American Protestantism, the example through which American Protestantism would be purified and renewed. The calling of the parish, he assured me, was to be the norm, in all essential realms of the Church's life, for the whole Church in American society. I recall replying, in more strenuous language than I will use here, that he was mistaken and that part of the reason he was mistaken in this ambition for the parish was contained in his manifest ignorance, along with others (though not all in the group ministry), about the life of the Church outside East Harlem. For the fact was that very few of the clergy of the parish at this time had any experience in the Church, apart from their special experience in East Harlem itself. Of the twenty or so members of the group ministry on the scene when I first came to the neighborhood and to the parish, only five of us – George Todd, Melvin Schoonover, Geoffrey Ainger, Donald De Young and myself – had had any significant involvement in the life of the Church outside East Harlem, especially in any ecumenical sense.

The dangerous aspects of the parish's attitude were not just its wholesale rejection of the Church outside East Harlem, not even its conviction that mission is dependent upon and follows charity. More important, the group ministry was intent on conformity to the world and too easily disposed to think of itself as the model of the Church in American society. Members of the group ministry were filled with stereotyped opinions about the condition of the Church outside the inner city, but, except for a few of us, none of them had ever lived in the Church outside or had any first-hand knowledge of any church other than the parish.

At this stage in the parish's struggle to survive and to become a responsible member of the Church, the parish – and specifically the group ministry – was in danger of becoming sectarian, in danger of becoming so conformed to their environment and so dominated by it that the understanding of the Church which was asserted had become essentially joined to the sort of place in the world in which the parish was established. The Church could be the Church, to put it plainly, only in the slums. That is sectarianism, no less than it is where a church is established on grounds of class or race or language or any other secular criteria.

But this is not only sectarianism, it is romanticism. East Harlem is a frontier of the Church, but it is no more a frontier of the Church than the university or suburbia or anywhere else. Fanfare and special pleading and self-serving propaganda about the inner city ministry are both misleading and obscene. East Harlem, the earlier emphasis of the parish there notwithstanding, is in itself no more a frontier than any other place in the world. A frontier is wherever the Church trusts the Gospel in the Gospel's inherent relevance to the whole of life in this world. A frontier is wherever the Church exercises the freedom which God gives the Church to share the burden of anyone, in order to make known how Christ bears all burdens of everyone everywhere and in all times.

The sectarianism of the parish at this period was perhaps particularly sensitive to my own presence in the group ministry because I am an Episcopalian, and before coming to the parish, I had had a certain experience not only within the Anglican Communion, but in the ecumenical movement, especially in the World's Student Christian Federation and in the World Council of Churches. From that background and experience I knew something of the ministry of the Church outside East Harlem and, frankly, I was not impressed with the ready assurances that the East Harlem Protestant Parish represented the prototype of the renewal of the Church in the world, as much as I instinctively admired the social concern of the members of the group ministry. Even before affiliating with the parish, I had not hesitated to be critical of my own denomination or of the churches at large. Indeed, on the basis of my own involvement in the Church outside of East Harlem, and in view of the lack of significant involvement in or commitment to the Church outside by most, save a few, members of the group ministry, I felt authorized to say within the group ministry that not only were they not the image of the "new Jerusalem" and more than likely were building a new sect, based upon their location in and concern for the inner city, but they were guilty of the same conformity to the world which characterizes the churches and sects that take their identity and task from their place and status in the suburbs or elsewhere.

As time went on, the controversy about the nature of the Church and about the mission of the Church became gravely intensified within the group ministry, and, over a period of months, it focused upon two principal issues, although there were many ancillary matters which were also involved from time to time.

The first was centered upon the significance of the Bible for Christian people and for the life of the Church. Some of the members of the group ministry were appallingly diffident toward the Bible; and those who were the most self-serious about the analysis of culture and society were most often the dilettantes in Bible study. Those professing condolence for people showed mostly indolence for the Bible. Apparently, some of the clergy felt that Bible study was unnecessary, since they had already learned all they needed to of the Bible in seminary.

To some others in the group ministry – and to myself – this seemed astonishing in the extreme, especially among Protestants who might be expected to recall that, historically, Protestants have been a people of the Word of God in the Bible. Surely, intimacy with the Word of God in the Bible, reliance upon the Word of God in the Bible, is a characteristic of the ordinary practice of the Christian life, it seemed to those of us who urged that the group ministry and the people of the congregations engage in some corporate Bible study each week. After much controversy about the matter, it was decided that the group would spend an hour or so in Bible study just before the regular weekly staff meetings. It was often an erratic, sparsely attended – or attended to – exercise, but it exposed the fundamental disunity within the group ministry as to the content of the Christian faith and the nature of the Church's life and work. In this Bible study, the minds of some were filled with notions of truth, ideas of good, with interesting hypotheses, strong sentiments, and current events – and these things were actually asserted to test the Word of God. But few seemed ready just to *listen* to the Word of God in the Bible, to ask: What *is* the Word of God? Now, later, much later, after many struggles and both indifference and resistance, with the counsel and nurture of such visitors to the parish as Suzanne de Dietrich, Hendrik Kraemer, and others, the Bible has been acknowledged as central in the life of the Church and, hence, of this parish – but only after much agony.

At the heart of the conflict and disunity regarding the place of the Bible in the Church – as in many other churches outside Harlem – was a fundamental misapprehension about what the Bible is. I have no inclination toward Biblical literalism, but neither do I think that the Bible can be neglected, as the liberal Protestants fondly do, save for the teachings of Jesus. I am no Biblical scholar, either, but I affirm the necessity for the most rigorous work of textual criticism and the like. I do not become greatly distressed by 'demythologizing' the Bible unless it is used as an excuse for banishing the Bible from contemporary life. None of these approaches to the Bible essentially affects the reliance upon the Bible of the ordinary Christian as a particular means through which the Word of God is uttered and may be heard by us no less today than in the earlier days of the Christian people. In other words, and without denigrating an appropriate place for Biblical scholarship and criticism, the characteristic approach to the Bible of the Christian is confessional. Christians confront the Bible in the expectancy that it is in and through the testimony of the Bible of God's presence and action in the common life of the world that they will behold the Word of God as such, that they will hear the Word of God in the objectivity, integrity, and serenity of God's own witness to Himself in this history, that they will confront the *living* Word. The Word of God, in this sense, mediated through the narrative, history, praise, testimony, and exhortation of the Bible, lives by God's own initiative and generosity in this world, apart from whether or not people listen to God's Word, apart from human wisdom and scholarship, apart from tampering with or manipulation of the Bible, apart from the interesting and even sometimes true views and opinions of individuals, apart from any hardness of heart. The Word of God, in this sense, which is mediated in and through the Bible, is the very same Word of God in which all life in the whole of creation originates, the same Word embodied and exposed in Jesus Christ, the same Word by which the world is judged and in which the world is fulfilled, the same Word of God present and active in the world in the present day and in each and every event and transaction of everyday life in the world. Thus, when Christians turn to the Bible in a confessional sense, they do so in the expectancy of discerning the same Word of God with which they are confronted in their involvement each day in the common life of the world. And in their experience of the Word of God in the Bible, on one hand, and in common life, on the other hand, each is confirmed by the other. This is the case, not because anyone is especially learned or wise or even diligent, but because the Word of God is indeed a living Word whose vitality is no less to be beheld and enjoyed in ordinary life today than in the saga of the Word of God in the history of the people Israel, in the Gospels of Christ's ministry, in the birth and beginnings of the Church, in the acts and testimonies of the first apostles and evangelists known to us through the Bible.

I count the diffidence toward the Bible in the group ministry, accompanied as it was by the neglect of reliance upon the Bible in preaching in the parish's congregations and in the liturgical practices of these congregations, as the reason for the gross misapprehension about theology in the group ministry in the days of which I speak. Somehow the parish clergy had come to think that theology is the theory of the Christian faith which, once comprehended and accepted, is to be applied and executed in practical action in the world. That is why, I suppose, that the honor given by some of us to the Bible as mediator of the living Word of God still at work in this world was unwelcome and received with such vigorous hostility by our colleagues in the group ministry. The role of humankind would be so much more important if we did not always have to watch for the presence and initiative of the Word of God in history. If this Word was not still active, God would be remote – if not, in fact, dead. Then, people could choose to justify themselves by their own words, and one could take or leave the Bible, as well as the inherited testimony of earlier Christians, according to one's own individual ethics or speculations. Carried to its logical extreme, such a position implies atheism. Although there are many sincere and honorable people who are atheists, there is no excuse for such people to masquerade as Christians.

The neglect, and in some instances outright suppression, of the Bible as a mediator of the Word of God gravely influenced the ministry of the parish in its day-to-day relations to the neighborhood around it. It meant, for one thing, a failure to respect the office of the laity in the parish congregations. For all practical purposes, they were excluded from the government of the parish – they had no authority in the calling of their own ministers, in determining the service of the parish to the community, in supporting the parish's ministry in a significant way; they were, in short, appendices of the group ministry, dependent upon the leadership and resources of the ecclesiastical authorities, objects of the ministry rather than participants in the total ministry of the Church in East Harlem. As has happened before, in the Church of Rome as well as in the churches of Protestantism, the group ministry at this time was becoming so overinstitutionalized, so large, so aggressive, and so self-contained that it took upon itself the prerogatives of a congregation. The group ministry not only met with great frequency – apart from the congregations – to make policy, raise and spend funds, plan tactics and the like, but it also met often, including Sunday mornings, to worship separately from the congregations. In practice, the esoteric life of the group ministry had become one which really claimed that the group ministry constituted the community of the faithful in this neighborhood, and that the people who were baptized and had been made members of the several congregations of the parish were consigned to some derivative and peripheral status in the ministry of the Church in East Harlem. The paradox of the group ministry, as it actually operated then, was that the group ministry itself was the chief and constant threat to the emergence of vital congregations among the people of East Harlem, while, at the same time, the emergence of some congregations in East Harlem was the most substantial threat to the group ministry as a congregation and as a paternalistic ecclesiastical institution.

The slothfulness of the group ministry in confronting such issues as these – the place of the Bible in the Church and the adjacent issues of preaching and liturgy and action in society, plus the office of the laity and its relationship to the ecclesiastical ministry – provoked some of us to leave the group ministry after a while. I resigned about fifteen months after first coming to the neighborhood, but decided to stay in East Harlem, living and working as a lawyer on my own thereafter, and so remained until 1962. My resignation, let it be said, by no means terminated communication or collaboration with the people – both lay and clergy – of the parish on specific issues concerning both the church and society, but, I trust, the decision permitted both the group ministry and myself to persevere in the work which each felt called to do in East Harlem, in society at large, and in the ministry of the Church.

Since that time it appears that there have been significant changes in the parish, among others the admission of the laity to a significant voice in the affairs of the parish and also a serious renewal in the parish in the recognition of the uniqueness of the Bible as an evidence and honoring of the Word of God in the world.

As I reflect upon these controversies, what they amounted to were reflections of the differences within American Protestantism at large as to the meaning of God's concern for and presence in this world. From my own vantage point and experience on that issue, the Christian faith is not about some god who is an abstract presence somewhere else, but about the living presence of God here and now, in this world, in *exactly* this world, as we know it and touch it and smell it and live and work in it.

That is why, incidentally, all the well-meant talk of "making the gospel relevant" to the life of the world is false and vulgar. It secretly assumes that God is a stranger among us, who has to be introduced to us and to our anxieties and triumphs and issues and efforts. The meaning of Jesus Christ is that the Word of God is addressed to people, to *all* people, in the very events and relationships, any and every one of them, which constitute our existence in this world. That is the theology of the Incarnation.

The Word of God is present among the poor as well as among all others, and what I have called earlier the piety of the poor conceals the Word of God. The piety of the poor is prophetic: In a funny, distorted, ambiguous way it anticipates the Gospel. This is confirmed every day in East Harlem. There is a boy in the neighborhood, for instance, who is addicted to narcotics and whom I have defended in some of his troubles with the law. He used to stop in often on Saturday mornings to shave and wash up, after having spent most of the week on the streets. He been addicted for a long time. His father threw him out about three years ago, when he was first arrested. He has contrived so many stories to induce clergy and social workers to give him money to support his habit that he is no longer believed when he asks for help. His addiction is heavy enough and has been prolonged enough so that he now shows symptoms of other trouble – his health is broken by years of undernourishment and insufficient sleep. He is dirty, ignorant, arrogant, dishonest, unemployable, broken, unreliable, ugly, rejected, alone. And he knows it. He knows at last that he has nothing to commend himself to another human being. He has nothing to offer. There is nothing about him that permits the love of another person for him. He is unlovable. Yet it is exactly in his own confession that he does not deserve the love of another that he represents all the rest of us. For none of us is different from him in this regard. We are *all* unlovable. More than that, the action of this boy's life points beyond itself, it points to the Gospel, to God who loves us though we hate Him, who loves us though we do not satisfy His love, who loves us though we do not please Him, who loves us not for our sake but for His own sake, who loves us freely, who accepts us though we have nothing acceptable to offer Him. Hidden in the obnoxious existence of this boy is the scandalous secret of the Word of God.

It is, after all, in Hell – in that estate where the presence of death is militant and pervasive – that the triumph of God over death in Jesus Christ is decisive and manifest.

The Word of God is secretly present in the life of the poor, as in the life of the whole world, but most of the poor do not know the Word of God. These two facts constitute the dialectic of the Church's mission among the poor. All that is required for the mission of the Church in Harlem is there already, save one thing: the presence of the community which has and exercises the power to discern the presence of the Word of God in the ordinary life of the poor as it is lived every day. What is requisite to mission, to the exposure of God's Word within the precarious and perishing existence of poverty, is the congregation which relies on and celebrates the resurrection. That which is essential for mission is confession of the faith – immediately, notoriously, and in whatever terms or symbols or actions are indigenous to the moment and place.

The characteristic of the life of God which the Church needs most to recall nowadays, I think, is how absurdly simple His action in the world already makes our witness to Him in the world.

The churches have been beset by a false notion of charity. They have supposed that the inner city must become much more like the outer city before the Gospel can be heard. They have thought that mission follows charity. They have favored crusades and abandoned mission. I am all for changing the face of Harlem, but the mission of the Church depends not on social reformation in the neighborhood, as desperately as that is needed, but upon the presence of the Word of God in the society of the poor as it is right now. If the mere Gospel is not a whole salvation for the most afflicted people, it is no comfort to other people in less affliction. Mission does *not* follow charity; faith does *not* follow works, either for donor or recipient. On the contrary, mission is *itself* the only charity which Christians have to offer the poor, the only work which Christians have to do.

The premise of most urban church work, it seems, is that in order for the Church to minister among the poor, the church has to be rich, that is, to have specially trained personnel, huge funds and many facilities, rummage to distribute, and a whole battery of social services. Just the opposite is the case. The Church must be free to be poor in order to minister among the poor. The Church must trust the Gospel enough to come among the poor with nothing to offer the poor except the Gospel, except the power to apprehend and the courage to reveal the Word of God as it is already mediated in the life of the poor.

When the Church has the freedom itself to be poor among the poor, it will know how to use what riches it has. When the Church has that freedom, it will be a missionary people again in all the world.

PART II

Reflections

Chapter Two

Honoring the Gift of Life

Andrew W. McThenia, Jr.[1]

Any discussion of Bill Stringfellow and vocation necessarily takes me to a consideration of his life; despite the fact that many of Stringfellow's sixteen books[2] dealt with vocation in a significant way, he was not a systematic theologian. During his lifetime he was often criticized in academic reviews because his writing was not nuanced or theoretical in the way that academic theology is supposed to be. One reviewer complained that his work reflects "a maddening lack of precision which leaves one puzzling" (Douglas, 1962). Nor was he generally concerned with offering a prescription for the world's ills. A reviewer said of *Dissenter in a Great Society* (Stringfellow, 1966) that while Stringfellow laid bare the soul of America, he worried "that there is not much guidance for translating moral commitment into effective political action" (Wilkins, 1967).

His writing, like his life, did not remain on the safe level of abstraction, but drew its power and strength from the world around him and from the Bible. Jim Wallis, the editor of *Sojourners*, has said that Stringfellow always wrote with the New York Times and a Bible on his desk. He was basically a witness; as did Peter and John in the Book of Acts, he most often spoke of what he had seen and heard.

When I look at his life I see a person who recognized early on that he was likely to march to a different drummer. Carolyn Heilbrun says that a biographer's job is to find that which is most compelling in a subject's life – "that special gift without name or definition" – to understand it and to explain it (Heilbrun, 1988:196). Certainly, Stringfellow's sense of vocation was a special gift. In *A Simplicity of Faith* (Stringfellow, 1982b) he wrote that "[biography] is rudimentary data for theology, and every biography is significant for the knowledge it yields of the Word of God incarnate in common life, whether or not the subject of the biography is aware of the significance of his or her own story" (Stringfellow, 1982b:21, Wylie-Kellermann, 1994:20). He went on to say that "vocation is the

[1]   My special thanks to Anthony and Jane Dancer. Anthony had the vision for the conference out of which this chapter emerged, and together he and Jane made it happen. It was a grace full event. Thanks also to Bill Wylie-Kellermann, my friend, mentor, and co-conspirator in so many Stringfellow projects, for comments on an earlier draft of this chapter.
[2]   For a complete bibliography of Stringfellow's work see Wylie-Kellermann (1994:416-426). This marvellous bibliography was first prepared by Rev. Paul D. West some years ago.

awareness of *that* significance of one's own biography" (Stringfellow, 1982b:21, Wylie-Kellermann, 1994:20).

The issue of vocation was a matter of life-long importance to Stringfellow. His vocation, he thought, was to be William Stringfellow, nothing more and nothing less. He understood that to be called by God is to be aware that the community of the church has been set apart from the rest of the world, not because it is somehow 'better' than other communities, but because its members have a different loyalty, a different citizenship, and a different set of norms which both hold the community together and determine how it will live in the larger world.

That was, for Stringfellow, a simple matter. Simple, but not easy. He knew we were called by the Word of God, and he knew that the object of the call was all of humanity. But it was the working out of the question, "what are we called to?", that was at the center of much of his life and writing (Wylie-Kellermann, 1994:19-111). Although he knew spiritually and intellectually what the concept of vocation was all about, grand theories never meant much to Stringfellow. For him, it was in the everydayness of life, in the particulars, in the nitty gritty, where important decisions were made.[3] Let me illustrate the very practical nature of Stringfellow's thought with two examples of vocational struggle in this life.

Both of these struggles came at a relatively early age. The first concerned his notion of a vocation in politics and his (unsuccessful) efforts to provide resources for guidance and direction in the preparation of such a ministry. That effort lasted about four years and came to a close as he embraced the question of vocation in the legal profession, a question that was to continue throughout his life.

The idea of a vocation in politics began early for Stringfellow. When he was studying at the London School of Economics he showed a remarkable clarity of thought and consistency with the New Testament in rejecting the notion, then (and I think still) widely held, that there is a hierarchy of vocations with ordained persons at the top of that ladder and the rest of us somewhere below the salt. And he was also clear in rejecting the notion that the matter of vocation was somehow only of importance to those in the so-called 'learned professions' like the priesthood, law, and medicine. He saw that sort of thinking as distancing, and one which drew lines of separation within the worshiping community. Writing in the Student Christian Movement (SCM) publication *Student World* he said that "it is possible to serve the Lord fully and devotedly not only as a priest, a missionary . . . but also as a teacher, a juggler, or a politician".[4] He worried that the concept of vocation had not been taken seriously by various church organizations, notably the SCM, with which he was then associated in a leadership capacity. His writing was an indictment of the various church bureaucracies for paying lip service to a

---

[3]   "Moreover in the Gospel, vocation always bears the implication of immediacy – there is really no such thing as preparing to undertake one's vocation when one grows up or when one graduates or when one attains a certain position or when one gets to a certain place. Vocation is always here and now, without anxiety where one might be tomorrow. . . . Vocation has to do with recognizing life as a gift and honoring that gift in living" (Wylie-Kellermann, 1994:71).

[4]   Student World, Volume XLIII, No. 2 p. 56 (1950).

genuine concept of vocation, but failing to provide some understanding of how one might live out that concept in the field of politics, agriculture, manufacturing, etc.

Beginning with his time in London and continuing through his years in the armed forces, he thought a great deal about how one might be fully human and live out a life in politics. In that connection he developed a research project at the London School of Economics on the impact of Christians on contemporary British politics.[5] He also prepared and circulated among various groups a proposal for an institute on ethics and politics (Rogers, 25 March 1953).[6] That proposal envisioned establishing an institute for persons considering lives in politics and public service in order that they might develop an understanding of the relationship of social science, ethics and Christian theology in a life of public service. His vision was that the institute be vocational; it was to be of assistance to Christians in politics so that they might live consistent with the Christian story. The proposal languished for the next two years while Stringfellow was in the armed forces, but on his return to the United States, he, together with some friends from old SCM days, revived it. Several academic institutions showed real interest in the concept, and within a year it had found a tentative home at Wesleyan University in Connecticut. A linchpin provision in the concept so far as Stringfellow was concerned was that the institute retain an intimate relationship with a worshiping community.

While Stringfellow was pleased with the interest shown by Wesleyan, he worried that too close a connection with a university would tend to abstract the institute from the realm of politics. "The old egghead label is a symbol of something very genuine which exists between those who talk politics and those [who] with their hands, so to speak – do politics" (Stringfellow, 26 March 1953). He was also worried lest the concept of such an institute lose its anchor with a worshiping community and get swept up in a sea of secularism.

The Institute of Ethics and Politics was established at Wesleyan University about the time he entered law school (Gessert, 1955). While day to day operations were taken over by an executive director, Stringfellow remained a board member for the next two years. Over the course of that period, the Institute became pretty thoroughly 'academized' and Stringfellow, believing that both of his fears – that the institute would become too abstract for the world of politics and that it would succumb to the pressures of secularization – had in fact become a reality, resigned from the Board in 1957 (Stringfellow, 8 August 1957).

That chapter reflects some pretty clear thinking about vocation, particularly for such a young man. He early on carved out a very different concept of vocation from that developed by Martin Luther. For Luther vocation was tied to one's station in life and it seems to involve something in the nature of a life-long

---

[5]   In particular, his work focused upon the work of William Temple and the Malvern Conference.

[6]   This conversation was continued in a series of letters between Rogers and Stringfellow at this time.

calling.[7] But Stringfellow did not, he said, "indulge in any fantasies that God called him to be a member of any profession or organization". Nor did the pursuit of vocation necessarily involve any permanency of occupation; it is "always here and now, without anxiety of where one might be tomorrow" (Wylie-Kellermann, 1994:71).

What seemed to happen with the experiment in the Institute for Politics was that instead of its becoming a place where Christians could be nourished in the implications of their baptismal vows, it began to create a separate class of professionals who looked to professional norms for moral decision making. Stringfellow worried that such professionalism put people in fundamentally different categories, and that what separated them from each other became more important for their social behavior than what they had in common in Christ. He considered the worshiping community an integral part of discerning the gifts of the Spirit and of forming identity. Anything less was apostasy and would lead to idolatry.

While he was approached about assuming the directorship of the Institute for Politics, he was already pretty disillusioned with the direction it was taking and decided to enter law school in the fall of 1953. As he was winding down his efforts with the Institute for Politics, his life seemed frantic. He was very much a loner during that time. Friends and former associates describe him as having almost boundless energy, but only one can recall where he lived. There are reports of his drinking heavily. While he spent a great deal of time looking for ways to finance his legal education, there is almost no evidence that he reflected on a life in the law as a matter of vocation. In the winter of 1953, as he awaited the beginning of the fall term in law school, he seemed either a young man in a hurry or one caught on a treadmill. Maybe there was no difference. In one of his more reflective moments he wrote of the dilemmas of American students recently discharged from the army. He spoke of the sense of abandonment by all institutions, including the church, that servicemen feel. "The impact of this sense of instability in all things upon which the individual is one which leads not simply to cynicism, and repudiation of participation in the community, an embitterment, but actually to a disintegration of personality – to a robbery of that upon which individual personality in America has so often depended for stability of purpose – a replacement for that which has been robbed by an oppressive but overwhelming sense of personal helplessness" (Stringfellow, February 1953).

That existential loneliness soon gave way to resistance when he enrolled in the first year class at Harvard Law School that fall.

> Initiation into the legal profession, as it is played out in a place like Harvard Law School, is, as one would expect, elaborately mythologized, asserts an aura of tradition, and retains a reputation for civility. All of these insinuate that the process is benign, though, both empirically and in principle, it is demonic...I suffered the overkill ethos of

---

[7] "There is the underlying assumption...for Martin Luther...that the moral content of the vocation's call is stable since society itself was assumed to be stable" (Stassen et al., 1996:78).

the Harvard Law School – I think – with enough poise as a human being to quietly, patiently, vigilantly resist becoming conformed to this world. (Stringfellow, 1982b:126-7)

Without question that resistance helped him become more aware spiritually and he began to make some extremely important and life-giving connections between vocation, baptism, and the powers and principalities.

To understand this confrontation between his continual search for vocation and the power and principality known as the legal profession, those who are unfamiliar with the High Temple of Legal Education in America, the Harvard Law School, might reflect on two lawyer stories closer to home, Dickens *Bleak House*, and Trollope's *Orley Farm*. Legal education in America has elements of both: a stultifying worship of tradition, and a professional morality which makes the lawyer answerable only to her client.

When Stringfellow entered law school, the legal profession was a very close knit affair. It was marked by well defined boundaries and was extremely hierarchical in nature. In many ways it still is. Several things help to ensure these distinctions in the profession, and among them, the place of one's legal education is not insignificant. Historically, the Harvard Law School has long been at or near the center of the legal culture in America.

In those post World War Two years when Stringfellow was at Harvard, there was a symbiotic relationship between the worldview of Harvard and the legal profession. Harvard was the center of legal process thinking. Law in action was a search for shared principles in the social order. That philosophy rested on the assumption of an expanding and progressive social order in which the majority of the citizenry shared the same underlying values, the values of enlightenment rationalism: the so-called neutral principles. Most crucial to this 'process school' was a shared belief in the competency of institutions, particularly courts, to decide how questions of policy would be answered.

The trick was to uncover the underlying neutral principles. And that search was to be guided by courts. Judges were by virtue of their training and station uniquely suited for this detached role. The nagging questions of how there could be objective values knitting together the citizens of a liberal democracy – a system premised on a pluralistic subjectivity of values – was for a long time ignored. However, it never fully disappeared (Mensch, 1990:32). This search for neutral principles left little room for asking whether the principles that undergird the law are all that neutral. Nor did it leave much room for asking questions about substantive justice. Law was process and justice was to be insured by procedural fairness. (One is reminded of Thomas Merton's observation that the end of the world will be quite legal.) And a lawyer's primary responsibility in that order was to assume a moral neutrality; to adopt a point of view of being point of view*less* on questions concerning the moral nature of a client's enterprise. The danger of relying on a concept that holds one's highest loyalty is to her client's autonomy calls a person away from real responsibility. It conceals from her the character of her conduct as her own direct responsibility (Barth, 1960:14).

Stringfellow arrived on the scene as the process school was gaining the high ground at Harvard. He commented on the failure to consider the relationship between law and *justice*:

> I also thought, while I was in law school, that *justice* is a suitable topic for consideration in practically every course or specialization. Alas, it was seldom mentioned, and the term itself evoked ridicule, as if justice were a subject beneath the sophistication of lawyers. (Stringfellow, 1982b:126-7)

Furthermore the process school left *no* room for questions of faith or for questions about the relationship between faith and law. The legal profession, with its faith in enlightenment rationalism, proceeded as if there had never been any connection between the western legal tradition and faith. The irony of all that was not lost on Stringfellow, who intuited that the faith that Judges could uncover underlying values was itself a religion – the religion of the intellectual. And that secular seminary known as the Harvard Law School was the primary defender of the faith.

The nexus between law and theology was simply disregarded as American law continued on a fiercely secular path. As a result of that process, law students came to see the connection between faith and law as mostly a disconnection; to the extent they considered that any nexus remained at all, they thought first of law not faith. Whatever vestiges of memory of faith communities students might have brought with them were generally transformed into notions of alien enterprises threatening the constitutional order of autonomous liberalism. In the legal academy religion was cabined off into the safe status of being merely 'private and subjective'. It is incredible that legal education was so successful in that effort. No wonder it became, and has remained, the trusted gatekeeper of the profession.

From the outset of his time at Harvard, Stringfellow seemed to know what the stakes were. While his working class background would have been an impediment to automatic membership in the elite of the patrician American legal establishment, as a Phi Beta Kappa graduate of an eastern college and former Rotary Fellow at the London School of Economics he could certainly have found a home at the Harvard Law School. Yet he never sought insider status. In fact, he spent the better part of three years resisting the process of professionalization. During that first year in law school he assembled a group of students and a few practicing lawyers to explore ways in which faith questions confronting prospective lawyers would not be overwhelmed by the elaborate professionalization rituals taking place in the law school. He even found one faculty member who was willing to join the group. That committee on vocation in the legal profession continued to meet during his entire time in law school and was an important venue of resistance to the deformation and bleaching by the powers of the profession.

On a list of his top five priorities in Cambridge (Massachusetts, that is), law school ranked a distant tenth. While he was a student he continued to take classes at the Episcopal Divinity School, taught rhetoric and coached debate at nearby Tufts University, traveled widely as a consultant to the World Student Christian Federation, and managed to check in at the law school about every two weeks.

By the time of his graduation he had been so successful in his resistance efforts that he could truthfully claim that "I emerged from the law school as someone virtually opposite of what a Harvard Law School graduate is projected by prevailing system to be" (Wylie-Kellermann, 1994:32).

To a great extent that posture of resistance allowed him to discern his next vocational move. While many of his classmates began their ascent on the ladder of the legal establishment by joining major Wall Street law firms, Stringfellow, in the first of many moves to the margin, joined the ministry of the East Harlem Protestant Parish in order to start a street law practice in New York's most densely populated and poorest neighborhood. That was an extraordinarily unusual commitment at that time and indeed an uncommon commitment today. He described his work in Harlem as providing representation "for people deprived of elementary rights: Blacks, Hispanics, Native Americans, political prisoners, homosexuals, the elderly, the handicapped" (Wylie-Kellermann, 1994:33-4).

The reason he went to East Harlem was not a political one. He did not use social location as a platform for some other agenda. That move to the margin was, in worldly terms, a bad career choice. It was for him a matter of vocation. He found himself there because that is where his vocational call led him. He later wrote that:

> To be concerned with the outcast is an echo, of course, of the gospel itself. Characteristically, the Christian is to be found in his work and witness in the world among those for whom no one else cares – the poor, the sick, the imprisoned, the misfits, the homeless, the orphans and beggars. The presence of the Christian among the outcast is the way in which the Christian represents, concretely the ubiquity and universality of the intercession of Christ for all. All human beings are encompassed in the ministry of the Christian to the least. (Wylie-Kellermann, 1994:41-2)

The move to East Harlem was significant on many counts. It represented an outright rejection of a traditional career path for a Harvard Law School graduate and a direct confrontation with the powers.[8] It also represented leaving the safe world of abstraction endemic to the legal academy of that period and entering the world of pain, death, and incarnational theology. It was the beginning of a new chapter in his education: his "deschooling" (Davis, 1996:52). But as much as anything else it was a deepening of vocation.

It was a deepening in a profound sense. Recall, if you will, my earlier description of the adversary system of American law as distancing a lawyer from her client. The conventional wisdom on the lawyer's role is that a lawyer owes near absolute loyalty to an ethic which exists to protect a client's autonomy. Any reservations the lawyer has about the client's proposed course of action or morality are, in large part, simply irrelevant. The lawyer is called to be morally neutral. Like most conventional wisdom, the support for this notion of lawyer neutrality comes in large part from the legal profession itself – and from few other places (which is

---

[8] For more on Stringfellow's relationship to the principalities and powers, see especially Chapter 5.

another way of saying that long entrenched absurdity has its own rationale). You will recall the problem that Anthony Trollope had with the adversary ethic in *Orley Farm*.

The novel revolves around the question as to whether Lady Mason forged the codicil to her husband's will. The climax is her trial for perjury in previously swearing that she saw the will properly executed and witnessed. Lady Mason, in fact, did lie about the execution of the will, because she herself had forged it. She is well defended by three lawyers who live with varying degrees of discomfort with the demands of the notion of professionalism. Mr. Chaffanbrass (some claim he is an early incarnation of Rumpole of the Bailey) is worried only about getting his guilty client off. Mr. Furnival, who appears rather astute, except for permitting his clerk attempt to buy off another, does his job with an uneasy conscience. The third, Felix Graham, worries so much that he is unable to do his job, but he does make off with Madeline Staveley, the judge's daughter.

Trollope was less than enthusiastic about the attitude of his lawyer characters who were uninterested in the question of guilt or innocence of their clients. Some time ago a publisher did an American edition of the book and had one of our more eminent lawyers and legal ethics scholars, Henry Drinker of Philadelphia, write an introduction. Drinker concluded that Trollope just didn't understand the functions of lawyers and stated that one of his greatest misconceptions was that he thought it unethical for a lawyer to take a case when he does not believe in the inherent justice of his client's cause. Drinker went on to lecture Trollope on the American Bar Association's Canons of Ethics. Drinker, the expert, had to educate the non-lawyer Trollope because he was an outsider.[9]

That is one of the major problems with professionalism. It separates us from our ordinary lives. We lawyers have adopted a morality of procedure. We are among the new ruling elite class of symbolic analysts.[10] We develop, impose, and interpret our own ethical standards. Outsiders like Trollope are incompetent to comment because they don't understand lawyers.

That entire line of thinking was morally repugnant to Stringfellow. He resolutely refused to surrender the demands of his faith to the 'bleaching' influence of professionalism. One of the major reasons he joined the East Harlem Protestant Parish was so that his work as a lawyer would be closely tied to a worshiping community.[11]

As I understand traditional Lutheran thought on vocation or 'station in life', the Christian who is a member of a profession would look to the profession for her

---

[9]   I am indebted to my friend Tom Shaffer for much of this discussion on Trollope (and for so much else). See Thomas Shaffer (1966).

[10]   The term 'symbolic analyst' is one given to people who process information in this new electronic post industrial age. Lawyers, journalists, and computer experts are among the new ruling class: a class which does not produce or govern but which processes and trades in valuable information.

[11]   He later encountered the power of professionalism in another guise in the East Harlem Protestant Parish, but that is another story, told in Stringfellow (1964c:85-97) or Wylie-Kellermann (1994:130-40).

standards of moral action. One will know how to act within a particular 'station', 'office', or 'profession' because of norms established *not* by a believing community but from the orders of creation and the profession itself. According to this concept of 'orders of creation', a soldier takes his direction from the role defined for soldiers in the world. Similarly a hangman does his job well when he does what the hangman's union tells him what a good hangman must do. Or a lawyer serves in accordance with the dictates of his profession and without regard to contrary teaching from a community of worship.

That line of thinking seeks to deny the reality of the Fall. As John Howard Yoder says, 'the way things are' is not the 'order of creation' (Yoder, 1989). Stringfellow told us so many times that institutions too are fallen. Our job as lawyers is to resist the pull of the profession which would have us set aside our faith claims. That is in large part what Stringfellow was talking about when he distinguished vocation from career. And I think that in joining the East Harlem Protestant Parish he sought to bring his vocational issues to the church, to the believing community, and not to surrender them to a professional ethic that separates brothers and sisters from each other and from their calling under God to be known as sinners saved by grace.

Stringfellow saw being a lawyer as a pastoral gift; he heard the call to be an advocate, to intercede for the need of another, to become vulnerable in the place of another – as gifts from God. At the same time he knew that living within the bounds of a profession that has, as its core reality, a morality based on an adversary system which separates people from one another and which is often at variance with the Christian story, would always be problematic. He wrote early in his life in the law that "I continue to be haunted by the ironic impression that I may have to renounce being a lawyer, the better to be an advocate" (Stringfellow, 1982a:17). He never escaped that tension; in truth he knew that he never could. Instead he faced it head on. Stringfellow had a unique ability to live into the contraries, contradictions, and paradoxes of life. I believe that was because he was continually attentive to the vocational call and the warrant that comes with baptism. He knew he was a sinner saved by grace. He knew the shape and structure of the world. He could be free in obedience in a world of uncertainty. He knew, as Archbishop Rowan Williams might put it, his own métier (Williams, 1995:95).

I will close with a final story from Stringfellow's practice in Harlem. In his early years in the law Stringfellow got some very important deschooling on the streets of East Harlem that opened his eyes to the awesome nature of the powers. Because he was so well grounded in his own vocation, he was on occasion successful in redeeming them. The story follows:

> There is a boy in the neighborhood...whom I have defended in some of his troubles with the law. He used to stop in often on Saturday mornings to shave and wash up, after having spent the week on the streets. He has been addicted for a long time. His father threw him out three years ago, when he was first arrested. He has contrived so many stories to induce clergy and social workers to give him money to support his habit that he is no longer believed when he asks for help...He is dirty, ignorant, arrogant, dishonest, unemployable, broken, unreliable, ugly, rejected, alone. And he knows it. He

knows at last that he has nothing to commend himself to another human being. He has nothing to offer. There is nothing about him that permits the love of another person for him. He is unlovable. Yet it is in his own confession that he does not deserve the love of another that he represents all the rest of us in this regard. We are all unlovable. More than that, the action of this boy's life points beyond itself, it points to the Gospel, to God who loves us though we hate Him, who loves us though we do not please Him, who loves us not for our sake but for his own sake, who loves us freely, who accepts us though we have nothing acceptable to offer Him. Hidden in the obnoxious existence of this boy is the scandalous secret of the Word of God. (Stringfellow, 1964c:97-8)

One of the significant things in the story for me is the clarity of Stringfellow's vision. It is interesting to contrast his view of the young man with the 'professional view'.

The professional response would be to urge a lofty detachment from this young man (and from his pain). Professionalism would treat him as a problem to be solved rather than a life to be treasured. The professional would ask how can we come to terms with the need to defend this worthless kid in his various scrapes with the law. The profession would take justifiable pride in its answer that we need to defend him *in spite of his worthlessness* in order to uphold the system of justice.

But what Stringfellow saw in the young man is "the scandalous secret of the Word of God". That mandates a radically different response. We need to stand with this young man not in spite of his worthlessness, but *precisely because* of it.

That vision is based not on something abstract like the system of justice, but on the reality of the resurrection. That reality leads one to compassion. Compassion is not willing to be altruistic, or generous, or tolerant, or charitable. Compassion is not willing at all. Compassion is surrender. It involves giving up on our notions of goodness and tolerance and accepting that we are precisely like the young man who the profession would hold at arm's length, alone and in need of God's saving grace.

It is in such moments of powerlessness that we come to experience the true power that liberates us and frees our imaginations from the need to draw lines which separate us from others in order to affirm our own goodness. It is in these moments that the grace of God transcends the injustice of the present age and agitates the resilience of those like Stringfellow who struggle now to expose and rebuke injustice.

In that act of seeing that young man through the eyes of compassion, Stringfellow rebuked the powers, and at least for that moment redeemed the legal professional to pursue its true vocation. Thanks be to God for the Gift of William Stringfellow.

Chapter Three

On Being a Prophet and a Theologian: Reflections on Stringfellow and the East Harlem Protestant Parish

Kenneth Leech

The years 1956-1964 were extremely critical years in Stringfellow's life, and also in mine. They were also critical years in the whole development of urban ministry in the United States and Britain, and it is some of the interconnections between people and movements in those formative years that I want to reflect on. In particular, I want to examine one facet of Stringfellow's life and explore what its implications might be for us all. That one facet is his quarrel with the East Harlem Protestant Parish, which led him to resign from it after only 18 months.[1]

Now in 1956, in the summer, at the age of 28, Stringfellow went to work in East Harlem, which for those of you who don't know it is the area between 5th Avenue and Madison Avenue, roughly north of 100th Street, and up to 112th, sometimes known as Spanish Harlem, or East Harlem, to distinguish it from Harlem itself. He didn't stay very long. He entered into a dispute with the Protestant parish and resigned, although he did stay in East Harlem practising as a lawyer for many years afterwards.

In 1956 I was 17 years old, and was just beginning to struggle with the question 'Can I be a Christian and remain an intelligent human being?' The person who helped me to answer that question in the affirmative was the philosopher Alasdair MacIntyre, who in those days was a member of a parish on the edge of Manchester which I also joined. In 1956 Macintyre gave me his first book *Marxism: An Interpretation* (MacIntyre, 1953), which has gone through a number of revisions. MacIntyre's book was a reflection on Christianity and Marxism, and it finished with the following paragraph:

A community committed alike to politics and prayer would serve in the renewal of the whole church, for it would bring to us a fresh understanding of that central act of the church's life, which is in humble thanksgiving to eat the body of a Lord who hungered

---

[1]   The East Harlem Protestant Parish was a pioneer and flagship experiment in Urban Ministry at that time, and highly regarded for it. It was formed in 1948 by Don Benedict, Archie Hargraves, and George Webber. The abbreviation EHPP will be used hereafter.

and thirsted, and to drink the blood of a Lord who the powers of Church and State combined to crucify outside the walls of the city. (MacIntyre, 1953:126)

Now anyone that reads that paragraph from MacIntyre will immediately recognise the affinity with both Stringfellow, who wrote much which was similar, and with the EHPP, one of whose founding aims being precisely to create a community committed alike to politics and prayer. Now having been influenced by MacIntyre, one of my central concerns in 1956 at the age of 17 (and it remains an equally important concern now) is how one creates communities and sustains communities which are committed alike to politics and prayer.

In 1958 I moved from Manchester to live in the east end of London, a quarter of a mile from where I live now. I found myself living in Cable Street, close to the London Docks (in the days when London had a Docks). There was a little cafe across the road called Little Harlem Cafe which did much to embody the very strong sense among the very racially mixed community of Cable Street that there was some kind of affinity between Cable Street and Harlem. In fact Cable Street was often referred to in the newspapers of the time as London's Harlem.

I lived in the Franciscan House, which had been a brothel, and which the friars, I thought rather unwisely, called a House of Hospitality. There, in Cable Street, in the basement chapel of this house we used to pray for people all over the world who were doing similar work, and I remember on Tuesdays in 1958 we used to pray for people in inner-city ministries in the United States. I remember the names, although I didn't know who they were: we always prayed for Norman Eddy, and Bill Webber in East Harlem, and we prayed for Bill Wendt and Kilmer Myers in the Lower East Side. There, on a Tuesday in prayer, the name of William Stringfellow first entered my hearing. There were many thousands of people in 1958 that I had never heard of, but there were two people in particular that I had never heard of: William Stringfellow and Dorothy Day. It was in Cable Street that I first heard of both of them.

Now William Stringfellow and Dorothy Day had a great deal in common. Not least, Dorothy Day founded the Catholic Worker Movement in 1933, and was as committed as Stringfellow was to solidarity with the poorest and most oppressed people and communities.

The reason I had not heard of William Stringfellow was probably due to the fact that his books were never published in this country. The reason I had not heard of Dorothy Day was because Cardinal Griffin, the Archbishop of Westminster, had banned the *Catholic Worker* from all the Catholic bookstores on the grounds that it was communist. Had he realized that in fact it wasn't communist, but anarchist, he would have had apoplexy. But the anarchist bookshop wouldn't sell it either because it was religious. So the only place you could get it was at Hyde Park Speakers Corner, where it was sold every week for a penny a copy by an Anglo-Catholic anarchist called Laurens Otter.

So, my conscious awareness that there were other people doing similar work, and that there was a kind of informal network of Christians in a variety of cities in Britain and the United States who were all in touch with each other and were influenced by each other, really came about in those early years in Cable Street. And at the heart of it was the EHPP.

Therefore, when I first went to the United States some years later it was to East Harlem that I went, on the way, curiously, to a drugs conference at the Haight-Ashbury free clinic in San Francisco. Now you may rightly point out that to go Haight-Ashbury via East Harlem is not the most direct route, but for some eight years all I knew of the United States and the church in the United States was Haight-Ashbury and East Harlem, and I knew nothing in between. As a consequence, I had a very curious image of what North America was like.

These years from 1956 to 1964 were crucial for Stringfellow: he came to East Harlem; he fell out with the Parish; he continued as a lawyer; and in 1964 he wrote what I still think is one of his greatest books, *Dissenter in a Great Society* (Stringfellow, 1966).

In Britain, the influence of the EHPP was very significant. In the early 1960s Bruce Kenrick, who had worked in East Harlem and was one of the key people in the formation of Shelter around the same time,[2] decided to write a book about East Harlem (Kenrick, 1962). Published as I was preparing for ordination, it was one of the books that really inspired me and shaped and formed me as a pastor. However, having been captivated by Kenrick's book, I was rather brought down to earth when I went to East Harlem and discovered that quite a number of ministers there didn't approve of it and said it was all wrong.

Yet it was one of those great and inspiring books which only appear about once a decade, and it set many people of my generation on the path to ministry in the urban areas. At the time, *Come Out the Wilderness* (Kenrick, 1962) was a very important book in raising the consciousness of Christians in Britain, not only about East Harlem, but of inner cities generally, long before things like *Faith in the City* (Harvey, 1989) and the Methodist Report were even gleams in their collective authors' eyes.

Linked with this was the influence that the EHPP had on ministry in Notting Hill. After the inter-racial conflicts of 1958,[3] Donald Soper, then president of the Methodist Conference, encouraged the formation of a ministry in the Lancaster Road area of Notting Hill based on the ministry in East Harlem. The three ministers who began that ministry in Notting Hill, Geoffrey Ainger, David Mason, and Norwyn Denny, had all worked in the EHPP with William Stringfellow. Now I mention all this because I think in these years there were all kinds of interconnections, and links, and influences, in this field of pastoral ministry. And Stringfellow, although most people had never heard of him in this country, was at the heart of the East Harlem work.

---

[2] Kenrick is one of the unsung heroes in fact – most people have not even heard of his name, but it was Bruce Kenrick who really founded Shelter arising out of the Notting Hill Housing trust work.

[3] These have erroneously gone down in history as the Notting Hill Riots although they didn't occur in Notting Hill, they occurred in Notting Dale, Shepherds Bush, and the Latimer Road area.

Although I never met Stringfellow, I was attracted first of all to his work by two things. The first was his commitment to work in East Harlem and his commitment to the kind of ministry I was beginning to get involved with in London. The second was that he seemed to have the same relationship with the Episcopal Church in the United States that I had with the Church of England; a relationship he described once as "benign disaffection". We both seemed to be rather marginal to the churches to which we belonged.

Stringfellow came to East Harlem when he was 28, and within a very short time Kenrick was writing about Stringfellow's belief that there was a radical failure to take the Bible and Christ seriously in the EHPP (Kenrick, 1962:124-125). Before examining this in more detail, we first need to look again at what Kenrick was doing in *Come Out the Wilderness*.

Kenrick talks about the importance in pastoral ministry of staying with suffering, recognizing that much of the time we have no easy answers and that we simply stay with the wounds and the pain, and that that process may go on for many years. He talks particularly about this in relation to the experience of heroin addiction. As I read him for the first time I had just met my first two heroin addicts who were the sons of my church warden in Shoreditch, and so I was just becoming familiar with the heroin scene in London.

Now, Kenrick reinforces this by saying: "the church must suffer and be crucified with those it seeks to serve; and...it must keep on being crucified even though the nails bite deep and the hope of resurrection is obscure" (Kenrick, 1962:155). This seems to me to be an important insight, and it's one I think we need to hold in our minds as we continue our discussion because I think it is quite crucial to what was going on in East Harlem, and it may be relevant to why Stringfellow got into dispute. I don't know for sure, but I want to raise the question.

Stringfellow described his relationship with the EHPP really in a very extreme form in his book *My People is the Enemy* (Stringfellow, 1964c). To my mind, there is one passage which is crucial to our reflection. It is this.

> They plunged into all sorts of social work and social action – narcotics, politics, neighborhood improvement, education, housing, and the rest. They instituted therapy and counseling for addicts, engaged in voter registration, lobbied for new playgrounds, organized PTAs, complained about slum landlords, made themselves a nuisance to those in power around the neighborhood. It was in many ways an admirable, if idealistic, and in Christian terms naive effort, but they neglected and postponed the proclamation and celebration of the Gospel in East Harlem. (Stringfellow, 1964c:88)[4]

That was the basis of his critique. Now when I read that, a number of contradictory and confused emotions go through me. One is to say yes, these are all the things we've been doing at St Botolphs for years and years and years; the parallels are very precise. Another bit of me says they are good things and they shouldn't be

---

[4]   For further reflection by Stringfellow upon EHPP see *Poverty, Charity and Mission: East Harlem Protestant Parish* in part one of this book.

written off as naive. And they're not just social work, and why should social work be used as a term of abuse anyway. Then part of me says yes, I've been saying this kind of thing to St Botolphs too. That there is a danger that churches become nothing more than what Tony Benn once called "intensive care for capitalism", and they do not challenge the powers at all, they simply act as a casualty station, a band-aid ministry, they pick up the pieces, they comfort the afflicted, but they don't afflict the comfortable, because if they did their government grant would be taken away. Yes, I know all that, and I feel very much that and in my role at St Botolphs I find myself saying many of the same things, so my heart goes out to Stringfellow. I say all this, yet I think looking back on it Stringfellow's remarks are grossly unfair. Grossly unfair to those people who are still in East Harlem today 50 years after the EHPP was formed.

During the writing of Kenrick's book correspondence between Stringfellow and Kenrick was generated. Some of it is very interesting, and worthy of our attention.

Based in Liverpool, Kenrick wrote to Stringfellow to say that he is going to write a book about East Harlem, and that he wants to deal with – this is Kenrick's phrase but it could be Stringfellow's – "the radical failure to take the bible and Christ seriously, and the desperate need for a ruthless, uncompromising, prophetic voice" (Kenrick, 19 October 1960). This was what Stringfellow apparently missed in East Harlem. Kenrick goes on to send Stringfellow his draft paragraph for Stringfellow's criticism.

> Into this unpromising situation came a slight, intense, immaculate lawyer in the spring of 1956. William Stringfellow was 30 years of age, and he lived and worked with the group for two years. Unlike the other members who shared his particular concern, he made no allowance whatever for the complex nature of the parish worker's problems. He ignored completely the feelings those who had been working there for eight years longer than he. And day after day, and week after week, he savaged the group without mercy for their neglect of the Word of God. He was rude, he was ruthless, he was rigid, and he was right. (Kenrick, 19 October 1960)

Stringfellow replies, and after making a few factual corrections he goes on to deal with the more fundamental points that Kenrick is making. "I did not ignore, nor was I ignorant of, the complex nature of the parish worker's problems. On the contrary, aware of them, I disregarded them as excuses for the indifference of the ministry to the gospel. I did not savage the group without mercy. I did so without pause, that is, persistently. But not without compassion or mercy. On the contrary, it was out of compassion that I was persistent in whatever harassment I was to the group. I don't mind your saying I was rude, ruthless etc. But perhaps you should add relentless" (Stringfellow, 26 October 1960).[5]

---

[5] In his reply to Stringfellow Kenrick made clear his cheerful willingness to incorporate the many changes and improvements Stringfellow suggested, with one main exception as it concerns our discussion here. Kenrick proposed to keep the phrase "without mercy", on "purely stylistic grounds" as "there will be few, if any, who will take the phrase...literally" (Kenrick, 24 November 1960).

So here is Stringfellow in dispute with this very important parish, and in one sense it is a classic conflict between the prophetic and the pastor, or if you like between the servant church and the prophetic church. Stringfellow is playing the role of the prophet, the role which Walter Brueggemann once described as a "destabilising presence in any community", a trouble maker, one who upsets the apple cart. But was it fair? Did he actually take seriously what the East Harlem ministers and workers were trying to do? One and a half years is not very long to give a parish a chance.[6] And in fact it is interesting that much of the critique that Stringfellow made was subsequently incorporated into the parish programme after he left.

Now what was it about Stringfellow which led him into dispute with this important experiment in urban ministry? I think there are a number of things which give us a clue. Stringfellow was a profoundly biblical person. He was *not* a fundamentalist, but he *was* steeped in the scriptures. He wished to develop what Jim Wallis, who was very much a disciple of his, later called an 'agenda for biblical people' (Wallis, 1976). He wished to develop, and did develop, a kind of biblical consciousness. He said on one occasion that he found himself reading more and more of the Bible, and when he thought his phone was being tapped by the FBI he used to read whole chunks of the prophet Amos across the phone. I have done that myself on occasions. And he felt that there was a neglect of the Bible and taking the Bible seriously in its challenge to the contemporary scene. He described the EHPP as a parish that was deeply conformed to the world (Stringfellow, 1964c:91).

Now again it is a dilemma which we have all been in. It is a dilemma which I live with at St Botolphs all the time. And I suppose one of the differences between Stringfellow and me, here, is that he found that the conflict was an impossible one to negotiate and he left after a year and a half, and I've stayed. But to stay is a very uncomfortable thing. And all the issues which McThenia raises about professionalism in Chapter Two, all the them-and-us, I-and-it relationships with people who are called clients, or problems, all those arise for me too.

I think that the neglect of the challenge of scripture was fundamental to Stringfellow's critique. He really did believe that the Protestant parish was playing down, and at times ignoring the prophetic and confrontational dimension of the Christian message. That it was in fact substituting the servant church with the prophetic church. I think it was Martin Luther King Jr. in one of his sermons who said that the role of the church is not to be the servant of the state, still less its master, but always its conscience. And it was that which I think Stringfellow found missing, rightly or wrongly (and I think in some respects he was wrong), in the EHPP.

---

[6]   Editor's note: For clarification, Stringfellow did not leave ministry in Harlem at this time, but did leave the Group Ministry team of the EHPP. There, his ministry continued among that community until 1963. His experiences there were deeply formative to his own life and work. "The decision [to resign] permitted both the group ministry and myself to persevere in the work which each felt called to do in East Harlem, in society at large, and in the ministry of the Church" (Stringfellow, 1964c:96).

Linked with that, and other people in this volume say much more about this, there was a strong apocalyptic dimension in Stringfellow. Now many people are, rightly, very wary of apocalyptic. When they think of apocalyptic in contemporary Christianity they think of Oklahoma and Waco, and vast numbers of millennium groupings which show no sign of abating, and one can sympathize with people like Rosemary Ruether who will say that apocalyptic is a dangerous form of Christian presence: something that Christians should be very wary of and have as little to do with as possible. I think Stringfellow helps us to see the radical potential in the apocalyptic vision, and the key text here for those of you who haven't read it, and for those of you who can get hold of it, is of course his book *Ethic for Christians and Other Aliens in a Strange Land* (Stringfellow, 1973). *Ethic* is based on the book of Revelation and is saturated in the imagery of Babylon, which itself is central to his understanding of the powers and principalities.

As is pointed out elsewhere, it was Stringfellow's grasp of the powers which led Walter Wink eventually to produce his three volume work on the powers. But Stringfellow's influence was in short spurts in a way. His books were short, they show all the signs of having been written straight off, they rarely have references, they sometimes don't have an index. This is street theology, theology in a hurry. Theology, in a sense, written prayerfully and passionately, with all the strengths and weaknesses that that style brings with it: a lack of balance very often, and one suspects at times an utter certainty that he has got it right and no one else has. When I spoke to Geoffrey Ainger, who had been in East Harlem with Stringfellow in the 1950s, his first comment was "he was always very dogmatic".

The apocalyptic strand in Stringfellow led him into dissent with East Harlem. He felt that they were picking up the pieces, they were doing good to broken people, they were not challenging Babylon. Linked with this is a third factor in Stringfellow's spirituality and approach to pastoral ministry: that he was essentially a dissenter – dissenter in a great society. He often spoke about resistance as the only way to live humanly, under a totalitarian regime.

He was very much a theologian of resistance, which is no doubt why Karl Barth in that memorable encounter with Stringfellow in the University of Chicago, pointed to *him*, ignoring Bob Grant, Martin Marty, Hans Frei and all the other academic theologians sitting in the same room, and said this is the man that America should be listening to. But there is a lot of affinity between Stringfellow and Barth, the emphasis very strongly upon proclamation and the relationship of proclamation with resistance. Stringfellow must have been one of the first American writers in the modern period to talk very clearly about the need for a confessing church, using that expression which comes out of the Nazi period in relationship to our situation now.

I think the fourth element of Stringfellow's theology which led him into dispute with East Harlem, was that he was completely taken up with, one could even say obsessed with, the question of death. When I spoke to Geoffrey Ainger he remembered a Bible study Stringfellow did very vividly in East Harlem in the 1950s on the Epistle to the Colossians. Apparently Stringfellow said that the "whole Epistle is about death". Ainger said that upon hearing this, everyone switched off.

But if you read Stringfellow's works the theme of the dominion of death is constantly coming up. Whether he is talking about the actual death of Anthony Towne, or whether he is talking about the experience of mourning and grief and bereavement, or whether he is talking about the actual relationship of the church to the world, death is central. The whole essence of Stringfellow's theology can be seen in terms of the conflict between the Kingdom of God and the dominion of death symbolized by Babylon. And he says in *Ethic*, that "the doom of Babylon, the great city, occasions celebration in heaven" (Stringfellow, 1973). Now again, he did not believe that the East Harlem parish was seriously confronting the dominion of death and seeking to bring about the new life of the resurrection, that in a sense they were making the dominion of death more humane, accommodating it, and making it more liveable with.

Now, back to the question of his criticism of the EHPP and his resignation. Although I have hinted that I was not entirely happy with Stringfellow's critique, was he right? Kenrick says he was. But part of me says no, this criticism of Stringfellow's is very impatient and very arrogant. There are other dimensions to pastoral ministry than constant polemic and confrontation. There are dimensions of gentleness, and care, and silence, and listening, and staying with the suffering. And there doesn't seem to be a lot in Stringfellow's writings about that. And it may well be that the EHPP had quite a bit to teach him about those dimensions, and he didn't stay long enough to learn.

And so I want to finish with some questions. I never met Stringfellow, all I know about his personality is what I have picked up from the books, and the odd tapes, and talking to people who knew him. But the story is a very familiar one. It's the story of the destabilizing presence in a community. It's the story of the clash between the prophetic and the pastoral. It's the story of what Richard Holloway has called the "antithetical preacher" who throws kerygmatic parcel bombs through the windows of those who are at ease in Zion. It is an old conflict which is going on still. I don't know how much of this was to do with incompatible theologies, different views of the relationship of church and world, different views indeed of what the church is, or how much of it was to do with personality.

I'm always worried about people like Stringfellow, Thomas Merton, Dorothy Day, and Conrad Noel and all these people who were always trouble makers when they were alive, because the moment they die they were sanitized. I think it is important when people are dead to look at them honestly, and to avoid eulogizing and sanitizing them. In doing so, there is one area that I worry about his work. When I look honestly at some of Stringfellow's work, I think there is a certain impetuousness, impatience, and an inability to understand the position of those less charismatic people who simply get on with the boring work, and are still in East Harlem now. So I want to finish by suggesting first of all that the EHPP were deeply grateful to Stringfellow, they learnt a lot from him, and they all hold him in the greatest affection.

The second point is this. As I look at Stringfellow I see a kind of modern monastic with a kind of twentieth century version of the monastic vows: he had this strong commitment to poverty; he had a single minded chaste vision; he knew very clearly what he was doing; and he had a strong sense of obedience which of course led to disobedience of and resistance to the principalities. But the one which seems to be perhaps missing and which was clearly present in some of the people he fell out with, was the Benedictine tradition of stability: of staying there and not moving, and saying God has put me here, and as far as I know hasn't told me to go, and here I stay. So when I realize now that next year the EHPP will be 50 years old (it's not called that anymore but the storefront churches are still there), and I realize that Norman Eddy is still living there, and Bill Webber who helped set up the ministry is spending his retirement training black Pentecostal ministers in Sing-Sing prison for the ordained ministry, then I look back at Stringfellow's critique and I have to ask: is he really being fair to these people who are still there 40 to 50 years on?

So I think my question – and it is a question, I don't know the answer to it – is this. In his prophetic ministry Stringfellow is quite rightly challenging a ministry which is missing out on some of the dimensions of ministry. What has he learnt from them?

Chapter Four

The Vocation of the Church of Jesus the Criminal[1]

Mark Thiessen Nation

Introduction: And the Truth Shall Make You Odd

The stairway smelled of piss.

The smells inside the tenement – number 18, 342 East 100th Street, Manhattan – were somewhat more ambiguous. They were a suffocating mixture of rotting food, rancid mattresses, dead rodents, dirt, and the stale odors of human life.

This was to be home. It had been home before: for a family of eight – five kids, three adults. Some of their belongings had been left behind. Some of their life had, too.

The place, altogether, was about 25 x 12 feet, with a wall separating the kitchen section from the rest. In the kitchen was a bathtub, a tiny, rusty sink, a refrigerator that didn't work, and an ancient gas range. In one corner was a toilet with a bowl without a seat. Water dripped perpetually from the box above the bowl. The other room was filled with two beds: two double-decker military cots, and a big ugly convertible sofa. There wasn't room for anything else. The walls and ceilings were mostly holes and patches and peeling paint, sheltering legions of cockroaches.

This was to be my home. I wondered, for a moment, why. Then I remembered that this is the sort of place in which most people live, in most of the world, for most of the time. This or something worse.

Then I was home. (Stringfellow, 1964c:2)

This was my first exposure to William Stringfellow. I knew when I read the opening passage from *My People is the Enemy* (Stringfellow, 1964c) that this was not 'typical' theology. I also knew that this was a theologian whose writings I must read. That was around 1974. In January 1976 I became a subscriber to *Sojourners*[2] magazine and thus became a regular reader of Stringfellow's frequent columns in that magazine. I also read four or five more of his books over the next few years.

Writing of the influence of Jacques Ellul and Stringfellow, Walter Wink says: "These two lawyer-theologians drew their followers from the fringes of the theological empire: from readers of *Sojourners* magazine, evangelical social activists, disillusioned liberals, discontented clergy, conscientized laity, and a

---

[1] An earlier version of this chapter can be found in Nation (1998).

[2] It was called *Post-American* at this time.

handful of oddball lawyers" (Wink, 1995:17). In the mid-70s as a theological seminary drop out and an ex-Baptist, I qualified in three or four of these categories. But what was it that attracted a variety of us to Stringfellow?

To begin with I think it was partly his person – who he was, or was perceived to be, by those who read him. I think it was, as we were reminded in the introduction to this book, that he "never really quite fit" (Hauerwas and Powell, 1995:31).[3] He seemed a personification of "Flannery O'Conner's paraphrase of the gospel: you shall know the truth, and the truth shall make you odd" (Shaffer, 1995:120). I am not, first of all, referring to his, shall we say, unusual fascination with the circus. Though I get a sense that his eccentricities and his gaunt appearance may have, for those who knew him, added to the mystique that was William Stringfellow. But I refer, rather, to the way in which his life was a living set of contrasts, the ways in which he didn't fit statistical averages. A man who lives in squalor in Harlem isn't supposed to be a Harvard-trained attorney or dress in a three-piece suit.[4] Nor is a graduate from Harvard Law School normally predisposed, on principle, to pursuing no career, proclaiming as did Stringfellow: "I died to the idea of career and to the whole typical array of mundane calculations, grandiose goals and appropriate schemes to reach them. I renounced, simultaneously, the embellishments – like money, power, success – associated with careers in American culture, along with the ethics requisite to obtaining such condiments" (Stringfellow, 1982b:125). He appeared as Mary Lou Suhor put it, as "a proper Episcopalian prophet in a three-piece suit" (Suhor, 1995:74). His oxymoronic nature – in combination with his serious Christian commitment – was precisely what endeared Stringfellow to many of us.

The Biblical Adventure Continues

A second compelling feature of Stringfellow was his approach to the Bible. Jim Wallis spoke for many when he said: "While liberals ignored the Bible and evangelicals fought over the various theories of its inspiration, William Stringfellow applied the biblical Word to our lives and times like no other contemporary Christian" (Wallis, 1995:91). At the beginning of 1976 Stringfellow wrote: "I spend most of my life now with the Bible, reading or, more precisely, listening. My mundane involvements, ostensibly distinguished from this vocation...more and more readily become incorporated into this main preoccupation so that I cannot really separate the one from the other any longer...The biblical adventure continues, I expect, forever and ever" (Stringfellow, 1976c:19). For many of us Stringfellow (among others) helped to rescue the Bible and helped us to see the continual reading of it as an adventure as well. Many of us desired to learn, with Stringfellow, "to understand America

---

[3]   Hauerwas and Powell's article appeared originally in Hauerwas and Powell (Hauerwas and Powell, 1994).

[4]   For more discussion, see Andrew McThenia's reflections on Stringfellow's vocation in Chapter 2.

biblically – *not* the other way around, *not*...to construe the Bible Americanly" (Stringfellow, 1973:13). Stringfellow appeared almost incapable of not thinking in a biblical idiom. He "used the Bible as the quarry from which he mined his thought, as editor Bob DeWitt put it" (Suhor, 1995:77).

'Keeper of the Word' is the image evoked by several as they write about William Stringfellow.[5] "To people across the religious spectrum," says Jim Wallis, "William Stringfellow offered simple advice – listen to the Word, trust the Word, discern the Word, live the Word" (Wallis, 1995:95). That the Word of God for Stringfellow was not, in a simple way, a term identical with the Scriptures was liberating for some of us who had grown uncomfortable with a narrow evangelical reading of God's involvement in the world.[6] However, Stringfellow still took reading and listening for the Word of God through the Bible seriously. In fact, as Bill Wylie-Kellermann reminds us, "the neglect, and in some cases outright suppression, of the Bible as mediator of the Word of God went to the heart of [Stringfellow's] disagreement, even with some he loved and respected dearly, about the nature of the church" (Wylie-Kellermann, 1995:65-6).

The Bible is Politics

Of course it was not just that William Stringfellow seemed to take the Bible very seriously (which he did), and that he could not easily be categorized in the way he read it (which was the case), but it was also what he became passionate about as he read the Bible. What he became passionate about was politics: biblical politics. But it was the particular way in which he approached politics that provides the third compelling dimension of Stringfellow.

It is significant that Stringfellow cared about the right issues (for those of us who matured in the 1960s and 1970s). Stringfellow said, that "Characteristically, the Christian is to be found in his work and witness in the world among those for whom no one else cares – the poor, the sick, the imprisoned, the misfits, the homeless, the orphans, and the beggars" (Stringfellow, 1964c:40). He also said that

> the church of Christ is called as the advocate of every victim of the rulers of the age, and that, not because the victim is right...but because the victim is a victim...Advocacy is...how the church lives in the efficacy of the resurrection amidst the reign of death in this world. (Stringfellow, 1977a:94-5).

Through his own experiences and relationships and because of his Christian sensitivities Stringfellow deplored the pervasive racism of the United States: "Racial discrimination and segregation, though often in ingenious guises, still mars

---

[5]   The image apparently originated with Daniel Berrigan when he spoke at Stringfellow's funeral (Wallis, 1985:6). The image is repeated in the title of that edition of *Sojourners*, the title of Jim Wallis's article (Wallis, 1995), and, finally, it is the title of the edited book of Stringfellow writings (Wylie-Kellermann, 1994).

[6]   That Stringfellow used the term "Word of God" more broadly than simply a term for the Scriptures see, among other places, Stringfellow (1964c:95-102).

the lives of most congregations of most denominations" (Stringfellow, 1964b:77-8). He knew these "ingenious guises" were often denied. In fact, he argued, "part of the pathology of American racism is that almost all white people have been reared for generations as white supremacists and do not even realize it" (Stringfellow, 1969:81-2). This rearing is so pervasive and profound among white Americans that Stringfellow described the results as "mass idolatry" (Stringfellow, 1969:80).

In addition to the violence of poverty and racism Stringfellow also addressed the violence of nationalism and, specifically, the Vietnam war. "For a Christian," said Stringfellow, "there is such a commitment as decent respect and open affection for the country of one's citizenship. But this is not the same as a patriotism which is idolatrous and deadly" (Stringfellow, 1969:101). And this is precisely what the war in Vietnam had become, according to Stringfellow (1969:92-102). Or, to put it differently, the war in Southeast Asia was a "grotesque example" of how death can become "enshrined as social purpose" (Stringfellow, 1973:67-75).

> But do not conclude therefore that this war has happened in a void or is somehow isolated from the rest of the American story. The power of death militant in America is neither unique to this nation (it is common to all nations) nor novel within this nation (it is a historic feature of the nation from its origins). (Stringfellow, 1973:74-5)

It was because he believed this enshrinement of death needed to be resisted that he supported acts of civil disobedience in response to the war in Vietnam, including a close, long-term friendship with Daniel Berrigan and others at Jonah House in Baltimore.[7]

Stringfellow was never slow to deal with specific ills in society, especially in his earlier writings. But his passions were more directly related to theology, the central idiom within which he related to social ills. In an open letter to Jimmy Carter, then presidential candidate, some of Stringfellow's recurring theological themes are present. "I affirm," said Stringfellow, "that we are called, as a vocation, to confess the active sovereignty of Jesus Christ as Lord in this world, and, in turn, to act in relation to the politics of this world in a way which honors and bespeaks the judgment of the Word of God over the politics of this world" (Stringfellow, 1976b:7). The action must be militant because, after all, we are dealing with the demonic institutionalized in "the principalities and powers" and, therefore, "biblical people" are engaged in "resistance to the purpose and power of death in the political realm" (Stringfellow, 1976b:8).

In the midst of his significant passion, Stringfellow never sought to remove the ambiguity from politics. "The ethics of biblical politics offers no basis for divining specific, unambiguous, narrow, or ordained solutions for any social issue. Biblical theology does not deduce 'the will of God' for political involvement or social action" (Stringfellow, 1973:54). But acknowledging ambiguity was never, for Stringfellow, an invitation to indifference. Quite the contrary. "In welcoming the

---

[7]   On this see: Stringfellow (1966:76-87); Stringfellow and Towne (1971); Polner and O'Grady (1997:204, 227-230); and McAlister (1995).

Word of God in the world...perhaps the first thing for both clergy and laity to keep in mind is that in this world there is no such thing as neutrality about any public issue" (Stringfellow, 1966:156).

Appreciation and Critique

How would I assess the significance of William Stringfellow almost twenty years after his death? All of the elements of Stringfellow's thought outlined above continue to have significance for me; however, what I most appreciate about Stringfellow's approach to Christian life as it relates to politics is well summarized at the end of his book, *Dissenter in a Great Society* (Stringfellow, 1966:161-4). The four words he uses there are realism, inconsistency, radicalism, and intercession.

By realism Stringfellow means an acknowledgment that God acts in the real world where we live. This implies taking seriously the history, the context, within which we are located. Of all people, says Stringfellow, the Christian "is free to face the world as it is without flinching, without shock, without fear, without surprise, without embarrassment, without sentimentality, without guile or disguise. [The Christian] is free to live in the world as it is" (Stringfellow, 1966:161).

To many observers Christians will appear inconsistent, and Christians should not be surprised by this, says Stringfellow. Their apparent inconsistency is because the Christian seeks to be non-ideological, seeking only to act under the label Christian and no other.

> And though the Christian acts in this world and in particular circumstances in a society for this or that cause, though the Christian takes his stand and speaks out specifically, he does so not as the servant of some race or class or political system or ideology but as an expression of his freedom from just such idols. (Stringfellow, 1966:162)

By radicalism Stringfellow means to make the claim that Christians always live as aliens in whatever society they live. "The Christian is perpetually in the position of complaining about the status quo, whatever it happens to be" (Stringfellow, 1966:162). This is not because Christians are by nature irritants or naysayers. It is rather that the Christian's "insight and experience of reconciliation in Christ are such that no estate in secular society can possibly correspond to, or much approximate, the true society of which he is a citizen in Christ" (Stringfellow, 1966:162). That is, on the one hand, Christians should not confuse the Kingdom of God with a given human culture or society and, on the other, their vision of the Reign of God gives a vantage point from which to critique society.

The fourth element of Stringfellow's political quadrilateral is intercession, by which Stringfellow refers to advocacy for the poor and oppressed.

> Characteristically, the sign of the inclusiveness and extremity of the Christian's concern is represented and embodied in his specific care for those who, in a given time in

society, are the least in that society, for those whom all the rest have ignored or forgotten or cast out or otherwise have abandoned to death. (Stringfellow, 1966:163)

It is the combination of the four – especially their creative interaction – that makes Stringfellow's approach to social ethics so profound. His refusal to separate, finally, the public from the private and his bold announcement that "the biblical topic *is* politics" are Stringfellow's attempts to ensure that the Gospel is not privatized and thereby, in reality, held captive to a nation's dominant culture (Stringfellow, 1966, 1973:14ff).

I must also, however, state some dissatisfaction with Stringfellow as I read him today. Those of us who share Stringfellow's passion for the Christian faith raise questions only while heeding the admonitions of Walter Wink: "Woe to those who propound his theology without incarnating it in their flesh. Woe to those who soberly debate his meaning without participating in his love for clowning. Woe to those who traffic in his thought as a commodity for scholarly advancement. It was not for this that William Stringfellow suffered the anguish and ecstasy of life on this good earth" (Wink, 1985:25). With these warnings in mind I proceed with my critique.

"The diligent reader of earlier books of mine," said Stringfellow in a posthumously published book fragment, "will have noticed that *theologically* I could fairly be described as a closet Anabaptist" (Wylie-Kellermann, 1994:158). I am not sure what William Stringfellow meant by identifying himself as a closet Anabaptist. But perhaps it is telling when in *Conscience and Obedience*, in his chapter on "The Vocation of the Church as the Holy Nation", he also mentions Anabaptists (and Quakers) (Stringfellow, 1977a:101). He appears to do so because he wants to make the claim that what he is writing is not simply for Christians as individuals but rather for the church "as an institution and society". As he looks across the American landscape these traditions seem to him to offer the best hope for understanding that the claims of the Gospel (especially in relation to 'biblical politics') are for the church and not just for individuals. As one *standing* within the Anabaptist tradition – that is, as an 'un-closeted Anabaptist', a Mennonite – I would like to name what makes me uneasy, so many years later, with some of what Stringfellow wrote. Ironically, much of what I will name, I would suggest, are impediments that hinder the appropriation of his writings by the larger church.

First, I would point to Stringfellow's way of using extreme language. Death, idolatry, apocalyptic, the Fall, and principalities and powers are terms that appear frequently in Stringfellow's writings. I believe Stanley Hauerwas and Jeff Powell have done as well as can be done in expressing appreciation for how this language functions, in their discussion of Stringfellow's use of apocalyptic language. They are right in saying that Stringfellow

wanted to help us see how apocalyptic language narrates our world in a manner that helps us not to be seduced by the world's ways of doing good…Apocalyptic for him always was a way of reminding us of the intrinsically political character of salvation…Apocalyptic is Stringfellow's…mode of taking seriously Christ's Lordship over the public, the social, the political. (Hauerwas and Powell, 1995:32-3)

Again they write,

> the nonapocalyptic vision of reality that dominates American public life tempts American Christians, like other Americans, to accept, with despair and relief, the inevitability and thus the goodness of things as they are. Christians, unlike other Americans, ought to know better. Our world lies under the shadow of the principalities and powers, but they are not its legitimate or ultimate lords. Our helplessness in their hands is merely one of the lies by which they deceive and seek to control us. Against their deceptions, the apocalyptic perspective invokes God's truth. (Hauerwas and Powell, 1995:40)

I believe they are right about what Stringfellow intended and what his language helps to accomplish. However, at what cost?

I believe Walter Wink has captured the heart of the problem. Stringfellow's approach, says Wink,

> was paradoxical in the extreme…While some are less lethal, corrupting, and venal than others, all [powers] are equally fallen, all seek their own survival as the highest good, all are complicit, therefore in idolatry, all have thus become demonic. There is no room here for amelioration, for a continuum between good and bad. The powers – all of them, without exception – participate in the kingdom of death. (Wink, 1995:18)

When one begins to compile a list of everything Stringfellow names as a principality and power it is difficult to think of any social entity that is missing (Wink, 1995:26). As Wink puts it,

> in short, the powers comprise all social, political, and corporate reality, in both visible and invisible manifestations. The list runs the danger, however, of including everything and therefore denoting nothing. Stringfellow himself provides greater precision by the pungent examples he uses, so the notion never empties into abstraction or becomes vapid. (Wink, 1995:26)

Such extreme, apocalyptic language can, after a while, become ignored by most of us. For most of us grow weary of reading the world in such extreme terms. After a while we wonder how language about everything partaking of the Fall, idolatry, and the principalities and powers relates to reality. I think Wink is right that Stringfellow (at least partially) helps redeem his language from abstraction by his use of pungent examples. However, another potential problem with such extreme language is that it can be taken too seriously. For example, for several years in the mid-1970s, I received the newsletter called *Year One* from Jonah House in Baltimore. I was also a part of a small group that Phil Berrigan, of Jonah House, came to address during the same period. The extreme language of the newsletter and Berrigan struck me as out of touch with reality and generally unhealthy.[8]

---

[8]   I write this only after some reflection. I deeply appreciate the commitment and the cost paid by those who are members of Jonah House; their commitment is remarkable (I also had good friends who were members of Jonah House for a brief time in the late 1970s). But

My second critique is about Stringfellow's view of the Church. Hauerwas and Powell say that "as a person identified with political radicalism, Stringfellow's sense of the importance of the church might well seem odd" (Hauerwas and Powell, 1995:37). I am not sure they are right about the importance of the church for Stringfellow. To be sure, there are passages in Stringfellow's writings that are positive about the church. And his frequent use of biblical and theological language presumes either a Christendom (which he deplores) or a church for whom this language is compelling. However, I find Stringfellow not only more critical than positive about the church but, also, inadequately appreciative of the need for ongoing structures and institutions to make the church possible. This makes sense given that Stringfellow says that "ideology is inherent in every institution, while institutional forms are implied in every ideology" (Stringfellow, 1969:45). It is consonant with his protest that Christianity is not a religion (Stringfellow, 1969:39,42, 1962:17-38).[9] I would be the last to make excuses for the abuses of churches and church hierarchies or the churches' far too frequent callousness regarding the poor and oppressed. But nonetheless, it is not at all clear that Stringfellow appreciates the need for traditions, structures, institutions that are a part of what make a church a church over time (Stringfellow, 1962:84ff, 1964b:116, 1982b:102-104). In fact it appears that Stringfellow, because of his understanding of principalities and powers, is unable to appreciate the need, in general, for traditions, institutions, and structures that make possible continuity and socialization.[10] We still need the prophetic voice of Stringfellow to remind us of the potential for abuse within social structures. But we also need to attend to the traditions, institutions, and structures that nurture us and make possible within us and among us the virtues that enable us to live in the way Stringfellow suggests.[11]

---

their overblown rhetoric – in the newsletter and personally – has too often struck me as untrue to reality and, sometimes, contradictory of their claim to love their enemies. I also have questions about some of their tactics, in terms of effectiveness and appropriateness. Bill Wylie-Kellermann has questioned whether it is appropriate to 'blame' Stringfellow for some of the excessive rhetoric that emanates from Jonah House. He might be right; it might not be. However, I tend to think it is fair for at least two reasons. First, Elizabeth McAlister, of Jonah House, says that Stringfellow's were among the books they "refer to most frequently" (1995: 41). And, second, their rhetoric though on occasion more excessive or acerbic than his, seems to be a fair extension of the logic offered in his writings.

[9]   Let me also say, I am familiar with the Barthian critique of religion and have sympathy with it. However, Stringfellow's critique of religion seems to fit too well with his general criticisms of the Church.

[10]   One can see Stringfellow's ambivalence about all of this in a passage in (1973:57ff). I believe a representative statement is the following: "if you look for the Jerusalem reality of Church among the established ecclesiastical and churchly bodies, what you will find is chaos" (Stringfellow, 1973:59).

[11]   I am conscious that this sort of critique, especially during Stringfellow's formative years, were often made by political and social conservatives. It would be interesting to know what Stringfellow would have made of the writings of people like Alasdair MacIntyre and Stanley Hauerwas, whose focus on these matters is not married to a conservative political agenda. Their writings were available when Stringfellow was alive, but he does not refer to

Another critique pertains to Stringfellow's disdain for ethical method – or, sometimes, simply ethics. Again, for Stringfellow, methodology in general comes in for criticism, for "ideology is inherent in methodology" (Stringfellow, 1977c:13). Furthermore, according to Stringfellow

> a Christian is not distinguished by his...moral decisions, or habitual conduct...A Christian is distinguished by his radical esteem for the Incarnation – to use the traditional jargon – by his reverence for the life of God in the whole of Creation, even and, in a sense, especially, Creation in the travail of sin. (Stringfellow, 1962:49)

In fact, "the claim of the church that it represents in history restored creation is not contingent at all upon virtue in the church but upon the freedom of the Word of God in this world" (Stringfellow, 1977a:32). "In the Bible, the ethical issue becomes simply: how can a person act humanly now" (Stringfellow, 1973:56)?

Aside from his aversion to methodology, what is it that causes Stringfellow to disavow both the importance of Christian moral behavior and the ability or need to discern the differences between good and evil, better and worse behaviors? For Stringfellow, there seem to be two central theological reasons for Stringfellow. First, in many places he utilizes what has often been a standard Protestant misunderstanding of Paul that makes a dichotomy between works and grace and worries that humans imagine they can justify themselves by their works. For example, he refers to ancient Israel's reception of the Ten Commandments. What happens, according to Stringfellow, is that the Israelites imagine they can earn their salvation by obeying the commands rather than relying on God's grace. But what is really true is that

> there is no [one] who is not liable to judgment, and there is none without need of forgiveness...The Word of God is belittled when in the Church or in one of the churches the Word is construed in a fashion that makes obedience to the Word of God not dependence upon grace but a convenient moralistic, pietistic, or ritualistic conformity. (Stringfellow, 1964b:112-3)

This is a caricature of Judaism and of the writings of Paul. It erroneously makes Judaism into a religion which routinely teaches that salvation can be earned. And it quite illegitimately pits good works against the grace of God in a way that fits neither Judaism nor the writings of Paul and other New Testament writings.[12]

---

them. I make the point precisely because, like Stringfellow, I do not want to advocate some ethic for heroes. I rather desire a church (as institution and community) that nurtures us in the habits of the Christian faith that would make it possible for us to resist those powers and forces that war against the Gospel of Jesus Christ.

[12] Long before Stringfellow died there were substantial writings that challenged many of these views, writings that, among other things, offer what is sometimes referred to as a 'new perspective' on Paul (and on the Judaism from which he came). For example, Yoder (1972) was already incorporating some of the newer perspectives on Paul as they relate to ethics. The major work by Sanders (1977) was published seven years before Stringfellow's death. However, to be fair, there has been a much greater volume of literature on this subject

Second, Stringfellow leaves the prerogative for judging in God's hands, reducing the rest of us to an equity of ontological sinfulness. As he puts it,

> the Biblical description of sin is not so much the designation of certain kinds of conduct as sin...as it is the usurpation by [humans] of the prerogative of God in judging all human decisions and actions. The Christian knows and confesses that in all things – in every act and decision – [people] are sinners and that in no way, by any ingenuity, piety, sanction, or social conformity, may a [person] escape from the full burden of the power of sin over his whole existence. (Stringfellow, 1963b:36)[13]

Moreover, Stringfellow believed, "it is of utmost importance to acknowledge that no [person] is the judge of any other...nor is a [person] even his own judge, nor is society the judge, nor, least of all, is the Church the judge of [anyone]" (Stringfellow, 1963b:29). This is the case even in relation to law officials who are grossly unjust and members of the Ku Klux Klan who employ violence and treachery (Stringfellow, 1966:133).

What is strange about Stringfellow's disavowal of ethics is that his writings are replete with moral pronouncements, usually cloaked in witness or advocacy language. But his disavowing of method, combined with his peculiar approach to making moral pronouncements, makes it difficult to discern what it is that operates normatively for Stringfellow in his ethical pronouncements. Furthermore, it is difficult for such an idiosyncratic language to serve as the moral language for a community which would seek to have accountability. Let me take one example: racism. Clearly Stringfellow was against racism. Why could he not say he was against it because it is immoral, on the basis of claiming Jesus is Lord or "there is no Jew or Gentile" or "love your neighbor as our self" – there would be various biblical and theological rationales to give as to why, for Christians, racism is immoral. Furthermore, the church would have theological and moral reasons to relate redemptively even to members of the Ku Klux Klan. But it would not be because we cannot judge behavior; Stringfellow does judge their behavior to be immoral! Rather it is because we as Christians not only name sins – like racism – but we also believe in loving our enemies; we believe in the possibility of reconciliation and forgiveness, etc.

As a fellow, but 'un-closeted Anabaptist' I have great sympathies with Stringfellow's project. We need prophetic voices like Stringfellow's and we need them for the whole church. I desire with Stringfellow not to let the biblical Word become captive to methodologism, whether ethical or otherwise. I want the apocalyptic Word to ring out from the Scriptures reminding us that Babylon constantly tempts us and we often fall prey; but not to the exclusion of the Word

---

since most of Stringfellow's writings had been written and, even more so, since his death. For an overview of some of the issues see Thielman (1999) and, for ethics, Matera (1996).

[13] These views are partly undergirded by Stringfellow's desire to protect his notion of the freedom of God (Stringfellow, 1964b). Karl Barth and Dietrich Bonhoeffer had a similar approach at this point. See the insightful critique of Barth in Yoder (1970:57-81) and Bonhoeffer in Rasmussen (1972:149ff).

that would help us distinguish between greater and lesser evils, greater and lesser approximations to what God desires from us. We need, sometimes desperately need, to be reminded of a gracious God, but not to the exclusion of a living relationship in which it matters whether our behaviors befit a faithful covenant with this gracious God. As a church we need to be reminded that the Jesus whom we proclaim Lord was convicted of "perverting the nation" – he was, in short, a criminal (Stringfellow and Towne, 1971:59-68). It is unquestionable that the institutional church has too often tamed and, sometimes, even distorted the Gospel by twisting it into something that fits far too comfortably with selfishness, greed, lust, racism, injustice, and violence. But the solution is not to talk as if all institutions are equally evil; it is rather to claim that this institution called the church is to be redeemed, is to be the body of Christ for the world. It is to be an institution supportive of communities who seek to follow this crucified Christ by living lives of faithful obedience. It is to equip us to live lives, rooted in Jesus Christ, that relate redemptively and prophetically to individuals, groups, and institutions who are outside the Church.

Yes, we need prophetic voices like Stringfellow's. But if Stringfellow's words are to continue to speak God's Word we must rescue them from some of their idiosyncrasies. It is not enough to live humanly during the Fall. We need the entire voice of the biblical idiom from Genesis to Revelation. We must reclaim the vocation of the Church – the whole Church and particular churches – to embody the Gospel of Jesus the criminal, serving as witness to the Word of God, as an advocate for the poor and oppressed, as a sign of the Eschaton toward which Stringfellow's Word continues to beckon.

Chapter Five

Not Vice Versa: Stringfellow, Hermeneutics, and the Principalities[1]

Bill Wylie-Kellermann

Proximate to the discernment of signs is the discernment of spirits. This gift enables the people of God to distinguish and recognize, identify and expose, report and rebuke the power of death incarnate in nations and institutions or other creatures, or possessing persons, while they also affirm the Word of God incarnate in all of life, exemplified preeminently in Jesus Christ. The discernment of spirits refers to the talent to recognize the Word of God in this world in principalities and persons despite the distortion of fallenness or transcending the moral reality of death permeating everything.

   This is the gift which exposes and rebukes idolatry. This is the gift which confounds and undoes blasphemy. Similar to the discernment of signs, the discernment of spirits is inherently political while in practice it has specifically to do with pastoral care, with healing, with the nurture of human life and with the fulfillment of all life. (Stringfellow, 1973:139, Wylie-Kellermann, 1994:302–3)

On Wednesday evening before Pentecost 1938 William Stringfellow sat; an anxious eleven year old waiting through the lections and hymns. He once confided that on account of his musical ineptitude he regularly refrained from singing but thereby focused all the more on the language and theology of the hymnal, first learning there the esoteric names of the principalities and powers and of their vocation to praise God. His own recounting of that day includes disillusionment that there was no secret to be revealed concerning the mysterious working of the Holy Spirit (actually not a bad day's work for a confirmation liturgy) (Stringfellow, 1984, Wylie-Kellermann, 1994:23–4). In any event, at the time appointed he stepped forward. As the original humans, Adam and Eve, presided from above in stained glass, Stringfellow soberly answered the bishop's queries. Yes, he renewed the baptismal promises first undertaken on his behalf and in his stead, among other things renouncing the devil and all his works.

   Some forty years later, as a rainstorm broke, he led a group of friends at his home on Block Island in a liturgical exorcism to banish from the place of his household the presence of death after his dearest friend and companion, the poet Anthony Towne, had died (Stringfellow, 1982b:54–8). For that liturgy he employed a rite, published by the Bishop of Exeter (Petitpierre, 1972), which

---

[1]   An earlier version of this chapter can be found in Wylie-Kellermann (1999).

Stringfellow had acquired and first utilized to publicly exorcise President Richard Nixon on the eve of his second inauguration.

Let no one consider these liturgical events either spooky or weird. Stringfellow enjoyed regarding them with deadly seriousness as inherently political while in practice having specifically to do with pastoral care and healing.

For present purposes it's noteworthy that his copy of that exorcism booklet is altered by his own hand consistently substituting "death" or "the power of death" (which he accounted a "living moral reality") where the prayers name "the devil" or "the enemy". These are synonyms I believe he would transpose back into his own confirmation and baptismal vows. Baptism always has about it an element of exorcism and for William Stringfellow it specifically celebrates and affirms freedom from the power of death and all its works – indeed from the principalities and powers of this world.

Apart from Anglican hymnology, the young Stringfellow's first real dose of powers theology came at the World Conference of Christian Youth in Oslo, Norway which he attended as a college sophomore in 1947. Under the theme of the "Lordship of Christ" there was plenty of room for the triumphalism which characterized the expansive postwar American ecumenism in which Stringfellow was a participant. However, the speakers at that conference bore their good news out from the shadow of death. They spoke out of Christian resistance movements under Nazi occupation. They were chastened and sober. Among them were Martin Niemoller of Germany, Bishop Belgrav of Norway, and Madeleine Barot of France.[2] Mme Barot, for example, was particularly lucid in identifying the "chaos of order" in which humanity had fallen slave to its own systems, to its own production and discovery, and to its own propaganda for which she saw the Babel story as emblematic (Macy, 1948:153–165). In *An Ethic for Christians and Other Aliens in a Strange Land* (Stringfellow, 1973), Stringfellow mentions that conference as the beginning of a conversation with those very people from whom he acknowledges learning two things: firstly that, in the overwhelming circumstance of Nazi possession and occupation, resistance (however symbolic, haphazard, and apparently futile) became the only way to live humanly, retaining sanity and conscience, and secondly that recourse to the bible in itself became a primary, practical, and essential tactic of resistance (Stringfellow, 1973:117–20, Wylie-Kellermann, 1994:173–4). This confluence, a kind of sequence or circle really – bible study, comprehension or discernment of the powers, and resistance for the sake of humanity – is hardly incidental. This marked a conversation seminal to his life and thinking.

Stringfellow (1973) begins by asserting that in the book, "[t]he task is to treat the nation within the tradition of biblical politics – to understand America biblically – *not* the other way around, *not* (to put it in an appropriately awkward way) to construe the Bible Americanly" (Stringfellow, 1973:13, Wylie-

---

[2]   Their speeches are found in Macy (1948). Other speakers included Reinhold Niebuhr, W. A. Visser't Hooft, Stephen Neill, and D.T. Niles.

Kellermann, 1994:173–4).[3] Notice what is being said here. Today, this might be said to acknowledge his contextual reading site and confess his own social location in imperial America, but more is suggested. Imperial America, its spirit and ethos, is held to assert itself as an active and aggressive agency in biblical interpretation, claiming the text as its own.

Not only are the powers a question of hermeneutics. For William Stringfellow, hermeneutics are a question of the powers.

It is almost as though American empire, sensing its exposure in the biblical Word, engages a pre-emptive literary strike, claiming, possessing and interpreting the bible in its own guise, for its own convenience, justifying itself as the divinely favored nation. Stringfellow calls this violence – and it is a violence virtually synonymous with the Native American genocide or the racism of American chattel slavery or the nuclear arsenal or the pyrotechnics of the Gulf War and the slow continuing siege of Iraq.

No doubt those on British soil will recognize the ways in which the bible is read Englishly or United Kingdomly – also suitably awkward terms. That was surely most prominent and exaggerated at the height of the colonial empire when imperial expansion and the Kingdom of God were most conspicuously confused, but it may also be as current as the civil liturgies of recent election campaigns.

That is to say, this powerly intervention is not a new or uniquely American process. In fact, for most of its history, the gods of this world have blinded the church to its own scriptures with respect to the "principalities and powers". In the hermeneutical history these terms have been excised, suppressed and obscured. One analysis ties the effectual disappearance and demise of the powers in Protestant theology to Luther and Calvin at the very beginning of the Reformation.[4] Stringfellow, however, locates that dissipation at an earlier juncture, with the "Constantinian Arrangement" of the fourth century. Beginning with that time, Christians had "forgotten or forsaken a worldview or, more precisely, doctrines of creation and fallen creation, similar to Paul's, in which political authority encompasses and conjoins the angelic powers and incumbent rulers" (Stringfellow, 1977a:48). Walter Wink, the New Testament scholar whose stunning trilogy on the powers was seeded by Stringfellow's work and who has thereby become the primary and practical American spokesperson on the theology of the principalities, concurs. The church

> soon found itself the darling of Constantine. Called on to legitimate the empire, the church abandoned much of its social critique. The Powers were soon divorced from political affairs and made airy spirits who preyed only on individuals. The state was thus freed of one of the most powerful brakes against idolatry. (Wink, 1984:113)

---

[3]   Acknowledging both its imprecision and chauvinism, I will continue here to use Stringfellow's term "American".

[4]   See Visser't Hooft (1948:15–31), who argues that the significance of the victorious cosmic Christ was lost in their attenuated struggle with apocalyptic sects of the time.

Rome was effectively pre-empting its own exposure by and vulnerability in the Word of God. The New Testament was being read Romanly as it were, the substance of the powers written into the oblivion of spiritual individualism.

When Stringfellow first began to speak and write on the powers in the early sixties, he went on the road stumping in colleges and universities. He identified the powers with institutions, images, and ideologies as creatures before God having an independent life and integrity of their own, whose vocation is to praise God and serve human life. In the estate of the fall, however, they are seen to be demonic powers. Their vocation is lost and distorted, in fact inverted: instead of praising God and serving human life they pretend to the place of God and enslave human life. This exposition, which became chapter three of *Free in Obedience* (Stringfellow, 1964b), met a strange mix of fascination and rebuff. He loved to tell the story of an early presentation, in fact two of them, given in Boston. Scheduled for similar talks the same day at Harvard Business School and at the Divinity School, he debated with himself about excising, from the business school version, any explicit biblical reference or language, but decided in the end to let it stand intact. The business school students it turned out, engaged him thoroughly, bending his ear long past the hour appointed, with numerous examples from their own experience of dominance and possession with respect to corporations and the commercial powers. Their experiences verified his own observations.

Later at the seminary, however, with the identical speech, he was ridiculed and written off. Ruling authorities, principalities, world rulers of the present darkness were viewed as the incidental vestige of a quaint and archaic language, an esoteric parlance now obsolete, with no real meaning in history or human life (Stringfellow, 1964b:51–2, Wylie-Kellermann, 1994: 192).

At the seminary not only did the consequences of the Constantinian comity reign, it was aided and abetted by yet another 'power', in this case the tyranny of the historical critical method. In Stringfellow's enumeration of the principalities he came to include not simply all institutions and all images, but also all ideologies and all methods. Historical criticism may be recognized as both. After imperial accommodation drove the majority of New Testament references to the powers off into longstanding spiritual abstraction, historical criticism with its cosmological commitment to scientific rationalism and materialism, wrote them off the New Testament map altogether.

Walter Wink has said an astonishing thing in precisely this regard. Commenting on the inability of several previous scholars working on the powers to confess their practical significance for a twentieth century Christian ethic, he notes:

> They were themselves caught in the principality of New Testament criticism, which had become as dogmatic and stultified as the religious orthodoxy it had been invented to overthrow. Not surprisingly, as a New Testament scholar, I found it necessary to perform a public exorcism of myself, hermeneutically, by writing *The Bible in Human Transformation*. (Wink, 1995:25)

A hermeneutical exorcism! Wink's scholarly little tract[5] declared historical criticism bankrupt. It named the myth of objectivism which fabricated an impassable gulf between text and reader, precluding commitment and engagement in either personal or social transformation. It exposed the idolatry of technique to which biblical studies had fallen prey. It identified the cult of expertise which severed scripture study from believing and worshiping communities. It got him 'black listed' in the scholarly guild and denied tenure at Union Seminary. And it freed him literally to write this remarkable trilogy on the powers.

Though there are several others, I would mention just one further way that Stringfellow seemed to regard the principalities as an agency aggressively intruding on bible study. He contended that the single most important credential required for comprehending scripture was to give oneself in vulnerability to listening to the Word. Yet in the present situation we are assaulted by a profusion of what he termed "babel": verbal inflation and inversion, the distortions of doublespeak and overtalk, spin doctoring, soundbytes, coded phrases, jargon, rhetorical wantonness, redundancy, exaggeration, incoherence, the chaos of voices, the violence of the repetitious lie (Stringfellow, 1973:97–107, Wylie-Kellermann, 1994:214–222). He argued that this verbal overload and incapacitation has become virtually the main method of political rule. To have ears to hear, to listen conscientiously to the bible is itself, as he learned from participants in the confessing movements of World War II, is to resist the assault of the powers (Wylie-Kellermann, 1994:182–2).

A striking omission from that list in *Ethic* of European Christian resistance mentors is Karl Barth. I'm not quite sure what to make of that. Jacques Ellul is listed as a subsequent conversant and there would be similar warrant for the inclusion of Barth as well.

It was virtually the gathering storm of World War II, an historical crisis, which urgently broke the hermeneutical impasse with respect to the powers. As Bonhoeffer wrote in 1932: "How can one close one's eyes at the fact that the demons themselves have taken over rule of the world, that it is the powers of darkness who have here made an awful conspiracy" (Dawn, 1992:12). Barth, of course, was an active participant in the confessing struggle – and he was a biblical spokesperson in the reclamation of powers theology. After Stringfellow's public questions to him concerning the powers at the 1962 University of Chicago panel, Barth whispered to him, "It's all in *Church and State*. It's all there."[6] Though Stringfellow is falsely accused of being a Barthian, friends do attest that he read a volume of Barth's dogmatics and he certainly read *Church and State*[7] wherein, among other things, Barth confirms and concedes the conjoining of rulers and the angelic powers in the state. In the main, however, Barth's primary role in Stringfellow's developing theology was simply to encourage and embolden his active pursuit of the powers. Karl Barth did it in two ways. First, by simply confirming Bill's articulation of the inquiry. Simply on the basis of his questions

---

5 See Wink (1973), and his sequel which outlines a new paradigm (Wink, 1980).

6 The reference is to Karl Barth *Church and State* (Barth, 1939).

7 His copy of that text in marked and annotated. He cites it in Stringfellow (1977a:36).

Barth replied, "I like to hear you speak as you do" and "I think we agree" – which then prompted him to turn and urge that audience, in an underscored aside, "Listen to this man."[8]

The other encouragement (and this is by no means incidental) was to conceive of the principalities as a broader category than the state alone. Barth in his reply to Stringfellow in Chicago specifically mentioned ideology, sport, fashion, religion, and sex as examples.

In the United States, of course, it was a different set of historical crises which broke open the powers biblically for reconsideration: not so much the context of National Socialism and World War II, but the racial crisis forced by the African American freedom struggle and the war in southeast Asia. The year following his public converse with Karl Barth, Stringfellow was back in Chicago in 1963 as a speaker at the first National Conference on Religion and Race where he created a small uproar. Chaired by Benjamin Mays and headlined among others by Martin King, Sargeant Shriver, and Abraham Heschel, the conference was the first major ecumenical and interfaith foray into the racial struggle. Stringfellow's remarks were a response to a major address by Dr. Heschel, the late Jewish scholar and theologian, which was itself remarkable for naming racism as idolatry, for identifying the exodus as a lead image in the struggle, and for outlining a prophetic response on the basis of the Hebrew scriptures. Stringfellow's responding comments were controversial in part because he excoriated the gathering as "too little, too late, and too lily white" (a phrase he would come regularly to employ in prodding the church), because he observed that the initiative in the struggle no longer resided with white folk, but had passed from white to black, and because he named voices (like Malcolm X and James Baldwin) who would not be heard at the gathering. However, his most remarkable observations were these:

> From the point of view of either biblical religion, the monstrous American heresy is in thinking that the whole drama of history takes place between God and humanity. But the truth, biblically and theologically and empirically is quite otherwise: the drama of this history takes place amongst God and humanity and the principalities and powers, the great institutions and ideologies active in the world. It is the corruption and shallowness of humanism which beguiles Jew or Christian into believing that human beings are masters of institution or ideology. Or to put it differently, racism is not an evil in human hearts or minds, racism is a principality, a demonic power, a representative image, an

---

8   From master tape recording of the event held by Word Record and Music Group, Nashville, TN. It is interesting that in the published transcript of that conversation, the University of Chicago Divinity School expunged both of those comments from the official record (University of Chicago Divinity School, 1963:22). In the foreword to *Evangelical Theology: An Introduction* (Barth, 1979), the lectures which Barth gave at the University of Chicago and Princeton University, he refers to "the conscientious and thoughtful New York attorney William Stringfellow who caught my attention more than any other person" (Barth, 1979:ix).

embodiment of death, over which human beings have little or no control, but which works its awful influence in their lives. (Stringfellow, February 21 1963:14)[9]

I can think of few such statements at once so precise and prescient. Since that day the legal apparatus of American apartheid has been all but dismantled. Yet no force or structure or spirit has proven more relentless and resilient than racism in our country. It is empirically a demon which rises up transmogrified in ever more beguiling forms and predatory guises. Many, including Dr. Heschel, heard in the dreadful realism of Stringfellow's statement, an invocation to despair. In fact, when Heschel reappeared at the podium he turned about directly to face him and said, "Mr. Stringfellow, if my ancestors had followed your advice, we would still be making bricks for the Pharaoh".[10]

Stringfellow, however, had not ended there. He continued:

This [racism] is the power with which Jesus Christ was confronted and which, at great and sufficient cost, he overcame. In other words, the issue here is not equality among human beings. The issue is not some common spiritual values, nor natural law, nor middle axioms. The issue is baptism. The issue is the unity of all humankind wrought by God in the life and work of Christ. Baptism is the sacrament of that unity of all humanity in God. (Stringfellow, February 21 1963: 14–15)

Apart from the commotion prompted among Jewish participants by this claim (to which Heschel, who may have listened more carefully, had not replied), this is an utterly remarkable confession of faith. White supremacy, a modern principality, was named as confronting Christ. And racism, as a demonic power beyond desperate human control, is declared overcome and defeated in Christ. Moreover, the emblem of that freedom from bondage is the unity, not of all Christians, but the unity of all humankind witnessed in baptism. Stringfellow couldn't be clearer that this radical hope of reconciliation was predicated on the cross and upon tears yet to come, but it is a true hope and a true freedom rooted both in his realism about the power and in his sacramental understanding of ethics.

Let me underscore that baptism is being named as a frontal assault upon the rule of the powers. That is true in the reconciled humanity to which it points. That is true in the allegiance to Christ which it asserts, obviating and mitigating every other claim or allegiance. And that is true in the freedom from death, literally the freedom to die, which it explicitly affirms.

For more on this latter, let's consider the other context which prompted a reawakened comprehension of the powers on the American scene: the war in southeast Asia. In Stringfellow's view the war represented a grotesque example of the demonic, of death virtually as social purpose. It demonstrated the variety of concrete ways in which the military powers (particularly the Pentagon and the technocratic state) had passed out of human control, propagating the war largely by

---

[9]   I have edited this quote for sexist language.

[10] As recalled vividly by Richard Taylor, a member of the audience. Interviewed by Bill Wylie-Kellermann, 26 November 1996.

extra-constitutional authorities beyond the accountability of democratic constraint. Military technology was a driving force with a necessary logic all its own, from the think tanks of corporate research and development, to the battlefield testing of firepower against human flesh.

At the height of the war in 1968 Stringfellow attended the trial of the Catonsville Nine. Dan and Phil Berrigan among others had burned draft files with homemade napalm in a liturgical act of protest against the war in Vietnam. Stringfellow would later refer to this as a "politically informed exorcism" (Stringfellow, 1973:150). Concurrent with the trial there was a festival of hope: music, poetry, and words of encouragement to continued resistance were offered in the sanctuary of a Baltimore church. Stringfellow who was about to undergo a risky life-threatening surgery to stem the deterioration of his health, could barely walk from pain. Summoned to the pulpit for a word, he offered an admonition, a benediction, an utterance of the gospel:

> Remember, now, that the State has only one power it can use against human beings: death. The State can persecute you, prosecute you, imprison you, exile you, execute you. All of these mean the same thing. The State can consign you to death. The grace of Jesus Christ in this life is that death fails. There is nothing the State can do to you, or to me, which we need fear. (Stringfellow, 1970c:33)

This was no idle or superfluous dispensation. The anti-war and freedom movements had been about to come together when Martin Luther King was killed. Malcolm X and a number of Black Panthers had been assassinated. Official guns would shortly be turned on college students at both Kent State and Jackson State Universities. The freedom to die, really the freedom of the resurrection, the freedom which baptism signals, that freedom to which Stringfellow testified was the very freedom on which continuing resistance to the powers needed to be grounded. If today, such movements are held in check more by the seductions of the market, than by the more blatant power of death, that is a shadow which nevertheless lingers yet over our land, holding its sway.

The Catonsville Nine, as it proved, were convicted, but several of them declined to submit readily to sentence. Daniel Berrigan went underground, speaking, writing, and playfully eluding the Federal authorities for several months. He was a walking festival of hope. When Berrigan was finally captured by the FBI it was at the Block Island home of William Stringfellow and Anthony Towne. In consequence the two were indicted with harboring a fugitive.

Though the indictment, clearly a political charge, was eventually quashed, this was a momentous event in Stringfellow's life. It was the first time he had personally suffered so bluntly the aggressions of the principalities. Given his state of health, it was indeed a bodily assault threatening death. But it was also his first experience of being victimized by the legal principalities which he had fought so vigorously on behalf of others, in East Harlem for example. In many respects the event seeded the energy of *Ethic* (Stringfellow, 1973). As it happened, Bill and Dan had sat at the dining room table discussing the biblical bases of that book (the Babylon texts of Revelation) while in all likelihood the FBI listened in by high powered directional microphone. Then came the indictment, a provocation further illuminating the texts, clarifying the mind. If the principalities and powers had known what they were doing, they would have let it slide. That book effected their complete exposure (becoming something of a theological handbook for the American resistance movement). Stringfellow claimed yet again the grace and freedom he commended. Legally and politically he was unintimidated, standing instead by his friendship with Berrigan.

Another influence on *Ethic* which must be mentioned, perhaps at some length, is Jacques Ellul, the French social historian and theologian.[11] *The Meaning of the City* (Ellul, 1970a) had only just been published in English. Stringfellow wrote to Ellul concerning the indictment against himself and Towne:

> It is difficult to put succinctly in a letter all that has happened and its background, growing out of the past several years in which this society has so much constricted and in which opposition to the regime has provoked a repression more serious and extensive than most people realize...There is not the slightest doubt in my mind that charges were brought against us because we have openly expressed our opposition to the barbarism in Indochina and the threatening totalitarianism in America. One might even say that we are attacked by the government because we are Christians, although I would not want to put it that way without a more complete designation of what that means. (Stringfellow, 23 February 1971)

Given the times, Stringfellow went on to press again his longstanding (and eternally pending) invitation that Ellul come to the States, though now with a more strenuous political urgency.

Such a trip had been arranged more than once. The two of them pursued for some thirty years a personal correspondence, though Stringfellow attributes to the Holy Spirit the coincidence that they would find themselves writing on similar biblical texts or with common reference to particular powers, since their letters never discussed what each would be working on next.

Consider these excerpts from an earlier letter of Ellul to Stringfellow:

> Bien Cher: I have just finished your book...with great emotion – the description you give of the current development of the USA is almost unbelievable. In Europe, no one pays attention at all to this reality...I often ask myself which is easier – on the one hand, to live, like me, in a country radically non-Christian, where the invocation of the Gospel means nothing to 'the person on the street' – or, on the other hand, like you to speak in an officially Christian country, to have the facility that the message of the Gospel is normally well received, but where it's a matter of breaking through the misunderstandings, the hypocrisies, and giving the Gospel its revolutionary power. I was terribly pleased with your last chapter. You and I are trying to transmit an insupportable truth – and I sense in your pages the same urgency, the same passion that I feel in myself. I don't know how to tell you how near I am to you, how much it consoles me to

---

[11]   For discussion on the similarities and differences between Stringfellow and Ellul, and more upon the nature of this important relationship, see Chapter 8.

know that there is, over there, a person chosen by God to carry on this combat which sometimes seems desperate to me. (Ellul, 16 November 1966)

Stringfellow's first brush with Jacques Ellul was actually a near miss. Ellul, just then emerging from participation in the French resistance movement, addressed a post-Oslo conference of the WSCF in 1947. Stringfellow, however, went off instead to a meeting of Anglican youth at Canterbury. So while Ellul was warning the worldwide student movement against elaborating organization and systems, Stringfellow was enjoying audiences with the Archbishop and Her Royal Highness and, several for that matter, with the famous 'Red Dean of Canterbury'. Stringfellow took considerable interest in Ellul's talk when it was published (Ellul, 1948).[12]

Their first direct contact came about in connection with a major conference on theology and law which Stringfellow organized in 1958. It marked the beginning of the perennially frustrated stateside invitation. The hugely successful conference was built, prepublication, around the English translation of Ellul's *The Theological Foundation of Law* (Ellul, 1960). That volume, a radical Christian critique of natural law which comported with Stringfellow's own position, is pertinent to the topic of principalities in a number of ways, though a noteworthy one is that he there identifies institutions theologically with the principalities, powers, thrones, and dominions of the creation hymn found in Col 1:15. That view is an anomaly in Ellul's writing, since he more generally rejects the view that the powers are creatures willed by the God of Jesus Christ which have been somehow deflected from their true and valid purpose. This is, however, precisely Stringfellow's view (and Wink's who followed him) and that view may have been nourished by Ellul (Ellul, 1960).

For Stringfellow the principalities are indeed creatures, which is to say they have a life and integrity of their own (Stringfellow, 1964b:52–3, 1973:78–80, 1977a:27–32). He references them to the Genesis story and the granting of human dominion (not domination he would stress). This is to say further that each power has a particular vocation to praise God and serve human life. Now this matter of 'vocation' can prove to be a very useful heuristic principle in analyzing a given principality.[13] It becomes actually quite a radical question to ask, as pastors and community activists in Detroit have recently with respect to a newspaper strike: What is the vocation of a newspaper? How does it praise God by serving human life? Or, as we also have been inquiring lately in Detroit: What is the vocation of a city? What is it called in the Word of God to be? Or, here's a radical one beyond unquestioned presumptions: What is the vocation of a bank? These are interrogations which Christians are authorized by baptism to make. They are queries of practical discernment with enormous political import. They entail "the talent to recognize the Word of God in this world in principalities and persons" (Stringfellow, 1973:139). Incidentally, this charismatic gift of discernment is substantially what Christians may bring to any struggle for social transformation,

---

[12] This paper was essentially chapter two of Ellul (1989).
[13] Walter Wink himself develops this for practical use (Wink, 1984:15–8).

where they are often working side by side in improvisational alliance with secular folks who have a lucid social analysis but who are effectively blind to half of social reality.

The creatureliness of the powers for Stringfellow underscores that they are not actually under human control, whatever naive misapprehension people hold in this regard. It emphasizes the vocational question, which also signifies their standing before the judgment of God. Stringfellow acknowledges that the exact origin of this creatureliness in the powers has about it a certain mystery. Human beings are obviously privy to the genesis of given institutions, but something more than human initiative comes into play.

In point of fact, though Ellul denies their creaturehood, his view is not all that different. Concerning the nature of the powers, he situates himself somewhere between two positions, sometimes emphasizing one aspect, sometimes the other: 1) that they are less precise powers than traditional demons, but still possessing "an existence, reality, and as one might say, objectivity of their own" and 2) that they are simple human dispositions, human factors which are constituted as powers by virtue of being exalted as such (Ellul, 1976:151–2). For example, he treats the city as a purely human creation, virtually an act of rebellion first by Cain against God. And yet on the basis of an etymological argument he observes that the word for city means also the Watching Angel, the Vengeance and Terror. "We must admit that the city is not just a collection of houses with ramparts, but also a spiritual power. I am not saying it is a being. But like an angel, it is a power on a spiritual plane" (Ellul, 1970a:9). Clearly, not a creature with a vocation, but a mystery to which humanity has some privity and initiative nevertheless.

When the English translation of *The Presence of the Kingdom*[14] was republished in 1967 (Ellul, 1967b, 1989), Ellul asked Stringfellow to provide an American foreword. The American wrote:

> Few books by American authors purporting to deal with theological ethics discern the presence and power of death in this world, in this day, even in America, as an essential clue, to nations and institutions as well as individuals, of their radical alienation from one another and from themselves, that is to say, of their fallenness. (Stringfellow, 1989:xvii)

On this matter of fallenness Stringfellow and Ellul were in absolute agreement. As far as Stringfellow was concerned American Christians were hopelessly (the word is used advisedly) naive concerning the depth and ubiquity of the fall. Fallen creation included for him the distortion, confusion, and, as already noted, inversion of vocation in the principalities. It means they are become, every one, demonic powers – dehumanizing, enslaving, and dominating human life. It means they place their own survival above service to human life. It means, among other things, they usurp the place of God.

---

[14] This was his post-war theological manifesto, which clearly charts the future course of his whole life's work.

The structure of the fall in Ellul's work bears prominently on the common observation that he wrote on two parallel tracks. He would do sociological or historical analyses of political authority, say, or propaganda, or technology and would match them with works of biblical theology, taking on II Kings, or Revelation, or a sweeping thematic study of the City in Scripture. For example, take the volume which arrived at Stringfellow's door, just as he had completed a first draft of *Ethic* (Stringfellow, 1973). Ellul's book, *The Meaning of the City* (Ellul, 1970a), so radically pessimistic about human works and radically hopeful about God's grace in history, is in fact the theological counterpoint to *The Technological Society* (Ellul, 1964) which is every bit as pessimistic about the tyranny of technique aggressively penetrating every aspect of human society. In this parallel process Ellul made a rigorous methodological commitment to keeping his sociological analysis free of religious reference. He clearly desired the scathing sociological works to stand on their own as analysis, but he also wanted Christian readers to live with the dialectical tension of the two tracks. For many secular academics, his biblical theology was utterly unknown or dismissed as little more than some quirky hobby. Many are nonplussed, dumbfounded would be more precise, to discover that he was a Christian, let alone that faith was the beginning and end of his work.

Now Stringfellow takes the opposite literary tact. In writing on the principalities he moves seamlessly between social analysis and scripture or theology. It is all one for him. That method was rooted, for him, in a radically incarnational theology which refuses any otherworldliness. By his lights, the genius of the biblical witness is that "the Bible deals with the very sanctification of the actual history of nations and of human beings in this world as it is while that history is being lived" (Stringfellow, 1973:47). It was theology which led Stringfellow to refuse the bifurcated approach. This is to say that if one took *Technological Society* and *Meaning of the City* and compressed them together under the weight of racial crisis and war-making in America, the dialectical sparks would fly upwards and a book very like *An Ethic for Christians and Other Aliens in a Strange Land* would appear.

Marva Dawn has shown that the concept of the powers is a point of departure for Jacques Ellul's social analysis and, in fact, the very tie between the two tracks (Dawn, 1992, 1996, Dawn and Ellul, 1997). What Ellul demonstrates empirically, is that particular powers prove to have a life of their own operating with an independence actually beyond human decision making and control. The virtual autonomy of technology in shaping the course of its own development is a prime example. When he slips into appearing to grant it a mythic kind of will, he steps back with a sociological qualification:

> It is obvious – and this comment holds for all the rest of this discussion – that when I say technology "does not admit", "wants", etc., I am not personifying in any way. I am simply using an accepted rhetorical shortcut. In reality, it is the technicians on all levels who make these judgments and have this attitude; but they are so imbued, so impregnated with the technological ideology, so integrated into the system, that their

vital judgments and attitudes are its direct expression. One can refer them to the system itself. (Ellul, 1980:335, footnote 2)

His sociological synonym for the fall is "the logic of necessity", a kind of analytical equivalent for "the law of sin and death". It is the web in which all are caught. He employs it to gather up, as Dawn put it, everything that "is unavoidable, the compulsion or constraint caused by circumstances or social conditions which make certain actions obligatory or inevitable" (Dawn, 1992). His genius is in uncovering what might be called the *stoicheia*, the building blocks or rudiments of that necessity. With respect to technique, these are the means choosing the means. With respect to political power or violence, the same. Having identified the laws or mechanisms by which violence operates, he concludes, "The order of violence is like the order of digestion or falling bodies or gravitation". Then who can fight against it? For Ellul and Stringfellow both, we are caught in a horrifying bondage – which they describe with such unflinching honesty that we are led to the brink of despair.

Nevertheless, beyond all imagining, they both proclaim a freedom from that bondage. Freedom from the logic of necessity is a kind of ethical Christian charism for Ellul. Stringfellow names it plainly: freedom from the power of death.

Actually and ironically, it is that freedom which I believe enabled Stringfellow to look the Beast in the face without flinching, turning aside, or going weak in the knees. He lived and wrote in the freedom of the resurrection, the freedom to die. He wrote as it were in the estate of justification – free to stand at any given moment before the judgment of God. Stringfellow commended thereby an ethic, without principle or program, which was sacramental, improvisational, incarnational and eschatological: an ethic of resurrection.

It was, as it were, an ethic rooted in his own baptism: renouncing Satan and all his works, which is to say, placing himself under the Lordship of Christ alone. William Stringfellow was simply convinced "that neither death, nor life, nor angels, nor principalities, nor things present, nor things to come, nor powers, nor height, nor depth, nor anything else in all creation will be able to separate us from the love of God in Christ Jesus our Lord" (Rom. 8:38-9).

Chapter Six

William Stringfellow's Apocalyptic Hermeneutics

Christopher Rowland

Introduction

I have been wrestling with William Stringfellow's work. I think I must have read Stringfellow when I was writing my first book on apocalyptic, but apart from the fact that I recall getting it out of the University library in Cambridge it made no impact upon me at all then. How very different when I read *An Ethic for Christians and Other Aliens in a Strange Land* (Stringfellow, 1973) in preparation for writing this chapter. As there are no copies of any of Stringfellow's books in Oxford University, I obtained copies of *Ethic* and also *Conscience and Obedience* (Stringfellow, 1977a) elsewhere. I remember distinctly the morning I got the books. I opened them, started reading, and could not put them down. Reading *Ethic* that morning was like water on a thirsty ground. It was something that at that particular moment I needed for spiritual nourishment in order to perhaps understand the reality in which I found myself. I also found myself resonating very warmly and thankfully for what was written in those one hundred and fifty pages.

What I am going to do here is share some of those one hundred and fifty pages with you, in order to explain something of Stringfellow's apocalyptic hermeneutics. It is in part a descriptive account of what you will find in *Ethic*, together with one brief passage from *Conscience and Obedience*. I will then go on to look at two ancestors of Stringfellow, before raising questions about how the particular perspective that we find in this book might relate to our own situation.

Ethic is about the book of Revelation. Revelation offers its readers the perception of things which are beyond human understanding, as an indispensable guide to their present situation and their eternal destiny as they struggled to live under the shadow of empire. Nevertheless how that divine perspective is construed has varied down the centuries. There have been a variety of ways of reading this enigmatic apocalyptic book, and Stringfellow's approach represents one very distinctive perspective on it, placing him with the mystics and political radicals who have found in these visions the equipment to read 'the signs of the times'.

The visions of Revelation have been related to their ancient, first century context. In this interpretative approach questions are concerned with the meaning for the original author and readers and with the need to decipher the complex symbolism and its relationship to the particular circumstances in which Christians in late first century AD in Asia Minor found themselves. Revelation, although it only occasionally prompts that quest for the meaning of the mysteries, (e.g. 17.9 cf. 1.20 and 4.3), has prompted scores of ingenious attempts to unlock its mysteries, most comprehensively in the interpretative tradition of Joseph Mede and Isaac Newton (Burdon, 1997). There has been a visionary appropriation of it in which the words offer the opportunity to 'see again' what had appeared to John of Patmos and become a means of prompting new visions whereby there can be a discernment of higher spiritual realities (Carey, 1999:169). There has been the 'actualizing' of Revelation in which particular visions are believed to be identified with, or embodied in, contemporary events. Related to that tradition of 'actualization', there has been an application of the text to an interpreter's own circumstances. Rather than the text of Revelation being 'decoded', so that the apocalyptic imagery is translated into a more prosaic narrative of persons and events, the imagery of Revelation is used as an interpretative lens with which to view history. In this way of using the text of the book of Revelation the interpretative perspective has ceased to be solely about the eschaton and becomes instead a means of interpreting every age of human existence. This is typical of Stringfellow's use of the Apocalypse, to quote his words; "Babylon is allegorical of the condition of death reigning in each and every nation or similar principality...The parable of the nation in the fullness of its apocalyptic reality...Babylon represents the principality in bondage to death in time – and time is actually a form of *that* bondage – Jerusalem means the emancipation of human life in society from the rule of death and breaks through time, transcends time, anticipates within time the abolition of time" (Stringfellow, 1973:49,50,60).

What follows then is an account of the way in which Stringfellow is using the book of Revelation in particular, and the Bible generally, in order to understand the particular history in which he found himself in the late 60s and early 70s, and offering to us I think a model for the way in which we can use the Bible to interpret the particular situation in which we find ourselves too.

Understanding Life Biblically

In chapter five Bill Wylie-Kellermann drew our attention to the way in which *An Ethic for Christians and Other Aliens in a Strange Land* is a book which is geared to enabling Stringfellow's audience, which he saw primarily as North American, to read their own country – to read America – biblically, rather than allow the culture and values of the United States of America to determine the way the Bible is read. Stringfellow makes it clear (and this is something I think it is important to hang onto) that he is not engaging in exegesis, by which I mean the minute attention to the detail of the text trying to work out what every word means. Exegesis as it is exemplified by Stringfellow's work is something more impressionistic and holistic, expository and rhetorical rather than analytical and 'scientific'. He says he is writing a tract that moves beyond analysis to ethics, to see how the text can impact upon an individual and a group as they look upon their own particular contemporary history.

At the heart of his method is this conviction that the Bible can assist one to understand a particular moment of time because it enables an enhanced vision of the reality that confronts one. And that, I think, comes across in the following quotation.

> Biblical living involves…a converted sense of time, a transposed perception of history. The biblical mind beholds history as the epoch of the Fall and recognizes time as a dimension of the death experience. Biblical faith…breaks out of the linear conceptions of time and confounds sequential doctrines of history…Biblical insight encompasses all things as in a moment. So in the same event, in any happening whatever, there is the moral reality of death and there is the incarnation of the Word of God, the demonic and the dehumanizing and the power of the resurrection, the portents of the Apocalypse impending and the signs of the imminence of the Eschaton. (Stringfellow, 1973:152)

What one notes here is the importance of attending to the Fall not just as some isolated past event or personal event, but a cosmic event. The following sentence is crucial: "Biblical faith breaks out of the linear conceptions of time and confounds sequential doctrine of history. Biblical insight encompasses all things as in a moment" (Stringfellow, 1973:152).

Now here one sees something which forms the key to the way in which he uses the book of Revelation: "biblical insight encompasses all things as in a moment". So one is concentrating upon a particular moment; one is not necessarily looking at the totality of history, but one is looking at one's own history in all its particularity and uniqueness and utilizing the Bible to interpret that. Once one does that, there can then be opened up in the humility before God a glimmering of the understanding of the moral reality of death and the recognition of the demonic and dehumanizing alongside the power of the resurrection which is at work. Stringfellow offers us as the pre-eminent moment, the crucifixion; this for him is the pre-eminent example of the transcendence of time, of the cosmic converging upon the momentary, of the integration of the ethical within the sacramental, of the dialectical 'no and yes', characteristic of the biblical witness. In it is the intercession for all human beings throughout history. So, this past event in history is seen as the key to all history, "Christ is crucified before one's eyes" to take Paul's words in Galatians. It offers the means whereby one can begin to understand the totality of one's own situation.

Stringfellow offers no neat answers and does not expect to go to the scriptures as if to a 'self-help' manual which will offer 'off the shelf' solutions. Nor is he interested in abstract principles or grand theories to apply to the situations in which we find ourselves. He emphasizes this on several occasions in *Ethic*, for example pointing out that biblical politics offers reorientation rather than 'right' or 'ultimate' answers to our questions (Stringfellow, 1973:53-57). The ethics of biblical people concern events not moral propositions: precedent and parable, not propositions or principle (Stringfellow, 1977a:24). There is no norm, no ideal, no grandiose principle from which hypothetical, preconceived or carefully worked out answers can be derived because there are no disincarnate issues.

In *Ethic*, he offers one example of this, and perhaps initially unexpectedly: in his discussion of pacifism he rejects the idea that you can have this abstract principle and a commitment to pacifism which as it were transcends any situation in which one may find oneself. By reference to the situation which Dietrich Bonhoeffer found himself in, he stresses how important it is to attend to our own incarnational time and place.

> This points to what is deficient in traditional pacifism or in any other attempt to ideologize the gospel, namely, the attempt to ascertain idealistically whether a projected action approximates the will of God...No decision, no deed, either violent or nonviolent, is capable of being confidently rationalized as a second-guessing of God's will. (Stringfellow, 1973:132)

Here is an example of him stressing the importance of one's context, and being able to read that context with a biblical faith.

Taking seriously the particularity of one's context in all its fallenness and its potential to manifest the signs of resurrection and the new heaven and earth means staying with that situation of fallenness and accept being subject (though not obedient to) the principalities and powers. In *Conscience* we note the importance which he attaches to Paul's injunction to Romans 13. Stringfellow stresses the vocation of the principalities and powers. Although he has some pretty stringent things to say about their unwillingness to fulfil their vocation, alongside that, there is the important emphasis on their integrity and their vocation under God. This comes out in the following passage from *Conscience*, where he is setting up the supposed contrast between Revelation 13 and Romans 13.

> The references in Romans...recall that political authority...has authenticity and fulfillment of its own integrity and capacity in life in worship, which is to say, in recognition and adoration of the sovereignty of the Word of God...On the other hand the profound distortion (though not obliteration) of that very vocation for the fallen political principalities is described, in Revelation, in the grotesque imagery of predatory beasts...assaulting those who profess and trust the sovereignty of the Word of God in this world. (Stringfellow, 1977a: 35)

Now I think both of those aspects need to be borne in mind, and the importance which Stringfellow clearly attaches to the vocation of the powers. They are not totally demonic.

The Book of Revelation in *Ethic for Christians*

What Stringfellow sets out to do in *Ethic* is, he says in the introduction, to answer the question posed by the Psalmist in Psalm 137 "How shall we sing the Lord's song in a strange land?" The answer: we can do that because the book of Revelation enables us to do it. Why? The book of Revelation is "a parable of the fallenness of the nations" (Stringfellow, 1973:21). The book's stark contrasts, not least that between Jerusalem and Babylon, offer an interpretative key to understand the cosmos under God. As a principality in bondage to death in time, Babylon is an allegory of the condition of death, and a description of every city. It is the focus of apocalyptic judgement. Jerusalem is concerned with the emancipation of human life from bondage to death and its rule. A parable of the church of prophecy, it anticipates the end of time, within time, whereby the history's end is revealed as the fulfilment of life at this time. Antichrist is a stylized way of talking about the idolatry of death in a nation. Antichrist mimics and displaces Christ. Antichrist is where the churchly institutions are banished or destroyed or converted into functionaries of the State (Stringfellow, 1973:49-50,60-61,114).

This contrast offers a way of looking at the world, a means of seeing things differently. Central to this, as we have seen, is the crucifixion of Jesus. So in Revelation 5 the lamb moves to centre stage. The one who is the victim actually becomes the one who shares the throne of God and transforms the way history and turns upside down the way in which reality is to be viewed. What comes out in the way in which the book of Revelation is used in *Ethic,* is that, rather than the book of Revelation being a kind of chronology of human history or of the future, Stringfellow sees the book as a kind of lens through which one might see one's own situation. The book of Revelation is apocalypse not so much as the cataclysmic destruction of the world, but as the means of insight or revelation. Stringfellow toys with the words 'apocalypse' and 'eschaton'. Apocalypse is the means whereby one gains insight into the fallenness of the particular historical situation and the powers which confront one. Eschaton is the hope, that alternative horizon which offers a different perspective. What is crucial is the way in which he says the apocalypse is not just for the community of the last days, but is applicable to every age. It offers a way of transcending time to see how in our history Eden and the Fall, Jerusalem and Babylon, all are to be found in the reality which confronts one.

Stringfellow takes seriously the principalities and powers. What he is also doing (and this relates to his attempts to use the apocalypse to interpret his own history) is to see this doomsday language as being imminent and relevant to his own situation, as well as being ultimate:

> So long as time lasts the apocalyptic reality impends upon each and every happening. In the very anarchy and futility that mark the fallen principalities and powers empirically the apocalypse is forecast and portended. (Stringfellow, 1977a:67)

The images of Babylon and Jerusalem have ceased merely to be eschatological future images, but relate to how one relates to one's reality here and now. Babylon as a description of every city, an allegory of the condition of death. It is the principality in bondage to death in time – the focus of apocalyptic judgement. Apocalyptic insight enables one to detect where Babylon is at work. On the other hand, there is another horizon which is represented by Jerusalem. This is about the emancipation of human life in society from the rule of death. It is a parable he says of the church of prophecy, an anticipation of the end of time. Daringly, Stringfellow applies the antichrist imagery to the situation which confronts him in the early 1970s. In this he is doing no differently from what we find in the New

Testament, where, as is well known, the only occurrences of the word Antichrist come in a situation where a community is trying to understand the reality of conflict and separation within its midst (see 1 John 2.20ff). In other words, Stringfellow is in touch with an apocalyptic hermeneutic which is not just talking about some eschatological figures, but real people of flesh and blood.

Stringfellow can talk about Antichrist as a stylized way of talking about the idolatry of death in a nation. Picking up ideas from the book of Revelation, he sees Antichrist as mimicking and displacing Christ. The church is in particular danger here, as such activity represents the moment when ecclesiastical institutions may find themselves converted into functionaries of the state, or banished if they fail to conform. For Stringfellow, there are always signs of that happening. In that situation, however, there are, under God's grace, always going to be found the marks and beginnings of Jerusalem. If I have read *Ethic* correctly, this will often be found in surprising places. Stringfellow describes the ideal, 'confessing' church. It is

> spontaneous, episodic, radically ecumenical, irregular in polity, zealous in living, extemporaneous in action, new and renewed, conscientious, meek, poor. (Stringfellow, 1973:122)

The role of the Confessing Church is to expose the reign of death while affirming the aspiration to a new life. Typical of such a church is the saint, who

> is just an exemplary human being, a mature and free person, a humanized human being; a prophet is one whose work is intercession for human life, the faithful public advocacy of human life in society, the proclamation and provocation of redemption. (Stringfellow, 1973:87)

In enabling a Confessing Church to be sustained, and indeed to come into existence, there is a constant need for resistance and recourse to the Bible. That is always going to be basic and an essential part of the tactic of resistance. Stringfellow speaks about the various activities of this sort of church: discernment, and prophecy. He mentions glossolalia as a characteristic feature and here picks up the contrast between the liberated witness as compared with the language of Babel. What comes across in his understanding of the Confessing Church is an understanding of the relationship between the Confessing Church and culture which is confrontational. What is required is the cultivation of a counter-culture. Indeed, in *Ethic* Stringfellow questions what he calls redemption by osmosis.

Stringfellow's Ancestors

Let me move on now, after that very rapid summary, to say a little about Stringfellow's ancestors. I think there are many one might look to, and in concentrating on two radicals I am aware that I *could* have talked about Stringfellow and Augustine. I think a lot of the way in which Stringfellow uses the book of Revelation echoes what one finds in the *City of God.* I have chosen to focus upon two radicals because I think in many ways, both in terms of their life, and in what they are doing with the book of Revelation and the Bible, there are many affinities with the work of William Stringfellow.

First of all, Gerard Winstanley. Those of you who have read Christopher Hill's book *The World Turned Upside Down* (Hill, 1972) will recall that after the beheading of Charles I and the beginnings of the commonwealth there was this turmoil in British society. The possibility was dreamt amongst all sorts of radical groups about a new kind of society being set up in seventeenth-century England. And one of the most remarkable of the writers who flourished, round about 1650, was Gerard Winstanley, who with a group of others set up a commune in order to establish common ownership of the common land of England for the ordinary people. His writing spans a very short period, 4-5 years at the most, and we hear very little of him thereafter. But in the writing we do have, what we find is the use of the Bible and in particular the use of the book of Revelation and the book of Daniel, which mirrors very much what we find in Stringfellow's work. Jerusalem and Babylon are either just past historical realities or eschatological hopes but represent the struggle at work in human history: the new Jerusalem is not to be seen only hereafter, but is seen and known within creation, now.

> When a man hath meat, and drink, and cloathes .. and all shall cheerfully put their hands to make these things that are needfull, one helping another ... This is the glory of Jerusalem ... when the covetousnesse and the selfish power is killed and cast out of heaven. (Winstanley and Sabine, 1941:184)

What comes out of this quotation is that the new Jerusalem is not to be seen only hereafter, but is something which is here and now, within creation. Here Winstanley is breaking away from dominant understandings of the book of Revelation and of future hope. There is here that appropriation of the Apocalypse and the application to contemporary historical experience, particularly of that group, but also of the possibilities which Winstanley thought were around at the time.

William Blake, who lived a century later than Winstanley and was heir to the same radical tradition, is, I think, very different from Stringfellow in one major respect – it is much more difficult to get at precisely what he is saying. I think the reasons for this are very deliberate; what Blake offers in his writings and his illuminated books is a way of reading the world and understanding reality which also recognizes the enormous difficulty confronting anyone who is reading as a result of how much they have imbibed of the dominant ideology of their day. What he is setting up all the time in his poetry, his paintings, and his designs are different attempts to challenge our illusions and enable us to see things differently. In his last great epic poem *Jerusalem*, Blake is doing something very similar to what we find in Stringfellow's *Ethic*. There the Jerusalem Babylon contrast is being used in order to interpret the deluded state which he sees as being typical of English life in his day.

What we now know as *Jerusalem* is in fact an introduction to some versions of Blake's poem *Milton*. This famous passage brings to gather several of the themes, which I have touched on already. The New Jerusalem is not something remote or far off but a possibility, something, which may be built in England's green and pleasant land. There is not a disjunction between human activity and divine activity. Nothing here about leaving it all to God, for the simple reason that God is involved through the imaginative and creative work of the artist. There is an application of the texts to the writer and his contemporaries. The vision of the New Jerusalem is one that is open to all and the task of building belongs to all. *Jerusalem* itself is based on a contrast between what is actually the case and what might be. The contrast between the implied question of the opening lines becomes explicit at the beginning of the second stanza and the hope for Jerusalem in this green and pleasant land. What is needed for that hope to be fulfilled is not just honest endeavour, but 'Mental Fight', reflecting Eph. 6.10. 'Mental Fight' is the process of challenging the way in which dominant patterns of thinking and behaving make it difficult for all God's people to be prophets. Elijah's chariot is not just part of past history but something which can be the inspiration of the poet as a new Elijah comes on the scene condemning the idolatries of Ahab and Jezebel and offering an alternative to the Baalism of a contemporary culture, which, according to Blake, had led to the capitulation of Christianity to a religion of rules and violence. Prophetic activity likewise is not just a thing of the past. It is the vocation of all people.

Now there are many quotations I could have offered you to illuminate the way in which Blake also is taking the book of Revelation and taking these images and as it were using them as lenses with which to view his particular history. He is doing this because he quite consciously thought of himself as a prophet. He wrote three prophecies. As far as Blake is concerned, a prophet is not someone who actually foretells the future. Rather it is somebody who actually has that insight into the nature of the fallenness of humanity and can enable somebody to see what is going on. It is a vocation, which is open to anyone. In an annotation to a book by a former Welsh Bishop, in fact the Bishop of Llandaff, in which the Bishop took issue with Tom Paine, William Blake leaps to Tom Paine's defence, and frequently throughout the book we find Blake's marginal comments on various points which have been made by Watson. In one, he talks about prophecy. He says:

Every honest man is a prophet. He utters his opinion both of private and public matters. Thus if you go on so the result is so, he never says such a thing shall happen, let you do what you will. A prophet is a seer not an arbitrary dictator. (Blake and Keynes, 1966:392)

There is much that could be said about Blake's understanding of the Bible, but I think with regard to Stringfellow I want to draw to your attention one passage which I think enables one to see how Blake and Stringfellow have so much in common in the way they view the bible and use it. This is a quotation from a letter he wrote around about 1800.

> The wisest of the ancients considered what is not too explicit as the fittest for
> instruction, because it rouses the faculties to act. (Blake and Keynes, 1966:793)

The Bible fits into this category. It is full of material that is "not too explicit". In
other words it leaves space, it enables the reader to use his or her own faculties to
interpret, and by means of the text actually to interpret the situation in which they
find themselves. That is precisely what one finds happening again and again in
Blake's use of scripture. It is being used as a lens both to create a new way of
understanding the principalities and powers through his own idiosyncratic
mythology, and his own way of understanding his own history.

    The other thing that I want to draw your attention to in Blake, which relates to
points that have been made throughout the day about Stringfellow, is Blake's
insistence on what he calls minute particulars. Blake resisted again and again
abstract general theorising. And so, in *Jerusalem* he says you "who wishes to see a
Vision; a perfect Whole / Must see it in its Minute Particulars". And then, with
regard to ethics, Blake writes, with a note of sarcasm, "he who would do good to
another, must do it in Minute Particulars / General Good is the plea of scoundrel,
hypocrite, and flatterer".

    This theme is what comes out again and again in *Ethic* (Stringfellow, 1973).
There is resistance to abstract principles being derived from the Bible; rather what
one is being asked to do again and again is incarnate oneself and to use the bible in
that particular context to interpret the situation in which one finds oneself. A
wonderful example of Blake engaging these minute particulars, in two poems from
his *Songs of Innocence and Experience*. What he does in this poem is take an
event, a regular event in the church's calendar, a service of thanksgiving, which
took place in St Paul's Cathedral. Through this ordinary event, the "minute
particulars" of this occasion, he sees beyond it and imbues this event with
apocalyptic significance by utilizing the language of the book of Revelation to shed
new light on it. The final words of the poem in *Songs of Innocence* open the way
the to the parallel poem in *Songs of Experience* also called *Holy Thursday*, which
reminds one that those people, those children in St Paul's, were the fortunate ones.

Songs of Innocence: Holy Thursday	**Songs of Experience: Holy Thursday**

'Twas on a Holy Thursday their
    innocent faces clean,
The children walking two & two in
    red & blue & green,
Grey headed beadles walk'd before
    with wands as white as snow,
Till into the high dome of Paul's
    they like Thames' waters flow.
	Is this a holy thing to see,
	In a rich and fruitful land,
	Babes reduc'd to misery,
	Fed with cold and usurous hand?

O what a multitude they seem'd,
    these flowers of London town!
Seated in companies they sit with
    radiance all their own.
The hum of multitudes was there,
	Is that trembling cry a song?
	Can it be a song of joy?
	And so many children poor?
	It is a land of poverty!

	And their sun does never shine. And their fields are bleak and bare. And their ways are fill'd with thorns It is eternal winter there.

but multitudes of lambs,
Thousands of little boys & girls
  raising their innocent hands.

Now like a mighty wind they
  raise to heaven the voice of song,
Or like harmonious thunderings
  the seats of heaven among.
Beneath them sit the aged men
  wise guardians of the poor;
Then cherish pity; lest you drive
  an angel from your door.
(Blake and Keynes, 1966:121)

For where'er the sun does shine,
And where'er the rain does fall:
Babe can never hunger there,
Nor poverty the mind appal.
(Blake and Keynes, 1966:211)

The Holy Thursday poems offer readers the opportunity to find allusions to these chapters of Revelation as the poet meditates upon a particular social event in eighteenth-century England. There is the focus on a moment, what Blake calls "a Minute Particular", when one may pierce behind the appearances of a well known event in the social calendar, to bring out its inner reality and the contrasting emotions and attitudes which it engenders. In the *Songs of Innocence* version of *Holy Thursday* Blake treats us to a heart-warming description of innocent orphan children processing to St Paul's cathedral in London. They have been beneficiaries of those generous hearted people who have pity on the poor. In reading one catches oneself sharing that sense of satisfaction that charitable concern for the less fortunate can often elicit. But outside the door of the great cathedral, a different story is to be told in the companion poem in *Songs of Experience*: the reality of what actually is the case for the majority of children in 'this green and pleasant land'. The juxtaposition of the two poems parallels the stark contrast in Rev. 6-7. In Revelation 6 death and pestilence stalk the earth, while in Rev. 7 the followers of the Lamb exult in their salvation. Allusions to Rev. 7 abound in the two poems. The body of children who raise their voice in praise are a small sample of that great multitude of victims, who have "washed their robes and made them white in the blood of the Lamb". The lambs, multitudes; grey headed beadels (= Revelation's elders, who in this poem are given a subordinate position to the children, "beneath them sit the aged men") all connect with Rev. 7. In the last stanza of the Songs of Experience poem, "Babe can never hunger there", echoes the more hopeful Rev. 7.16 ("they will hunger no more").[1] As in Rev. 7 the children of the *Holy Thursday* poem are not merely passive recipients of the charity of the wealthy. The poet indicates their peculiar quality in the words "with radiance all their own" and in the "mighty wind of their song", echoing Rev. 19.6. Their praise is an assertive moment, a voice of voiceless, when, on this religious occasion, they are allowed to raise their voice and in Blake's perspective of the event dominate the proceedings. But the sense of pride and satisfaction at generosity exercised and innocent praise is given a rude shock at the end of the evocation of thanksgiving and charity in the *Songs of Innocence* version. There is the veiled threat and challenge in the words

---

[1]   A parallel noted by Glen (1983:173).

"Then cherish pity, lest you drive an angel from your door". Apocalypse lurks, like the Son of Man outside, knocking at the door of the Laodicean church in Rev 3.20, disturbing the wisdom, order and life of comfortable London.

Conclusion

There is more to be said, on Blake and Stringfellow. I hope I have just given you a sample of the importance of relating these two remarkable people. But let me conclude with a few things about what Stringfellow is saying to us in *Ethic* and our own situation, because I think any remembrance of Stringfellow requires more than discussion of him as merely the subject of an academic debate. So, I ask myself about the continuing effect of this particular apocalyptic hermeneutic; and I think he offers me two challenges.

In terms of contemporary theology Stringfellow's work has many affinities with Latin American liberation theology, particularly as it is reflected in the life of the Basic Ecclesial Communities. Compare the way in which Stringfellow sets about his biblical interpretation with what I think typifies the way in which the Bible has been and is being used in grassroots communities in Latin America. Here is a quotation from an influential little collection by someone who has been at the heart of the liberation theology project with the grassroots in Brazil:

> the emphasis is placed not on the text itself but rather on the meaning the text has for the people reading it...understanding life by means of the Bible...The discovery of meaning is not the product of scholarship alone, of human reasoning, but is also a gift of God through the Spirit. (Mesters, 1989)

It is possible to see reflected in these words some of the same sorts of characteristics that are evident in Stringfellow's work. We notice the importance which is attached to the worshipping community for that understanding.

Both the wisdom of the Basic Ecclesial Communities and that of William Stringfellow offer the chance to educate the paralysed consciences of those of us who are part of comfortable Britain. Stringfellow sets out the challenge to middle America in particular, and those who are in situations of leadership. He posed the question "How can we act humanly amidst the fall?" and "How can we sing the Lord's song in a strange land?", and answers "I hear that in the book of Revelation's response to the question posed in this Psalm" (Stringfellow, 1973:28). That poses the uncomfortable question about what the consequence might be if we were to begin to use the lens of Jerusalem and Babylon living in the situation in which we do. We are thereby reminded that there is a powerful tradition within the Bible of the notion of exile, a situation in which one might enter, literally or spiritually, to see things differently. That may include those in the corridors of power as well as on the margins, "by the waters of Babylon".

In the book of Daniel we find a distinguished person, not sitting by the waters of Babylon playing his harp, but in the palace of King Nebuchadnezzar, struggling to work out some kind of way of life in which he as an alien in a strange land can live and work in this sort of context. That kind of vision engages me. On that morning when I read *Ethic* it engaged me here in Oxford and prompted me to think about how it is I live and work in this particular place. I link the book of Daniel with Stringfellow's work, to explore all those grey areas, the limits of compromise, what to protest about and what to keep quiet about, how to act prophetically, and how – as I do more often than not – to avoid just taking the line of least resistance. One of the problems with this talk about an ethic of resistance is that there is the constant need to resist that self-righteous spirit of being one of the elect of the holy city who has got it right. When I read *Ethic* and *Conscience* I think Stringfellow has got a clear grasp on the need to grapple with that issue. Whatever may have been the case in his life I think in what he *writes* he is not asserting he has got the answers – far from it. There is that ongoing need to emphasize the particularities of every situation.

There is one other thing about resistance. Stringfellow tells us that it is in resistance that persons live most humanly e.g. (Stringfellow, 1973:138). Yes, but there is also a danger: resisting can, without due care, lead not to living more humanly either for oneself or for others, but to a human shrivelling and diminution of human flourishing. One must find ways of dealing with that. It is an ongoing, contextual task for which there are no simple answers from the scriptures but a resource to inform the struggle to interpret the particulars:

> The issue of biblical ethics is not expressed in vain efforts to divine the will of God in this or that particular situation. On the contrary, biblical ethic asks how to live humanly in the midst of death's reign. And biblical politics, therefore, as it manifests resistance to the power of death, is, at once, celebration of human life in society. Or, by parable, biblical politics means the practice of the vocation to live as Jerusalem, the holy nation, amidst Babylon. (Stringfellow, 1973:151)

Chapter Seven

William Stringfellow and the Politics of Liturgy

Mark D. Chapman

Stringfellow as 'Sacramental Socialist'

One theme appears over and over again in Stringfellow's writings: that of the materiality or sacramentality of the Christian religion. Quite simply, true religion – that is, religion which has to do with God and which is not simply focused purely in on itself – is a worldly activity; and that is true even in its most profoundly spiritual moments. For Stringfellow, it is in the liturgy that this materiality, this worldliness, is expressed most fully, and that is because the church's liturgy functions as a microcosm of the whole Christian experience of the world. The gathering of the congregation for worship is the counterpart to the dispersal of that same congregation in the world in its life of witness. Thus Stringfellow could write in *Dissenter in a Great Society*: "in the broadest sense all of life is liturgical" (Stringfellow, 1966:150). Worship and life were integrated in a Christianity rooted in the incarnation. Consequently, liturgy was not something confined to the sanctuary, it was neither "spooky" nor "lucky", but rather was "a dramatic form of the ethical witness of Christians in this world" (Stringfellow, 1966:151).

This chapter interprets Stringfellow in the light of a broader sacramental tradition, seeing his theology as firmly located in the depths of ordinary human experience and leading to ethical activity within the concrete realities of the world, which is dramatized in the worship life of the church. "Theology," he writes, "is about the knowledge God gives men of Himself in and through the life of mankind and the world's existence" (Stringfellow, 1962:51). Furthermore, by discussing Stringfellow's thought in dialogue with other writers in the Anglican sacramental tradition, his explicitly experiential theology is seen as a fundamentally *political* theology which can be fruitfully compared to the radical tradition pioneered by English Anglo-Catholic socialists in the early years of the twentieth-century, which similarly emphasized the transformative role of the sacraments. It is not without some justification that Stringfellow can be called the 'sacramental socialist' *par excellence* of the second half of the twentieth-century.[1] Like so many of these pioneers Stringfellow was uncomfortable with the institutional church, often

---

[1]   On 'sacramental socialism' see part two of Jones (1968); Cf. part two of Gray (1986).

calling it back to a radical rethink of its priorities. He can rightly be described as a prophet, and in many ways he resembles the outsiders and mavericks who pricked at the complacency of the Church of England early in the twentieth-century. In his often purple pronouncements on the hypocrisy and self-centredness of the church, together with his integrated picture of liturgy and life, Stringfellow's writings are often strikingly reminiscent of some of the earlier generations of Anglican political thinkers.

For instance, the eccentric monk of the Community of the Resurrection, J.N. Figgis (1866-1919), could write in 1917 that "the Church of England at the close of the nineteenth century was the most respectable institution ever known in the annals of the human race" (Figgis, 1917:40).[2] However, Figgis maintained, it was through the rediscovery of worship of a God who simply could not be controlled by Christians that the church could rise up against "mere tradition or outward respectability" (Figgis, 1914:83). In this way the church could again begin to exist for those who were scandalized by decent society. In a prophetic statement Figgis thus claimed that "[u]nless we can be the Church of the poor, we had far better cease to be a Church at all...More and more does it appear that no correctness of dogma, no beauty of Catholic ritual, no sentiment of devotion, no piety esoteric and aloof can secure the Church from collapse, unless she gain a 'change of heart' in regard to the relations of wealth and poverty" (Figgis, 1914:99-100). Similarly, he claimed: "We may stumble on hard paths; but I cannot for the life of me understand why Christian people of this day should have such a nervous fear of error when it comes to siding with the poor – in this back-slum scrimmage we call 'civilisation' – while it was the danger of subserviency to the rich that seems to have inspired the Epistle of St James" (Figgis, 1914:103). For Figgis, the sacraments, as the corporate life of those committed to service in the world, took on a profoundly political dimension.

In a similar manner, and for similar reasons, Stringfellow also sees the sacraments as fundamentally political. Thus he claims that baptism and communion "far from being esoteric, religious rituals – are most concretely political and social in character" (Stringfellow, 1966:149). In a powerful statement which reveals something of his integrated picture of the union of church and world, of eschatological hope and revealed promise, Stringfellow could write: "The liturgy...is a living, political event. The very example of salvation, it is the festival of life which foretells the fulfilment and maturity of all of life for all of time in *this* time. The liturgy *is* social action because it is the characteristic style of life for human beings in this world" (Stringfellow, 1966:149). Politics or social action was no mere bolt-on extra for the Christian religion, but rather Christianity was social and political or it was nothing. As the religion of the incarnation, Christianity simply could not avoid being political. Again there are close points of contact with an earlier tradition: for instance, in the original set of objectives of one of the early Christian Socialist organizations, Stewart Headlam's Guild of St Matthew of the late nineteenth-century, sacraments and the reformation of society were intimately related: the *raison d'être* of the Guild was the study and rectification of social ill in

---

[2]   On Figgis see Chapman (2001a).

the light of the incarnation, coupled with a renewal of the sacraments and frequent participation in holy communion.[3]

This strong sense of incarnationalism – of the Gospel present in the depths of human experience – which has typified so much Anglican socialism[4] provides the counterpart to Stringfellow's often bitter criticism of religion in the name of the Gospel. It is the incarnation that offers the basis for hope: however much the Gospel might stand over and against all cultures, in exposing evil and the dominion of principalities and powers, the incarnation, God's complete identification with humanity, together with the recognition of the utter giftedness of creation, allows Christians to pursue the imperatives of the Gospel in the here and now. There is simply no place apart from God, no place is forbidden: the incarnation and the Holy Spirit allow the Christian "to deal with history in this world just as it is" (Stringfellow, 1964b:127). The squalor of the Harlem ghetto is every bit as pervaded with God's presence as the most profound forms of liturgy. Thus, Stringfellow wrote in *A Private and Public Faith*, the "confidence of the Christian task" is that there is "nowhere an escape from the Word of God. The joy of the Christian life is that nowhere is the Word of God absent...The characteristic place to find a Christian is among his very enemies. The first place to look for Christ is in Hell" (Stringfellow, 1962:47,49).[5] The scandal of the incarnation is the good news of God's presence in what appears to be most distant from God: "I do not care – I do not mean to be impudent, but I, for one, do not care – if God lives somewhere and someplace else. But I care a lot when I hear – in the Bible, or in the church, or in the presence of a Christian, or in the ordinary happenings of my own life – that God is with us now, anyway and already, and even, thank God, before we call upon Him. I care a lot, in other words, when I hear the news of Jesus Christ" (Stringfellow, 1962:22). It is from this starting point of the incarnation that Stringfellow develops his theology of sacramentality, his theology of radical worldliness.

The World

Although Stringfellow is remembered principally as the theologian of principalities and powers, as a prophet calling the church to rediscover its essence in the gospel of repentance, he was at the same time a theologian for the world: the church is not set over and against the world but instead it has a responsibility to serve and transform the world. The church might be counter-cultural, but it did not set itself

---

[3]   On Stewart Headlam (1847-1924) and the Guild of St Matthew see Jones (1968:114-5).

[4]   On the differing traditions of Anglican socialism see Norman (1976); Bryant (1996); Wilkinson (1998).

[5]   See also Stringfellow (1962:64-68) where, in discussing *West Side Story*, Stringfellow comments: "The Word of God – the same Word uttered and observed in the sanctuary – is hidden in the ordinary life of these boys in gang society" (Stringfellow, 1962:67).

against the world: the world was good, created by God and capable of transformation. Stringfellow's theology is no theology for the sect, but is a radically catholic theology which focuses on worldly transformation. Consequently, it is, according to Stringfellow, the "interpenetration of his secular and religious lives which identifies the Christian" (Stringfellow, 1962:51). The Church *needs* the world since it is precisely *in* the world that the Church is to bear witness to the Gospel, and it is that very same world that the church is called upon to serve. Without the world the church is as nothing. "That is to say, the Christian must live in this world, where Christ lives: he must live in this world *in* Christ" (Stringfellow, 1962:80, cf. 1964c:32, 1966:141).

In this emphasis on the world, Stringfellow stands in a tradition which reaches from the pioneer Christian Socialist, F.D. Maurice, through to Michael Ramsey, but which also embraces many others from outside the mainstream, including socialist mavericks like Conrad Noel. On the one hand, such an understanding of the world, which provides a point of contact between these many different thinkers, is opposed to a Calvinism which emphasizes the doctrine of election, of total separation of the saints from the world. On the other hand, however, it is also quite opposed to those catholic models of the church which similarly emphasize the separation of the church and the world in an ever greater clamour for holiness. As Maurice himself often repeated, the world and the church were coterminous. In a famous phrase he remarked: "The world contains the elements of which the Church is composed. In the Church, these elements are penetrated by a uniting, reconciling power. The Church is, therefore, human society in its normal state; the World, that same society irregular and abnormal. The world is the Church without God; the Church is the world restored to its relation with God, taken back by him into the state for which he created it" (Maurice, 1849:403). For Maurice there simply could not be a contradiction between church and world, a point he made in a sermon with more than a hint of irony: "The Father loves the world, the Son dies for the world, the Holy Ghost convinces the world that it has a Deliverer and a Righteous Lord, and that he has taken out of the hands of a usurper; and the Church, which is sealed with his name, is not to love the world, not to save the world, not to convince the world, but to set itself up as a rival competitor to the world, to plot against the world, to undermine the world!" (Maurice, 1849).

At the deepest level, Stringfellow's theology is also a worldly theology standing in this tradition: it stresses the incarnation, the reconciliation of the world and God in the person of Jesus Christ. It is thus the history of *this* world which is to be changed by the Christian ethic: "The most notorious, plain, and victorious truth of God is that God participates in our history – even yours and mine. Our history – all our anxieties – have become the scene of his presence and the matter of His care" (Stringfellow, 1962:72). History is at one and the same time the arena of human activity, that place where lives are lived and where destinies are shared (Stringfellow, 1964c:28),[6] but also that place redeemed by Jesus Christ. "From my own vantage point," Stringfellow writes, "the Christian faith is not about some god

---

[6]   This theme of the interdependence of all people, both rich and poor, is a major theme of *Dissenter in a Great Society* (Stringfellow, 1966).

who is an abstract presence somewhere else, but about the living presence of God here and now, in this world, in *exactly* this world ... That is why, incidentally, all the well-meant talk of 'making the gospel relevant' to the life of the world is false and vulgar. It secretly assumes that God is a stranger among us, who has to be introduced to us and to our anxieties and triumphs and issues and efforts. The meaning of Jesus Christ is that the Word of God is addressed to men, to *all* men, in the very events and relationships in this world. That is the theology of the Incarnation" (Stringfellow, 1964c:97). Drawing from this strong sense of incarnationalism, Stringfellow's own political witness as "radical lawyer and exemplary Christian" (McThenia, 1995) becomes for him the worldly expression of the power of Christ in history. The world of politics is thus "the scene of God's work and the subject of God's love" (Stringfellow, 1966:159).

In *Free in Obedience*, Stringfellow sees the "real issues of faith" as having to do "with the everyday needs of men in the world and with the care for and service of those needs" (Stringfellow, 1964b:17). In a programmatic passage later in the same book, he again emphasizes the unity of liturgy and life, commenting on the importance of engaging with the world as nothing less than the "renewal of the sacramental integrity of the churches" against the "fictional theology which now entraps the churches and their people". Although the Christian might be helpless against the principalities and powers which control the world, this does not lead to hopelessness. On the contrary, claims Stringfellow, "the Christian hope becomes manifest in the very event in which a people or a man confess utter helplessness, for that confession *is* the first and free and most reckless acknowledgement of God's life and presence in the world" (Stringfellow, 1964b:17). The Christian life is thus about the discernment of God's presence which in turn will lead to a validation of the sacraments: "the celebrations at the altar of God's awful and fearsome, splendid and victorious presence in the world will be validated in mission to the city. Then the city will hear that it is God who builds the City of Salvation" (Stringfellow, 1964b:29).

In his later works this theme of the heavenly city again looms large, and once again the task of the Christian is to discern the presence of life amidst death, however powerful the forces of Babylon.[7] Against an ethic of escape he stresses an ethic of sanctification: the Bible, he writes in *An Ethic for Christians and Other Aliens in a Strange Land*, "deals with the sanctification of the actual history of nations and of human beings in this world as it is while that history is being lived" (Stringfellow, 1973:47). Although the ruling powers might be under the dominion of oppressive forces, it is nevertheless *within* the world itself, rather than in any parallel spiritual domain, that the Christian Ethic takes root: the eschatological hope shapes the world as it is, despite the Babylonian forces and crises at work in society (Stringfellow, 1973:53). Thus, Stringfellow asks, "how can a person act humanly now? ... How can the Church of Jesus Christ celebrate human life in society now?" (Stringfellow, 1973:56,57). Or in biblical terms, "how shall we sing the Lord's song in a strange Land?" (Stringfellow, 1973:156). The ethics of radical

---

[7]   Interestingly Figgis also devotes a chapter to the Babylon of the modern world in his cultural critique (Figgis, 1912:65-120).

resistance may issue in destruction and chaos, and yet it is in such a worldly situation that new life emerges (cf. Stringfellow, 1973:118,142). As the Christian sets about recovering the essential humanity from which he or she has been robbed in the death of the Babylonian exile, so at the same time the Christian understands and celebrates life as the gift which emerges from God in even the most hostile circumstances. "In the event," writes Stringfellow, "the *no* which issues against death *is* at once the *yes* which celebrates life as a gift" (Stringfellow, 1973:64). Whatever the power of evil, the incarnation confirms the fundamental goodness and giftedness of all creation. And to resist evil is at one and the same time to embrace a life which stands against the "certitude of death – of moral death, of the death to one's humanity, of death to sanity and conscience, of the death which possesses humans profoundly ungrateful for the lives of others" (Stringfellow, 1973:119-20). And that gratitude is vindicated by the power of the resurrected Christ which confirms the presence of God in the midst of the principalities and powers. It is the resurrection of Christ that "means the possibility of living in this life, in the very midst of death's works, safe and free from death" (Stringfellow, 1964b:72). In the power of the resurrection sainthood is life accepted as gift (Stringfellow, 1966:47).

Witness and Worship

It is in this context of living Christianly in a hostile environment that the Christian witnesses prophetically to life as a divine gift: discerning the signs of life is at one and the same time "related to the possibility of celebration in a sacramental sense, to the vitality of that worship of the people and the quality of that worship for coherence and significance as the worship of God rather than hoax or superstition" (Stringfellow, 1973:139, cf. 1977a: 67). It is in this situation that the gifts of the Spirit, particularly that of discernment, take on a political significance: prophecy is about the unmasking of idolatry, pointing out where life is being obliterated by the "violence of Babel" (Stringfellow, 1973:141, cf. 1964b: 63). Thus Stringfellow exhorts his readers: "In the middle of chaos, celebrate the Word. Amidst Babel, I repeat, speak the truth. Confront the noise and verbiage and falsehood of death with the truth and potency and efficacy of the Word of God" (Stringfellow, 1973:142-3, cf. 1966:40). The charismatic gifts of the Spirit are seen to be about the recovery of life in a situation of death, thereby enhancing the church's "servanthood or priesthood on behalf of the world", in order to "disclose the *political* significance of the gifts and their uses" (1973:144). Against the aggressive power of the principalities of this world, the gifts stand in opposition, dispelling idolatry and allowing human beings to "celebrate Creation, which is, biblically speaking, integral to the worship of God. These gifts equip persons to live humanly in the midst of the fall" (Stringfellow, 1973:145). It is in this context that Stringfellow can speak of "politically informed exorcisms" (Stringfellow, 1973:150) as Christians confront political circumstances by exposing the idolatry of the nation. It was to this end that Stringfellow once prayed for the restoration of

Richard Nixon's humanity, a shocking reminder of the measure of the outreach of biblical witness (Stringfellow, 1977a:98-9).

Sacramental activity in the world is thus a witness of the renewal of creation which flows beyond the sanctuary and the narrowly religious life into life in the wider world. Consequently, according to Stringfellow, when the Catonsville Nine burned their draft records in May 1968, they were acting against the violence of the nation in a "direct outreach of the renewal of the sacramental activity of the sanctuary, a liturgy transposed from altar or kitchen table to a sidewalk outside a Selective Service Board" (Stringfellow, 1973:151). Recalling the rediscovery of the social dimension of the mass at Vatican II, Stringfellow points to ethical activity as "a portrayal and communication of the Jerusalem reality of the Church of Christ loving and serving the world" (Stringfellow, 1973:151).

This sacramental witness in the world is a constant theme in Stringfellow's work: it is in the humdrum life of the everyday world that the Christian uses whatever gifts are available to him or her. Consequently, Stringfellow claims, "The daily witness of the Christian in the world is essentially sacramental, rather than moralistic. The public witness of the Christian is a symbol and communication of his death in Christ every day in each situation in which he finds himself. He thereby demonstrates his faith in God's triumph over death in Christ. The ethics of witness to redemption are sacramental ethics of grace, rather than of prudence or law" (Stringfellow, 1964b:39). Having unmasked the forces of death, Christians are able to enter fully into the world free in the knowledge that they will not be overwhelmed or controlled by these hostile forces: everything can therefore be placed at the disposal of the world without asking for anything whatsoever in return. And again the reason for this is simple: "Because of his comprehension of the Incarnation – the entrance into and participation in human existence of God himself – the Christian must simply be there, no matter how unpleasant that may be" (Stringfellow, 1964b:40-41). And that involves a listening and a discernment rather than an alienating moralism (cf. Stringfellow, 1962:97). As an example of such 'sacramental' activity, Stringfellow tells the story of a young Harlem addict whose only possessions were the clothes on his back. Seeing Stringfellow freezing to death, dressed only in a shirt, chinos and sneakers, he offered him his coat. "That," claimed Stringfellow, "is what is known as a sacrament" (Stringfellow, 1964c:43).

Here there are obvious similarities with Frank Weston (1871-1924), bishop of Zanzibar in the early decades of the twentieth-century and surprising leader of the Anglo-Catholics in England after the First World War. In his famous commission to the assembled Anglo-Catholics at the 1923 Congress at the Royal Albert Hall in London he emphasized that for the liturgy to be meaningful it needed to flow from the church to the world and back again. Christ was present in the sacrament, but it was the very same Christ who was also present in the faces of the poor. For Weston, although "Christ is in and amid matter, God in flesh, God in sacrament", he was also present in the people, in the poor and the outcast. Thus he proclaimed, "You cannot claim to worship Jesus in the tabernacle if you do not pity Jesus in the slum...go out into the highways and hedges, and look for Jesus in the ragged and the naked, in the oppressed and the sweated, in those who have lost hope and in those who are struggling to make good. Look for Jesus in them; and, when you find Him, gird yourselves with His towel of fellowship, and wash his feet in the person of His brethren" (Weston, 1923:34-5).[8] To be meaningful liturgy could not be contained in worship and adoration, but had to flow out into the world.

If, for both Stringfellow and Weston, sacramentality flows out from the liturgy into service in the world, the ethics of witness also serves to unearth the idolatry of the world, leading the Christian to live a style of life with the express purpose of exposing the "transience of death's power in the world"; it is a form of life that will never be satisfied with the status quo. This theme is repeated through the course of Stringfellow's works. Thus he wrote in *Private and Public Faith*: "the biblical image of the Church is *never* one of an innocuous, isolationist religious society cut off from the actual affairs of men and nations in the world" (Stringfellow, 1962:25). That means the Christian will always be in some sense an outsider, an alien, (Stringfellow, 1962:25, 1966:162) one who knows that no secular reform will ever completely remove the "reign of death" (Stringfellow, 1964b:44). And this is simply because, by witnessing to Christ as the true Lord of history, the Christian also exposes "the false lords of history" (Stringfellow, 1964b:73). For this reason, he claimed in *Conscience and Obedience*, biblical politics is always in tension and opposition to the prevalent system, always "alienated from the politics of this age" (Stringfellow, 1977a:13). The Church as witnessing community becomes the worshipping community pointing the world forward towards its true end: it is a herald of the end, "the trustee of the society which the world, now subjected to the power of death, is to be on that last day when the world is fulfilled in all things in God" (Stringfellow, 1966:142). The combination of world and church, however, means that the church exists for the sake of the world in so far as it "beseeches" the end. Its "authorization" is thus constant complaint: "By the mercy of God, the inherent, invariable, unavoidable, intentional, unrelenting posture of the Church in the world is one of radical protest and profound dissent toward the prevailing status quo of secular society, whatever that may be at any given time, however much men boast that theirs is a great society" (Stringfellow, 1966:143). For this reason the Christian, claims Stringfellow, "is the most blunt and relentless realist" (Stringfellow, 1962:161) who is nevertheless always "in protest" (Stringfellow, 1962:162). And it is because of its constant living beyond the world as a witness to the true society, that the Church becomes the "only society worthily named great" (Stringfellow, 1962:164).

Concluding his discussion of witness in *Free in Obedience*, Stringfellow reminds his readers that authentic witness of the gospel is "an inherently sacramental event – a confession and celebration of God's freely given and wholly sufficient reconciling action in Christ, to which nothing can be added or amended nor anything compromised or taken away" (Stringfellow, 1964b:117). Again the witness of the Christian is inter-related to his or her worship. Indeed, the sacramental life rests in the unity of being and doing where the church is gathered for worship: there is a recalling, a pointing back in remembrance of all that God has done, and also at the same time there is a sense of expectation as the church

---

[8]   On Weston see my reappraisal in Chapman (Chapman, 2003).

"anticipates with gladness and eagerness the final reconciliation of the whole of creation" (Stringfellow, 1964b:118). The dominical sacraments of baptism and eucharist, as well as the act of preaching, become festivals of reconciliation between past and future, as focal points for the Gospel of reconciliation and anticipation. There is, however, the constant temptation in the sacraments to separate being from doing. Consequently "it is imperative to be concrete about what happens in the celebration of the gospel in the common sacraments" (Stringfellow, 1964b:120).

The Sacraments

Although Stringfellow's thought is refreshingly unsystematic, his thoughts on the sacraments reflect the broader themes that have already been outlined. In speaking of baptism, his principal concern is with the power of the presence of God to overcome death. Baptism is thus the sign of the new life, the life lived away from death and towards God. Consequently the adult who is baptized publicly announces "to the world that he has been freed in his own life from the power of death by the grace of God for him". Similarly infant baptism is the public proclamation of the power of God to raise the dead (Stringfellow, 1964b:63). And in turn baptism is seen as the political authorization for action in the world as all Christians share in the ministry of the church to witness in the world. Baptism consequently "bestows the power to live in Christ as a servant of the world" (Stringfellow, 1966:154). For those baptized in Christ, the world, created by God and a gift of God, becomes precious.

Similarly, at the heart of the eucharist there is the notion of thanksgiving. According to Stringfellow, it is the celebration of the gift which God has given us, the remembering of who God is and what he has done for us. The vocation of the Christian is seen as something defined by worship understood as the response of gratitude and gratefulness for the generosity of God in creation, the celebration of life as gift; worship is offered for the sake of the perfection of creation as it is pointed to its origin (Stringfellow, 1977a:30). The eucharist is thus understood as the celebration of this giftedness of life (Stringfellow, 1977a:65). In turn, the eucharist also focuses the prayers of the people for the world. Consequently, when the congregation intercedes for the world, Stringfellow claims, it becomes "with particular clarity, the Body of Christ sharing his ministry, for Christ has made the consummate intercession for the whole world" (Stringfellow, 1964b:121). As a petition for God's will to be done, so intercession becomes the means by which the congregation acknowledge their identity as human beings, and where human beings in the whole of their life are represented to God (Stringfellow, 1962:75). In this way the Holy Communion becomes the "oblation of the congregation, the offering to God, in the only full and appropriate response of men to his redemptive gift of himself" (Stringfellow, 1964b:122).

In *Dissenter in a Great Society* Stringfellow points to the liturgy, and primarily the eucharist, as the dramatic response to the ethical life of the Christian in the world. The liturgy of the Gospel thereby becomes the "theatricalization of the biblical saga of God's action in this world, thus relating the ubiquity of the Word of God in history to the consummation of the Word of God in history to the consummation of the Word of God in Jesus Christ" (Stringfellow, 1966:151). Liturgy is the celebration of the death and resurrection of Christ recalled and rehearsed in the hope for the world. As the gifts of God are returned to God, so "*the very event*" of God's reconciliation of the world to himself is taking place: "God is with his people, and his people worship him as God" (Stringfellow, 1964b:122 original emphasis, McThenia, 1995). Thus Stringfellow claims, "the new community in Christ, the Christian society is manifest in history as over against all other nations and all the societies men make as a witness that the true hope for community is in Christ" (Stringfellow, 1964b:123). The liturgy is the "normative and conclusive ethical commitment of the Christian people to the world. ... All authentic witness in the name of Christ, exemplifying in the world the virtue of Christ, which Christians undertake in their dispersion in the practical life of the world, is portrayed in the liturgy celebrated in the gathered congregation" (Stringfellow, 1966:152).

The Authentication of Worship

Equally important for Stringfellow, however, is the worldly counterpart to worship: the gathered congregation also lives in dispersion throughout the world, playing its part in ordinary life and work. Indeed, it is this life in the world that vindicates the liturgy: "Worship at the altar is thus authenticated by the constant involvement of the people of the church in the world's life and by the public witness of the church in the world" (Stringfellow, 1966:160-1).[9] In this life the Christian thus becomes increasingly aware of the tension between Christ and Caesar, between grace and law, between sin and salvation. Again the solution is to embrace the dichotomies in the life of discipleship: "to live in that tension worship in the congregation and witness in the world must be integral to one another" (Stringfellow, 1964b:123). Just as there can be no solitary worship, so there can be no solitary witness in the world: all people depend on, and inter-relate with, one another. The Christian is thus always a member of congregation gaining support and strength from his or her participation in both liturgy and life wherever he or she may be. Consequently, the "whole of Christian life, both that within the gathered congregation and that in dispersion in the world, is sacramental, and the structure, relationships, meaning, and style of life are the same whether the Christian is participating in the esoteric life of the congregation in worship or is involved in the practical life of the world" (Stringfellow, 1964b:125). In turn, the split between church and world is overcome

---

[9]   In this emphasis on the materiality of the sacraments, Stringfellow shares something with Conrad Noel in his attacks on the prissiness of much Anglo-Catholic religion. Thus Noel writes: "The Mass...is the manifestation of an all-pervading God in a common act and through material things, rather than the bringing down of an absent God into alien matter, so that as the drama of the eucharist unfolds itself, Christ is more and more manifest among us. This, then, is the 'Magic of the Mass'" (Noel, 1939:218).

as the sacramental expression of life as a continual offering to God and world spreads out equally from the one into the other, each authorizing and authenticating the other (Stringfellow, 1964b:126). "The Christian goes about – whatever he be, which may be anywhere, whomever he is with, which may be anyone – edified and upheld by the sacramental community which is the Church in the congregation. ... He is confident that the Word of God has already gone before him" liberating "all men, all principalities, all things from bondage to death" (Stringfellow, 1964b:128). The sacraments of the church, according to Stringfellow, thus become the means whereby the congregation points beyond itself to God and the world: it is the same Word of God encountered in the sanctuary who is met in the faces of the poor in the world. As he writes in *A Private and Public Faith*, "to celebrate the Word of God in the sacramental worship of the congregation is an anticipation of the discernment of the same Word of God in the common life of the world". There is a reciprocity between church and world guaranteed by the sacraments: "To be in the presence of the Word of God while in the world authenticates the practice of sacramental life within the congregation. One confirms and is confirmed by the other" (Stringfellow, 1962:63).

From a similar point of view, Stringfellow is keen to engage in criticism of those forms of worship which fail in the double task of worshipping God and of service in the world. Speaking from his own sense of embarrassment when he accompanied a friend to a service where the Word of God had been parodied in what was little more than an alumni rite for a church anniversary, he observes that the main failing was that the service failed in the real task of preaching, which was "a kind of dialogue between the Word of God beheld in the Bible and the liturgy, on the one hand, and on the other the Word of God as it may be seen and heard within the common lives of the people of the congregation" (Stringfellow, 1962:42). Not surprisingly, Stringfellow is deeply critical of a church negligent of both the Word of God and the world, a church which becomes self-obsessed or which simply seeks to domesticate its Gospel. The liturgical life consequently becomes the means whereby the Christian is reminded both of the confession of faith, as well as the need to confess sin: the celebration of the congregation produces that situation where no secret can remain hidden and consequently confession becomes the beginning of worship (Stringfellow, 1962:56). Life is thus lived in the raw in the worship of the Christian who acknowledges his or her failings as the starting point for witness in the world.

Stringfellow and the Sacramental Socialist Tradition

For Stringfellow, then, life and liturgy are united in the life of Christian witness lived out sacramentally in a hostile world. The similarities with the earlier tradition are obvious. What is more, Stringfellow was as much an outsider as most of those of the earlier generation. Like Stringfellow, few of the sacramental socialists seemed to fit into the structures: a methodological hostility to hierarchy and ecclesiasticism could hardly be accommodated in a church established either by parliament, prestige or wealth. Figgis, for instance, sensed the need for mystery to prevent the absolutizing of what he called the Athenaeum Club gospel: Christ called us beyond the smugness of the present. Christianity, he claimed, did not exist for "respectable people living in the suburbs of London and of University towns. ... It was made for bad people...it is a mockery and a lie to give this bloodless professorial abstraction the place of the living, loving Saviour who rose from the dead and gives Himself in the Eucharist" (Figgis, 1913:29). For Figgis, and for Stringfellow after him (cf. Stringfellow, 1962:53), the professor's Christ was not the Christ worth knowing; instead they both sought that strange and subversive Christ who died on the Cross, who rose again and who lives in the poor, and who simply could not be contained by our systems.

Stringfellow was a thorn in the flesh – he was no polite suburban Anglo-Catholic revelling in liturgical reform; instead liturgy and life were contained together in a world-shaking message that challenged the church and forced it to pay attention to the world around it. And at the heart of his disturbing message was the very simple recognition that the worship of God was inevitably political as it exposed idolatry. And this political meaning of the liturgy was something that had been recognized by a whole collection of socialist thorns who punctured the flesh of the comfortable church. Thus for Conrad Noel (1869-1942), the radical vicar of Thaxted in Essex, "politics in the wider sense of social justice, are part and parcel of the Gospel of Christ, and to ignore them is to be false to His teaching." Indeed, he went on, "worship divorced from social righteousness is an abomination to God" (Noel, 1945:91).[10] Figgis, Frank Weston and Conrad Noel all provoked hostility for preaching an unsettling and disrupting Gospel, quite divorced as they saw it from the message proclaimed by the church compromised as it was by riches and establishment. And the problem seems equally present at the turn of the millennium. Luxury might have given way to managerialism, but still the church seems equally distant from the unsettling message exposed by the political power of the liturgy. But it is precisely that message that needs to be heard in every generation: for it is the message which will banish evil and point the world to worship and to witness to its creator in gratitude, humility and service. Furthermore, it is hard to know whether such a message will be heard in a church fixated on adapting itself and its Gospel to a world under the dominion of all manner of principalities and powers.

---

[10] On Noel see Chapman (Chapman, 2001b).

Chapter Eight

Kindred Minds, Prophetic Voices

Andrew Goddard

Introduction

Of the many influences upon William Stringfellow's thought, one of the most significant was his friendship with the French lay theologian Jacques Ellul. Stringfellow first became aware of Ellul's work through his involvement in the World Student Christian Federation and his ecumenical activities in Europe in the late 1940s and early 1950s. It was then that Ellul's classic text *The Presence of the Kingdom* was recommended to him and became a book which he "read and re-read with enthusiasm" (Stringfellow, 1970b:26).[1]

The two men first met each other during an ecumenical conference at Bièvres in the mid 1950s. In their short meeting the establishment of a lifelong friendship was sealed with a remarkable experience which revealed the close bond that already existed between them. Ellul had organized for a translator because he felt his spoken English was poor and Stringfellow found that "hearing French spoken was, at best, a pleasant hardship which left me enjoying the sounds but not comprehending very many words" (Stringfellow, 1970b:27). Fifteen years later, although Stringfellow was unable to recall the substance of their afternoon's discussion, the meeting itself was clear in his memory:

> I recall vividly that, after awhile, perhaps half an hour, it was recognized between us that we did not need a translator, though Ellul was speaking French and I English. There was, simply, this remarkable rapport – absolute unhindered and uncompromised communication. As he would begin to speak I would know what he was saying before the words were translated. He manifestly had the same intuitive insight whenever I started to talk...It was a most astonishing experience. (Stringfellow, 1970b:27)

As a result of this bond, Stringfellow began reading Ellul's books in the original French long before they were translated into English. His enthusiasm for Ellul's first published book (Ellul, 1946) led him to organise a national conference on

---

[1]   Ellul's *Presence of the Kingdom* originated as talks to the WCC Ecumenical Institute at Bossey in 1946. It appeared in French as *Présence au monde moderne: problèmes de la civilisation post-chrétienne* in 1948 and SCM published the first English edition in 1951. Stringfellow himself wrote the introduction to the 1967 edition which reappears in the most recent reprint of the book (Ellul, 1989).

theology and law in Chicago in 1957. Although Ellul did not attend this in person, it was inspired by his work and he contributed an important article to the proceedings.[2] Despite doubts about the book on the part of both publishers and academics, Stringfellow succeeded in securing an English translation in 1960 (Ellul, 1960).[3] He continued to correspond with Ellul and helped to persuade Eerdmans both to translate many of his books into English[4] and to publish the first major study of his work in 1970 (Holloway, 1970).[5]

Ellul and Stringfellow both recognized that they shared a common vision and task. Stringfellow acknowledged this publicly in a number of articles about Ellul:

> Our views are quite similar...in our respective books in the realm of theological ethics there appears a very strong topical parallelism...I attribute this correlation in our writing to the prompting of the Holy Spirit, though some may think it mere coincidence, since Ellul and I have never had prior consultations about what each has been thinking and publishing. (Stringfellow, 1977b)

This chapter highlights three of the central themes which unite Stringfellow and Ellul's work and make their contribution to contemporary Christian ethics so significant. Before doing so, however, it is helpful to set Ellul in context by offering an introductory biographical and bibliographical sketch which also highlights the number of significant parallels between his own life and Stringfellow's.[6]

Jacques Ellul: A Biographical and Bibliographical Sketch

> One reason that Ellul's thinking has been provocative...is that his theological insights are authenticated...by the intense involvement of the man in the very social crises that he seeks to address theologically...In Ellul one finds that ideas and acts are so integral one

---

[2] This was the first of numerous unsuccessful attempts by Stringfellow over two decades to attract Ellul to speak in the United States.

[3] Stringfellow's correspondence includes a stinging 1959 letter to the University of Chicago Press in response to their rejection of the manuscript (because it was too close to 'fundamentalism' and did not show any knowledge of the secular literature of law) (Stringfellow, 10 April 1959). He finally informed Ellul in April 1960 that, "The Doubleday edition of your book is scheduled to be published in September. I have shared the manuscript with Professor John Bennett, Dean of Union Theological Seminary here. He was scandalized by it. You should regard that as a very great compliment" (Stringfellow, 19 April 1960).

[4] On the cover of *The Meaning of the City* (Ellul, 1970a), which influenced his own *Ethic for Christians and Other Aliens in a Strange Land* (Stringfellow, 1973), Stringfellow writes, "Ellul's *The Meaning of the City* has startling significance...It should rank beside Reinhold Niebuhr's *Moral Man & Immoral Society* as a work of truly momentous potential..." (Ellul, 1970a).

[5] This study includes a short piece by Stringfellow (Stringfellow, 1970a).

[6] A fuller account can be found in Goddard (1996) and Goddard (2002).

to the other that his decisions and actions in actual life are an incarnation of what he thinks and writes. His witness as a Christian has been nurtured in danger and turbulence. (Stringfellow, 1989:xvi).

Jacques Ellul was born in 1912 in Bordeaux, the city which, despite the pull of Paris for most leading French academics, was to be home for most of his life. An only child, many of his school years were marked by poverty as his father was frequently unemployed. On leaving school he studied law at Bordeaux University, completing a doctorate in an aspect of Roman law in 1936.[7] It was during these university years in the 1930s that three major events occurred which were to shape his life.

Ellul's home had had little religious education because, although his mother was a Christian, his father was a Voltarian sceptic. However, around the time of entering university he had a powerful conversion experience through reading the Bible and subsequently joined the French Reformed Church. There, not least through his friendship with Jean Bosc, he was heavily influenced by the renewed interest in Kierkegaard's thought and the work of Barth.

In his second year at university he also discovered the writing of Karl Marx whose methods of social and economic analysis were to continue to be so important in his later work. It was nothing short of a revelatory experience for the young Ellul whose family were suffering from the Depression:

All at once I felt as if I had discovered something totally unexpected and totally stupefying, precisely because it related directly to my practical experience...I felt that at last I knew why my father was out of work, at last I knew why we were destitute...Marx was an astonishing discovery of the reality of the world. (Ellul, 1981:4)

Although his initiation into Marx's thought led Ellul into his life-long struggle for revolutionary social and political change, this did not take the form of joining a left-wing political party. Instead, along with his fellow student and life-long friend Bernard Charbonneau, he became involved in a branch of the French personalist movement. There he began to develop his radical critique of both the developments within modern society and the main political movements (fascism, communism, and capitalist liberal democracy) on offer to the public.

Ellul's first major confrontation with the establishment came in 1940 when, following a public attack on the collaborationist Vichy regime, he was sacked from his teaching post and then had to flee Bordeaux. He spent the rest of the war farming in a small hamlet from where he participated in the Resistance until, at the end of the war, he was invited to serve as Bordeaux's Deputy Mayor on the liberation city council.[8] His term of office was short and the frustrations he

---

[7]   Like Stringfellow, Ellul, despite his expertise in law, was often uneasy about being classed as 'a lawyer' and, although he was Professor in a Law Faculty, his legal writings are only a small (and much neglected) proportion of his literary output.

[8]   Stringfellow held a post with a similar level of political responsibility, as Second Warden or Vice-Mayor of Block Island from 1976.

discovered in attempting to secure radical change through holding political office determined much of his later critical analysis of the political and bureaucratic world. He returned to a full-time academic post as Professor of the History and Sociology of Institutions in Bordeaux University's Law Faculty and Professor in the Institute of Political Studies, positions he held until his retirement in 1980.

Throughout his life, Ellul was active in church and society. Like Stringfellow, he was an early participant in the ecumenical movement, contributing to the first WCC Conference in Amsterdam in 1948. He also played a leading and often controversial role in the French Reformed Church. Among his achievements were reforms to the church's system of theological education where Ellul sought to encourage lay people to engage in theological study. For a number of years he also pastored a largely working-class congregation in his home town of Pessac.

Convinced, like Stringfellow, of the need to act locally while thinking globally, Pessac also provided the context for Ellul's long-standing involvement with work among young delinquents. He was one of the pioneers of this movement in the 1950s and eventually headed up a National Committee for Unity between Clubs and Teams of Prevention until retiring from the work in 1977. It was also local circumstances which re-kindled his environmentalist beliefs and led him, along with Charbonneau, to organize and co-ordinate (from 1968 onwards) protest groups in the Aquitaine region which opposed government 'development' plans.[9]

In the midst of all this activity, Ellul was also a prolific writer. By the time of his death in 1994 he had published 50 volumes (30 of them are available in English translation) and over 1,000 articles.[10] The majority of his books form part of a massive project of research and writing which he mapped out for himself while in exile from Bordeaux during the war. They self-consciously take the form of two strands of writing which are in dialogue with each other: historical/sociological and theological/ethical.

The historical/sociological series of Ellul's works aims to enable readers to understand and question the world in which they live so that they can then act to change it. These books have little or no explicit Christian content and their analysis derives from ideas first developed in unpublished writings for the personalist groups of the 1930s. At their heart is the conviction that the twentieth-century world is undergoing a crisis of civilization as a result of the dominance of Technique which now shapes our whole society including its politics, communication, law, art, and religion.[11]

---

[9]   Similar concerns about planning regulations and development played an important role in Stringfellow's activities in Block Island in the 1970s.

[10]   Joyce Hanks has, through the journal *Research in Philosophy and Technology*, produced three extensive and invaluable bibliographies (in 1984, 1991, 1995) of Ellul's work and secondary material relating to Ellul and a full bibliography of primary texts is now available (Hanks, 2000).

[11]   The most important work is obviously Ellul's seminal *The Technological Society* (Ellul, 1964). Other important English titles in this strand of his work include Ellul (1965, 1967a, 1971a, 1975, 1978, 1980, 1990b).

It is, of course, Ellul's theological and ethical works which show the closest relationship to Stringfellow's writing. Ellul, like Stringfellow, wrote extensively as a lay Christian with the aim of helping his fellow Christians hear and live out God's word within the world which his sociological studies analysed. These works can be classed into three broad categories. A number of volumes focus on either a particular area of life in the world or a central aspect of Christian life and discipleship (see Ellul, 1969b, 1970a, 1970b, 1973, 1983, 1985, 1991).

There are also important studies of individual biblical books in which the living Word addresses us in our contemporary context (see Ellul, 1971b, 1972b, 1977, 1990a). Finally, there are the books which develop Ellul's ethic for Christians.[12]

Although only a brief sketch has been offered here of Ellul's life, the truth of the opening quotation from Stringfellow should be evident: Ellul, like Stringfellow himself, was a revolutionary dissenter in both church and society, a true 'protestant' who wrote out of what he lived and lived out what he wrote.

Ellul and Stringfellow: Their Common Contributions to Contemporary Christian Ethics

Central to both Stringfellow and Ellul are three features which constitute their major common contributions to the task of contemporary Christian ethics. These are their devotion and fidelity to Scripture, their critical and realistic analysis of their own social and political worlds through using the biblical witness to principalities and powers, and their commitment to a revolutionary Christian lifestyle within the world. Each of these hallmarks of their work needs to be examined in turn.

The Centrality of Scripture

In his appreciative articles about Ellul, Stringfellow regularly refers to his Scriptural faithfulness as crucial to his work. He sees Ellul's thinking as provocative because "his theological insights are authenticated by diligence in biblical study" (Stringfellow, 1989:xvi) and he writes of Ellul's "exemplary use of the Bible" (Stringfellow, 1977b).

In attempting to interpret the remarkable experience they had on their first encounter, Stringfellow acknowledges different ways in which the gift of transcending the language barrier could be described but, although he does not deny these, his own conclusion is more "definite and concrete":

---

[12]　The first of these is the work mentioned above, *The Presence of the Kingdom* (1989, originally 1951) whose subject matter is addressed again in Ellul (1972a). The introduction to Ellul's ethics is *To Will and To Do* (1969a) and the major volume, whose title demonstrates the links with Stringfellow's theology discussed in earlier papers is Ellul (1976).

Such an experience originates in that which the participants have shared in common before they ever met. The pre-experience in which Ellul and I had already partaken was and is the Bible. (Stringfellow, 1970b:28)

That this should be the primary appeal of Ellul to Stringfellow is not surprising. His own commitment to Scripture is clear in his writing and was central to his life and character. Those who knew him well found it infectious. They bear witness to the fact that "the constant of Stringfellow's identity and language was its biblical character" (Wylie-Kellermann, 1994:9) and that "Bill loved the Bible and was one of its most diligent students" (Wallis, 1995:89). Shortly before his death his self-description to a reporter was, "I've been trying to live as a biblical person and understand the nation and the world in a biblical way" (Wallis, 1995:89).

This devotion to Scripture which marked both men was certainly not, however, a simple, conservative, proof-texting fundamentalism. In terms of theological groupings, Ellul and Stringfellow could be seen as having much in common (but never being fully in tune) with two significant strands of recent thinking. They share many of the concerns of those 'neo-evangelicals' who combine an affection for Barth with a desire for radical social and political Christian witness while being unhappy with some of the narrow dogmatism and shibboleths of traditional evangelicalism. They are also in many ways pre-cursors of the more recent post-liberal school with its strong commitment to the text of Scripture but emphatic distancing of itself from both traditional liberal modernist scepticism and conservative concerns to defend Scripture's historicity and to develop elaborate systems of doctrine which then can distort Scripture itself.[13] What undoubtedly lies at the heart of both Ellul and Stringfellow's life and thought is the shared conviction that Scripture must be central to Christian discipleship and hence any ethic for Christians.

More precisely, it was the living Word of God which was determinative for Ellul and Stringfellow. As with Barth, this Word is mediated to us today through the Bible and its witness to Jesus Christ, the incarnate Word of God, but it is not reducible to the Bible. The Bible is therefore not to be read in the way any other text might be read. It does not have to be dissected and subjected to techniques of historical, critical analysis or elaborate hermeneutical tools in order to yield its meaning to us.

Indeed, that approach is ultimately useless for Christian faith

It is indeed permissible to treat the biblical text like any other document, but we are sure in this way never to grasp *anything*. I do not say to grasp a little something that would be the basis of a possibility for faith. I say *nothing*...From the viewpoint of faith, what can be grasped by means of a lay hermeneutic is nothing since it is not the central object, the

---

[13]   Perhaps the best exponent of this approach in biblical studies is Walter Brueggemann. It should be noted, however, that in contrast to Brueggemann, Ellul has much more sympathy for 'canonical readings' (as in Childs' work) and always reads the Old Testament as a witness to Christ. Others in this school are Hauerwas (ethics) and Lindbeck (doctrine).

goal, the real content, the hidden sense, the life-giving spark of the text. (Dawn and Ellul, 1997:198)[14]

Scripture must, instead, be read as a whole and from within a faith-commitment to Jesus Christ. It must, above all, be *listened* to in order that through its words we may hear God's Word. This Word reveals to us the reality of ourselves and our world and also God's redemptive work in and for the world. It also is a Word which, more than giving us answers, puts us and our world into question and demands from us a response. At the heart of such true listening is therefore response in faithful obedience so that the Word of God becomes living and active in us, for us and through us as we both listen to Scripture and incarnate the Word in our common everyday life in the world (Wylie-Kellermann, 1994:167-83).

It is this confessional relationship with the Word of God heard in the Bible which is determinative for the other two key characteristics of their Christian ethics. Because, like the early Barth, they have discovered and fallen in love with that strange, new world which is in the Bible, the world of God (Barth, 1928), Ellul and Stringfellow now look at the world in which they live through different eyes.

Rather than following Bultmann so that our modern world judges and demythologizes the world of Scripture, Ellul and Stringfellow reverse that process and let the world of Scripture judge and demythologize our modern world. Their view of Scripture also leads to their conviction that at the heart of Christian discipleship is faithfulness to the Word of God and they both, in turn, firmly believe that Scripture reveals that such a pattern of life will result in a radical non-conformity to the ways of the fallen world in which we live.

A Realistic Approach to the World and the Powers

In Ellul's writings, one of the most important consequences of life in Christ and commitment to the Word of God is that Christians are enabled to face the world as it really is:

> Christianity teaches us first that we ought to see things as they really are...Christianity pushes us to discover what is – in me, in my neighbour, in the world. Without deforming it and without judging it, because that which is corresponds exactly to what God reveals to us about our human situation and about God's action regarding it in the world...Concrete reality must not frighten us; we must not veil it... (Dawn and Ellul, 1997:72-3)

Ellul's resoluteness in applying this led him to be regularly accused of implacable and unwarrantable pessimism (Dawn and Ellul, 1997:94-109). In fact, the heart of his Christian realism is summed up in Stringfellow's glad acknowledgment that Ellul troubled Americans because "he does not flinch from naming Satan as the apparent ruler of this world" (Stringfellow, 1989:xvii). Here, in this reference to 'Satan', also lies one of the most important insights shared by Stringfellow and

---

[14]   This is the first English translation of Ellul's important 1968 article on hermeneutics which is fully discussed in Ray (1979).

Ellul: the importance of the biblical witness to the existence and work of the principalities and powers in the fallen world for any understanding of our contemporary world.

For Ellul, the key to the world's current situation is the biblical story of the Fall or, as he preferred to refer to it, *la rupture*. This reveals to us that our world has ruptured the communion with God for which it was made and that man is now set about creating his own world (symbolized for Ellul by the city). As a result, this world in its totality is marked by the polar opposites of the features which God desires. Instead of enjoying diversity and otherness, there is a quest for unity and closure. Instead of self-giving agape love, there is Eros which is the will to power. Instead of freedom, there is necessity and bondage. Instead of life, there is death.[15] These four characteristics are found in human beings and all their works (by which Ellul does not mean simply individual sinful works but all our concrete, cultural and political works). They are, however, most dangerously present in the fallen world whenever the principalities and powers are active.

Ellul is at his weakest in his brief attempts to describe the origin and ontology of the powers. Here again he seeks a middle path between traditional evangelical/fundamentalist views and those of mainstream liberalism (Ellul, 1976:151-2) but his own settled view is neither clear nor consistent. In his earlier writings he tends to see the powers as having an existence of their own (although not in the traditional sense of 'demons'). However, as his work progresses, they are increasingly viewed as human dispositions which 'exist' by human determination. Here it is supremely man's quest for self-justification through his works which instantiates the powers. They 'exist' because man invests his limited works with love, faith and devotion and so the works cease to be relative and, through becoming ultimate and sacred, become the locus of the powers and the source of our slavery, alienation and destruction.

Ellul is at his strongest in discerning the concrete contemporary forms of the powers and demonstrating (as did Stringfellow) the stranglehold they have over the modern world by his focused and detailed sociological and theological analysis of such phenomena as Technique, the State, Mammon and the City.

Although both Ellul and Stringfellow undoubtedly at times presented too one-sided and negative an account of the powers and the present state of the world, they have one great strength often lacking in contemporary Christian ethics. This realistic perspective and conception of the powers enabled them to detach themselves from the commonplace perspectives of their own societies and cultures and instead to view them in a critical and discerning manner. And, because these acts of discernment were ultimately derived from listening to God's voice in Scripture, they found that they were often applicable in both the French and

---

[15] 'Death' is not as central within Ellul's theology and ethic as in Stringfellow's but it is, nevertheless, an important feature of the fallen world. He firmly believed (in his powerful and prophetic words which grace the cover of the new edition of *The Presence of the Kingdom*) that, "if we let ourselves drift along the stream of history, without knowing it, we shall have chosen the power of suicide, which is at the heart of the world..." (Ellul, 1989).

American contexts. So, in July 1970, Stringfellow wrote to Ellul concerning *The Meaning of the City*:

> I marvel that something so cogent for the American crisis can be written by one not an American until I remember that you are writing just as a biblical person, not particularly as a Frenchman, and the issue of relevance has nothing much to do with nationality, but rather has to do with our humanity in Christ. (Stringfellow, 30 July 1970)

If at times they failed to acknowledge the relative advantages of living in a liberal democratic society (as opposed to, say, a communist or Nazi dictatorship) at least they did not fail to recognize the real powers of death and evil at work in their own nations. In contrast to many Western Christians they did not see the enemy at work only in their personal private struggles against temptation or in the public actions of foreign nations and alternative political systems. They knew and sought to persuade others that, despite the relative freedom and comfortable lifestyle enjoyed by most American and French Christians, their own societies remained part of the fallen world in rebellion against God. As a result, they could both see that, in reality, "the situation here is now both very grave and very dangerous for anyone who cares about human life in society" (Stringfellow, 30 July 1970).

A Revolutionary Christian Lifestyle in the World

In the book which first introduced Stringfellow to Ellul's work, the second chapter is entitled "Revolutionary Christianity". Such a concept is not strange today but Ellul's insistence on its significance in the immediate post-war period has led to him being classed as "the original liberation theologian" (Hanks, 1985). His conception of the character of a true Christian lifestyle was clear:

> The situation of the Christian in the world is a revolutionary situation. His or her share in the preservation of the world is to be an inexhaustible revolutionary force in the midst of the world. (Ellul, 1989:31)

This clearly marks a radical break with a conformist, establishment "Christendom" conception of the Christian's situation in the world. It is a stance which Stringfellow (who once described himself as "theologically...a closet Anabaptist" (Wylie-Kellermann, 1994:158)) fully embraced. For him, one of the major challenges facing the contemporary church was that, despite the obvious disintegration of the church's traditional powerful stance in Western society, too many Christians were still devoted to what he referred to as the "Constantinian Accommodation".[16] The importance of this theme is evident from the fact that (along with the principalities and powers) it was the subject he chose for his famous exchange with Karl Barth in which he observed that "the churches do not

---

[16]   Stringfellow defined this as the church's situation in Western Christendom whereby "the church, refuting apostolic precedent, acquired a radical, vested interest in the established order and became culpably identified with the institutional status quo in culture and society..." (Wylie-Kellermann, 1994:149).

commonly exercise a vitally critical attitude towards politics, public policy, or the nation's actual life and culture" (Wylie-Kellermann, 1994:188).

This view of the Christian's calling to be a critical and revolutionary voice within the world clearly has much to support it in Scripture's witness to the works of God and the general ethos of the teaching of both the Old Testament prophets and Jesus himself. By making it central to their work, both Ellul and Stringfellow produced an exhortative, prophetic style of ethical writing. Instead of detailed exegesis of specific Scriptural commands, careful casuistic counsel, or elaborate engagement with moral philosophy and debate over the definition of ethical concepts, their ethical writing is more in the form of an impassioned call to develop a critical Christian conscience which will discern, protest against, and seek to resist the powers of the fallen world.

The major difficulty with such an emphasis is, that by focusing so much on the *character* of the Christian calling as one which, *vis-à-vis* the world, is revolutionary and critical, the *content* of the ethic can become problematic. Paradoxically, by stressing that the Christian has to be an "inexhaustible revolutionary force" (Ellul), exercising "a vitally critical attitude" (Stringfellow) to the world, this form of ethic easily has its whole agenda set by the world and can even find its specific content shaped by a reaction to the world rather than by God's Word.

To be fair to them, both Stringfellow and Ellul were well aware of these dangers. Indeed, their desire to resist replacing the voice of God in Scripture with the voice of other revolutionary and critical forces in the world often led them into trouble with their natural supporters both inside and outside the church.

For Stringfellow, this is perhaps most evident in his experience in Harlem parish in 1956-7. Here he joined those Christians who were at the forefront of combating the then largely ignored evils of racism and poverty in American society. And yet, within a year he had left them with a stinging attack upon their methods which, though revolutionary and critical compared to the dominant ideology of the time, made (Stringfellow believed) the same mistake as the church had always made in relation to the world:

> The church is much tempted by conformity to the world, by accommodating the message and mission to the particular society in which the church happens to be, in the slums and in the suburbs...This temptation beguiled the group ministry of the East Harlem Protestant Parish. They plunged into all sorts of social work and social action – narcotics, politics, neighborhood improvement, education, housing, and the rest...But they neglected and postponed the proclamation and celebration of the gospel in East Harlem. In the congregation of the parish, the Bible was closed; in the group ministry there was even scorn for the Bible as a means through which the Word of God is communicated in contemporary society. (Wylie-Kellermann, 1994:133)

Similarly, Ellul, in his desire to avoid being captured by the world's agendas, not only developed his own original analysis and critique of contemporary Western society, he also focused much of his attention on critiquing those who, in many ways, appeared to be his natural allies in seeking revolutionary change. His numerous assaults on Christian Marxists and liberation theologians (Ellul, 1988), and his polemical attacks upon many of the "revolutionary" political stances taken by his own French Reformed Church and the World Council of Churches,[17] alienated many from his work, not least because he failed to mount similar thorough critiques against reactionary Christian movements which defended the status quo.

In developing their vision of a radical Christian pattern of discipleship, Ellul and Stringfellow were (as the previous sections have shown) aware of the need to listen to both the Word and the world. They were, however, also both determined not to let themselves become captive to revolutionary powers in the way that the church historically fell prey to establishment powers. They therefore emphasized the need to let the Word of God in Scripture be the driving and shaping force of their lives and their ethic; and both knew that it was a serious error to assume that all those who opposed dominant ideologies and powerful institutions were to be welcomed as agents of God's Word in history. Nevertheless, despite their awareness of this potential trap, the polemical and highly political nature of their writing means that the moves they made from Scripture to contemporary Christian ethics were at times opaque. As a result, those Christians who disagree with their specific conclusions (even if they agree with the general tenor of their ethic) will often find them difficult dialogue partners in constructive ethical debate on specific subjects.[18]

Conclusion: Beyond Ellul and Stringfellow

This chapter has brought together the lives and works of Jacques Ellul and William Stringfellow. It has traced the personal links between them, drawn attention to some of the similarities in their biographies, and highlighted three common features of their ethic for Christians.

Although both Ellul and Stringfellow were viewed by many as prophetic figures, neither would have appreciated the formation of a school of prophets who simply repeated their own words of exhortation or judgement. While much of their analysis and critique remains of value today, much more also needs to be said and done if the church is to have an ethic which is both truly contemporary and truly Christian. In seeking to develop such an ethic, it is vital that their contribution is built upon rather than being ignored or forgotten. Their approach to the task of contemporary Christian ethics has left many important questions to struggle with:

---

[17]   Ellul (1972a) is in large part a protest against those radical Christians who have distorted his concept of 'revolutionary Christianity' expounded in Ellul (1989).

[18]   As has already been noted, Ellul and Stringfellow almost always saw to eye-to-eye and so this problem rarely arises in comparing their writing. Nevertheless, in the area of sexuality an interesting divergence appears with Ellul taking a much more conservative, almost biblicist line. It would be interesting to consider how on this important subject the two usually like-minded lay theologians would interact with each other and to judge which is being most faithful to their shared convictions discussed here.

How are we faithfully to listen to God speaking in and through Scripture without simply slipping into naive biblicism? How are we to understand and identify the reality of the principalities and powers at work in our world? How are we to determine the concrete implications of the call to live a revolutionary Christian lifestyle in this world?

Finding and agreeing upon answers to such questions will be no easy task. The difficulties of such an enterprise should not, however, weaken the resolve to undertake it. As Western civilization enters a new post-modern, increasingly post-Christian millennium, Ellul and Stringfellow together provide important guides to the way forward for Christian ethics: a constant and careful listening to God's Word in Scripture alongside a critical examination of our contemporary world in order to discern and live out the Christian's revolutionary calling to be salt and light, aliens and strangers, in the world, here and now, where God has placed us.

Chapter Nine

Speaking Nonsense to Power:
The Mission of William Stringfellow

Simon Barrow[1]

Introduction

William Stringfellow has provided waymarks on many a pilgrim journey towards
the outer edges of church and the conflict-ridden margins of society. I first came
across him in the pages of *Sojourners* magazine in the mid-1980s, applying his
sharp political analysis and angular biblical reading to the disturbing realities of the
Reagan-Thatcher years. At that time I was wrestling with the tension between deep
immersion in the secular world of social action and the call to Christian
authenticity. I found Stringfellow the ideal companion in this struggle to discover a
creative, authentic synergy between faith and ferment.

Later, of course, the questions came. Was his overall perspective not too fideist
in its emphasis on the Word overcoming the world? Was the apocalypticism of his
social critique not overstated? Was there any functional meeting point between
Stringfellow's biblical-prophetic stance and the world of practical politics? Could
any church live up to his vision of its call to be 'a holy nation' in a largely apostate
age? How is the intense theological realism of his appropriation of St Paul's
language about principalities and powers really sustainable in a materialist climate?

I still think that these are valid questions. Indeed I own them more strongly now
than I did when I first came across Stringfellow's writings. But I have also learned
more: about theology as an imaginative, provocative, untidy 'refiguring of the
world' (not just as an exercise in creating convenient coherence); about faith as a
call to ultimately risky living and thinking;[2] and about William Stringfellow as a
passionate, difficult, committed human being whose whole *raison d'etre* was to
speak uncommon sense – non-sense in their limited terms – to the powers that be.
Unless all that is appreciated, with whatever qualifications of hindsight,
Stringfellow will remain little more than a stranger at the gates making rude, rather
discordant noises against our complacency.

So in this chapter what I want to do is temporarily to suspend disbelief and to
offer not 'a critique' but 'a response' – a positive, critically engaged reaction to his

---

[1]   I am grateful to Dr Nick Adams of New College, Edinburgh, for his comments on
this essay.
[2]   As Fuller puts it, to "dare to be naïve" (Fuller, 1975).

continuing provocations. This response will be conditioned by three interlocking concerns: how we might act responsibly in face of the multiple lesions of the world, the particular vocation of Christian mission, and the overall scope of the ecumenical vision. As we proceed I will refer to some of the wider challenges I have outlined in the light of my reading of what Stringfellow has to offer. As he once observed: "By all means, if you will, raise these questions, but, first, *listen to the Word*" (Stringfellow, 1967:17).

Word and World Turned Upside-Down

To comb through a set of essays and articles by William Stringfellow (Wylie-Kellermann, 1994) is to immerse yourself in a world and a Word turned upside down (cf. Acts 17.6). Whereas the whole twentieth-century Christian theological project has been conditioned by multiple arguments about how biblical texts can fit in to our way of seeing things (whether that way is one circumscribed by autonomous secular reason or by pluralistic religious expressivism), Stringfellow's point of departure is to transform existing procedures and to invite us to re-encounter the world narrated biblically. As he said in his Preface to *An Ethic for Christians and Other Strangers in a Strange Land* (Stringfellow, 1973), and has been pointed out elsewhere in this book, his purpose was to construe America biblically, not to construe the Bible Americanly.

In broader perspective this means seeing ourselves afresh as part of a world nexus emerging from the freedom of God, as a humanity stumbling (sometimes crashing) into the redeeming love of God in the midst of the world's glorious messiness, and as people ultimately destined for the transformed fullness of life in God. All this, of course, is mediated by life-changing stories about of the words, actions, death and risen life of Jesus Christ, in whom the promise of a new community beyond want and oppression is enfleshed and anticipatorily realized.

These events in turn produce a body of people sufficiently lacking in wisdom and prudence to put their trust in such unlikely events, and who then proceed to challenge the principalities and powers of earthly dominion in the name of a Lord who disavowed the might usually associated with such title. All this is recorded for us in a set of ancient minutes which are, shall we say, still in dispute – since the actual direction of the church was much more in line with national interests (the Constantinian turn) and sometimes indistinguishable from the will of the powerful whom the Magnificat eschatologically describes as tumbling from their thrones.

This account of the world, focused on the contested events surrounding an obscure Mediterranean peasant in the backwater of an ancient empire, is at first entirely baffling from the perspective of the same world described by early twenty-first century techno-science. But such shock is, Stringfellow would claim, the only way the world can regain its soul. I am sure he is right. Even so, I have just summarized the Christian narrative in soothing interpretative cadences which are still far removed from the forceful, unapologetic approach of Stringfellow himself, who once wrote:

> If one cares to discern the Word of God in the Bible, then one must listen to the Bible in the Bible's own context and not deal with the Bible in a random, perfunctory, smattering fashion. Some will think this a naive approach to the Word of God in the Bible. I suppose it is just that. It is one that simply affirms that the Word of God has content, integrity, and life that belongs to God and that this can be received and comprehended by ordinary human beings (Stringfellow, 1967:17-18).

Unbounded hermeneutical confidence of this kind has been substantially lost in the two decades after Stringfellow's death. But you do not have to be indifferent to the pitfalls of reading a single over-arching narrative out of a very diverse set of biblical texts in order to remain fully alive to the inspiring trajectory of this world-transforming counter-story, and to its instantiation in endless lively encounters between what appear to us to be the fragments of daily life and the fragments of the Word in the world. Such encounters are the principal fabric of Stringfellow's approach, a continual, creative, difficult confrontation between worldly realism and eschatological realism which is far more nuanced in detail than its detractors read from the headlines.

And where he has dared to tread, others, notably John Howard Yoder (1972) Walter Brueggemann (1993), Ched Myers (1989) and Walter Wink (1998), have followed – mitigating some of the over-ambition of 'biblical theology', and showing how the Gospel as encountered, lived and spoken by a late twentieth-century activist-theologian like Stringfellow can be re-appropriated again and again for our continually changing times.

This is as it should be, because in spite of his avowedly confessional concern for the Bible, Stringfellow's approach to the text was not naively literalistic (Ochs, 1999). It was antithetical to the ideological concerns of Christian fundamentalism and could actually be surprisingly eclectic (Stringfellow, 1964c:92-94, 1967:13-20). Moreover, he saw 'biblical witness' as an ongoing process, founded by, but not restricted to, the texts themselves. In all this he was much more 'modern' than he sometimes appears in his rhetoric.

Talking Un-Common Sense

None of the foregoing should be allowed to mitigate the basic offence to 'common sense' of Stringfellow's message, of course. According to a friend who heard him, he once spoke of *glossolalia* in the New Testament as "strange speech and utterance in resistance to the Beast". My shorthand for this is 'speaking nonsense to power'. In a way all his advocacy and writing was like that. The forces of death in the economic, social, cultural, political and religious worlds are so constituted, he said, to render incomprehensible the message of life and hope to all in their thrall. And yet the whole point of the Christian Gospel is that the Word has already broken into human history and has communicated with the lowly and the unwise. Thus his distinctly protestant conviction that the biblical narrative can and will cut through to ordinary human beings in ways that its scholarly and ecclesiastical guardians cannot fully fathom.

Stringfellow believed fiercely (and tenderly) that the redemptive self-giving embodied in Jesus Christ, not violence, might and manipulation, is the most powerful force in the universe. This conviction shines through his counter-intuitive approach to almost every subject. But he was the first to see what non-sense it is given the present constitution of the world and the naturally comforting instincts of traditional religion. In *Conscience and Obedience* he wrote:

> A most obstinate misconception associated with the gospel of Jesus Christ is that the gospel is welcome in this world. The conviction – endemic among churchfolk – persists that, if problems of misapprehension and misrepresentation are overcome and the gospel can be heard in its own integrity, the gospel will be found attractive to people, become popular, and, even, be a success of some sort. This idea is both curious and ironical because it is bluntly contradicted in Scripture and in the experience of the continuing biblical witness in history from the event of Pentecost unto the present moment. (Stringfellow, 1977a:109-12)

In a *Homily on the Defeat of the Saints*, Stringfellow goes on to describe the way in which "Christians are authorized to recall political authority to the vocation of worship" (by which is understood the right value or worth-ship of all things in relation to God) and to "reclaim dominion over creation for humanity". This calling, inevitably, produces conflict. But even here the approach of the Christian must confound expectations: "To bless the powers that be, in the midst of persecution, exposes and confounds their blasphemous status more cogently and fearlessly than a curse" (Wylie-Kellermann, 1994:349). Paul's injunction (Romans 12.14) and Jesus' practice of enemy-loving are rendered politically operative in an unsentimental but only *un*commonly sensible way. This is an ethic for an eschatological people who share none of the conventional assumptions about success, power, popularity, progress or effectiveness – and few if any of the privileges and investments these assumptions confer.

If Christ the Fool presides at the Feast of the Kingdom, as Stringfellow suggested through his love of circuses, then the company of Jesus will be equally ridiculous – and death-defying. So it is no surprise that this East Harlem lawyer consorted with the fractious, the disturbingly single-minded and the disobedient – an uncomfortable *ekklesia* of persons, church-going or not, whose whole business consisted in publicly not bowing the knee to the gods of the age. The Berrigan brothers, who he met in the mid-1960s, are among the best known of these consorts.

Christ as the Meaning of the World

But who is this Christ who keeps such odd company, calls us to peculiarity, and justifies blatantly strange behaviour and speech? He is none other than the One who reveals to us the true nature of the world, says Stringfellow:

> The meaning of Jesus Christ is God's concern for and presence in this world. The Christian faith is not about some god who is an abstract presence somewhere else, but

about the living presence of God here and now, in this world, in exactly this world, as people know it, and see it, and touch it, and smell it, and live and work in it. That is why, incidentally, all the well meant talk of 'making the gospel relevant' to the life of the world is obscene: it secretly assumes that God is a stranger among us, who has to be introduced to us and to our anxieties and triumph and issues and efforts. The meaning of Jesus Christ is that the Word of God is addressed to people, to all people, in the very events and relationships, any and every one of them which constitute our existence in this world. That is the theology of the incarnation. (Stringfellow, 1961:585)

What we have here is a particularity that issues in universality, a local that brings a global hope into a specific horizon without absorbing or dominating it:

Jesus Christ is the assurance that all of life, the life of every human and of the rest of creation, originates in and ends in the life of God. Your life, or mine, or that of anybody, issues from the word of God. This is and remains the essential truth about you or me or anybody, no matter whatever else may seem to be true. (Stringfellow, 1963a:7)

This viewpoint is at once characteristically Christian and also affirming of human diversity – another Stringfellow distinctive in an age where the fruitless intra-theological battle over the 'uniqueness' or 'finality' of Jesus Christ continues to confuse the particularity of obedience in the now with the kind of ambition about universal systems that is actually contrary to a truly eschatological reading. By contrast, for Stringfellow God is decisively Christ like, but this in no way predisposes him to judge others too readily, to hijack Christ for one community only (even the one that names him), or to fall prey to the idea that the Word issues in a closed system. Like Stanley Hauerwas he sees Christians as 'resident aliens', but his ethic is more open to the 'others' too (Stringfellow, 1973), and his best practice of discipleship consists of strangers making friends rather than enemies.

God's Freedom and Ours

What is at stake in all this is the relationship between the freedom of God and the freedom of human beings. This was Barth's theme, of course, and while Stringfellow enjoyed a natural affinity with the great Swiss theologian's thought, his own provocations are too untidy and episodic to fall prey to that "positivism of revelation" which Bonhoeffer deduced would result from Barth being turned into too much of a Barthian (DeGruchy, 2000). There is, indeed, something very akin to Bonhoeffer's unswerving commitment to the freedom of the world as realizable within the freedom of God in Stringfellow's assertion that:

Christians must live in the world – and not for their own sake, and not for the sake of the Church, much less for the sake of any of the churches, not even for God's sake, but for the sake of the world. That is to say, the Christian must live in this world, where Christ lives: the Christian must live in this world *in* Christ (Stringfellow, 1962:74).

Stringfellow's concern for the personal and individual Christian and their creatureliness was also political and cosmic in scope. Against those who have read into his work a mere political reductionism, this points to the deep spirituality which infuses his writing – born of much pain and personal turmoil. As Edwin Robertson once spoke of Bishop Bell, "nothing human was alien to him". This resulted not in a rejection of ethics but in a refiguring of the ethical challenge to live humanly in the face of inhuman forces, above all through a realization of the transforming grace and judgement of God which goes far deeper than even our (his) most confident moral pronouncements. Just as Jesus contended with the religious authorities in his day who wished to usurp to themselves the power to bless and curse, so Stringfellow refused to judge his enemies, even as he opposed them. Here too the freedom of God transforms but does not absorb or obliterate human freedom.

Advocacy as Mission

Stringfellow's approach to mission is also radical. In *Conscience and Obedience* he argues that "in this age the church of Christ is called as the advocate of every victim of the rulers of the age, and that, not because the victim is right, for the church does not know how any are judged in the Word of God, but because the victim is a victim" (Stringfellow, 1977a:94). It is vital to understand that what he is saying here is not that 'victimhood' is blessed, that oppression should be internalized in self-sacrifice, or that those who are victims should be sympathized with, but that the Christian vocation is to struggle with victims against the whole culture and institution of victimization – in politics, economy, religion, culture and society. The logic of this, of course, is that we should cease to be victims, objects, and act as free citizens, subjects, of a new zone of being – what Peter Selby calls "the commonwealth of God" (Selby, 1997) and Walter Wink "God's domination-free order" (Wink, 1998).

This mission of God is furthered, says Stringfellow, not by elaborate strategies that parallel the tactics of those who currently lord it in this world, but by a faithful and responsible willingness to stand with Christ the Victim in actual places of victimization, and to name his victimhood as the one which truly exposes the bankruptcy of principalities and powers in contrast to the true *unlordly* lordship of God's Christ. In this sense, advocacy becomes evangelistic and evangelism demands advocacy, because good news exposes the real character of bad news and vice versa. The world is named (but not conquered) in the Name of the Coming One, the one whose time is promised in and beyond the contingency of the world (Stringfellow, 1963a, Hoedemaker, 1998). Moreover the delimiting territoriality of the world is reclaimed as the spacious territoriality of the kingdom of God.

> This advocacy, in its ecumenical scope as well as its actual specificity, constitutes the church's political task, but simultaneously, exemplifies the church's worship of God, as intercession for anyone in need, and for the need of the whole of creation, which

exposes and confounds the blasphemy of predatory political authority. (Stringfellow, 1977a:94)

In this approach the all too commonly encountered way of presenting the 'tension' between missiology and ecclesiology (does mission create the church, or does the church create mission?) becomes redundant. Both are generated in response to "the extraordinary presence of the Word of God in the world in Jesus Christ" alongside its victims. All this implies a major relocation of the *ekklesia* away from its preoccupation with a certain reductive chaplaincy to power, ritual purity and proximity to worldly influence – the comfortable places which make evangelism and advocacy unnecessary and therefore deeply problematic. For Stringfellow, placing ourselves rightly in the world, at the disposal of the Word, is what mission is all about:

> When the church has the freedom itself to be poor among the poor, it will know how to use what riches it has. When the church has that freedom, it will be a missionary people again in all the world. (Stringfellow, 1962:80-81)

For me this parallels Bonhoeffer's clarity of insight on the vocation of church (alongside prayer, justice and living humanly) as he approached his own end (Bonhoeffer, 1962:166). In practical terms it means raising difficult questions about the common sense dictated by institutional logic and operational power at the cutting edge of engagement. So, for example:

> The premise of most urban church work, it seems, is that in order for the church to minister among the poor, the church has to be rich, that is, to have specially trained personnel, huge funds and many facilities, rummage to distribute and a whole battery of social services. Just the opposite is the case. The church must be free to be poor with nothing to offer the poor except the gospel, except the power to discern and the courage to expose the gospel as it is already mediated in the life of the poor. (Stringfellow, 1962:80)

There is a sense and non-sense in that, as Stringfellow well knows. His demand is that we live the tension fully, not resolve it short of its demand.

Church as Counter-Institution

But what sort of church could actually sustain the kind of transformative encounter between God and the world mediated in Jesus Christ and in the continuing task of missional advocacy alongside those pushed to the margins? Unlike some more recent writers Stringfellow was not tempted to reify the church as a realm apart in an attempt to make it live up to the terrifying Gospel vision. He was acutely aware of its sin and failing, and he was also far too hard headed to fall either for the idea of ecclesial perfectibility or for the perfectibility of an ecclesial idea. Instead, as an Episcopalian who was sometimes rejected by its authorities and who often raged against both ecclesiastical authority and the soft-centredness of episcopacy

(Stringfellow, 1971:1-3), Stringfellow managed the important trick of being more a low church catholic than either a low or high-church protestant. He valued the church (against those who sought to dismiss it), but he valued it as present event not just as past pattern (against those who sought to preserve it), and he saw it as an instrument of divine purpose, not a vehicle to rescue a few good souls from a damned world.

So, while perceiving in real, living churches the infection of mere religiosity, the danger of introspection, the captivity of Constantinianism and the temptation of blasphemous quietism, Stringfellow still adhered to the central gift of church as exemplified in its odd diversity, unexpected courage and prophetic awkwardness: namely its calling as an "exemplary or pioneer or holy institution" freed "from primary or controlling concern about her own survival" (Stringfellow, 1970c:148). This high calling becomes plausible in his theology and practice because the church is a community that explicitly acknowledges its only foundation as being within the limitless creativity of God. It can therefore allow itself to be nourished by prayer, renewed by forgiveness and sustained by hope in the face of impossible odds. If it so chooses.

For Stringfellow, then, the essential catholicity of the church does not subsist in inherited structures, a priestly caste, historic formularies or divine privilege. In one way or another he questioned or denied all these, and in the Preface to his unpublished book *Grieve Not the Holy Spirit* he roundly denounced the usurpation of the Word "by the idolatrous mystique attributed to the churchly institution as custodian of extraordinary secrets or as mediator of assorted dispensations and practically magical gratuities" (Wylie-Kellermann, 1994:318). Instead, the church is catholic, universal, because it exists for the redemption of humanity not for itself. Its vocation is to be the risen body of Christ given for a broken world – in institutional form. This last twist is vital. The very institutional nature of church life which makes it (in Stringfellow's version of the Pauline typology) a principality prone to demonic distortion also enables it to strive towards being a redeemed and redeeming organization.

> So ideas of a non-institutional church or a deinstitutionalized church or uninstitutionalized church seem to me to be as nebulous as the Greek philosophy from which such ideas come and contrary to the biblical precedent. That does not temper my critique of the inherited church institutions; in fact it sharpens it and makes it more urgent. (Stringfellow, 1970c:148)

It is this combination of vision and realism, nourished by the actualities of East Harlem Protestant Parish and Chambers Memorial Church, which still distinguishes Stringfellow's ecclesiology from both churchy romanticism and anti-church individualism. In his writing and practice the church is a collective way of, as I would now put it, 'living beyond our means' – finding the resources of the crucified and risen life which can alone make possible a confrontation with the forces of destruction and death. But, just as the true church does not have a life of its own (it owes its existence to God) so also it cannot remain alienated from the threads of humanity which God assumes in Christ; it is not itself the kingdom of

God but a means towards that new creation – rather than some reformulated version of 'the Christian society'. This distinction seems significantly clearer in Stringfellow than it is in some recent writings of Stanley Hauerwas, whose underlying affinity with revised versions of Christendom has recently become evident (Hauerwas and Fodor, 1997:214).

Ec-centric Ecumenism

Last but by no means least, then, comes ecumenism. Though he saw Christian division as a scandal and the practical task of unity as essential (Stringfellow, 1964d), Stringfellow had little interest in ecclesiastical joinery, the ascendancy of "proud, independent, complacent confessional blocs", an entomological tendency to feed on decay (Stringfellow, 1964a), or an over-precious approach to tradition. For most of these reasons, he turned down a good job with WCC in Geneva in 1959.

Rather, since the church exists as a sacrament (rather than for the sacraments) only by virtue of being convened in the world through the Word, the world and the Word come first. And the New Testament word *oikumene*, from which we get our term ecumenism, denotes, indeed, the saving love of God for the whole inhabited earth, not some hobbyist preoccupation with uniting churches.

I do not know whether Stringfellow ever made that point in quite that way, but he certainly lived it. A convinced member of the laity he opposed clericalism and churchliness (as principalities) every bit as much as he supported a new international expression of the Spirit in and through church institutions which (as we have noted) he believed could signify both a challenge and an alternative to other principalities in this world. What we have at work here, once again, is a useful and demanding paradox (a studied non-sense) between the visionary and the pragmatic. But at every point the incarnation of God in the world is the defining centre. That is ecumenism – an ec-centric unity with the impoverished, marginalized and oppressed in which a new community is created, and a new society becomes visible.

And in the midst of these painful birth-pangs of God's new age there remains, for Stringfellow, celebration and life. It doesn't often appear that he or his partner Anthony Towne found church 'fun', despite their deep commitment. But their joy was certainly complete when they spent time with the circus, which Stringfellow described using the language of the old Latin motet, *O Sacrum Convivium*:

> This principality, this art, this veritable liturgy, this common enterprise of multifarious creatures called the circus enacts a hope, in an immediate and historic sense, and simultaneously embodies an ecumenical foresight of radical and wondrous splendour, encompassing, as it does both empirically and symbolically, the scope and diversity of creation. (Stringfellow, 1982b:87-8)

When I read that remarkable paean to a friend, she commented that with the addition of a little bread and wine, what we have here is the Eucharist, the eschatological banquet – something that will be a particular pleasure for William Stringfellow in his capacity as one of the clown princes of the circus of heaven.

Chapter Ten

Being Biblical Persons

Rowan Williams

I am taking a text from Exodus. Moses said to the Lord: "O Lord I have never been eloquent, neither in the past nor since you have spoken to your servant. I am slow of speech and tongue. The Lord said to him: 'Who gave you your mouth? Who makes you deaf or mute? Who gives sight or makes blind? Is it not I the Lord?' " (Exodus 4: 10-11).

Stringfellow speaks of being a biblical person, and he distinguishes being a biblical person from being a religious person. Here is a fundamental distinction that we ought to spend some time with. To be a religious person is actually very like being a secular person. The religious person, like the secular person, lives in one world. The disagreement is only about how many things there are in it. The religious person happens to think there are extra things in it called 'religious things', but there is one world. For the religious, there is an area of that world properly talked about in religious language, and there is a religious object called God. For the secular person there isn't, but what's a little disagreement between friends? The religious and the secular are the mirror image of one another; but the *biblical* is something different.

To say that the biblical person lives in something other than one world is certainly not to say that the biblical person escapes from one world into another. The truth is far more difficult and far more challenging. The biblical person lives in one world, which is constantly under judgement, under seduction, under question from another. Do we call it another world? Another frame of reference? Another language? We could just call it God.

The religious person looks at his or her one world and seeks to interpret it, as the secular person seeks to interpret it; to make sense. The biblical person puts himself or herself in the way of being interpreted, 'being made sense of'. The biblical person risks being vulnerable, because to put yourself in the way of being made sense of is to become vulnerable. The interpreter is the person with power, the person with the categories to organize the world. The person being interpreted is the person whose hands and heart are open to receive a very worrying and not always welcome gift, because the sense being made of us may not be the sense we would like to make. Or to put it more bluntly, the way God sees us may not be the way we would like to see ourselves.

Moses, whatever his feelings on that famous occasion in Exodus, was at least being tactically quite sensible, in saying to the Lord "I'd rather not say anything about this, if it is all the same to you". Moses knows he is in the middle of a process by which God is making sense of him, and his whole community, and that is a very disorientating process. It would have been very much easier if Moses had been able to say "I've got the message. I'll pass it on". But Moses is vulnerable. Moses lets himself be interpreted.

Perhaps, picking up on another theme in Stringfellow, that has something to do with being baptised. When you are baptised, sense is made of you: the sense of Jesus Christ. Your meaning, what you communicate, is bound in with what Jesus Christ is and is doing. You are interpreted by Christ in baptism, and that, far from being something which gives a sense of oppression or enclosure, is the ground of that freedom that is central to Stringfellow's theology – the freedom to know that the sense that God makes of you is not going to be shaken by any other kinds of sense, not even by the common-sense of the world.

Stringfellow sometimes comes over refreshingly as someone very short on common sense. He had massive imagination, massive depth, and in some ways very little self-protective sense. What the world calls common sense was uncommonly lacking in much of what he did. This is characteristic of many of the servants of Jesus Christ throughout the ages, because it is not common sense which they are interested in, it is the uncommon sense of Christ himself.

Being baptised and being called are about being interpreted. The name by which God calls you is what makes sense of you, that hidden, obstinate, mysterious self which God seeks to draw out of your acts and your thoughts and your struggles. A phrase powerfully used by a recent American philosopher is that the self is an integrity struggling to come into being, not something given in advance; and that integrity struggling to come into being is for Christians an integrity residing in Jesus Christ.

So, the biblical person is that vulnerable person, trying to find what her name is in the mouth of God, a person being cautious about the words which will be easy, which will make a sense that God has not given. Do we say that the biblical person lives in one world or two? Who knows how to answer that? The biblical person lives in the world, but the world under God. God, the Kingdom, the truth are making inroads all the time upon the world where we live. God, the Kingdom, and the truth are looking for transformation, or if you want to put it more dramatically, exorcism, of the world in which we live, and the biblical person lives uncomfortably in the world under that judgement.

The biblical person is not then either somebody who lives in one world, making sense of it, or in one world but with a citizenship to which they can always escape in another, but a person living in sovereign freedom, in a world that is being transfigured. The biblical person knows that their life is a text, a communication, a work of art that will speak. But it will speak when the concern about interpreting, making sense, is surrendered. Some of that I suppose is what Stringfellow speaks of when he describes how the issue of your own self acceptance is bound up with the freedom to be accepted by a community. To be accepted by a community, to live in a community, is in fact something far more demanding, and far more unusual than our common rhetoric, our rather glib rhetoric, might suggest. It is to live in a costly and engaged respectfulness for each other's creativity. It is to be aware how idolatry of every kind subjects some persons to the agendas of others.

And to live as a biblical person is to live in freedom from all that, and so necessarily to live with others in justice.

The question has come up in this book about how we live in the church, a church whose integrity or freedom is not always blindingly obvious even to those who love the church most and are most profoundly involved in its business. But if Stringfellow is right, being a biblical person is something very different from being a church person. The church should be what happens to biblical persons in life together. But because of our constant urge to move from the biblical to the religious the church becomes something which is another item in the world, in that world upon which God and the Kingdom and the truth are seeking to make an impact. There are many tightropes involved in walking the way of discipleship, and living in the Church certainly involves walking various kinds of tightropes (living as an Archbishop in the church is perhaps even more of a delicate acrobatic act than most).

But let's go back to the basic point – being a biblical person and therefore to live in community, in the acceptance of one another's creativity, and in systematic hostility to everything that flattens out or freezes this world into the unity of the religious or the secular, is the most fundamental calling that God can give us. The Bible is about how persons are made and shaped and driven together and woven together by God. It's about how our strength comes from our surrender to that reality directed and shaped by God. As Stringfellow says in speaking about biography as theology, it's about how human lives become texts of power, because they show how God makes sense of us.

At the end of this book then, when we have been reflecting upon theology and freedom, we can rightly open ourselves to the hope of that particular and rather paradoxical kind of freedom which Stringfellow speaks of in the name of the Bible. We can ask to be delivered from the tyranny of one world. How pervasive that is: the new world order, the system which will end history, whether it has a left or right label on it. The oneness of the world, which will offer the solution of problems, the provision of identity, and at the end of the day the annihilation of what is other. That kind of oneness is what we need to be delivered from.

The American literary critic and biblical critic Regina Schwartz has published recently a very provoking and very delightful book called "The Curse of Cain". It's about what she calls the "evil legacy of monotheism". How very easy, she is saying, to take the one God and make of the one God the ultimate reinforcement of *your* plans for unity, your nation, your self, your programme. Against that, she says, against that sort of monotheism, the Bible provides another vision of God, a vision in which otherness is always joy and gift, a vision of abundance or of generosity as opposed to the pinched and narrow vision of that kind of oneness.

The in-breaking of the otherness of God and the Kingdom and the truth, condemns us in many ways to a world of unfinished business. It blocks off the way to a unity, a resolution, which will stop us struggling, or growing; and therefore the in-breaking of God and the Kingdom and the truth obliges us to be biblical persons in the process of coming to terms with the other among ourselves, and rejecting false unities, sacred canopies that block out the real heaven.

We pray then to stop being religious and to be made biblical. We pray for the sense of living in the world under God's judgement, for the energy of that gift which will make us able to live with the painful processes of transformation, and commit ourselves to God, the Kingdom and the truth, as the energy of transformation for us. And we thank God for biblical persons we have known, and particularly for William Stringfellow.

Praise God from whom all blessings flow
Praise him all creatures here below
Praise him above the heavenly host
Praise Father Son and Holy Ghost.

Bibliography

Barth, Karl (1928) 'The Strange New World within the Bible', in *The Word of God and the Word of Man*, Hodder & Stoughton, London, pp. 28-50.

— (1939) *Church and State*, G. Ronald Howe, London.

— (1960) *Church Dogmatics: Vol. 3.4*, ET ed, T & T Clark, Edinburgh.

— (1979) *Evangelical Theology*, T & T Clark, Edinburgh.

Blake, William and Keynes, Geoffrey (1966) *The Complete Writings of William Blake*, New ed, OUP, Oxford.

Bonhoeffer, Dietrich (1962) *Letters and Papers from Prison*, Fontana, Glasgow.

Brueggemann, Walter (1993) *The Bible and Postmodern Imagination: Texts under Negotiation*, SCM, London.

Bryant, Chris (1996) *Possible Dreams: A Personal History of Christian Socialists*, Hodder & Stoughton, London.

Burdon, Christopher (1997) *The Apocalypse in England: Revelation Unravelling, 1700-1834*, St. Martin's Press, New York.

Carey, Frances (1999) *The Apocalypse and the Shape of Things to Come*, University of Toronto Press, Toronto.

Chapman, Mark (2001a) *The Coming Crisis: The Impact of Eschatology in Edwardian England*, Sheffield Academic Press, Sheffield.

— (2001b) *Liturgy, Socialism and Life: The Legacy of Conrad Noel*, DLT, London.

— (2003) "Christ and the Gethsemane of Mind: Frank Weston Then and Now", *Anglican Theological Review*, Vol.85, pp.281-308.

Crites, Stephen (1971) "The Narrative Quality of Experience", *Journal of the American Academy of Religion*, Vol.39, pp.291-311.

Dalferth, Ingolf (1988) *Theology and Philosophy*, Blackwell, Oxford.

— (1999) "Creation - Style of the World", *International Journal of Systematic Theology*, Vol.1, pp.119-37.

Dancer, Anthony (2001) *Theology in the Life of William Stringfellow*, D.Phil, Faculty of Theology, University of Oxford.

Davis, Murphy (1996) 'A Conversation on Biblical Politics', in *The Legacy of William Stringfellow*, (Eds. Andrew McThenia Jr and Bill Wylie-Kellermann), Washington and Lee University, Lexington VA, pp. 50-56.

Dawn, Marva (1992) *The Concept of the Principalities and Powers in the Works of Jacques Ellul*, Ph.D, Theology & Religious Studies, University of Notre Dame.

— (1996) "Powers and Principalities: Yoder Points to Ellul", *Faith and Freedom*, Vol.5, pp.54-59.

Dawn, Marva and Ellul, Jacques (1997) *Sources and Trajectories: Eight Early Articles by Jacques Ellul That Set the Stage*, Eerdmans, Grand Rapids.

DeGruchy, John (2000) *The Cambridge Companion to Dietrich Bonhoeffer*, CUP, Cambridge.

Douglas, J.D. (1962) "Review of a Private and Public Faith", *Evangelical Quarterly*, Vol.35, pp.118.

Ellul, Jacques (16 November 1966) 'Letter to William Stringfellow', in *William Stringfellow Papers, #4438*, Division of Rare and Manuscript Collections, Cornell University Library, Box 9.

— (1946) *Le Fondement Théologique Du Droit*, Delachaux et Niestlé, Neuchâtel.

— (1948) "The Christian as Revolutionary", *The Student World*, Vol.61, pp.221-6.

— (1960) *The Theological Foundation of Law*, Doubleday & Company, New York.

— (1964) *The Technological Society*, Alfred Knopf, New York.

— (1965) *Propaganda*, Alfred Knopf, New York.

— (1967a) *The Political Illusion*, Alfred Knopf, New York.

— (1967b) *The Presence of the Kingdom*, New York.

— (1969a) *To Will and to Do: An Ethical Research for Christians*, Pilgrim, Philadelphia.

— (1969b) *Violence*, Seabury, New York.

— (1970a) *The Meaning of the City*, Eerdmans, Grand Rapids.

— (1970b) *Prayer and Modern Man*, Seabury, New York.

— (1971a) *Autopsy of Revolution*, Alfred Knopf, New York.

— (1971b) *The Judgment of Jonah*, Eerdmans, Grand Rapids.

— (1972a) *False Presence of the Kingdom*, Seabury, New York.

— (1972b) *The Politics of God and the Politics of Man*, Eerdmans, Grand Rapids.

— (1973) *Hope in Time of Abandonment*, Seabury, New York.

— (1975) *The New Demons*, Seabury, New York.

— (1976) *The Ethics of Freedom*, Mowbray, London.

— (1977) *Apocalypse: The Book of Revelation*, Seabury, New York.

— (1978) *The Betrayal of the West*, Seabury, New York.

— (1980) *The Technological System*, Continuum, New York.

— (1981) *Perspectives on Our Age*, Seabury, New York.

— (1983) *Living Faith: Belief and Doubt in a Perilous World*, Harper and Row, San Francisco.

— (1985) *The Humiliation of the Word*, Eerdmans, Grand Rapids.

— (1988) *Jesus and Marx: From Gospel to Ideology*, Eerdmans, Grand Rapids.

— (1989) *The Presence of the Kingdom*, 2nd ed, Helmers & Howard, Colorado Springs.

— (1990a) *Reason for Being: A Meditation on Ecclesiastes*, Eerdmans, Grand Rapids.

— (1990b) *The Technological Bluff*, Eerdmans, Grand Rapids.

— (1991) *Anarchy and Christianity*, Eerdmans, Grand Rapids.

Figgis, J.N. (1912) *Civilisation at the Crossroads*, Longmans, London.

— (1913) *Antichrist and Other Sermons*, Longmans, London.

— (1914) *The Fellowship of the Mystery Being the Bishop Paddock Lectures Delivered at the General Theological Seminary, New York, During Lent 1913*, Longmans, London.

— (1917) *Some Defects of English Religion and Other Sermons*, Robert Scott, London.

Frei, Hans (1974) *The Eclipse of Biblical Narrative : A Study in Eighteenth and Nineteenth Century Hermeneutics*, Yale University Press, New Haven.

— (1975) *The Identity of Jesus Christ : The Hermeneutical Bases of Dogmatic Theology*, Fortress Press, Philadelphia.

— (1993) *Theology & Narrative: Selected Essays*, OUP, Oxford.

Frei, Hans, Hunsinger, George and Placher, William C. (1992) *Types of Christian Theology*, Yale University Press, New Haven.

Fuller, R. Buckminster (1975) *Synergetics: Explorations in the Geometry of Thinking*, Macmillan, New York.

Gessert, Robert (1955) "Christianity and Society: The Institute of Ethics and Politics", *Christianity and Society*, Vol.20.

Glen, Heather (1983) *Vision and Disenchantment : Blake's Songs and Wordsworth's Lyrical Ballads*, CUP, Cambridge.

Goddard, Andrew (1996) "Jacques Ellul: Obituary", *Studies in Christian Ethics*, Vol.9, pp.140-53.

— (2002) *Living the Word, Resisting the World: The Life and Thought of Jacques Ellul*, Paternoster Press, Carlisle.

Gray, Donald (1986) *Earth and Altar: The Evolution of the Parish Communion in the Church of England to 1945*, Canterbury Press, Norwich.

Green, Garrett (1987) *Scriptural Authority and Narrative Interpretation*, Fortress Press, Philadelphia.

Hanks, Joyce (2000) *Jacques Ellul: An Annotated Bibliography of Primary Works*, JAI Press, Stamford.

Hanks, Tom (1985) "The Original 'Liberation Theologian'?" *Cross Currents*, Vol.35, pp.17-32.

Harvey, Anthony (Ed.) (1989) *Faith in the City*, SPCK, London.

Hauerwas, Stanley and Fodor, James (1997) 'Remaining in Babylon: Oliver O'donovan's Defense of Christendom', in *Wilderness Wanderings: Probing Twentieth Century Theology and Philosophy*, Westview Press, Boulder CO.

Hauerwas, Stanley and Powell, Jeff (1994) 'Creation as Apocalyptic: A Homage to William Stringfellow', in *Despatches from the Front*, (Eds. Stanley Hauerwas and Jeff Powell), Duke University Press, Durham, NC, pp. 31-40.

— (1995) 'Creation as Apocalyptic: A Homage to William Stringfellow', in *Radical Christian and Exemplary Lawyer*, (Ed. Andrew McThenia), Grand Rapids, pp. 31-40.

Heilbrun, C (1988) *Writing a Woman's Life*, Norton, New York.

Hill, Christopher (1972) *The World Turned Upside Down: Radical Ideas During the English Revolution*, Temple Smith, London.

Hoedemaker, Bert (1998) "Naming the World in the Name of the Coming One: Changing Relations between Mission, Modernity and Eschatology", *Exchange: A Journal of Missiological and Ecumenical Thought*, Vol.27.

Holloway, James (Ed.) (1970) *Introducing Jacques Ellul*, Eerdmans, Grand Rapids.

Jones, Peter d'Alroy (1968) *The Christian Socialist Revival, 1877-1914*, Princeton University Press, Princeton.

Kenrick, Bruce (19 October 1960) 'Letter to William Stringfellow', in *William Stringfellow Papers, #4438*, Division of Rare and Manuscript Collections, Cornell University Library, Box 4.

— (24 November 1960) 'Letter to William Stringfellow', in *William Stringfellow Papers, #4438*, Division of Rare and Manuscript Collections, Cornell University Library, Box 4.

— (1962) *Come out the Wilderness*, Collins, London.

Lindbeck, George A. (1984) *The Nature of Doctrine: Religion and Theology in a Postliberal Age*, 1st ed, Westminster Press, Philadelphia.

Loder, James E. and Neidhardt, W. Jim (1992) *The Knight's Move : The Relational Logic of the Spirit in Theology and Science*, Helmers & Howard, Colorado Springs.

MacIntyre, Alasdair (1953) *Marxism: An Interpretation*, SCM, London.

Macy, Paul Griswald (Ed.) (1948) *The Report of the Second World Conference of Christian Youth*, WCC, Geneva.

Matera, Frank (1996) *New Testament Ethics: The Legacies of Jesus and Paul*, Westminster/John Knox Press, Louisville, KY.

Maurice, F.D. (1849) *Lincoln's Inn Sermons*, J.W. Parker, London.

McAlister, Elizabeth (1995) 'William Stringfellow: Continuing Clarification of Ethic and Action', in *Radical Christian and Exemplary Lawyer*, (Ed. Andrew McThenia), Eerdmans, Grand Rapids, pp. 41-47.

McClendon, James William (1974) *Biography as Theology: How Life Stories Can Remake Today's Theology*, Abingdon Press, Nashville.

McThenia, Andrew W. (Ed.) (1995) *Radical Christian and Exemplary Lawyer*, Eerdmans, Grand Rapids.

Mensch, Elizabeth (1990) 'The History of Mainstream Legal Thought', in *The Politics of Law*, (Ed. D. Kairys), revised ed, Pantheon, New York, pp. 13-37.

Mesters, Carlos (1989) *Defenseless Flower: A New Reading of the Bible*, Orbis Books, Maryknoll.

Myers, Ched (1989) *Binding the Srong Man: A Political Reading of Mark's Gospel*, Orbis, Maryknoll, NY.

Nation, Mark Thiessen (1998) "The Vocation of the Church of Jesus the Criminal:Reflections on the Writings of William Stringfellow by an Un-Closeted Anabaptist", *Faith and Freedom: A Journal of Christian Ethics*, Vol.6, pp.17-24.

Noel, Conrad (1939) *Jesus the Heretic*, J.M. Dent, London.

— (1945) *An Autobiography*, J.M. Dent, London.

Norman, E.R. (1976) *Church and Society in England 1770-1970: A Historical Study*, Clarendon Press, Oxford.

Ochs, Peter (1999) *Pierce, Pragmatism and the Logic of Scripture*, CUP, Cambridge.

Petitpierre, Dom Robert (Ed.) (1972) *Exorcism: The Report of a Commission Convened by the Bishop of Exeter*, SPCK, London.

Polner, Murray and O'Grady, Jim (1997) *Disarmed and Dangerous: The Radical Lives and Times of Daniel and Philip Berrigan*, Holt, Rinehart and Winston, New York.

Rasmussen, Larry L. (1972) *Dietrich Bonhoeffer: Reality and Resistance*, Abingdon, Nashville, TN.

Ray, Ronald (1979) "Jacques Ellul's Innocent Notes on Hermeneutics", *Interpretation*, Vol.33, pp.262-82.

Rogers, Bill (25 March 1953) 'Letter to William Stringfellow', in *William Stringfellow Papers, #4438*, Division of Rare and Manuscript Collections, Cornell University Library, Box 2.

Rowland, Christopher (1988) *Radical Christianity: A Reading of Recovery*, Orbis Books, Maryknoll.

Russell, Bertrand (1921) *The Analysis of Mind*, Allen & Unwin, London.

Sanders, E.P. (1977) *Paul and Palestinian Judaism*, Fortress Press, Philadelphia.

Selby, Peter (1997) *Rescue: Jesus and Salvation Today*, SPCK, London.

Shaffer, Thomas (1966) "The Christian Lawyer - an Oxymoron", *America*, Vol.175, pp.12-17.

— (1995) 'The Church and the Law', in *Radical Christian and Exemplary Lawyer*, (Ed. Andrew McThenia), Eerdmans, Grand Rapids, pp. 103-21.

Slocum, Robert (Ed.) (1997) *Prophet of Justice, Prophet of Life*, Church Publishing Incorporated, New York.

Stassen, Glenn, Yeager, D.M. and Yoder, John Howard (1996) *Authentic Transformation*, Abingdon Press, Nashville.

Stringfellow, William (8 August 1957) 'Letter to Victor Butterfield', in *William Stringfellow Papers, #4438*, Division of Rare and Manuscript Collections, Cornell University Library, Box 2.

— (10 April 1959) 'Letter to Alexander Morin, University of Chicago Press', in *William Stringfellow Papers, #4438*, Division of Rare and Manuscript Collections, Cornell University Library, Box 4.

— (19 April 1960) 'Letter to Jacques Ellul', in *William Stringfellow Papers, #4438*, Division of Rare and Manuscript Collections, Cornell University Library, Box 4.

— (23 February 1971) 'Letter to Jacques Ellul', in *William Stringfellow Papers, #4438*, Division of Rare and Manuscript Collections, Cornell University Library, Box 15.

— (26 March 1953) 'Letter to John Turnball', in *William Stringfellow Papers, #4438*, Division of Rare and Manuscript Collections, Cornell University Library, Box 2.

— (26 October 1960) 'Letter to William Stringfellow', in *William Stringfellow Papers, #4438*, Division of Rare and Manuscript Collections, Cornell University Library, Box 4.

— (30 July 1970) 'Letter to Jacques Ellul', in *William Stringfellow Papers, #4438*, Division of Rare and Manuscript Collections, Cornell University Library, Box 15.

— (1961) "Poverty, Piety, Charity and Mission", *The Christian Century*, Vol.78, pp.584-86.

— (1962) *A Private and Public Faith*, Eerdmans, Grand Rapids.
— (1963a) "Evangelism and Conversion", *International Journal of Religious Education*, pp.6-7,22.
— (1963b) *Instead of Death*, Seabury Press, New York.
— (1964a) "Ecumenicity and Entomology: New Church Problem", *The Christian Century*, Vol.81, pp.1239-41.
— (1964b) *Free in Obedience*, Seabury, New York.
— (1964c) *My People Is the Enemy: An Autobiographical Polemic*, Holt, Rinehart and Winston, New York.
— (1964d) "The Unity of the Church as the Witness of the Church", *Anglican Theological Review*, Vol.46, pp.394-400.
— (1966) *Dissenter in a Great Society*, Holt, Rinehart and Winston, New York.
— (1967) *Count It All Joy: Reflections on Faith, Doubt, and Temptation*, Eerdmans, Grand Rapids.
— (1969) *Imposters of God: Inquiries into Favorite Idols*, Witness Books, New York.
— (1970a) 'The American Importance of Jacques Ellul', in *Introducing Jacques Ellul*, (Ed. James Holloway), Eerdmans, Grand Rapids, pp. 135-8.
— (1970b) "Jacques Ellul: Layman as Moral Theologian", *Messenger*, Vol.119.
— (1970c) *A Second Birthday*, Doubleday & Company, New York.
— (1971) "Why Are There No Bishops in Jail?" *The Fourth Quadrant, St Clement's Episcopal Church*.
— (1973) *An Ethic for Christians and Other Aliens in a Strange Land*, Word, Waco.
— (1976a) *Instead of Death*, 2nd ed, Seabury Press, New York.
— (1976b) "Open Letter to Jimmy Carter", *Sojourners*, Vol.5, pp.7-8.
— (1976c) "Untitled Column", *Sojourners*, Vol.5, pp.19.
— (1977a) *Conscience and Obedience: The Politics of Romans 13 and Revelation 13 in Light of the Second Coming*, Word Books, Waco.
— (1977b) "Kindred Mind and Brother", *Sojourners*, Vol.6, pp.12.
— (1977c) "Myths, Endless Genealogies, the Promotion of Speculations and the Vain Discussion Thereof", *Sojourners*, Vol.13, pp.12-13.
— (1982a) "A Lawyer's Work", *Christian Legal Society Quarterly*, Vol.3, pp.17,19.
— (1982b) *A Simplicity of Faith: My Experience in Mourning*, Abingdon, Nashville.
— (1984) *The Politics of Spirituality*, Westminster Press, Philadelphia.
— (1989) 'Foreword to the 1967 Edition', In *The Presence of the Kingdom*, (Jacques Ellul), 2nd ed, Helmers & Howard, Colorado Springs, pp. xv-xix.
— (c.1959-1960) 'Handwritten Notes for Speech', in *William Stringfellow Papers, #4438*, Division of Rare and Manuscript Collections, Cornell University Library, Box 4.
— (February 21 1963) "Care Enough to Weep", *The Witness*, pp.13-15.
— (February 1953) 'Remarks Made in a Panel Discussion at a Student Christian Movement Gathering', in *William Stringfellow Papers, #4438*, Division of Rare and Manuscript Collections, Cornell University Library, Box 2.

Stringfellow, William and Towne, Anthony (1971) *Suspect Tenderness: The Ethics of the Berrigan Witness*, Holt Rinehart and Winston, New York.

Stroup, George (1981) *The Promise of Narrative Theology*, SCM, London.

Suhor, Mary Lou (1995) 'Bill – Recollections of an Editor', in *Radical Christian and Exemplary Lawyer*, (Ed. Andrew McThenia), Eerdmans, Grand Rapids, pp. 74-87.

Sykes, Stephen (1985) "The Grammar of Narrative and Making Sense of Life", *Anglican Theological Review*, Vol.67, pp.117-26.

Thielman, Frank (1999) *The Law and the New Testament: The Question of Continuity*, Crossroad, New York.

University of Chicago Divinity School (1963) "Introduction to Theology: Questions to and Discussions with Dr. Karl Barth", *Criterion*, Vol.2, pp.3-24.

Visser't Hooft, W.A. (1948) *The Kingship of Christ*, Harper and Row, New York.

Wallis, Jim (1976) *Agenda for Biblical People*, Harper & Row, New York.

— (1985) "A Holy Humility", *Sojourners*, Vol.14, pp.4-6.

— (1995) 'Keeper of the Word', in *Radical Christian and Exemplary Lawyer*, (Ed. Andrew McThenia Jr.), Eerdmans, Grand Rapids, pp. 88-97.

Weston, Frank (1923) *In Defence of the English Catholic*, Mowbray, London.

Wilkins, Lewis (1967) "Review of Dissenter in a Great Society", *The Ecumenical Review*, Vol.19, pp.488-9.

Wilkinson, Alan (1998) *Christian Socialism: Scott Holland to Tony Blair*, SCM, London.

Williams, Rowan (1995) *Ray of Darkness*, Cowley, Cambridge, Mass.

Wink, Walter (1973) *The Bible in Human Transformation*, Fortress Press, Philadelphia.

— (1980) *Transforming Bible Study*, Abingdon, Nashville, TN.

— (1984) *Naming the Powers: The Language of Power in the New Testament*, Fortress Press, Philadelphia.

— (1985) "A Mind Full of Surprises", *Sojourners*, Vol.14, pp.25.

— (1995) 'Stringfellow on the Powers', in *Radical Christian and Exemplary Lawyer*, (Ed. Andrew McThenia), Grand Rapids, pp. 17-30.

— (1998) *The Powers That Be: Theology for a New Millennium*, Doubleday, New York.

Winstanley, Gerrard and Sabine, George Holland (1941) *The Works of Gerrard Winstanley*, Cornell University Press, Ithaca.

Wood, Charles M. (1987) 'Hermeneutics and the Authority of Scripture', in *Scriptural Authority and Narrative Interpretation*, (Ed. Garrett Green), Fortress Press, Philadelphia, pp. 3-20.

Wylie-Kellermann, Bill (Ed.) (1994) *A Keeper of the Word: Selected Writings of William Stringfellow*, Eerdmans, Grand Rapids.

— (1995) 'Bill, the Bible, and the Seminary Underground', in *Radical Christian and Exemplary Lawyer*, (Ed. Andrew McThenia), Grand Rapids, pp. 56-72.

— (1999) "Not Vice Versa. Reading the Power Biblically: Stringfellow, Hermeneutics, and the Principalities", *Anglican Theological Review*, Vol.81, pp.665-82.

Yoder, John H. (1970) *Karl Barth and the Problem of War*, Abingdon, Nashville, TN.

Yoder, John Howard (1972) *The Politics of Jesus*, Eerdmans, Grand Rapids.

— (1989) *Body Politics*, Discipleship Resources, Nashville TN.

Index

ORGANISATION FOR
ECONOMIC CO-OPERATION AND DEVELOPMENT

FROM MARSHALL PLAN TO GLOBAL INTERDEPENDENCE

NEW CHALLENGES
FOR
THE INDUSTRIALIZED
NATIONS

The opinions expressed in this publication
are the responsibility of the authors
and do not necessarily represent those of the OECD.

TABLE OF CONTENTS

3

---

1. Addresses at the Marshall Plan Commemoration Dinner, offered by the Secretary-General of the OECD to participants in the Conference, at the Château de la Muette, Paris, June 2, 1977.

FOREWORD

by Lincoln Gordon
Conference Co-Chairman

In December of 1975, inquiries were made simultaneously to me in Washington and to Robert Marjolin in Paris by Former Ambassadors Fred L. Hadsel, Executive Director of the George C. Marshall Research Foundation, and John W. Tuthill, then Director General of the Atlantic Institute for International Affairs. The question was whether the two of us (each contingent upon the acceptance of the other) would agree to serve as co-chairmen of a conference proposed for June, 1977, to mark the thirtieth anniversary of the speech at Harvard by the American Secretary of State which launched what later came to be known and celebrated as the Marshall Plan.

The sponsors acknowledged that thirtieth anniversaries are rarely noted. Pearl has scarcely won a place alongside the silver and gold associated with twenty-five and fifty years. In favor of the proposal, they made three persuasive arguments:

  a) thirty years was close to the maximum for bringing together persons who had played important roles in carrying out the Marshall Plan;
  b) the industrial countries joined in the OECD were encountering severe new challenges, both domestic and external; and
  c) elections were imminent in several of the member countries, including the largest one, which meant that by 1977 many political leaders would be working with relatively new mandates from their constituencies.

From the time of the earliest discussions, it was specified that any such conference should not be limited to the history of the Marshall Plan period, and should certainly not be a mere exercise in nostalgia among superannuated veterans. To be worth the effort, the project would have to relate history to the present and future; to include the newer generations; and to comprise a serious effort at appraisal of the opportunities and obstacles which confront the industrial nations in shaping individual and collective policies.

With those conditions understood, Robert Marjolin and I quickly accepted the invitation. At the Organisation for Economic Co-operation and Development, Secretary-General van Lennep enthusiastically welcomed the initiative and, with the endorsement of the OECD Council, offered the hospitality of the Château de la Muette and the administrative services of the

5

Organisation. The German Marshall Fund of the United States provided financial support for conference planning and for commissioning papers by a group of six distinguished experts, papers which were circulated in advance to the conference participants. In addition, the co-chairmen recruited two or three highly qualified panelists to lead the discussion on each paper. The sponsoring organizations and Marshall Plan veterans from a number of member countries assisted in preparing lists of proposed participants. On June 2 and 3, 1977, three working sessions were held for presentation and discussion of the papers, punctuated by a bountiful Marshall Plan Commemoration Dinner at the Château de la Muette addressed by the OECD Secretary-General and by authoritative representatives of the French and United States governments.

The results of this undertaking are presented herein: six remarkably penetrating papers; comments by experienced and knowledgeable panelists; and lively general discussion; together with the thought-provoking addresses delivered at the dinner of June 2.

*
* *

During the planning phase, we formulated the objectives of the conference in the following terms:

"Although building on the historic experience of the Marshall initiative of 1947 and what its success has signified for subsequent developments over the following three decades, the main emphasis of the conference is intended to be forward-looking. Its central thrust is to seek a renewed sense of common purpose among the industrial democracies, identifying the challenges and opportunities they face in the last quarter of the twentieth century, both in their mutual relations and in the global context."

We were thus proposing two interconnected motifs: historical and contemporary, with the principal weight on the latter.

On the side of historical perspective, a number of new insights were provided by the two authors from the " Marshall Plan generation, " Lord Franks and Professor Kindleberger, and in the comments of Dr. van der Beugel, Mrs. Camps, Minister Brofoss, Ambassador Ortona, and Lord Roll, as well as by several " veterans " among the general participants. Their observations helped to place the Marshall Plan in the wider global setting of its own time, and also to identify the elements in the nature and conduct of the enterprise which made it so phenomenal a success.

There was general concurrence with my own remarks, in opening the conference, that the oft-heard plea for " another Marshall Plan " to deal with new international problems reflects a failure to understand the Marshall Plan itself or the loose application of a false analogy. That is especially the case with respect to relations between industrial and developing countries—the " North-South " issues of today. In the words of Robert Marjolin: " There was only *one* Marshall Plan; there will never be another, because

6

the Marshall Plan sprang from historically determined, special circumstances, which will never be repeated as such. "

At the same time, there was eloquent testimony to the influence of the Marshall Plan's success on the course of subsequent events in both the political and economic domains, including the preservation of democratic institutions in Europe and the movement for integration culminating in the formation and later enlargement of the European Communities. The institutional innovations have also left their enduring mark on international relationships, not only in the OECD itself—a lineal descendant of the OEEC and the Marshall Plan—but in the working methods of other international organizations, both regional and global.

Contrasts were sharply drawn by some participants between the circumstances of the late 1940s and the late 1970s, in an effort to account for the capacity in the earlier period to respond to challenges with speed and vigor. With most of those contrasts I would concur: the conviction then that the alternative to prompt action was chaos; the sense of the presence of a common enemy; the high quality of post-war leadership in most countries; and the unchallenged preponderance of the role of the United States. But there is one point on which my first-hand recollections do not confirm the observations of several participants (especially younger ones)—the alleged " simplicity " of the issues of that time compared to today. I detect in that view a kind of retrospective mythologizing, as if a set of policies which led to such consummate success must have been seen in advance to be obviously correct. In fact, the success was hoped for but not unambiguously foreseen. There was at times a sense of desperation—as during the run on sterling before the devaluation of 1949, or the " utterly intractable " problem of the German Federal Republic's unemployment and balance-of-payments deficits, thought to be the structural consequences of the refugee inflow from the East and the loss of food-exporting provinces. One might add the supposedly incurable " world dollar shortage, " about which economists of the highest distinction were writing solemn treatises published precisely when the United States was entering its long phase of external deficits!

Nor were the policies all thought through in advance. The major components of European self-help and mutual help, backed by North American support (for Canada supplemented the American effort on several fronts), were the essence of the Plan, but some of the most important specific measures emerged only after the operation was well under way. Cardinal examples were the arrangements for intra-European trade liberalization and the European Payments Union. Far from being " obviously correct, " the EPU had to with-stand strenuous attacks on two fronts: from globalists who feared that a European currency bloc would defer indefinitely the general convertibility envisaged at Bretton Woods and undermine the International Monetary Fund beyond repair; and from sub-regionalists who preferred a tight monetary confederation called FINEBEL (or sometimes, less euphoniously, FRITA-LUX)—a kind of anticipation of the European Economic Community of Six, but lacking both the political and the economic advantages of including Germany. Yet, in retrospect, the EPU seems to have been ideally designed as a transitional stage between the constrictive bilateralism of immediate post-war Europe and the broader interdependence of the industrial democracies which marked the decade of the 1960s.

In the forging of these measures, the OEEC played an heroic part, stretching to the limit the creative potential of an intergovernmental institution whose constitutional structure, as emphasized in Lord Franks' paper, was designed to minimize its powers. Within the wider success of the Marshall Plan, the success of the OEEC is a special chapter, which I hope will be written in detail one day by Robert Marjolin. As Secretary-General during the critical period, he transformed a constitutionally weak position into a very considerable *de facto* influence by force of personality and intellect. One of his instruments was an informal group he flatteringly designated as his " brains trust. " The members were drawn from the permanent delegations of the key countries, and met once or twice a month (usually over excellent meals) to discuss the next set of problems confronting the ongoing processes of European recovery and the wider international economic framework— problems still over the horizon and not yet on the agenda of the Executive Committee or the Council, much less ripe for negotiation among Ministers. Without prejudicing the positions of their respective governments, and working without documents, minutes, or transcripts, the group helped to give form to the issues and to potential solutions which maximized the elements of mutual gain. Marjolin's own thinking was thus filtered back to the governments which retained the power to act, and often returned later as formal governmental initiatives incorporating his ideas. Among many happy recollections of the Marshall Plan years. I place special value on the privilege of having participated in that group.

*
* *

In its historical aspects, the hopes of the conference planners were fulfilled. On the contemporary side, however, it would be misleading to claim that we found answers to the search for " a renewed sense of common purpose among the industrial democracies. " A reading of the three complementary papers by sociologist Crozier, economist Lindbeck, and political scientist Hoffmann will reveal a common vein of pessimism concerning the capacity of the advanced societies to come to grips with their internal problems of growth, economic stability, and social harmony; or even to conserve the terrain already won, to say nothing of further advances, in European integration and broader interdependence. The papers by Kindleberger on North-South and Knirsch on East-West economic relationships show clearly what was underscored by many speakers during the conference: that the management of interdependence must now take account of all parts of the globe, with the welfare of the OECD countries becoming increasingly dependent on external as well as mutual relationships.

The undertone of pessimism in part reflected immediate circumstances. Coincident with our meetings, the official North-South dialogue known as the Conference on International Economic Cooperation (CIEC) was winding

8

down only a few blocks away to an ambiguous close. There were neither the fireworks of celebration nor the artillery of confrontational collapse—merely the whimper of non-agreement on unfulfilled, and probably unfulfillable, aspirations. Recent elections in some OECD countries and opinion polls in others were signalling widespread public dissatisfaction with governments in office, but not decisive swings to opposition forces.

A major contributing cause of this malaise is obviously the continuation of exceptional levels of unemployment in most industrial countries, paradoxically matched by continued inflation. How to overcome this "stagflation" was the central question before the OECD's McCracken Committee, whose report *Towards Full Employment and Price Stability* was completed ust prior to the Marshall Plan Conference and several of whose members participated in our discussions. Directly related to this baffling internal problem, which has undermined confidence in macroeconomic policy-making at the national level, is the transformation in the international economic environment since 1971-73, which has unleashed the strongest pressures for protectionist barriers against trade and capital movements witnessed since the Great Depression of the 1930s.

Our discussions touched repeatedly on these circumstances, including their baneful effects on the European integration movement, on relations among industrial countries as a whole, and on prospects for harmonious development of North-South and East-West relations. Underlying those references, however, was a more profound set of questions, bearing on social discontents, group and national tensions, and conflicting non-economic as well as economic aspirations, which appear to be by-products of affluence and are resistant to the simple solvent of economic growth. Even if some magic wand could recreate the full employment and price stability of the 1960s, it was implied, many of those concerns would remain and would continue to pose serious difficulties for international economic relationships. A full exploration of such difficult and complex issues would have required much more time than was available to us. Their structural aspects are the central concern of the OECD's long-term project, known as "Interfutures," whose report is expected in 1979.

In any event, it is clear that the course of international economic cooperation can no longer proceed on the easy assumption that the free movement of goods and capital, supplemented by *ad hoc* macroeconomic policy coordination among the strongest economies, is the invincible wave of the future, propelled by its contributions to global welfare and the efficient allocation of resources. As the Lindbeck and Hoffmann papers make uncomfortably evident, qualifications to the liberal thesis itself, coupled with distributive conflicts and increasing desires for "public goods" and non-economic goals not readily served by market forces, are bound either to complicate the international agenda or to eventuate in chimerical and impoverishing efforts to "recapture" national automony. It would, after all, be very surprising if pure liberalism could be retained as the guiding principle for international relations among countries whose domestic policies include an increasing array of governmental interventions to serve a host of democratically imposed objectives.

9

This dilemma underlay the three "alternative strategies" presented in the concluding section of Professor Lindbeck's paper, to which conference participants frequently reverted. The strategies were:

1. a retreat from internationalization;
2. more automatic national adjustments to a highly internationalized system, and
3. more energetic international coordination and cooperation in an effort to bring national political actions into closer accord with the international character of the economic system.

Professor Lindbeck's own preferences were for a combination of the second and third strategies although his realistic expectations were for compromise policies incorporating elements of all three into " a kind of semi-organized anarchy. " Without exception, other participants joined him in rejecting the first alternative as a costly retrogression, which might well sacrifice the gains from an improved international division of labor without securing the supposed national benefits of freedom from interdependence.

As between the second and third choices, the variety of opinions reflected a cleavage which (as pointed out in Professor Kindleberger's paper) runs all the way back to the initiation of the Marshall Plan. In oversimplified terms, it is the clash between free marketeers and economic planners. In my own view, the capacity of the industrialized nations to deal effectively with their common internal and external problems will depend on their ability to bridge that cleavage—to find ways of providing public goods, correcting market failures and distortions, and pursuing non-economic objectives without losing the unrivaled power of market forces as allocators of scarce resources and stimuli to innovation.

Deification of the market is no less absurd than faith in all-embracing planning. The market should be accorded due respect in its proper place, and sectoral planning should seek to use market forces for public purposes, rather than to fight then frontally—and usually vainly. For many sectors, planning is neither necessary nor useful; for others, it is indispensable. And when interdependence can either reinforce or frustrate national plans, or when a floor of agreed minimum standards is essential to acceptable competitive behavior, there is a *prima facie* case for selective international cooperation, with its precise scope and intensity depending on the specific issues at hand.

It is much easier to recite general principles of this sort than to apply them to the tough issues of national and international politics. As the domestic and international dimensions of many policies in sector after sector become increasingly intertwined, however, the institutions of intergovernmental cooperation—and those few charged with supranational administration—will be constantly confronted with the need to balance and reconcile the market and planning components of their actions. To quote once more my colleague Robert Marjolin, that process will require " a great deal of intelligence [I would add *disciplined* intelligence] and a total absence of dogmatism. "

Thirty years after the initiation of the Marshall Plan, the environment is evidently not propitious for grand designs or all-embracing new international orders or heroic leaps to regional or global political confederations. New orders, after all, generally arise out of the supreme crises of global conflict, military or economic—crises which mankind can now scarcely afford. But reflection on what has been accomplished over these last decades should provide some reassurance to the industrial democracies, notwithstanding the discontents of the day. Their resilience should not be underestimated, nor should the near-revolutionary consequences of cumulative incremental change, which is the characteristic mode of democratic and open societies. They have not yet learned to treat common problems with the fortitude and resolve inspired by common enemies, but they have made a good start in building the institutions and inculcating the attitudes to help them do so when the painful alternatives to such cooperation become better understood. Those institutions and attitudes are the permanent legacy of the Marshall Plan.

*
* *

Several organizations and many individuals contributed to the realization of the Marshall Plan Commemoration Conference. The George C. Marshall Foundation, in Lexington, Kentucky, and the Atlantic Institute for International Affairs, in Paris, originated the project and assisted at several stages in its implementation. The financial support of the German Marshall Fund of the United States played an indispensable role. Administrative support and hospitality were admirably handled by the Organisation for Economic Co-operation and Development, where special thanks are due to Secretary-General Emile van Lennep, Deputy Secretary-General Charles G. Wootton, and the External Relations Division staff led by Thierry Monnier with the able assistance of Liz Millar.

In editing the proceedings and preparing them for publication, I have been assisted by Liz Cecelski with translations from the French and by my secretary Debbie Hemphill in successive stages of revising and assembling the materials. For the remaining errors, including those of translation or of possible misinterpretation in summarizing the thoughts of conference participants, the responsibility is mine.

Lincoln Gordon.

Washington, D.C.
January, 1978

I

LESSONS OF THE
MARSHALL PLAN EXPERIENCE

1

WELCOME

by Jonkheer Emile van Lennep,
Secretary-General, OECD

It gives me great pleasure to welcome you all to OECD on the occasion of this Conference, which has been arranged to commemorate the thirtieth anniversary of General Marshall's Harvard speech. In greeting you today, I should like first of all to pay tribute to the George C. Marshall Foundation and the Atlantic Institute for International Affairs for their fine initiative in organising the Conference.

It is now two years since we were first visited by the Executive Director of the Marshall Foundation, Ambassador Fred Hadsel, and the idea of a commemorative conference at OECD took form. And I know you would also wish me to express our collective and particular appreciation to the two co-chairmen, Ambassador Lincoln Gordon and M. Robert Marjolin for the considerable preparatory work they have undertaken.

This commemoration is a very special one. We are now thirty years on from the Harvard speech that not only launched the Marshall Plan but also sowed the seeds of co-operation in Europe that have flourished and grown stronger with successive years, and it is difficult to speak to you on this occasion without some feeling of emotion. Marshall was a man of great perception. He recognised that to reconstruct Europe more than just material aid was needed. The future was at stake. A decisive commitment to a new era of co-operation was required. He gave the European countries an opportunity to determine their future and they took it. The Marshall Plan provided the impulse for a new approach to co-operation in policy-making. It is this common approach to problem-solving that has evolved steadily throughout the past thirty years in OEEC and later in OECD. I think that Marshall would not be at all unhappy to see the fruits of his ideas now.

Our conference is perhaps a novel way to commemorate this occasion. The organisers have brought together, here at the Château de la Muette, a group of eminent personalities whose interest in and knowledge of international affairs and interdependence is indeed considerable. The themes that have been chosen evoke the basic concept of Marshall's original approach to the European problem: interdependence. It is therefore most fitting that you should have gathered at OECD to discuss these topics, the challenges that face modern industrial society, since these same challenges are very much the preoccupations of this Organisation. Even more interesting from my point of view is that the papers and the discussions should give us at OECD an important and perhaps slightly different perspective on the problems of interdependence that are at the heart of our tasks here.

Interdependence is a reality and our aim should be to strengthen it. Co-operation among countries must be the first essential ingredient of any interdependence. Interdependence is not only a function of the relationships between countries that are members of OECD but also the relationship of OECD countries with all other countries of the world and particularly with the developing countries, where there are very special problems. Perhaps in solving them, or at least working together in a realistic and balanced way to solve them, we will begin to recognise and implement the true meaning of co-operation and interdependence.

Marshall looked to the future with ideas from which we in Europe have greatly benefitted. That is the tradition we should follow. It is to the future that we must continue to direct our attention and we in OECD are attempting to do this. I am sure that in the Organisation we shall find useful many of the ideas that will emerge from this Conference.

2

INTRODUCTION TO THE CONFERENCE

by Dr. Lincoln Gordon,
Conference Co-Chairman

In discussions of public policy in the United States (and I dare say in other countries as well) during the past quarter century, it has become almost a cliché for someone to say: " What we really need is a Marshall Plan for our cities, " or " a Marshall Plan to abolish poverty, " or " a Marshall Plan for energy, " or " a Marshall Plan for Africa, " or Latin America, or whatever other objective the speaker may have in mind. That cliché has become an almost unconscious tribute to the European Recovery Program launched by Secretary of State George Marshall thirty years ago. The Marshall Plan indeed deserves the tribute. Perhaps alone among large-scale international ventures of recent times, it accomplished greater results, it cost less, and it was completed more rapidly than its initiators hoped or expected.

The cliché is generally misplaced, however, since the kinds of problems referred to, whether domestic or international, generally do not lend themselves to solution by a concentrated four-year effort. Yet the tribute reflects a yearning to emulate other aspects of the Marshall Plan which may indeed be relevant: clarity of diagnosis, adequacy of resources applied, and the vision and political leadership capable of setting aside short-term conflicts of interest, and even historic rivalries, in favor of longer-term but by no means Utopian mutual gains.

When Robert Marjolin and I were invited to organize a program for this conference, and to commission papers for discussion, we accepted on condition that the discussions not be focussed simply on those magic years of 1947-52, but rather seek from the past such illumination as might be relevant to the present and future. In my first memorandum on the Conference in March 1976, I suggested that " it should reflect the need for a renewed sense of common purpose among the industrial democracies through the identification of challenges and opportunities they face in the last quarter of the twentieth century, both in their mutual relations and in the global context. It need not, and probably should not, draw blueprints for new ' grand designs, ' but it could help to recreate a sense of direction and to identify critical agenda items for the coming decade. The Conference might thus contribute modestly

15

but significantly to the badly needed restoration of self-confidence in the 'First World'." I hope that our discussions in these two days will be guided by that objective.

There is little doubt about the need for a restoration of confidence. That was the keynote of the Downing Street Summit communiqué a month ago. Today's widespread pessimism seems paradoxical when one compares the present condition of the industrialized democracies with that of Europe or Japan, or even North America or Australasia, thirty years ago. We have all enjoyed prodigious economic growth, at higher rates and with fewer interruptions than ever before in history. Poverty is greatly reduced and social mobility increased. Yet neither public contentment nor respect for economic management shows corresponding improvement. The effectiveness of domestic economic policies is under strong political attack everywhere. The validity of international cooperation and the readiness to yield some degree of national autonomy are being severely questioned.

In particular, there is no longer a general belief, either by governors or governed, that the art of macro-economic demand management has become a virtual science—a science whose frontiers are concerned only with marginal refinements quaintly labelled "fine tuning." It is likewise recognized that the networks of international and transnational economic relationships create much more complex problems than merely avoiding the frustration of national demand management by inadvertent importation of unemployment or inflation from abroad. Yet the belief persists—and I consider it justified—that even if we must continue to grope in a condition of half knowledge and half ignorance, we will do better to grope together than each nation on its own.

It would, of course, be good to reduce the proportion of ignorance. The papers before us are designed to assist in that task. It is noteworthy that the several authors, writing entirely independently, converge on significant points. They all see much to be done in strengthening the structure and content of international collaboration, but they eschew grand institutional designs and simplistically doctrinaire policies. They appreciate the tensions between particularist pressures, whether functional or regional or national, and the wider potential gains from interdependence. They respect the power of market forces as allocators of resources and spurs to efficient management, but they also recognize the limitations of markets and the need for coherent relationships between market actions and decisions of public policy. They seek the mutual gain inherent in international economic cooperation without denying the existence of zero-sum, competitive elements which are also inherent in those relationships. They point to the fragilities and vulnerabilities, as well as the strengths, in the structures that have been developed during these thirty years, and the need for deliberate action to protect against those vulnerabilities. And in every case their discussions place cooperation among the industrial democracies in the wider framework of rapidly changing global relationships.

It was an outstanding characteristic of the Marshall Plan that, while the initiative came from the United States, its development into operational form and its subsequent implementation were joint products of trans-Atlantic

16

political, intellectual, and administrative collaboration. The collaborators were more concerned about pushing the program forward toward effective results than they were about who got the credit. That may be one reason for the quiet pride in the experience shared by those of us fortunate enough to have been participants. It is singularly appropriate that we should begin our proceedings with a review by one of the master architects of the Marshall Plan as a going concern. Lord Franks was chairman of the Committee on European Economic Cooperation which prepared the combined European response to Secretary Marshall during the summer of 1947. He is too well known to need an elaborate introduction today—a man equally at home in Embassies and Chancellories, in Lombard Street and Downing Street, in Whitehall and in the quadrangles of Oxford colleges. He will launch our Conference by introducing the topic: " Lessons of the Marshall Plan Experience. "

LESSONS OF THE MARSHALL PLAN EXPERIENCE

by Lord Franks, P.C., G.C.M.G., K.C.B.

Time is a great leveller. When we look back over thirty years to the Marshall Plan, a full generation of human life, it seems naturally to take its place in the history of the Western World since the Second World War, and we can easily fail to grasp its exceptional quality and significance.

No part of the story of the Marshall Plan—its conception, its execution, or its consequences—is remotely conceivable in relation to the twenty years between the First and the Second World Wars. Then the United States had withdrawn in isolation, while the nations of Western Europe each pursued their own national policies. When the Great Depression afflicted all, no collective effort of economic collaboration to accelerate recovery was possible. What a contrast is presented by the concerted activity and collaboration of 1947 and the immediately following years: in the spring of 1947 the economic and social state of Western Europe was far graver than in the thirties. Help was offered to Europe by the United States: in his speech of 5th June at Harvard General Marshall stressed its concern and involvement. " Any government, " he said, " that is willing to assist in the task of recovery will find full co-operation, I am sure, on the part of the United States government. " In the summer of 1947 the Committee of European Co-operation in response to the Harvard speech drew up a joint programme for economic recovery in which the needs of particular countries were not specified. Its successor, the Organisation for European Economic Co-operation, was able by unanimous agreement to divide the aid given by the United States and later to carry out major reforms in the fields of trade restriction and monetary policy. The Marshall Plan, in its conception and execution, gave rise to the idea of unity in Western Europe.

Everyone knows that the Marshall Plan was a success. I shall not burden you with an account of the stages of recovery. It is enough to say that as early as the second half of 1950 in the member countries of the Organisation for European Economic Co-operation industrial production was 25 per cent greater than in 1938, while steel was two thirds greater and agricultural production one third greater than in 1947. The deficit on dollar account had been reduced from $ 8.5 billion in 1947 to $ 1 billion in 1950.

I wish rather to invite your attention to two elements which, as I look back, seem to me to have been critical in the success achieved and which remain relevant to the issues of the present day.

The first was the initiative taken by the Americans. The formulation of policy was enlightened, generous, resolute, and swift. Its general aim may be illustrated by two short quotations, the first from Dean Acheson's speech on May 8th, 1947, at Cleveland, Mississipi, the other from the Harvard address itself. With characteristically austere eloquence Dean Acheson said: " Not only do human beings and nations exist in narrow economic margins, but also human dignity, human freedom, and democratic institutions. It is one of the principal aims of our foreign policy to-day to use our economic and financial resources to widen these margins. It is necessary if we are to preserve our own freedoms and our own democratic institutions. It is necessary for our national security. And it is our privilege and duty as human beings. " At Harvard General Marshall said: " Our policy is not directed against any country or doctrine but against hunger, poverty, desperation, and chaos. Its purpose should be the revival of a working economy in the world so as to permit the emergence of political and social conditions in which free institutions can exist. " In the policy of the United States government were blended enlightened self-interest and generosity of spirit.

Apart from preliminaries, the making of the policy began on April 28th when General Marshall returned from the Council of Foreign Ministers in Moscow. Those at work, besides the Secretary of State, were Dean Acheson, Will Clayton, George Kennan, Chip Bohlen, and Ben Cohen. The policy was announced in just over five weeks. So much for speed.

Throughout these weeks there was the will to act. It sprang particularly from General Marshall himself and Will Clayton. When the Secretary of State got back from Moscow he said in his radio address to the nation: " We were faced with immediate issues which vitally concerned the impoverished and suffering people of Europe who are crying for help, for coal, for food, and for most of the necessities of life... The patient is sinking while the doctors deliberate... action cannot await compromise through exhaustion. " When the next day he summoned George Kennan and put the Policy Planning Staff to work on the plan of action, his only advice was " Avoid trivia. " At the crucial meeting on May 28th, when the Secretary of State received the Policy Planning Staff's memorandum, " It would be folly, " he said, " to sit back and do nothing. " Will Clayton wrote two powerful memoranda, one in March, the other in May. In the first he spoke of hunger, economic misery, and frustration, and argued that prompt and effective aid was essential to the security of the United States; in the second he stated that for Europe to survive it must receive two and a half billion dollars annually of coal, bread grains, and shipping services: the facts were well known and there was no need for further study. I remember from my own experience the moral force with which Will Clayton, when convinced, put a case. His powers of persuasion were not easy to resist.

The Americans were far-sighted in the conditions they attached to their offer of help. The offer was made to Europe, not just to Western Europe.

19

They did not wish to divide Europe; responsibility for that must lie with the Russians, if they refused to accept, as they did. The programme for recovery must be drawn up, not by the Americans, but by the European nations who would therefore be responsible for it. The Americans foresaw that otherwise blame for any failure in the programme would rest with them; the initiative must come from Europe. Any European recovery programme must be a joint one for which all the participating nations took collective responsibility. A series of national programmes—a set of shopping lists—could do nothing, in the American belief, to alleviate in the longer run the fragmentation of the European economy and the absence of a large market. Lastly, the Americans saw clearly that without recovery in Germany there could not be recovery in Europe. They were aware of the feelings about Germany then prevalent in many countries of Europe, but were convinced that recovery in Europe required the revival of German productivity.

The policy of the government of the United States is the first critical element in the Marshall Plan. The American people were dominant and the peoples of Western Europe dependent on the United States for their future. But the Americans did not assert dominance over Europe by the formulation of the Marshall Plan; they impelled the Europeans in response to their offer to initiate action and together recreate Europe with American support.

The second critical element in my view was an idea, the idea of unity in Europe, in Western Europe, once Eastern Europe had withdrawn. It was alive in American thinking. It was in the mind of George Kennan as he drafted the report of the Policy Planning Staff for General Marshall: the insistence on a joint programme initiated by Europeans, so that they began to think like Europeans and move towards a larger, less fragmented market. When the Three Wise Men, Will Clayton, Lew Douglas and Jefferson Caffery, met the Committee of European Co-operation in session, I remember Will Clayton advocating the advantages of Customs Unions and their propriety under the GATT. It occurs in the statement of policy in the American Economic Co-operation Act: " Mindful of the advantages which the United States has enjoyed through the existence of a large domestic market with no internal trade barriers, and believing that similar advantages can accrue to the countries of Europe, it is declared to be the policy of the United States to encourage these countries through a joint organisation to exert sustained common efforts as set forth in the report of the Committee of European Co-operation. "

The idea of working towards unity in Europe was also alive in the thoughts of the European delegations to the Committee of European Economic Co-operation. The report itself is a European recovery programme, not merely a series of bids by and for particular countries. It states that " the controlling principle of the Committee's work has been the interdependence of the national economies of the countries concerned and, if these countries are to proceed quickly along the road to recovery, they must proceed together. " Again, " The Committee believes that, if means for carrying out the report are made available, a joint organisation to review progress achieved will be necessary.

This organisation will ensure, to the fullest extent possible by joint action, the realisation of the economic conditions necessary to enable the joint objectives to which each country has pledged itself to be effectively achieved. " The chapter of the report " On Economic Co-operation " refers to Customs Unions. It speaks of the progress already made by the three Benelux countries and refers to preliminary moves by the four Scandinavian countries. Most of the participating countries express their decision to set up a study group to examine the possibility of a Customs Union or Unions, while France, with Italy in association, recognises that the present division of Europe into small economic units does not correspond to the needs of modern competition and that it will be possible with the help of Customs Unions to construct larger units: France therefore stands ready to negotiate with any European governments sharing these views.

All these varying ways of seeking to give some expression to the idea of unity in Europe are to be found in the report of the CEEC, but only when the Committee drafted the Convention which set up the OEEC were alternative versions of the idea clarified and argued. In effect there were two concepts: the French were protagonists of one, the British of the other. The French wished the structure of the OEEC to have considerable power and authority at the centre. They wanted a strong executive board with power to act between the larger conferences of all the member countries. The Secretary-General of the international secretariat was to have authority to co-ordinate the activities of member countries and have the power to take major initiatives in policy. The British wished the OEEC to be under the control of the participating governments with the national delegations to the OEEC taking the leading role. It was to be an instrument of inter-governmental co-operation. There was a real issue. For the French, the idea of unity in Europe involved the admission in principle of a limitation on sovereign independence. The British would not accept in principle any such limitation.

The OEEC as set up by the Convention was broadly on the lines of the British rather than the French model: it was inter-governmental in character and decisions were reached by agreement. By the irony of history what was affirmed in principle was denied in practice. The Organisation was in permanent session. It possessed a permanent secretariat which implemented the decisions of the Council and continuously studied the European economy. This gave the OEEC an identity of its own. The national delegations, resident in Paris and working closely with the secretariat, built up an OEEC point of view, while keeping their governments fully informed. They and the secretariat together devised a number of techniques to persuade governments to a common view. Sir Eric Roll, who served with distinction in the British delegation, has summed it up: " The techniques of questionnaire and the mutual analysis of replies, the cross-examination of one's expectations and plans by one's peers, have had a powerful effect in moulding national policies. At the very least they have created a general readiness to ' look over one's shoulder ' before taking any major step in foreign policy, to ask what consequences it might have for one's partners, and how any adverse results might be mitigated. Subtler in its working, often as powerful, and sometimes even more so, than more rigorous constitutional obligations, this habit of consultation and co-operation has resulted in a real limitation of national sovereignty in economic matters. "

But the French thesis lived on in men's minds as an alternative approach. The French believed that unity in Europe should be institutionalised and that international institutions could be created which in one way or another recognised a limitation on national sovereignty. Inspiration and life were given by Jean Monnet and Robert Schuman. Jean Monnet, as a result of his experience in the First World War, was convinced that any group concerned with an international problem was strongly influenced by the structure within which it worked. An institution with a declared international purpose and agreed procedures changed the outlook of those who worked for it: they became international in their approach. Robert Schuman, a man from the Carolingian Middle Kingdom, believed in the unity of Europe but saw its foundation in the reconciliation of the two old enemies, France and Germany.

These convictions produced the proposal of 9th May 1950: " to place Franco-German production of coal and steel as a whole under a common higher authority, within the framework of an organisation open to the participation of other countries of Europe. " Further, " by pooling basic production and by instituting a new higher authority, whose decisions will bind France, Germany and other member countries, these proposals will lay the first concrete foundations of a European federation which is indispensable to the preservation of peace. " This constituted a radical new departure in the way of life of Western Europe. Six countries—France, Germany, Italy, Holland, Belgium, and Luxembourg—joined the European Coal and Steel Community, but the United Kingdom remained outside, adhering to its views on unity in Europe. The reason for refusing to join was made clear by the National Executive of the Labour Party then in power: it was the binding effect of the High Authority's decisions and the consequent limitation of sovereign independence.

As all know, this success of the French thesis had consequences. As a result of the Messina Conference of the Six, treaties establishing two new communities were signed in Rome in the spring of 1957: the European Economic Community and the European Atomic Energy Community came into being. Once again the United Kingdom stayed outside but British opinion slowly changed until a national referendum on 5th June 1975 showed that the people by a decisive majority wished to join the Communities. The British Government then accepted the negotiated conditions of entry and became a member, so closing a long chapter in the debate on the way in which unity in Europe should be pursued.

It would be false to maintain that all the member countries have at all times shown unwavering allegiance to the Communities. France, for instance, under General de Gaulle exhibited a resurgence of the spirit of national independence. The British have yet fully to learn the habits of thought and action natural to life in the European Community. But two things stand out from this long history since 1947. The idea of unity in Europe, which was embodied in American policy for the Marshall Plan, which was alive and obtained expression in the CEEC and the OEEC, as it worked in men's minds over time, has changed the face of Western Europe. And, secondly, this is due, not solely but first and foremost, to France whose leaders had the inspiration to devise an acceptable vision of a new order of life in this part of the world.

Machiavelli thought that the study of history afforded examples of politically relevant knowledge. Can this be true as we look back after thirty years at the Marshall Plan: in particular can it be true of the two critical elements in it, the nature and quality of American foreign policy and the idea of unity in Europe? The world of 1977 is different from that of 1947. Then the United States stood forth preeminent in power and wealth; the rest of the world was exhausted by the consequences of victory or defeat. Now there are two great powers, the United States and the Soviet Union, each equipped with the means to destroy industrial civilisation, and a third, China, prepares to join them. Germany and Japan through their manufactures and trade are strong and prosperous nations. The long post-war boom ended about ten years ago and since then stable patterns in the international exchange of money and goods have been hard to achieve. Complaints are heard that the economically stronger nations pursue monetary and fiscal policies which are relatively deflationary and impede the advance of the weaker, and it is asserted that the weaker are not willing to discipline themselves and put their houses in order.

Certainly the world has changed but not, I think, so much that the two critical elements I have picked out in the whole enterprise of the Marshall Plan no longer have relevance to contemporary problems and preoccupations. The Plan originated in a declaration by the United States that it was concerned for Europe and involved in its future. In 1947, the countries of Western Europe were dependent on the United States for the continuance of their social and economic life. Now Western Europe is a going concern, some peoples being more prosperous, others less so, but, taken as a whole, it is vigorous and enjoys high standards of living. Does this mean that the old relationship is outmoded and has become irrelevant? I do not think this is the case. Western Europe, the European Economic Community, is still dependent upon the United States for its security, and its prosperity is directly linked to that of the United States. Many of the younger generation do not wish to accept this fact. Too young to remember the Marshall Plan, their minds are coloured by memories of the war in Vietnam and of Watergate. They do not trust America or American foreign policy. But these aberrations are only part of the story; in the same years the strength of democratic institutions in the United States was sufficient to prevail on one President not to offer himself for re-election and to cause another President to resign. And the facts are unchanged: in the existing global constellation of power Western Europe depends on the United States. I remain confident that the reliance is not misplaced. It Western Europe needs the United States, the United States needs Western Europe and the European Community. On this side of the Atlantic there are several hundreds of millions of creative, able, and industrious people who collectively are of major weight and influence in world affairs. It is, and will continue to be, a vital interest of the United

States that these people, to paraphrase the words of General Marshall at Harvard, should continue to enjoy the political and social conditions in which free institutions can exist. As in 1947, so in 1977, it is the common interest of the United States and Western Europe that the concern and involvement of the United States in Western Europe and the European Economic Community should continue.

The second critical element was the idea of unity in Europe, an idea present from the beginning of the Marshall Plan. No one could assert that to-day this idea is outmoded or outworn. The institutions we see existing and functioning, the Coal and Steel Community, the Economic Community, and the Atomic Energy Community are compelling evidence of the vitality and power of the idea. What is there to be learned for the future as we look back on the history of these developments? The first point to make is that, as I have pointed out, they sprang from the French thesis about the way to unity. I wish to draw your attention to two constituents of the thesis which are present in the first creation, the Coal and Steel Community. On the one hand, the Community is declared to be a first stage towards a political end, the federation of Europe. On the other, the sphere of action of the Community is expressly limited to one main sector of the economies concerned, coal and steel. The proposal for the Community exhibited a practical, down-to-earth approach in singling out for the experiment one sector, admittedly of the highest importance and containing the potentiality of political conflict. Both constituents were well put in the original announcement of the French Government: " Europe will not be made all at once, or according to a single, general plan. It will be built through concrete achievements, which first create a *de facto* solidarity. "

Looking back to this historical event in the spirit of Machiavelli, I hold that we can learn from it in relation to present problems. It is true that the idea of unity in Europe points in the end to a political federation of Western European peoples. Their nations are accustomed to play a role in world affairs. They wish to be in the room when great decisions are taken and have a voice in the deliberations. The larger nations of Western Europe have up to sixty million citizens. What chance is there that any of them alone will be able to exert influence and have an effective voice in a world of super-powers? Alone, any one European nation is unimportant. It is only if together and able to speak with one voice that the peoples can make an effective contribution and have a voice in their own destinies. And while they have not, it is not only they who are frustated but the world is the poorer. The ultimate condition of Western Europe playing its due part in the world is a political federation able to declare a united policy.

But the proposers of the Coal and Steel Community were both realistic and wise. They knew that in 1950 Western Europe was not ready for political federation. Progress towards that end entailed a series of limited, practical experiments in the art of living and working together and developing an international point of view. Hence the sector approach. The success of the Coal and Steel Community was the precondition of the next step, the customs union of the Economic Community. It is still the case that in 1977

24

Western Europe is not ready for political federation. But this does not mean that further advances are not possible. Indeed it is imperative that they should be made, for life and its institutions cannot stand still; there must either be progress and growth or there will be decline and decay. The potentialities of the Economic Community are far from exhausted and, if we look back on the model which history presents to us, vigorous and constructive advance can be made through the sector approach.

It seems obvious that progress should be made in three directions. Each involves the exertion of political will and is difficult, though not impossible, just as the original Coal and Steel Community was the creation of a sustained act of will which, inspired by the vision of unity, overcame the difficulties, material and historical, between France and Germany.

The first is agriculture. The existing agricultural policies of the Community are unsuccessful. This failure is symbolised by the so-called mountain of butter, evidence of the inability to prevent the systematic overproduction of milk. Policy appears to have got lost in a morass of bureaucracy and to be smothered by mounds of paper. Of course, the difficulties in overcoming the existing inertia are real; each member country has political problems about its own agriculture, and the Community as a whole has problems with the world at large. But I recall the English proverb: " Where there is a will, there is a way. " The opportunity and the need are clear. Agriculture presents a major, critical, but limited problem; a constructive solution is overdue.

Then there is energy. It is asserted that in thirty years or so the production of oil will be falling while demand increases. The United States over the next decades will certainly be importing large and increasing quantities of oil to offset the progressive shortfall in its domestic production. Oil from the North Sea has, it is predicted, a limited duration. Now and in the near future the Economic Community is heavily dependent on oil for energy. If over the next thirty years the availability of oil is likely to diminish and the price exacted by foreign suppliers to rise yet more steeply, the issue is whether alternative sources of energy can be enlarged to fill the gap. It is not certain that the production of coal can be sufficiently increased nor is it possible to be sure that men will be willing to go underground to mine it at wage costs that the Community can afford. There is bound to be serious consideration of major programmes for the production of nuclear energy. But at present there is not agreement in the high technology of this form of energy about the plants which are the best and most efficient, or the safest, to build. And any major programme would involve problems in the disposal of radioactive waste which raise social, environmental, and indeed philosophical issues. Now is not too soon for the reason and will of the Community to be put to work on a constructive and unified energy policy.

Lastly I come to the most difficult and politically the most challenging sector, that of monetary policy. Long ago in the field of money and payments the OEEC was able by stages to forge the European Payments Union despite objections and difficulties urged perhaps in particular by the United Kingdom, but the Payments Union worked well and to the benefit of all. Action, common policy and action, was possible in the field of money. But monetary policy itself is a great challenge. Every government believes that monetary policy is an important instrument in the control of the economy. Every government tends to shrink from allowing the use of this instrument to be inhibited or subjected to a discipline which it does not itself impose. Yet governments are not as free as they would like to think in devising their monetary policies: the external pressures of international trade and the balance of payments severely restrict their scope of manœuvre. Response to these pressures is not in fact a positive decision. It is an illusion for governments to assert that by themselves they can individually decide what they will do on monetary matters. In the early years of the OEEC liberalisation of trade and of monetary arrangements went hand in hand and were complementary to each other. Together with the essential support of Marshall Aid they constituted the foundation of the prosperity that Western Europe has achieved. The European Community through its Common Market has achieved a great liberalisation of trade. That large step forward awaits and needs its complement, a common monetary policy, if the potential for productivity and prosperity of the Community and its members is fully to be realised.

4

COMMENT

by Dr. Ernst van der Beugel (Netherlands)

Lord Franks in his admirable paper brought us back to what certainly for many of us will remain one of the most exciting and constructive periods of our working life. He rightly points out that in the summer of 1947 in the Petit Palais in 90° without air conditioning the basis was laid for the restructuring of the Western world. Imaginitive and bold.

Those who were to speak with Dean Acheson, present at the creation, will never forget it. Nor will they forget that these meetings were chaired by Sir Oliver Franks. My generation was spoilt for the rest of our lives by serving under the very best chairmen in the very beginning of our careers.

The Marshall Plan was what the London *Economist* called, in 1948, " an act without peer in history. " And in the same article the *Economist* wrote: " This week it is fitting that the peoples of Western Europe should attempt to renew their capacity to wonder so that they can return to the United States a gratitude in some way commensurate with the act they are about to receive. " One more quote more than anything else symbolises for me the element of generosity in the Marshall Plan to which Lord Franks so rightly refers.

In its final report, the Select Committee on Foreign Aid of the United States House of Representatives, known as the Herter Committee, wrote: " If we undertake the proposed European Recovery Programme, we are in effect assuming the responsibility for the economic revival of Western Europe. Responsibility without power is a situation generally avoided by cautious people, but the alternative in terms of human lives, human misery, and human slavery is perhaps too frightful to permit us the luxury of being cautious. "

In the fashionable " debunking " exercise of United States foreign policy, it is often said that the United States adopted the policy of the Marshall Plan out of sheer self interest. I find this a rather absurd argument. No nation—and certainly no powerful nation—can base its foreign policy on anything else than its own interest. The relevant question is whether the interpretation of self interest is narrow and short-term, or constructive, imaginative, and focused on long term trends. The policy of the major

27

European powers in the 1930s are an example of the first; the Marshall Plan was a superb example of the latter.

So much for the past. Today we should not be overwhelmed by our nostalgia but should face the present. The least one can say is that the world has become much more complicated. Trotsky was right when he said in 1917 that anyone desiring a quiet life had done badly to be born in the 20th Century. After all, life in 1947 was relatively simple. It seems to me that the main characteristics of the first fifteen to twenty post-war years were: First, that the Western system was guided and managed by the United States in a position of near monopoly of political, economic, and military strength. The American leadership was accepted in Europe and (let us not forget) in the United States. Second, it was assumed that the process of European unification would in a relatively short time, and rather automatically, lead to the creation of a single political and economic actor of major importance on the world scene. The interests and policies of Europe and the United States would be roughly parallel. Third, the international system was dominated by the adverse relationship between the United States and the Soviet Union; the United States still enjoyed military superiority. Fourth, the economic assumptions, both domestically and internationally, were liberal and neo-classical. The international system was based on GATT, the International Monetary Fund, fixed parities, and the predominance of the dollar. The Western world, both internationally and domestically, believed in free market forces. Welfare was equated with growth and efficient production. And the United States acted as the leader of the economic game—or at least as its referee.

Fifth and finally, these facts, values, and assumptions were shared by the overwhelming majority of those who made and influenced policies on both sides of the ocean. In other words, there existed a near consensus on the leadership of the United States, the assumptions of the process of European integration, the adverse relationship with the Soviet Union, and the rules of the economic game.

Time does not permit me to elaborate what has changed in these five characteristics of the first fifteen to twenty post-war years. Those were the years of which Henry Kissinger said that the consequences of our mistakes were still manageable.

United States leadership was affected by the growing strength of Japan and Western Europe and domestically by the combination of Vietnam and Watergate. Fortunately—and miraculously—the United States has overcome the traumatic effects of these last events. Traumatic because if there is a difference between Americans and Europeans (and I am always rather reluctant to register differences between Americans and Europeans) one could perhaps say that in general Americans live in the expectation of success and Europeans live in the expectation of disaster.

The position of military superiority of the United States has been gradually replaced by military parity between the United States and the Soviet Union, and the consensus about the relationship with the Soviet Union has been gravely affected. Furthermore, there is no longer consensus on the basic rules of the economic game. Both internationally and domestically, the preponderance of free market forces is in jeopardy.

Let me focus my comments briefly on what has changed in two of the main characteristics of the early post-war years: the assumptions concerning the automatic character of European integration and the near consensus about the main elements of foreign policy in the policy-making establishment of the Western world.

A few facts have become very clear. First, in our efforts to structure the Western world, we have gravely underestimated—especially in Europe—the toughness and tenacity of the nation-state. In other words, we have been wrong in assuming that the preponderance of domestic political and economic structures was on the way out. The malaise of European integration is not primarily caused by incidental foreign policy acts of different European governments but by a much deeper phenomenon: the toughness of the domestic structure, the preponderance of the nation-state—which is something quite different from old fashioned nationalism. The failure of Europeans to achieve greater unity among themselves has been mainly due to their conflicting outlooks on what is reasonable, responsible, and realistic in terms of their internal political situations.

This preponderance of the domestic structures has been increased by two other phenomena. Most European countries have governments which rule by slight majorities or coalitions or both. Most of them are weak. One gets the impression that not men but events are the present masters of Europe. And weak governments are very sensitive to domestic pressures when they formulate their foreign policies. The interaction between domestic and foreign policy is infinitely greater now than in the early post-war period.

A second factor which increases the preponderance of the domestic structure over foreign policy considerations is the growing and vastly increasing role of governments in the economic and social life of our countries. The welfare state, the *état providence*, is a national animal and the nation becomes —more than we ever expected—the natural framework of loyalty and dependence of the average citizen.

This does not imply for a moment that I find myself in disagreement with Lord Franks' statement that the two critical elements of the Marshall Plan—the reliance on the United States and the idea of European unity—have not lost their great and lasting validity. On the contrary. But the changes which have taken place do imply, it seems to me, that we should patiently adapt ourselves to new forms of interdependence rather than cling to what we thought and hoped was the ideal structure of the Atlantic world thirty or even fifteen years ago.

Miriam Camps has given us the keyword—" the management of interdependence "—and there we have a long and difficult road to follow. If we keep in mind, however, that in a changed world the two critical elements of the Marshall Plan are as valid as they were thirty years ago, we might have a chance to succeed.

5

COMMENT

by Mrs. Miriam Camps (United States)

I find it very difficult to disagree with Lord Franks that the crucial elements in the success of the Marshall Plan were the character of the US initiative and the idea of European unity. But I think it worth underlining that Lord Franks characterized American policy not only as " enlightened and generous " but also as " resolute and swift. " The same could, of course, be said for the nature of the European response. Secretary Marshall made his speech in June 1947. By September the Committee for European Economic Co-operation, headed by Lord Franks, had drawn up the joint European programme and was discussing it in Washington. By April of 1948 the Economic Co-operation Act had become law and the Charter of the OEEC had been signed.

An elapsed time of about ten months is not bad for a programme that was expected to cost the United States $ 16 billion (and they were *1948* dollars) and which committed sixteen European countries to a wholly new kind of collective action. Contrast that with the response to the energy crisis. The The Arabs imposed their embargo in October 1973, and the OPEC countries raised the price of oil shortly thereafter. Yet only now has the United States begun serious consideration of anything that can honestly be called an energy policy; and the record of the European Community, as Lord Franks has pointed out, is not much better. Why is it that large ideas could be translated into action so much more quickly then than they can now? Are the issues really so much more complex or are we simply more aware of their complexity? Is it more sophistication or less confidence that tends to make swift and resolute action so difficult today?

Mr Crozier's paper deals with this central problem and we shall discuss it in more detail later. Certainly those of us who were involved in the early days of the Marshall Plan—on both sides of the Atlantic—were not only full of confidence but undoubtedly rather simplistic in our tackling of large problems; sometimes we had little but enthusiasm to guide us. But I wonder whether those who are responsible today do not suffer from too rich a diet of facts and theories. If it is impossible to take any decision until all the available data have been collected and analysed and all the paths of interconnectedness and feedback traced through, too much information can be as bad in its own way as too little information. And if in the future American and European policies are to be not only " enlightened and generous " but also " swift and resolute, " we shall have to learn how to master a superabundance of knowledge and find new ways to speed up the process of government decision-making.

The second critical factor identified by Lord Franks, the idea of European unity, was at that time an imprecise and controversial idea. It still is. As a junior officer in the State Department concerned with European questions, I participated in seemingly endless meetings about what the Europeans meant when they talked of unity or unification, about what we thought they should mean, about how far it was appropriate for us to support one concept rather than another, and whether we should push or simply support. In one memorable incident, we in the State Department suggested to the ECA that they use the phrase " integration of Europe " instead of " unification of Europe. " We felt " integration " was less precise, sounded more economic and less political and was, therefore, likely to be more readily acceptable to all the countries concerned. The phrase stuck, but the ambiguity remains. Rather ironically, in a book written by a European a few years ago, the American use of the word " integration " instead of " unification " was applauded for giving precision to an inchoate idea.

One of the more interesting speculations of the " what would have happened if " variety, is whether or not things would be appreciably different today had the British government (and some of the other European governments that shared their views) agreed to include in the original charter of the OEEC a firm commitment to form a customs union, as various European and American leaders were then urging be done. At that time, there were sixteen countries in the OEEC; shortly, if the present applicants are admitted, there will be twelve members of the European community, and one or two further additions seem probable. Would the inventiveness and energy that found expression in the Schuman plan and in the early days of the European Economic Community have been channelled instead into forming the wider customs union and developing it into a true economic union? Would things be in better shape today if the long years of negotiation—first on the abortive free trade area in the late 'fifties and then, in the early 'sixties and again in the early 'seventies—on British entry into the Community had been rendered unnecessary and the amazing intellectual capital invested in those three sets of negotiations used instead to solve the problems of the European economy? Or would the attempt to form a European customs union in tandem with putting into effect the other aspects of the European recovery programme have been too big a step, causing both enterprises to founder? These are intriguing avenues for speculation. But the past cannot be replayed, and whether better paths to the present might have been taken is a less important question than where we should go from here.

In his opening comments, Lord Franks singled out agriculture, energy, and money as the three areas in which renewed European efforts to define and pursue common policies are needed. The reform of the common agri-

31

cultural policy and the development of a European energy policy, although very difficult to bring about, do not, perhaps, raise quite the same kind of problem as the third—monetary union. There are those, and some of them are in this room, who argue that the need for deeper and more frequent co-ordination of monetary and other macro-economic policies among the core countries of the industrialised world—Western Europe, the United States and Canada, and Japan—has rendered obsolete the need for further progress towards economic union in Europe. Like Lord Franks, I question this view. But I do think that the consultations on monetary policy that are now taking place—not only in the OECD and the IMF but also with increasing frequency at a very high level in the Groups of Five, Six, or sometimes Seven— have reduced the scope for certain kinds of Community action.

The half-way house of policy consultation and harmonization has been pre-empted. There is room for some useful additional action on a Community basis, but there is not *much* room *unless* the countries of the Community are really prepared to accept economic and monetary union as their eventual goal. And, despite the continuing rhetorical commitment to this goal, the reality of the commitment seems to me still to be in doubt. Given the discrepancy in rates of inflation, in economic performance, in standards of living, monetary union is obviously not for today. But if monetary union really were the long-term objective, this would have implications, in the short-term, for regional policy, for the way Community funds are fed and used, for the way Community currencies relate to the " snake, " and for the way Community countries act in wider forums. In none of these areas is there much evidence of the kinds of action one might assume would flow from a firm commitment to the eventual goal of monetary union.

Monetary union, like European union, means different things to different people. What it is sensible for the Community countries to aim at, and how Community action might reinforce or cut across action in the monetary field that is now needed on a broader basis, are very large and difficult subjects. We shall inevitably come back to them later when we turn to the discussion of the relationships among the industrialised countries.

In the few minutes remaining to me, let me summarise, very briefly, my own views about the topic before us: the continuing relevance of the Marshall Plan. I think it gave an essential impulse to three interlocking processes. First, the process of organising Europe; second, the process of establishing an enduring U.S.-European relationship; and third, the process of establishing a functioning international economic system. All three processes are still needed.

Despite all the ambiguities that surrounded and still surround the concept of integration or unification, I think it was of central significance that Secretary Marshall asked for a European initiative and that the response was a European programme, not sixteen separate national programmes. Mutual assistance on a European basis was built into the programme from the start; the various European payments arrangements, culminating in the EPU, were designed to ensure that American aid was a residual, drawn on after European resources had been used more effectively. The Marshall Plan and the OEEC were not the first, nor were they the most ambitious, efforts to pull Europe together, but they were undoubtedly landmarks in the process of " thinking European. "

As Lord Franks pointed out, the Marshall Plan committed the U.S. to Europe in a way that was historically unprecedented. It made the even more far-reaching commitment to NATO easier than might otherwise have been the case, and it made the later transformation of the OEEC into the OECD a logical development. The concept of an Atlantic Community as an alternative to the European Community has beguiled, and in my view distracted, some people at some times; and perhaps it still does. It is unfortunate that the same word—community—has been used to describe what are two quite different kinds of relationship. A close and enduring relationship between the United States and an organised Europe has been for the last thirty years central to the policies of governments on both sides of the Atlantic. It continues to be truly fundamental. But the Atlantic process is one of co-operation and co-ordination, not, as is the European process, one that envisages the progressive substitution of common policies for separate national policies. Moreover, as the addition of Japan, Australia, and New Zealand to the OECD has shown, the Atlantic relationship, at least in its economic dimension, is increasingly becoming a relationship shared by all the highly developed industrialised democracies.

The third process, that of establishing a functioning international economic system, was also given a critically important impulse by the Marshall Plan. The phrase in Marshall's speech about the " revival of a working economy in the world " clearly had a more limited meaning to most people in 1947 than the same words have today—more limited both in geographic scope and in terms of the extent and intensity of the interactions that go to making up a working international economy. But the Marshall Plan was always an outward-looking conception, perhaps at times rather too outward-looking for some of the more impatient " Europeans " on both sides of the Atlantic. Tension between the two objectives of encouraging the emergence of a strong, healthy European economy and of strengthening the global system was inevitable. But as the history of the EPU and the Code of Trade Liberalization demonstrated, the two objectives need not conflict but can be mutually sustaining.

The recovery of Europe was obviously an end that was eminently worth seeking on its own; but it was also a necessary step in a wider process. And it seems to me that today we must view the tasks before the industrial democracies in rather similar terms: there is much they need to do to deal with the problems posed by their own interconnectedness and their openness and vulnerability to each others actions. But the OECD, like the OEEC before it, is not a closed system and it should not seek to be one. Now even more than then, the management of our own interrelationships must be complemented by an awareness of and a concern for the broader system. And it is in their dual role as the motor and the balance wheel of a global economy and an emerging world economic system that is efficient, equitable, and flexible enough to respond rapidly to new problems that those countries that made a resounding success of the Marshall Plan will find their main challenge in the years ahead.

One brief final reflection. Thirty years ago we had no doubt that economics was politics and *vice versa*. For a time in the intervening years there has been a tendency to think that the two could be kept in separate boxes and that economic problems could be solved by brains and money, if applied in adequate quantities. We are at last shedding that illusion and realising, once again, that it is political economy, after all, which we must try to understand.

6

SUMMARY OF THE DISCUSSION

The discussion revolved around two main themes: the outlook for further development of the European Communities and the relations between Western Europe and wider geographical frameworks—other industrial countries, developing countries, and global.

With respect to Western Europe, all speakers concurred that the roots of the European Communities lay in the Marshall Plan itself and in the intra-European trade and payments arrangements developed through the OEEC. There were differences of view, however, concerning the conceptual significance and the political obstacles involved in further moves toward economic and monetary union. One former Commissioner of the European Economic Community saw a fundamental difference between the achievement of a customs union, relinquishing tariffs and other trade barriers, and a move to monetary unity, which would require a pooling of all instruments of domestic economic and financial policy, and therefore a pooled political sovereignty. In today's circumstances, he saw no early prospect of such a move, since European governments and peoples are not now prepared to relinquish control over domestic economic policy. None the less, he continued to believe in European political unity as an ultimate goal, necessary for the preservation of freedom as well as for an adequate role on the world scene.

Another former Commissioner, on the other hand, supported a more incremental view. He explained that the "commitment" to European economic and monetary union at the summit meeting of 1969 at The Hague was based on the premise that the maintenance even of a customs union required arrangements for the reconciliation of national economic and financial policies, in addition to a common trade policy. In his view, the plan for economic and monetary union worked out at that time might have come into being had it not been disrupted by the "dollar crisis" of August, 1971.

Other speakers emphasized that Western Europe is too limited an area to deal effectively with many contemporary problems of economic policy. That was the case in each of the three major sectors identified by Lord Franks—agriculture, energy, and monetary policy. Reform of Europe's unsatisfactory "common agricultural policy" could be effectively undertaken only as part of a global system of coordination of food and agricultural policies. International energy cooperation must extend at least to the entire

35

industrialized world represented in the OECD, and ideally also to the oil exporters, the less developed oil-importing countries, and the communist countries. On monetary policy, so long as Western Europe fell short of monetary unification, harmonization with the other international financial giants, notably the United States and Japan, was at least as important as harmonization within the European Community itself.

Note was also taken of the difficulties often experienced in achieving common positions within the Community on matters other than trade and agriculture, and the resulting tendency for those matters to be negotiated directly between individual national European governments and outside governments. In most of the comments, however, there was some endorsement of Mrs. Camps' view that Western Europe still had the potential of a closer degree of integration of economic policies—and perhaps an ultimate fusion of sovereignties—than the wider " OECD community, " even though that wider community was not very distant from a customs union in industrial goods and was increasingly engaged in efforts at harmonization of macroeconomic policies.

Several references were made to relations between industrial and developing countries—the " North-South " issues under official review in the Paris meeting of the Conference on International Economic Cooperation just drawing to a close. No one considered the Marshall Plan a directly relevant precedent for handling those issues in operational terms, but an historical connection was noted in the principle of rich countries accepting some responsibility for assisting the economic development of poorer countries.

Finally, there was concurrence with the contrast drawn by Mrs. Camps between the " resolute and swift " action taken in 1947-48 to set Europe on the road to economic recovery, and the seeming paralysis of today in many aspects of domestic affairs as well as in international cooperation. One speaker attributed the contrast to the felt presence of a common enemy thirty years ago, while others believed that fear of economic collapse had been the main motivation, with the Cold War becoming an important factor only in 1949-50. Today, the problems themselves seem more intractable; international issues are inextricably mixed with domestic issues of vital concern to insecure governments; and the catalyst of a common enemy or common fear of economic catastrophe is lacking. The economic recession and inflationary stagnation of recent years have undermined confidence in the management of macroeconomic policies domestically and internationally. Yet interdependence is an objective reality which is too precious to be abandoned. The hope was expressed by a Japanese spokesman that common positive objectives would become a sufficient basis—without requiring a common enemy—for reconciling differences in domestic policies which reflect differing cultures and values. The Marshall Plan had succeeded in that objective as between North America and Western Europe; a similar achievement was now required on a world-wide scale.

II

STRUCTURAL EVOLUTION
IN INDUSTRIALIZED SOCIETIES

by Professor Michel Crozier

I

Before coming to the substance of the question I have been asked to deal with, two preliminary remarks seem to me to be called for, one concerning the concept of structure and the other the concept of evolution.

The concept of structure which was dominant in the past seems to me to be ill-suited to our present situation. It evoked of course the determinism of organised hierarchies, underlying trends, and behavioural factors. It had the advantage of providing reassurance by offering the simplest and most efficient support for the arguments of forecasters. But it was an easy target for criticism and even for the most radical contestation: the overemphasis on rigidities and conditioning that it denoted called attention to conformist tendencies and feelings of alienation which were then in their turn to be overemphasized.

Now, on the contrary, it seems clear to me that it is the confusion rather than the ridigity of structures, their weakness and vulnerability rather than their capacity for manipulation, that henceforth constitute the problem.

So I shall use the term structures in its broadest sense, that is to say as the aggregate of the arrangements which enable people to maintain fruitful coope- rative relationships, and not in its narrow sense of hierarchical apparatuses and social determinisms. And the question I propose to examine will be about means, not ends: given the minimum objectives of economic efficiency and social peace that a society must set itself, are our structures adequate, or will they pose problems?

My second remark has to do with the significance of the concept of evolution. I believe that we have been much too obsessed with macro- economic or macrosocial methods of reasoning which highlight continuities more apparent at aggregate level, and minimize the partial crises which are masked by the smoothness of the curves, and are quite inadequate for giving early warning of problems, thus leading to major crises and breakdowns.

Extrapolation of development curves is indeed an excellent means of projection, for the short term, at least. But if carried on too long, it inevitably

37

leads to absurdities. Not only do phenomena change in time, but their relations inter se do too, as does the structuring of the field of which they form part. Hence it is no longer possible to integrate them in the same way into a viable whole, and if a fresh effort is not made to bring the systems or subsystems in question under control once more, crisis and decline are unavoidable.

The increasingly uncertain context in which we have to live makes us more keenly aware in this perspective that the evolution of structures cannot be dealt with, as there was too great a tendency to do, as a problem of observation—of identifying the underlying trends, if not indeed the laws of development, or as a problem of sound planning—as if people could freely decide on their future and model the social systems of which they form part accordingly. We are necessarily reduced to a much more pragmatic attitude: what we must try to do is to anticipate the problems and develop in time the capacities needed to resolve them.

II

Instead of analysing trends and prognosticating about future development, I should now like to try to present, starting from these opening remarks, a sociological diagnosis of the problems which industrialized societies, and more especially the European societies, will henceforth encounter.

My thesis can be summed up as follows: the economic growth of the past three decades has entailed a much more than proportional increase in the complexity of human relationships and the decisional systems coordinating them. Correlatively, it has entailed partial disintegration of the traditional instruments of social control, and more particularly of the structures for containing and controlling incompatibility and conflict.

Despite the instinctive reactions of the social corpus, which spontaneously generates many important initiatives, we can observe in all our societies that the capacity for command and control of our social complexes and decision systems has weakened appreciably at the very time when demand by individuals has strengthened. The result is not only the vague uneasiness we are already experiencing, but threats of coming crisis and decline. The societies of western Europe are particularly exposed to these dangers. This situation will persist as long as we have not succeeded in developing means of social control and decision systems better suited to the infinitely more complex problems with which we are now faced.

III

First let us tackle the problem of decision-making. At the most commonplace level, it is characterized by cumbersomeness. Everywhere and at all levels, the number of participants, the number of persons, groups, and institutions which have to be consulted or which may be involved has expanded

38

exponentially. The number of operations required has become considerable and in spite of all efforts the time needed to carry them out seems to make action impossible.

The superiority of democracies has often been ascribed to their basic openness. Open systems, however, give better returns only under certain conditions. They are threatened by entropy if they cannot maintain or develop proper regulation.

European democracies have been only partially and sometimes theoretically open. Their regulations were built on a subtle screening of participants and demands; and if we can talk of overload, notwithstanding the progress made in handling complexity, it is because this traditional model of screening and government at a distance has gradually broken down to the point that the necessary regulations have all but disappeared.

Let me take an example I have recently studied: the comparison made between two similar decisions made in Paris in the 1890's and in the 1960's: the decision to build the first Parisian subway and the decision to build the new regional express transit system. This comparison shows a dramatic decline between the two periods in the capacity to take rational decisions. The 1890 decision gave rise to a very difficult but lively political debate and was a slow decision-making sequence, but it was arrived at on sound premises financially, economically, and socially. The 1960 decision was made in conditions of semisecrecy, without open political debate, but with a tremendous amount of lobbying and intrabureaucratic conflict. Its results, when one analyses the outcomes, were strikingly poorer in terms of social, economic, and financial returns. It seems that the elite professional decision-makers backed up by sophisticated tools could not do as well as their less brilliant predecessors, while the technical complexity of the decision was certainly not greater. The only striking difference is the tremendous increase in the level of complexity of the system and its dramatic overload due to its confusing centralization.

There are a number of interrelated reasons for this situation. First of all, scientific and technical progress has made it necessary to mobilize a great many more different authorities for the same single project. Second, social and economic developments have made it possible for a great many more groups and interests to coalesce. Third, the information explosion has made it difficult if not impossible to maintain the traditional distance that was deemed necessary to govern. Fourth, the democratic ethos makes it difficult to prevent access and to restrict information, while the persistence of the bureaucratic processes which had been associated with the traditional governing systems makes it impossible to handle them at a low enough level. Because of the instant information model, and because of this lack of self-regulating subsystems, any kind of minor conflict becomes a governmental problem.

These convergences and contradictions have given rise to a growing paradox. While it has been traditionally believed that the power of the state depended on the number of decisions it could take, the more decisions the modern state has to handle, the more helpless it becomes. Decisions do not only bring power; they also bring vulnerability. The modern State's

39

basic weakness is its susceptibility to blackmailing tactics. This is especially damaging in Western Europe, where it is also gradually developing within many other institutions: large-scale industrial organisations, trade unions, hospitals and churches for example.

Another series of factors tending to overload all industrial or post-industrial social systems develops from the natural complexity which is the result of organisational growth, systemic interdependence, and the shrinking of a world where fewer consequences can be treated as acceptable externalities. European societies not only do not escape this general trend; they also do not face it with the necessary increase of governing capacities. Politicians and administrators have found it easier and more expedient to give in to complexity. They tend to adjust to it and even to employ it as a useful smokescreen. One can give access to more groups and more demands without having to say " no " and one can maintain and expand one's own freedom of action or, in more unpleasant terms, one's own irresponsibility.

Beyond a certain degree of complexity, however, nobody can control the outcomes of one system; government credibility declines; decisions come from nowhere; citizens' alienation develops and irresponsible blackmail increases, and a vicious circle thus develops. One might argue that the Lindblom model of partisan mutual adjustment would give a natural order to this chaotic bargaining, but this does not seem to be the case because the fields are at one and the same time poorly structured and not regulated.

One might also wonder why European nations should suffer more complexity and more overload than the United States, which obviously was a more complex system open to more participants. But overload and complexity are only relative to the capacity to handle them; and the present weakness of the European nations comes from the fact that their capacity is much lower because their tradition has not enabled them to build decision-making systems based on these premises. This judgment about the European nation-states' decision-making capabilities may be surprising since European countries, like Britain and France, pride themselves on having the best possible élite corps of professional decision-makers, in many ways better trained or at least better selected than their American counterparts. The seeming paradox can be understood if one accepts the idea that decision-making is not done only by top civil servants and politicians but is the product of bureaucratic processes taking place in complex organisations and systems. If these processes are routine-oriented and cumbersome, and these organisations and systems overly rigid, communications will be difficult, no regulation will prevent blackmail, and the defects of the structure will increase the overload. For all their sophistication, modern decision-making techniques do not so far seem to have helped very much because the problem is political or systemic and not a technical one.

Recent developments have forced us to face up to the results of the underlying trend of the last thirty years. Everywhere in the industrialised democratic societies we are living a climate of bureaucratic crisis.

In Europe especially there are increasing areas where governments' capacity to act and to meet the challenge of citizens' demands has been drastically

40

impaired. Almost everywhere secondary education and the universities, and in many cases, metropolitan government, land use, and urban renewal as well, are adversely affected. This impairment of capacities is becoming prevalent in more countries in bargaining among groups, income redistribution, and the handling of inflation.

Why has complexity grown so much and so rapidly? From a sociologist's point of view, it is the consequence of the basic explosion of social interaction and of communication. In every developed industrial or post-industrial society man has become much more a social animal than before. The social texture of human life has become and is becoming more and more complex because in all activities more people interact with an increasing number of others. Exchange of goods and of activities is also an exchange between people. There can be no economic growth without such a social premise. There are, indeed, limits that depend on the sheer capacity of people to handle these interactions. But the choices people make are of a very different nature from those they had to make in the past. This is quite clear in the case of the exponential growth of communications. The basic rule on these matters seems to me to be the following: from a leader's point of view people never know what they should know, nor what they should have seen in the mass of papers they process. But what they should *not* know they know immediately. As a result dispersion, fragmentation, and simple ranking tend to be replaced by concentration, interdependence, and a complex texture. There seems to have been much more order in the fragmented universe of the past, and there is much more confusion in the more integrated one of today.

IV

Now let us try and see the other side of the problem. Why is it so hard to cope with the inevitable complexity? Why does it take so long to discover the means of social control, the modes of government that could master it?

Quite simply because it is almost impossible to distinguish the complexity of the problem from the weakness or rather the inadequacy of the means for dealing with it. Mastery presupposes simplification and ordering. Complexity is reduced by development of new means or rather new methods. What is happening now? The structures of authority seem to be crumbling in all countries and in all fields: businesses, government bodies, religious and even scientific institutions, trade unions, the political parties themselves. These facts are usually interpreted in terms of values. I am not convinced that that is the right approach. The problem appears to me to be simpler and more concrete. The increase in exchanges and interactions among people entails, in the free-enterprise context of Western Europe, an extraordinary expansion of freedom of choice of which we have not really become aware. It is that freedom of choice which is the major source of tension undermining the authority relationship. Freedom of choice means for each individual a larger set of alternatives, hence the possibility of playing several games at the same time, and therefore no longer being really dependent on someone else.

41

Negotiation between superior and subordinate is radically altered if the subordinate has reasonable alternatives available to him at any time. A leader who depends on his subordinates for achieving his objective and who cannot constrain them because they can easily leave him, no longer has the same powers as his predecessor, who enjoyed a quasi-monopoly or at least reigned over a captive audience. True, he may find other ways of taking action in order to gain the upper hand over this complexity of activities beyond his control. But he will have no prospect of winning if he confines himself to reaffirming the traditional model of values. To succeed, he must on the contrary rely on the reality of the game and seek to turn it to his own purposes. The problem is then no longer one of values but of social organisation.

This phenomenon is quite general.

Everywhere in the West the freedom of choice of the individual has increased tremendously. With the crumbling of old barriers everything seems to be possible. Not only can people choose their jobs, their friends, and their mates without being constrained by earlier conventions, but they can drop those relationships more easily. People whose range of opportunities is greater and whose freedom of change is also greater, can be much more demanding and cannot accept being bound by lifelong relationships.

This is of course much more true for young people. It has further been compounded by the development of sexual freedom and by the questioning of women's place in society. In such a context traditional authority was bound to be brought into question. Not only did it run counter to the tremendous new wave of individual assertion, but at the same time it was losing the capacity which it had maintained for far too long of controlling people who had no alternatives.

If this is true, the problem is not one of reasserting old values of respect and decency as against the growing tide of barbarism nor of trying once again to reconstruct the world according to a single set of values, even if they are those of unlimited freedom and self-expression. We must find new regulations for a completely different social game. New patterns of conflicting values will emerge in due time.

V

Now we come to our central problem of social control and governability. Our system of government, not only in politics, but in other institutions, was developed around some strong sociological features: fragmentation of categories and situation, social and professional barriers, difficulty in communicating. Authority could therefore rely on distance and on secrecy and captive audiences. But when barriers crumble and competition develops, authority must move to completely new ground. This is all the more necessary since it had in the past been counterbalanced by the right of dissent and the possibility of using alternative channels to obtain redress. But when authority collapses, dissent is no longer rewarding, and conflict which cannot be regulated becomes neurotic.

42

It is useless to delude ourselves by supposing that a return to, or modernization of, fundamental values can provide us with a solution. We have to realize that for this to occur we would also have to prevent people from communicating with one another, and reconstitute the social barriers and fragmentation between territorial and occupational units.

On the other hand many writers, notably Ivan Illich, consider that we could dispense with a lot of government. If the veritable role of institutions is analysed dispassionately, most of them lose much of their utility. But the pressure to keep and expand them is irresistible because every demand for intervention—in fact every question put by the individual to society as a whole—becomes an institutional pressure. The protection of each individual citizen implies control over all other citizens.

The dominant feature of our societies is that the collective fabric is much denser and that this fabric is a human construct which necessitates constant intervention. Developing and administering a collective fabric as the essential condition for social development is tending to become one of the basic activities. It can be simplified; it cannot be dispensed with. And it can be simplified only by a persistent effort to acquire a deeper understanding of its characteristics and usefulness.

VI

These problems exist everywhere in the industrialized countries, and even in the socialist countries. But Western Europe is suffering from them in a particularly acute form. Western Europe is in a very special situation because it has a long record of traditional social control imposed upon the individual by collective authorities, especially the state, and by hierarchical religious institutions. Admittedly these authorities and institutions have been liberalized over the centuries since the epoch of absolutism. Nevertheless, a strong association between social control and hierarchical values still persists, which means that a basic contradiction tends to reappear. Citizens make incompatible claims. Because they press for more action to meet the problems they have to face, they require more social control. At the same time, they resist any kind of social control that is associated with the hierarchical values they have learned to discard and reject. The problem may be worldwide, but it is exacerbated in Europe, where social discipline is not worshipped as it still is in Japan, and where more indirect forms of social control have not developed as in North America.

European countries, therefore, have more difficult problems to overcome to go beyond a certain level of complexity in their politico-administrative, social, and even economic systems. There are differences in each country, each one having maintained a very distinctive collective system of social control. But each one of these systems now appears to be insufficient to solve the problems of the time. This is as true for Britain, which was considered to have mastered the art of government for all time, as it is for Italy, which could have been an example of stable " nongovernment ". France also has a centralized apparatus less and less adequate for managing modern complex systems and is therefore becoming more vulnerable. To some extent Germany benefits from the deep trauma of nazism, which has forced more basic change in the management of its social texture, but it is nevertheless under the same kind of strains.

A second problem is the increasing difference between the decision-making game and the implementation game. Completely different rationales are at work at one level and at the other. In the decision-making game, the capacity to master a successful coalition for a final and finite agreement is a function of the nature and rules of the game in which the decision is one outcome. Since the same participants are playing the same game for quite a number of crucial decisions, the nature of their game, the participants' resources, and the power relationships between them may have as much validity in determining outcomes as the substance of the problem and its possible rational solution. In the implementation game, however, completely different actors appear whose frames of reference have nothing to do with national decision-making bargaining and whose game is heavily influenced by the power structure and modes of relationship in the bureaucracy on the one hand, and in the politico-administrative system in which the decision is to be implemented on the other. Quite frequently the two games work differently and may even be completely at odds. A gap can therefore exist between the rationality of the decision-makers and the outcomes of their activity, which means that collective regulation of human activities in a complex system is basically frustrating.

Such a situation, which develops in most large-scale organisations and institutions, is reproduced and exemplified at the upper political level where all modern democratic systems suffer from a general separation between an electoral coalition and the process of government. Completely different sets of alliances are necessary to get an electoral majority and to face the problems of government. The United States and Japan also have these problems, but they are especially acute in West European countries because of the fragmentation of social systems, the great difficulties of communication, and the barriers between different subsystems which tend to turn in on themselves and operate in isolation.

It is true that there are many differences among the European countries in this respect and one should not talk too hastily of common European conditions. There is quite a strong contrast, for example, between a country like Sweden, which has developed an impressive capability for handling complex problems by relieving ministerial staffs of the burden of administrative and technical decisions and by allocating considerable decision-making powers to strengthened local authorities, and a country like Italy, where a very weak bureaucracy and an unstable political system cannot take decisions and cannot facilitate the achievement of any kind of adjustment. The majority of European countries, however, are somewhat closer to the Italian model, and Sweden seems for the moment to be a striking exception. This does not seem to be due to the size or type of problems since small countries, like Belgium, or even the Netherlands and Denmark, are also victims of overload

44

and complexity due to the rigidity and complexity of group allegiances and to the fragmentation of the polity.

In order to get a genuinely more balanced view one may have to play down the differences between the consensual countries of North Western Europe and the conflict-ridden authoritarian Latin cultures.

A general drift toward alienation, irresponsibility, and breakdown of consensus seems to prevail everywhere, even in Sweden. With the passage of time, group bargaining has become more and more routinized, that is, more and more bureaucratic, and workers, if not citizens generally, have also tended in moderate North West Europe to feel as alienated as those in the traditionally revolutionary Latin countries. In Denmark, the Netherlands, and Britain, the social democratic consensus is breaking down while the relationships between groups have become so complex and erratic that citizens are more and more frustrated. Politics become divorced from the citizens' feelings and even from reality. Vicious circles therefore tend to develop which bring these countries much closer than ever before to the countries of continental Europe.

All these problems are certainly multiplied by the new dimension of international problems which has made the European national state a somewhat obsolete entity. One could obviously conceive of a federal European system which could rely on strong decentralized local and regional decision-making systems, thus reducing the overload at the top, the bureaucratic nature of the intermediary processes, and the citizens' alienation. But efforts at unification have tended to reinforce the national bureaucratic apparatuses as if these traditional nerve centres of European affairs could not help but harden again. Thus, Western Europe faces one of its most impossible dilemmas. Its problems are more and more European in nature, but its capacity to face them relies on institutional instruments of a national and bureaucratic nature that are more and more inadequate but that tend at the same time to strengthen their hold on the system.

Present European problems are not intractable and European societies, whatever their weaknesses, do still possess a lot of resources that can be mobilized when wanted. They have already shown during the contemporary period considerable resilience and an unexpected capacity to adapt, to adjust, and to invent. Right now they still manage to maintain democratic stability against very difficult odds. And during the past twenty years, they have carried through a very impressive mutation that few observers would have trusted them to accomplish. If there was no external constraint, there would be no reason to believe they could not accomplish the second mutation that seems necessary now.

The basic situation, therefore, that should concern us is not so much the intractability of the problems and the incapacity of European societies to meet the challenge; it is the vulnerability of Europe. Indeed, all European nations have to live through the same impossible situation: they have to carry through a basic mutation in their patterns of government and their mode of social control while facing at the same time a crisis from within and a crisis from without.

The crisis from within revolves basically of course around economic and social instability. Inflation at the rate it has reached increases the tensions it had alleviated formerly. Its disruptive effects undermine the basis of the social bond because of the loss of trust and the impossibility of planning ahead. But too much deflation would mean an impossible reallocation of resources and/or raise unemployment to an unacceptable level. Countries are therefore in an intolerable vicious circle which it is very difficult for them to break without going into a deeper depression, and whose risks seem impossible to accept in view of the fragility of their social fabric.

Managing such a crisis imposes the need to give priority to short-term considerations, and makes it all the more difficult to meet the more basic challenge of the necessary mutation of social controls.

This is, of course, compounded by the consequences of the crisis from without, which is not only the crisis of energy and the crisis of the balance of payments but the relative situation of weakness of the European nations whose welfare is for the first time directly dependent on outside pressures from non-Western powers.

Such a contradiction makes Western Europe vulnerable. Drifting to a chaotic kind of state socialism that would guarantee employment could be an easy solution temporarily for some countries but would raise more problems for the future. A regression to more authoritarian patterns is not impossible at a later point, in particular as a consequence of the lack of governability associated with the state socialism formula.

VII

To prevent this drift and this risk, European nations should try to transcend their present dire constraints and face the challenges of the future by investing their resources more wisely according to a more thoughtful strategy.

They should try especially to accelerate the shift away from their old model of fragmentation, stratification, secrecy, and distance, which in the past produced an acceptable balance between democratic processes, bureaucratic authority, and some aristocratic tradition, and experiment with more flexible models that could produce more social control with less coercive pressure. Such experimentation, which is bound to succeed in the long run, looks dangerous in the present vulnerable situation, when we naturally hesitate to jeopardize what remains of the old means of social control so long as we are not sure of the quality of the new means. Innovation, nevertheless, seems to be absolutely indispensable. It has to be careful innovation, but it is the only possible answer to Europe's dilemma.

The problem of *means* therefore seems to be more important than the problem of ends. European societies should invest in the development of these means which represent its basic capacities.

First of all, they should invest in new experiments in organisational or systemic arrangements which can introduce new self-regulating mechanisms within the gigantic, confused, impersonal bureaucratic systems, whether at the organisational or at the market level. What is needed is not grandiose schemes or constraining state regulations but practical local experiments. Observation of what is taking place now shows spontaneous development of a lot more innovations than Utopian thinkers may believe.

Secondly, investment in practical knowledge is even more fundamental. Knowing the actual rationale of existing arrangements and systems seems to be vitally important, not only for innovation but to help people make decisions on any issue. The lack of understanding of the basic regulations of any subsystem and of course of the larger system is appalling. Western European societies badly need a lot more intellectual input to understand their social fabrics. This is not idle dreaming but the most essential element for practical action.

Thirdly, in order to experiment they not only need to know, they also must have a capacity to face up to new and more difficult situations and to play new and more complicated games. Decentralization and self-management always fail because people cannot face the psychological tensions involved in dealing with problems more directly. One of the main investments to be made in our societies should therefore be to train their members to improve their capacity to deal with conflicts and tensions more directly.

Finally, our intellectual training does not seem to be adequate. We seem to perpetuate in our schools and universities the model of bureaucratic rationality that prevents people from learning from experience or even understanding the reality of complex human problems. New training models are available. They could change the dominant rationality which the elites perpetuate and which plays a decisive role in preventing the necessary mutations from taking place.

2

COMMENT

by Professor Anne O. Krueger (United States)

When I agreed to discuss Professor Crozier's paper, I was curious as to whether an economist would be able to comment usefully on a sociologist's paper and what the area of common concern and insights might be. His excellent paper surpassed my highest expectations in a variety of ways.

Fiest, the social concerns that Professor Crozier expresses, namely that modern decision-making mechanisms seem increasingly unable to cope with pressing political and economic problems, are issues that are starting to worry economists. Secondly, it seems to me that economists have some insights into the same questions that Professor Crozier analyzes, and that it may be useful to attempt an economist's interpretation of some of the phenomena he discusses. Finally, I found his paper extremely stimulating, and congratulate him on it.

In recent years, concern with the political process has begun to emerge as a major question in economics. The word " political economy " has moved back into the discipline. Prior to that, economists built models in which the political process was regarded as exogenous, and in which private decision makers reacted to the autonomous policy actions undertaken by the government. Those actions were viewed as something outside the pale of economic analysis. Recently, however, studies have begun as to the ways in which economic and political forces interact in political and economic decision-making.

In this regard, there is, it seems to me, a real question as to what the " increased rationality in decision-making " that Professor Crozier pleads for really is. From the perception of an economist, one of the phenomena which has given rise to the " overload of the system " is simply the fact that it is considerably more complex because the role that governments are expected to perform has increased so markedly.

I would be very interested to see the comparison of transport decisions in Paris in the 1890's with those of recent years to which Professor Crozier referred. I would guess, however, that one of the significant differences is that higher incomes in recent years have resulted in higher aspirations. Concerns with the environment, with noise and air pollution, and with the

48

" quality of life " in general, are in large part concerns that we can afford because we are rich societies. Insofar as these issues are becoming more and more important, we are asking governments to resolve questions that were previously determined by the market (by neglect, perhaps, as in the case of air pollution) and not by the political process.

Everyone can see a common interest in law and order, diplomatic representation abroad, and related issues. To the extent that nineteenth century governments were concerned more exclusively with those sorts of functions, the degree to which the political process was called upon to resolve conflicting claims was proportionately, as well as absolutely, smaller than it is today. Increasing affluence has resulted in pushing issues to center stage which revolve around trade-offs between the interests of different groups. Political concerns, in other words, have shifted from almost exclusive focus on those issues on which consensus could be reached, to a wider domain in which the political process must, to a much greater extent, concern itself with resolving conflicting claims and interests.

An illustration of this is inflation. In one sense, inflation can be viewed as resulting from the inability of the political process to come to grips with these conflicting claims. When politicians are unable to resolve them, their default is reflected in government budget deficits. Each group gets part of what it wants some of the time only to lose it again when inflation erodes it as the next group has its demand (temporarily) satisfied.

As a parenthetical comment related to this, I was pleased and surprised to read that Professor Crozier does not believe that the United States is as badly off as Western Europe. To me, Professor Crozier's description and analysis of the problem sounded uncomfortably familiar.

If my perception—that the crisis is in large part the result of the demand that the political process resolve conflicting claims—is sound, I am not entirely confident that Professor Crozier is correct in his suggestion that more education may provide a solution. Indeed, it could even be argued that more education might result in more intelligent defenses of self-interest by all concerned groups and thus a greater degree of impasse.

Nonetheless, there is undoubtedly an important role that education can play. It is probably useful to distinguish several levels at which one might want rationality. On one level there are clearly instances in all countries of decisions being made where, if the advocates of those decisions could have foreseen the (predictable) outcomes, they would not have supported them. This is the case of the simple mistake, in which the individual or group does not understand its own immediate self-interest. At this level, greater education can help to provide a better decision-making process immediately. One wonders, however, how many such simple mistakes there are. It seems a reasonable conjecture that their frequency may be diminishing over time, as increased experience with the political process teaches the participants more about their own self-interest.

The second level at which one might hope for rationality is that in which advocates correctly perceive their direct self-interest, but where, if different interest groups could negotiate a different set of decisions, all would be better

49

off. This correct perception of " narrow " self-interest is, it seems to me, far more challenging, and on this level I am skeptical as to how much " education " can accomplish. It is in this dimension that there is a need for new mechanisms, of which Professor Crozier speaks.

Among economists, there has been discussion for the past several years of the need for a " social contract " as a means of breaking inflation. The basic concept is that negotiations among various interest groups—labor unions, management, government, farmers, and others—might determine a package under which price and wage increases could be restrained and all would be better off. Such packages are certainly possible, although no one seems yet to have devised a mechanism for arranging them.

In this regard, I feel impelled to question one of Professor Crozier's suggestions—namely that experiments with small groups might yield insights into possible new societal decision-making mechanisms. My skepticism is based upon the premise that much of the current malaise really stems from a perception of society that is shared by a vast majority of people. These perceptions arise in part out of affluence, and in part out of modern communications (themselves a function of our wealth) which convey the same information to the participants in many countries simultaneously. Under those conditions, I am not really convinced that an experiment with a smaller group or one sort of decision-making apparatus in one place can tell us very much, given the interdependence among communities. A related aspect is, of course, that our decision-making units are very big, and that is surely part of the problem. To the extent that experiments could be conducted at all, they could be undertaken only with small groups again a distinct limitation on their applicability to the general situation.

As the above remarks suggest, I found Professor Crozier's paper extremely stimulating and one that will continue to influence my thinking for some time to come. I would like to close by commenting upon the applicability of his discussion to the theme of this conference, namely, the implications for interdependence. As an international trade economist concerned very much with pressures for protection, both tariffs and quotas, against imports in the United States, I could not help but reflect that, insofar as the political process is increasingly perceived as a means by which different economic groups can press their claim, it is almost inevitable that some aspects of international economic life are bound to suffer. Given the sorts of political mechanisms we now have, it seems natural that domestic producer interests are likely to dominate over domestic consumer interests. If that is accepted, then issues of domestic versus foreign interests seem to fall within the second class of cases I was discussing earlier, namely, ones where a negotiated package might make all better off than the results of our present decision-making processes. The lack of a mechanism for such negotiation is very threatening to the future of the international economy. One can only hope that diplomatic pressures among countries are more effective than some domestic political mechanisms when it comes to arranging the international economy.

3

COMMENT

by Professor Hideaki Okamoto (Japan)[1]

I would like to comment on three points. First, I endorse and support with great respect almost all the points made by Professor Crozier. I think his paper is a remarkable contribution, pointing out explicitly the trend toward bureaucratic crisis in our highly industrialized societies. Coming from Japan, I can identify similar examples of almost all the points he made. For example, there are close similarities in decision-making for the transport system, such as the now famous problem of the second airport for Tokyo.

Secondly, however, I would like to say something about another basic current, which he touched on in his paper but did not emphasize enough. There are so many impressionably convincing examples of the bureaucratic crisis that we may be tempted to overlook the opposing current, that is, the trend on the part of some types of organization to become more responsive to the changing social texture of modern society. In many large organizations, I even see a trend toward *debureaucratization*, in the sense that the social texture is moving away from a rigid bureaucratic structure and gaining in elasticity and in potential for further decentralization and democratization. To make my point more clear, let me mention some of the dimensions of what I am calling debureaucratization.

In contrast with the traditional methods, for example, in many large organizations one now sees a tendency to assign a project instead of a narrowly defined job to the persons involved, even down to the production workers. There are also tendencies to emphasize the need for autonomy and self-accountability, instead of emphasizing control and discipline. There are tendencies to introduce " feed forward " rather than " feed back ", that is to say, decisions are not based on precedent or pre-established manuals, but are rather made by systems of concepts, utilizing behavior signs and information technology. There are also trends toward giving greater weight to performance rather than credentials or formal qualifications. This leads to the wider use of internal education mechanisms after experience on the job, while formal academic and vocational education are increasingly losing their significance as preparatory

---

1. Revised text prepared by the Editor on the basis of the verbatim transcript of the Conference.

mechanisms. There is also a trend, in my view, toward merit rating as an organizational control mechanism rather than educational variations. All this implies that it is less the formal hierarchy of bureaucratic desks which tends to dictate the dynamics of organization, and more the staff individuals who are sitting at those desks. If we may term this a " staffocracy ", it still has a substantial bureaucratic element, but it may also have a potential to be more adaptive to a changing environment with respect both to efficiency and to democratic participation.

Thirdly, there are structural factors in the industrialized societies which make this kind of change more feasible and probable. The advancing educational standard within the general population may foster the change toward debureaucratization. The prevalence of a basic minimum standard of social welfare may be another facilitating factor. Viewed on the whole, there is a trend for organizational changes to be quite rapid and to help overcome what Professor Crozier calls the problems of fragmentation and stratification. So I would tend to say that, if it is true that Europe is suffering more than other regions from these organizational problems (which I doubt), one underlying reason may be Europe's success in achieving these related improvements in structural conditions.

Because of that, while I agree with Professor Crozier's proposal for expanding the amount of experimentation and research on the organization of decision-making processes, I also think it very important to have a deeper understanding of the functions of the organizational structures—a field in which we can learn a great deal from international comparisons. This is another respect in which international cooperation is needed in order to maintain economic prosperity along with the further democratization of our social structures.

4

COMMENT

by Mr. David Watt (United Kingdom)

Let me begin as my colleagues have done by saying how much I admire Professor Crozier's essay, and also how much political students and observers in England as elsewhere have learnt from him in general. He has illuminated a whole field of what one might call bureaucratic sociology for many years. The fact that most of us are familiar with some of the ideas contained in the paper we are discussing this morning is a tribute to Professor Crozier's very wide influence.

The picture he paints certainly bears a remarkable likeness in my view to the situation as we see it in Britain. There could hardly be a better description of the classic virtues which are supposed to reside in that system than Professor Crozier's phrase " an acceptable balance between democratic processes, bureaucratic authority, and some aristocratic tradition." (And now I come to think of it, perhaps that is rather a good description of Lord Franks.) Nor is there a better summing up of the present reality than his observation that the social democratic process is breaking down while the relationships between groups have become so complex and erratic that citizens are more and more frustrated. That I think is certainly true of Britain. The argument that lies between these points is very complicated, very subtle, and in detail constantly illuminating. I know some of it to be true and I suspect, although I think neither I nor Professor Crozier could prove it, that much of it is true.

That part of the thesis on which I have reservations is really concerned with the future. Professor Crozier, if I read him rightly, takes a pretty gloomy view, not only about the present situation but also about the ability of existing institutions to evolve in order to cope with the future in the limited time available before a major calamity. I am not quite so sceptical myself and I might put my rather tentative optimism in the form of four specific points.

First then, why have the phenomena that Professor Crozier describes occurred in precisely the way that they have? He himself has some tentative explanations and in the case of Britain ascribes these developments to the strength and power of our institutions which are unfortunately moulded by the old set of rules, as he calls them. This diagnosis is all right so far as it goes but it doesn't actually explain the question of timing. You see, up to 1965 if there was any complaint about the British political system, and on the whole there wasn't, it was that it was too consensual, too effective, and too good at resolving conflicts in what one might call a boring and dull kind of way. Why at that precise moment did things fly apart from the centre rather than at some other time? The conventional explanation offered by British political scientists has had to do with a range of psychological traumas rather different from the Crozier ones. These are, first, the loss of the British Empire, which was much more deeply woven into the texture of British life than it was into the texture of some other European countries with empires; and second the combined pressures on the British economy of external competition and internal industrial inefficiency, this last being a phenomenon whose origins go back far beyond the limits of Professor Crozier's thesis. I am not sure myself that this conventional wisdom doesn't have something in it. I don't think that that necessarily invalidates all Professor Crozier is saying in general or what he implies about Britain in particular, but it at least suggests to me that there are some national psychological conditions in which it is easier to cope with Professor Crozier's problems and other national psychological conditions in which it is harder.

This brings me to my second observation. It seems to me that Professor Crozier is in danger of falling into the trap against which he warns us at the beginning of his essay, that of extrapolating from existing trends. The most fashionable current of political thought in Britain at the moment is that of Mrs. Thatcher and Sir Keith Joseph and the revised *laisser faire* economic school. They would maintain that there is nothing inevitable at all about some of the trends on which the Crozier thesis is based. Inflation and high unemployment, they would contend, exercise their own disciplines, and it is possible that instead of forcing us to adapt our institutions in the way that Crozier suggests they might simply stop us in our tracks. They might, for instance, cause us to opt for slower economic growth or even lower living standards and it is by no means certain that that tradeoff would be so unsatisfactory as to cause eventual breakdown of the system. Again, inflation and high unemployment might once more cause industrial workers to embrace, even if only grudgingly, the authority of politicians which is said to have been lost. The partial success of incomes policy in Britain over the last decade suggests that they may to some extent have had this effect. There is another associated problem here which is this. Supposing we do extrapolate the trends, where do they finally lead us? If we follow Professor Crozier's prescriptions and adapt our institutions to the new social rules, will not continuing economic growth and technological progress and all the complexities that he rightly says flow from them simply catch up with the new system and pose the same dilemmas at a different level? And if Crozier replies that there is a limit to these complexities, how do we know that it hasn't nearly been reached now and that the failsafe mechanisms of our present system are not about to work?

My third point is that if the situation is exactly as Professor Crozier describes, I am a bit doubtful about the significance of his recommendations for action. It is not that there is anything foolish about trying to invest in political experiments, or practical knowledge, or training for new and more complicated games. It is simply that in real life things tend not to happen like that. The society in aggregate is either capable of adapting itself to endogenous pressure or it isn't; and the deliberate activities of politicians, sociologists, and political journalists will not by themselves be the main determinants of what happens. General Marshall and Jean Monnet might be said to have changed history and we are celebrating that change today, but as Miriam Camps replied in her remark to Stanley Hoffmann, the climate of the times was already hatching the idea and the political system of the US was already organised to respond to perceptions of enlightened self-interest.

I very much agree with Professor Okamoto when he talks about the many signs of organisational adaptation today, and I would say that there are some encouraging signs of political adaptation as well. Let me take two British examples. The idea of independence for Scotland has been around for three or four centuries, if not longer, and has been revived in response to just the kind of pressures that Professor Crozier is concerned with. The British Government at Westminster naturally reacts to this pressure which affects, as one would expect, their political situation within the existing party rules. The Scottish National Party is a very discomforting and effective pressure group. The final compromise on Scotland has yet to emerge, but it will certainly look remarkably like an example of the kind of new experiment that Crozier desires.

Another example is the reform of the British electoral system. As you know, at present our Members of Parliament are elected as the representatives of single member geographical constituencies on a straight majority basis. This system has tended to produce strong central government, but it has been brought under attack because it also tends to entrench the power of large, arthritic political parties and gives them a license to impose alternating and one-sided solutions upon conflicts of interest. To change this system is clearly against the short-term interest of the major parties and most of the politicians. But in the end it will change, I believe, and the reason is not so much theoretical system building as the fact that the existing parties, particularly the Labour Party, are simply losing public credibility. Their membership is declining; their votes are declining; and their ability to deliver the goods is declining. This alerts the enlightened self-interest of politicians in casting about for wider support by restructuring their coalitions. Proportional representation has already been introduced in Northern Ireland in order to produce a non-sectarian coalition; and the desire of the old parties to cut down the disproportionate power of the Scottish National Party will almost certainly lead to its introduction in elections to a new Scottish Assembly. The Westminster Parliament will take longer, but the forces in favour of moving in that direction are undoubtedly growing. To that extent, our present arrangements can be said to be justified since they are generating change themselves.

Finally, I don't think Professor Crozier should kid us, as he seems to be doing at one point, that he is talking about institutions and not about values.

The choice of a democratic rather than a totalitarian system, which he makes implicitly towards the end of his essay, is a striking example of a moral stance. He says, " a regression to a more authoritarian pattern is not impossible at a later point, " and it is the word *regression* that gives him away. For at the very least it implies that democracy is higher on some evolutionary scale than totalitarianism. As a matter of fact, one might say in passing that authoritarian regimes are having their own acute troubles as a result of a lot of the factors that Professor Crozier is talking about. Decision-making is not at all easy these days even for dictators. And one could well argue that if one takes the situation in say, Russia, as one's starting point, the complexities of a modern, highly industrialised state are beneficial and tend to produce a loosening and a more open society. In other words, it seems to me that the factors outlined in Crozier's essay may be tending to make both our own system and the Communist one converge on the other Crozier option, namely, a chaotic kind of state socialism.

In the face of these pressures our own concern is to preserve open, democratic forms of government because we believe certain things about the human spirit and what it needs in order to maximise its essence and its potentiality. If it turns out that very large numbers of human spirits and their corporeal envelopes are incapable of coexisting except in conditions which limit freedom below the minimum we have come to regard as essential, it will be more than just depressing. It will force us to abandon altogether the view of man that has been the essence and the glory of Western civilisation since the Renaissance. Personally, I hope and believe that this will not be necessary. I also believe that our societies will in fact fight desperately to prevent it.

5

SUMMARY OF THE DISCUSSION

The available time permitted only a brief general discussion. One speaker, concurring with Professor Crozier's contrast between the ability of political coalitions to secure election to office and their inability to implement a coherent program, emphasized the importance of legislative assemblies in democratic countries. Legislatures often seem irrelevant nowadays, and a determined effort is needed to reinvigorate them, since they can take a national view, help reconcile regional and sectoral conflicts, and disseminate the results of any consensus. On the other hand, since so many of today's issues are transnational, perhaps there is an important role for the European Parliament.

Another speaker endorsed the broad sweep of Professor Crozier's thesis, but felt that he may have generalized excessively from the French case and given too little credit to ameliorating factors in many countries. In his view, for example, there has been less weakening of traditional values and social controls in the United States and Japan than in the Catholic countries of Europe; some societies are more effective than others in resolving issues without recourse to government; and government itself is more effective in some countries than others, partly because of federal arrangements for decentralization. Moreover, the degree of " ideologization " of issues varies from country to country.

A third speaker asked Professor Crozier whether there was a danger that " debureaucratization " might result in such a degree of fragmentation that societies would become incapable of implementing central decisions. On this point, Professor Crozier replied that bureaucratic organization is always softened by human adjustments, and he felt some concern that efforts to reform bureaucratic structures might risk the elimination of such informal human accommodations. On balance, however, he felt that our societies suffer from an excess of centralization in the State and other large organizations, and that there is need to create a larger number of poles of decision-making.

Replying to Professor Krueger's comments, Professor Crozier emphasized the modest scope of his call for greater rationality: it involves the readiness to trade off some apparent short-term gains for more important, even though admittedly more uncertain, longer term advantages. On the matter of small scale social experimentation, he agreed that it has limited objectives and cannot cope with large decisions, which must be taken at the center, but he hopes to relieve the burden of overcentralization through improvements in the base—for example, by constituting new kinds of markets for decision-making. There are many examples of central decisions which fail to get implemented because of inadequate understanding of what is really going on at the base. Professor Crozier, however, is not arguing the thesis of the universal superiority of decentralization for all purposes.

On the issue of whether the United States is less affected than Europe by the structural issues described in his paper, Professor Crozier feels that the United States does enjoy advantages of time, space, and resources which give it greater flexibility and resilience than the European countries. In Europe, there is a feeling of much tighter constraints of time within which to find solutions.

Replying to Professor Okamoto's comments, Professor Crozier agreed that Japan (and also the United States) does present many examples corresponding to the case of the Paris " Metro. " He also saw important differences in the manner in which different countries respond to similar problems, and agreed that careful international comparative studies would be very rewarding. On the question of " debureaucratization, " he acknowledged that there are tendencies in that direction, but saw a danger of being misled in this field by exaggerated claims for new methods of organizing work and taking other social decisions. The reality is not always what the words allege.

Replying to Mr. Watt, Professor Crozier recognized the complexities of the British example, but emphasized that during the last decade, the United Kingdom has faced a number of problems whose severity had been underestimated both within and outside of Britain. For example, the decolonization of the British empire was rightly judged a remarkable success, but it also involved costs within British society which were not adequately recognized. As to future prospects in Britain and elsewhere, Professor Crozier was very cautious in making any kind of prediction, but he did believe that new types of adjustment and social invention were more probable than any effort simply to go backwards or to freeze the social order. He was therefore somewhat less pessimistic than the impression apparently conveyed by his paper as a whole. He did, however, remain concerned about the danger of a regression in Europe from democratic and liberal values, as happened in the 1930s, and he believed that Europeans must be alert to that danger and should give serious thought to means of averting it.

Concluding his comment on other points arising in the general discussion, Professor Crozier concurred on the importance of legislative bodies and the need for renewing their vitality. Concerning the matter of variations in structural issues from country to country, he agreed on their importance, but on balance he had been impressed more by the similarities of experiences elsewhere with those in France. As to the broad outlines of structural malaise, he felt that there was a relative convergence in modern industrial societies generally.

III

ECONOMIC DEPENDENCE
AND INTERDEPENDENCE
IN THE INDUSTRIALIZED WORLD[1]

by Professor Assar Lindbeck

From the point of view of economic analysis, we may look upon the consolidation of the national states during the centuries following the medieval period as an adjustment of the political system of the presently industrialized world to some basic changes in the economic system, requiring larger integrated areas for markets of commodities, factors of production, credit, and entrepreneurship. The potential efficiency of expanded geographical domains for markets could be fully realized only if the political jurisdiction domain also expanded accordingly, by way of the substitution of national for local systems of currencies, tariffs, infrastructure, and official laws and regulations of economic activities and transactions.

As we know, the geographical domain of markets did not stop expanding at the national borders, but was extended to ever larger areas, generating a more and more internationally integrated, or " internationalized, " economic system. The driving forces behind this process of internationalization of the economic system are numerous: [2] technological development, by being biased in favor of communication and transport, drastically reduced the costs of sending goods and messages over large distances, relative to other costs, and it also made some of the externalities of the production and consumption process international in character; accentuation of the returns to scale in some industries forced small and medium-sized countries to specialize in a more and more narrow range of products; the increased role of technology in production and management stimulated trade in technology, which resulted not only in an expansion of trade in patents and machines but also, due to the complementarity between technology and management, in an internationalization of entrepreneurship; the rapid growth of raw-material-scarce areas, such as Europe and Japan (and more recently also the U.S.), increased

---

1. Some slightly technical sections, in fine print, may be skipped without loss of the continuity of the paper.
2. For a more detailed discussion of this point see (Lindbeck, 1973].
The author is Professor of International Economics at the University of Stockholm and Director of the Institute for International Economic Studies. This paper was written while the author was Irving Fisher Visiting Professor at Yale University.

59

the skewness in the geographical location of consumption relative to production of raw materials and fuel; and finally, the high income elasticity for product differentiation of consumption, and the increased similarity of per capita income and preferences among developed countries, led in combination with returns to scale to an enormous expansion of intra-industry trade.

However, in addition to these technical and economic factors, the economic internationalization process has also been stimulated by political decisions, and therewith connected institutional changes. The "victory" of the idea of free trade at about the middle of the nineteenth century is an obvious example. Another example is the activities after the Second World War of organizations such as GATT, IMF, EEC, EFTA, OECD and other global and regional organizations for economic cooperation. In particular, the agreements on the liberalization of trade and the creation of considerable convertibility of national currencies were crucial prerequisites for much of the subsequent internationalization of markets for goods, credit, and entrepreneurship during the post World War II period.

However, when the politicians by their own decisions contributed to an internationalization of the economic system, they released, like " the Sorcerer's Apprentice, " forces which were beyond their own powers to control. The national state has therefore, in field after field, become a less efficient unit of policy-making than before, because of increased international economic dependence and interdependence. Many problems of the world of today can fruitfully be seen in the light of the tensions that have thereby been created between a strongly internationalized economic system and a political system that is still based on the notion of sovereign national states.

This paper deals with exactly these tensions, and the attempts of the national states to deal with them.

WHAT IS " NEW "?

International economic integration is, of course, nothing new in the economic history of the western world. Schematically speaking, perhaps we can say that it started at about the same time as modern economic growth, i.e. approximately in the middle of the nineteenth century [Kuznets 1967]. The increasingly international character of the economic system during the course of the post-World War II period is, to some extent, only a catch-up to conditions already prevailing before the First World War, and at the end of the nineteen twenties, after the international disintegration during the two world wars and the Great Depression. [3] (In other words, the period 1913-1945, with some reservation for the twenties, may be regarded as a *deviation* from the long-term trend to increased international economic integration.) There are, nevertheless, some new features of international economic integration.

---

3. For an extensive discussion of the history of the concept and doctrine of economic integration, see [Machlup, 1977]. Discussions about *international* economic integration are pursued in *inter alia* [Cooper, 1968 and 1974; Lindbeck, 1973; Salant, 1977A].

In particular, the revolutionary development of technology in the communication of messages has made markets in different countries integrated to a much larger extent than previously, in the sense of a *higher short-term substitutability and mobility* of goods and (mainly short-term) assets in different countries in response to changes in circumstances.

Another new feature is the farreaching internationalization of *entrepreneurship and technology*, and hence the expansion of direct foreign investment, this development also facilitated by the revolution in the transmission of information over large distances, which has made it possible to operate global organizations efficiently.

Moreover, even though the aggregate ratio of trade to GNP in many countries is not much higher today than in, for instance, 1913 and 1929, there has been an increase in the trade shares within practically all *private* production sectors, including a number of sectors which were earlier usually classified as " non-tradables, " such as building construction and a number of private services, e.g. insurance, recreation (as reflected in tourism), and consulting. This dramatic internationalization within most private sectors of economic activity is largely " missed " if we only look at figures concerning aggregate trade ratios, which have been prevented from increasing more dramatically because of the rapid expansion of the low-trade public sector, and in particular in nominal terms because of relative price increases for services.

In addition, and this is one of the most drastic new developments, the most important *external effects* of production and consumption today are " external " to nations and not only, as earlier, to firms and households, as witnessed by air and ocean pollution and by competition among nations for the riches of the oceans and the seabed. Increased international " demonstration effects " in the spheres of private consumption and public policy are other examples of international external effects.

These new features of international economic integration allow us to regard the present economic system, in particular the private sector, as considerably more " internationalized " than the economic system in previous periods, in spite of the fact that aggregate international trade flows, capital flows, and labor flows were nearly as large as today (sometimes even larger) in the early twentieth century—relative to the size of the industrialized market economies.

It is also likely that the general *awareness* of international interdependence has increased recently—among economists, politicians, and the general public —partly because of the dramatic events in the seventies related to more violent world-wide macroeconomic instability (unemployment and inflation), the global crop failures in 1972-73, the policies of the oil cartel in 1973-74, and the international confrontations about jurisdiction over the oceans and the seabed and between developed and less developed countries.

A more fundamental reason for the increased awareness of international economic interdependence is that the tension between international economic forces and domestic policy ambitions is much more strongly felt today than in earlier periods because the domestic political objectives have become so much

61

more numerous, detailed, and ambitious. Economic interdependence was not a serious economic policy problem before governments established targets concerning domestic variables such as employment, growth, inflation, income distribution, and the allocation of resources. [4]

GENERAL CONSEQUENCES
FOR NATIONAL ECONOMIC POLICY

What are, then, the general consequences for national economic policy of this internationalization process, and the related dependence and interdependence among the economies of different countries? On a rather abstract and general level of analysis, I would hypothesize the following six consequences: [5]

1. Changes in domestic aggregate demand—whether brought about by economic policy actions or by shifts in private behavior—would, as a rule, be expected to have *smaller* effects on the domestic economy than before, as an increased share of the effects would tend to " leak abroad " via the current and the capital accounts of the balance of payments, as well as via intercountry migration of labor. Examples of policy actions for which this point is particularly relevant are variations in income taxes, transfer payments, sales taxes, and open market operations; it holds also for (nondiscriminatory) government purchases of tradables. [6]

2. Changes in relative prices between countries, including changes brought about by way of policy actions, would as a rule be expected to have *greater* effects on the domestic economy than before, since increased substitutability between domestic and foreign goods is an important part of the internationalization process. Examples of policy tools for which this point is relevant are exchange rates and taxes and subsidies on trade, financial assets, and the production of tradables. [7] There are counterexamples, however. Attempts to influence the domestic distribution of income, by way of changes in relative factor prices (after taxes and subsidies), will be less effective the higher the international mobility of labor—as illustrated by the " brain-drain " problem.

3. When changes in aggregate demand and/or relative prices occur *abroad*, the effects on the domestic economy would, as a rule, be expected to be *stronger* than before, because of " spillover " effects of variations in foreign

---

4. The increased role of international transactions over time, relative to *total* economic activity (market *plus* nonmarket), is probably underestimated in the national accounts before the Second World War because of the trendwise fall in the partly unreported (domestic) do-it-yourself sector. It is conceivable that a bias in the opposite direction exists in the statistics for recent decades in some countries because of do-it-yourself activities related to more leisure time and higher marginal tax rates.

5. For an elaboration of some of these points see [Lindbeck 1976].

6. For an attempt to establish empirically a positive relation between " economic openness " and "spillover" effects across the national borders of aggregate demand management, see [Whitman, 1969].

7. Open market operations are here regarded as " demand management " in the bond market, whereas selective taxes or subsidies on the holdings of financial assets in different currency denominations are regarded as " relative price policies. "

aggregate demand and because of the earlier mentioned increased substitutions between goods from different countries in response to changes in relative prices between countries.

4. The *uncertainty* about the effects of changes in domestic and foreign policy instruments would be expected to increase, as the economic system becomes more complex, more difficult to model realistically, and therefore also more unpredictable, due to the tighter linkages with foreign countries. [8]

5. For the same general reasons, the *uncertainty* will also be expected to increase with respect to the domestic effects of various domestic and foreign (" exogenous ") *non-policy* shocks.

6. Even if the *effects* on the domestic economy of foreign disturbances are likely to increase and be more uncertain as a result of tighter international economic dependence and interdependence, it is more hazardous to hypothesize about the " character " (distribution) of these disturbances themselves. In general, if a country experiences increased economic integration with nations that are *more* stable than its previous " partners, " we would expect that the integration process will *reduce* the variance of " relevant " net disturbances from abroad. The variance of such disturbances *may* increase in the opposite case; the reason why I say " may " rather than " will " is that the " law of large numbers " may help to reduce net foreign disturbances in increasingly internationalized economies if the disturbances in different countries are *independent* (uncorrelated), as they might be in some cases (such as political disturbances, strikes, and sometimes also embargoes). In that event, an expanded integrated area will function like an insurance system with risk-pooling.

By way of summary, in slightly technical terms, we may say that the mean size of " own-country multipliers " tends to *fall* in the case of demand changes, but *rise* in the case of relative price changes; that the mean size of " foreign country multipliers " on the domestic economy tends to *rise;* and that the variance and covariance for all multipliers tends to *rise*.

If by the term " high effectiveness " of national policy instruments we mean that (the mean of) the multipliers of the domestic policy instruments are large and have a small variance and covariance, we may conclude that increased international economic dependence and interdependence reduces the effectiveness of aggregate demand management. The consequences for the effectiveness of policy instruments that change relative prices, by contrast, are ambiguous, as the mean of the coefficients rises, at the same time as the variance and covariance of the multiplier goes up, thus making the effects both stronger and more uncertain. [9]

Of course, " high effectiveness " as defined here is not enough for a successful stabilization policy, as the national target variables are influenced not only by the policy instruments but by non-policy parameters as well.

---

8. I assume that this factor is not fully compensated for by the falling costs of obtaining information from other countries.

9. If the *coefficient of variation* of the multipliers is used as a measure of the effectiveness, there will be an increased effectiveness if the variance increase less than the mean of the coefficient.

For that reason, it may be useful to supplement the concept of " effectiveness " with the concept of " controllability ", borrowed from optimum control theory. (See, for instance, Nyberg-Viotti, 1976.) The degree of controllability will here be rather heuristically defined as the degree to which the authorities are able, in principle, to control the time-path of the domestic target variables by manipulating the policy instruments. When general policy discussions refer to *autonomy* of national economic policy, perhaps this can be interpreted approximately as " controllability " in this sense.

More specifically, by " high " *de facto* national autonomy (controllability) of economic policy let us mean that three conditions are fulfilled:

1. *de jure* national government control of certain policy instruments, as determined by national laws and international agreements;
2. " high effectiveness " of these policy instruments, as defined above; and
3. the absence of strong, unpredictable, domestic and foreign disturbances that push national target variables radically off course.

Thus, except for the increased size of (the mean of) the multipliers of national " relative price instruments, " for the reduced size of (the mean of) the multipliers of domestic exogenous disturbances, and for the possibility of reduced variance of foreign disturbances by way of integration with stable countries or the exploitation of the law of large numbers of independent shocks, an increasingly internationalized economic system tends to result in a reduction in the *de facto* autonomy of national economic policy—by way of less *de jure* control of certain instruments (via international agreements), a lower *effectiveness* of the national policy instruments available, and larger and more unpredictable *effects* (multipliers) of foreign disturbances.

The discussion above is based on the following type of formalization, where the (vector of) target variables (T) are assumed to have been solved out as reduced form equations in terms of (vectors of) national demand management instruments (I_{nd}), national relative price policy instruments (I_{np}), national exogenous non-policy parameters (E_n), foreign policy instruments (I_f), foreign endogenous variables (V_f), and foreign (exogenous) non-policy parameters (E_f) :

$$(1) \qquad T = aI_{nd} + bI_{np} + cE_n + dI_f (+ eV_f) + fE_f,$$

the coefficients (the vectors $a, \ldots, f$) expressing the total multiplier effects on the (vector of) target variables. Of course, V_f is dependent on I_f and E_f, which would create problems of estimating equation (1) *if* V_f is included.

This formulation of the problem is appropriate mainly for small countries, for which it is reasonable to treat foreign endogenous variables (V_f) as " parametrically " given from outside. Thus, the formulation in this equation expresses *dependence* rather than *interdependence*. For large countries it is more relevant to use models with a simultaneous determination of both domestic and foreign endogenous variables. This would, of course, mean that the (vector) variable V_f would drop out from the reduced form equation, which is the reason for putting this term in parentheses in equation (1).

" High effectiveness " of domestic policy may now be defined as a large mean value and a low variance and covariance around the mean of the estimates of the coefficients a and b. " High controllability " requires, in addition, that the mean value and the variance and covariance of the other variables and parameters in the reduced form equation (E_n, I_f, V_f and E_f), and their respective multipliers (c, d, e, and f), are small.

The hypotheses presented above about the consequences of increased international integration for a country implied that all coefficients excepts a would increase, and that the variance (and covariance) of the coefficients would also go up, whereas the consequences for the variance (and covariance) of the variables I_f, V_f), and E_f would depend on the correlation between the various shocks in other countries, and the (relative) stability of the countries with which more integration is brought about.

These considerations are, of course, far from the "whole truth" of the theory of national autonomy of economic policy. In particular, foreign governments would sometimes be expected to change their policy instruments in direct response to "domestic" policy changes, thus generating oligopolistic, or game-theoretic, situations. This may be the case in particular in response to domestic policy measures that change the relative price drastically between some important goods and/or factors between countries, as such tools often have strong cross-country effects—simply another side of the strong domestic effects in highly open economies. (Formally, in the context of equation (1) above, I_f would now become dependent on I_{nd} and I_{np}; and I_f would then drop out from reduced form equations that are based on models with "reaction functions" for foreign policy decisions.)

GENERAL POLICY CONCLUSIONS

What, then, are the general policy conclusions of these considerations? I would like to stress three points.

First of all, if, for the time being, we neglect the policy reactions of foreign governments to domestic policy changes, we have seen that increased economic dependence and interdependence would as a rule be expected to raise the *relative* effectiveness of policy instruments that rely on relative price changes (between countries), i.e. "demand switching" policies, as compared to "demand varying" policies (if the uncertainty does not increase more for the former than for the latter type of policy instrument).

Secondly, the increased uncertainty about the effects of domestic policy instruments is, as a rule, an argument both for using the policy instruments rather carefully—what is often called "gradualism" by contrast to "big bangs"—if the economy is not very far from full capacity utilization, and for using "packages" of policy instruments in order to bring about some pooling of risks. [10]

Thirdly, the generally reduced autonomy of national economic policy and the increased interdependence of policy instruments are matched by increased potential gains from policy coordination with other countries. There are several reasons for this:

a) the reduced effectiveness of some policy instruments, mainly aggregate demand policies for small countries, make supporting actions by foreign governments potentially useful;

b) increased multiplier effects of policies abroad, mainly policies in large countries, create strong "externalities" (in a vague meaning of the term) of policy actions by individual countries, and hence make a "cosmopolitan" case for considering the effects on other countries when policies are decided in one specific (in particular large) country; and

---

10. For the general case of using many policy instruments in order to pool risks, see [Brainard 1967].

c) the interdependence of the policy actions themselves may make cooperative solutions preferable for all parties (including the large countries).

All these complications do not, of course, mean that international economic integration would necessarily be " bad " from the point of view of economic welfare of the domestic citizens of a national state. Increased efficiency in resource allocation, and increased international transmission of technology, are well known potential plus items from international economic integration. Moreover, actions by national governments in fact often damage rather than improve the welfare of their domestic citizens, in particular perhaps in a long run perspective—because of limited competence of governments, the short time-horizon of most policies, and the enormous difficulties of assessing long-term effects. From that point of view, *reduced* autonomy of national economic policy may sometimes prevent governments from damaging the welfare of their own citizens. For instance, increased international integration of markets may create higher standards for the performance not only of firms but also of national public authorities, and also make domestic restrictive practices by public authorities, or publicly regulated firms, less effective. Moreover, international agreements may prevent governments from implementing restrictions on trade and payments with long-term damaging effects. In fact, this point is often accepted by central banks and governments themselves, when they favor international *de jure* " straitjackets, " such as fixed exchange rates (for instance in the case of the small " snake " countries) and rules against the use of tariffs, partly because such arrangements make it easier for governments to withstand domestic political pressures for higher spending, higher wages, and the preservation of economically obsolete industries.

It could perhaps also be argued that easier movements of labor across national borders, by giving individuals the chance to " vote with their feet, " are not only an obstacle to national income redistribution policies, but also a way of preventing governments from taking actions that damage highly qualified minority groups, perhaps with long-term disadvantages for the population as a whole.

However, to advance in the analysis of the consequences for economic policy, let us look more in detail at two specific branches of national economic policy: stabilization policy and allocation policy.

CONSEQUENCES FOR STABILIZATION POLICY

The postwar principles of stabilization policy, based on Keynesian macro theory, were strongly colored by the historical circumstances during the period when the principles emerged, i.e. the 1930's and 40's. The fact that these were periods with strong autarkic tendencies, due to the Great Depression and the Second World War, is probably a main reason why Keynesian stabilization policy has largely been conceived in a national perspective, with a minimum of consideration for the international environment.

However, as always, " reality kicked back ". This holds for both policy instruments and target variables. First of all, it was found by experience that some domestic *instruments* of stabilization policy [i.e. some of the I_{na}'s and I_{np}'s in equation (1)] either were difficult to change, or did not influence the variables that the governments wanted to affect (such as domestic activity variables), or influenced variables that the governments did *not* want to affect (such as, in some cases, the balance of payments). For instance, countries trying, like the U.S. in the early 60's, to fight unemployment by way of low interest rates experienced, at fixed exchange rates, a deterioration in the balance of payments, with monetary disturbances for other countries as well; and in a system of floating exchange rates, governments experienced currency depreciations and associated price increases for tradables, as illustrated by developments in by the U.K. and Italy.

By contrast, countries trying to fight inflation with higher interest rates, like West Germany in the 60's, found out that, at fixed exchange rates, domestic policy was partly aborted by capital inflows and associated consequences for the domestic credit market. Thus, whereas expansionist monetary policy may generate balance of payments problems, contractive monetary policy may not have the intended effects on the domestic economy—at fixed exchange rates.

However, with floating rates a restrictive monetary policy is rather ideal from he point of view of fighting inflation, as the tendency of the exchange rate to appreciate helps stabilize prices for tradables. It is, of course, these circumstances, in combination with occasional tendencies for exchange rates to " overshoot, " that has stimulated the talk about " vicious " and " virtuous " circles under floating exchange rate regimes.

Experience during the post-World War II period has also shown that strategic domestic stabilization policy *target variables* are strongly influenced by fluctuations abroad in output and prices—not only in fixed but also in floating exchange rate systems, as only good luck would guarantee that short-term changes in exchange rates that equilibriate stock-demand and stock-supply of financial assets in various currency denominations also *eliminate* the short-term effects of foreign fluctuations on domestic output and prices.

All this illustrates, of course, the need of conceiving both macro analysis and stabilization policy in an international context.

A global analysis

The most popular approach to " international " macro analysis in recent years has been to study various transmission mechanisms between nations: Keynesian export-multipliers; direct price effects on tradables (the so called " commodity arbitrage mechanisms "); wealth effects via current account surpluses (or deficits); capital flows and associated interest rate effects; inter-country flows of labor and tendencies to wage rate arbitrage; inter-country transmissions of expectations and aspirations, etc. This " transmission-mechanism " approach is, of course, in stark contrast to the way economists traditionally analyze highly integrated areas *within* nations. For instance, the conventional way to pursue macro-economic analysis for the U.S. is certainly not to make separate analyses for individual states, and then study the "transmission mechanisms" between the states, but rather to study aggregates for the U.S. as a whole.

In the highly internationalized world economy of today, it is quite conceivable that, as a first approximation, an aggregate approach for the *group* of industrial market economies (such as the whole OECD area) is useful. For instance, in the context of a general equilibrium (or general disequilibrium) approach, aggregate excess demand functions for the world economy as a whole might be postulated for commodities, labor, credit instruments, and money, in order to explain the time path of output, prices, wage rates, and interest rates for the world economy as an integrated system.

However, to simplify matters, let us combine the commodity and labor markets into one equation, designed to express the rate of inflation as a function of capacity utilization, reflecting both "direct" effects on prices via excess demand for commodities, and indirect effects via excess demand for labor, which means, in fact, that the "real" part of the model is consolidated into one function. Moreover, as excess demand functions for credit are extremely difficult to construct empirically, it is convenient to drop the credit market (by Walras law), and instead retain an aggregate money market. This means, in fact, that the analysis is consolidated into one "real market" and one "monetary market".

Let us do some further violence to the general equilibrium approach, by trying *as one alternative* to explain the paths of nominal national income through the money market function, in conformity with monetarist thinking, and *as an alternative approach* to explain the price path through the function with aggregate capacity utilization as the independent variable, reflecting a "Keynes-Phillips" type approach. It is, of course, also possible to *combine* these two approaches.

The "monetary approach" is illustrated in chart 1, showing the rate of change of international reserves, national money stocks (approximately M_1) and nominal national income (nominal GDP). From this chart it is difficult to see any relation during the period 1960-68 that would suggest a causal interpretation like international reserves → national money stocks → nominal income. The chart looks more "friendly" to that interpretation for the "dramatic" period 1969-75—again relying on "eye-econometrics". [11]

Let us then turn to the "Keynes-Phillips" approach, letting capacity utilization be measured as the percentage deviation of actual output from

---

11. As the relation among the three time series differs so much between the two periods, and as we have very little *a priori* knowledge about the time lags—which may very well be strongly variable—it is not clear that a formal statistical estimation of the asserted functions is warranted.

However, if some regressions are tried, with constant time-lags, reasonably good statistical fits are obtained. In general, it would seem that a one percent increase in reserves is associated with about a 1/3 or 1/2 percent (later) increase in domestic money stocks, and that a one percent increase in domestic money stocks is associated with a 2/3 percent or perhaps slightly less than one percent (later) increase in nominal income—with the time lags in the "best" fits of some one or two years (if discrete time-lags are assumed).

The good statistical fits depend entirely on the observations from the latter part of the period (1969-76).

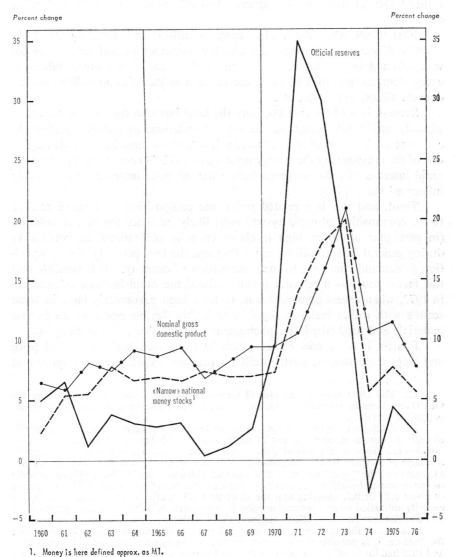

Chart 1

MONETARY VARIABLES AND GDP

Current Prices

OECD AREA AGGREGATES

Annual Data

Chart based on official OECD statistics

Percent change

Percent change

Official reserves

Nominal gross
domestic product

«Narrow» national
money stocks[1]

1960 61 62 63 64 1965 66 67 68 69 1970 71 72 73 74 1975 76

1. Money is here defined approx. as M1.

potential (full capacity) output in the OECD area as a whole (chart 2). [12] The chart " looks " no doubt quite consistent with the hypothesis that not only the unemployment rate but also, with a variable time lag, the rate of inflation is rather systematically related to the degree of unused capacity, both for 5-10 year trends and for major short- and medium-term fluctuations in capacity utilization. [13]

However, even if this " superaggregative " approach is useful, it is certainly not enough, when trying to explain the rate of " world inflation "—or rather " OECD inflation "—and even less of course inflation in individual countries.

First of all, when the level of capacity utilization is alrready quite high, additional increases of excess demand for commodities and factors are not well reflected in the degree of capacity utilization. Some other indices of excess demand may then be more useful, such as statistics on unfilled orders, delivery times, quit rates, etc.

Second, it is likely that not only the level but also the rate of change of capacity utilization influences the rate of inflation, as sectoral bottlenecks are more likely to occur in fast than in slow business upswings. This may be one of the reasons why the speedy upswing of 1972-73 resulted in an unusually rapid increase of inflation (even before the oil price increase, which mainly influenced the 1974 figures).

Third, and this is a related point, the composition of demand relative to the composition of capacity will most likely influence the rate of inflation (in particular at rather high levels of capacity utilization), as bottlenecks during general booms will be more frequent the less perfectly the composition of demand conforms to the composition of capacity. It is possible that this factor too was a relevant feature behind the rapid increase of inflation in 1973, when excess demand seems to have been particularly large in some sectors with rather inelastic supply and highly flexible prices—such as raw materials and food (the latter phenomenon largely due to crop failures).

Fourth, it is by now rather generally recognized that inertia and price and wage expectations, partly built on previous experiences, are important

---

12. The chart is based on OECD statistics; potential output is estimated by the OECD secretariat by way of a production function with available labor and capital as independent variables.

13. As the time lags are not well known, and possibly strongly variable, it is not feasible to make a rigorous econometric test of the hypothesis. However assuming that the rate of inflation is a function of the GNP-gap, with a constant time-lag, as well as of inflation in a number of previous periods—the latter variable expressing inertia or some kind of adaptive expectations—the " best " statistical fit is obtained with a time lag (for the GNP-gap variable) of one or one-and-a-half years, usually giving a coefficient in front of the GNP-gap variable of about 0.25 or 0.5, implying that the short-term effect, after a time-lag, of a change in capacity utilization by one percentage point is one quarter or half a percentage point on the rate of inflation—*plus* later effects via inertia or inflationary expectations.

It is conceivable that the response of inflation to capacity utilization is non-linear; for instance, it is possible that the dramatic changes in capacity utilization between 1972 and 1975 had larger effects on inflation than had previous, more modest variations in capacity utilization. For previous attempts to apply a global approach to international inflation, by way of global capacity utilization, see [Duck, et al., 1974] and [Lindbeck, 1975], the latter exposition using only graphic and verbal methods of analysis. For a more general discussion, see [Salant, 1977B].

Chart 2

OECD
UNEMPLOYMENT RATE (PERCENT OF CIVILIAN LABOR FORCE),
CHANGES IN CONSUMER PRICES AT ANNUAL RATES AND GNP-GAP
Semi-annual Data 1955-1976

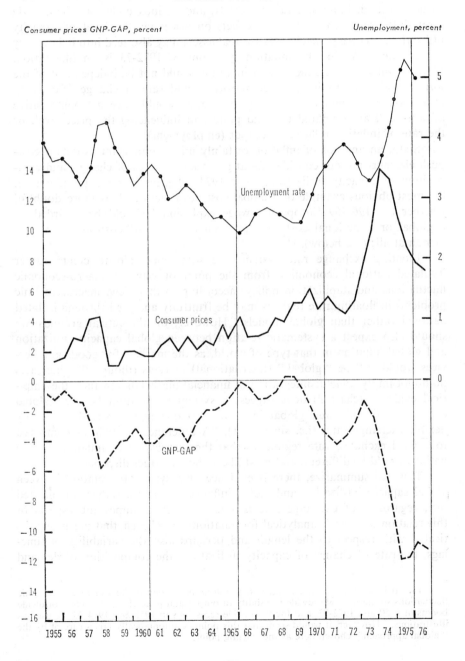

Consumer prices GNP-GAP, percent

Unemployment, percent

Unemployment rate

Consumer prices

GNP-GAP

71

determinants of inflation, which most likely is an important reason why inflation was greater in the deep 1974-76 recession than in the earlier much milder recessions. It is probably also a reason why inflation was greater in the 1971 recession than in the 1966 recession.

A somewhat related, fifth point is that a " world-wide " expansionary monetary policy may have a rather " direct " effect on prices of real assets —such as land, buildings, raw materials, and various collector's items—via asset shifts, quite apart from the effects on prices via the level of capacity utilization. These price changes for real assets may also feed into inflationary expectations. Again, the inflationary boom of 1972-73 is an illustration. If this point is correct, the rate of inflation would not be independent of the *way* in which a certain level, composition, and rate of change of capacity utilization is brought about; monetary policy would have a " comparative advantage ", as compared to fiscal policy, in influencing the price level, or the rate of inflation relative to output (employment).

Sixth, an analysis of inflation certainly misses important aspects if cost-push elements are not considered—at given levels, rates of change, and composition of capacity utilization. The 1974 oil price increase is, of course, the most obvious example of a global cost-push factor. It is more doubtful whether the 1968-69 European " wage explosion " should be regarded as a global or a national cost-push phenomenon—or a " cost-push " phenomenon at all; (see below). [14]

Floating exchange rate systems are sometimes said to create rather insulated national economies, from the point of view of macro-economic fluctuations and stabilization policy; according to that view, macroeconomic problems in floating rate regimes may be fruitfully analyzed through isolated national rather than global models. However, on theoretical grounds we should also expect a systematic relation between global capacity utilization and global inflation in that type of world, as the markets for goods and services would still be " global " (international) markets (though floating rates no doubt imply *some* disintegration of financial markets). In fact, the empirical evidence (chart 2) does suggest a systematic relation between global capacity utilization and global inflation also during the period of highly flexible exchange rates (i.e. since 1971). A difference, though, as compared to a fixed exchange rate regime, is that the *distribution* of inflation among nations would be different, and most likely show a larger dispersion.

Thus, to summarize, there is evidence of a systematic relation between global capacity utilization and global inflation, though a rather complicated one, regardless of exchange rate regime. However, important aspects of this relation are lost if analytical formulations are chosen that are unsophisticated with respect to the length and perhaps also the variability of time-lags, the rate of change of capacity utilization, the composition of demand

---

14. It is often also argued that a *synchronization* among nations of macroeconomic fluctuations strengthens worldwide instability of output and price changes. The worldwide booms in 1950 and 1972-73, and the worldwide recessions in 1958 and 1974-75 are used as illustrations. However, it would seem that this point is automatically taken care of by the " global approach " chosen here as the starting point.

relative to capacity, exchange rate changes, cost-push elements, and the role of inflationary expectations and asset shifts.

Acceleration versus non-acceleration

Chart 2 raises the important question whether the increased capacity utilization from the late fifties to the late sixties " only " meant that the rate of inflation was moved to a higher level, the " non-acceleration hypothesis, " or if instead a rate of capacity utilization was reached where the price trend tended to accelerate, the " acceleration hypothesis ".

Some light might be shed on this issue by looking at the OECD area *excluding* the U.S., as in that area no trendwise increase in capacity utilization occurred during the period in question; and up to about 1969 there was not any trend to higher inflation either. In other words, a " high " level of capacity utilization was sustained in that area for a very long period without any apparent tendency for the price trend to accelerate. The later increase in the rate of inflation in that area, from about 1969, may then be interpreted as an " import " of (additional) inflation from the U.S., when prices for tradables in the U.S. started to go up more rapidly, and when international liquidity " exploded " due to deficits in the U.S. balance of payments. The dramatic price development of 1973-75 can, of course, be explained by the specific historical features of that period, as mentioned above.

On the basis of these experiences, I do not think that we are entitled to argue, as some people do, that the permanent rather high level of capacity utilization in the non-U.S. part of the OECD area from the mid-fifties to the late sixties was *bound* to result in an acceleration of the price trend. It is still possible to argue, in view of available evidence, that the high level of capacity utilization in Europe and Japan during that period—often with not more than about 2 percent registered unemployment—may very well be consistent with a non-accelerating price trend. However, this statement needs some modifications. One is that a prerequisite for a non-accelerating price trend is that the exploitation of market power by strong organized groups in our societies, mainly the labor unions, does not force the authorities to accommodate even faster increases in nominal factor prices; however, that may happen at nearly *any* level of capacity utilization, except possibly in deep depressions. Another modification is that changes in the composition of the labor force, or higher voluntarily chosen " search unemployment, " partly a result of more liberal rules of unemployment compensation, may increase the level of registered unemployment for any given level of capacity utilization. A third modification, finally, is that inflationary " shocks " that hit a high-capacity utilization economy may tend to create prolonged periods of increasing inflation due to price-wage and wage-wage spirals, inflationary inertia, inflationary expectations, and a cost-accommodating demand management policy. Thus, a high-capacity utilization economy is easily pushed into steeper inflationary trends, because of the absence of shock-absorbers, in particular if the booms are highly synchronized among countries, so that supply elasticities for the world as a whole become small.

73

National differences

The fact that it may be useful, as a first approximation, to analyze fluctuations in output and prices in the OECD area as a whole by a " global " model does not, of course, mean that macroeconomic instability and inflation in individual countries are unrelated to specific conditions within these countries. There are several reasons for this: the labor market is usually rather national; tradable commodities and credit instruments from different countries are often far from perfect substitutes; a substantial part of GNP consists of commodities that may approximately be classified as " nontradables "; and a substantial fraction of domestically issued credit instruments may also be approximately classified as " nontradables ". The experience during the post-World War II period amply illustrates that domestic conditions *are* important, even in quite small countries. This certainly holds for fluctuations in output and employment. For instance, during the 1974-76 worldwide recession, countries pursuing domestic expansionary (employment-creating) policies, such as a number of small European countries, were indeed able to avoid heavy increases in unemployment, though they could not prevent some fall in the output of tradables. However, the policy was not without serious problems. Many of these countries experienced drastic increases in their current account deficits. It would also seem that in 1974-76, inflation dropped much more slowly in these countries than in countries where capacity utilization fell dramatically, such as the U.S., West Germany, Japan, and Canada, which probably illustrates that the domestic rates of wage and price increases are indeed influenced by domestic aggregate demand management—even among countries that are connected with fixed exchange rates (such as the countries in the D-mark zone). [15] Of course, sooner or later such deviations in the price trends will have consequences for the exchange rates, if heavy unemployment in the tradable sector is to be avoided. (Most of the small countries in the D-mark zone were, in fact, forced to devalue against the D-mark in late 1976 and early 1977.)

Thus, the national autonomy of stabilization policy for individual countries is a complex and multi-faceted problem, with an important role for *both* global and national forces.

The need for a fixed point

Inflation has been seen here as a very complex phenomenon, related to the level, rate of change, and composition of global and national demand relative to productive capacity; price expectations; and also the activities of organizations with strong market powers. However, rather than going

---

15. Again, rigorous estimates are difficult, because of ignorance about the time lags. This difficulty is accentuated by the fact that policy in some countries has been " swinging " back and forth between expansionary and restrictive actions. I have therefore abstained from formal estimation. However, in general I think that we are entitled to say that the size of unused capacity increased relatively much, and inflation went down much more rapidly, in the four countries mentioned in the text than in most other countries. See *OECD Outlook*, December 1976, Table 16, and information in other sections of that report on changes in capacity utilization.

further into the interrelations among these various factors, I would like to emphasize a specific feature of our economic system which contributes to the observed inflationary bias. I am thinking about the apparent lack of some " fixed point " that pins down the values of nominal magnitudes in the international and national economic systems.

It is well known that, in the context of general equilibrium theory, we can determine not only relative but also absolute prices if some *nominal* entity in the excess demand functions is exogenously determined. It is usually assumed that the exogenously determined variable in such models is the quantity of money, which then makes it possible to solve out not only relative prices but also the general price level [Patinkin 1956]. However, formally we could alternatively fix the price for some specific good such as labor or foreign exchange, which also makes it formally possible to determine the general price level.

To illustrate the point, let us assume a general equilibrium model with n " goods ", the nth being fiat money (m), and the prices of the other goods being denoted p_i. The excess demand functions are written f_i, in relative commodity prices and real money balances, where $\mathbf{P} = \sum_{i=1}^{n-1} \mu_i p_i$ is the general price level:

$$ f_i \left(\frac{p_1}{p_{n-1}}, \ldots, \frac{p_{n-2}}{p_{n-1}}, \frac{m}{\mathbf{P}} \right) = 0, \qquad i = 1, \ldots, n-1 $$

and where the nth market (for money) has been formally excluded by Walras' law. The system consists of $n-1$ endogenous variables—the relative prices $p_1\big/_{p_{n-1}}, \ldots, p_{n-2}\big/_{p_{n-1}}$, and $m/\mathbf{P}$—as well as of $n-1$ equations. Assuming that the system has all the mathematical properties that are required for a unique and economically meaningful solution in these variables, the system determines not only relative prices but also the general price level: from the solution for real money balances, $(\overline{m}/\mathbf{P}) = \alpha$, we derive $\mathbf{P} = \alpha/\overline{m}$, if m is exogenously given $(\overline{m})$.

If instead m is endogenous in the model, we can still solve out the real value of money balances $(m/\mathbf{P})$, but not the general price level separately. However, that can be done formally if some price of the model is exogenous, such as the price for labor. Let $p_1 = \overline{w}$ be the exogenously determined wage rate, and solve out the relative price $(\overline{w}/p_{n-1} = \beta)$, which gives $p_{n-1} = \overline{w}/\beta$; this makes it possible to calculate also all other absolute prices $p_2, \ldots, p_{n-2}$, and hence the general price level, $\mathbf{P}$. Alternatively, the exchange rate (e) may be exogenously given in a model where prices for tradable goods are formed on world markets, whereas other prices are formed on national markets. Formally prices for tradables are $p_t = \overline{e}p_t^*$. If world market prices (p_t^*) are *given* for the individual country, p_t is a parameter $\overline{p}_t = \overline{e}p_t^*$, and may be treated analytically in the same way as $\overline{w}$ above.

This somewhat esoteric point has some bearing on an understanding of the national and international economic systems of the real world. During the period of the gold standard, both the international and the national price levels were " tied down " by the fixed price of gold, and by the " discipline " on national government policies that was brought about by way of the effects of domestic inflation on the balance of payments (gold flows), and therefore on the money stock. We " learned " during the twenties and thirties that the straitjacket of the gold standard is " irrational, " because it limits the autonomy of national stabilization policy. However, perhaps we can say that the requirement of a balanced government budget, and thus also the net financial claims on the government, was still assumed by many politicians, and some economists, to serve as a constraint against inflationary policies. However, after having tasted " the Keynesian fruit of knowledge, " we economists abandoned the balanced budget as well; we were also, somewhat reluctantly, followed by politicians and the general public.

However, many politicians, administrators, and economists obviously still felt that *some* fixed point was necessary to " tie down " nominal variables, and hence provide some discipline over inflationary policies. In the absence of both the gold standard and the balanced budget, perhaps we could say that during the post-World War II period, the system of fixed exchange rates functioned as such a fixed (or quasi-fixed) point, except for the reserve currency country, the U.S., which was supposed to discipline itself (even before the abandonment of gold convertibility), and thereby also to be responsible for the world price level. In retrospect, this system did not function badly as long as the U.S. price level (for tradables) was steady, and as long as speculation in the value of the dollar did not generate strong capital outflows from the U.S. However, as we all know in hindsight, and some people saw in advance, the " fixed point " disappeared when these conditions, in particular during the last half of the sixties, were no longer fulfilled.

As a consequence of all these events, we seem to have created an international economic system without a fixed point that can determine the price level—thus leaving the determination of the price level in each country, and the world as a whole, to the discipline, or lack of it, i.e. to the *discretionary policy* of various individual governments, in interaction with the central banks and various strongly organized groups in our societies, mainly of course labor unions. After tasting " the fruit of knowledge " we have all, like Adam and Eve, been expelled for our sins from the Paradise of Price Stability. A cynic would perhaps say that in our attempts to remove various irrationalities of our economic and political system, we have in fact created the great irrationality of an indeterminate price level.

Our " sins " have, of course, not passed unnoticed by the various Political Churches of the world, who each have their own prescriptions on how to improve upon the situation. The monetarists want us to tie down the price level in each country, or group of countries, by an exogenous path of the quantity of money and/or international reserves—hoping that wages, prices, and (floating) exchange rates will adjust accordingly. The incomes policy advocates want us to make wage rates the fixed point of the system, by way of voluntary agreements or compulsory rules for wage (and possibly price) formation—letting perhaps the money stock adjust to an exogenously determined wage and price trend. And the advocates of fixed exchange rates, whom we find mainly among bankers but to some extent also among economists, have resumed the earlier lost mission. Various ecumenical churches have tried different combinations of these various gospels. An eclectic, like myself, probably has to join the ecumenical movement.

CONSEQUENCES FOR ALLOCATION POLICY

The public discussion of the consequences for national economic policy of increased international dependence and interdependence has focused on stabilization policy aspects. However, there are important consequences for allocation policy as well.

The most obvious consequence is perhaps the increased vulnerability of the domestic economy to supply disturbances for specific goods abroad — for instance due to strikes, political unrest, actions by cartels, embargoes, or other "non-market" disturbances. However, there are also some more "ordinary" market effects on the domestic economy. A natural starting point for a discussion of this aspect is the observation that international economic integration means that firms in various countries as a rule will be confronted with stiffer and more "impersonal" competition—at least during an adjustment period—as trade restrictions are removed and the geographical market domain widens, and the degree of monopoly is reduced. Analytically, firms will often experience flatter demand curves, less security in their markets against intrusion of rivals, and increased difficulties in bringing about agreements to restrict competition. On the basis of this broad hypothesis, several subhypotheses may be inferred. I would like to mention five such subhypotheses that seem to be of particular relevance for allocation policy.

1. First of all, profit margins, and the rate of return on physical assets, would be expected to fall, as a rule. [16] A basic difficulty in testing this hypothesis is, of course, that profit margins may fall for many reasons other than increased international competition, such as increased aggressiveness of labor unions, as indicated above. Moreover, in countries where the currency has become increasingly overvalued, a fall in profit margin may be regarded as the result of a "collision" between exchange rate policy and wage developments, rather than as an expression of stiffer international competition. However, by looking at a large number of countries, including those for which the exchange rate has become increasingly undervalued, the risk of this particular misinterpretation would be minimized. We could also compare the development of profit margins in sectors with different trends in the degree of competitiveness. What has been said here does not mean that the entire incidence of increased competition is assumed to fall on profit. Particularly scarce factors (i.e. factors with inelastic supply) in general in individual countries will experience a fall in relative factor prices when trade is liberalized— along the lines of the factor price equalization theorem.

2. Stiffer international competition would also, at least for a while, be expected to result in a more rapid rate of change in the comparative advantages among nations, as new countries enter as active competitors. However, the concept of comparative advantage is not easy to measure empirically, though indirectly we might be able to say something about the issue by looking at, for instance, the development of the size of net exports relative to output in various sectors.

3. A more rapid rate of change in comparative advantage, in turn, would be expected to result in a more rapid rate of structural change. This hypothesis might be investigated by looking at the rate of change of the com-

---

16. Some firms, for which new market opportunities are opened, may in a short and medium-term perspective experience increased profit however, when they invade earlier protected markets.

position of output and/or employment in the economy as a whole. However, as the most dramatic expansion of trade during the post-war period has taken place within rather than between sectors, except for sectors such as textiles, we would not expect that the internationalization process (so far) has had much of an influence on the rate of structural change between sectors. However, we would expect substantial effects on the structure of firms within sectors, such as the size distribution of firms, as a more rapid rate of structural change within a sector would be expected to show up in more mergers. We would also expect strong effects on the assortments of products within firms. If in the future the manufacturing sector of the less developed countries will become increasingly important for the supply of goods in the developed countries, the reallocation of resources between sectors in the latter countries will be more pronounced—and painful.

4. Insofar as a more rapid rate of structural change has been brought about, we would also expect a tendency to more frictional and structural unemployment, as measured by, for instance, the long-term trend of the *sum* of unemployment and openings (relative to the labor force). As different regions within a country often specialize in different industries, we would expect increased frictional and structural unemployment also to show up as increased regional dispersion of unemployment. However, as many factors other than international competition also may generate frictional and structural unemployment—regulation of relative wage rates " against market forces, " liberalization of the rules for unemployment compensation, etc.—it will in practice be difficult to identify the influence of increased international competition.

5. The squeeze on profit margins would also be expected to result in a tendency toward a fall in the growth rate of private investment, and therefore also in long-term economic growth, at least if profitability is already below a certain level, so that factors other than profitability and internal funds do not constitute the effective constraints on private investment. If this development of profits is a combined effect of stiffer international competition and more aggressive wage policy, so that not only does the profitability of investment fall, but also the real wage rate rises relative to real capital costs, we would not only expect investments to fall, but also that the investments actually undertaken would become more capital-intensive than otherwise. There is then a risk that full capacity utilization of the capital stock will be reached before full capacity utilization of the labor force—an obvious possibility in several countries during the cyclical upswing after the 1974-75 recession. However, in countries where the cost of energy has increased greatly relative to labor costs (such as in the US), no such increase in the costs of labor relative to capital may have taken place during the period 1974-1978, and perhaps later as well.

There are not enough empirical studies so far available to give us confidence in the empirical relevance of these various hypotheses. However, even a rather casual look at easily available statistics suggests that the relevant time series have at least moved in the directions asserted by the hypotheses. This seems to be the case in particular for profit margins, the speed of structural

78

change (in particular mergers), structural unemployment, and the tendencies concerning the volume of private investment. [Lindbeck, 1973.]

The reason why hypotheses like these are difficult to test is not only that the asserted developments may be the result of changes in the economic system other than increased international competition, but also that the asserted tendencies refer to *hypothetical* developments with unchanged policies, whereas in reality economic policy would be expected to react to the asserted tendencies.

In fact, the reactions of governments to the asserted effects are one of the most interesting aspects of the whole process. Governments cannot avoid reacting in some way to developments like these, in particular in view of the recent tendencies of governments in many countries to raise and differentiate their policy ambitions, for instance with respect to employment opportunities, income distribution, and environmental quality. In fact, it would seem that governments are no longer satisfied with a " generally " high level of employment, incomes, and environmental quality, but are increasingly concerned with the unemployment, income, and environmental situation for various subgroups of the population, such as the elderly, the young, the handicapped, and various other minority groups; most recently with the employment situation in specific firms and regions—sometimes perhaps in particular in regions with voters of substantial marginal importance for the next election.

INDUSTRIAL POLICY, NEOMERCANTILISM, AND NEOPROTECTIONISM

Thus to summarize: at the same time that national governments have become more anxious to control the domestic economies—in terms of stabilization, allocation, and distribution policies—the autonomy of national economic policy has fallen. (In some countries, the autonomy of national governments is also challenged by demands for regionalization, or federalization, within the national states.)

All this constitutes an important part of the background for recent attempts by national governments to develop new policy tools, or revitalize some old ones, in order to restore some of the autonomy of the national state, and hence to make it easier to achieve the ever more ambitious policy targets. The " new industrial policies, " or the emerging " neomercantilism " and " neoprotectionism, " can fruitfully be seen in this light. Obvious examples are the implementation of strongly *selective* policy instruments, such as selective fees on imports and selective subsidies on exports; subsidies on production, employment, and research and development; public capital grants and subsidized credit; tying of foreign aid; protectionism in government purchases; the exploitation of regulations of product standards for protectionist purposes; and regulation of the competition of foreign enterprises, by way of so called voluntary agreements on exports as well as regulation of the entry of " alien " production units.

Thus we have in recent years experienced the historically rather unique situation that national governments simultaneously have introduced liberalization of tariffs and increased intervention in the domestic economies. Many interesting economic and political problems today are related to these divergent trends.

PROBLEMS CONNECTED WITH THE NEW POLICIES

What, then, are the main problems connected with these more interventionist and selective domestic policies?

As the new policies mainly rely on methods that influence price relations and the composition of demand—for reasons discussed at the beginning of the paper—it is natural to focus the analysis on the effects on relative prices, or more specifically on the information and incentive content of the price system, and on the allocation of resources.

In certain cases, the selective measures undertaken may, no doubt, *improve* the information and incentive content of the price system, and hence the allocation of resources, from the point of view of economic efficiency and optimality. Obvious examples are taxes on environmental disturbances and wage subsidies to elderly and handicapped people who otherwise, at prevailing wage rates, would be unemployed, and perhaps also general subsidies on the use of labor in unemployment areas and taxes on employment in " overheated " areas—if we regard stickiness of relative wage rates and limited mobility of labor as " given ". However, a large (and I would say *major*) part of the new allocation policy, such as strongly selective production and investment subsidies, cannot easily be defended on these grounds.

To illustrate the problems of investment stimulus, let us, in the conventional way, assume that new investment can be arranged along a scale of falling rate of return, i.e. along a marginal efficiency of investment curve (Chart 3). Let us also assume that the curve is originally II. If capital costs are r_1, the investment volume is i_f, which is also assumed to be the " desired " volume, in the view of the authorities; let us simply call it " the full employment investment volume ". Now suppose that the rate of return curve falls to $I'I'$, for instance due to stiffer international competition, tending to result in an investment volume of i_1. In order to restore the investment volume to the initial level, i_f, i.e. to what is required for full employment, several alternative policies are possible, in principle.

One possibility would be to use a rather general type of stimulus, by reducing capital costs across the board to r_2. This may be achieved for instance by a reduction in interest rates or by a *general* subsidization of investment expenditures (or a reduction in a possibly existing investment tax). In a highly open economy, the latter approach may in many cases be superior, as the governments may want to reserve monetary policy for balance of payments purposes (in a fixed exchange rate country) or to influence the exchange rate (in a floating rate regime). For an individual country, a devaluation is an alternative, or complementary, approach.

However, several countries have in recent years chosen strongly selective ways of stimulating investment expenditures. One reason may be the existence of political targets concerning the allocation of investment expenditures, sometimes connected to social targets concerning for instance housing, sometimes to prestigious high-technology projects in manufacturing, or simply to short-term vote-getting considerations, as politicians seem to believe that political payoffs are greater if the government can take credit for specific projects —a new factory or some specific jobs that are rescued—rather than general improvements in production and employment opportunities. Another reason may be a desire to stimulate investment only in fields with some amply available factors of production, such as unemployed labor in certain regions or production sectors. A third reason, finally, may be

80

Chart 3

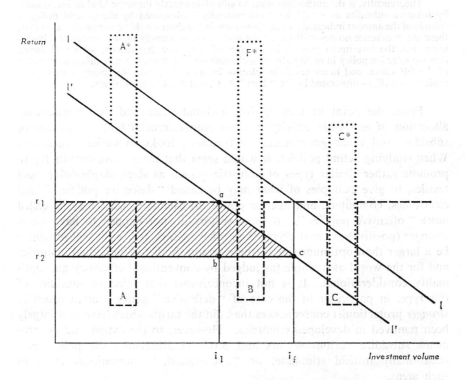

income distribution considerations, or more specifically an unwillingness to accept a general increase in profits, which would (at least temporarily) be the result of a genreral reduction in capital costs; in the context of chart 3, this increase in profits is illustrated by the shaded area.

On the basis of some of these reasons, several alternative policies might be implemented. One possibility would be to reduce capital costs in a selective way; in the context of Chart 3, we would then get a discontinuous capital cost curve, as illustrated for instance by the broken (step) surve in the chart.   As a consequence, investments with quite different rates of return (before the subsidy) will be brought about—some investment that would have come about anyway (illustrated by the horizontal segment of the bar denoted *A*); some which are among the " marginal " investments that would have been brought aobut by a general reduction in capital costs (illustrated by the horizontal segment of the bar denoted *B*); and some with a very low rate of return (illustrated by the horizontal segment of the bar *C*).   In fact, it is quite conceivable that a number of projects with negative rates of return (before subsidies) would also come about.

A rather similar result can be brought about if the authorities, as an alternative, sub-sidize in a selective way outputs or factors of production other than capital.   In the context of chart 3, we would then get a new discontinuous marginal efficiency jof investment curve—I'I' modified by the discontinuous deviations as illustrated by the contours of the dotted bars.   The horizontal segments of the bars A*, B*, and C* then denote the invest-ments which will receive such subsidies.

Instead of a general increase in profits, there will in both cases be selective increases in profits for some investment projects.   Depending on the exact design of the policy, this selective profit increase may be smaller or greater than the general profit increase in the case of a general reduction in capital costs.   It is likely, however, that the authorities would at least try to make the total increase in profit smaller in the case of selective subsidies, as the policy often in fact is motivated by a desire to limit the income redistribution in favor of profits.

Theoretically, if the authorities want to stimulate exactly the same kind of investments by selective subsidies as would be "automatically" stimulated by the general policy, a subsidy of the amount indicated by the triangle abc in the chart would be required. However, there are in practice no possibilities for the authorities to identify these "marginal" investments (i.e. the investment projects in the interval bc). For that reason, we would expect that the selective policy in reality always will subsidize investments at *very* different branches of the I^hI^h curve, and hence result in selective increases in profits for many nonmarginal projects as well, as illustrated by the "bars" A, C, and A*, C*, respectively.

From the point of view of international trade and the international allocation of economic activity it is, of course, crucial how the *pattern* of subsidies and other government interventions looks in various countries. When studying actual policies, it would seem that many governments try to promote rather similar types of industries—such as steel, shipbuilding, and textiles, to give examples of what may be called "defensive policies," and electronics, computers, and nuclear power, to exemplify what may be called more "offensive policies". If these sectors do not happen to have much stronger (positive) external effects than other sectors, the result will of course be a larger than optimum size of these sectors both for individual countries and for the world as a whole (as judged by conventional efficiency and optimality considerations). It is not inconceivable that selective subsidies of this type, in particular in the case of "defensive" actions, often result in *stronger* protectionist consequences than did the tariffs which have now largely been removed in developed countries. However, to the extent that governments subsidize various sectors and products differently, the policy may occasionally instead stimulate, or "overexpand," international trade in such areas.

Thus, to summarize, many of the new selective interventions, partly induced by increased international competition and increased international disturbances in general, in combination with more ambitious and more detailed policy targets and more aggressive wage bargaining, constitute a serious threat to efficiency in the allocation of resources in the world economy, probably even more so than the tariffs which have been removed, as tariffs often were more *general* types of interventions. From that point of view, it could reasonably be argued that future conferences on international trade should perhaps concentrate on reducing these various selective subsidies and similar interventions in the allocation of resources rather than on cutting tariffs. That would have the additional effect of perhaps stopping, or even reversing, the enormous concentration of economic powers in the hands of central planning administrators and politicians, which is perhaps the major consequence for our societies of the ever more selective interventions.

Traditionally in economic theory, subsidies of production are usually regarded as less distorting for the allocation of resources than tariffs, as the latter change relative prices not only for producers but also for consumers, which has been analyzed as an "excess burden" of tariffs for consumers. (See [Corden, 1974].) However, that conclusion rests on a comparison of tariffs and subsidies with about the same "structure" among goods. When in the present exposition tariffs are regarded as usually *less* distorting than subsidies, the reason is that the pattern of subsidies, in my judgment, nowadays tends to be more uneven among sectors than tariffs (with subsidies of perhaps 25 or even 50 percent of production costs in some sectors, and zero in others); that subsidies are usually implemented in a more interventionist fashion, with different levels of subsidies for different firms; and often also that subsidies create bargaining situations between individual firms and public officials which means that " the parametric function " of prices will be destroyed, and that firms will find that bargaining with public officials often gives a much higher rate of return than do market activities, such as cost reductions and innovations. For these reasons, the proliferation of selective subsidies tends today, in many countries, to erode the information and incentive content of the price system.

ALTERNATIVE STRATEGIES

There are, in principle, several alternative and partly complementary strategies to deal with the problems created for national states by the internationalization process; by the increasingly ambitious and detailed policy targets of governments; and by associated tendencies for governments to use more selective policy tools, which by their nature tend to disturb other countries.

I. One strategy is a *retreat* from the internationalization process, by way of more protectionism. This would, in fact, mean that we would try to adjust the economic system to the national character of the political system. I have argued here that a return to higher tariffs probably would be a less distorting way to achieve this end than is the new type of selective " industrial policy " that is now pursued in various countries. Tariffs are also more consistent with a decentralized market economy than are highly selective and very detailed interventions in the decision-making in individual branches and firms by administrators and politicians—without apparent competence in production, marketing, or innovation activities.

II. A second strategy would be to accept a highly internationalized economic system, but try to *reconcile* it with nationally based political systems, either by way of more efficient automatic adjustment mechanisms between countries, such as freely floating exchange rates and more perfectly functioning international capital markets, *or* by way of the deployment of domestic policy tools, with a minimum of " distorting " cross-country effects, such as general subsidies (taxes) on investment and on the employment of handicapped or poorly trained labor, income compensating schemes, and measures that promote factor mobility within countries. These policies would be in stark contrast with the present trend to highly selective interventions by way of subsidies, capital grants, and regulations in individual industries and even individual firms. However, to the extent that low domestic profitability is a consequence of aggressive wage bargaining, it is quite possible that labor will " seize " the subsidies to investment by way of additional wage increases, which would mean that there may be no easy " policy fix " for the profitability problem, if labor unions do not accept a profitability level that is necessary for high levels of investment.

III. A third strategy, finally, would be to try more energetically the difficult road of international *coordination and cooperation* of economic policy, i.e. to try to adjust, to some extent, the political system to the international character of the economic system. Such coordination could, of course, take many different forms, the most modest version being simply exchange of information among governments so that (iterative) decisions by individual governments are made with the best possible knowledge about what other governments are up to.

A more ambitious form of coordination would be coordination of the actual use of certain policy instruments, largely for the purpose of preventing strong cross-country policy disturbances, escalations in the " world level " of some instruments, or " cobweb " patterns of policies in various countries. International agreements about the level and structure of interest rates, monetary growth rates, and exchange rates are, of course, obvious candidates for such concerted actions.

An even more ambitious form of policy coordination would be the coordination of basic policy targets, which however would require a considerable homogeneity of preferences among governments and voters in various countries. However, in deep international recessions and in pronounced international booms it may be possible at least for the major countries to agree about the direction in which to influence aggregate demand, to avoid " prisoners' dilemma " type situations where everybody either is waiting for export-led expansions generated by expansionary policies in other countries or is hoping for reduced inflation in world markets. The problem is, of course, much more difficult when the world economy is simultaneously plagued with both unemployment and inflation, as in the 1974-77 period. My judgment is that the best policy action in such a situation is a temporary reduction in indirect taxes on goods and services in several countries—consumer goods as well as capital goods. Such a policy both stimulates spending, partly by way of substitution between periods, and reduces immediately the short-term rate of inflation. I have always been surprised that governments have not much tried this type of policy, preferably in international cooperation.

Policy coordination discussed so far could perhaps be called " positive coordination, " in the sense of trying to achieve coordinated actions by governments. A somewhat different type of policy coordination—perhaps it could be called " negative coordination "—is agreements among governments about rules and guidelines for non-acceptable, and/or acceptable, uses of policy instruments (what sometimes is called " policy harmonization "). This has been tried with considerable success in the case of tariffs, with less success for exchange rates, and with very little success for subsidies and similar interventions in production and trade.

We may ask what type of international economic system can be expected as an outcome of future agreements about such rules and guidelines. If we want to be realistic, we should obviously not expect that future rules about the *exchange rate system* will be based on a system of fixed rates (adjust-

84

able pegs). The rather successful performance of that system during the first one or two decades after the Second World War was based on quite unique historical circumstances that made the disequilibrium in the market for foreign exchange, that necessarily follows from price control on foreign exchange, a very special one. That system was bound to break down when the deficit of the main reserve currency country (the U.S.) no longer happened to coincide with the desire of the outside world to accumulate reserves; when the confidence of the real value of the reserve currency was eroded by increased inflation and an ever larger volume of debt of the U.S.; and when the increased size of foreign held assets in general in the world, in combination with partially restored convertibility, made capital markets much too integrated to permit uncoordinated national policies without highly speculative capital movements.

In other words, the very specific historical circumstances that made the system of fixed exchange rates work have disappeared. One of the main consequences is that the supply of international reserves no longer is determined, to the same extent as earlier, by the economic policy of the U.S. and by the expectations about the dollar exchange rate; it results instead from the joint effect of monetary policy in a great number of countries. Thus, there is no *central* control over the supply of international liquidity and international reserves, which even become difficult to define. However, the risk of an explosion of international liquidity as in 1970-72 is less likely now when the main reserve currency country is floating.

It may also be difficult to retain the liberal *trade system* that has been one of the main achievements of international diplomacy during the post-World War II period. I am here thinking not only about the demands from governments in some LDC's to replace free trade with international price regulation, cartellization, and state regulated trade, but also about the previously discussed tendencies of governments in developed countries to intervene drastically and in detail in the allocation of resources and hence also in trade flows by way of " new industrial policies, " which is often simply a euphemism for protectionism and mercantilism. The likelihood of such developments is accentuated if the adjustment mechanisms of the balance of payments, in particular the current account, do not work reasonably well, for instance because of stickiness of real wages in the tradable sector, even in the case of exchange rate changes.

It is, of course, possible that governments in practice will try all or most of these various strategies simultaneously: retreats from the internationalization process, largely by way of highly selective protectionist interventions; development of policy instruments designed to reconcile international economic forces with domestic political ambitions; and attempts to achieve some policy coordination—the most probable result of all this being *permanent crises*, and *ad hoc* policies to deal with them. Most likely, this is what we should expect of the future, in view of the complexity of the problems at hand, the varying conceptions and understanding of the real world, and the different interests of citizens among and within various countries.

In other words, it is probably realistic to expect a continuation of the kind of " semi-organized anarchy " which has always characterized inter-

85

national relations, but which has, in fact, allowed a remarkable improvement in material well-being in the industrialized world during the last century, and in particular after the Second World War. The optimist may hope for something better, but the pessimist (if he has rather traditional " liberal " values) could certainly imagine something much worse, such as strongly centralized, government-operated national economies, in economic warfare with each other. I did not say that I am a pessimist.

REFERENCES

Brainard, W. [1967], " Uncertainty and the Effectiveness of Policy, " *American Economic Review*, Papers and Proceedings, May 1967, *57*, pp. 411-25.

Calmfors, L. and Herin, J. [1977], " Price-Formation and Open Economies—A Case Study for Sweden, " Institute for International Economic Studies, Stockholm (forthcoming).

Cooper, R. [1968], *The Economics of Interdependence*, New York.

Cooper, R. [1974], *Economic Mobility and National Economic Policy*, Wiksell Lectures, Stockholm.

Corden, M. [1974], *Trade Policies and Economic Welfare*, Oxford, 1974.

Duck, N., Parkin, M., Rose, D., and Zis, G. [1976], " The Determinants of Wages and Prices in the Fixed Exchange Rate World, 1956-71, " in Parkin, M., and Zis, G. (eds.), *Inflation in the World Economy*, Manchester, 1976, pp. 113-43.

Kuznets, S. [1967], " Quantitative Aspects of the Economic Growth of Nations Level and Structure of Foreign Trade: Long Term Trends, " *Economic Development and Culture Change*, vol. 15, no. 2, Part II.

Lindbeck, A. [1973], " The National State in an Internationalized World Economy, " Seminar Paper no. 26, Institute for International Economic Studies, University of Stockholm.

Lindbeck, A. [1976], " Stabilization Policy in Open Economies with Endogenous Politicians, " *American Economic Review*, May 1976.

Lindbeck, A. [1975], " Business Cycles, Politics, and International Economic Dependence, " *Skandinaviska Enskilda Banken Quarterly Review*, no. 2, 1975.

Machlup, F. [1977], *A History of Thought on Economic Integration* (forthcoming).

Nyberg, L. and Viotti, S. [1976], " Controllability and the Theory of Economic Policy: A Critical Note, " Institute for International Economic Studies, University of Stockholm, Seminar Paper no. 61.

Patinkin, D. [1956], *Money, Interest, and Prices*, Evanston, Illinois.

Salant, W. [1977A], " The International Transmission of Inflation, " in *Worldwide Inflation*, Brookings Institution (forthcoming).

Salant, W. [1977B], " A Supernational Approach to the Analysis of World Inflation, " in *Worldwide Inflation*, Brookings Institution (forthcoming).

Whitman, M. v. N., " Economic Openness and International Financial Flows, " *Journal of Money, Credit, and Banking*, vol. 1, no. 4 (Nov. 1969).

2

COMMENT

by Professor W. Max Corden (Australia)

Professor Lindbeck has given us a thoughtful, comprehensive, and also quite original paper. It focuses on the internationalisation of the economies of the industrialised world and the limits this has created for national policy-making. He ends by listing three alternative strategies for the future, namely: first, retreat into protectionism; secondly, reconciling international economic integration with national political systems; and thirdly, relying on international co-ordination and co-operation. Clearly, all three policies are being followed to some extent, and the question is what weight is being given or should be given to each. Rather than take up particular points in Professor Lindbeck's paper—and I really have no particular disagreements— I should like to make some general remarks on the broad issues he raises.

The post-war recovery of Europe and Japan, greatly helped by generous and imaginative American assistance in both cases, inaugurated a period of unparalleled growth in standards of living in the industrialised world, notably of course in Japan and in continental Europe. While there were fluctuations, especially the Korean boom and slump episodes, until 1973 it was essentially a period of uninterrupted growth. It was a great success story, certainly not predicted during or immediately after the war. This growth success coincided with the internationalisation of the OECD world as described by Professor Lindbeck. An interesting issue is whether this internationalisation was a significant contributory cause of growth, or rather, whether it was a consequence. The answer is probably that it was both. That it is likely to have been a *cause* follows from general economic principles—the gains from specialization and comparative advantage and from increased competition. It must also to some extent have been a *consequence*: it is easier to reduce restrictions in trade and capital movements in an environment of general growth.

This high and steady growth came to an end in 1973 or early 1974, and reasonable price stability came to an end a few years earlier. Now, in all the OECD countries in varying degrees there is unemployment that is much higher than it used to be, and with a few notable exceptions there are high rates of inflation. The unpleasant figures will be known to everybody here.

87

From the point of view of the issues of this paper, this raises two questions: first, can one blame the internationalisation of the OECD economies, as described by Professor Lindbeck, for these troubles? Secondly, to deal with these difficulties now that we have them, whatever the reasons, is it necessarily desirable to retreat from internationalism, to *de-link* the economies to some extent? These are the big issues and obviously I cannot go fully into them here. Professor Lindbeck has given us some partial answers.

To turn to the first question: can one blame the internationalisation of the OECD economies for our troubles? Broadly, while it is true that there has been in the early 1970s an international transmission of inflation, there was plenty of scope for countries to counteract the transmission effects. Above all, countries were free to appreciate their exchange rates. The fact that the disturbances happened everywhere certainly suggests that there was an international process. Inflation can be generated by relative price changes —the rise in the price of oil and, to a lesser extent, of other primary commodities—and these relative price changes affected all countries. But there is no clear evidence that the more protectionist countries, like Australia, suffered less than the more open economies, like the Scandinavian countries. What mattered rather were the domestic policy responses, including exchange rate adjustments, and these depended on social attitudes, historical considerations, and so on.

To turn to the second question, is de-linking now desirable to deal with these problems? The answers would seem to be fairly clear. For some individual countries to be free to counter inflation more effectively than others, a de-linking of exchange rates is certainly necessary. But there is no need to retreat into protectionism or fragmentation of the international markets for capital, technology, and so on.

Again, this is admittedly a large issue and one must qualify any answer. In many countries, the forces of protectionism are currently very strong. There is a widespread feeling that if a government is to take the problems firmly in hand it needs independence from foreign disturbances and foreign constraints. But it can go a long way with exchange rate flexibility, which is necessary but not sufficient to deal with its domestic inflation independently of what other countries do, and with flexibility of fiscal policy, including the ability to adjust indirect taxes and various subsidies.

Then there is the unemployment problem, a problem common to all our countries. Can protection or de-linking help here? It is now, I suspect in a number of countries at least, generally a problem of excessively high real wages for certain categories of people, notably the young and the unskilled. It is not a problem to be dealt with by traditional Keynesian means. De-linking, even of exchange rates, will have little effect here. Even protection of particular labour-intensive industries, such as textiles, will not go to the root of the problem. That would have locally favourable effects on employment, but the problem is more widespread. Furthermore, it would be a way of shifting the unemployment from the developed to the developing countries.

Let me return to Professor Lindbeck's three alternative strategies for the future.

Perhaps a retreat into protectionism—in Europe under the euphemism of " industrial policy "—is inevitable at a time of slump and excessively high wages of some workers. But I doubt that there is either evidence or logical argument to suggest that it would significantly help to solve the problem, and its long-term costs are well known.

Professor Lindbeck's third alternative—international co-ordination and co-operation—is obviously desirable. But it has familiar limits. There are of course particular benefits in the exchange of information about common problems, and that is what OECD is all about. I would suggest the heaviest reliance will have to be placed upon—and indeed *is* being placed upon—his second alternative, namely " to accept a highly internationalised economic system but to try and reconcile it with nationally-based political systems ". The nation-state is a reality and national thinking still dominates attitudes in most if not all our countries. Given this, we must try and preserve the economic integration in the flows of trade, capital, and technology that have been achieved. But countries will wish to have independent monetary and fiscal policies, and so some exchange rate flexibility will be needed to make these compatible. Perhaps, if we can survive these unfortunate few years (I hope few years) without long-term harm—that is without a retreat into protectionism—ready to move into another era of prosperity, and having learnt a few lessons meanwhile, we should be grateful.

3

COMMENT

by Dr. Giorgio La Malfa (Italy) [1]

Professor Lindbeck's paper is a most stimulating reflection on the problems of internationalisation of economic activities versus national economic policy tools. The paper leads naturally to some difficult questions which we have to tackle in our discussion.

His argument is that the effectiveness (in the sense he defines it) of national economic policy tools, measured by their ability to reach assigned targets, has been greatly reduced by the integration of markets for tradable commodities. In the second place, he claims that greater international competition has had allocative effects, among which the most notable is a fall in profit margins, or in the rate of profit from most tradable commodities, which in turn entails a fall in investment incentives in most industrial countries. Out of this framework, which Professor Lindbeck has set forth very clearly, comes a basic choice among three alternatives which he mentions in his paper: namely, retreat into protectionism; reconciling international economic integration with the national political system; and, third, relying on international coordination and cooperation.

I find of particular interest the observation that protectionism is now appearing in disguise in most industrial countries, in the sense that it takes the form of an apparently legitimate industrial policy, trying to subsidise particular investment or employment situations of special groups in our countries. That, as Professor Lindbeck justly observes, is going to cost even more in terms of efficiency and welfare than a traditional tariff system, and it contains all the dangers of protectionism as such.

I find the paper very pessimistic in attitude but, unfortunately, a quite realistic assessment of where the international economic situation is leading nowadays. I would like, so to speak, to add some further gloom to the abundant amounts of gloom which we have been pouring forth in our conference, by recalling that Professor Lindbeck does not mention or analyze the further consequences of the oil crisis which has been developing over the past four years in the world. If we take into account the kind of developments which

---

1. Revised text prepared by the Editor on the basis of the verbatim transcript of the Conference.

followed from the oil crisis, we are likely to get a picture in which elements of protectionism will tend to be even more widespread and more readily adopted.

In 1974, OECD countries had some $ 20 billion balance-of-payments deficit on current account, and in 1975 this figure was smaller due only to the serious recession which took place in most of our countries. In 1976, the deficit is back to where it was in 1974, and now the consensus among economists seems to be that it will stay there for many years to come unless we project another period of recession as serious as the one we went through in 1975. Doubts are now being very frequently voiced about the banking system's ability to manage the OPEC surpluses by funnelling them into deficit countries through the kind of recycling of which we heard quite a lot in 1974 and do not hear so much nowadays. Even to think about triangular schemes of financing now seems very difficult—schemes which have been discussed over the past three years, in which OPEC countries lend to developing non-oil-producing countries, either directly or through the channel of international organisations, and then these less developed non-oil-producing countries purchase commodities from industrial countries, and these finally would pay back their oil bills to the OPEC countries through the income from sales to underdeveloped countries. That would be a cooperative scheme in which we could both sustain industrial activity in industrial countries and improve the prospect for development of less developed countries; but of such schemes, we do not hear very much now. They seem to be very difficult to work out.

It seems to me that for OECD countries as a whole, and even for the Common Market countries, it would be possible to cope with the problem of energy in real terms, namely, with some combination of energy savings with a search for alternative sources of energy, and with pressure on oil-producing countries to lower their prices. In some sense, it would even be possible to face the problem of current account balance-of-payments deficits in monetary terms; namely, we could all together accept the existence of a deficit for the OECD countries as a whole without worrying too much. Yet nothing of this sort is done. The real intervention through investment in energy is not taking place, nor has any solidarity been developing among oil-consuming countries over the last three years, notwithstanding the many talks that have taken place on this matter. So what we are doing (without saying it out loud) is simply trying to shift the deficit around among industrialised countries. We are each trying every year to close the gap in the balance-of-payments by moving it to some other industrial country. And this situation is introducing (I think Professor Lindbeck is right in general and would be especially right in this matter) elements of protectionism, open or hidden protectionism, in most of our economic policy decisions and is bound to increase the amount of protectionism generally.

The second point which I would briefly mention is inflation. Here I disagree somewhat with Professor Corden's comments. I consider that in most industrial countries—and obviously I think mainly of the experience of my own country, Italy, but also of a country like England—there has been either open indexation of money incomes or *de facto* indexation of incomes

91

through wage bargains. Such a situation is going to make almost impossible the use of exchange rate changes as a tool for coping with inflation. In other words, a movement in exchange rates tends to get into prices through various indexation schemes, and then leads to further imbalance in the balance-of-payments and further devaluation. That prevents, in most medium-sized industrial countries, the use of exchange rates as a viable tool for coping with inflationary pressures.

Not only energy but also inflation is a question which has to be tackled at an international level. It has to be tackled jointly by most industrial countries—both the countries which are suffering from inflation and those which have been freer from inflation, like Germany or the United States. In some sense, what we need in this area is an international policy which is jointly a policy to reduce inflationary pressures through guidelines on incomes or stringent directions on public finance and monetary policy, together with some stimulus to recovery which has to be introduced in the international economy as a whole. We now have countries, like Germany, which have almost totally solved the problem of inflation, but which are not willing to provide any support to other countries' levels of activity. I can see many good reasons for a country like Germany not wanting to risk more internal inflation simply in order to help the recovery of other countries. Yet there are many countries in which social problems are serious. In a country like Italy, where there are problems of regions which are less developed and where unemployment is still very high, the danger of fighting inflation through an increase in unemployment is so paralysing to governments that they would rather have more inflation than risk more unemployment. Therefore, in this field of inflation we either get a common policy, which together creates greater discipline in terms of monetary and fiscal and incomes policies, plus some policy of international stimulus to industrial investment and industrial recovery, or each country is going to try to face the problem alone, which entails for some countries a state of hyperinflation but for most countries more inflation and more unemployment as well.

These are the two main comments I wanted to add to Professor Lindbeck's excellent paper. The conclusion is that we need political action at this point. Political action means not merely accepting the second alternative of Professor Lindbeck's three, as Professor Corden seems to favour. We need to move towards internationalisation of the political system in which we function. We have to take up the problem of further political integration at least on a regional level—at the level of Western European countries. I agree on this point with the comment this morning that the existence of a common enemy may help towards solving the problem. Yet the problem today is not that there is no common enemy, but rather that we do not see very clearly where it is or what the dangers of the situation are. It takes better politicans than we generally have in industrial countries nowadays to see the dangers of what lies ahead for our countries.

John Maynard Keynes, during the discussions of the peace treaties after the first World War, was able to see very clearly where the peace treaties would lead most European countries. He was able a few years later, in

1926, to foresee the economic consequences of Mr. Churchill's policies. Unfortunately, no politican at that time was as far-sighted as John Maynard Keynes, and we have been going through very serious troubles because myopia seems to be the rule for politicans.

4

COMMENT

by Professor Dr. André J. Vlerick (Belgium)

May 1 say first of all how glad I am to participate in this conference, being myself a survivor of the Marshall Plan.   I started my career as responsible for the operations under the Marshall Plan for the Belgium-Luxembourg economic union, and I am happy to see here many colleagues I worked with at that time.

I read with the greatest interest and studied, because it is not so easy a text, the paper of Professor Lindbeck, and I agree with the general line and with his conclusion.   My comments therefore will be more on specific points and also on what he said about alternative strategies.

First of all Professor Lindbeck says that the trade shares have remained stable in relation to the GNP.   I don't think it is very appropriate to compare trade to GNP; he himself recognises this point when he says that, of course, GNP has risen much more because of the non-tradable public sector, " which is indeed the case.   Even if we exclude the public sector and services in general and look at the world statistics of the United Nations, we find that the growth rate in production of goods, value added in agriculture and industry, from 1955 to 1972, was 5.7 per cent per year; but trade was growing in volume in that same period by 7.0 per cent.   In the period 1966/72, production rose annually by 5.5 per cent whereas trade rose by 8 per cent.   If we look at manufactures: from 1955 to 1972 the average annual rise in production was 6.4 per cent, but in trade it was 8.2 per cent.   From 1966 to 1972 it was 6.3 per cent in production and 9.5 per cent in trade, which is 50 per cent more. So certainly, as far as production of goods of agricultural and industrial origin are concerned, there has been a very important increase in world trade share.

Even if we take the GNP as a base, trade has increased as a share of GNP, in countries with a very open economy like, let us say, the Benelux countries.   If I take the example of the Belgium-Luxembourg economic union, the exports were in 1953 29.7 per cent of GNP but in 1975 were 53.3 per cent.   They have gone up steadily: in 1960, 35 per cent; 1965, 38 per cent; 1970, 47 per cent; and now, above 53 per cent.   This shows that even in relation to the GNP trade has become much more important.

A second remark I would like to make is that Prof. Lindbeck's study is, limited to the OECD countries. When we study internationalisation and interdependence of our economies we can't of course forget the less developed countries, if we want to avoid important mistakes in our conclusions. If we look at the evolution of world trade in the three great regions of the world, the developed market economy countries, the less developed countries, and the socialist countries, we find very different figures. For all goods taken together, in 1955, 64.7 percent of all exports come from the market economy countries, and 71.7 per cent in 1972. For the less developed countries the share decreased in the some period from 25.4 to 18.1 per cent. For the socialist countries it has remained fairly stable at 10 per cent. There is of course an important conclusion to be drawn from that, especially if we study further the different rates of growth of exports and imports and compare these for the various regions of the world and even for the various areas in the developed region. In the case of the OECD countries, we find that in the EEC group the annual rate of growth in exports has been 9.4 per cent between 1955 and 1972, in the EFTA countries 5.9, in the United States 4.7, and in Japan 14.7.

This remark about less developed countries not being taken into account in the paper is, of course, not a criticism; the author deliberately limited himself to the OECD countries. Considering our trade relations with the less developed countries seems all the more important when we bear in mind the second report to the Club of Rome, which shows some dramatic projections of what the world will be like if we don't undertake a much more important development aid. We were told this morning that the word " Marshall Plan " has been used very often, and this was in fact a tribute to the Marshall Plan, in order to characterise a new policy which might be started for instance for Africa or for Latin America. I really think that, if we believe the scenario developed by the second club of Rome report, on the necessity of helping the underdeveloped countries to become real partners in a truly internationalised economy, we the developed countries ought to embark on a real Marshall Plan for developing to a very great extent aid to the less developed countries. This means that we ought to agree not on stopping the growth of national product, but on stabilizing our welfare, halting our personal income growth and giving all of our surplus production, which will continue with the rise in productivity, to the developing countries. This aid should be given, however, in the appropriate form consistent with autonomous development; that means development which can be supported further by the local markets themselves.

A third remark is that the role of transnational enterprises could be stressed more than it has been in the paper. I read that in the United Kingdom 80 per cent of the exports, at this moment, are for the account of multinational companies, and 70 per cent of the exports stem from such companies in the United States. It is certain that we have to look into the fact that multinational companies, notwithstanding governments' industrial policies which Professor Lindbeck talked about, are pursuing their economic logic of development. They are actually developing a sort of international division of labour which is no longer the horizontal division of labour, but the division of labour

95

between various stages of the industrial process. Basic elements of goods, let us say in electronics, may be shipped to an Eastern European country, and be exported again in a semi-assembled form, to be assembled finally in Belgium where the quality control will take place. Another example is shoes, the most labour intensive part of the production is being done in Tunisia, and the assembling afterwards in Northern Europe. This is an important fact governments should take into account because, as Professor Lindbeck said clearly, " we have released all these forces and now they are beyond our control. " We should know that this is to go on, whatever governments do.

I have some doubts about the validity and especially about the usefulness of the macro-economic analysis, where Professor Lindbeck relates the world money reserves, the money volume, and the rates of inflation, on the one hand, and on the other hand the unused capacity and unemployment rates. I think that, when we take such large aggregates, we are bound to find this sort of systematic coincidence and that it is not helpful in drawing conclusions for economic policy.

A fifth comment concerns the new policies, the " industrial policies " as governments like to call them. I think that more stress should be put on the existing non-tariff barriers than has been done up to now. We all know that the EEC has achieved a customs union, certainly, but non-tariff barriers still exist for more than 250 products; there are that many files waiting for study and decision at the European Commission. Nobody talks about that; everybody prefers to ignore it; but we know that, although at their origin those national regulations may not have had a pro- tectionist goal, they have in fact a protectionist effect, and in some cases are also applied with a protectionist intention. The national regulations on food products, for instance, or safety requirements for electrical equipment, differ widely even between countries very closely connected within the EEC. Pharmaceuticals are a very good example of how little our markets may be integrated for some products where government regulations intervene. We have all known that the United States Department of Agriculture has often succeeded in using the agricultural health requirements as a means to prevent European agricultural goods from entering the American market. This is still something very important in international integration, which very few people talk about.

Another aspect of the same problem is the progression in state owner- ship of firms through nationalisation or otherwise, on the initiative of governments. All state owned firms have a degree of nationalist bureaucracy at the head, and, of course, this is the source of a hidden protectionism. We know we have very little chance as a Dutchman or a Belgian to sell equipment to the French Régie des Tabacs which has always been a French state enterprise. We have to take into account that with the current crisis the tendency towards protectionism is growing. It has come down by getting rid of tariffs, as Professor Lindbeck said, but we have built up some other protectionist measures which become stronger and stronger every day.

The same applies to the public sector in general, which in many European countries means more than 50 per cent of the total national product. The public sector has a tendency to be nationalist, perhaps less in countries like Belgium and Holland, which are too small and would be punished immediately, being so international in their economic activity. In larger countries, we see that foreign participation in tenders for important public works, even in their former colonies, is practically impossible.

In the sixth place, a comment on the alternative strategies. I think that we all agree that retreating from internationalisation doesn't mean much. The facts are there, the reality will kick back anyway, we are in an internationalised world because of the technology, because of the technology of communications, as Professor Lindbeck stressed very well. Going back to tariffs would, I think be a very bad thing, even if Professor Lindbeck may be right when he states that some of the other measures have a more distorting effect than tariffs. Certainly we have to consider the abolition of tariffs as something which has been achieved and tackle further the problem of non-tariff barriers. Reconciling the national political system with the international character of the economy isn't a very clear alternative to me. I think there is a great danger that, if we define it, we come to something very near to those new policies. Who will fix the rules? Who will define exactly the sort of measures? Therefore, my preference certainly goes to the third alternative —co-operation and integration—a co-operation going beyond what we have reached up to now, so as to follow the economic reality which has to develop in that line.

My last point will be that we have indeed a need for a fixed point. I may be in disagreement there with my colleagues, but we have such a need, and I think that fixed rates of exchange were such a fixed point. Very easily we say now, that, after all, floating rates are a convenient method of adapting our economies, but doesn't that really mean that we refuse the discipline which was formerly imposed by the fixed exchange rates, to go back to what?—to something which is undefined and which will come down to various undefined and unforeseeable " new industrial policies. " I am in favour of going back to fixed currencies for the Western World and certainly in the EEC.

The European Economic Community should go further. I have defended years ago the idea of a common monetary unit, one single monetary currency unit for Europe, and I am still convinced that this was a rather easy thing to achieve. Nothing prevented us from having a common currency unit defined in terms of Special Drawing Rights, or whatever it may be, to which all European currencies would be related. That common currency could be used gradually more and more in intra-European trade, for floating intra-European loans, etc. European loans in the Euro-bond markets might have been expressed in that currency, instead of what we have been trying to do for so many years, using abstract notions of a Unit of Account based either on the former European Payments Union unit or on various sorts of combinations or baskets of currencies. If we had agreed to accept the discipline of one common money, each European country would have had the obligation of adapting itself to the European economy, finding itself in the some position as an individual state in the United States, which has to adapt itself to the U.S. economy. If the United States had so many currencies as we have in

Europe, they would have a monetary problem every month, and it is incredible that we talk so much about integration and that we have gone back from the European Payments Union to the present chaos. Mr. Chairman [M. Marjolin], this morning in a reply to my question you said, and this was quite right, that the OECD, or the OEEC at that time, had achieved with the European Payments Union something very important for intra-European trade and integration. I think that in the line of monetary cooperation among the European countries, we are now not as far any more as we stood under the European Payments Union system. Therefore, my final word is a plea for all Europeans to tackle again that problem of a common European currency.

5

SUPPLEMENTARY COMMENT

by Minister Eric Brofoss (Norway) [1]

In his technically brilliant paper, Professor Lindbeck points to and reflects on a correlation he maintains can be established between the rate of inflation and the rate of utilization of productive capacity. The policy conclusion that can be inferred is that, as inflation is still with us, let us keep the rate of utilization down.

Most countries certainly obey that doctor's order. The figure of unemployment among the OECD countries amounts to more than 17 million. When we include their families, a number of people equal to the population of France are on the dole in this OECD area.

These people will ask the question: Are these hardships really necessary and unavoidable?

The veterans of the Marshall Plan period can take pride in having been soldiers in a most successful campaign against desperation and chaos-the targets for attack in Mr. Marshall's memorable Harvard speech.

However, when looking around in the world today, I find no ground for complacency: Is the state of affairs I just referred to the proper response to Mr. Marshall's visions? Does it make the world safe for democracy as another great statesman so eloquently described his goals?

These are not rhetorical questions; they point to serious issues at this juncture when we meet not only to commemorate and pay tribute to the memory of Mr. Marshall, but also to reflect on the challenges confronting the industrialized countries.

Let me start my observations by referring to some facts that cannot be disputed:

If one draws a chart similar to No. 1 in Professor Lindbeck's presentation, but for the period 1947-1957, we would find a different kind of correlation: full employment, full utilization of productive resources, great improvements in productivity, a remarkable economic growth in all our countries,

---

1. During the general discussion of Professor Lindbeck's paper, Dr. Erik Brofoss, former Planning Minister and Governor of the Bank of Norway, delivered a condensed version of these comments. He later transmitted the full text to the co-chairmen, with a request that it be included in the proceedings.

and at the same time a price stability vastly better than the performance in the present state of deliberate deflation.

From these data, one might infer a policy conclusion dramatically opposite to Mr. Lindbeck's. I do not do so myself; I only want to voice a word of caution against the tendency prevailing among econometricians to draw policy conclusions from statistical correlations that in a time perspective might be purely accidental.

My second set of data is this: Since the end of the Marshall Plan period proper in 1952, the purchasing power of most currencies has declined by at least 50 per cent, in many countries much more. Yet, in spite of a doubling of prices, real income, in terms of goods and services, has also doubled.

Now, again, do not let us jump to the policy conclusion that there is a simple way out of the present stagflation, but let these data serve as another reminder of the fallacy of using correlations as a basis for policy formulation.

We shall not be able to overcome all our present problems just by adding fuel to inflationary forces.

However, instead of being against the sin of inflation in general, we should take a closer look at some aspects not only of inflation but also of deflation.

We all recognize that inflation carries with it inequities and injustice, in particular to the old and other groups with fixed nominal incomes.

But it is no real solution to try to correct one inequity by creating new ones hitting other groups. That is what deflation does when it deliberately causes unemployment which hits individuals indiscriminately. Within the OECD area, it means a loss of real income equal to the GNP of United Kingdom in a world where perhaps as many as two-thirds of its people live below subsistance levels.

Such a policy is tantamount to a collective reprisal against workers with the purpose of forcing the trade unions to submission.

I read in the paper this morning that blanket bombing is to be banned in warfare. Yet it is to be retained and used aggressively in the field of economic policy.

Is is no satisfactory answer to the complaints of the victims that there are various systems that compensate for the loss of income. The vast majority of people want to earn a decent living by doing honest work.

Neither is it an answer to say that 5 percent unemployment is a low figure. People do not tolerate being treated merely as a number in a compilation of statistics and in a numbers game.

Some of the speakers have commented upon the fragility of the fabric of our institutional systems, both internationally and domestically. Therefore, it is a dangerous argument to say that such an unemployment rate is needed to make the system work.

The reaction may easily be: let us scrap the system!

A retreat from the international system of interdependence would be a serious blow to our ideas of international cooperation. Everywhere, there are cries for more protection.

It would, however, be far more serious if our system of national democratic government itself would be questioned. When we praise achievements thirty years ago, we should also heed the lessons of the failures of the interwar period.

The young people are particularly hard hit by unemployment. Let us not forget that in the future our countries will be governed by the young generation of today. That is a generation that increasingly feels victimized and frustrated.

Instead of submitting to the tenets of the " dismal science "—as economics was called a century ago and it still is no misnomer for some of today's practitioners of the profession—I urge that we address ourselves to the fundamental issue of how to modernize our political institutions. That is the real challenge with which the industrialized nations are confronted today. I am positive that the system of decision-making processes can be improved upon so as to make it able to cope with the complexities of our modern society.

I may be allowed to refer briefly to our experience in Norway in the first post-war period. We suffered serious losses of real wealth and the German occupation authorities played havoc upon our monetary system. In spite of this legacy of great inflationary pressures, we were able to keep the price level practically stable from 1945 to 1950. Over the whole period of 5 years the consumer price level only rose by 2 percent, which is no more than what some countries experience in one month today.

Instrumental in the implementation of that stabilization policy was the establishment of an Economic Coordination Council, with representatives of the main government agencies and not only the trade unions but also all the principal organizations of trade and industries. It was a forum for a confrontation, where the inconsistencies of claims and their incompatibility with a stable price level could be demonstrated.

I am confident that full employment, economic growth, and stability can be achieved simultaneously. Let us at this commemorative conference face that challenge by reaffirming our belief in one of the fundamental aims as laid down in the OEEC charter, that of full employment.

6

SUMMARY OF THE DISCUSSION

The general discussion focussed mainly on the alternative strategies presented in the concluding section of Professor Lindbeck's paper. All speakers rejected the first alternative of a retreat from internationalization, although it was also recognized by all that protectionist attitudes and pressures are growing throughout the industrialized world. There were, however, significant differences in emphasis on the relative merits of the second and third alternatives, and on the kinds of governmental intervention in economic affairs which could be reconciled with maintenance of the efficiencies and welfare gains from economic interdependence.

One speaker suggested that the three strategies are not incompatible alternatives, and that governments will probably combine elements of some protectionism, some increase in cooperation, and some reconcilation of national policies with greater internationalization. In his view, the increased intervention of governments in economic affairs cannot simply be shrugged off as " neo-mercantilism "; there are recognized " legitimate " grounds for intervention to deal with externalities, defense, security, protection of health and environment, and promotion of long-term goals, such as conservation of depletable resources, which are inadequately served by market forces. Some forms of intervention anticipate future market developments instead of conflicting with market forces. The task of international cooperation, therefore, is not simply to assure open and competitive markets, but also to reconcile potentially contradictory types of intervention and to minimize resulting distortions.

Other speakers pressed Professor Lindbeck to clarify his own preferences, especially between his second and third alternatives. One felt that " semi-organized anarchy " was more or less equivalent to " *ad hoc* crisis management, " which since 1974 has meant sliding backwards into increased protectionism; it threatens to go further unless universal high growth rates without inflation can be resumed—an unlikely prospect. Another speaker wondered whether common rules and standards in some major sectors, including monetary policy, agriculture, energy, and the broad shape of industrial structures, might not provide the missing " fixed points " and constitute a framework within which market forces could then operate fairly freely. Another speaker, with experience in international business, pointed to the dilemma now faced

102

by multinational corporations, which in the 1950s and 1960s thought they were both responding and adding momentum to the movement for international economic integration. Now they were being challenged by governments, labor unions, and other interest groups, which make it increasingly difficult to optimize the use of resources on a worldwide basis. Unless means can be found to avoid further delinking of national economies, business investments will increasingly be made to serve disintegrated national markets, with lasting bad effects upon production patterns.

Another speaker endorsed vigorously the third Lindbeck alternative of increased coordination and cooperation, partly because of the unresolved problem of energy deficit financing. In his view, continued reliance on the private banking system for petrodollar recycling might lead to an international financial crisis like that of the 1930s, with recessionary consequences far worse than 1974-75. The problem of energy supply alternatives and energy deficit financing, therefore, should be tackled as a serious common problem (if not a common enemy), in the same spirit as the Marshall Plan, including oil-importing developing countries as well as OECD member countries.

In his reply to the general discussion, Professor Lindbeck first dealt with several analytical points. Concerning the relative vulnerability of more open or more closed economies to the international transmission of inflationary pressures, he agreed with Professor Corden that the outcome depends mainly on the kinds of policies adopted by governments rather than the degree of " openness. " For this purpose, however, he emphasized that the international spread of inflation is related more to the proportion of *tradables* to GNP than the proportion of actual *trade*. Concerning the relation between exchange rate changes and domestic price levels, he argued that the spreading tendencies toward indexation make exchange rate adjustments very efficient as means of influencing price levels, although they admittedly weaken the effect of such adjustments on trade.

On the policy issues, Professor Lindbeck stated his preference for a combination of the second and third alternative strategies. That would involve a maximum of automatic adjustment mechanisms among countries, such as flexible exchange rates and easier capital flows, but would also include adjustment assistance and compensation to disadvantaged groups, including retraining and other measures to enhance factor mobility.

On the critical issue of price stability and full employment raised by Minister Brofoss, Professor Lindbeck said that this topic was too important to be dealt with adequately in a paper focussed on economic interdependence. He pointed out that inflation itselfs leads ultimately to unemployment and that the ideal prescription would be not to let the inflation get started. At the same time, he agreed that present levels of unemployment are unacceptably high in relation to the improvements in price stability. He felt that a policy of cutting indirect taxes might have combined stimulus to greater employment with a reduction in prices and inflationary expectations. He regarded Norway's success with incomes policy as exceptional rather than typical.

IV

THE OECD
AND THE THIRD WORLD

by Professor Charles P. Kindleberger

Introduction

Many young people in the United States today believe that age 30, rather than 18 or 21, marks the rites of passage from youth to adulthood. Thirty years is also the standard length of a full generation. On the thirtieth anniversary of the conception or birth of the OECD, therefore, it may be useful to look at the history of the organization, its present problems, and to peer briefly into the uncertain future. My assignment is to undertake these tasks with respect to the so-called Third World, often referred to as developing countries, the South, or LDCs. To a small degree, it should be noted, this is an intra-OECD topic as well as one of external relations, insofar as parts of some countries, notably Southern Italy, and all of others, i.e. Greece and Turkey, in 1947, and today Portugal, belong to the category of developing countries or regions rather than developed.

History

At the end of World War II there were two views of how to deal with world economic problems, the dominant *global* approach, embodied in the United Nations (UN), the United Nations Relief and Rehabilitation Agency (UNRRA), the abortive International Trade Organization (ITO), later replaced by the General Agreement on Tariffs and Trade (GATT), the International Bank for Reconstruction and Development (IBRD), and the International Monetary Fund (IMF), not to mention specialized agencies in food, health, education, weather, aviation, etc.; and the so-called *key-currency*, or *key-country* approach, that recommended if not relieving and rehabilitating, at least reconstructing and developing one country at a time, in an order that started a process that spread from the center out. The key-currency approach was enunciated mainly by John H. Williams in his testimony before Congress in opposition to the Bretton Woods agreement, and especially to the IMF. [1]

---

1. John H. Williams, *Postwar Curency Plans and Other Essays*, New York, Knopf, 1944.

As a United States member of the Preparatory Commission of the League of Nations for the World Economic Conference of 1933, he had advanced the key-country notion as early as 1932. [2] The contrast between the global and the key-country notion is similar to that between " balanced " and " unbalanced " growth. Balanced growth is summed up in the view of the London *Economist* some time ago, that because of interdependencies among industries, demand creating supply, and supply creating demand, " you cannot do anything until you do everything. " [3] In contrast, unbalanced growth as enunciated by Albert Hirschman is a theory that rests on the proposition that one thing leads to another, and that economic recovery and development are best achieved by breaking successive bottlenecks, each bottleneck being obvious at a given time, and its breaking leading to more recovery and growth through what Hirschman called " linkages. " [4]

As often happens when two diametrically opposed policies come into contention, the world blurs the experiment needed to determine which is correct by undertaking both simultaneously. The UN was created, and UNRRA, the IBRD, GATT, and the IMF, but along with these global organizations, there followed an Anglo-American Financial Agreement in 1946, covering a $ 3 750 000 000 loan from the United States to the United Kingdom for the purpose of restoring convertibility to the pound sterling, a key currency. This experiment was unsuccessful, and convertibility was ultimately abandoned in July 1947. The winter of 1946-47 revealed, however, that the global approach of UNRRA, post-UNRRA relief, together with the initial credits advanced to Europe by the IBRD and the IMF, would also prove inadequate. A new effort was necessary, and this, the Marshall Plan, based on Secretary George C. Marshall's speech of June 1947, was another key-country, or rather key-region, proposal, seeking to restore world recovery and ultimately development through the recovery of a strategic continent. There were echoes of a key-country approach within the key region : it is not generally remembered that when William L. Clayton and Lewis Douglas visited the British Foreign Secretary Ernest Bevin on behalf of the United States on June 24, 1947, Mr. Bevin proposed that the Marshall Plan be applied first to Britain, and then by Britain and the United States in partnership to the Continent of Europe. [5] The " special relationship " between the United Kingdom and the United States proved not to be this special.

The Third World entered into the initial European Recovery Program in various ways. As noted above, there was an internal Third-World component. The program that the Italian government had for its South—including

---

2. See *Documents diplomatiques français*, 1932-39, 1re série, 1932-35, Paris, Imprimerie Nationale 1966, Tome II, para. 180, Geneva to Paris, p. 386.
    3. See e.g. " India's Crucial Plan, " *The Economist*, February 25, 1956, pp. 516-517: " In an underveloped economy every thing has to be got going at once, so that the various sectors can provide each other with markets and complementary facilities; a lag in any one part destroys the balance of the plan. "
    4. See Albert O. Hirschman, *The Strategy of Economic Development*, New Haven, Conn., Yale University Press, 1958.
    5. *Foreign Relations of the United States, 1947*, Vol. III, *The British Commonwealth, Europe*, Washington, D.C., U.S. Government Printing Office, 1972, p. 269.

the 10-year Vanoni plan for economic development and the investments of the Cassa del Mezzogiorno—was folded into the recovery effort of that country. Greece and Turkey were included in industrial Europe. This last is largely the result of historical accident. In February 1947, President Truman had enunciated a program of defense for Greece and Turkey which were under pressure from infiltrating Communist forces and the Soviet Union, respectively, and which, in the case of Greece, the United Kingdom was no longer able to assist. The so-called Truman plan was largely military in purpose and outline, though the program of road construction in Turkey had an economic component insofar as roads designed for moving troops and materiel also served, with limited extension, to connect farm and market. But the Truman plan was unpopular in the United States. It was regarded as negative, rather than positive. A clear domestic political gain was achieved by consolidating the military plans for Greece and Turkey into the wider European recovery effort.

Economic recovery is a somewhat ambivalent concept. In its objectives, the Marshall Plan was a highly practical mixture of restoring the *status quo ante* and correcting it to the extent it was unsatisfactory, both within the limits of feasibility. For Southern Italy, Greece, and Turkey the Marshall Plan represented development rather than reconstruction. Professor Gottfried Haberler of Harvard University enjoyed telling the story that when the Turkish delegate to the first OEEC meeting brought in his country's request for assistance, he was taken aside by the United States representative, and told that the program was excessively modest and should be increased. Similar technical assistance was not required of the more developed countries, anxious to return as quickly as possible to old standards of living. On the contrary, the $30 billions in the initial calculation of needs was scaled down by Messrs. Clayton and Douglas to $16 billion, a figure believed to come more nearly within United States capabilities.

The OEEC plans did not explicitly provide safeguards against "backwash effects," such as was later done in the Treaty of Rome setting up the European Economic Community of the Six. Like customs unions, stimulated recovery has largely benign effects on trading partners, and on separate regions within them. Under certain circumstances, however, it can be harmful by drawing away resources from the periphery, or diverting demand elsewhere. The Treaty of Rome established a European Social Fund, a European Investment Bank, and an Overseas investment Fund to meet the problems of particular regions or sectors within member countries or former colonies, that were adversely affected by recovery at the center. This impact of recovery in Europe in the early days of the Marshall Plan seems not to have been so powerful. On the contrary, under the so-called (W. Arthur) Lewis model of "growth with unlimited supplies of labor," the movement of disguised unemployed labor from, say, the agricultural to the industrial sector stimulates both. Given an initial increase in demand or reduction in costs, the industrial sector gains from massive inward transfers of labor through the expansion of production without sharp increases in wages; in turn, the agricultural sector gains in income per capita of those remaining, since output drops less than the input of labor, if at all, and farmers may find it worthwhile to invest in machinery and new productive methods. [6]

The Europe of 1947 was very different from that of 1939 in its relations with large sections of Asia and Africa, and some portions of South and Central America, plus the West Indies, which had been dependent on European powers. Colonial ties were breaking or were about to break. The economic impact of this process was misperceived on both sides. The European colonial powers thought that they would suffer great economic losses from the independence of their former possessions. At the same time, the former colonies believed for more than a decade that throwing off the economic exactions of Europe would make then instantly rich. The notion was a familiar one. Germany had complained about the loss of its colonies under the Treaty of Versailles until the eve of World War II. [7] In addition, the occupying powers and West Germany thought after World War II that West Germany would go hungry because of the loss of grain-producing areas of Pomerania, Brandenburg, Mecklenburg, and East Prussia behind the Iron Curtain. Neither of these primitive ideas rooted in the fallacy of misplaced concreteness had much validity. On the whole, and with only a few exceptions such as the Belgian Congo, colonies were a net burden to their European masters. The richest countries in Europe, Sweden and Switzerland, were not colonial powers. The loss of the grain-producing areas of Eastern Germany improved, rather than worsened, the economic position of West Germany over time by allowing it to buy cheap world wheat instead of the heavily protected and inefficiently produced cereals from the East.

The failure of independence to bring instant wealth to former European colonies had a more sustained impact. In due course, the notion developed that political differed from economic independence, and that the former did not necessarily lead to the latter. In place of imperialism and colonialism, political independence might bring only neo-imperialism and neo-colonialism, or *dependencia* suffered also by the many countries of Latin America which obtained political independence from Spain and Portugal early in the 19th century. These last notions were vague in outline and content. It was not clear how they applied separately to the varied experience with decolonization of Britain, which granted independence to large segments of Asia and Africa, after having prepared them for it in varying degrees; to Belgium and the Netherlands which were expelled from the Congo (Zaire) and the former Netherlands East Indies (Indonesia) respectively, and to France which replaced colonial ties with most of her African colonies with voluntary support for administration and especially teaching, as foreign aid, or perhaps in exchange for continued adherence to the francophone area, but was belatedly and forcibly expelled from Algeria in Africa and Indo-China in the Far East.

A significant relation between Europe and the Third World involved in the key recovery of Europe turned on the complex monetary connections

---

6. See my *Europe's Postwar Growth: The Role of the Labor Supply*, Cambridge, Mass., Harvard University Press, 1967.

7. Hjalmar Schacht was especially bemused by such thoughts. See H.H.G. Schacht, " Germany's Colonial Demands, " *Foreign Affairs*, January 1937, pp. 233-34.

between former colonies and dependent states with France to some degree, but especially with Britain. Under the Anglo-American Financial Agreement, Britain had agreed to seek to scale down and/or to fund into long-term debt the large sterling debts represented by the accumulations of her currency by dependent allies in payment for troops and for services provided to troops, notably by India, Egypt, Iran, and Iraq. The independent members of the British Commonwealth—Canada, Australia, New Zealand, and the Union of South Africa—had voluntarily reduced their accumulated wartime claims on Britain, and the settlement of Britain's Lend-lease obligations to the United States had been readily achieved. Reduction and forced funding of the claims of dependent territories and less developed countries proved more difficult, for Britain to propose as it would have been for the countries concerned to accept. In consequence, Britain failed even to negotiate with these countries. Under the Marshall Plan, no new pressure was applied to the settlement of these debts, but the recovery experienced by Europe, plus the extension of the sterling area in other directions, enabled a start to be made in paying them off.

The extension of the sterling area through the currency boards of former African colonies such as Ghana, or independent Malaysia—the former Malay States—has been misinterpreted, even by such a distinguished economist as Dennis Robertson. [8] The monetary systems of many of these colonies, not always replaced by central banks when they became independent, rested on the issuance of domestic currency on a one-for-one basis against a reserve of sterling balances held in London. Numerous observers like Robertson believed that Britain was exploiting these colonies by requiring them to lend to her in order to obtain money for use within the colony. But the money supply could be expanded otherwise than by building an export surplus into holdings of sterling. Sterling could be acquired as well by borrowing. Many of these colonies, later independent countries, borrowed in London, held the proceeds in sterling securities and balances, and issued new money against these holdings. Such a system involved little expense—the difference between the cost of borrowing and the return on government securities and balances—and had the advantage of funding an import surplus, should one occur, in advance.

One further financial connection ran between the Marshall Plan and the Third World, and afforded an interesting parallel between the British loan and the European Payments Union (EPU), both representing key-currency approaches to world recovery. The European Payments Union of 1950, it will be recalled, was a device to prevent decline in intra-European trade arising from the attempts of various countries in Europe to earn dollars from one another to pay for imports from the United States. Supported by an initial credit from Marshall Plan funds, and by subventions from the United States to make up the cash required of persistent debtors, it enabled the participants to balance their accounts overall in Europe, giving and receiving credit, along with dollars, and eliminated the incentive to build surpluses in Europe to

---

8. Dennis Robertson, *Britain in the World Economy*, London, Allen and Unwin, 1954.

pay for deficits outside, an incentive that was leading progressively to declines in imports and in total intra-European trade. But balancing trade with Europe would not have been optimal from a world point of view. I forebear from tedious demonstration of this proposition, except by reference to the well-known studies of Folke Hilgerdt, *The Network of World Trade* and *Europe's Trade*, written for the League of Nations as part of that institution's preparation for the postwar. [9] Hilgerdt showed that some countries like Germany typically earned surpluses within Europe needed to pay for net imports from overseas areas, whereas others, like Britain, had large export surpluses in extra-European trade that, together with overseas investment income, enabled them to requite import surpluses with the United States and Western Europe. To force intra-European current payments into balance would distort this efficient pattern of multilateral balancing. The way out of the dilemma was to enlarge the concept of European trade to include sterling and franc-area payments within the framework of the EPU, along with those of Britain and France. By this act, the bulk of world payments outside of dollars were included in European settlements, and the distortion to world payments theoretically implicit in EPU was minimized.

Finally, in the early history of the Marshall Plan, it is well to note an ambiguity that has persisted over the full thirty years of the relations within Europe and those between the OECD countries and the Third World. To the Americans, and especially to Messrs. Clayton and Douglas, the purpose of the Marshall Plan was to restore the economies of Europe to the point where free markets could function efficiently. These ideas were also held strongly by the Germans under the leadership of Adenauer and Erhard. To much of the rest of Europe, however, and implicit in some of the language of Secretary Marshall's speech and in the presentation made by the Department of State to the Congress, the Marshall Plan represented a move by Europe to international economic planning with the aid of outside resources provided by the United States. The OEEC report and the Department of State documents which projected the balances of payments of 17 countries for $4\frac{1}{4}$ years, specifically noting exports and imports within Europe and with the outside world in 26 separate commodities or commodity groups, bespoke planning. The emphasis given by Clayton and Douglas and later by Paul Hoffman to larger markets, reduced discrimination, abolition of quotas, and the like moved in the direction of free markets. A quarter of a century later the issue had not been fully resolved. The French government proposed, albeit in the vaguest of terms, that the New International Economic Order demanded by the Third World should represent an attempt at world planning for prices and quantities of commodities, balances of payments, foreign aid, and other magnitudes in international economic relations, this at the same time when French internal planning had lost some of its mystique and *planification* was giving way to *déplanification*.

A major shift occured in 1951 when the Labor Party under Attlee was

---

9. League of Nations, *The Network of World Trade*, Princeton, N.J., 1944, and League of Nations, *Europe's Trade*, Princeton, N.J., 1945.

defeated in Britain and was replaced by a Conservative government. Labor had embraced a policy of international commodity agreements in which governments would commit themselves to buying or selling given quantities of particular products at stated prices over periods as long as five years. In theory, such arrangements provided assurances for the buyer that it could obtain desired supplies, and for the seller that it had certain outlets. So highly prized were the latter regarded in Britain, as a result of the experience of the depression, that it was felt that the seller could afford, with assured outlets, to undertake cost-reducing investments and to sell at below-world-market prices.

The outbreak of the war in Korea gave a sharp boost to raw-material and food prices, and ended the interest of suppliers in such arrangements. Countries such as Denmark and Argentina that supplied large quantities of foodstuffs to Britain under commodity agreements felt aggrieved that their prices were held down by agreements with time still to run, when those of the rest of the world moved sharply upward. Britain was asked for voluntary adjustment and refused it. The international commodity agreements were unlikely to have been renewed by the supplying nations, had not the Conservative victory ended the policy in favor of freer markets. The Korean war dampened the complaints of the LDCs, led by the brilliant Executive Secretary of the Economic Commission for Latin America, Raúl Prebisch, that the terms of trade were moving inexorably against developing countries. At the same time it made them impatient with international commodity arrangements that held prices down rather than up.

In the initial OEEC stage, perhaps the only sector that was thoroughly planned was that of petroleum, where governments depended for guidance on the international oil companies. It did not last long. Neither the European Coal and Steel Community (ECSC), which sought to plan coal from 1950 but fell back finally on national solutions before being absorbed into the EEC, nor the OECD, ever succeeded in the postwar period in achieving a coherent energy policy. In oil the initial start by the companies gave way before divergent Italian and French policies, that sought to establish national companies, serving national political as well as economic interests. In particular, France staked heavily on buying high-cost Algerian oil through its national companies, rather than cheaper Middle-East oil sold by American and British companies. Ultimate independence for Algeria in 1961 raised questions as to the wisdom of the policy. The failure of the EEC and the OECD to achieve unity on energy foreshadowed the chaotic response to the Yom Kippur embargo of November 1973, discussed below.

An unsuspected contribution of the early OEEC period to today's Third World, recently mentioned by Hollis Chenery at the Eastern Economic Association Hartford meeting in April 1977, lay in the development in Southern Italy, Greece, and Turkey of techniques for guiding national economic growth. Requests for aid under the Marshall Plan were required to stress the uses to which it would be put, and to couch the statement in terms of national-income accounts that were just coming into general use in the framing of economic policies. The Cassa del Mezzogiorno that carried out development policies

111

in Southern Italy under the Vanoni plan was furnished with Marshall Plan counterpart funds, arising from the sales of delivered goods. The IBRD was embarking slowly on project planning. The OEEC pioneered in program planning for economic development inside Europe, to develop techniques of later worldwide significance.

The OECD Period

The conversion of the OEEC to the Organization for Economic Cooperation and Development in 1960 marked a new stage in Europe's external economic relations. Symbolically, the word " Europe " was eliminated from the organization's title; the word " development " was added. The key region was changed to a key class, developed countries, inclusive of the United States, Canada, Japan, and later Australia and New Zealand, creating perhaps a precedent that countries might develop sufficiently to be graduated into OECD ranks. [10] The European mantle of the OEEC was taken over by the EEC, later enlarged from the Six to the Nine. Much of the time of the OECD was engaged in the work, of great importance for the developing world, of planning macro-economic policy among developed countries so as to sustain world income. Along with the EEC it concerned itself with North-South European problems, such as the regulation of migration from the Mediterranean littoral to the industrialized countries of Europe. In the majority of its work, however, dealing with trade, aid, technology, and the multi-national corporation, it found itself centrally concerned with issues of world development. In trade, the OECD occupied only a portion of the world stage, sharing it with GATT and the United Nations Conference on Trade and Development (UNCTAD). In development, again, the major role was assigned to the IBRD and its fellow organizations, the International Development Agency (IDA) for soft loans and the International Finance Corporation (IFC) for equity finance; to the regional development banks for Asia, Africa, and Latin America; and to United Nations agencies such as the U.N. Development Programme (UNDP). OECD's role in the multi-national corporation was shared, to a degree, by the United Nations Commission on the Transnational Corporation. In monitoring aid, the Development Assistance Committee (DAC) of the OECD operated largely alone. To provide support to its own developing members, the OECD established a special programme, which during the 1960's rendered classical technical assistance along the lines of other international and national organisations. Latterly this programme has been transformed to undertake a more distinctively co-operative approach as a tangible expression of solidarity between industrialized and industrializing countries. So far as I am aware, the Organization played no particular role in discussion of the so-called

---

10. It is of some interest that an American group under the editorial direction of William Yandell Elliott, proposed an " Atlantic " orientation of U.S. foreign policy along OECD lines, with Japan included with Europe, Canada, and the United States as an honorary Atlantic power. See William Y. Elliott, ed., *The Political Economy of American Foreign Policy*, New York, Holt, 1955.

" link, " i.e. the linking of issues of new international money (Special Drawing Rights or SDRs) to foreign aid, to make the " seignorage " from the issuance of international money available to the developing countries. These issues were discussed in the special circuit of experts dealing with purely monetary issues—the Group of 10, the International Monetary Fund, the Bank for International Settlements, and most recently the 27-country Conference on International Economic Cooperation which is also seized with several other topics on the development agenda: stabilization of international commodity prices, compensation for fluctuations in export proceeds, and, an issue raised by the Group of 77 (actually 113 countries) at its Manila meeting in May 1976, rescheduling of the international debts of developing nations.

The issue of North-South trade continued to play a role in OECD deliberations after the developing countries became disenchanted with GATT, and founded their own United Nations Conference on Trade and Development (UNCTAD), that first met in Delhi in 1964. This left GATT more or less a rich man's club, although some developing countries continued to be active in it. One of the first requests of UNCTAD was for generalized preferences for developing countries as an exception to the GATT rules of non-discrimination and reciprocity in tariff treatment. Generalized differ from regional preferences (and reverse) preferences, which had been a continuous subject of disagreement between the United States and the EEC, and of discussion primarily in GATT but also in the OECD. The preferences that the United States objected to were those accorded to former European colonies in the EEC. These were most significant in the period before Britain joined the Common Market, when especially the French *Communauté* obtained preferences in the EEC as a whole, and especially in Germany, at the expense of former British colonies in Africa and the less developed countries of Latin America. The United States also found objectionable the reverse preferences of former colonial powers in the markets of former colonies. With the extension of the EEC from the Six to the Nine, and reductions in tariffs under the Kennedy Round, these issues lost critical significance. At Lomé the arrangements concluded between the enlarged EEC and former colonies provided compensation on the grounds of discrimination while reverse preferences were abandoned.

Generalized preferences represented tariff discrimination by developed countries mainly in manufactured products in favor of developing countries. They were generalized because they applied in principle to all developing countries—though the line between developed and developing countries was difficult to draw—and not just to those with particular political associations. For a long time the developed countries resisted the demand on the ground of the principle of non-discrimination, until finally one by one they conceded, the United States and Germany giving up last. The concessions were surrounded with such limitations as to quantities, however, that the preferences were worth little.

The developing countries had a strong case that they had been discriminated against. Import quotas, tariff items held out of the bargaining of the Dillon, Kennedy, and the continuing Nixon rounds of GATT multilateral negotiations, the special agreements for export limitations in textiles, and especially the provision of the Kennedy Round that allowed for free trade only in tariff categories produced 80 per cent by a limited list of countries—the EEC and the United States—made very apparent that the developed countries were unwilling to reduce tariffs seriously, if at all, in the labor-intensive products that developing countries had a chance of producing cheaply for export to world markets.

As it happened, the 80 per cent provision of the Kennedy round authorizations amounted to very little when President de Gaulle vetoed British admission to the Common Market in January 1963. Without Britain as a member of the EEC, very few items qualified for 100 per cent reduction. The legislation nonetheless revealed the reluctance of the developed countries to make a place for imports competitive with the lower-paid workers in their societies. The issue was internal to the OECD countries as well as between them and the members of UNCTAD, as difficulties in making a place for Japanese manufactured exports and the pressure applied to Japan to adopt voluntary restrictions showed.

In economic theory, of course, generalized preferences are inferior to free trade or reduced tariffs, insofar as they permit countries to maintain substantial levels of protection for their inefficiently-allocated resources, if somewhat less protection for developing than for developed competitors. Adopted as an expedient of *Realpolitik*, it has become defused as an issue because of its limited application, and the more pressing issues of resisting tariff and quota increases.

The OECD role was much larger in foreign aid, the multinational corporation, and within the Continent of Europe, migration from South to North, than in trade preferences. In aid, the Development Assistance Committee (DAC) played largely an informational role, compiling data, making comparisons, publishing annual reports, and discussing subjects of interest to donors. It endorsed the UNCTAD target that developed countries should make available in total flows to economic development one per cent of gross national product, later supplemented by the target of 0.7 per cent for official aid as defined by DAC in the more meaningful but still excessively ambitious demand of the Group of 77 and in the UN resolutions of the Second Development Decade. It also pressed hard, and with some success, for softer financial terms.

Utopian critics could easily find fault with the work of DAC, which in its early stages appeared to accept as " aid " virtually everything that the member countries chose to regard as aid. In theory, there is a continuum between a strictly commercial transaction, with no element of aid, and a pure gift, with no element of *quid pro quo*, which is aid. Every transaction between North and South could find a place on this continuum and the proportion of aid to " business " could be theoretically at least calculated. DAC included with aid some German short-term commercial credits to developing countries at market rates of interest, and French support for former colonies in the *Communauté* that represented an attempt to maintain close administrative and cultural ties between these countries and France, and

114

were part of foreign policy rather than disinterested assistance. Admittedly the distinctions are difficult to draw. A similar utopian objection could be leveled at the proportional target of foreign aid by developed countries which failed to take account of either income per capita or of relative contributions to other approved international undertakings. International income redistribution is clearly at a very rudimentary stage. Like the celebrated woman preacher of Dr. Johnson or the dog of Mark Twain that walked on its hind legs, the OECD is perhaps more properly applauded for doing it at all than for its crude and unsophisticated performance.

In the multinational corporation, the OECD has proceeded slowly. In 1976 it produced a code of conduct, voluntary rather than mandatory, and dealing essentially with problems of corporate subsidiaries in developed countries—questions of anti-trust, taxation, obligations with respect to employment, illegal payments, and the like. The range of issues is different from those discussed in UNCTAD, which has been concerned with restrictive business practices, the patent system, and the limitations imposed by head offices on their subsidiaries to export; and from those dealt with by the United Nations Assembly which has passed a number of resolutions concerning the permanent sovereignty of developing countries over their own resources, the inherent right of countries to renegotiate outstanding contracts when they so choose, and which finally established a United Nations Commission on the Transnational Corporation, to serve as a clearing house for information on the subject and to prepare a code of rights and duties for host countries and transnational corporations. Developed countries are members of the UN Commission on the Transnational Commission, but are outnumbered, as is true of most UN organizations, by the representatives of developing countries. These latter dominated the report of the Committee of Experts which proposed the Commission on the Transnational Corporation, and gave a developing-country flavor to the report, emphasizing principally the rights of host countries and the duties of foreign corporations. Emphasis on the Permanent Sovereignty of Developing Countries over the natural resources within their boundaries—a right not in question—conveys a suggestion that nationalization need not entail " prompt, adequate, and effective " compensation as called for in the United States interpretation of international law, or that such compensation can be reduced by devices of taxes or fines for past " misconduct " levied retroactively.

Multinational corporate activities in developing countries are inevitably an item on the North-South agenda in the years ahead. In the judgment of this observer, however, there is so little meeting of minds between North and South that it is useless to try to agree on a common code that would paper over the cracks but fail to yield operational guidance. The OECD should continue to work on the problems of multinational firms among the developed countries, strengthening its code, giving it the teeth now said by the *Economist* to be lacking, leaving it open to adherence by countries of all levels of income and stages of development that want to accept it, but urging it on none. At the same time, developed countries should be wary about undertaking commitments in the UN Commission on the Transnational Corporation that mean something different to the developing countries than the evident language. Foreign direct investment in the developing countries is shrinking, and the reasons are evident: the present discounted value of potential benefits is exceeded by the value of the risk. I have elsewhere recommended that the United States withdraw its guarantees of and insurance for United States direct investment abroad, on the ground that they unnecessarily convert business into political disputes. [11] United States firms are sophisticated enough to appraise the risks of foreign investment as well as the government. Losses abroad are already made good up to 48 per cent, to the extent that the investing firm has profits on which it pays income taxes in the United States. If developing countries do not want foreign investment, there is no reason why the United States or any other developed-country government should insist that they have it. On the other hand, if they want it, there is something to be said for the position that they must create a climate in which developed-country business can operate with assurance. In this area, in my judgment, little purpose is served by the attempt to negotiate codes embracing North and South, as contrasted with rules of conduct for firms within the developed world, or those regarding LDC treatment of foreign firms, such as that reached in the Andes Pact.

In commodity problems, the OECD record is dominated by the major failure in November 1973 to take effective action in response to the Arab OPEC embargo and the general OPEC price hike, and to respond to the widespread fear echoing the reaction at the outbreak of the Korean War in June 1950, that commodity prices would rise sharply again. The failure was shared by the EEC and by the developed countries acting through normal political channels. The increase in the price of oil was applauded by developing countries as a victory for the class of countries, even though it affected many of them adversely, and as a forerunner of further commodity price increases. The failure, of course, was to ration scarce oil among the countries affected by the embargo, and especially to take care of the needs of the Netherlands, which was subjected to an embargo of 100 per cent, as opposed to the 25 per cent cut affecting other OECD members (except the United States, an oil producer, the 100 per cent embargo of which by Arab producers was not of critical importance).

The Netherlands energy position was alleviated firstly by its possession of North Sea gas, that covered 40 per cent of its energy requirements, and then by the reallocation by international oil companies of Iranian supplies from normal customers to the Netherlands. In this respect, private companies performed what may be regarded as a governmental task, that is, sharing out scarce goods. This private discharge of a public task was required because the OECD and EEC governments, allies of the Netherlands, were each setting about to solve its energy problem in a national way, such as by offering special inducements for oil to Iran, rather than taking orderly joint steps to meet the crisis. Earlier, the United States had placed an export embargo on soybeans, on which its ally Japan was dependent, to issue the

---

11. See my " World Populism, " *Atlantic Economic Journal*, November 1975, pp. 1-13.

second Nixon shock to that country. Later Japan, exposed more than most of the countries of OECD by reason of its dependence on imports of raw materials, went into what appeared very close to panic, as it undertook to make special deals, not only for oil but also for copper, iron ore, and other materials. The OECD inability to respond swiftly to the crisis by the sharing of petroleum was only the last step in a series of failures in the energy field since the earliest Marshall Plan days, the most serious of which doubtless was the inability to agree on and finance, prior to 1973, a program of accumulating and storing supplies of oil for an extended period. A 90 day supply had been agreed but not widely implemented. If it had been possible to accumulate supplies for a year, or perhaps only for six months, as oil experts had recommended, the low vulnerability of Europe to the Arab OPEC embargo and price hike might well have forestalled it.

North-South Relations within the OECD

The major North-South issue within the OECD of which I am aware is the problem created for especially Turkey and Portugal by the actions of West Germany, France, and Switzerland in halting further immigration of workers from Mediterranean countries. The issue is a complex one, with social and political as well as economic dimensions. Demographic conditions in Turkey especially, but also in Portugal, which has an additional employment problem posed by the return flow of its citizens from former possessions in Africa now independent, ensure that there will be serious unemployment in these countries stretching far into the future. These countries believe that this unemployment might be effectively alleviated, with benefits for national income, the balance of payments, savings, investment, and economic growth, if migrant workers could continue to go to OECD countries, but especially France, West Germany, and Switzerland to work, after recovery from the recession of 1975-76 has been accomplished. Greece, it should be noted, is not as interested in promoting worker emigration, as its own recovery has proceeded sufficiently far to make it anxious to retain its present work force, to attract back especially skilled workers in Northern Europe, and even to attract foreign workers itself. Yugoslavia has interests similar to those of Turkey and Portugal, but is not a full member of the OECD. Southern Italy is guaranteed free access to the labor markets of France and West Germany under the Rome Treaty of the EEC, but not to that of Switzerland. France, West Germany, and Switzerland restricted further immigration of workers in 1973 and 1974, ostensibly on the basis of a short-run decline in jobs, but more and more, as it appears, for social reasons, fearing that they are unable to assimilate such workers in larger numbers. For humanitarian reasons, both France and West Germany are continuing to permit resident foreign workers to remain, even though unemployed, in contrast with the expulsion practiced in the 1930s, and to bring in dependent members of their families. They seem to be resolved, however, to limit increases in the proportion of the labor force represented by Mediterranean workers, even at a cost in economic growth and in inflation. OECD commitments calling for equity of treatment of citizens of any country by other members may not be proof against the intensity of concern in France, West Germany, and Switzerland over the problems created by large numbers of difficult-to-assimilate foreigners.   By the same token the fact of citizenship in the British Commonwealth was not sufficient to prevent a Labor Government of Britain from requiring Indians, Pakistani, and West Indians to have a job before migrating, thereby effectively cutting off their immigration.   To the economist, world welfare is improved by moving labor from where it is cheap to where it can earn a higher return, provided always that the Malthusian revolution has been accomplished in the country of emigration and that the migrant is not immediately replaced by the natural increase of population.   But as in so many aspects of the world, the optimal economic and the optimal social solution to the migration problem would diverge even if the countries of emigration had adopted effective family limitation, as most of them have not.   As the world gets smaller, and information on differences in levels of living is more widely disseminated, the question of international migration threatens to transcend the OECD context.   It is already important for Yugoslavs in Europe, and for Puerto Ricans and Mexicans in the United States.   The Mexican/United States instance demonstrates, moreover, that legal barriers to migration may not be effective.

The New International Economic Order

The demands of the Third World for stabilized commodity prices, trade preferences, foreign aid amounting to 0.7 per cent of the GNP of developed countries, the link to the SDR, new rules for the multinational corporation, free use of the North's technology, without restrictive business practices, plus rescheduling of accumulated debts, more stable exchange rates among developed countries, and a share in any profits derived from exploitation of the ocean seabed pose many problems for the OECD countries at various levels.   Among them are whether these problems should be treated in one great big package deal, as called for by the developing countries in the sixth and seventh special sessions of the General Assembly of the United Nations and sought in the Paris Conference on International Economic Cooperation with its four commissions on commodities, energy, finance, and development; or one at a time, commodity by commodity rather than eighteen commodities at once, and rescheduling the debts of countries as required, along previous lines of the so-called Paris Club, rather than in one grand bankruptcy proceeding; whether the OECD countries should enter negotiations with the developing world with agreed positions, vote as a bloc, caucus on new propositions, or by and large take independent national positions and run the risk of being overcome through divisions; whether to seek generally market solutions to economic problems, or to embark on a system of world planning; whether to accept the proposition implicit in the NIEO demands of the Group of 77, the Non-Aligned Group, the UN majority, and others, that a change in institutional arrangements will make possible significant increases in the levels of living of the Third World, as they admittedly did for the OPEC countries and for the coffee-growers outside of frost-stricken Brazil, without increases in productivity and output; whether in fact the need of the moment is not for less negotiation, less integration, fewer North-South agreements, and more for what is coming to be known as " decoupling. "

In this writer's judgment, to put the matter bluntly, the OECD and the developed world can make their greatest contribution to the development of currently LDCs by:

1. maintaining their own stability and growth, including relatively full employment, avoidance of inflation, and balance-of-payments equilibrium;

2. maintaining free markets, with readiness to accept LDC imports and to adjust domestic resources to them. In the short run " market disruption " may require limited intervention. Over periods as long as five years the economic health of LDCs and DCs alike requires making room for emerging LDC exports of manufactures;

3. maintaining and expanding foreign aid through multilateral agencies;

4. abandoning governmental pressure to force LDCs to accept direct investment and encouragement to such investment through guarantees and insurance;

5. tolerating LDC attempts to raise prices of commodities along lines of the success of OPEC in oil, but neither endorsing them nor retaliating. It should be enough to remind developing countries of the lesson of economics that in the long run, equilibrium market-clearing prices must prevail, and that attempts to raise them higher will sooner or later fail, as the example of sugar in 1974 and 1975 so conclusively shows.

This is a difficult and trying course of action for the developed countries, and especially the sharing of the pain of making room for LDC exports of manufactures, of the deficit that is the obverse of the OPEC balance-of-payments surplus, of the monetary and fiscal expansion needed to keep world income growing steadily, and of providing the aid. Such burden-sharing is essential if the task of maintaining world stability is going to be accomplished. It is far more important than the difficult, probably impossible, task of negotiating the demands of the New International Economic Order in an enormous package.

This is not doctrinaire *laissez-faire*. The writer happens to believe that markets are generally right, but sometimes wrong, and that when they are wrong they should not be depended on. He believes that the private good of efficient resource allocation through well-functioning markets can be achieved only against the provision of the public goods of macro-economic stability, policing of markets against monopoly, and intervention as needed when from time to time, as happens, normally well-functioning markets break down. In times of acute shortage, scarce commodities must be allocated. In times of acute glut, redundant supplies should be taken off the market. Such provisions differ fundamentally from the view that the market is always wrong and needs to be supplanted by mechanisms of planning, allocation, and redistribution. When capital markets function poorly they should be supplemented by governmental aid, to assist redistribution as well as foreign resource flows, and by capital provided as a public good through the IBRD and IDA.

One " public good " which the developed world seems to be unable to provide itself, but the absence of which is particularly painful to the LDCs, is international money, or what amounts to the same thing, the stability of exchange rates among leading currencies. Developed countries have adopted floating rates because of inability to harmonize their own monetary, fiscal, price, and employment policies. The decision imposes a substantial burden on the LDCs which must decide, as each change in the relationship among major currencies takes place, whether to move with the dollar or the mark, the franc or the yen. It is sometimes suggested that each LDC should fix its money to a major currency, and abandon the direction of the external value of its money to it. Such advice fails to address the reality that LDCs typically have a number of trading partners, and resent subservience to any. LDCs have a hard enough task fixing the value of their currencies to a stable DC network. When the DC currencies are themselves unstable, the difficulties are compounded. The needs of the LDCs in this regard are perhaps not sufficient reason to alter DC policies on floating. In the writer's judgment, however, they provide a further argument to already compelling ones in behalf of international money.

Finally, there should be a lender of last resort to support situations of financial breakdown. For the LDCs, it should be the Paris Club. But the LDCs themselves have a stake in seeing that the DC financial system remains strong. The OPEC countries seem finally to have realized their vital interest in a flourishing world.

Within these limits of provision of the public international goods of world stability, open markets, and international money, and intervention to come to the rescue in case of breakdown, trade, commodities, and multinational corporations should separately be permitted to take care of themselves. This is not decoupling, as it assumes continued North-South interdependence. It may be attacked as " trickle-down " help, though I would prefer to characterize it as emphasizing the key role of Japan, the United States, and Western Europe in world prosperity—necessary, but not sufficient, to enable LDCs to grow of their own efforts, with foreign aid. It does imply an attempt to defuse issues of political economy by letting markets work out continuously evolving solutions except where they are clearly incapable of doing so.

The Big Package in which all international economic issues are rolled together into a tremendously complex and endlessly ramified agreement seems to appeal to diplomats and political scientists. It fails to attract this economist. There are examples of past successes, such as the peace of Vienna in 1815. It seems dubious that this can be repeated in the economic sphere. I see nothing in theory, and little in practice beyond the incredibly difficult multinational negotiations under GATT, to suggest that 18 commodity agreements can be concluded simultaneously when it is frequently impossible to conclude one.

The OPEC embargo and price hike were strongly dysfunctional for the world, not only because they plunged the world into recession but because they spread throughout the developing world the illusion that instant wealth was a realistic prospect. In my judgment, the instant wealth of OPEC, like political independence for former colonial possessions, fails to solve the political and economic problems which these countries must overcome one at a time, and constitutes only a limited example of the path to be followed to development. Like most poor individuals, most poor countries can reach affluence only by learning how to become productive. The prospect of striking it rich, winning a lottery, finding a pot of gold is delusive and sub-versive. Development is a slow, painful, frequently disheartening process, in which different countries move at different paces. Currently developed countries can help by foreign aid, by making room in international markets for newcomers as they learn to produce efficiently, and by opening the ranks of the OECD and other developed country groupings to those countries making the grade and wanting admission. When individual countries are overwhelmed by debt, they should be forgiven in bankruptcy proceedings of the Paris Club type. The foremost task, however, and the one that eases every problem of the developing countries from commodity prices, balances of payments, debt service, to entry into new markets, is to maintain real income in the developed world growing. The most important work of the OECD in North-South economic relations is that of Working Party No. 3, and the economic summit planned for May 1977, among the developed countries themselves.

121

2

COMMENT

by Dr. Attila Karaosmanoglu (Turkey)

I feel especially privileged to speak here, as a result of the historical accident which Professor Kindleberger has mentioned. Had Turkey not been accepted as a result of that accident I would not have had the chance of addressing this distinguished group. I feel, however, at a disadvantage after such an eloquent presentation by Professor Kindleberger, since I was going to express the hope that his views are not shared by the people attending this gathering. At least, having listened to Professor Vlerick, I know that there is one person who does not share them, and I hope there are many more.

I also hope that there is a willingness to depart from the ambiguity which Professor Kindleberger observes in the relations between the OECD and the Third World for the last thirty years. This should be in a direction where benefits from the recognition of global interdependency and efforts for global cooperation could be realized, and the conditions for an equitable growth for the world economy could be defined.

The paper describes the evolution from a political to an economic dependence for newly independent countries, but it fails to confront the fact that it is now time to recognize the interdependencies between the OECD and the Third World.

My differences with Professor Kindleberger arise not only because I am from a developing country, which in his account happened to have become a member of the OECD as the result of an historical accident, but also because I do not think that we are confronted with a zero-sum game. If we are concerned with the plight of the masses, who do not get an equitable share from the fruits of world economic growth, and who are not able to use their potential for a positive contribution towards it; and if we accept the fact that the situation they are in is not entirely of their own making; and if we also have the political will to do something about it, then it should be possible to make some institutional arrangements to ensure a better flow of world trade; more stable remuneration and better terms of trade for commodity producers; and a larger and more efficient flow of financial resources and technology to the Third World. By arriving at a better worldwide allocation of resources, and mobilizing underutilized human and natural resources in

122

the developing countries, we can make development efforts work to the benefit of all parties.

I see history—even within the confines of Kindleberger's analysis—differently. Almost half of his paper is devoted to reviewing the history of the corrective institutional arrangements that were needed in the heart of industrial Europe to " meet the problems of particular regions or sectors within member countries or former colonies that were adversely affected by recovery at the center. " His examples reveal these countries' concern that growth and its benefits are not automatically spread through demand for factors of production or needs to extend markets, even within national boundaries of one country. That the institutional arrangements broke down does not necessarily mean they were superfluous. It may instead reflect lack of foresight and the domination of short-term, narrow national interest or, more simply, their having fulfilled their functions.

I don't want to argue, in the short time available for my comments, with Professor Kindleberger on what I consider such disputable statements as:
> " On the whole, and with only a few exceptions such as the Belgian
> Congo, colonies were a net burden to their European masters, " or,
> " OPEC embargo and price hike... plunged the world into recession... "

At least on the latter point, I should like to remind him that several OECD studies have concluded that though the oil embargo and the price hike contributed to the severity of the recession, they did not cause it.

Before I try to identify what are the important issues missing in Professor Kindleberger's paper, I would like to review very briefly, mostly in his own words, his conclusions as to the issues on the international agenda.

On Aid

Professor Kindleberger finds the 0.7 per cent aid target " excessively ambitious. " What he does not mention is the fact that at least two countries have met the target and some others committed themselves to do so. He accepts that " international income redistribution is clearly at a very rudimentary stage, " but he finds satisfaction in his reference to Boswell's *Life of Johnson* that it is done at all. He does not recognize that this issue merits close attention because of the long-term risks (such as social disruption) inherent in not taking adequate action.

On Multinational Corporations

Rather than trying to understand the position of the developing countries on this issue, he concludes that " little purpose is served by the attempt to negotiate codes embracing North and South as contrasted with rules of conduct for firms within the developed world. "

On Commodity Problems

Professor Kindleberger states that OECD's record is dominated by a major failure in November 1973 to take effective action in response to the Arab OPEC embargo and the general OPEC price hike. He thinks that the failure is caused by " acting through normal political channels. " He believes in sharing and rationing among the OECD countries. But I am afraid he does not extend his belief outside this community very generously.

On North-South Relations within the OECD

According to Professor Kindleberger, the only issue of major significance is the halting of further immigration by West Germany, France, and Switzerland. He considers that in " continuing to permit resident workers to remain, even though unemployed, in contrast with the expulsion practices in the 1930s, " France and West Germany are making a humanitarian gesture. But his account makes no reference to the use of the less developed OECD countries as shock absorbers to modify the effects of fluctuations in the more developed economies by importing or expelling workers or halting immigration.

On the International Economic Order

After warning the OECD countries against, by and large, taking " independent positions and running the risk of being overcome through divisions, " he suggests " less negotiation, less integration, fewer North-South agreements " and more " decoupling " of issues. In his judgment " OECD and the developed world can make their contribution to the development of currently less developed countries by maintaining their own stability and growth with free markets, readiness to accept LDC imports and to adjust domestic resources to them, slackening off the effort to reach agreements on arrangements which are untried, probably cannot be carried out, and where blame for failure will be laid at the door of neo-imperialism or neo-colonialism. " He objects that the new proposals are being advanced in the form of a package as though they were a toy for a child. But I think that evades the real issue. The real issue is one of willingness to tackle these problems—whether in the form of a package or separately in a purposive way—so that the policies are formulated, agencies which are to implement them are identified, and the implementation started.

On what the Developed Countries can do to help the Third World

Professor Kindleberger has a short and simple package which includes:
— foreign aid;
— making room in international markets as developing countries learn to produce efficiently;
— opening the ranks of OECD and other developed country groupings to those countries making the grade and wanting admission;
— bankruptcy proceedings for countries overwhelmed by debt, and most importantly;
— to maintain the growth of real income in the developed world.

I am glad to acknowledge that, even at the political level, the OECD countries have a more progressive stance than Professor Kindleberger has in this paper. The Appendix to the Communiqué of the Economic Summit

124

Meeting on World Economic Prospects definitely goes farther in its recognition of interdependency and its promise to work towards a better framework for cooperation between the OECD and the Third World. Though I understand that Professor Kindleberger believes that they really do not go beyond words, I should like to be more optimistic than he is.

There should be no doubt and, coming from a developing country, I should be the first to emphasize, that the primary responsibility for development rests with the developing countries themselves and in many countries development performance could definitely be better. But better performance, either in terms of growth or its distribution, requires support through financial resources and access to the markets of industrial countries. There is a real need for the creation of what Mr. McNamara, President of the World Bank, calls a " global compact. " This should adopt a strategy towards the alleviation of poverty within a reasonable period of time, and it should identify additional aid and trade support to be provided by the developed countries, as well as pressing for an undertaking by the developing countries for policy reforms and structural changes to eradicate poverty and improve efficiency of resource utilization.

Professor Kindleberger finds virtue in bluntness and, as I quoted earlier, sees the greatest contribution the OECD could make as the maintenance of its own stability and growth.

Allow me to ask with the same degree of bluntness the following questions:

— Could OECD maintain its real income growing without uninterrupted access to resources from the developing countries, and without significant growth in the markets in those countries?
— Isn't the growth of the exports of the LDCs at least as much a demand question as a supply question? If so, why make room in international markets only as they learn to produce efficiently? If they are not producing efficiently why do they pose a threat? If some are producing efficiently why wait any longer? and
— Most importantly, perhaps, what is the significance of " making the grade " to be accepted to the ranks of the OECD?

I hope such attitudes do not mean that interdependency is only a dream until countries can " make the grade " and become acceptable as members of the OECD community.

After hard-earned experience as a practicing development economist for nearly a quarter of a century, I agree with Professor Kindleberger that development is a slow, painful, and frequently disheartening process, but I think there are real benefits to be obtained from a greater recognition of global interdependency. To realize them, the OECD countries need to take certain more positive steps by:

1. Recognizing differences in the needs and interests of different groups of developing countries;
2. For low income countries, providing increased amounts of concessionary assistance, to help diversify their economies while increasing the availability of food for their people;

3. For middle income countries, improving the possibilities for access to the markets of the developed world.

In the very short time remaining, let me at least make a list of what the developed countries can reasonably do in the field of trade:

— Prevent the introduction of new import restrictions, and clarify and tighten rules regarding the " safeguard " or emergency use of quantitative restrictions and administration of import licences where these exist;
— Liberalize trade in textiles and clothing;
— Cut tariffs in the current multilateral trade negotiations;
— Allow the introduction of domestic pricing and support arrangements to be discussed in negotiations on agricultural trade;
— Reduce existing non-tariff barriers;
— Relax selectively present rules regarding export subsidies;
— Establish graduation rules for countries enjoying special benefits and privileges regarding export subsidies, exemptions from tariff-cutting procedures, GSP preferences, or special freedom in using quantitative restrictions;
— Establish adjustment assistance schemes to help shift resources out of sectors which are no longer competitive;
— Help to diversify the economies of the developing countries.

If there is a real desire and determination to benefit from the fruits of global interdependence, I think, with an effort similar in enlightened long-term self-interest to the Marshall Plan, we can do quite a lot.

3

COMMENT

by Professor Thierry de Montbrial (France)

My comments on the paper by Professor Kindleberger, which is rich in detail and closely argued, will be organized under four headings.

Firstly, the lessons of the Marshall Plan for action today. I shall not attempt to deal with the purely historical aspects of the Marshall Plan, on which I am not an expert.

The second group of comments will concern the specific topic of energy, which is referred to by Professor Kindleberger several times in his paper.

I shall then move on to the general problem of the approach to North-South relationships.

Finally, my fourth group of comments will deal with a somewhat more general problem—and here I apologize for possibly overlapping with the previous discussion—that of international economic cooperation as a whole.

Lessons of the Marshall Plan for Today

I shall examine this question from the viewpoint of North-South relations. As Mr. Gordon remarked when he opened the conference, the need for some kind of Marshall Plan has become a cliché used in many different contexts nowadays.

With respect to North-South relations, we hear two contradictory propositions: according to the first, the rich countries should organize a Marshall Plan to help the poor countries; while the other proposition is that the poor countries (or rather the newly rich OPEC countries) should organize a Marshall Plan to help the rich countries!

As to the first proposition—a Marshall Plan of the rich countries to benefit the poor countries—I would rule it out entirely for the simple reason that the original Marshall Plan was a kind of pump-priming operation; all the human capital was already there, and once the pump was primed, the machinery would once again operate. The situation is manifestly entirely different in the case of development problems.

On the other hand, the idea of a Marshall Plan established by the new rich countries in regard to the old rich (or industrialized) countries, deserves serious attention, since just as after the war the purpose was to avoid cutthroat competition among the European countries, so today the problem is to avoid the same kind of rivalry, with each country striving to restore equilibrium in its commercial balance or balance-of-payments at the expense of the others.

It follows that it would be entirely logical to envisage a genuine Marshall Plan among the OPEC countries to provide capital to the industrialized countries, either directly or through purchasing power distributed among the poor countries. To some extent, this thought is the basis of the so-called " Witteveen facility " in the International Monetary Fund, and in my view the idea could be put forward directly and clearly.

Energy

Professor Kindleberger lays considerable stress on the failure of energy policy, both at the level of the European economic community and at the level of the OECD.

In this regard, one wonders whether quite profound underlying causes are not at work. Without developing the point in detail, my thought is that these causes lie in a very serious divergence of interests between Europe and the United States on the one hand, and within Europe on the other, where the positions taken are far from being compatible or coherent.

That brings me to an observation on the crisis of the autumn of 1973. Professor Kindleberger refers to the attitude of the industrialized countries, especially in Europe, with respect to the Netherlands. He seems to regret that we did not display an attitude of greater solidarity with our Netherlands ally.

Let me first observe, as Professor Kindleberger himself noted, that the Netherlands did not really suffer. We were well aware at the time that the oil companies were in fact supplying petroleum to the Netherlands. The problem was therefore much more political than physical. As to whether we should or could have had a more cooperative attitude, the brief sentence in his paper on this point raises a host of questions. The paper uses the term " ally, " but the alliances in which we participate, and foremost the Atlantic Alliance, are not directed at the kind of situation we faced in the autumn of 1973. Besides, the oil case posed a challenge of " crisis management " for which we were in no way prepared. The issue of lack of solidarity with the Netherlands, therefore, cannot be treated in so summary a fashion. It is essentially a political issue.

Still on the issue of the crisis of October 1973, Professer Kindleberger refers to the mistake made by developing countries who thought they were going to become rich overnight. In some respects, of course, they were mistaken, but in others they were certainly not. Without any doubt, the OPEC countries themselves worked out an excellent deal, if only on the political level. They have gained a degree of power which they most decidedly did not have previously. As to the non-oil-producing developing countries, to be sure they were among the principal victims of the operation, but their calculation—that oil was the only weapon which could indirectly lead the developed countries to take more interest in them—was not entirely absurd, as demonstrated by subsequent events, notably the Conference on International Economic Cooperation which is just coming to a close and which would scarcely have taken place without the crisis of 1973. In my mind, therefore, the calculation was not as unreasonable as Professor Kindleberger suggests. I might add that, while certain developing countries may have deceived themselves, the industrialized countries certainly made an error of judgment when they put their faith in economists who forecast the collapse of the oil cartel within six months!

All of this indicates that the oil problem is fundamentally both political and economic. But that subject warrants a much more extended discussion.

The Approach to North-South Relations

I agree entirely with the thought that the colonial powers were mistaken in thinking that the loss of their colonies would be a tragedy inevitably leading them to decline or decadence, while the developing countries also had many illusions in believing that economic independence would necessarily lead them into a glorious future.

But I think that there are two very important problems, then as now, and that Professor Kindleberger's paper does not do justice to these two points. The first is the problem of economic security. This is a real problem, especially for Europeans and also for the Japanese. It is the problem of security of supplies, and I think this is what Dr. Karaosmanoglu had in mind when he asked whether growth could continue as such in our countries if there were interruptions in the supplies of raw materials. Then, beyond economic security, there is security in general; or, to put the problem in very general terms: to avoid encirclement, or to spare Europe problems such as that of Cuba for the United States in 1962.

These two concerns, I think, are essentially European in character; they are not felt by Americans, or at least not to the same degree. For this reason, I do not entirely agree with the idea so strongly put forth in Professor Kindleberger's paper that, if the developing countries had no desire for foreign investment, then we have no reason to force it on them and it is up to them to accept whatever terms are offered.

This idea has consistently figured in American policy. If I am not mistaken, it appeared in the famous speech of Dr. Kissinger to the United Nations on September 1, 1975 and it still appears in the attitudes expressed by Mr. Vance at the Paris North-South conference in recent days. I would agree with this approach were it not for this problem of security which is very substantial, especially for us Europeans and for the Japanese.

This leads me to the conclusion that, now as in the past, one must look at North-South relations from the global viewpoint with regard to their scope, and from the regional viewpoint with regard to their application.

When I say " global in scope, " I mean that North-South relations involve the management of trade in goods and services and the problem of assistance in the broadest sense—and I use deliberately the word " assistance " rather than " aid. " At the same time, North-South relations should be looked at on a regional basis. This would be consistent with some of the propositions contained in Professor Kindleberger's paper concerning the " key

129

country " approach, and also with the idea that not everything can be done multilaterally. Relationships taking account of specific geographical and historical features are often more fruitful. I believe that it is that attitude which has inspired the policy of the European Community, and at the political level has inspired a recent action such as the Franco-Moroccan operation in Zaïre.

My own conception of North-South relations, therefore, fits within a more global concept of international economic relations, somewhat in the matter of a " nest of dolls " or concentric circles. There must be relations from nation to nation; there must be relations from region to region, for example the European Community with the Associated States; and there must be multilateral and global relations. Each of these levels has its proper place in the whole.

For example, for all the reasons I have briefly presented, the European Community has a natural vocation of strengthening its relations with the African countries, or at least with some of them, and with the Arab countries.

On two fundamental points, I am in agreement with Professor Kindleberger. The first is the importance for the South of the prosperity of the North. The oil affair has brought about an almost universal recognition—even if it is not always said aloud for obvious reasons—of the damage which an excessive, and especially a very sudden, increase in oil prices can cause to the developing countries by way of its effects on the industrialized countries. The second point, which comes down to " God helps those who help themselves, " is one which we must have the courage to state and keep on stating —that the problem of development is first and foremost a problem for the developing countries themselves. The extreme example, of course, is that of China, which makes it a point of honor not to depend on any other country. I believe that quite often the radical rhetoric of the Third World simply hides a degree of inability to deal with their own problems. A general cooperative effort is called for, but the most important part of that effort must be undertaken by the developing countries themselves.

International Economic Cooperation

From the methodological point of view, the problems are fundamentally similar whether one is dealing with North-South relations, with international microeconomic cooperation, with coordination of macroeconomic policies, or with many other subjects. One comes back to the two conceptions of the Marshall Plan set forth in Professor Kindleberger's paper: a return to liberalism, on the one hand, and a beginning of international economic planning, on the other.

Consider first the matter of free trade. Professor Kindleberger does recognize some exceptions to the laws of the market, but they are exceptions, while the rule favors the law of the market. Let me here make a point concerning economic theory, which teaches that the conditions required for the effective working of the market are in fact extraordinarily stringent. The amazing thing is that the market works at all! This is not just a question of such frequently mentioned conditions as the absence of externalities.

130

There is also the matter of perfect foresight, a complete system of futures markets for all goods, the absence of increasing returns, and a whole series of other such assumptions including the absence of indivisibilities. But, in practice, everyone knows that in the real world increasing returns are more the rule than the exception.

From the theoretical viewpoint, therefore, I would argue that the law of the market is more the exception than the rule. That having been said, the test of the market comes in the fact that in practice it has not worked so badly, and indeed empirically is probably one of the least bad solutions that has been found so far for the problems of economic exchange, notwithstanding the theory!

In any case, no one can deny that with respect to raw materials, organized commodity arrangements are much more satisfactory than uncontrolled markets, at least in principle. If experiments in this field so far have generally failed, the reasons rest in large measure in the ill-will or non-participation of certain essential participants.

To be sure, the idea of moving directly to eighteen raw materials, when one has not been able to make a satisfactory arrangement for a single one, is scarcely reasonable. But I repeat that, in principle, the idea of organized commodity arrangements for raw materials must be recognized as a good idea.

With respect to energy, that seems to me in principle a typical field for the application of the idea of organized trade, since there has never been a real market in oil except perhaps at the moment of the great discoveries toward the end of the nineteenth century. By one means or another, there has always been interference with market forces.

Let me now turn briefly to the nature of interdependence and the " controllability " of international economic relations. This is directly relevant to what Professor Michel Crozier was saying this morning. International economic relations have become so complex that interdependence is no longer under control. To use a biological metaphor, we have a body in which the interdependence of the various organs has developed a good deal, but the brain has not grown in the same proportions.

As a result, we run the risk that some organs will become hypertrophied, and it is well known that when a biological system as a whole does not grow harmoniously, sooner or later the system will die. Whence a question; are we able to make the brain grow in proportion to the interdependence of the organism? If the answer is affirmative, that becomes a worthwhile objective; but if we do not have that capacity, we should have the courage to admit that some limitations on interdependence are necessary; because if one permits interdependence to develop without control, it will ultimately lead to crisis and death.

My next comment is a bit theoretical, and deals with the difficulty of finding satisfactory solutions to problems of cooperation in general. In this game of cooperation, as played in 1977, there are many actors, without any one of them being predominant, while in 1947 there were only a few players, with one predominant one who was able to police the system (in the best sense of that word). That makes it very difficult to arrive at cooperative

131

solutions under present conditions, since examples of the " prisoners' dilemma " (as mentioned in Professor Lindbeck's paper) are much more likely to occur than in the past. Only a long process of experimentation, therefore, will make it possible to arrive at a satisfactory organizational formula.

My final point is an attempt at concrete application of the preceding ideas. We must think again about the concept of " organized liberalism. " Now what is meant by organized liberalism? The element of liberalism means that the objective should remain the freest possible international trade, and that goes especially for North-South relations, but the element of organization is necessary precisely to avoid loss of control of the system. I would suggest three fields of application for this idea of organization (coming back to my nest of dolls, combining a degree of regionalism with a degree of multilateralism). First is the organization of certain markets, in some cases to improve competition or to manage recessions, and in other cases (sometimes associated with the first), to deal with situations where increasing returns to scale make it impossible for markets to function. Examples would be shipbuilding or iron and steel.

Then there is the related idea of a *gradual* change in market shares—that is, that changes in international trade take place in accordance with the principle of the international division of labor, but in a sufficiently gradual manner to avoid provoking protectionist reactions.

Finally, all this is entirely consistent with Professor Kindleberger's rejection—with which I entirely agree—of the " big package, " an idea which can be attractive only among ivory tower intellectuals. But it is essential to have a relatively clear idea of the direction we want to take and the means for moving in that direction, leaving the rest to common sense.

4

SUMMARY OF THE DISCUSSION

During the general discussion, several speakers enlarged on the role of the OECD in relation to developing countries, supplementing the points in Professor Kindleberger's paper. A former chairman of the Development Assistance Committee (DAC) pointed to three aspects of the OECD's institutional role in North-South relations. First, the OECD secretariat and committee structure assist member countries in orderly negotiations with developing countries in UNCTAD, specialized UN conferences, and (most recently) the Conference on International Economic Cooperation; he believed that the " Group of 77 " (developing countries) would have benefited from a similar organization on their side. Second, the OECD Development Centre had done pioneering work on important aspects of development strategy, including trade policy and the problem of adequate employment opportunities—the latter topic subsequently being picked up by the International Labor Office's world employment program. The Development Centre also provided a forum for informal meetings between governmental and private representatives of both industrialized and developing countries, for example on issues of population policy. Jointly with the OECD secretariat, the Centre had done important work on science and technology for development. Third, the work of the DAC itself extended well beyond mere exchange of information. Each year, the aid program of every member country was reviewed in depth, with the conclusions set forth in widely circulated letters from the chairman, covering not only economic development in the narrow sense but also social issues. These had included questions of basic needs and equity in development several years before the recent wave of popular interest. The annual reviews constitute a form of pressure on aid donors in addition to their role as means for the exchange of information. The original precedent for such mutual reviews of individual country programs by the group as a whole had been set in the Marshall Plan itself; it was later followed by the NATO " Wise Men " of 1951; then by DAC; and in the 1960s by the Inter-American Committee on the Alliance for Progress (CIAP).

Another speaker emphasized the growing activity of the International Energy Agency, working within the framework of the OECD and dealing with several issues specially mentioned in Professor Kindleberger's paper. He referred to the emergency oil import sharing program, designed to avoid

133

a repetition of the events of 1973-74, and also the plans for longer-term cooperation in energy conservation and the development of alternative energy sources.

Another speaker called attention to the long-term study project recently initiated by the OECD under the title " Interfutures. " The purpose of that project is to assist in developing concepts of desirable and feasible shapes of the world of the future, with special emphasis on harmonious growth extending both to developing and to industrialized countries. The developing countries, in his view, would not be able to find solutions entirely through collective self-reliance, since most relevant scientific and technical expertise is found in the industrialized countries. It was a new and most important role for the OECD to seek means of harmonizing the policies and actions of countries with different cultural backgrounds and at differing stages of economic development.

Two other speakers challenged some aspects of Professor de Montbrial's exposition. One was especially skeptical of the feasibility of organizing commodity markets effectively, and in any event considered such market organization a poor means of assisting development in comparison with direct resource transfers and improved access for developing countries in the markets of industrialized countries. Professor de Montbrial's biological metaphor was also challenged on the ground that it assumed the need for a system with central control, whereas in nature many complex systems, especially ecological systems, are self-regulating and completely decentralized. The speaker saw a partial analogy with economic systems, where markets bring about huge numbers of individual decisions coordinated by the decentralized system, thus relieving the burden on central administration. For that reason, he felt, it was not self-evident that the " brain " (which he interpreted to mean central bureaucracies) needs to expand in proportion to the complexity of the system.

Finally, one speaker raised a specific question concerning freedom of movement of labor, to which Professor Kindleberger replied at the close. Professor Kindleberger's view, there was no prospect of bringing about the same degree of freedom for migration as can be achieved for trade in goods, because the optimum areas for human organization in social and political affairs are much smaller than the optimum economic areas. Many problems flow from conflicts between the optimum social and optimum economic areas. Professor Kindleberger sympathized both with Turkey's desire for continuing work opportunities in Germany and with Germany's concern for the resulting social difficulties. This kind of problem should be discussed between the governments concerned, with serious efforts to avoid taking action as if the other party did not count. But, to some extent, the conflicts are inescapable, and there is no general optimum solution which will remove all of them.

V

INTERDEPENDENCE IN THE EAST-WEST ECONOMIC RELATIONS

by Professor Peter Knirsch

FOREWORD

It is no simple matter nowadays to develop any particularly new thoughts on East-West economic relations. Too much has been written about problems in this area in the last twenty years. Politicians and economists have vied with each other in extolling East-West trade in the various stages of the East-West political conflict as an instrument for weakening the other side or as an important means of improving political relations, with the result that the literature on the subject, amplified by diligently collected statistics, has become almost unmanageable.

Perhaps it will help to avoid misunderstandings if I start by saying what this paper cannot and does not intend to do. It is not intended to be a detailed history of East-West economic relations, nor a synopsis of all the literature on the subject, nor an empirical quantitative description of these relations, nor yet a stock-taking of the institutional arrangements which have been of importance for East-West economic relations in the last thirty years. These approaches to the study of the question are indeed the basis of my paper, but I do not propose to report on them in detail or to duplicate them. Instead I shall try to summarize the identifiable longer-term trends in East-West economic relations, pick out the more influential factors and their effects, and take a new look at them in a wider historical perspective. In dealing with a subject both experts and journalists have written about at such length it may be not only worth-while making a more general summary and trying to see, not only the trees, but also the whole of the wood. With the aid of this overview I shall conclude with the much more difficult task of trying to deduce the determinants of the future course of East-West economic relations

DEFINITIONS

It may make things clearer if I briefly explain the terms I use. By *East* is meant the " socialist countries of Eastern Europe, " principally the East European Member countries of the " Council for Mutual Economic

135

Assistance " (CMEA, often called COMECON in the West), i.e. seven countries, namely the Soviet Union, Poland, the German Democratic Republic,[1] Czechoslovakia, Hungary, Romania, and Bulgaria. Unless otherwise stated, our analysis will be confined to this group of countries.

It should be mentioned here that the group is very heterogeneous, as the Soviet Union's size, economic potential, and political influence clearly give it a dominating position compared with the six other CMEA countries, but as regards economic development and standard of living the German Democratic Republic and Czechoslovakia are at the top of the group, while Romania's and Bulgaria's backwardness in these respects is very marked.

Looking further afield, a more detailed analysis would have to include the economically less developed CMEA Member countries of Cuba and Mongolia in the group, and also the non-CMEA countries of Yugoslavia, Albania, the People's Republic of China, North Korea, Vietnam, and perhaps also Laos and Angola.[2] This list makes it clear that the geographical term " East " is a very incomplete description of a group comprising such widely differing economic and political features. This use of the term in fact dates from a time when the group consisted entirely of the Soviet Union and the smaller East European countries.

The composition of the " West " is almost more complicated. It consists essentially of the developed industrialized countries of Western Europe together with the USA, Canada, and Japan, but for our purposes we shall include in it all the OECD Member countries including Australia and New Zealand. It will be clear that the term " West " serves here only as an abbreviation and has no geographical connotation.

The expression " economic relations " also calls for clarification. In connection with East-West relations the most important factor is *trade* and, unless otherwise stated, our remarks will always refer to East-West trade. There are also *capital movements* in the form of commercial and investment loans, *invisible trade*, and direct *economic co-operation* in the form of inter-governmental or industrial co-operation in which trade is not the primary consideration.

HISTORY OF DEVELOPMENT
OF EAST-WEST ECONOMIC RELATIONS

The starting point

Until the Second World War, the smaller East European countries' foreign trade relations were mainly with the West European industrialized countries, while the Soviet Union's foreign trade both with its East European

---

1. Apart from the political question whether the economic relations between the two parts of Germany should be regarded as foreign trade, the Federal Republic of Germany and the German Democratic Republic have been classified as West and East respectively and the trade between them, unless otherwise stated, has been counted as East-West trade.
2. The inclusion of the two last-mentioned countries among the " socialist countries " is admittedly open to question. The presence of observers from them at the Thirtieth Conference of the COMECON in July, 1976 in Berlin might be taken as a criterion. However, this question has no bearing on the rest of the paper.

neighbours and with the West, was relatively unimportant owing to its basic policy of economic self-sufficiency. In 1938, the share of world trade held by today's socialist countries in Eastern Europe was only 6.4 per cent, [3] mainly because of the low level of economic development in most of them. After the Second World War, it looked at first as if this traditional level of trade would be restored despite all the political and structural changes which had occurred (especially in Czechoslovakia), in addition to which much closer economic relations had developed between the Soviet Union and the countries occupied by its troops or, like Yugoslavia, ideologically close to it.

It is difficult for people of my generation to discover to what extent the victorious Western powers and the Soviet Union placed any hopes in a balanced East-West relationship as a continuation of the wartime alliance—such a prospect would of course have included the possibility of closer economic relations. What we do know is that the wartime alliance broke up very quickly and that *the Soviet Union became isolated from the economy of the Western world* no less quickly. Connected with this was the equally rapid consolidation of Soviet domination of the occupied countries of East and Central Europe and, sometimes after a period of very one-sided economic relations in the form of dismantling plant and reparations, the attempt to bind these satellite countries as closely as possible to the Soviet Union, not only politically but also economically. A side effect of these efforts was that those countries' traditional trade with the West never got going again or was very soon broken off.

In historical perspective, however, this *process of " the partitioning of Europe "* [4] and the birth of a " Second World " had more than the negative effect of separating populations and destroying historically developed economic relations. The process also inevitably meant that the Soviet Union began to abandon its basic policy of economic self-sufficiency. Although the Soviet Union thought at the time that it would strengthen its external economic relations only with politically dependent countries, and at first was certainly swayed by the prospect of unilateral advantage, the " establishment of a socialist world market " as these relations were somewhat pompously called, [5] was the beginning of a more effective inclusion of external economic relations in the Soviet economic development model. This led at first to increased inter-relationships among the East European countries' economies, themselves,

---

3. Figure calculated by J. Wilczynski in: " The Economics and Politics of East-West Trade. " A Study of Trade Between Developed Market Economies and Centrally Planned Economies in a Changing World ", London 1969, page 52. For details of the development of Eastern Europe's foreign trade relations in the post-war period, see Nicolas Spulber, " The Economies of Communist Eastern Europe ," New York and London 1957, pages 409-454.
4. This description is used by Wolfgang Wagner in " Die Teilung Europas " (The Partitioning of Europe), Stuttgart 1959.
5. The theory of the " disintegration of the single world market " was propounded by Stalin. J. W. Stalin, " Ökonomische Probleme des Sozialismus in der UdSSR " (Economic Problems of Socialism in the USSR), German translation, East Berlin 1952, pages 31-33. See also Eugen Varga, " Grundfragen der Ökonomik und Politik des Imperialismus (nach dem Zweiten Weltkrieg) " [Basic Issues in the Economics and Politics of Imperialism (after the Second World War)], German translation, East Berlin 1955, pages 37-42.

137

but also made it possible in the sixties for the " East " to seek more economic contacts with the " West. "

The nadir of East-West economic relations

That last observation, however, takes us much too far ahead in our historical review. In 1947, a further attempt was indeed made to arrest the above-mentioned decline in East-West economic relations. On 28th March, 1947, the " Economic Commission for Europe (ECE) " was established by the Economic and Social Council of the United Nations, with the object of establishing and promoting economic cooperation among member countries both in the West and in the East. But political conditions made it impossible for that body, in the early years of its existence, even to halt the growing economic division between East and West, let alone contribute to strengthening relations between them. Nevertheless, the ECE deserves mention here, because in those days when East-West economic relations were almost completely barren, it was the only important economic forum in which West and East European countries co-operated at all and tried to solve jointly minor technical problems of post-war reconstruction. [6]

A little later, on 12th July, 1947, the " Organisation (or first " Committee ") for European Economic Co-operation " (OEEC), later the OECD, was founded in connection with the United States' offer on 5th June, 1947, of aid for European economic recovery. Both the Marshall Plan and the OEEC were originally conceived as open to the East European countries. [7] But viewed historically this development was a major step towards splitting the world economy into East and West, because the seeds of the separation of Eastern Europe were countained both in the USA's pronounced domination of the OEEC and in the latter's parallelism with the ECE, which in principle could on an all-European scale have performed tasks exactly like those of the OEEC, having been set up with United States participation as the " Economic Commission *for* Europe " and not " *of* Europe ". Nor should it be overlooked that much earlier, after the foundation of the " International Bank for Reconstruction and Development " and the " International Monetary Fund " (IMF) in 1944 in Bretton Woods, and subsequently at the World Trade Conference in Havana from November, 1947 to March, 1948, the Soviet Union had dissociated itself from the attempts to reform the system of world trade. In retrospect, the split would seem to have been foreshadowed long in advance, and was inevitable in the constellation of that time. [8]

Against this longer-term background, the serious deterioration in East-West economic relations which developed rapidly after 1947 was largely the

---

6. Economic Commission for Europe, Geneva (publisher): ECE, A Key to Economic Co-operation, New York 1975 (Inf/ECE/1/75), which states in this connection that in the early years following the establishment of the Commission in 1947, governments used the ECE for solving urgent problems of post-war European reconstruction; shortages of coal, electric power, and industrial raw materials, as well as transport difficulties and shortages of housing.
7. See H.B. Price, The Marshall Plan and Its Meaning, Ithaca, New York 1955.
8. For Soviet post-war policy, see Zbigniew K. Brzezinski: The Soviet Bloc—Unity and Conflict, Harvard, Cambridge, Mass. 1960.

result of *current political events.* On 2nd July, 1947, at the Foreign Ministers' Conference in Paris, the Soviet Foreign Minister, Molotov, firmly rejected the Marshall Plan on behalf of the Soviet Union and gave warning of an impending division of Europe. Czechoslovakia and Poland, the only East European countries which had expressed interest in receiving Marshall Plan Aid, had to withdraw their declarations of support under Soviet pressure. From then on, the " Cold War " soon led to the paralysis of East-West trade and at the end of 1947 and beginning of 1948, the USA took its first embargo action against Eastern Europe. [9] The monetary reform in the three Western-occupied zones of Germany and the Berlin blockade which followed caused a dramatic worsening of political relations between the USA and the Soviet Union, which found economic expression in the Export Control Act of February, 1949, and the establishment of an agency for coordinating Western trade policy towards Eastern Europe in November, 1949, namely the " Co-ordinating Committee " (COCOM). This Agency drew up embargo lists of strategic goods which led to a drastic reduction in economic relations with Eastern Europe. During the Korean War, the USA tried, by passing the " Battle Act " in 1951, to make all countries receiving American aid enforce the embargo more strictly.

The Western measures outlined above were an attempt to use economic pressure by the West, whose economic potential was far superior to that of the East European countries, to influence the political behaviour of the communist countries. It is difficult to say after the lapse of time to what extent Western politicians believed they could thereby bring about the economic and political collapse of the Soviet Union and its satellites.

These last paragraphs may give the false impression that the disruption of the world economy resulted entirely from economic *measures taken by the West in the Cold War.* At that time, if I am not mistaken, the initiative in the actual steps taken lay in fact with the West, although they were basically reactions to political measures taken by the Soviet Union. In addition, however, the Soviet Union and the other communist countries, which it then controlled very closely, were themselves trying at least to some extent to isolate themselves from the world economy. We have already mentioned their early dissociation from the Bretton Woods decisions. The next clear step towards " demarcation, " although this word was not yet used then, was in September, 1947 when the Cominform was set up and in January, 1949 when the " Council for Mutual Economic Assistance (CMEA), " often called the COMECON in the West, was founded, which is described by writers as a direct reaction to the integrating effect of Marshall Plan aid on Western Europe. [10] The Soviet Union's withdrawal from the world market reflected at that time its basic policy of self-sufficiency, and there is good reason to

9. According to Hanns-Dieter Jacobsen, " Die wirtschaftlichen Beziehungen zwischen West und Ost. Strukturen, Formen, Interessen, Auswirkungen " (Economic Relations between West and East: Structures, Forms, Interests, and Effects), Reinbeck bei Hamburg 1975, (rororo study 79), page 14. Also Gunnar Adler-Karlsson, Western Economic Warfare 1947-1967, Stockholm 1968, pages 22-82.
10. See for example Peter J.D. Wiles, Communist International Economics, Oxford 1968, pages 311 ff.

assume that the world market would have been split in two even without the embargo action taken by the West.

Irrespective of these speculations, the result was quite clear. From 1949 to 1954, East-West economic relations were at an extraordinarily low level and reached their nadir in 1953 with a 1.3 per cent share of world trade. [11]

The return to a modest normality

The next period in East-West economic relations lasted roughly from 1954 to 1965. During that time, East-West trade grew about fourfold, but in view of its very low starting level that still meant quite a low level by the end of the period. The share of East-West trade in world trade only just doubled from 1.3 per cent in 1953 to 2.6 per cent in 1965 [12] but the importance of the events of this period in determining the scope for further developments in East-West economic relations should not be underestimated. On the political side of the relationships between the two systems, there was the gradual abatement of the Cold War. Several circumstances had made this possible, among which the *developments in Eastern Europe* seem to me to have been decisive. After the Second World War, the West was clearly shocked by the vehemence of Soviet expansionism, which succeeded within three years in establishing communist regimes in eight European countries. In reacting to it, the stand taken by the West in the Berlin question and in Korea was correspondingly tough, with the above-mentioned effects on East-West economic relations, but in the fifties it became apparent that what the Soviet Union could achieve politically was by no means unlimited. The first sign of this was the ideological and political conflict with Yugoslavia as early as June, 1948, and in the fifties the Soviet power structure was exposed to *serious strains*. The rising in the German Democratic Republic on 17th June, 1953, the disturbances in Poland in October, 1956, and the Hungarian revolution in November, 1956 made it increasingly clear that there were limits to the exercise of Soviet power. Here *political changes inside the Soviet Union* were of decisive importance. Stalin's death in March, 1953 and the " de-Stalinisation " introduced by Krushchev's secret speech at the Twentieth Party Conference of the Soviet Union Communist Party in February, 1956 were key factors in bringing about changes in the Soviet Union's domestic and foreign policies which, although slow, had an important cumulative effect.

The continuation of this period saw the ideological and political dispute with the People's Republic of China and Albania in 1960-61, and the start of Romania's struggle for independence in 1962. The Soviet-Chinese conflict dealt a most serious blow to the USSR's claim to hegemony over the communist countries.

Parallel with this internal weakening, there was an increase in the Soviet Union's military might, and when it drew level in atomic weapons the " balance of terror " was established and its external security and self-confidence were considerably strengthened.

---

11. This figure is given by Wilczynski in *op. cit.*, page 52.
12. *Ibid.*, page 52.

These political developments in the " East, " which are of course only roughly outlined here, also had an important influence on the factors which later decisively affected trends in East-West economic relations. For one thing, they reduced the West's anxiety about Soviet expansionism, and the Cold War and the embargo policy gradually came to be regarded as less important than before. Indeed in some Western circles during this period, extreme *optimism* developed regarding the possible future development of East and West towards an evolutionary solution to the division of the world into two: in 1961 the *theory of convergence*, whose leading exponent was Jan Tinbergen, went a long way in that direction. Apart from the question as to how realistic these ideas were, they made the public ready, and with it Western policy, to regard closer economic relations with Eastern Europe as not only politically acceptable, but perhaps even politically desirable as a contribution to further internal changes in Eastern Europe. [13]

It would probably be fair to describe the political result in the West of these developments as a *recognition of the status quo*, which was at first reluctant and then gradually accepted the changed political facts in Europe, while in the East Krushchev tried to sum up the change in East-West political relations in the concept of " peaceful coexistence. " Despite the West's clear military superiority, its attitude was now one of passive compliance, and only in extreme situations like the Cuba crisis of 1962 dit it take up a firmer stance. As a result, the West came to recognize the Soviet sphere of influence, at least in Europe, both during the Hungarian uprising in 1956 and also when the Berlin Wall was erected in 1961. Later, when the Soviets intervened in Czechoslovakia in August, 1968, the West was neither willing nor able to oppose in any way these measures for consolidating Soviet dominance in Eastern Europe. For East-West economic relations, however, the result of this development was to *moderate the hostile attitude* which had emerged soon after 1945 and to *make East-West political relations more stable*, both of which changes later facilitated the development of economic relations between the two blocks.

Another development in this period was that the West managed to achieve considerable economic consolidation. The reconstruction carried out after the Second World War led in most countries of the Western world to continuing expansion, interrupted on the whole by few fluctuations, and as a consequence to a signifiant *increase in the economic potential and general prosperity* of these countries. Meanwhile, it was clear that although the communist countries of Eastern Europe could also boast of very rapid economic growth, the gap between them and the West in economic and technological development was still very wide and Krushchev's boastful claim about soon overtaking the USA was quite unrealistic in the foreseeable future. Thus along with increased political self-confidence went a more conscious economic self-confidence, to which Europe may have contributed by all the high hopes connected with the establishment of the European Economic Community in March, 1957. This changed attitude and situation in the West led in due

---

13. See the analysis by Zbigniew K. Brzezinski, Alternative to Partition, New York 1965.

course to the abatement of objections to economic relations with the East and to a much more positive policy towards East-West trade.

However, the great importance of this period for East-West economic relations was due not only to the political changes in Eastern Europe mentioned above, but also to the *changes in economic thinking* and in the level of economic development taking place in the East. After the Second World War, the Soviet Union had reverted to a basic policy of self-sufficiency in its foreign trade relations with the West [14] and had imposed this policy on the smaller East European countries.

Here an important part was played by the efforts to achieve *economic independence* from the developed Western industrialized or " capitalist " countries, which were regarded as hostile. This reflected Soviet Russia's early experiences in the civil war after 1917, but it is no accident either that in Eastern Europe to this day people still remember the West's embargo policy after 1947, which is used as proof economic relations with the West must never be allowed to become so close that they would make the East European countries economically dependent. [15]

In addition to these political reasons, the prevailing *differences between the economic systems* made the East disinclined to take part in world trade. Central planning was only to a limited extent able to adjust to the sometimes violent fluctuations of the world market, especially as far as prices and possible volume of sales were concerned. It was simpler, therefore, for the planning authorities to keep trade relations with the Western world market at as low a level as possible, at any rate as long as the domestic shortage of goods was very serious and there were hardly any reserves. As a result of these considerations, trade with the West had dwindled to a residual item, being based on the minimum of imports needed to supplement home production and on attempts to export the amount required to balance the accounts.

The Soviet Union was able to operate this *autarkic system* without undue economic sacrifice because, like the USA, its need for foreign trade was small owing to the size of its own economy. Moreover, the policy of self-sufficiency was encouraged by the Soviet Union's relatively low level of development which hampered its ability to sell on the world market. But the policy posed serious problems for the smaller socialist countries, which were heavily dependent on foreign trade to supplement their own economic structures. It soon became clear, moreover, that this situation could not be changed by copying the Soviet policy of creating as diversified an economic structure as possible. It was no accident that the first arguments against an autarkic policy were put forward by the Hungarians as early as 1953 and 1954, [16] and were taken up in subsequent years by economists in the German Democratic Republic and Poland.

---

14. This was still so according to Stalin's latest writings, see Josef W. Stalin, Ökonomische Probleme des Sozialismus in der UdSSR, *op. cit.*, page 32. Note the very different treatment of this problem by Peter Wiles, *op. cit.*, pages 419-453.
15. Repeated in a more recent Soviet publication on our theme; see A. M. Voinov, V. Ja. Iochin, and L. A. Rodina, " Ekonomičeskie otnošenija meždu socialističenskimi i razvitymi kapitalističeskimi stranami, " Moscow 1975, pages 14-16.
16. Stated by Wiles, *op. cit.*, page 22.

There was also another way in which the period from 1954 to 1965 prepared the way for greater participation by Eastern Europe in the world economy. The discussion, again initiated by Stalin, on the relationship between planning and the market led to the so-called " discussion on the law of value " at the end of the fifties, and then to an intensive reappraisal by economists at a theoretical level concerning the constituent elements of the planning system, with particularly important contributions by Polish economists after 1956 and Czechoslovak economists after 1964. As a result, the door was no longer closed to including in the system of internal controls a more decentralized *planning system supplemented by market economy elements,* and in the reforms of the sixties attempts were made in varying degrees to institute such a system. [17] The consequence of these discussions for East-West economic relations was as follows: the realization that the influence of economic planning was very limited even inside a socialist country allayed the reluctance of having economic relations with the world market where planning did not apply, and the risks to the planned economies of Eastern Europe from trade with the West were balanced against its possible advantages.

In my estimation, these changes in economic thinking in Eastern Europe were a most important starting point for a *new orientation of economic policy* in favour of closer economic relations with the West. The new intellectual currents were strengthened by a change in the economic constellation in the East. There too, the post-war period by and large was one of rapid economic growth up to about 1960, although apart from the German Democratic Republic and Czechoslovakia the level of economic development in Eastern Europe was relatively low. The growth was based mainly on utilizing additional factors of production, especially by increasing the industrial workforce and by new investment in industry. By about 1960, however, there was no further scope for continuing this extensive growth in most East European countries and *economic growth slowed down* considerably. It proved extremely difficult, if not impossible, to make the transition to intensive forms of growth under the conditions of the existing system and, as economic policy relied on rapid growth for achieving its aims, ways out of the difficulty were sought. For the domestic economy, the above-mentioned reforms were an attempt to find a way out, but at the same time the economic policy-makers turned their attention to *foreign trade as a possible growth factor.* As the results of co-operation among the socialist countries in the COMECON were not very impressive, and provided little scope for overcoming the emerging growth difficulties, the economic policy-makers inevitably became more interested in trade with the West. [18]

Thus on closer inspection the period from 1954 to 1965 was by no means as unimportant in the development of East-West economic relations as the

17. See Peter Knirsch, " Aspekte der Wirtschaftsreformen in Osteuropa " (Aspects o-Economic Reforms in Eastern Europe), in Hamburger Jahrbuch für Wirtschafts- und Gesellf schaftspolitik (Hamburg Yearbook for Economic and Social policy), 15th year, Tübingen 1970, pages 101-118.
18. See Imre Vajda, The Role of Foreign Trade in A Socialist Economy, Budapest 1965, page 298.

modest trade figures at first suggest. It seems to me that what most influenced the readiness of the West to do more trade with the East was the political changes in Eastern Europe, while what most changed the attitude of Eastern Europe toward trade with the West was the changes in economic thinking and also the changes in economic policy imposed by the increasingly difficult economic situation.

Experiences and problems of earlier periods

Before continuing our historical review it may be useful, apart from describing the political and macro-economic factors, to consider the general course and problems of East-West economic relations in the first 20 years after the Second World War. The period from 1954 to 1965 was of great importance for the further development of East-West economic relations in that the *practical experience* was gained then which provided the basis for a much more significant expansion of East-West economic relations in the seventies. It may now scarcely be possible for the younger generation to realize how cut off the East European countries, and especially the Soviet Union itself, still were from the West in the fifties. Few Western businessmen went to Eastern Europe in those years and hardly any tourists. *Information* on political, social, and economic conditions in the West was very scanty, at least in the Soviet Union, and was badly distorted by propaganda. Here I might mention a personal impression. When I made my first extended tour of the Soviet Union in 1960, I was regarded as a curiosity, at least in the provinces, as much as in the People's Republic of China in 1976.

However, it was not only the Soviet population which had little information in the fifties about the West, and still less correct information. The West also was dominated by fantastic ideas about living conditions in the Socialist countries. The Federal Republic of Germany, for example, had taken over the Nazi picture of Bolshevism almost unaffected by de-Nazification and re-education and kept it during the Cold War.

In the sixties, this distorted state of information on both sides underwent substantial changes which were of great importance for the further development of economic relations. While the East as a whole, with the exception to some extent of Hungary and Poland, remained very unwilling to allow its citizens to travel to the West, tourists from Western countries were actively encouraged to visit Eastern Europe, and some countries like Romania and Bulgaria deliberately promoted this traffic as a source of hard currencies. This, combined with more lenient police action against contacts with Western travellers and receiving information from the West, gave the populations of Eastern Europe a wider and more objective knowledge of conditions in the West. At the same time, the West's knowledge of Eastern Europe was increased by the evidence of its own eyes and by fuller reporting, to which the East itself also contributed. As regards economic information on Eastern Europe, it should be remembered that statistical yearbooks did not reappear in the Soviet Union and the German Democratic Republic until 1956, but that since then *information of reliable analytical value* on Eastern Europe has greatly increased.

144

A direct contribution to East-West economic relations came from *business contacts* which were made in the fifties and sixties in connection with the gradual growth of East-West trade. Western businessmen had to learn through a rather difficult process the special conditions governing exporting to the State trading countries; negotiations with the State foreign trade authorities were unduly lengthy and tiresome by Western standards and the associated red tape, not only in the East but to some extent also in the West, was much worse than in normal foreign trade transactions. Very often a Western supplier of capital goods did not get to know the actual recipient of his products in the East, but only the superintending Ministry or competent foreign trade agency, which tried to safeguard itself by pitching its technical specifications too high.

From the start, trade with the East was hampered by the East European countries' shortage of hard currency, a shortage which was and still is mainly due to structural weaknesses in their production system, which could sell only raw materials and semi-manufactures on the world market, and much less finished industrial and agricultural products, because the latter were usually inferior to the products of the developed Western countries in quality and technology. For a long time Eastern foreign trade officials thought, and probably many of them still think, that the simplest way out of this situation consisted in *compensation deals*, whereby the problem and risk of marketing the counterpart goods was shifted onto the Western trading partner. Amusing though it may be to hear of world-famous Western engineering firms suddenly having to sell Russian vodka or caviar, it was certainly a highly inefficient way, from an economic point of view, of widening East-West economic relations. The above-mentioned changes in economic thinking in Eastern Europe may have been one reason why these forms of trading came to be recognized there also as too expensive and became less sought after

Shortly thereafter, *credits* from Western suppliers began to be obtained for financing East-West trade and the terms of these credits quickly became a decisive factor in East-West business deals. Competition between Western firms for export business to Eastern Europe was largely governed, not only by the quality of their offers and the prices they quoted, but also by the terms of their supplier credits. In order to promote their foreign trade, most Western exporting countries had introduced government-supported systems for insuring and subsidizing export credits. In the early sixties, these led in some cases to a *credit race* among Western exporters to Eastern Europe, in which some credits granted to East European countries were on considerably more favourable terms than those recommended by the Berne Union. [19] We shall revert later to the problems of Western credits to the East, but at any rate in the sixties they contributed a good deal, mostly through medium-term supplier credits, to developing East-West trade, although they hampered the evolution of a uniform Western policy.

Meanwhile, this period of comparatively slow but steady growth in East-West trade gave the East valuable experience. While in the fifties it

19. For details see Wilczynski, *op. cit.*, pages 229-232.

could still happen that an *Eastern trading partner* was only ready to do business with his Western " class enemy " with important ideological reservations, and often knew little about the realities of the Western market and perhaps little about the technical standard of the products he wanted to buy or sell, representatives of the State trading countries gradually acquired the knowledge necessary for successful business negotiations. Although to this day East-West business is fraught with an unusual amount of red tape, adequately trained negotiating partners were increasingly found in the East who tried to do their job as *technocrats* without wearing large ideological blinkers.

Among the experiences of this period was the increasing familiarity of each side with the other side's *philosophy and institutions*. The Western businessmen who specialized in " red trade " gradually came to know the complicated pattern of responsibility in the East's foreign trade machinery. They learned that in State trading countries, apart from economic calculations, " everything was possible " if one had the right connections, and in many cases they fell in all too well with this system and collaborated in corrupt practices, some of which were already well established. The Eastern side had to learn that there was a great gulf between State trading agreements and their implementation through transactions with private firms, and that Western governments were better able to hinder foreign trade than to promote it effectively.

All in all, this relatively long period of slowly developing East-West economic relations hardly brought the two ideological and political standpoints closer together, but it considerably widened each side's knowledge of the other's economic peculiarities and requirements, thereby laying a valuable foundation for the expansion of East-West economic relations.

The increasing intensification of East-West economic relations (1965-1976)

As we come nearer to the present in our rough division into time phases, we can observe a steady *acceleration in the growth of East-West trade*. Whereas, from 1961 to 1965, the average growth in CMEA countries' imports from western countries was 8.6 per cent, and in their exports to those countries 9.2 per cent, the corresponding figures for 1966 to 1970 were 12.4 and 10.7 per cent respectively; 22.2 and 18.1 per cent for 1971 to 1973; no less than 40.0 and 42.0 per cent for 1974; and 36.5 and 6.5 per cent for 1975. [20] Whereas the trend discernible in the early sixties continued between 1966 and 1971, only at a faster pace, East-West trade expanded at an unprecedented and extremely rapid rate from 1972 to 1975 even if we eliminate the distortions caused by price increases on the world market and exchange rate changes, and consider growth in real terms.

Firstly, however, a *general warning* seems called for: the high growth rates over the last five years could easily lead to on overestimate of the impor-

---

20. Cf. Benedikt Askanas, Halina Askanas, and Friedrich Levcik: Der Aussenhandel der RGW-Länder 1960-1974 (External trade of CMEA Countries, 1960-1974); in: Österreichisches Institut für Wirtschaftsforschung, Monatsberichte, Vienna, 1974, No. 11.
Economic Commission for Europe: Economic Survey of Europe in 1975, Part I (Prepublication text ECE XXXI/1 Add. 1), Table 5.1.

tance of East-West trade. In fact, on the international scale, the significance of East-West trade is still very small: by the mid-seventies its share in world trade was about 2.5 per cent although the East European countries accounted for some 30 per cent of world industrial production at that time. So the mutual involvement between the East European countries and the western industrialized countries is very slight in spite of this steep upward trend.

Although there is this need to keep things in proportion, the acceleration in the progress of East-West economic relations is highly significant for the topic we are discussing and we will now examine the factors that have brought about this striking change.

1. First in importance is the *improvement in East-West political relations.* We have shown earlier how, after Stalin's death, there was a shift away from Cold War attitudes. In the late sixties began the process that became generally known as " détente " in East-West relations. In spite of the continuing presence of very big differences in political ideology between the Western democracies and the communist countries of Eastern Europe, negotiations on arms limitations and on possible areas for disarmament, the Four Power Berlin Pact, and the Treaties signed between the Federal Republic of Germany and the USSR and Poland generated a climate of political security, even reciprocal trust, such as had never existed before. Even setbacks like the Soviet invasion of Czechoslovakia or developments in Vietnam, Laos, and Cambodia failed to have any lasting negative effect. This political détente was a basic condition for the rapid development of East-West economic relations in the first half of the seventies.

2. Readiness to trade with the West had increased considerably in all East European countries and particularly in the Soviet Union itself. This was not merely a quantitative matter of doing more business, but a *qualitative change in attitude.* We have shown how the basic doctrine of economic self-sufficiency gradually came to be questioned in the East and how, from about 1965 on, the importance of external economic relations was generally recognized, in economic theory and economic policy, as a factor of growth. From then on, attitudes toward trade with the West became distinctly more positive.

3. From the facts we know today, it is impossible to say to what extent this political détente was bound up with the East European wish to increase its trade with the West, but there is good reason for supposing that East European efforts to improve the political climate between East and West are, to a large extent, to be explained in terms of economic need.

4. This is certainly the impression we get if we take a closer look at the *motivations of the East.* So far we have spoken only very generally about the difficulties experienced in switching from extensive to intensive growth, which opened Eastern European eyes to the economic policy attractions of foreign trade as a growth factor. This is true for all foreign economic relations in general. At the same time as relations were developed with the West, efforts were also made to intensify economic relations among the CMEA countries themselves. The CMEA " complex programme " of 1971 was

147

the most important external measure taken to arrive at more rational forms of division of labour and economic integration in the East. [21]

There are, however, more specific reasons for the changed attitude toward economic relations with the West. One major cause of the growth problems in all East European countries consisted in the difficulties of their political and economic systems in the *industrial exploitation of scientific and technical progress*. [22] For modern industrial economies, this is by far the most important growth factor and this was increasingly understood in the planned economies of Eastern Europe. [23] Since the East European systems, in their present form, are not yet efficient enough in this respect, it has to be replaced by economic relations with the West and the transfer of industrially applicable modern technologies, primarily in the form of imported plant and machinery. This, in my view, is the main reason for the rapid expansion in East-West economic relations after 1971.

The earlier importance of trade with the West as a *stopgap* for production and supply bottlenecks in East Europe was in no way diminished by the new policy. In recent years this reason for trade has become even more important, since not only has it been a question, more than previously, of supplying the special products that the CMEA countries, for national or technical reasons, could not produce (or not in sufficient quantity), but in addition a more or less regular process began of making up for shortfalls by importing from the West, with the state planning authorities taking increasing account of consumer needs. The best known examples in this connection have been the Soviet Union's regular purchases of grain in the West, but meat and butter have also been imported in significant quantities.

5. Given the kind of system that the CMEA countries have, it must be assumed that this far-reaching change of course by all the Eastern bloc countries in their economic relations with the West was not a spontaneous process but rather *a carefully considered political decision*. This is a reasonable assumption today, since the attitude of the East European countries has not changed for a number of years now, however sceptical a view one takes of the rationality of political decisions even in East Europe. We know nothing about how this decision came to be taken and whether the reasons we have given were in fact behind it, but the results are clearly recognizable: from about 1965, and quite definitely from 1971, the CMEA countries were ready:

---

21. (No author's name given): Komplexprogramm für die weitere Vertiefung and Vervollkommnung der Zusammenarbeit und Entwicklung der sozialistischen ökonomischen Integration der Mitgliedslän derdes RGW (Complex programme for the further intensification and improvement of the co-operation and development of the socialist economic integration of the Member States of the COMECON); German text in: Neues Deutschland, Berlin (East), 30th July 1971.

22. Cf. Peter Knirsch: Technischer Fortshritt und zentrale Planwirtschaft (Technical Progress and Centrally Planned Economies); in: Werner Markert (Publisher): Osteuropa-Handbuch. Sowjetunion. Das Wirtschaftssystem, Cologne, Graz 1965, pages 213-235.

E. Zaleski, J. P. Kozlowski, H. Wienert, and others: Science Policy in the USSR OECD, Paris, 1969.

23. Last year, at the 25th Conference of the Soviet Union Communist Party, Brezhnev and Kosygin among others again strongly stressed the importance of technological progress. Prâvda, Moscow, 25th February, 1976 and 2nd March, 1976.

— to expand their economic relations with the industrialized countries of the West considerably,
— to increase their imports substantially, particularly of capital goods,
— to incur considerable longer-term indebtedness with the West to finance these imports, and
— to look for new types of economic relations with the West, such as industrial co-operation, so as to ensure a more efficient transfer of modern technology.

6. East-West economic relations are not a one-sided affair; the East European efforts we have described depended on a reciprocal *Western readiness* to trade with the East. I have tried to show how political objections and material obstacles in the way of trade with the East were broken down in the 60s. There were, of course, developments in the other direction: West European integration in the European Economic Community and its Common Agricultural Policy reduced the markets for traditional East European exports considerably. These developments must have been unwelcome at the time but they were not the result of political hostility, and in the long run the resulting changes in the patterns of East European exports could produce economically advantageous results. Overall, the policy of the Western industrialized nations during this period was, and still is, favourable towards economic relations with the East, as is proved by the many bilateral government trade treaties and agreements on economic and technological co-operation and the negotiations on " Basket No. 2 " at the Conference on Security and Co-operation in Europe. At least equally important, in practical terms, was the continuing readiness of the Western governments to help banks and suppliers bear the burden of Eastern indebtedness by means of guarantees or official credits.

These political conditions on the Western side were certainly an important factor in the rapid expansion of East-West economic relations, but with conditions as they are in the market economy countries of the West, private firms could only be encouraged, not forced, to trade with the East. It is in the nature of the market economy that the readiness of private enterprise to do business is not amenable to direct political control. This may often have been a source of irritation for policy-makers. In East-West relations, for example, they had had to deal with the attempts of business to beat the COCOM embargo rules. The improvement in East-West political relations affected decisions in the business world to the extent that the *political risk* of such trade was reduced. However, the West's readiness to trade, which fundamentally was always there, has been given an additional stimulus over the last ten years by the economic recession affecting many Western industrialized countries, with its two low points in 1967 and 1974/75. The efforts of Western firms in this situation to find markets in East Europe and their willingness to grant credit were greater than before. [24]

---

24. Jan Stankovsky: Bestimmungsgründe des Ost-West-Handels (Determinants of East-West trade); in: Österreichisches Institut für Wirtschaftsforschung, Monatsberichte, Vienna, 1972, Vol. 10, pages 412-424.

Thus, all in all, political and economic conditions during the period 1965-1976 were particularly favourable for the development of East-West economic relations. In my view, the most important feature was the policy decision taken in East Europe substantially to increase their imports of Western capital goods at the cost of a high level of indebtedness. Whether the détente came before this decision or was politically necessary for its success, I am not—as an economist—in a position to say. All the other factors I have mentioned, however, would seem to be secondary compared with this basic economic and political decision by the East.

CURRENT PROBLEMS IN EAST-WEST ECONOMIC RELATIONS

This study is not intended as a piece of research into economic history. Our retrospect over the last thirty years of East-West relations is intended purely as a basis on which to assess present problems and likely developments in the foreseeable future. The following paragraphs deal with those viewpoints that seem particularly significant at the present time.

The political dimension in East-West economic relations

Up to now, as we have shown, economic relations between East and West have depended to a large extent on the political relations between the two. In very simplified terms, it may be said that the Cold War greatly limited economic relations and that détente provided a basis for their rapid expansion. But although it is important to stress these influences, they should not be given undue weight. The importance of these political factors has to be qualified to the extent that all international economic relations, not merely those between East and West, are subject to political influence. This applies even to trade between allies or friendly nations including, for example, those in the European Community, and this fact is brought out particularly clearly at the present time in the economic relations between the industrialized countries of the West and the Third World. To that extent, the political dimension of East-West economic relations is not as unique as is often assumed, although it is particularly conspicuous in their case.

In this connection, a view worth studying is the thesis that these political influences have *lost some of their weight* during the course of time. It is certainly not an inflexible law of nature. In view of the major differences in political ideology between East and West, it would seem perfectly possible, at any moment in time, for East-West economic relations to be severely curtailed or broken off altogether for political reasons. The big unknown in the way of any predictions in this area is the element of irrationality in politics, but apart from this basic indeterminacy, due to special situations which may arise, there are various factors to suggest that East-West economic relations may become relatively independent of political developments.

For most East European countries, economic relations with the Western industrialized countries have assumed too great an importance in quantitative, and still more in qualitative, terms for them to be at the mercy of political

150

vagaries. The economic policy objectives in these countries give high priority to economic growth and any impairment of economic relations with the West would, in present circumstances, seriously compromise the realization of this objective for a considerable time. But there are other respects in which the East is no longer wholly free in its political decisions. With advancing industrialization, the claims of the population to a higher standard of living have become more insistent, and internal peace and labour productivity depend on that standard of living being maintained. Economic relations with the West are contributing more and more to this maintenance of living standards, directly by supplementing food supply resources and indirectly through their contribution to expanding industrial production. For both reasons, therefore, I conclude that at the present time the East European countries are interested in the greatest possible *undisturbed continuance* of economic relations with the West, not only for economic but also for political reasons. To some extent, economic factors have gained the ascendancy over politics in East Europe in recent years, and it is only in relatively extreme situations that they could revert to the customary precedence of politics over economics that has always been assumed to apply in the East.

In a similar way, but perhaps less clearly, the economic side of East-West economic relations has become independent of politics in the West. Admittedly, as we shall see, the overall significance of East-West trade is still very small, but for many industries, particularly the capital goods sector, exports to East Europe, as was far from being the case in—say—1948, are now very important in terms of maintaining the level of employment. Western governments too would meet with considerable internal resistance from these pressure groups if they attempted to place any drastic restrictions on economic relations with the East without serious justification apparent to all concerned.

Structural problems limiting East-West economic relations

So far we have considered only the overall development of East-West economic relations. We now need to supplement this by taking a look at basic structural factors. So far East-West trade has largely been *complementary in nature*. Put simply, Western finished goods, primarily capital goods (SITC 5-8), are supplied to East Europe and East European raw materials, fuels, and agricultural products (SITC 0-4) are supplied to the West. [25] Admittedly, this *one-sided pattern* has, in the long run, improved and become generally more balanced, but there still seems a long way to go before any kind of substitution in foreign trade is reached, particularly in the Soviet Union's case. One of the reasons for this is the stop-gap function of trade with the West referred to earlier, a function that has by no means completely disappeared. Another, however, is the big differences in productivity between West and East which make East European finished industrial products poor

---

25. Cf. Askanas, Askanas and Levcik, loc. cit. Entwicklung und Struktur des Ost-West-Handels im Jahrzehnt 1960/70 (Development and Pattern of East-West Trade in the Decade 1960/70); in: DIW-Wochenbericht, Berlin (West), 1972, No. 10, page 82.

competitors on world markets. [26]   In practice, the quality level of industrial products from East Europe, their technological standard, presentation, and packing and, last but not least, the inadequate or total lack of marketing and the unsatisfactory after-sales service hold back any expansion on world markets.

This one-sided product pattern severely restricts expansion potential in East-West trade.   The relatively small range of competitive products available from the East European countries soon limits the volume that export trade can reach.   Since the import requirements of the East European countries for qualitatively and technologically high-grade Western industrial products has so far been practically infinite, only two possibilities are left for economic relations with the West.   If the East European countries want equilibrium in their balance of payments—apart from the Soviet Union this is roughly the same as having equilibrium in the balance of trade—trade with the West will have to be kept to a relatively low level because of the limitation equilibirum would place on exports.   The second possibility, allowing greater freedom of imports, would be to accept a deficit in the balance of trade and to cover this by credit or loans from the West.

The one-sided product pattern of East-West trade has, in the past, had a particularly bad effect on East European countries' trade balances, because the terms of trade developed unfavourably for the East's main exports (raw materials and agricultural products) as compared with the capital goods that were its chief imports, and this demanded further efforts to expand export trade.   It was not until about 1973 that this negative factor became less significant: since then price ratios have, generally speaking, become more favourable for the pattern of the East European countries' export trade, but the relatively close dependence of East European exports on economic developments in the West, particularly marked in the 1974-1976 recession, remains.

Economic policy-makers in the East European countries are well aware of the unfavourable effects of this one-sided export pattern.   Overall, the possibility of bringing about any rapid change in this situation unfortunately seems limited.   The reasons for it lie partly in the different levels of industrialization in the East and West.   It is not by chance that the GDR and Czechoslovakia, the most industrialized of the East European countries, also export the largest proportion of finished industrial products to the West.   As things stand, the only hope is that increasing industrialization will, in the longer term, change matters.   Another factor, however, is the fact that the economic system in East Europe is relatively ill-suited to producing qualitatively and technologically high-grade industrial goods, and, in spite of all the discussion on reform and the attempts that have been made in that direction, there is as yet no hint of how this problem might be satisfactorily solved in the foreseeable future.

The smaller East European countries dependent on export trade, like Hungary and Poland, suffer especially because of the limitations imposed

---

26.   Rolf Krengel gives an excellent analysis of these problems in: Die Bedeutung des Ost-West-Handels für die Ost-West-Beziehungen (Significance of East-West Trade for East-West Relations).   Göttingen, 1967, pages 100-102.

on trade with the West by their limited export possibilities. Their greater readiness for far-reaching economic reforms stems at least partly from their eagerness to find an answer to this problem. In addition, there is the pursuit of export-based growth as part of their economic policy. These considerations played an important part in the modernization of Poland's industrial facilities between 1971 and 1975.

The solution of financing problems as the main cause of the expansion in East-West economic relations

We have already pointed out that there is a way around the limiting effect of restricted export opportunities on the expansion of East-West economic relations; that is for East European imports to be financed by loans from the West. In a more detailed analysis, of course, the possible contribution to the balance of payments of a surplus in invisibles should also be taken into account, but in practice, even in the tourism-oriented countries in the Eastern bloc like Romania and Bulgaria, this has not overcome the general shortage of hard currency [27]. Specific factors would also have to be considered: for example the GDR's balance-of-payments situation has always been somewhat more favourable because of the particular pattern of internal German trade and proceeds from tourist traffic; Poland has benefited from West German reparation payments; and the Soviet Union has resources to help its balance of payments in the form of gold reserves whose real level, however, we do not know. In spite of these particularities, *borrowing from the West* is the best short-term solution for all the CMEA countries to increase their imports in the light of the export problems that have been described.

Up to the beginning of the sixties, Western credit to East European countries was on a very small scale, but as the Cold War gradually abated and interest grew in trade with the East, the Western industrialized nations became more willing to allow credit. At the same time, the East European countries gave up the principle of keeping their balance of payments in equilibrium as far as possible and began to incur debts with the West. In the sixties credit facilities, mainly in the form of supplier credits for specific deals, gave considerable impetus to the expansion of East-West trade. In particular, very large contracts, like the supplies of West German piping to the Soviet Union or the car factory built by FIAT in Togliattigrad, would have been out of the question without credit.

Even so, East European indebtedness to the West was still relatively limited up to 1970. By 1968 the accrued figure was given as US $ 1.7 billion, which financed some 25 per cent of exports from the West. [28] Experience with credit financing was clearly favourable on both sides—the West, in

---

27. Revenue from external trade was estimated at about US $ 200 million for 1971 (not including the Soviet Union). Edwin M. Snell: Eastern Europe's Trade and Payments with the Industrial West; in: Joint Economic Committee, Congress of the United States (Ed.): Reorientation and Commercial Relations of the Economies of Eastern Europe. Washington, D.C., 1974, page 688.

28. Wilczynski, *loc. cit.*, page 226. The trade balance figures for trade with the West are given in: Entwicklung und Struktur des Ost-West-Handels... *loc. cit.*, page 80.

particular, is continually commending its East European customers as reliable payers.

We have discussed the circumstances in which the economic policy decision for large-scale development in economic relations was taken in East Europe in the second half of the sixties. Since the governments of these countries were certainly aware that any rapid expansion in exports to the West was out of the question, acceptance of greatly increased indebtedness to the West must have been decided at the same time. In any case, the actual trend of events implies that this was so. Between 1970 and 1975, imports increased far more steeply than exports to the West; the CMEA countries' trade balances with the West were all in deficit; and by the end of 1976, their cumulative debt to the West totalled some US $ 38-40 billion. [29] In 1970-1973, the volume of imports from the West ranged between 10 per cent (Hungary) and 38 per cent (GDR) higher than that of East European exports to the West, and trade balance deficits had to be covered up to about 50 per cent by credit. [30]

What is interesting here is not only the rapid increase and high level reached by East European indebtedness, but also its *changed form*. In addition to the supplier and bank credits for individual deals, the only facility originally given, there was a steady increase in untied bank loans, borrowing on the Eurodollar market, and the raising of loans in Western capital markets.[31] On the East European side, the borrowers involved were the state banks of the individual countries and their subsidiaries in the West, and also the two CMEA banking institutes.

The importance of new forms of East-West economic relations; long-term compensation deals and industrial co-operation

Borrowing in the West was certainly the most important step toward expanding East-West economic relations, but there were other measures as well. While straight compensation deals by no means disappeared from East-West trade (although their importance has dwindled in recent years because of the steep increase in the volume of trade), new forms of economic relations arose alongside trade relations in their simplest form which continued to account for by far the largest share. The first, chronologically, was a change in compensation trade itself. To varying extents, compensation deals in the 60s ceased to be the direct exchange of goods, and were converted into *long-term compensation projects* through a system of bridging loans. A supplier in the West, or a consortium in the case of big projects, would supply

---

29. Börsen- und Wirtschafts-Handbuch, 1977, Frankfurt-am-Main, 1977. There are no official statistics on the COMECON countries' debt to the West. The figure given, therefore, can be only a rough estimate. ECE, Economic Survey of Europe in 1976, Geneva, 1977, Part A (Pre-publication text ECE XXXII/1 Add. 1), Chapter 2, page 62 gives a cumulative debtor balance of US $ 32-35 billion and quotes an estimate of US $ 38 billion. According to a Chase Manhattan Bank estimate the deficit in Spring 1977 must have been US $ 45.8 billion. Cf. New York Herald Tribune, 5th March, 1977.

30. Askanas, Askanas, and Levcik, *loc. cit.*

31. ECE, Economic Survey 1975, *loc. cit.*, pages 84 and seq.; ECE, Economic Survey 1976, loc. cit., page 61.

East Europe with large consignments of goods or complete plants, payment for which would be made only several years later in the form of supplies of goods preferably produced in plants installed with the help of these Western supplies to East Europe. The best-known transaction of this kind in the Federal Republic of Germany was the deal with the Soviet Union to exchange pipe for natural gas, but many other examples could be cited from basic and manufacturing industries.

However, *credit financing* was a component part of long-term compensation deals and only differs from normal loans in the special agreements concerning repayments. From about 1965, *industrial co-operation* as a new form of East-West economic relations was a qualitative step forward compared with straightforward trading. In its strict sense the term covers long-term co-operation between firms in the East and West in production, research and development, and marketing. [32] The role of the Western partner is usually to supply the plant, capital goods, and technological know-how, while joint production facilities are located in the East European country, using mainly indigenous manpower. Payment for the Western contribution is made in the form of goods supplied out of joint production to the firm concerned.

In industrial co-operation, the Western partner is far more concerned than in the case of straight-forward trade supplies, that the production facilities he has installed in the East European country should be put to *as productive a use as possible*, because his chances of making a profit from the co-operative deal depend on the quality of joint production. For the East European side, this private enterprise motivation in the West guarantees more efficient economic application of modern technology than could be achieved through its own research and development or by state imports of Western capital goods. In addition, this formula is a sound economic proposition for the Eastern side, because it generally implies that the financing of the preparatory work is settled in the West and because the problem of marketing the goods there is shouldered by the Western partner.

In the early seventies, industrial co-operation was expected to supply considerable momentum for the expansion of East-West economic relations, with hopes in some of the smaller East European countries running particularly high. Co-operation deals between Western firms and Hungary, Romania, and Poland increased in volume relatively quickly between 1971 and 1973. A major reason for the Western firms involved was to expand capacity in this boom period with the help of East European labour. The recession that followed brought this new form of East-West relations largely to a standstill and, compared with total trade between East and West, the share of industrial co-operation, at under 5 per cent, was never very significant.

---

32. For details see: Peter Knirsch: Vom Ost-West-Handel zur Wirtschaftskooperation? (From East-West Trade to Economic Co-operation?); in: Europa-Archiv, 28th year, Bonn 1973, No. 2, pages 61-69. ECE, Analytical report on industrial co-operation between ECE countries, Geneva 1973 (E/ECE/844/Rev. 1). F. Levick and Jan Stankovsky: Industrielle Kooperation zwischen Ost und West (Industrial Co-operation between East and West), Vienna and New York, 1977 (Studien über Wirtschafts- und Systemvergleiche, Vol. 8).

This overall quantitative judgement, however, does not do justice to the new phenomenon. At the moment, some 17 per cent of Western machinery deliveries are accounted for by co-operation deals and apart from that the efficiency of technology transfer and the indirect effects of co-operation, particularly in improving the pattern of East European exports, are certainly greater than in the case of ordinary trading. [33]

Up to now, co-operation deals in the form of *Western shareholding* in joint ventures in East Europe have always been on a very small scale. The few cases in Romania and Hungary are exceptions and at most are interesting as symptomatic of the changing ideological thinking in those countries. At the moment, there are no signs that this form of co-operation can attain any great significance in East-West economic relations.

The role of institutional factors

Institutional factors have always had a strong influence on the development of East-West economic relations, and even without any special attention being drawn to them they have cropped up time and again in our historical review. In general, it may be said that, with the passage of time, the significance of institutional regulations with a *restrictive* effect on East-West economic relations has diminished, facilitating the development of those relations. The originally very extensive *embargo lists* banning the export of strategic goods to East Europe were already being cut down in the fifties, the West European industrialized nations outpacing the USA in this process. [34] The *quantitative quotas* originally imposed on imports from East Europe had fallen during the sixties in most Western countries to a small number of imported products—the " hard core "—and at present the large majority of East European imports are liberalized. The bilateral *clearing agreements* that used to apply between West and East have been replaced by settlements in convertible currency, with bilateral trade agreements now only to a limited extent providing a relatively loose framework for reciprocal trading. The initial restrictions on granting credit to communist countries were largely lifted during the sixties. The offering of *most favoured nation* treatment to the CMEA countries was a slower process. When Poland, Hungary, and Romania joined the GATT, and Romania the IMF, in the early seventies, further institutional obstacles were overcome. There remain the trade restrictions stemming from West European integration in the EEC, particularly on agricultural imports from East Europe.

Thus, overall, the quantitative restrictions still applying in the West relate to relatively few goods imported from East Europe, though they are

---

33. ECE, Economic Survey 1975, *loc. cit.*, page 81; ECE, Economic Survey 1976, *loc. cit.* page 65.
34. See Bonnie M. Pounds and Mona F. Levine: Legislative, Institutional, and Negotiating Aspects of United States-East European Trade and Economic Relations; in: Joint Economic Committee, Congress of the United States (Ed.): Reorientation and Commercial Relations of the Economies of Eastern Europe. Washington, D.C., 1974, pp. 531-555. Thomas A. Wolf: New Elements in U.S.-East Trade Policy, Vienna, 1974 (Forschungsberichte 1974).

important from the trade policy viewpoint, and some East European countries are still not given most favoured nation treatment in customs tariffs. By comparison with the original institutional restrictions, the increasing liberalization of East-West trade is unmistakeable, and such restrictions as do exist would appear amenable to negotiation. For the EEC countries, after the transfer of sovereignty in trade matters to the Community institutions in 1975, one outstanding problem is the recognition of the EEC by the East European countries and the subsequent elevation of the CMEA to the status of negotiating partner. [35]

This, very briefly, is how the institutional aspects of East-West trade are portrayed in both Western and Eastern literature. Possibly because of the particular field in which I work, this way of looking at things, limited to events in the West, does not seem to me to give the whole picture. Personally, I would attribute at least equal responsibility, as regards the development of East-West economic relations, to the *institutional regulations in East Europe*. Institutional restrictions due to the planned economy systems in East Europe, however, take a different form. Because of the state monopoly in foreign trade and general currency control in these countries, all foreign trade transactions have to be authorized by the state and the effect on imports is the same as that of an all-embracing quota system. In principle, the foreign trade agencies in state trading countries are wholly responsible for deciding the detailed pattern and range of authorized foreign trade business. With the systems prevailing in these countries, there is certainly no easy way of eliminating these institutional limitations on the Eastern side, but an effort could be made to smooth out some of the bureaucratic difficulties involved in this foreign trade system. This would seem possible to the extent that the controls on foreign trade relations required by the system could be exercised in other forms. If the appropriate changes were made, trade with the West could be not only expanded but also organised far more favourably as regards costs. In the sixties, when economic reforms were introduced, projects along these lines were discussed in East Europe and some attempts made to introduce them. In a number of CMEA countries, e.g. Poland, Hungary, Romania, and Bulgaria, several industrial enterprises of importance in terms of foreign trade were granted independent foreign trading rights which reduced the work that has to be done by the foreign trade agencies. Though not in a position to go into details, I would say that there is a significant potential for increasing the efficiency of East-West economic relations along these lines that has not yet been exploited.

Current trends of developments in East-West economic relations

We pointed out earlier how, during the first half of the seventies, East-West economic relations developed very rapidly on the basis of Western credit.

---

35. In spite of its importance for East-West economic relations, the complex of relations between the EEC and the COMECON cannot be discussed here. Cf. Charles Ransom: The European Community and Eastern Europe. London, 1973. Ieuan G. John (Ed.): EEC Policy towards Eastern Europe, Westmead, 1975.

For a study of long-term developments and possible new trends, however, it would seem necessary to take into account certain *changes which have occurred during the last few years*. Whereas trade in both directions between East Europe and the West continued to increase very rapidly in 1974, at a rate of over 40 per cent, the pattern began to change in 1975 with Western exports still increasing very steeply (30 per cent) but imports from East Europe growing at a rate of only 6 per cent. For 1976, figures are available only for the first nine months. They show a considerable slow-down (to 7 per cent) in the growth of Western exports, whereas growth in imports from East Europe speeded up to about 16 per cent. [36]

Various reasons can be advanced for these latest developments. The sudden drop in *Western imports* from East Europe in 1975 was primarily due to the world-wide *economic recession*, which meant a severe contraction of the markets for East European exports. In 1976 the East European countries were clearly successful, by means of special export drives, in increasing their sales considerably to the Western industrial countries in spite of the still relatively unfavourable economic situation in the West. These effects on East-West economic relations of the short-term economic situation in the West are not in fact of a lasting nature, but they may have a long-term influence on East European attitudes toward economic relations with the West. Like inflation and currency crises in the West, cyclical fluctuations are major factors of uncertainty for the Eastern planned economies. We have shown how central economic planning basically took a very reticent stand with regard to external economic relations because of their incompatibility with the planning system. It could well happen that, given greater economic interpenetration with the West, planning problems could become so great that autarkistic attitudes might reassert themselves.

The other feature of 1976 was the considerably slower growth in *East European imports* from the West. Admittedly, East-West trade has always been characterized by relatively large short-term fluctuations, and incomplete figures for one year should not be interpreted straightaway as evidence of a change in trend. Even so, there seems to be some indication of efforts to prevent the indebtedness to the West, that has grown so swiftly in recent years, from growing at the same rate, or even to reduce it. The East's export efforts and successes in 1976 to which we have referred fit this same picture, with Eastern products obviously also capable of improving sales potential on world market on the basis of earlier imports of capital goods from the West. In any case, the trend towards a greater balance in the patterns of East-West export and import trade is gaining ground. This process has been made easier, at least for the Soviet Union, by the improvement in the terms of trade in relation to the West in recent years, which has led to some easing of the foreign currency situation. The possibility that the East may now be less willing to be indebted to the West will, in any case, need to be taken into account when we consider future prospects for the development of East-West economic relations.

---

36. ECE, Economic Survey, 1976, *loc. cit.*, page 58.

EAST-WEST ECONOMIC RELATIONS
DEPENDENCE OR INTERDEPENDENCE?

The relative importance of East-West economic relations for the two sides

East-West economic relations are of quite *different relative importance* for the Western industrial countries and for the East European countries. For the West, economic exchanges with the East, in spite of their rapid expansion in recent years, are still of hardly more than marginal significance. For the OECD countries, the proportion of their total foreign trade done with the East is on average about 3.5 per cent. For the EEC countries, the proportion of total trade done with the CMEA area is at present 5 per cent. For the Federal Republic of Germany, the proportion is above average—about 6 per cent. The United States, only 1 per cent of whose total foreign trade is with the CMEA countries, is far below the average, while on the other hand Austria has a much above average share, 15 per cent of its total foreign trade being with the Eastern countries. These figures for shares apply roughly to the years 1973-1975. The picture does not change very much if we take a closer look at figures for individual countries, or their relatively short period fluctuations, or if we consider the various foreign trade ratios in relation to gross national products. The overall result remains the same, namely that economic relations with Eastern Europe are of relatively small importance to the overall economic picture. In the case of the Federal Republic of Germany, with an economic involvement with the East which is above the Western average, total trade with the European socialist countries, that is to say including Yugoslavia, amounted to about 2.4 per cent of GNP (out of a total foreign trade turnover of 38.9 per cent), the share of exports to these countries in GNP terms amounting to 1.5 per cent. Another calculation (not entirely convincing) suggests that out of a total of 4.6 million jobs in the Federal Republic of Germany which depend on exports, about 320 000 result from economic relations with the CMEA countries. [37]

Taken all in all, the total economic significance of economic relations with Eastern Europe is certainly quite small for the developed Western industrial countries. Nevertheless, if we take the above-mentioned figure for the employment effect seriously, at least as an indication of the order of magnitude, then these relations are not insignificant for some Western countries. This impression is reinforced if we consider the significance for *certain branches of industry* for which exports to the East are above average. Taking the Federal Republic of Germany once more as an example, for the iron and steel industry exports to the East account for 8.4 per cent of total sales and 24.7 per cent of sales abroad, while the corresponding figures for machinery are 5.9 and 13.5 per cent—quite high figures. [38] It can be said, therefore, that for some branches of industry exports to Eastern Europe are significantly more important

---

37. RGW-Länder vermindern Handelsbilanzungleichgewich (CMEA countries reduce trade balance deficits), Deutsches Institut für Wirtschaftsforschung (DIW), Wochenbericht, Berlin (West) 1977, No. 12, page 105.
38. Ibid.

than for the Western economies as a whole, and the overall economic effect of trade with the East, in conjunction with certain cyclical situations, is more significant for economic policy in some circumstances than the global figures might at first sight lead one to expect.

On the other hand, there is no doubt that trade with the West is of considerably greater significance for the CMEA countries. This is true above all for the share in total foreign trade, which for all CMEA countries together was 30 per cent in 1975. Taking individual country figures for the share of Western trade in total foreign trade turnover, Poland with 41.3 per cent, Romania with 36.7 per cent, and the Soviet Union with 31.3 per cent are at the top of the table, while Bulgaria with 17 per cent is at the bottom. [39] Because of the imbalances in foreign trade referred to above, the significance of imports from the West is still greater. For Poland in 1975 they accounted for 49.3 per cent of total imports, for Romania 41 per cent, and for the Soviet Union 36.4 per cent, while even for Bulgaria they amounted to 23.6 per cent of total imports. As we have already explained, foreign trade as a percentage of GNP is relatively low in the East European countries, which diminishes the overall economic significance of these relatively high shares of trade with the West. It is of course not easy to compare the gross national products of the CMEA countries with corresponding Western figures or with total foreign trade figures. But the following rough picture can be said to apply: for the Soviet Union, which because of its large total potential has the greatest share in East-West trade (in 1975 its turnover with Western industrial countries was 41.9 per cent of the total CMEA turnover with these countries), foreign trade is of only relatively small overall economic significance. For 1973 the ratio of total foreign trade turnover to GNP was estimated at 8.4 per cent. Within this, the share of trade with the industrial West was 2.2 per cent of GNP, and of imports from the West about 1.2 per cent of GNP. The foreign trade involvement of all the other CMEA countries is considerably higher, and the importance of trade with the West correspondingly greater. The share of imports from the West in GNP terms in 1973 for the smaller CMEA countries was of the order of magnitude of 3 to 6 per cent of GNP. [40] However questionable these figures may be, they do indicate clearly that the significance of economic relations with the West is quite considerable for all CMEA countries in terms of the quantitative share in foreign trade, while in terms of the share of imports from the West in GNP, it is at least not insignificant for the smaller CMEA countries. And in any case this quantitative significance is considerably greater than for the Western trading partners.

For the East European countries much more than for their Western trading partners, it is safe to assume that this quantitative importance is consid-

---

39. SEV Secretariat: Statističeskij ežegodnik stran-členov SEV 1976, Moscow 1976, page 341 and authors calculations.

40. On the basis of estimated foreign trade ratios of CMEA countries, Askanas, Askanas, Levcik op. cit. Table 1, and western export shares for 1973 according to the SEV Secretariat: Statističeskij ežegodnik stran-členov SEV 1974, Moscow 1975, pp. 331 and 333, imports from the West were 3.2 per cent of GNP for Bulgaria, 5.1 per cent for Hungary, 5.8 per cent for the GDR, 4.6 per cent for Poland, 4.2 per cent for Romania ,and 3.8 per cent for Czechoslovakia.

erably enhanced by *qualitative considerations*. Over 80 per cent of imports from the West consist of industrial finished products, which it can generally be assumed help to fill important gaps in supplies in Eastern Europe. In particular, under the heading " machinery and vehicles, " which accounts for about 40 per cent of imports, it can be assumed that the products in question are of great importance for the building up of industry in East Europe, but cannot in the foreseeable future be produced in the socialist countries themselves in sufficient quantities, and above all not to the same technical level and corresponding quality. The importance of imports from the West, moreover, is also greater than the quantitative ratios would suggest, since by means of them the centrally planned economic systems of Eastern Europe can overcome part of their built-in rigidity and become more elastic and flexible. This is also true, indeed perhaps particularly true, for the Soviet Union, with its relatively small quantitative dependence on foreign trade. The Soviet purchases of grain in the West over the last ten to fifteen years provide the best example of this.

The question of independence or interdependence

The difference in the importance of East-West economic relations for the two sides could easily lead one to conclude that the East has become *economically dependent on the West*. The political consequences of such a view could be quite far-reaching on both sides. Politicians in the West might come to the conclusion that these economic relations could be used to reinforce political demands on communist countries. Policy makers in the East, fearful that such dependence might be misused, could try to bring about a drastic limitation of these economic relations between the two systems.

I believe that in this " either-or " form, the question is not being properly put. We must remember that between the developed Western industrial countries and the socialist countries of Eastern Europe there are profound ideological and political differences, which cannot be reconciled in the foreseeable future and which contribute, with other things, to a state of affairs in which all relations between the systems, including economic relations, are subject to constant careful supervision by both sides. But besides these elements of division and " demarcation " which subsist in spite of all policies for détente, there are also—and we should never forget this—important *elements tending to unite the East and the West*. The common cultural and historical roots, and the civilizing influences common to both systems imparted by conditions in the age of industrialization, constitute a broader common basis than we are often inclined to think when we are under the influence of political conflicts. In addition, there is *a political pragmatism* which makes the avoidance of open or exaggerated conflicts, i.e. " coexistence, " almost axiomatic for both sides in the interest of their own survival.

In these circumstances, East-West economic relations form a very concrete part of the links between the two systems. As I see it, the political and ideological differences prevent the development of onesided situations of dependence with serious political implications, but they equally prevent the emergence of situations of excessively intensive interdependency. The political distance between the systems sets the limits for any exaggerated growing together of the two economic blocs. In other words, it might be said that in the East as in the West the economic relations between the two systems can at present be regarded as useful, and that each side would regard any disturbance of those relations as harmful for its own rising living standards and would in its own interest try to prevent it wherever practicable. On this basis, *interdependence* of the economies in the East and in the West exists, and this interdependence has certainly grown greater in the last ten years. This interdependence is, however, limited by the primacy accorded to political differences. It is possible that the interdependence which has emerged could, in concrete situations, lead to limited political concessions by one or the other side in the interests of preserving East-West relations. The political and ideological differences are, however, at least for the present still too great for either of the two sides to feel obliged to make any essential policy changes in the interest of economic relations.

Under these conditions, the political significance of the *asymmetrical nature of East-West economic relations* described above is not particularly great. It could give the West the comforting conviction that there can be no question of any serious economic dependence of the West on the East resulting from the vigorous growth of economic relations with Eastern Europe. From the global economic point of view, the shares of this trade are still much too small. There also seems to be no justification for the fear that, through the one-sided pattern of imports from Eastern Europe in regard to particular forms of energy or raw materials, any dependence on these supplies might have developed. In the Federal Republic of Germany, for example, Soviet deliveries of natural gas amount to about 9 per cent of total imports of natural gas. On the other hand, the economic policies of some Western countries, considering the counter-cyclical stabilizing effects which exports to Eastern Europe have and their significance for some branches of industry or some big firms, are certainly favourable to maintaining economic relations or developing them further. But there is nothing that " compels " them to do so.

For the Eastern European countries, imports from the West are of greater immediate importance, if we consider the economic policy efforts to bring about an acceleration of economic growth as a decisive motive for importing modern Western techniques. Naturally this means that the East has a positive interest in maintaining economic relations with the West, and this interest may be more concrete and stronger than in the West. [41] But this does not mean that there is any dependence which can be decisive for the character of the policies. Rather, it must be expected that the policies of communist countries also include a readiness to make sacrifices if they regard these as necessary for the achievement of political aims. In this connection, the economic potential already achieved and the industrial stage of development of the Eastern European countries are of relevance. Unlike the developing countries, such as for example the People's Republic of China, they can afford to make such sacrifices if necessary.

---

41. Snell, *op. cit.*, pages 682-724.

This argument of limited dependence may disappoint some observers. It dampens excessive hopes for a policy of détente or of readiness to co-operate based on economic considerations, but it also dampens naïve hopes for the achievement of political aims by means of economic pressures. It seems to me, however, that for East-West economic relations this argument is not only realistic but also necessary. Such a view of present realities makes it possible for both sides to continue developing these relationships without political complications and without illusions.

One-sided or mutual advantage in East-West economic relations

Closely related to the question of dependence is the much-discussed question of whether East-West economic relations do not confer benefits on only one side and, in view of the basic ideological and political differences, whether they do not contribute to weaken one's own position. As far as I can see, this argument is only to be found in the West, where it is indeed the most important argument against the further development of East-West relations. More recently it is being used first and foremost to oppose promotion measures by governments and the extensive granting of credits. [42]

At first sight, economists find this argument difficult to accept. Economic transactions between West and East are on the Western side generally undertaken by private enterprises, and on the Eastern side by State agencies for foreign trade. The resulting contracts are made according to conditions prevailing in the Western world market. Neither party is compelled to enter into these contracts. Assuming rational behaviour by the parties concerned, such contracts can only be concluded if both sides regard the transaction as advantageous. Of course the criteria for reaching this decision can be different, or can depend on special factors. For the Western partner the expected profit is the major factor for this decision and his individual profit, possibly reinforced by induced employment and income effects, contributes to increasing the prosperity of the economy. Insofar as there is government intervention through subsidies, particularly in the form of lower interest rates for the financing of these transactions, these costs to the economy as a whole must be subtracted from the increased profits accruing to the private sector. It seems highly unlikely that the net balance of transactions with the East —which cannot of course be calculated statistically—has so far been negative in any of the Western industrial countries. From the global economic point of view, trade with the East has so far certainly resulted in an increase in the prosperity of the Western economies.

I assume that thus far the proponents of this argument can hardly but agree. Their point is simply that the increase in prosperity which the East gets from these transactions is greater than that in the West. That argument can, in my opinion, be neither proved nor disproved. In its favour it can be said that the East, in trading with the West, receives goods which it would

---

42. E.g. Ulrich Wagner: Der Western finanziert seine Bedroher. (The West is financing its enemies), in Frankfurter Allgemeine Zeitung, Frankfurt am Main, 5th February, 1977, page 13.

either not be able to produce at all or only at high cost, which means that for the East the goods have a very high (or even infinitely high) value. It is also true that, as a result, economic development in Eastern Europe proceeds faster—we have already mentioned growth problems as the reason for the East European readiness to expand trade with the West. It is also true that the East can use this easing of its development problems, which is of course greatly increased when financed through loans, to divert additional resources to armaments, which are in the last analysis directed against the West, or to a better supply of consumer goods for the political satisfaction of its population. But with all this, it should not be forgotten that the East does not receive the Western goods for nothing. To the extent that it pays for the deliveries directly, it must forego corresponding goods for domestic use. In view of the weak position of all East European countries on the world market, they cannot pay much attention to whether these products are easy to forego at home, and the prices which they can obtain on the world market will often be unfavourable. What in the West appears to be dumping is often only a desperate attempt to sell something in order to earn foreign currency. Even Soviet oil and natural gas have had to be sold in the West at below the world price. [43] On the other hand, there is much evidence to support the assumption that the State trading countries pay relatively high prices for their imports from the West. The Western supplier must include in his price the special costs of business with the East, including ultimately the costs caused by the Eastern foreign trade bureaucracy, and also the special political risk attached to this kind of business. In addition, the still to some extent unsatisfactory marketing knowledge of the Eastern foreign trade partners, and also possibly their lack of business interest or skill in negotiation, also tend to put up the price they have to pay. Western wariness of competition also means that the East can by no means always obtain the most modern technology from the West. The financing of loans does not fundamentally alter these basic factors, since the Eastern side must ultimately pay for the cost of credit either directly or through the final price. All in all, for political, structural, and system-related reasons, the terms of trade for East European State trading countries in trade with the West are probably less favourable than under " normal " world market conditions, and any one-sided advantage seems, to say the least, very questionable.

The one-sided advantage argument is, however, also put forward in the West in quite a different sense. According to this, closer economic relations should be used by the West to bring about a change in the basic features of society and ultimately the system as a whole in Eastern Europe. Some advocates of this thesis of " change through rapprochement, " which incidentally is not limited to economic relations, argue either that more intensive relations can have the immediate effect of bringing about a change in the system, or alternatively that an economic strengthening of the East should be

---

43. In 1976 the delivery price of Soviet oil was about 8 per cent, and that of natural gas about 20 per cent, below the average import prices of these products in the Federal Republic of Germany. DIW-Wochenbericht 1977/12, *op. cit.*, page 102.

deliberately promoted in the hope that in this way the advancing industrialization process will bring about corresponding changes in the system.

A more detailed examination of this thesis, which found support among advocates of détente policies some years ago, is unfortunately not possible here. For anyone who has spent a long time studying the economic and social problems of Eastern Europe, it seems, to say the least, extremely speculative. Admittedly, increasing contacts with the West—and of course economic relations play a large part in these—have an important influence on social and political development in the East. I would regard this influence as so important as to justify the demand that the West should do everything possible not to reduce and certainly not to break off these relations. However, in view of the political power structures in Eastern Europe, it seems to me unrealistic to expect such far-reaching changes to result from the naturally very limited stimuli which could arise from economic relations with the West.

FUTURE PROSPECTS FOR EAST-WEST ECONOMIC RELATIONS

On the basis of the foregoing historical and problem-oriented considerations, we shall now try to conclude by formulating a set of propositions concerning currently recognizable possibilities for the development of East-West economic relations. In the context of this study, it is naturally not possible to work out a reasoned prognosis; all we can do is to indicate probable tendencies.

1. East-West economic relations will continue in the future to be very strongly influenced in their possibilities by the development of political relations between East and West. What follows is based on the assumption that significant political antagonisms between the East and the West will continue to exist in the future because of differences in ideology and in the social and economic systems. These antagonisms will mean that both sides will proceed cautiously in their relations with each other, but we assume nevertheless that this will only lead to fluctuations in intensity, not to any breaking off of relations and certainly not to open conflict.

2. The main factor in the development of East-West economic relationships in recent years has been the decision of the East European political leaders *considerably to intensify those relationships* and in so doing to incur a *high degree of indebtedness.* The main motive for this decision is to be found in the efforts to bring about by this means transfers of advanced Western technology and in so doing to step up their own technical development, thus overcoming the built-in restraints of their own systems with their unfavourable effects on growth. This motive appears to be very strong, and the corresponding reorientation in attitudes to Western trade has been going on now for the last seven to ten years. The desired economic results have so far been only very partially achieved, but the determination to achieve those results remains unchanged. Since there seems to be no alternative goal to put in place of this *transfer of technology from the West,* I would expect that this positive basic attitude toward trade with the West will be maintained for a long time to come, that is to say at least another few years.

165

3. Since the growth problems in the CMEA countries can hardly be overcome in the current five-year plan period 1976 to 1980, to judge by the way the plans themselves are drawn up, there seems likely to be a tendency toward continuation of the rapid expansion in economic relations with the West. Because of the difficulties which have emerged in those relations I would, moreover, assume that in the coming years trade with the West *will not grow more than proportionally*, but at a rate of the same order as the expansion in total foreign trade, or even perhaps more slowly than intra-CMEA trade itself. Differences among the individual CMEA countries in this respect seem likely.

4. The main obstacle to the further development of East-West economic relations is the *unfavourable balance-of-payments position* of the CMEA countries with the West. *Western credits* have in recent years made up this deficit and have been decisive in making possible the rapid increase in trade. At present, no final limit for Western readiness to grant credit is in sight. It does look, however, as if the Eastern European countries, in the light of the foreseeable future burden on their balances of payments, are no longer as willing as they have been in recent years to accept Western credits. I assume that the East European *indebtedness* in coming years *will grow at a slower* rate, and that the further development of East-West economic relations will depend on other factors.

5. Of these, the *success of the East European exports* will be of decisive importance. Quite apart from the question of whether indebtedness to the West does in fact slow down, as I have supposed, in the long term the only thing that can improve the balance-of-payments positions of the CMEA countries in regard to the West is an improvement in the pattern of exports, with a higher proportion of industrial finished products, and greatly increased efforts to find markets in the West. If these efforts do not succeed, then it can be expected that at some time or other a shrinking process will set in in East-West economic relations.

6. All in all, the possibilities of an increase in East European exports to the West appear to be *more favourable* at present than in the past. Industrial reconstruction with the help of Western technology, and greater familiarity with the conditions of the world market improve the chances of this happening. Also, the direct tying of future exports to Western deliveries, as provided under the long-term arrangements for compensation and industrial co-operation, must also have certain positive effects in this direction. At the same time, however, there are *negative factors* which must not be overlooked. In the past, the greatest obstacles to successful foreign trading activities by State trading countries arose from the economic systems operated in those countries. It is hard to see how any substantial change in this respect could come about without more fundamental economic reforms. At present, there are no apparent signs of political readiness to introduce reforms to facilitate foreign trade in the next few years.

7. If the last mentioned limitation is realistic, it would mean that *in the long run* one must make a *pessimistic estimate* of the future development of East-West economic relations. The possibilities for increasing indebtedness

must at some time or other come up against a ceiling, and the expansion and structural improvement in European exports are unlikely to occur under the existing conditions of the system. If on the other hand, it is assumed that in Eastern Europe in coming years far-reaching changes are going to be made in the planning system, it would be possible to make a much more positive forecast for the future of East-West economic relations, and beyond that for the integration of Eastern Europe into the world economy.

8. There are only limited possibilities for the West to contribute to the future expansion of East-West economic relations by *facilitating East European exports*. Abolition of the final vestiges of quotas and granting most favoured nation treatment would seem to be possible measures at the present time. Progress in this direction may be possible in the next few years, but its significance for the further development of East-West economic relations should not be overestimated.

9. Of great importance for the future development of East-West economic relations is *future economic development in the West* and the *general condition of the world economy*. Greater stability in the world economy will, in the long run, have a favourable effect on East-West economic relations. It would seem possible that the socialist countries will in future play a more active role in the management of world economic problems, since their increased involvement in world trade means that they are directly affected by those problems. Institutions such as the GATT or the International Monetary Fund may therefore gain in importance for East-West economic relations.

10. It is difficult at present to see how the *North-South conflict* will influence East-West economic relations. There is, on the one hand, a danger that it could lead to greater political tensions between East and West. On the other hand, the overcoming of underdevelopment could provide strong motives for increased economic co-operation between East and West in trilateral projects, and stimulate East-West economic relations in completely new ways.

It can be seen that the future development of East-West economic relations cannot be predicted in more than very vague outlines. Judging by the history of those relations over the last thirty years, we can see that, besides the developments which to-day seem probable, the possibility of completely surprising, unpredictable turns of events cannot be excluded. Cautious though we should be, it cannot be denied that the involvement of the East European countries in the world economy to-day is very much greater than at any time since the Second World War. I have tried to indicate the political limits of the interdependence which has emerged in consequence. If through the efforts of both sides it proves possible to keep the political East-West relationship within reasonable bounds, the limits to economic interdependence can be drawn very broadly and provide additional opportunities for improving the prosperity of both East and West.

2

COMMENT

by Mr. Peter C. Dobell (Canada)

Dr. Knirsch has dealt fully with the history of East-West economic relations. I know that the other two commentators will elaborate on his analysis more expertly than I could. I propose instead to comment on the non-economic elements of those relations which represent at this stage the more dynamic sector in East-West relations.

The major event of this decade in the field of East-West political relations has been the negotiation and signature of the final act of the Conference on Security and Cooperation in Europe (CSCE). To the Soviet Government in 1975, this act appeared as the successful conclusion of two decades of effort to secure international acceptance of the division of Germany and confirmation of the division of Europe. Since the establishment of communist regimes in all the countries of Eastern Europe, the Soviet hold on the region has been disturbed by popular uprisings, beginning with the one in East Berlin in 1953. Although these disturbances derived mainly from indigenous unrest, in the early years the Dulles doctrine of liberation undoubtedly added to the combustible situation. The Hungarian uprising of 1956 demonstrated on the one hand the limits to which the Russians could be challenged while on the other hand it showed that Western support would be restricted to exhortation.

In spite of these two reinforcing lessons, Czechoslovakia suffered invasion in 1968, and with that event the Soviet desire for international endorsement of the *status quo* was given new urgency. The prior condition to the holding of the CSCE was the election of a social democratic government in the Federal German Republic, ready to negotiate a *modus vivendi* with the GDR. The two essential elements were a four-power agreement on Berlin and the basic treaty between the two Germanies which was ratified in May, 1973. These opened the way for a serious negotiation in the CSCE.

The Final Act was a much broader document than the USSR had sought. The Russians did achieve what they wanted: an elaboration of the principles of *détente*, such as non-interference in the internal affairs of other states, codification of ground rules on economic cooperation, and endorsement of the physical *status quo*. But negotiation by consensus was probably to their disadvantage and they had to pay a considerable price for agreement, such as accepting the elaboration of a number of principles of conduct in the Final Act including respect for human rights and self-determination. They had, moreover, to agree to cooperate in the resolution of humanitarian problems and to accept that frontiers might be modified by agreement. Most importantly, by signing the Final Act they created an international platform for the advocacy of human rights and they acknowledged that Soviet conduct became the business of the other signatories.

Apart from their own aspirations, the USSR was urged on by some of its Eastern European allies, who believed that the Final Act could bring them a measure of protection against Soviet interference in their affairs. Such was the satisfaction of all the members of the Soviet bloc at the successful conclusion of the negotiations that they proceeded to publicize widely within their own countries the full text of the Final Act, much more widely in fact than it was publicized in Western countries. The Soviet and Eastern European leaders are now paying for their enthusiams, because the standards of the Final Act are being used by their own people to judge the conduct of their governments.

The most comprehensive response has been the formulation within Czechoslovakia of a document known as Charter 77. Comparable if less formal action has been taken, often by disaffected Marxists, in other Eastern European countries. Poland and Hungary have had their share of agitation. Even in the USSR, an informal group is monitoring Soviet performance under the criteria endorsed in Helsinki, and critics led by Andrei Sakharov have been speaking out on the question of human rights.

These internal responses have been matched and aggravated by external developments. President Carter's encouragement to those fighting for human rights in the Soviet Union has attracted most publicity, but there has been public pressure in all Western countries for Soviet bloc countries to extend human rights. Bukovsky and Solzhenitsyn and other Russians in exile have also been speaking out strongly.

The prominent Western European Communist parties, especially those in Italy and Spain, have become a very interesting source of criticism of conditions in Eastern Europe. Their response has been particularly troubling to the Russians. For example, an Italian communist publisher brought out Zdenek Mlynar's *Prague—Open Question*, and a member of the central committee of the Italian Communist Party wrote a foreword to that book. Eastern European dissidents have turned to the Euro-Communists for support and they have not been denied. Indeed, their fates are to some extent linked, since what happens in Eastern Europe has some effect on the image of the Euro-Communists. At the same time, the Italian and Spanish Communist parties in particular are resisting the formulation of Soviet-dictated communiqués at international meetings of Communist parties and declining to sign them.

These developments have in turn begun seriously to affect the politics of some nations in Western Europe. They have helped the Communist parties of France and Italy to increase their popular support. This trend could have very broad and uncertain implications for the future. If Communist parties in Western Europe should come to power through the ballot box, how will they exercise it? Will they ever voluntarily relinquish the levers of power if a subsequent election goes against them?

Lest it be felt that this is the main effect of the Final Act in the West, it should be noted that the Soviet Union and its allies have let it be known that they are ready to respond to charges on human rights questions by counterattacking—challenging the United States and Canada, for example, over the treatment of their native peoples or charging Britain for actions against those detained in Northern Ireland. The main problem for the West is how to handle the situation produced by the CSCE. The first test arises in June in Belgrade. How hard should the West push the USSR? Bukovsky has been advocating reversion to a policy of virtual political isolation of the USSR. But what would that achieve? It seems more prudent to make clear to the Russians that their treatment of peoples in terms of human rights is deficient, while not losing sight of the limits of Western influence. It is particularly important to avoid linking separate policy issues. The Jackson-Vanik Amendment provoked the Russians into denouncing a trade agreement with the United States and the number of Jews subsequently permitted to emigrate from the USSR has also drapped.

Human rights can best be pursued as part of a policy of " peaceful engagement, " to use the phrase which Brzezinski coined for President Johnson. It seems wise that an American emphasis on the observance of human rights in Eastern Europe and in the Soviet Union should be linked with a forthcoming U.S. approach in several fields: in the SALT negotiations; in efforts to resolve tensions in parts of the world particularly dependent on the Soviet Union, notably Cuba; and in the whole area of economic relations. These are issues to be faced very soon. A more significant test will come when and if a Communist Party is legally elected to office in Western Europe. It is difficult to anticipate the full implications of such an event, but clearly they would be enormous and incalculable and potentially as disturbing for the USSR as for the countries of the West.

My time has been short and therefore these remarks have been skimpy and superficial. They indicate that in the non-economic sector, East-West interaction has reached a level inconceivable only a few years ago. The prospect is for a situation which will become increasingly dynamic.

3

COMMENT

by Professor Alec Nove (United Kingdom)

In the time available I really will be brief, and begin by expressing pretty wholehearted agreement with the line taken by Professor Knirsch in his excellent paper. Perhaps on the historical side I may be allowed one small disagreement, entirely one of emphasis. It is thirty years, we have been reminded, since the Marshall Plan; it is twenty-five years since Stalin spoke of the existence of two separate world markets. A lot has changed since then. The Russian interpretation of the change lays great stress on the decisive nature of the alteration during this period, not so much of Soviet as of Western attitudes. There is a very interesting book on the subject published in Moscow last year, and although Soviet analyses of the political causes of the cold war are, to put it mildly, slanted and twisted, on the origins of the economic cold war history will be largely on their side. It is we who were in a position to do them damage, and we tried, thereby forcing them into a greater degree of autarky than they themselves possibly wished even under Stalin. The change in recent years, then, has brought East-West trade to more natural levels so to speak. As the Russian book puts it, " the de-politicisation of East-West trade " is largely due to changes on the Western side. I do not think that the Soviets have altered their policy towards *détente* in order to import technology; it is rather that Western changes in attitudes, including the recognition of the GDR, recognition of the *status quo* in Europe on the political side, and Western changes in their willingness to grant credits, have provided the Soviet Union and its allies with new opportunities in the economic field, including the import of technology, which they have of course taken. While not for a moment suggesting that Dr. Knirsch didn't mention this, I would perhaps give it more emphasis than he did as a factor. I agree with him entirely that their economic situation, possibly with Poland as an exception, is not sufficiently desperate for us to be able to utilise the economic weapon in a manner which might not be (from our point of view) counterproductive. There, I am very much on his side.

Moving to the present situation, I have circulated a set of tables, which underline a point which in Dr. Knirsch's necessarily brief presentation is perhaps obscured; that is the great differences among the different countries of Eastern Europe in recent years in the degree of their indebtedness, their vulnerability, and indeed in the economic policies pursued. In the case of the Soviet Union, 1974, was a magnificent year for exports to the West, an increase of 66 per cent in one year in value terms due, of course, primarily to a very sharp improvement in terms of trade. Probably the overoptimism to which this gave rise led them to place a large number of orders for capiatl goods in the West. Then recession in the West in 1975, the fall in the gold price, and the poor harvest leading to a sharp increase in grain imports, put the Soviets heavily in deficit, but this was not due to any particularly unsound internal policies.

It is otherwise in the case of Poland. The crisis in Poland was largely due to an internal policy of an extremely adventurous kind, which the Polish authorities deliberately sustained by incurring relatively the biggest debts to the West. The policy included an increase in investments by 125 per cent in five years, and an increase in money wages of 60 per cent in the same period. This very inflationary policy was likely to lead, and has in fact led, Poland to a situation which makes them very vulnerable, not only because of the level of their foreign indebtedness but also politically vulnerable to internal trouble. When we speak of factors making for instability in the West, we sometimes silently assume that the great totalitarian system of the East is inherently stable. It may will be so in Russia, but surely not in Poland.

If we move on to the other countries, one must mention the fact that, whereas Poland did not suffer on balance a worsening in the terms of trade because she is a big exporter of coal, the other countries' troubles were due very largely to adverse terms of trade rather than to any particularly unsound policies which they have been following. Therefore, as I am sure Professor Knirsch would agree, some differentiation is desirable. The vulnerability of these countries varies greatly, and this also affects our judgment of prospects.

Obviously the East's substantial indebtedness and the imbalance of their trade will compel them to moderate imports and press exports, and it is worth studying in some detail what their prospects are for developing exports, at least in the medium term. For the Soviet Union, well over two thirds of her exports are fuel and raw materials; 40 per cent of Soviet exports to the West consist of oil and petroleum products alone. Therefore, such very important matters as a correct estimate of their output and export prospects for oil become decisive in the medium term in judging their likely ability to pay for imports. Another key question is : are they going to be compelled still to import grain? This is a problem in both Russia and Poland; their imports of grain are partly a function of an absurdly low price for meat, which stimulates demand for meat and compels them to try to expand livestock herds. When the Poles tried to correct this ridiculous price—and it is ridiculous—they had riots on their hands, twice, in 1970 and 1976, reminding us of the interconnections between politics and economics.

It is also the case that they have difficulty in designing and marketing products of adequate quality to the West. Both the Soviet Union and especially the more industrialised countries of Eastern Europe must develop exports to the West of manufactures, including machinery and equipment, and they have great difficulty in doing this. Their poor technology, therefore, not only affects their balance of payments by compelling them to import more, but also inhibits what otherwise would be a fairly natural export for countries like East Germany and Czechoslovakia. A Czech once gave me the explanation for poor quality that " it is too easy to sell rubbish to the Soviet Union. " It is worth bearing in mind the effects on all these countries of the ease with which they can fulfill trade targets by exchanging mediocre goods with each other. In the longer run, the Soviet Union has Siberia, the greatest underdeveloped area of the world containing immense riches, very difficult and very expensive to develop quickly. But when we go into the 1980s, though there is a dispute between experts about their prospects for oil, the fact remains that the opportunities are very big.

Finally, before I run out of time, a word on the whole issue of inter-dependence. There are two schools of thought here. One, represented by Bukovsky, Solzhenitsyn, Sakharov, a number of American Senators, and quite a wide range of opinion, considers that interdependence in the sense of expanding our exchanges with them benefits *them* more than us, that therefore " *détente* is a one-way street. " Are we strengthening them by trade? The answer, of course, is yes. They buy that which they consider strengthens them. This is true. An American once said, " since all imports free resources for other purposes, including military purposes all Soviet imports are strategic, except bubble gum. " He was wrong; in *this* sense bubble gum too is a stra-tegic import. Of course, anything they buy is either of direct use for their civilian economy or for their production of weaponry, or it releases resources that might be used for this purpose. Therefore, it follows that we should only sell them what they do not wish to buy. This does not seem to me to make a great deal of sense. I cannot believe that mutually beneficial trade benefits them more than us.

I would like to end with an instance in which their system, which is in many respects irrational, may actually be more rational than ours. We had a butter mountain in Western Europe and we sold part of it to the Soviet Union very cheaply. Plainly they were glad of a bargain. But when *they* try and sell cheap, we regard this as dumping and insist on their selling dear. Perhaps in this respect at least they are not more irrational than we are.

To conclude, I would have thought that interdependence, which would cause loss to both sides in the event of a break, plus more extensive contacts, is probably on balance a more optimistic and even a more realistic policy than the reverse, though I do not for a moment imagine that the evil aspects of the Soviet System will be removed simply because they buy more from us or sell more to us.

4

COMMENT

by Professor Richard Portes (United States)

Professor Knirsch's paper is an excellent historical narrative and analysis of the underlying forces which have operated in East-West economic relations since the war. I have nothing to add to the story up to the turn of the current decade. I shall, however, expand somewhat on events since then, focusing in particular on the East European debt to the West. [1]

First, on the reasons behind the extremely rapid expansion of East-West trade and the East European debt: Eastern Europe's *economic need*, stressed by Professor Knirsch, reflects what I would call a structural hard currency balance-of-trade deficit. What they have come to regard as essential levels of imports from the West cannot be covered because of a shortage of exports which could be sold at acceptable prices. These essential imports have become so large since 1972, not only because of the technology gap, but also as a result of increasing internal demands from consumers, a substantial deterioration of the terms of trade of all countries except the USSR and Poland, and the continuing pressure for rapid growth exerted by the central planners.

It is important, I think, to note that overall the Eastern European deficit has not been an oil deficit; the region as a whole is a net exporter of oil, due of course to the USSR. Rather, this structural deficit is perhaps analogous to the early post-war West European dollar shortage. It is likely, I think, to be much more persistent. When Western economies are growing slowly they are reluctant to take more Eastern European goods, and they invoke anti-dumping provisions when East European exporters cut prices to try to sell their exports in the West. But if Western growth accelerates, the technological gap will widen.

Although I agree with Professor Knirsch that the primary initiative for the recent expansion of East-West trade has come from the East, I would emphasise more than he the active search by Western exporters, private firms, and governments for markets in Eastern Europe, and by Western banks for borrowers to whom they could lend Eurodollar funds. The recession beginning in 1974 gave a strong impetus along both lines. A good Marxist

---

1. For further details, see my paper, " East Europe's Debt to the West, " *Foreign Affairs*, July 1977, pp. 751-782.

(but not an Eastern European) might say that this initiative from Western businessmen came because the mature capitalist economies required a vent for surplus, both financial and real, and East Europe was just as attractive a market as the LDCs. I myself would not wish to conclude that we can simply relax and let " monopoly capitalist imperialism exploit " the socialist countries. I do think there are a few problems.

The most visible problem is the East European hard currency debt, which is just now approaching $ 50 billion gross. Of this, about half is now Euromarket debt. Eastern Europe financed almost 60 per cent of its hard currency deficits over the past three years in the Euromarket. As recently as 1970, it would have taken remarkable foresight to predict that the East would be willing to borrow from the West, and the West to lend to the East, sums of this order of magnitude. Are the last few years exceptional, or will it continue?

The current East European deficit has to be met by some combination of adjustment and finance. I agree with Professor Knirsch that we should not expect any major internal changes in Eastern Europe which might reduce their structural hard currency deficit by increasing their capacity to produce manufactured exports which they could sell easily in the West. There will be no significant market-oriented economic reforms, nor any move towards currency convertibility, no matter how much Western economists may urge them. On the other hand, I do not see, as he does, any significant reluctance in Eastern Europe to incur more hard currency debt. Provided we are willing to continue lending, I think they will continue to borrow. The current Hungarian Five Year Plan, for example, projects substantial hard currency deficits continuing at least until 1980.

I therefore will direct the rest of my comments to Western policy, in particular, to the question whether we are or should be willing to continue to lend on the scale of the past few years. Professor Knirsch says there must be some ceiling to the East European debt, but so far, it would be difficult to identify any constraints on the expansion of Euromarket finance. Yet, without some institutional developments, can we really suppose that further credit will be forthcoming in the amount of, says $ 25 to $ 40 billion up to the end of 1980? Would this be possible without much more substantial direct government involvement in guaranteeing commercial bank loans and official export financing? Would this be prudent without some international co-ordination? But could Western governments or international organisations deal with financing East European deficits in the existing institutional framework? And would any overt policy initiatives harm the confidence of the financial markets? If the problems of financing balance-of-payments deficits do become more severe, we might see a greater role developing for the IMF or for governments or central banks through the European Community, the OECD, or the BIS, but how could this apply to Eastern Europe? East European countries do not belong to these organization; only Romania is even a member of the IMF. And if the debt of an East European country were to become unmanageable, what would be the political implications of debt rescheduling? A " Paris Club " format, with explicit and detailed consideration and surveillance of the debtor's economic policies, would be very difficult for any East European country to accept. Will the East Europeans ask for debt relief if we give it to the LDCs? What leverage would Western creditors have over East European debtors, and what broader problems, both political and economic, would be raised by any attempt to exert such leverage? Can we envisage IMF missions to Warsaw, Budapest, and Sofia, prescibing stabilisation plans? And where would the Euromarket banks be at that point?

The East European debt to the West has created a new dimension of East-West interdependence, and it is not clear how either side will be able to cope with it. If the pressures of meeting debt service obligations do require East European countries to cut back on all but essential Western imports, they will thereby be forced into greater reliance on each other. And this will in particular push the smaller countries into more dependence on the USSR. I believe that centripetal forces in CMEA will in fact be very strong indeed over the next decade, partly just because the debt and debt service will limit hard currency import capacity. East-West trade was promoted in part as a means for breaking up the economic cohesion of Eastern Europe and the USSR, but the resulting accumulation of debt (or alternatively our unwillingness to buy enough of Eastern Europe's exports) has now made this unlikely. Indeed, our lending may have indirectly financed investment by other Eastern European countries in Soviet raw material extraction.

On the Western side, both banks and governments now seriously fear the possibility that East European countries may be unable to meet their debt repayment schedules around the end of this decade. But this simply means that they are likely to make every effort to continue to lend, in order to protect the loans they have previously made. This in turn creates leverage for East European debtors, which is reinforced by the political and economic factors hindering Western co-ordination of policies. The competitive desires for loan markets, capital goods markets, raw materials supplies, and political influence impede common trade or credit policies and even the simple exchange of information.

Almost exactly a year ago, here at OECD, Henry Kissinger warned that Eastern Europe might " play off the industrial democracies against each other. " But we don't need any outside help. France, for example, observing that the U.S. Congress has already restricted Eximbank lending to Eastern Europe, sees a " sour grapes " reaction in any American initiative which might be interpreted as seeking a more restrictive overall Western policy.

In my view, it is quite possible that at least Poland and perhaps other Eastern European countries will have to reschedule their hard currency debts around 1980. If business conditions and import demand do pick up in the West, then Euromarket lending will become much tighter. If not, East European hard currency exports to the West on the scale necessary to keep the debt managable will encounter stiff market resistance, while an enforced drastic cutback of Eastern imports from the West would seriously hurt both sides.

There would seem to me to be two possible policies to meet the problems created by our creditor relationship with Eastern Europe. One would be to accept a fairly rapid growth of the debt and to co-ordinate its financing much more actively. This might be done through international organisations or by the Euromarket banks themselves. Alternatively, the West could try to keep the debt down by operating on trade flows. This would involve reducing trade restrictions, stopping the application of anti-dumping laws, and possibly an agreement by major surplus countries to buy much of the manufactured goods which East Europe has so far been unable to sell to the West.

In any case, a range of choice will arise for the West between its economic relations with Eastern Europe and with the LDCs. The two areas will to some extent compete for our markets and for our financial support. It is, however, unlikely that we shall see a new Marshall Plan for either.

5

SUMMARY OF THE DISCUSSION

The brief general discussion, limited by the shortage of time, showed warm appreciation for the expert review of East-West economic relationships and general agreement that those relationships will continue to be important, but still subordinate to political and security issues.

One former diplomat with long experience in Eastern Europe commented on an historical question raised early in Professor Knirsch's paper, namely the extent to which the Western allies had looked forward at the end of World War II to a balanced post-war relationship. In his view, that was clearly the hope of the American administration as the war was ending and for a short time thereafter. The British were more skeptical, reflecting the well-known doubts of Winston Churchill. But it was the Russians who made any such hope unrealizable, Stalin taking the line that with the defeat of Germany and Japan, the British and Americans must now be regarded as enemies of the Soviet Union.

The speaker also emphasized the continuing importance of security relationships between East and West. The recent NATO summit meeting in London had pointed to the dangers implicit in the growing relative military strength on the Soviet side, with overtones of a possible revival of an East-West arms race if effective limitations could not be negotiated. Any such developments would inevitably raise questions concerning continued expansion of credits to the East and other aspects of the economic relationships. Concurring with the view that the Russians have a strong desire to secure more western technology, he wondered whether the resulting leverage, even though not enormous, might not be used to persuade the Soviet Union to reduce its arms sales to the Third World and to increase its development assistance.

Another speaker emphasized the importance of industrial cooperation agreements as an instrument in East-West economic relationships. He pointed out that such agreements are self-financing; they permit western firms to negotiate directly with eastern industrial " firms " instead of the difficult foreign trade monopoly agencies; they fit well with planning arrangements on the eastern side and commercial practices on the western side; and they automatically avoid allegations of dumping. He suggested that their scope was likely to expand even if East-West trade as a whole ceases to do so.

Other speakers commented on the issue of increasing East-West indebtedness. One wondered whether the eastern response might not be to push exports at cut-rate prices, creating widespread charges of dumping and market disruption and consequent tensions in East-West economic relationships. Another asked whether the eastern bloc might not be able to keep credit expansion within bounds by controlling imports, which is presumably easier for planned economies than for more open market economies. A third speaker, with extensive banking connections, confirmed that authorities in the eastern countries are concerned about possible western measures to reduce credits to them, including the possible linkage of this issue with political, security, or human rights issues. The Soviet Union has been pressing heavily for more liberal official credits from the United States and also exploring the availability of bank credits in smaller cities apart from the traditional metropolitan centers of international finance. He also ventured the thought that, if the West came to desire a concerted policy in this field, the central banks could strongly influence the actions of commercial banks through informal means.

Concerning the scale of East European indebtedness, Professor Portes responded that there has indeed been a dramatic increase since 1970, in real terms and in proportion to GNP and total trade, as well as in nominal terms. Available information on the maturity structure of the debt is inadequate, but he foresaw the prospect of severe pressure in the period 1979-81. Concerning import control as a means of limiting the debt burden, he pointed to the experience in Poland as illustrative of the political difficulties in limiting consumer goods imports (meat and grains), while limitation of producer goods and technology might be seriously disrupting to the economic development plans of the eastern countries.

In a brief general reply, Professor Knirsch noted that in recent discussions with Swiss bankers, he had found increasing concerns in their minds about the growing scale of East European indebtedness, but still no reluctance in practice to go on making loans. On the other hand, economists from the East European countries appear increasingly worried about the future burden of debt servicing on their balances-of-payments. Professor Knirsch therefore expects that there will be some effort to reduce imports from the West and strong efforts to increase exports to the West. Over the next five years, he believes that western exporters will find eastern markets somewhat more difficult than during the last decade. With respect to industrial cooperation agreements, Professor Knirsch had explored this arrangement intensively over several years, since in principle it constitutes a new kind of economic relationship between East and West which contains promising elements. On the other hand, its magnitude is still quite small, representing only 3 to 5 per cent of total trade, so that its importance ought not to be exaggerated.

VI

DOMESTIC POLITICS
AND INTERDEPENDENCE

by Professor Stanley Hoffmann

The study of international relations tends to follow the agenda of statesmen. In the sixties, both were dominated by strategic issues. In the past ten years, scholars and officials have devoted much of their attention to the problems raised by the interpenetration of societies and the interconnection of state policies in the world economy—the problems to which the term interdependence has been applied. On the one hand, students of world politics have tried to evaluate the extent to which interdependence changes the traditional, distinctive features of interstate relations, what Raymond Aron has called the logic of behavior of states competing in a " state of nature. " More specifically, the question to which scholars have addressed themselves is whether the particular imperatives or constraints of interdependence merely provide new opportunities and some new detours for the age-old contest of sovereign units trying to reach their goals in a world without either substantive consensus or central power, or whether the new characteristics transform the game of nations so deeply that it begins to resemble what we are familiar with in domestic politics. Are we still in " the state of war, " or already in " global politics "? On the other hand, conferences of statesmen, and meetings of members of national " establishments, " have tried to find solutions to a vast number of highly complex problems, in the relations between OECD countries, in North-South relations, and in East-West relations. Reports of think tanks and of groups like the Trilateral Commission have laid out alternatives for the monetary system, for East-West trade, for energy and commodities, for the law of the seas, for food or technology transfers, for aid to and trade with the developing countries, etc. What has been strangely lacking in all these efforts is a consideration of the domestic realities, which determine which of these alternatives is most likely to be adopted, and indeed dictate the goals of the players. Nicholas Wahl, writing about American-West European relations, has stated that their " professional analysis... has left little role for a separate, autonomous weight to the internal dimension. " [1] There are two different but convergent

---

1. In James Chace and Earl Ravenal, eds, *Atlantis Lost*, New York, New York University Press, 1976, p. 230.

reasons for this neglect. The traditional model of world politics is the "realist" paradigm, which looks at the state as a rational actor whose ends are shaped by its geo-political position on the map: the National Interest is supposed to have a quasi-objective reality, and indeed the concept itself entails, as one of its functions, insulating foreign policy from the vagaries of domestic politics. The primacy of foreign policy is one of the dogmas of the "realist" model. To be sure, some allowance is made for fundamental variations among regimes: it would not be realistic to discard the difference between the way in which a totalitarian state like Nazi Germany sets and seeks its goals, and the way in which democracies behave. Yet even there the emphasis is on continuity, and the scrutiny of domestic factors does not go very deep. As for what might be called the "modernist" model, which looks at the interdependent world from the perspective of global politics, it tends to suffer from a double bias. Analytically, its focus is on the factors, inherent in economic development, which weave the different state strands into a single tapestry; normatively, its preference goes to "one world" solutions, to collective methods for the management of common problems. As a result, the literature of political science still falls into two different compartments. Books on domestic political systems say rather little about foreign policy. Books on the foreign policy of a nation, or on international issues, say rather little about domestic factors.

The purpose of this paper is obviously not to bridge the gap. It is to raise a few questions about the interactions between domestic politics and interdependence, in the light of our experience since the days of the Marshall Plan, and given the problems which the industrial nations face in the coming years. I will begin with some remarks about the meaning of interdependence for domestic politics; then, I will look at some typical state responses to interdependence, determined by domestic factors; I will present what I consider to be the key issues raised by those interactions; and I will end with some considerations about the future.

II

Interdependence can be described as a *condition*. It refers to a situation of mutual sensitivity and vulnerability which affects all states, because of the inability of each of them to reach its national objectives in autarky. Either they cannot be achieved unless other states or societies provide the goods and services that are missing at home; or else the policies followed by others abroad are capable of disrupting those undertaken at home; or else the costs that would have to be paid for liberating oneself from such dependencies and insulating the nation from such disruptions would be so prohibitive as to entail important sacrifices of national goals and values. It is because of this condition that one often hears about "all of us in the same boat," or about "spaceship earth." But this is not an adequate way of looking at world politics. For the common condition tells us nothing about the individual situations. In particular, it tells us nothing about the two central ques-

182

tions of politics: who commands and who benefits? It is clear that the balance of gains and losses from interdependence varies from country to country, that some are less vulnerable than others, and that the universal condition covers both states which are able, so to speak, to spread dependencies all around and to export more disruptions than they import, and states that are in a plight of one-sided dependence on a dominant master or partner. Moreover, there are also vast variations in the distribution of the gains from interdependence across the population of a given state, or in the location of the losses incurred within a society, depending on the domestic and external strategies adopted by the governments.

It therefore makes more sense to analyze interdependence as a *process*, or as a set of processes. From the viewpoint of this paper, this is doubly relevant—positively and negatively.

1. Interdependence is a process which enhances the importance of domestic factors in international politics. The agenda of world politics is no longer filled by traditional strategic-diplomatic issues (although these remain essential). It tends to be occupied by the very issues that are central to domestic politics, i.e. issues of economic growth and social welfare. Foreign policy becomes the external projection of domestic needs and drives, international politics the confrontation and conciliation of domestic *projets*. As a result, the constituencies of foreign policy have broadened: to the traditional and specialized " establishments " of foreign policy experts and " military-industrial complexes, " one must now add all the groups whose interests are affected by what happens abroad. The scope of these groups depends, of course, on the issues, on the nature of the regime (is it one that allows for the expression of separate interests?), and on the degree of participation of the nation in the world economy. If we look at the OECD countries, that scope is pretty broad. It is true that in the past, and particularly in the pre-1914 world economy, citizens of these countries were already deeply affected by external economic events. But the connection was much less sharply perceived, both because fewer of the issues were the subject-matter of state policies, i.e. the responsibility of the governments and the concern of interstate politics, and because " the integration of the pre-1914 world economy was something of an illusion, "[2] due to the barriers imposed by nature (communications). Some groups, directly affected by free trade or by protectionism, were always part of the foreign policy constituency.

What is new is the susceptibility of all citizens, as producers or consumers, to becoming members of that constituency. This, in turn, corresponds to the end of the specialization of the foreign policy actors (decision-makers and enforcers). To the soldier and the diplomat, characteristic of the strategic-diplomatic chessboard, we now must add the functional departments and agencies (agriculture, industry, space, Treasury, etc.) which tend to have foreign policies of their own—not to mention the heads of multinational corporations, within their sphere of autonomous decision.

---

2. Richard Cooper, *The Economics of Interdependence*, New York, McGraw Hill, 1968, p. 152.

When we talk about domestic players in matters of interdependence, we must be careful to distinguish between constituencies and decision-makers. For while economic interdependence tends to enlarge both spheres, the broadening of the constituencies is tied to the nature of the political regime, that of the decision-makers' sphere to the degree of bureaucratic development (a key aspect of what is sometimes called modernization). A totalitarian regime which muzzles or shapes interest groups or ideological forces is, however revolutionary its goals, most able to stay close to the old model of the separation between domestic politics and foreign policy. A barely constituted state is likely to have a highly specialized foreign policy personnel. And yet, even when the constituencies are tightly controlled by the state, or when that personnel remains very small, the nature of the issues raised by interdependence will oblige leaders to pay close attention to domestic factors in their definition of the state's foreign policy.

2. To say that interdependence is a process, or a set of processes, is a way of saying that it is not a goal, or a set of goals. We should not speak of the "imperatives" of interdependence, and constrast them with the "obstacles" raised by domestic politics. For a given state, the imperatives consist in the goals which it has set, and which, in large part, emerge from domestic realities. Concerning these goals, two remarks are essential. First, for every government, they form a whole; while one can analytically distinguish domestic and foreign objectives, the two sets are intertwined. Every government, even (or especially) in authoritarian or totalitarian regimes, must legitimize its domestic power—in order to get reelected, or not to lose its bases of support; thus, the social groups that provide its lifeblood must be kept reasonably satisfied materially as well as ideologically— and this often entails the setting of *foreign* policy objectives (as in the case of French agricultural policy, or of West German industrial policy, or in the form of measures aimed at preventing inflation from being imported from abroad, or worsened by external commitments; if we switch from the material to the ideological realm, we can mention the British Labour party's rejection of European unity schemes, after World War II, or on the contrary the ardent embrace of such schemes by the Italian Christian Democrats). Conversely, even governments which seem to attach a much higher priority to foreign than to domestic affairs (say, the Nixon Administration) cannot help shaping their foreign policy in the light of their domestic problems (as in 1971). Governments look at the issues created by interdependence through the lenses shaped by their domestic experience (cf. Americas' and West Germany's preference for free market solutions to North-South problems). Foreign policy tends to be the extension of this experience.

Secondly, insofar as the foreign policy objectives are concerned, while it is impossible to put much order into the bewildering variety displayed by an ever growing number of states, one may, analytically, want to distinguish two ideal-types (if only in order to see to which one any given nation is closer). There is the ideal-type of the nation whose primary concern is its own internal development, or transformation, or conservation. Since it lives in an interdependent world, since it is likely to need some external goods or services (material or psychological), it will, of course, pursue a foreign policy, but of a primarily instrumental nature. Then, there is the ideal-type of the nation whose primary concern is its figure, influence, and role on the world stage, and which tends to tailor its internal make-up to the needs of that role. One may well ask why such a distinction is relevant, since interdependence can be either an obstacle or a springboard for states in either category. Nevertheless, from the viewpoint of world order, it is the second group that is the most awesome. The states closest to the first ideal-type, even when their actions appear disruptive (through protectionism, or the expropriation of foreign capital, or claims on offshore resources, for instance), are above all interested in scoring absolute gains. The states in the second category, even when their policies are cooperative and seem to stress the possibility of joint gains, are mostly eager for relative advantages over rivals; and even when this drive does not make them overtly more aggressive or disruptive, it is likely to elicit their desire for a bigger share of the joint gain, and to provoke the resistance of others to such uneven solutions: this is the contagion of competitiveness, so well analyzed by Jean-Jacques Rousseau.

In the history of the OECD countries, the smaller nations (such as Belgium, Holland, or Norway) are close to the first ideal-type; the United States and Gaullist France to the second. Among the middle powers, Italy has chosen the first alternative; its foreign policy has aimed above all at buttressing the internal balance of political forces (i.e. the " hegemonic bloc " around the Christian Democrats), and at serving its economic and social post-war transformation. France since 1969, and Britain gradually, have moved from the second category toward the first. In the cases of West Germany and Japan, the very success achieved, in the fifties and sixties, by concentrating on absolute gains and on the economic dimensions of foreign policy, *and* the high degree of dependence on outside markets and sources of energy or raw materials, have combined in recent years at least to raise the question of a possible shift from the first to the second category; both nations seem to hesitate around the dividing line—with Japan still on the threshold, but Bonn perhaps already on the other side...

The process of interdependence affects each state both as a set of *restraints* on, and as a set of *opportunities* for, its domestic objectives and interests. These is no need to repeat Richard Cooper's classic analysis of the way in which interdependence constrains domestic autonomy. He and others have shown how such classical tools of statecraft as macroeconomic monetary, credit, and taxation policies have been impaired in a world of rapid capital movements and " quick responsiveness to differential earning opportunities. " [3] A state trying to control inflation by raising the interest rate, and thus attracting foreign capital; a state trying to reduce demand by cutting imports, and producing not a return to balance or surplus, but a recession, because of the effect of such cuts on the clients of its exports; a state whose attempt to orient foreign investments results in their emigration to other, more liberal countries;

---

3. Richard Cooper, *The Economics of Interdependences*, New York, McGraw Hill, 1968, p. 152.

a state whose economic future is jeopardized by another power's, or group of powers', decision to change the rules of the monetary or energy games: these are all examples from the recent past. Decisions made in one country, by the government or by private economic agents, affect that country's partners immediately.

The ability of governments to limit the loss of autonomy varies, of course, greatly. The critique of the monetary system of the 1960's by France was based on the indictment of America's privileged capacity to get other nations to finance its balance of payments deficits—and to buy foreign enterprises with its overvalued dollars. And yet the United States did not escape all restraints: insofar as " the privileged dollar was a subsidy to European economic expansion, "[4] and the overvalued dollar favored the European and Japanese export industries over America's, various domestic American interests were hurt. The United States could appease them by changing the rules, in 1971—but in turn OPEC changed those of oil in 1973, and thus deepened the very recession which the need to check the American inflation of the 1960's had finally produced. Americans react with dismay at their vulnerability to outside trends and decisions because, unlike the Europeans and the Japanese, the experience of dependence is new to them. Still, in the balance of constraints, Western Europe and Japan do more poorly than the United States, both because of a higher ratio of trade to GNP, and because of their greater dependence on energy imports. And Western Europe has done more poorly than Japan, insofar as the fragmentation of Western Europe, and also, often, an obsession with the size of firms rather than with their efficiency, has played havoc with various important European industries.

As for the opportunities which interdependence provides, they range from the formidable development of industries geared to export, especially in Japan and West Germany, to the high profits and world-wide expansion of multinational corporations, which are actually national enterprises operating abroad, to the skillful promotion of domestic interests by governments eager to take advantage either of a privileged position (let us think of French agriculture within the Common Market, of American sales of wheat, or of Iran's oil policy) or of an asset desired by others (Brazilian uranium, in the West German-Brazilian deal). The opportunities provided by external markets may lead to the expansion of an industry far beyond the domestic needs that fostered its creation, as in the case of the French aircraft or the West German nuclear industries. And governments often find that the best way of exploiting an opportunity is to withhold their support on an issue of importance to others, until the interest they want to promote is satisfied: a tactic used by France in the EEC's agricultural policy, and later by Britain, both in order to obtain subsidies for its consumers of EEC farm products and in order to get regional development aid from its partners. Sometimes, a government can find in interdependence an opportunity for desirable domestic changes, as in the case of France opening her borders to her European partners

---

4. David S. Landes, (ed.), in *Western Europe: Trials of Partnership*, Lexington, Heath, 1977, p. 8.

in the 1950's and 1960's, thus transforming the outlook of a previously " Malthusian " business community, and finding in open competition across borders a powerful leverage for further industrialization and growth.

Sometimes, paradoxically, it is the restraint which is the opportunity. Whereas the loss of domestic autonomy provoked by interdependence usually compounds the restrictions on governmental freedom of maneuver already created by the necessities of domestic politics—the narrowness or composition of the electoral base, ideological and class tensions, bureaucratic inefficiency, etc.—there are cases when the external constraints actually result in a lifting of domestic obstacles, and may be deliberately sought by a government eager to remove these without direct internal collision. The recent negotiations between the IMF and the British and Italian governments have resulted, after much bargaining, in the former " imposing " on the latter, in exchange for the money loaned, conditions of budgetary and social policy which partly liberated these governments from the grip of left-wing socialist ideologues in one case, and a host of pressure groups in the other. Inversely, it is often the external opportunity created by interdependence which makes it possible for a government either to obtain or to impose domestic restraints. It was the need for France to make full use of the industrial opportunities provided by the Common Market, i.e. to be competitive, which justified the restrictive policies followed, in the 1960's, with respect to wage increases; more recently, the argument used by the Japanese government to obtain the cooperation of the labor unions in the fight against inflation was the preservation of Japan's huge exporting capabilities.

So far, we have only mentioned the opportunities provided by interdependence for domestic interests within the nation that is acting on the world scene. But we must add the possibility for the nation to affect domestic forces elsewhere, thanks to interdependence. For its processes facilitate access to political and economic élites in the " target country, " and thus extend the sphere of manipulation abroad—in two ways at least: more foreign groups can be affected, given the nature of the issues; and, within the acting nation, more groups can try to affect the foreign target. Sometimes, these machinations take rather scandalous forms: businessmen bribing foreign intermediaries or prospective clients, or trying to contribute to the overthrow of a hostile regime. But there are many other transnational links—between parties, or professional associations, or intellectuals—which can be used for the manipulation of a foreign society. As in the case of the restraints, such opportunities are unevenly distributed—along lines of might *and* skill: both are needed, neither can entirely substitute for the other. Insofar as so much of international politics today is the manipulation of interdependence—to minimize its restraints or to maximize its opportunities—without resort to the use of force, the most successful are likely to be those who know best how to affect, not only the governments with whom they have to deal, but the political and social forces to whose opinions and interests these governments must pay attention.

187

How have states reacted to the restraints and exploited the opportunities provided by interdependence? Let us examine two questions: the kinds of policies followed in response to domestic factors, and the kinds of domestic forces that have influenced these policies.

Minimizing constraints on domestic forces and policy instruments, and maximizing opportunities for such forces and interests, have come in two forms. One has been the setting up of procedures of cooperation that are meant to allow states to pursue their goals without endangering, and even by tightening, the network of economic interdependence. Other papers prepared for this conference study the development of this network in the past thirty years. I will only add a remark about the circumstances of its growth. There have been three main groupings. The "Atlantic" one (which includes Japan and corresponds to OECD, but also to the management of the monetary system) was set up largely along the lines laid out by the one power for whom the balance of restraints and opportunities was most clearly positive—the United States. Washington's privileged position allowed it, throughout the sixties, to put off the domestic constraints which balance-of-payments deficits entail for "ordinary" states. Indeed, the move from fixed rates to floating rates, imposed by Washington, meant an overt repudiation of such externally imposed domestic discipline, and a recovery of dwidling opportunities. Other nations accepted the Atlantic bargain both because of the extraordinary possibilities it offered for economic growth (including liquidity to finance it) and also military security, and because the United States allowed, in diverse ways, both Western Europe and Japan to protect their domestic markets from an unlimited invasion of American goods (and also, in the case of Japan, from the implantation of American multinationals behind the tariff barrier). The West European network was built by states, all of which, for different reasons, had come to the conclusion that national autonomy provided fewer opportunities for domestic development and external influence than the establishment of a common market and some common policies; as for the constraints that would result from these, they were seen either as bearable because of countervailing economic or foreign policy gains, or as actually desirable for domestic reasons, or as susceptible to renegotiation or alleviation. The third network is the quasi-global one, which covers "First World-Third World" relations. It is the one that has suffered the most, precisely because of Third World complaints about the unfairness of the balance of restraints and opportunities, shaped by the advanced nations: insufficient opportunities to fashion their own development plans because of heavy debts, or the paucity of aid, or the prevalence of multinationals; insufficient opportunities to ship their agricultural or industrial goods to the developed countries; excessive restraints imposed by price fluctuations affecting both their imports and their main export products, etc. It is important to note that the challenge to this network has mainly come, not from those domestic forces that have least benefited from post-war economic development in the Third World—the peasants, the workers uprooted from the land and moved to urban slums—but from the very élites of the new states.

More interesting for the purposes of this paper is the other kind of behavior: policies that, deliberately or not, loosen or rift interdependence on behalf of domestic goals—either because they aim at increasing or restoring domestic autonomy or at shoring up domestic forces threatened by interdependence, or else because the manipulation of ties of mutual interest to make them more advantageous to the nation results in the weakening or destruction of these bonds. Recent years have presented us with a multitude of examples, which fall into three categories.

1. State *actions* of self-enhancement, or state actions taken for domestic reasons, but detrimental to interdependence. Most prominent in the former case are the OPEC decisions of 1973 and after, with their enormous effects on the world economy; the decisions of states to enlarge their sphere of control beyond the territorial seas; and the establishment by many states of vast arms industries that depend for their profitability or survival on exports of conventional, often highly sophisticated, weaponry abroad—at the risk of multiplying opportunities for turning conflicts into wars, whose effects on economic interdependence are likely to be disastrous. The drive to export nuclear technologies that could be used for the production of nuclear weapons may be even more dangerous. It is interesting to note that the nuclear energy industries of Europe, which have developed simultaneously with the institutions of the Community, have always proceeded on a national basis (except for limited cooperative ventures); there has been no real attempt to devise a common nuclear policy, despite the shadowy existence of Euratom. Among policies taken for domestic reasons that result in a disruption of interdependence, one can list the new American food policy of 1972, which shifted to reliance on the market mechanism, and resulted in a depletion of grain reserves.

2. State *reactions* against the constraints of interdependence. We have already mentioned the " international coup d'état " constituted by the August, 1971 decisions of Nixon and Connally and by subsequent demands presented to the West Europeans and the Japanese, aimed at turning the American payments deficit into a surplus. The generalization of floating rates represents a weakening of the disciplining of domestic economies through the balance of payments; and while it can be presented as a way of saving interdependence from a breakdown into competitive devaluations or monetary blocs comparable to the disasters of the 1930's, it is nevertheless a factor of uncertainty for the world economy. It has led to a growing discrepancy between weak and strong currencies, which in turn has contributed to the relative anemia of the EEC. One may argue that the world economy, and the EEC, suffer less from a drastic decline in British imports due to the depreciation of the pound sterling, than from a similar reduction that would have been obtained through protectionism. But the recession of the mid-1970's, and either the balance-of-payments difficulties of some countries (such as Italy) or the plight of specific industries hit by foreign competition (in the United States or in Western Europe) have led to a resurgence of protectionist pressures, in the United States against both Japanese and West European imports, in Western Europe

against imports from Japan and from developing countries, and also to import control measures taken by Italy. It becomes more difficult to ward off such pressures, or to avoid such measures, when the opportunities for compensatory gains, or for temporary domestic austerity measures—comparable to those adopted in France in 1958-9 and again in the autumn of 1968—are wiped out or reduced by the state of the world economy. Another reaction to the recent crisis, apparently less destructive of the network of free trade, has been the adoption by the major industrial powers of policies of export-led growth; but, as many observers have pointed out, this is tantamount to a zero-sum game: not all countries can increase their exports simultaneously. Among the reactions against the costs of interdependence, one must also mention moves by developing nations to gain greater control over the activities of foreign enterprises.

3. State *inaction* due to domestic factors, yet dangerous for economic interdependence. The most striking example may well be the utter failure of the EEC in the realm of common industrial policy (even in the case of coal and steel). Neither earlier arguments about the technology gap, nor the failure of " national champion " policies, nor the growing preponderance of American computers, weapons, and civilian aircraft has led the separate members of EEC to give up often [fleeting national control: the gains from common policies that would go beyond *à la carte* arrangements have not seemed big or probable enough to offset the loss of control. The fiasco of the EEC's common energy policy has been particularly remarkable—before 1973 and after: here, national interests and practices have been too diverse, and the exploitation of the North Sea oil by Britain has obviously given London little incentive for a common strategy that could constrain its moves or limit its gains. The slowness of the United States Congress in adopting a national energy policy that would aim, not at impossible energy independence, but at making inevitable interdependence with OPEC less uneven, has been caused by the combined resistance of consumers and special interest groups. Protracted French inaction about inflation, due to the priority given to full employment, accelerated industrialization, and higher exports, in the period 1969-1973, first kept France from joining the common float of European currencies proposed by Bonn in 1971, and later, twice, led to France having to quit the West European experiment in monetary cooperation. Earlier, American policy-makers' " benign neglect " of the growing world monetary crisis, and their reliance on other nations' willingness to absorb dollars rather than on domestic measures to eliminate the payments deficits, had led to the breakdown of the Bretton Woods system.

We have been talking about state moves. It is necessary to be more precise in defining the domestic factors that take part in the attempts to curtail or to reshape interdependence. Here again, there are three components.

1. There is, in the first place, the *government* itself, as the force in charge of protecting and promoting what it considers the national interest. It is the government which integrates external and domestic concerns. As a result, even when several governments agree on the need to preserve economic interdependence, or on the imperative of avoiding a return to the conditions of

the 1930's, there will, in all likelihood, be a contest about the specific institutional shape and about the scope which cooperation ought to have—a contest in which domestic and foreign policy considerations are inextricably mixed. *All* French governments have, since the late 1940's, "tilted" in favor of European as against more Atlantic structures (the biggest difference among these governments has been over the respective scope of European versus *national* control). The reasons for this have to do not only with considerations of power-in-the-world (i.e., minimizing dependence on the United States), but also with the fear of the economic consequences, for French industry and agriculture, of an Atlantic design that would lead to a huge free trade area without any buffer between American goods and the French market. Again for a mixture of domestic and external reasons, Britain and West Germany have leaned more in the Atlantic direction, and this was precisely the reason for France's long opposition to British entry into the EEC except on French terms (the story begins in 1950, not in 1958). The Franco-American battle over the monetary system, in the 1960's, can be seen as a contest between one government eager and able to exploit the rules of the game so as to export much of its inflation (and to preserve its external freedom of maneuver despite payments deficits), and another government eager to keep out inflation, hard pressed to control it (as Bonn was doing) by primarily domestic means, and hostile to much of what Washington was doing around the world; each one was keen to preserve internal as well as external autonomy, each one was accusing the other of undermining interdependence. The same struggle about institutional shape and scope goes on today in North-South relations.

2. It is necessary to look at the importance and the role of bureaucratic structures and bureaucratic processes of decision in different countries; for they have a major, often very specific influence in shaping the state's policy on issues of interdependence. One can document, for instance, the existence of an American "Treasury view" of considerable effectiveness, both in the monetary turmoil of 1971-3, and in resisting Kissinger's attempts at moving away from the free market ideology toward some concessions to Third World demands in 1975-6. In the case of France, a long tradition of *colbertisme*, and the development of state institutions and procedures for post-war economic and social change, have resulted in an energy policy aimed at insuring maximum autonomy from foreign companies and from Middle Eastern oil, even at high prices—something which partly explains the resistance opposed by France to Kissinger's International Energy Agnecy, with its supranational features. [5] France also has a much more regulatory attitude toward monetary transactions and foreign investments than many of her partners. On the contrary, the Japanese bureaucracy has interpreted its role as one of supporting the formidable export drive of industry, hence of preserving an open world economy (while slowing down the dismantling of Japan's own protective mechanisms). As for bureaucratic processes, only agencies in charge of

---

5. Cf. Peter J. Katzenstein, " International Relations and Domestic Structures: Foreign Economic Policies of Advanced Industrial States, " *International Organization*, Winter 1976, vol. 30, no. 1.

domestic interests were involved in the American monetary and trade decisions of the summer of 1971, and later in the soybean embargo; this explains why the bad effects on other countries were, in one case, deliberately accepted, and, in the second case, neglected. [6]

3. Finally, specific interests, parties, and ideologies do influence the decisions of the statesmen. The switch of the American labor movement to protectionism cannot fail to affect the international trade policies of a Democratic administration, however strong its commitment to free trade: compromises will have to be found between the principles in which it believes (and which it also believes to be beneficial to the American economy as a whole in the long run) and the demands presented by politically important groups. It is a combination of disparate interests—coastal water fishermen, petroleum and hard mineral industries, marine researchers—which contributed to the United States' change of position regarding the two-hundred mile economic zone in the oceans, after the initial " internationalist " proposal of 1970 [7] favored by the Defense Department; and various industrial interests are still clearly in favor of a breakdown of the Law of the Seas Conference, rather than having an International Authority for the seabeds of the high seas that could seriously curtail the advantages enjoyed by United States technology in the exploitation of seabed resources. Radical ideologies that prevail among the élites of various Third World countries do not facilitate accommodation at UNCTAD, CIEC, or the United Nations, or at the Law of the Seas Conference. And many observers have wondered what the consequences for European and Atlantic cooperation would be if, in France, a leftwing coalition came to power and collided with economic interdependence. There are two reasons for this fear. One is the ideological hostility of the Parti Communiste Français and of a fraction of the Parti Socialiste to international structures dominated by " capitalist " states and principles, and their belief that the constraints of interdependence (especially insofar as capital movements are concerned) could seriously hamper domestic social reform but should not be allowed to do so—a belief expressed previously by the British Labour party in the days of the Coal and Steel Community. The other reason is the possible resort by the Left to protectionist moves or to safeguard provisions of international agreements such as the Treaty of Rome, as a result of economic and financial mismanagement. But radicals and Reds are not the only forces whose ideological fervor can try to affect the choice of specific structures of cooperation, or to restrict its scope, or otherwise to play havoc with interdependence. In France, the Gaullists have, over the years, resisted the institutionalization of interdependence and, insofar as it appeared necessary, preferred formulas that would give France a possibility of leadership—for instance, European as against Atlantic intergovernmental cooperation, and " Euro-Arab " arrangements for energy rather than the American-dominated

---

6. Cf. Graham Allison and Peter Szanton, *Remaking Foreign Policy*, New York, Basic Books, 1976; and Commission on the Organization of the Government for the Conduct of Foreign Policy, June 1975, Appendices, vol. 3.
7. Cf. Ann. L. Hollick, " Seabeds make Strange Politics, " *Foreign Policy*, 9, Winter 1972-3.

IEA; and they continue to resist the institutionalization of the summits of the advanced nations' leaders. Let us move across the Atlantic. Whatever one may think about who, in the long run, is likely to gain more from East-West trade, such commerce is an attempt at creating a network of mutual opportunities and restraints where none existed before. The Jackson amendment, voted by the United States Congress in 1973 at the request of a combination of "cold warriors" and Jewish organizations, brought the attempt, if not to a halt, at least down to very modest proportions.

IV

The problem of the interactions between domestic imperatives and the process of interdependence can be examined at two levels. At the highest level of generality, one can argue that there is an inherent contradiction between a global world economy, between the existence of problems which cry out for global solutions, on the one hand, and the fragmentation of the world into sovereign states on the other. As long as a small number of advanced nations seemed capable of playing a kind of collective steering role, the disadvantages of this tension could be reduced or disregarded. But the challenge from the Third World has put in question the legitimacy of this steering role. On key issues: energy, oceans, investments, trade, arms restraint, no solutions are conceivable without Third World participation. On some of these and on other major issues: food, arms, oil, trade, the participation of the Communist countries will also become increasingly necessary. Moreover, as the power discrepancies among the members of the steering group have fluctuated or sharpened, agreement among them along the lines of American policy has become less likely. Hence the need for a kind of leap "beyond the nation-state," either toward a world government or toward a considerable strengthening and broadening of collective institutions, endowed with substantial powers of management and decision. [8]

The problem with this analysis lies in the clash between diagnosis and prescription. If the diagnosis is correct (as indeed it is), how will the actors be led to the wholesale *auto-da-fé* of their residual powers of control—especially in a world in which many of them are new states whose first concern is to *create* domestic authority, and no consensus exists on the nature of the global solutions? Governments continue to derive their legitimacy from their home turf, however much their grip over it may have weakened. Most of the world is in the hands of governments which consider their first duty to be either the preservation of their control from external, ideologically hostile or economically exploitative intrusions, or else the establishment of their control over populations and resources still recently under the rule of colonial powers. This makes a leap or a sudden mutation perfectly implausible.

Let us therefore climb down to a more modest and realistic level. We

---

8. This is the position of the participants in the World Order Models Project; cf. Richard Falk, *A Study of Future Worlds*, New York, Free Press, 1975.

can note that the contradiction between global issues and state fragmentation has so far been managed, by trial and error, partly because of the very restraints which interdependence imposes and which states observe in their own self-interest, and partly because of the opportunities for absolute, joint, or even relative gains which its exploitation provides. But there are three reasons for concern—which have become evident in the past seven or eight years.

1. The relatively successful management of the past was related to two conditions, both of which have changed. The first was regular economic growth—insufficient to close or even narrow the gap between the rich and the poor, but sufficient to provide absolute gains to most nations. The promise of constant growth is flickering, less because of the " limits to growth " or the population explosion than because of its inflationary consequences. For most states have neither the internal means to curb inflation (cf. below), nor the possibility of preventing its import from abroad without cutting themselves off thereby from the benefits of interdependence, nor the desire to establish a stringent monetary system that would oblige them not to live above their means, because of internal resistances and of fear that such a system would not provide enough liquidity for growth. And yet, the need to act against inflation, once it begins endangering either the fabric of domestic society or the competitivity of the nation, leads to recurrent recessions which reduce the ability of states to cooperate, and shifts the governments' attention to domestic priorities and pressures. The second condition was the preponderance of the United States, Washington's role as the leader of the steering group.

2. The willingness of states to bear the intrusive costs of interdependence is being severely strained by two phenomena inherent in interdependence. One is the permanent manipulation of all by all; for it means an enlarged capacity of foreign states to affect, accidentally (through their own domestic policies) or intentionally (through their foreign economic policies), the domestic affairs of others, and a similar capacity for foreign, private holders of capital. This in turn means that the state is at the mercy of foreign-induced crises, which require emergency " solutions " that fully satisfy no one, and in fact prepare further crises. Moreover, this manipulation entails the ability of states (or non-state actors), if they are in a position of power, to harm others either by refusing or by unilaterally changing the rules of the game.

Secondly, such manipulation, and indeed the very existence of constraining ties, puts into stark relief the unevenness of power. The closer the bonds, the more troublesome is inequality: for there will be a permanent temptation to exploit or to reverse it. Interdependence among unequals is likely to be recurrently unbearable both to the very strong and to the very weak. It will be unacceptable to the very strong, if they are constantly summoned to make sacrifices on behalf of the weak and, so to speak, to subsidize them in order to prevent the system's unraveling, especially if such help would either save the weak from having to shape up, or allow them to challenge their benefactor—an experience which many Americans resented in the 60's, and which led to the reassertion of national power of 1971; an experience many

194

West Germans resent now, in dealings with their EEC partners or in North-South relations. And the terms of interdependence will be unacceptable to the weak, if they have means of redress, either through the exploitation of an oligopoly (OPEC), or through coalition-building. The growing discrepancy between Bonn and its partners within the EEC has resulted, if not in a breakdown of a Community that continues to serve the interests of all its members (Bonn has to keep its weaker partners from imposing unilateral trade restrictions or from undergoing drastic political upheavals through economic disruption), at least in a virtual stoppage of attempts at common policies.

The two factors converge in the following way: the international economy, manipulated by its members, operates as a constant but unpredictable system of double redistribution—of incomes, jobs, status within nations, and wealth and power among nations. But the domestic victims of this redistribution do not acknowledge the legitimacy of a haphazard or shifty mechanism that is external to the nation, and competes or conflicts with the internal redistributive schemes that have been legitimately, authoritatively, or imperatively set up within the confines of the nation.

3. Conversely, the capacity of states to withstand domestic pressures that amount to a rebellion against the constraints of interdependence and a withering away of its opportunities, is also in doubt. Here again, there are two factors. One is the radical increase in the functions of states (not only in advanced societies): they have undertaken the roles of " creators—as well as redistributors—of the common wealth " [9]; they have the responsibility for welfare, full employment, cultural identity, the promotion of national technology or elites, etc. : tasks that often squeeze them between their obvious interest in increasing wealth thanks to the benefits from trade and foreign investment (or from investment abroad), and the threats which free trade and free capital movements create for national autonomy or for specific sectors. [10] The other factor is the growing self-assertion of domestic groups, either hostile to foreign control or competition, or unwilling to limit the growth of their incomes to whatever may be compatible with the monetary discipline or the external competitivity of national goods, which participation in an open world economy requires. In the developing countries, the pressure on governments frequently comes from élites that complain about the lopsided development which openness to foreign capital induces; they argue for a " basic needs " strategy that would entail greater efforts at self-reliance and less resort to trade with the advanced nations or to foreign investments in exportable commodities or modern industry.

---

9. Edward L. Morse, *Modernization and the Transformation of International Relations*, New York, Free Press, 1976, p. 98.

10. The *New York Times* of April 30, 1977 describes Mr. Carter's dilemma over one aspect of his energy plan. Should he give rebates to buyers of foreign cars that consume relatively little fuel, at a time of high unemployment among American automobile workers? Obviously, interdependence, in the form of increased imports of such cars, would thus contribute to the national conservation effort. But it would also provoke violent resistance from United States car manufacturers and labor leaders. On the other hand, discriminating in the application of the rebate, at the expense of foreign cars, would violate the rules of GATT.

The two factors converge in overloading the agendas of governments, in obligind them to spend more time on domestic coalition-building and negotiating than on international bargaining, and in making societies live above their means. Of course, here again, some nations are better off than others: the famed crisis of ungovernability affects Japan or West Germany less than Britain, France, Italy, or the pre-Carter United States. But what has been called " the dilemma of rising demands and insufficient resources " [11] is a widespread phenomenon—it seems to affect even some of the newly oil-rich nations, such as Iran. And the consequences are likely to be either a retreat from interdependence, if its constraints are deemed unbearable, or the kind of hazardous manipulation aimed at improving the balance of restraints and opportunities which submits the world economy to dangerous shocks.

Thus, we are left with two paradoxes. One is the contradiction between the universal desire for development and growth, which leaves room for huge disagreements about the best strategy (capitalist versus Communist, " basic needs " versus the benefits of rapid industrialization, liberalism versus planning, etc.), yet rules out autarky in most cases, and the revolt against the costs, inequities and strains of interdependence which has just been described: a revolt which results both from widespread trends in the domestic make-up of nations, and from increasing power discrepancies which play havoc with interdependence. The other is the contradiction between the fact that most governments, especially in complex societies, find it difficult to move in ways other than marginal or incremental, given the weight and delicate balance of domestic obligations, and the fact that, nevertheless, international compacts, especially in the economic realm, are likely to be subjected to rapid erosion or disruption. In the absence of a central executive, legislator, or judge capable of enforcing them despite changes in the respective positions of the partners, and given the unlikeliness of a resort to force to impose enforcement over most of these issues, such compacts are at the mercy of the more daring —the least encumbered by domestic burdens, or on the contrary, the most hard-pressed by domestic demands, or simply the most ambitions. Crises thus appear as altogether inevitable, useful insofar as they force governments to cope with essential issues left unattended by incrementalism—and dangerous because of the strain they put on the international system.

V

What can be done to prevent domestic priorities and concerns from destroying interdependence? Let us return to an earlier point. There is little to be gained by exhorting statesmen not to kill the golden goose, or the golden calf, even if it threatens to move from the backyard into the living room. Their primary responsibility is to their nation, and they will " respect interdependence " only as long as it serves the national interest. Nor are they likely to sacrifice an economic policy, geared to their assessment of national needs and moods, to outside demands for a different policy more

---

11. Harold and Margaret Sprout, quoted in Morse, *op. cit.*, p. 98.

profitable to other nations at least in the short run (cf. West German resistance to pleas for a more expansionist policy that would accelerate its partners' recovery). The problem of world order, in this realm as in others, is to insure the compatibility of *national* objectives. For what, to an outside observer, looks like a clash between national and global considerations, appears to the statesman like a contest between different national interests.

A recent debate about future prospects has offered contrasting views. [12] Marina von N. Whitman has suggested that the best way to deal with " the darker side, " the " vulnerability aspect " of interdependence—given the need to avoid a " widespread retreat into protectionism " and the fact that flexible exchange rates have not provided much " insulation from external disturbances "—is to match " the increase in integration at the market level with some increase in coordination at the policy level "; and she suggests both positive coordination of macroeconomic policies among the advanced countries, and negative coordination (primarily in trade) between advanced and developing nations. Thierry de Montbrial has expressed skepticism about the prospects of positive coordination: nation-states are not ready to accept limits on their " freedom about domestic economic policy in the name of global interdependence. " The logical conclusion, he says, is that " interdependence should be somewhat reduced, " or contained. In particular, there must be limitations to the free trade principle (and many exist already, in agriculture or commodity agreements). In fact, there is far less of a contradiction between these views than a superficial reading suggests. Both are concerned with saving the global world economy, and eager to provide states and individuals with a modicum of order and predictability. Both realize that it is necessary to " preserve the scope for countries to pursue legitimately different objectives with respect to their domestic economies. " Mrs. Whitman acknowledges the need to " cushion the shocks of change " (in trade patterns, which create formidable adjustment problems) in the short run. Mr. de Montbrial would, I am sure, be willing to recognize that even a state that refuses, for example, to " bring deflation at home, in the name of international interdependence, " would be well advised, in setting its domestic economic policies, to take into account likely effects on others that could boomerang (as when the American soybean embargo led to a loss of subsequent soybean exports), or other nations' policies that could vitiate the effectiveness of its own. And he might also recognize that the orderly limitation of the free trade principle would require a great deal of bargaining and coordination (he himself mentions the Lomé Stabex formula, and agriculture).

The fact is that few nations want to retreat from interdependence altogether, and face the losses of wealth or the foregoing of gains which would result. The real choice is not between decoupling the domestic polity from the world economy, and ever increasing interdependence. It is between a disorderly and crisis-ridden approach, and an orderly one which reconciles different domestic imperatives in an interdependent world. Such reconcilia-

---

12. *Trialogue* (published by the Trilateral Commission), Winter 1976-7, no. 13, pp. 2-7.

tion can occur only through bargaining and cooperation. But these, in turn, will be successful only if ways are found both to reduce the costs and to increase the benefits of interdependence for the nations. Some of these ways will have to be explored jointly, as the goals and outcomes of cooperation. But some will have to be found through individual, domestic action, that would make the nation capable of orderly international cooperation. In other, clearer words, the problem discussed here can be solved only if states follow two, apparently divergent yet complementary directions. One is a self-imposed national reduction of vulnerability, aimed at reducing, so to speak, the pressure from the outside—at limiting the risks of interdependence (which is, however, one way of *improving* the balance of costs and opportunities). It may well entail, as Montbrial suggests, a curtailing, or a slowing down, or a cushioning of interdependence; for the nations as well as for individuals, constant and total manipulation from the outside is simply not tolerable. The other direction is the search for common solutions to global problems, by states eager both to prevent those external disruptions that starkly expose their loss of domestic autonomy (and thus bring about revolts against interdependence), and to maximize joint gains.

The reduction of vulnerability, at the cost of some sacrifice of interdependence, yet as the only way to avoid a far worse retreat from it, can take many forms. Three should be mentioned here.

1. Improved domestic management of the national economy is the best prerequisite for orderly cooperation, the best method for minimizing the impact of external shocks. This means, essentially, for the advanced countries, a sound anti-inflationary policy at home; endemic inflation, at inevitably uneven rates, disturbs trade patterns among advanced countries, provokes reactions which disrupt them even more (for in periods of recession and high unemployment, the loss of domestic jobs to foreign competition is particularly resented), and incites developing nations to try to raise in turn the prices of their own commodities, so as to protect their export earnings. To be sure, the international monetary system is often accused of contributing to inflation (the only debate seems to be about whether floating rates are less inflationary than the system of the sixties). However, certain countries such as West Germany have shown skill in controlling inflation nevertheless. What seems necessary is either a domestic system that opposes no insurmountable obstacles to the occasional decline of real wages, as in the United States, or one that allows for an incomes policy agreed upon between the government and the labor unions (which does not imply that domestic inflation is due only to the push of wages; but that has been a major factor in recent years). [13] For the developing countries, improved management that reduces vulnerability could take the form of a partial switch to a " basic needs " strategy, which would both reduce the need to gain massive access for industrial products on the markets of the advanced nations, and the need to let foreign enterprises shape the development of the national economy.

---

13. See the reflections of Raymond Aron, in *Plaidoyer pour l'Europe décadente*, Paris, Robert Laffont, 1977, Ch. VII.

2. A second necessary action is the deliberate effort to thwart external black-mailing possibilities, or to reduce dependence on outside suppliers capable of extracting an exorbitant economic or political price for their supplies. I am referring to the need, in the advanced countries, for domestic energy conservation and development measures, and for the creation of stockpiles of fuel and other essential materials; to the need for reserves of food in countries threatened with shortages; to the need, for many developing countries, to regulate and orient the activities of foreign enterprises, especially when these control vital national resources.

3. Limiting vulnerability through national action must also take the form of more effective and farsighted domestic policies of adjustment to losses from trade and from the changes in the international division of labor that trade brings about. Adjustment assistance schemes are obviously inadequate in periods of mass unemployment. But, on the one hand, they can never be a substitute for the combination of domestic management and international cooperation that alone could perhaps avoid the disaster of huge lay-offs; and on the other hand, the choice governments face is between a policy of internal " concertation " with representatives of potentially threatened sectors, aimed at orderly adjustment and reconversion, and a policy of resistance to external competition (or to the elimination of obstacles to third world exports toward industrial countries) with dangerous consequences either for economic efficiency or for world order.

However, such domestic measures will be of no avail if the onslaught of interdependence is such as to make internal disruptions inevitable. Hence the need for cooperative solutions, aimed at making interdependence both generally bearable and mutually profitable. It would take several volumes to sketch out such schemes, issue by issue. [14] Again, here, three points will suffice.

1. There must be cooperative attempts at mutual damege limitation. It is not in the interest of exporting countries to threaten simultaneously, in a given country (say, the United States), a number of industries that employ large quantities of workers, for such a threat would provoke irresistible demands for protection. It may not be in the interest of developing nations to press demands for preferential access to the markets of developed countries, if the granting of preferences is compensated by an escalating resort to escape clauses and safeguards. [15] Agreements which would entail, not permanent voluntary restraints on competition but a *spacing* of it (over time and place), or assurances of equal access to the markets of industrial states without the latter's resort to escape provisions, would be preferable. Similarly, especially in periods of recession, agreements against beggar-thy-neighbor policies, or policy coordination aimed at avoiding the simultaneous resort to deflationary measures in the leading economies, or more effective attempts at " managing " floating

14. For a sketch of a sketch (l'esquisse d'une esquisse) see the author's forthcoming book, *The Lure of Primary and the Logic of Interdependence*, to be published by McGraw Hill.
15. Cf. Richard Cooper, " A New International Economic Order for Mutual Gain, " *Foreign Policy* 26, Spring 1977, pp. 100, 118.

rates so as to avoid major or manipulative fluctuations, according to common guidelines, would belong in this category. So would case-by-case agreements on the debts of Third World countries, to avoid the damage that would result, either from the total cancellation of all debts (a heavy blow to their own prospects for further credit, and to further profitable " Northern " involvement), or from the bankruptcy of the poorer and needier of these nations.

2. The major task will be the search for areas of mutual or joint gain. Among the industrial powers, the most productive area may well be that of trade—the gradual reduction of non-tariff barriers, given the demonstrated mutual benefits derived, for economic growth, from the huge expansion of international trade since the Second World War. Between advanced and developing countries, there do exist, within the limits discussed above, profitable mutual prospects in trade: advanced nations will be able to sell more goods and services to the developing countries, if they provide these with the means to pays for such imports, either through direct aid or through the granting of access to their markets for the goods produced, thanks to the technology and capital equipment provided by the industrial states. But even in the realm of commodity agreements, there may be room for mutuality: one side accepting to pay for measures aimed at stabilizing prices, in exchange for guarantees of access to supply; and in the exploitation of the world's commons, there is ample room for joint gains. It is only if these occur that the populations of the industrial nations will be willing to make the quite considerable sacrifices entailed, for them, by the so-called new international economic order, or rather by a new international division of labor.

3. I have mentioned above the fragility of such compacts in a world of competing calculations, where the reciprocity of interests is never complete, and each side fears gaining less, or keeps trying to gain more, than the other. The bargains that have proved most durable are those which are founded either on a common concern for military security (and the preponderance of one provider of this public good), or on a common political will that both promotes and transcends the economic calculations. It is difficult to see new " common wills " comparable to that which animated, whatever their ambiguities, ambivalences, and animosities, all the champions of the European enterprise; and as for American military predominance, it is made less effective as an integrating force both by detente and by Washington's increasing reluctance to play world policeman. One may see in growing Arab interdependence a kind of replica of the European movement—but the latter was based on a will to reconciliation (especially between France and Germany); the former is based on a will to revenge.

We may well be doomed to imperfect deals between brittle bargaining structures, regional or ideological alignments of states with limited common interests. But even these would be imperiled if, on the strategic-diplomatic chessboard of world politics, states used their resources for, and tried to achieve mutual gains through, the development of vast weapons arsenals and industries. Ultimately, economic interdependence itself depends on moderation on, and successful management of, that chessboard. It is here, above all, that damage limitation is essential. For it is the precondition to all the cooperative enterprises necessary for damage limitation and joint gains in the economic realm. And while, as we have seen, domestic goals and pressures often submit interdependence to excessive stresses, economic interdependence does ultimately place on state power restraints that do not exist in any comparable way in the strategic-diplomatic realm. It is there that the model of world politics as a zero-sum game remains most valid; and it is therefore there that the conflict between domestic ambitions and world order risks, as in the past, being the most inexpiable. The resources devoted to traditional security concerns weigh heavily on governments and sharply reduce the gains from economic interdependence; these concerns often make the loss of domestic autonomy appear intolerable. In the short run, the extension of interdependence to the trade in arms may seem like an idyllic way of reconciling national objectives, of making interdependence compatible with domestic politics; but in the long run this may turn out to be the most self-destructive of delusions—and the area where there is both the greatest need and the greatest difficulty for cooperation in removing regional or global time bombs.

2

COMMENT

by Ambassador Egidio Ortona (Italy)

I have listened with the greatest interest to what has been said since yesterday and I have been asking myself what my participation should be as a discussant for the excellent paper of Professor Hoffmann. As one of those Europeans who were engaged quite a lot in the Marshall Plan implementation, I can look at what has been written and what I have heard from the double angle of my personal experience and what I would call the naitonal experience of my country in this particular process. It might even be helpful for me to illustrate the theoretical approach about the problems of interdependence with examples of experiences and events in which I have participated. Let me say that my first reaction in considering the Marshall Plan in the frame of this Conference is that, because of the way in which it was conceived, the inspiration which was behind it, and the conditions inherent to it, the Marshall Plan represented the first open and declared consecration of the phenomenon of interdependence.

The speakers yesterday and today have dealt extensively with the inception and history of the Marshall Plan, but I would like to add that, in transferring to the European countries the responsibility of apportioning American aid and of administering the recovery program, the American Government promoted willingly and advertently, as far back as thirty years ago, the concept of interdependence which has become today the most imperative element of international relations. The policy behind the Plan was so simply stated: " to sustain and strengthen principles of individual liberty, free institutions, and genuine independence in Europe through assistance to those countries of Europe which participate in a joint recovery program based upon self-help and mutual co-operation. " All the ingredients of what has been so brilliantly presented in the paper by Professor Hoffmann as the content of interdependence can be traced back and found in the phenomena which I saw engaging the work of governments and the attention of public opinion in the United States and Europe during the lifespan of the Marshall Plan. I refer to the interplay of restraints and opportunities, to states' attempts at self-enhancement, to states' reaction against outside impositions, and to states' inaction due to domestic factors. Not to speak of the components needed for the carrying out of the plan: governments, bureaucratic structures, specific interests, parties, and ideologies. Anybody who has had to advise his government on its actions, as I had the responsibility of doing, and to perceive and analyze the attitude of this country's public opinion, cannot help recalling vividly the inducement into interdependence which was inherent in the philosophy and conduct of the Marshall Plan and the role that it played in influencing the destiny of his own country. It was a successful venture because of the existence of two fundamental conditions, so well underlined by the paper of Professor Hoffmann: on the one side, the existing and developing trend of economic growth; and on the other side, the natural and accepted preponderance of a leader—the United States.

The awareness in the United States of such a responsibility was certainly the element which made the Plan such a striking success. This sense of responsibility revealed itself through the notion that, in its relations with Europe, the United States should move only in association with real European efforts; through the recurrent surge of humanitarianism coupled with the feeling that the United States could not prosper if it was encircled by poverty; through growing acceptance that the solution of the problem of Germany could be found only in terms of a unified Europe.

Let me now put forward some reflections related to the effects of interdependence on the national venture of my own country. Professor Hoffmann has noted that " interdependence is a process which enhances the importance of domestic factors in international politics " and that " foreign policy becomes the external projection of domestic needs and drives. " Let me recall at this point that exactly thirty years and six days ago, on May 29th, 1947, a new government was formed in Italy for the first time since the end of the war without the participation of the Leftist Parties. The Marshall Plan had not yet been formally launched, but the international arena was already aware of its oncoming announcement. One of those " present at the creation, " the Under-Secretary of State at the time, Dean Acheson, on May 8th in a celebrated speech at Cleveland on American foreign economic policy had recognized that the measures taken up to that time by the United States in support of European reconstruction had been inadequate because of the crisis reflected in the European balance-of-payments deficits, and had indicated that the U.S. Government was prepared to play an important part in European reconstruction in association with European countries.

The Italian Premier of the time, Alcide de Gasperi, had sensed the opportunities offered by the new American trend in a visit which he had made to Washington in the preceding month of January. The atmosphere prevailing then in Washington was permeated by the initiatives being taken (UNRRA, Bretton Woods, FAO, grant-in-aid, interim-aid) and by the studies made by American officials, scholars, and political leaders passionately engaged in the preparation of new vistas and formulas for aid. Being already in Washington at that time, I had tried my best to describe the implications of these American efforts and attitudes to my authorities. It was against this background that Signor de Gasperi found the strength and stamina to develop a line of action intended to exclude the parties of the Left—Socialists and Communists—from his Government. The inspiration and inducement behind this momentous decision, the effects of which have lasted for more than thirty years, was the conviction that Italy needed to be linked to countries which could help promote not only its economic recovery but also its political transformation along democratic lines.

Professor Hoffmann has included Italy in the category of those countries whose primary concern, within a process of interdependence, is their own internal development; because of the need for external goods and services, that implies the pursuance of a foreign policy mainly of an instrumental nature. The effect of such a situation was the building of the " hegemonic bloc, " as it is called by Professor Hoffmann, of the Christian Democratic Party in Italy. I do not contest this analysis, but would like to add that it was precisely the prospective benefits of interdependence with countries with democratic leadings and strong economic potentialities which led to the dismissal from the Government of Italy of those parties which that kind of interdependence would have jeopardized. Today, of course, there are differing views about the advantages brought to Italy by that decision. The attack is directed against the effects of conservatism that it implied, delaying necessary and pressing social openings, and against the so-called " clientelism " that a long permanence in power entails. But, whatever may be the retrospective judgment, one can maintain that in choosing the course of interdependence with those democratic nations, Italy took a step which at least allowed her to play an important role in the Institutions and Agencies through which the Western World has since affirmed its supremacy.

Now thirty years have elapsed, and it is certainly not a sterile exercise to assess the present situation in the light of the potentialities of interdependence, but now taking into consideration the more recent developments in the United States and (if you will allow me again a reference to my country) also the new modulations in the internal political patterns in Italy which can offer interesting and important reasons for meditation.

Of course, interdependence, in this generational lapse of thirty years, has assumed new characteristics and responded to new developments in the world arena. We can summarize them as a new series of realities: nuclear war as a practical risk; an indivisible international market for goods and supporting economic and financial services; revolutionary changes in electronic and physical communications; growing and decisive awareness by the countries of the Third World of their possible contributions and/or impositions. The recent meeting of the London Summit and the meetings which preceded and followed, in spite of all the difficulties and snags which have characterized the North-South dialogue, are at the same time proof and consequence of a growing interdependence among peoples and states: growing both in intensity and in the enlargement of its geographical scope to a global dimension.

The results of the Conference in Paris (CIEC) of the last three days, disappointing as they may have been, can nevertheless be considered not a denial but a confimation of that interdependence.

Professor Hoffmann, in pointing out the now prevailing reasons for concern, after the successful management of interdependence in the past, has mentioned *inter alia* the decline of the preponderance of the United States and of its role as leader of the so-called " steering group " of nations. Let me point out at this juncture that, while the validity of this assumption is undeniable, new hopes might be nurtured, at least if one takes note of recent statements emanating from the American Government.

The speech of President Carter at South Bend on May 22nd is certainly an eloquent expression of a new trend in Washington, which is as exalting as it is engaging and problematic. This speech had the merit of leaving behind the tortures of the moral crises that the United States has endured because of Vietnam and Watergate, and boldly opening new perspectives and commitments. " We can no longer separate the traditional issues of war and peace, " Carter said, " from the new global questions of justice, equity, and human rights. " At the conclusion of his speech, President Carter defined the vision of an American role as follows: " It is derived from a larger view of global change; it is rooted in moral values; it is reinforced by material wealth and military power. " The mainstream of the speech flows into a reaffirmation of democratic values and the American sense of responsibility. Will the determination exuding from these remarks overcome in the American Congress and public opinion what Professor Hoffmann calls " the reluctance to play the role of world policeman "? I would put it more mildly, in terms of the reluctance to continue exercising the responsibility of leadership around the world.

Alexis de Toqueville wrote 130 years ago in his famous *Democracy in America*, that " while democracy was suitable for the conduct of domestic affairs, the United States by location, temperament, organisation, and tradition should have stayed out of foreign affairs. The foreign policy of the United States is eminently expectant "; he said, " it consists more of abstaining than acting. " This was because, as he put it, a democracy can only with great difficulty regulate the details of an important undertaking, persevere in a fixed design, and work out its execution in spite of serious obstacles.

Even if one has to grant that the ups and downs of international cooperation among democracies in the last thirty years might find some explanation in what de Tocqueville stated, what the United States did with the Marshall Plan and thereafter can lead us to consider that prediction of the French writer as the only one in his famous book which was not confirmed by events. There certainly have been subsequent periods of turmoil, and years in which impulses were slowed up and programs scaled down. Nevertheless, the interdependence created by the Marshall Plan and the mechanisms adopted for its implementation have resisted the erosion of time. Moreover, as was said yesterday, some of the models of action and behavior of the Plan have also been adopted by other International Organizations. Now the new American administration seems to be determined again to work with a sense of purpose and a sense of history, which means that, as a nation endowed with the attributes of leadership, the United States must divine the significance of the present and heighten the perception of the needs and opportunities of the future.

Three decades after the launching of the most elaborate and intelligent

205

program of aid and collaboration, which constituted the Marshall Plan, the world finds itself again at a turning point. The pressure of the under-developed countries is on us just as new attitudes are shaping up in the domestic situations and political patterns of many of our nations.

In my own country, if I am allowed to revert again to it, we have to take note that the hegemonic bloc around the Christian Democrats is undergoing a process of retrogression. Eurocommunism, whatever that means—or, let us say Communism in my country and in other European countries—seems to be leaning towards new modulations and new nuances of behavior which apparently contain some traces of deviation, like the one mentioned by Mr. Dobell this morning, i.e., the refusal to follow certain Russian dictates. In examining Eurocommunism, however, we must exercice the utmost prudence: in fact, whenever this new from of Communism is described as a kind of new social democracy, the reactions from Communist quarters show that in these new political entities, the links and fundamental allegiances to the Communist ideology and the preponderance of Moscow are far from being abandoned. On the other side of the coin, dissension in Eastern European countries is producing unbalances in their midst and attempts at destabilization. On top of all that, détente is now somewhat of a compulsory permanent feature of the international setup, whatever shape it may take, even if we adopt in Clausewitz fashion the idea that détente in fact is the continuation of tension by other means.

What interdependence will entail in this new, more intense, and globalized phase is for all of us, who are anxiously following the developments of our domestic policies and our international commitments, a question mark of monumental magnitude. The conclusions reached by Professor Hoffmann in his paper seem to reflect such broad preoccupations. But I would like to emphasize, in relation to his final paragraphs, the importance of this new phase of interdependence as a promoter of actions and reactions within the domestic policies of our nations. Very much is implied in those elements of positive and negative coordination illustrated by Marina Whitman and recalled by Professor Hoffmann. On the other hand, I think that what emerges from our two days of discussion is the importance of cultivating the third alternative put forward to us by Professor Lindbeck: " to try more energetically the difficult road of international co-operation and co-ordina-tion. " The events of the North-South conference have certainly proved that the road is a difficult one, insofar, as it implies redistribution of wealth, imposition of new burdens, and changes in living standards.

Because of this, while the new trends which we can perceive in United States policies, with the declared intention of resuming responsibilities of leadership, are of extreme importance, it is clear that we cannot expect American leadership to be exercised again as at the time of the Marshall Plan. We have to be aware that the need is for common efforts, and that participation in future ventures must also engage vigorously new areas, not only European but also Arab. This new phase of interdependence will without doubt have extremely important effects on the domestic scene of countries like mine, which might be called upon more than others to endure the imposition of negative coordination and to develop new patterns of political expression. Without falling into the trap of rhetoric, I can only say that, because of the interplay of so many factors stemming out of growing interdependence, we must hope that in this arduous game the awareness of the need to uphold liberty and justice may prevail. That must signify keeping up the democratic system, either through continued control, in the exercise of power, of those forces which would oppose it, or in bringing it about that the impact of such lofty purposes leads to revisions of approach and of allegiances in the attitudes of those same forces. For this reason, let me conclude by saying that the value of interdependence in the world of today can never be enhanced too much, and that all efforts must be undertaken to make it the central purpose of human behavior in the future.

3

COMMENT

by Sir Eric Roll (United Kingdom) [1]

Speaking at very short notice and so late in the programme, one has the disadvantage that it is very difficult to say anything that hasn't been said already. But it has the compensating advantage that very likely there will not be time for anyone to argue against anything that I may have to say.

I am delighted to be able first of all to add my word of praise on Stanley Hoffmann's paper. I think it is a brilliant summing up. It embraces, very appropriately, all the papers we have reviewed during the course of this Conference, and it has some extremely wise remarks which I hope those in charge of affairs will study and take to heart. As I see it, the essence of his paper is to assert what is very often just acknowledged without being thoroughly taken into account, and that is, the primacy of domestic politics—including or adding the fact that human life is limited, that the active life of politicians is relatively short, that the life of governments is shorter still, and that therefore the need to be re-elected (to which he draws attention) tends to overshadow all other objectives. He analyses in a brilliant way the basic problem of how to secure international co-operation for recognised or accepted common objectives, regardless of whether this is to be on a European or other regional basis, or on a world wide basis, and regardless of whether it is to be achieved by intergovernmental or by supranational machinery. He also indicates the objective effects on domestic problems of the fact of interdependence and the interaction between the two.

In this process he draws up what to my mind is a very useful distinction between two ideal types of states, those which are out for " real gains " and those which are primarily concerned to cut a dash in international affairs, for whom bella figura is the most important aspect. I agree that this is a useful distinction but, of course, there is a twofold difficulty here. First of all, as he himself recognises, states tend to move from one category to another, sometimes in response to real changes in their effective strength, whether it is economic or military or political, sometimes in response to what they conceive to be, rightly or wrongly, a change in their strength. This imposes

---

1. A few days after the Conference, Sir Eric Roll was appointed to a life peerage under the title Lord Roll of Ipsden.

a certain limitation and makes it difficult to speak of any fixed pattern which would enable one to predict in advance how France will react or Italy will react or the United Kingdom will react: they may move from one category to another. And the second point—which perhaps he doesn't bring out so strongly in his paper, although he did refer to it this morning—is that there is often a very great difference between what one could analyse as the objective interest of a country in any given situation and the subjective picture in the minds of politicians, administrators, bureaucrats and so on, of what the real interests are at any one time. If I may just for a moment follow Egidio Ortona's example and be a little personal: if I look back on my own involvement in many international exercises and negotiations, I am filled with a mixture of amazement, shame, and perhaps sheer hilariousness over some of the points on which I did battle, often all through the night, on the instructions of my government and the total insignificance of the result when I look back upon it. All of us around this table will have had that experience, and this seems to be a subject worthy of further analysis in the light of the pattern laid down by Stanley Hoffmann.

So, as a result of this movement of states from one category to another and of the different conceptions they sometimes have of their real interests and of what it is they have to fight for or not fight for, we have in these last thirty years been dancing a sort of infernal square dance in which positions have been changing, partners have been changing, and never have we had the opportunity really to get together on a common programme. In this regard, certainly as far as the Marshall Plan, its *sequelae*, and Europe are concerned, the two principal culprits undoubtedly are the United Kingdom and France. And since confession is good for the soul, I am quite willing to say *mea culpa* on behalf of the British element in all this and to admit, for example, that in connection with the Marshall Plan and in connection with the early negotiations for the coal and steel community, we were thoroughly misguided, not only about the ultimate objectives of policy (on which anybody can be excused for not being clear) but on what our real interests were. Lord Franks, in his paper, has drawn attention to the difference in conception between inter-governmental and supra-national or supra-governmental machinery right at the beginning of the Marshall Plan. And very properly he didn't go far in analysing or assigning blame, but there is no doubt when you look back—and I admit it readily and I hope my French friends will be equally outspoken—I readily confess that we were wrong. The British were wrong in resisting to the extent we did the attempts to introduce more inter-governmental supra-national machinery, more power for the Secretariat of the OEEC, and so on, and the French were on the whole more correct in their assessment at that time. Of course that situation didn't last very long, and the period of 1958-69 is perhaps one in which our French friends might equally say *mea culpa* as far as European development is concerned.

Nevertheless, to revert to the Marshall Plan, it did succeed, though admittedly it didn't even get as far as a customs union, as Robert Marjolin reminded us yesterday, and it took the whole apparatus of the Treaty of Rome and setting up the European Economic Community to bring about a customs union. That is, perhaps, apart from the agricultural policy on which one may have different views, its only lasting achievement, as he again reminded us yesterday. It took a very long time to bring even that about, and that is not strictly a supranational matter at all, as again he told us yesterday. There is an enormous difference between a customs union and a monetary and economic union. The *légèreté* with which people speak of monetary and economic union deserves to be properly branded as such. Why, nevertheless did the Marshall Plan succeed even if it wasn't as seminal as it might have been. Stanley Hoffmann said yesterday that it succeeded because we had a common enemy and now we do not. He was immediately contradicted by Miriam Camps, who drew attention to at least one problem, namely energy, and Oliver Franks mentioned various others in his paper; and also by Giovanni Malagodi who made, I think, an extremely important intervention on that particular point when he spoke about the reaction of industrialised countries to the oil revolution—this quadrupling and later quintupling of the oil price—and the developments in the financial markets as a result of that. I think on that point future historians will write one of the most ignoble pages in the history of the industrialised countries of the world. By that I don't mean that we should have " ganged up ," not only because even had that been possible it would have been self-defeating, since I happen to believe that some change in the relation between the raw material producing and the industrialised countries was long overdue, more particularly as far as the oil producing countries are concerned. I hold this view because I believe that this problem required as large an act of imagination as the Marshall Plan did to produce something in the nature of a common policy, which would also have had very important effects in avoiding some of the problems that have arisen in the international financial sphere.

If I may again be slightly reminiscent, I did approach some of our authorities in the United Kingdom (obviously I addressed myself to the wrong department of state because I got a raspberry for an answer), suggesting that perhaps this was a case for a Marshall Plan type concept to bring together the requirements for development and investment of the oil-producing countries and of the industrialised countries for energy. I still believe that a great opportunity was missed here. I want to draw your attention also to the fact that the then Secretary of State, Henry Kissinger, at a dinner in London at which I was present, openly invited the industrialised countries to join with the United States in an attempt of that kind. That was not taken up, and I dare say Stanley Hoffmann's paper gives us the explanation of why it wasn't taken up. It was because the different states concerned took very different views of what they could achieve on their own and what their real interests were. We have managed to survive this period. The Euromarkets have managed to produce the recycling that was necessary, but with what lasting consequences remains to be seen. When you add to the problem created by the oil surpluses the horrendous figures that Professor Portes mentioned this morning on the indebtedness of the Eastern bloc, the financial future seems quite obscure.

I may remind you that somebody drew attention (I think it was Malagodi yesterday) to the 1930s in that regard, and to Keynes. If you look up the *Treatise on Money* to see what Keynes had to say about what was at that time called the international short loan fund, what we nowadays would call the Euromarket, he spoke of it having achieved what then seamed the enormous figure of one billion dollars. This is now estimated at three hundred billion, or more. The problem to which Keynes drew attention is still there, and I don't think the industrialised Western democracies have shown themselves particularly apt in dealing with it.

Another common enemy, if you like, is one to which Erik Brofoss has drawn attention, and that is the large volume of unemployment. I don't want to go into that since there are all kinds of problems of analysis in assessing what it means and whether it is going to continue; but it is undoubtedly, a very serious problem—particularly the unemployment of young people, to which the Summit Conference recently drew attention. If you recall the period of the 1920s and 1930s, this is a problem which should also give one pause, because any prolonged unemployment of the young will produce social and political consequences which, if not irreversible, certainly will be reversible only over a considerable period of time and the full consequences of which we can't quite gauge at the moment. Well, in Lenin's words, "What is to be done?" Stanley Hoffmann has given us some remedies. I hope he won't mind if I say that in the light of his diagnosis, the remedies don't quite measure up to the maladies; but I haven't anything better to suggest myself and I think this is a case of (as they used to say in Western saloons): "don't shoot the pianist; he is doing his best." What he has said is probably all that can be said at this stage. I don't know whether this infernal quadrille which we have been dancing will come to an end, or whether it will forever be a case of Browning's "Never the time and the place and the loved one altogether," but I feel that what he has proposed, basing himself on Marina Whitman and others, is probably the best we can do. The biblical injunction, "Weary not in well doing!" is the only advice we can give our statesmen.

Maybe the greater involvement of those who analyse, who write about these matters in actual affairs, which is a relatively new phenomenon in international matters, will be of some help. It hasn't very notably helped yet and the presence of economists, I regret to say, in the councils of government has not been a notable success in avoiding the problems of stagflation. But their presence is a new phenomenon both in international matters and in domestic policy and perhaps in the end it will produce some results.

211

4

SUMMARY OF THE DISCUSSION

The general discussion was limited to brief interventions, owing to the shortage of time. One speaker noted the close connection between Professor Hoffmann's analysis of relationships between internal economic policies and domestic political pressures and Professor Lindbeck's emphasis on the ways in which increasingly ambitious domestic policy goals affect the international transmission of economic conditions (inflation, unemployment, etc.). He also called attention to an additional aspect of shifting attitudes in industrial societies, namely an increasingly widespread resistance to change of all sorts. Thus there is resistance by industrial employees to new technologies; labor resistance to changing jobs or to changing the location of work; resistance on environmental grounds to many kinds of change, including some alternative forms of energy supplies; and resistance to alterations in geographical and architectural urban patterns. All this creates a kind of straitjacket of resistance to every type of specific change but one, to which there is no resistance at all: i.e., growth in real incomes.

In his view, however, the policy conclusions should not take the form of increased protectionism, or an effort to confine policy to macroeconomic measures. Selective measures are also needed, but they should be designed to fit with international integration and interdependence. He felt somewhat more optimistic than Professor Hoffmann on these possibilities because of the underlying convergence of interests. For example, the disproportionately rapid economic expansion in countries with strong basic economies, but experiencing temporary stagnation or slow growth, would be of benefit to them as well as to their partners. Measures to add flexibility to the labor market and to help people shift from declining into growing industries are to everyone's benefit. The same is true of investments in energy production and conservation and in other sectors where bottlenecks might impede the next wave of general economic growth. What is needed is to set higher sights for international policy cooperation, based on these underlying harmonies. The international division of labor remains a valid concept, and national actions conflicting with it are contrary to national as well as global interests. To secure better understanding of these issues by publics-at-large and by politicians is the task of economists and of political leaders.

Another speaker, while acknowledging that the road to interdependence is long and difficult, felt that the industrial world—and, indeed, mankind as a whole—really has no choice. He saw an irreversible process moving toward global unity, a process which might be delayed but could not be destroyed. The choice lies between an organized process of managed interdependence, or chaos. The vulnerability of interdependence should be reduced by building the international dimension more effectively into national management. Some of the arrangements within the European Community recognized this principle of reducing vulnerability. For example, since it was anticipated that free trade might be disadvantageous to some peripheral regions, deliberate measures to counterbalance those effects had been provided in the regional development policies, without sacrificing the goal of interdependence. He believed that further progress in European integration was still possible by small steps, recognizing that the time is not now propitious for great leaps forward.

A third speaker, referring to Professor Hoffmann's observations on bureaucratic resistance to interdependence, pointed out that bureaucratic forces can work in both directions. In his view, the bureaucracies in foreign offices and in trade ministries often favor interdependence for bureaucratic as well as policy reasons.

A fourth speaker suggested that the list of " common enemies " which call for international cooperation could well have global poverty added to it. He called for political leaders to act more like " statesmen " in pointing out to their publics the wide gains from interdependence to their societies, helping to overcome pressures from narrow, adversely affected interests.

Professor Hoffmann, in a very brief reply, suggested that leaders who assume the mantle of " statesmanship " often resort to the historically proven tenets of nationalism, which may be an easier solvent for domestic conflicts than interdependence. That has certainly been the road chosen by many leaders in newly independent nations. By the same token, he felt that the fact that mankind may face a choice between organized interdependence and nationalist chaos does not itself guarantee that chaos may not come out on top. The shortsightedness of nationalist politicians is all too apparent—a problem which poses the dilemma of either concentrating on weak and tepid remedies, because they alone seem feasible, or looking for grand Utopian designs, which would solve everything but have no prospect of realization. But that *is* the dilemma faced today by the industrialized nations.

213

5

CONCLUDING OBSERVATIONS

by Mr. Robert Marjolin, Conference Co-Chairman [1]

It is clearly impossible to pull together in a few words the conclusions of a conference such as ours during these two days, with their great scope and variety. It is even less possible to do justice individually to each of the participants: authors of papers, commentators, and discussants; but I thank them collectively for the important contribution they have all made to these discussions.

I will limit myself to a few closing remarks. I apologize in advance given the shortage of time, for the summary character of these remarks—without nuance, peremptory, and perhaps a bit severe.

A first observation that emerges clearly is the extremely positive character of what I will call " the Marshall Plan, " summarizing in that term a great variety of things. The Marshall Plan was the starting point, for Western Europe especially and for other countries as well—for Japan a little later—of twenty-five years of extraordinary prosperity, such as the capitalist world had never known before.

Can one give credit for this extraordinary success to the Marshall Plan alone? It would be very bold to say so. It is probable, in reality, that had there not been a Marshall Plan, Europe would have recovered just the same, but she would have rebuilt more slowly, with great difficulty and probably within a different economic and political framework.

I will therefore characterize the Marshall Plan, as was done at last night's dinner, as an extraordinary combination of lucidity and generosity on the part of the American people with solidarity and self-help on the side of Europe.

My second remark concerns present or future proposals that might try to copy the Marshall Plan. There was only *one* Marshall Plan. There will never be another, because the Marshall Plan sprang from historically determined, special circumstances, which will never be repeated as such. In particular, when I examine the North-South problem—the problem of development of the still underdeveloped countries—it is not a Marshall Plan

---

1. Translated from the French original.

214

that is needed; it is something else, a different combination of ideas and actions.

The Marshall Plan consisted of returning to motion a European economy which had been paralyzed but which continued to exist, notably possessing a well-educated population, highly qualified from the technical standpoint. The development of underdeveloped countries is someting quite different; it requires the building of industry and creation of a body of skilled manpower which in essence does not yet exist.

My third remark is to state that the West—since for all practical purposes the OECD is the West, even if one includes several countries which are not geographically located there—faces today a new challenge, both less dramatic and much more difficult to confront than the one we dealt with thirty years ago. The problem is less dramatic because no one is suffering as Europeans suffered on the morrow of the war; but at the same time more difficult because there took place all of a sudden, in 1973-74, in circumstances still poorly understood, a rupture in the economic history of the world—the replacement of a virtuous circle by what I would call a vicious circle.

The virtuous circle was the combination of economic growth with full employment, relative price stability, and the absence of major difficulties in the balance of payments. Today, in many countries, there are simultaneously economic stagnation, unemployment, inflation, and substantial deficits in the external accounts.

I am not sure that we are able today to deal with these problems, even on the intellectual plane. In addition, the situation has been worsened by a profound deterioration in the political climate of most European countries.

What I find striking is the diminution of governmental authority in practically all countries, at least in the more important European countries. Not only are the problems very difficult, but governments rarely have the strength to confront them; the public support which they used to enjoy a few years back is now too often lacking.

Today, if elections were held all over Europe at the same time, it is probable that, at least in the four most important countries—France, Italy, Britain, and Germany—governments would either be swept out of office or greatly weakened. This is not a matter of ideological reaction. In Germany and Britain, governments leaning toward the left would lose power; in France, a relatively conservative coalition would lose; the Christian Democrats would probably be set back in Italy.

We evidently face a vicious circle. Governments are unable to deal with the economic difficulties, and the persistence of those difficulties is further weakening the governments.

How to break out of that circle? I honestly do not know. It will take a great deal of intelligence and a total absence of dogmatism. To all these problems, one must add another: that of the developing countries, which can no longer be evaded and for which our governments have still not found an answer, assuming that they are really seeking one.

It is customary to close this kind of conference on an optimistic note, but I shall not do so. I will say simply that we need all the efforts we can muster to keep the difficulties from getting worse. I am reminded of an episode from *Alice in Wonderland* (or is it from *Through the Looking Glass?*). Alice meets the Red Queen, who takes her by the hand and starts to run very quickly, until Alice loses her breath and stops. The Red Queen says, as I recall: " You see, this is an amazing country. You have to run with all your strength just to stay in the same place; and if you want to move forward you have to run at least twice as fast. "

I fear that the world in which we live may be rather like Alice's Wonderland.

I have nothing more to say. Let me simply end these remarks by thanking Mr. van Lennep, his colleagues, and the entire OECD staff for the admirable fashion in which they have organized these two days. Without them, the conference could not have taken place, so I express appreciation on behalf of all the participants. (Applause.)

VII

REFLECTIONS ON THE MARSHALL PLAN AND GLOBAL INTERDEPENDENCE

1

ADDRESS

by Jonkheer Emile van Lennep,
Secretary-General
of the Organisation for Economic Co-operation and Development,
at the Marshall Plan Commemoration Dinner, Château de la Muette, Paris,
June 2, 1977

It gives me great pleasure to welcome you all here this evening at the Château de la Muette. It is a distinct honour for the OECD, and for me personally, to be able to greet such a distinguished gathering. And your presence here this evening is a most fitting tribute to General Marshall.

There are many people in this room who knew Secretary of State Marshall well, and who were very much part of the operation of his Plan. There are also many of you who were intimately involved in the implementation of national policies that resulted from the Marshall Plan. It is also most gratifying to see the " newer " Members of OECD, if you will allow me to describe you in this way, so well represented here this evening. Tonight we have, I think, the rather special opportunity to honour the 30th Anniversary of the speech of General Marshall. Just as in June 1947, we are today at a critical moment in the evolution of our industrialized, market-oriented, free nations and—to emphasize an important new dimension—in their relations with the rest of the world.

In a very real sense, General Marshall's speech that day at Harvard was a Declaration of Interdependence by the United States of America. To those of us in devastated Europe, such a concept could hardly be grasped at that time—only our dependence was evident. Yet, already in 1947, General Marshall recognised America's interdependence with Europe and set in train the programme of assistance which, indeed, brought great mutual benefit.

The intervening years have not been free of turbulence. With all the crises that we faced, we nevertheless experienced a growing awareness of our interdependence, and, especially here in Europe, undertook major initiatives to accelerate the processes by which our societies were, and still are, intermeshing. Your papers and comments today have raised questions about the processes—have they gone too far? Are governments intervening unilaterally to thwart them? Would it be realistic to imagine, in Professor Lindbeck's words, " strongly centralised, government-operated national economies, in economic warfare with each other? "

The malaise underlying these questions points up the timeliness of your meeting. The dangers for the United States and for the world order as a whole inherent in the prostrate state of the economy of Europe in 1947 were the genesis of General Marshall's " Declaration of Interdependence ". And now we face new dangers. What can we do about the serious unemployment and the inflation, and huge balance of payments imbalances? The last few years have shown only too clearly how vulnerable the world economy is to sharp fluctuations in demand and supply. The phenomenon of interdependence is not limited to the relations amongst OECD countries but also to our relations with the developing world and its special problems. In this latter case, an important new aspect is the growing number of developing countries emerging as important exporters through rapid industrial development. However, the most critical issue we and the developing countries should tackle together is the persistent and frightful poverty of hundreds of millions of people whose urgent, basic needs are simply not being met.

There is no turning back from the processes of interdependence. What is required is renewed commitment to far-sighted policies of co-operation, as the Marshall Plan epitomised in its day, to make our interdependent global system work more effectively. Interdependence calls for co-operation. Increased interdependence demands increased co-operation. In seeking to deepen interdependence, we are seeking to minimise vulnerabilities, to reduce uncertainties and to provide a stable basis on which to build the world economy.

Reduction of vulnerabilities and uncertainties can only be achieved by common agreement on a predictable development path, and on concerted policies. These will not simply emerge of their own accord: we shall have to make up our minds that certain aspects of international life can only be sustained on the basis of a co-operative approach. Domestic economic policies can no longer be considered as a separate method from those of the international scene. Interdependence means that domestic and international policies must interlock in a coherent and sustainable formula for stability and progress.

*
* *

[The following passages are translated from the French original—*Editor*.]

The results of the Marshall Plan constituted one of the greatest successes in the history of international cooperation. The reason was that General Marshall gave to Europe the opportunity for recapturing control of its own

218

destiny and taking the difficult decisions which its future demanded. In this respect, the Marshall Plan was genuinely innovative. New methods of cooperation were worked out at the OEEC. That cooperation resulted from close consultation among the makers of policy, working together on the basis of a common evaluation of the facts. This process of working together, looking toward joint action, was the essential element in the success of that undertaking. The recipe for that success, orginating in the OEEC, continues to function in full force at the OECD today. We have carried on with the task and, in my view, made some improvements in the traditional methods, but we must not let ourselves become complacent. We must remain constantly ready to respond to new developments in events and in the environment. The need for innovation remains.

When our governments work together to find a joint consensus on how to deal with the difficult economic problems of these times, each must do so on the basis of a solid national consensus. Beyond what each government must do to achieve that consensus, it is also essential to intensify the interactions among our societies, so that problems will be understood and solutions set in motion with intelligence and realism within the inter-governmental framework. It falls to our Organization increasingly to find ways of responding to these new requirements for international cooperation. The presence this evening of a number of members of parliament from various countries underscores their interest in the problems of interdependence and their implications.

On our side, in the OECD, I believe that we must study carefully ways of securing more active involvement of parliamentarians from our twenty-four member countries in the issues which concern us within the framework of this Organization.

Your Excellencies, Ladies and Gentlemen: the Château de la Muette has been the scene of numerous memorable events. Many of you will have noticed in the hall the bronze plaques which commemorate the tenth anniversary of General Marshall's Harvard speech. Our conference these days will, I believe, leave behind the imprint of your contribution toward a new vision of international cooperation, bringing together all nations for active participation in the management of our global system.

2

ADDRESS

of Mr. Robert Boulin,
French Minister of Economy and Finance,
at the Marshall Plan Commemoration Dinner, Château de la Muette, Paris,
June 2, 1977

Prime Minister Raymond Barre, whose official duties have made it impossible for him to attend this dinner, has asked me to express his regrets and to say a few words in his place.

It should first be emphasized that it is very rare for any economic events to have their anniversaries celebrated. When memories last as long as the thirtieth anniversary, they must be very special events indeed. If so many countries, notwithstanding this natural tendency to forgetfulness, have felt it desirable to come together on the occasion of this present anniversary, that is because the beneficiaries of the Marshall Plan recognize that it was a most exceptional success.

The new economic difficulties which are presently challenging us help recall to our minds the manner in which the Marshall Plan was able to set countries, destroyed by the war, on the road to a long period of prosperity. We are also led to inquire once again what were the real causes of its success. For my part, I see two major ones:

First was the combining of two wills: the readiness of the United States, then enjoying unrivaled strength, to bring assistance to a less fortunate group of countries was matched by the determination of this latter group to dedicate all their energies to their own reconstruction. It does not disparage the scope of the American action to declare that the success did not flow solely from American aid, but rather from the combination of aid and self-help.

The second cause was the way in which the effort was organized. The United States had made it a condition of their help that a joint program be worked out by the beneficiary countries. By leading the European nations to ensure the coherence of their program, the U.S. helped lay the foundations for a new type of growth. What was undertaken was not the reconstruction of the old and compartmentalized national economies; it was directed to a single economy, already European in scope.

220

The Marshall Plan also set in motion a movement which has never since been halted: creation of the OEEC, and later of the OECD, which started a form of cooperation which is being constantly reinforced and which now extends far beyond the merely economic domain.

The same causes which yesterday led to the success of the Marshall Plan are, in my view, the necessary conditions today for new successes.

First, with respect to our own problems, the persistence of inflation and of external disequilibrium weighs heavily, as we all know, on growth and levels of employment. The experience of the past thirty years shows us clearly that the way to cure these problems does not lie in turning inwards on ourselves or reviving protectionism; it lies rather in pursuing our cooperation and our openness to the outside world. Experience also demonstrates that such cooperation is not truly effective if it simply consists of leaning on one's neighbors; it must be complemented by measures of domestic reform.

Turning to the developing countries, even if the condition of our economies is not as firm today as a few years ago, we must keep in mind our duty of solidarity with the developing world. The Marshall Plan showed us that the development of one group necessarily helps the development of others. The interests of the industrialized countries, just as much as those of the developing countries, call for the establishment of those arrangements required for organized growth.

However, just as European reconstruction was made possible by the self-help of the European countries, so the development of the poor countries will depend in large measure on their own efforts. It would be an illusion to believe in the effectiveness of arrangements seeking to place the entire responsibility on the industrialized countries.

Ladies and Gentlemen: the lesson of the Marshall Plan remains valid today. An alliance between generosity and self-help, in my opinion, is the only means which can lead the countries of the world as a whole into a new phase of development.

3

ADDRESS

of Mr. Warren Christopher,
Deputy Secretary of State of the United States,
at the Marshall Plan Commemoration Dinner,
Château de la Muette, Paris, June 2, 1977

It is a pleasure to participate this evening in a ceremony that honors both the memory of a great man, General George Marshall, and the monument he built, the first successful attempt at broad-based European economic cooperation.

As I begin, however, I would like to bring you a personal message from President Carter. It reads as follows:

" Thirty years ago one of our greatest statesmen, George Catlett Marshall, spoke to an audience of graduating students at Harvard University of the condition of Europe in the wake of war. World War II had brought devastation upon Europe, he said, yet the " physical destruction was probably less serious than the dislocation of the entire European economy. " In bold, generous, and practical terms he proposed a cooperative European effort, in which the United States would participate, to rebuild the European economy laid waste by the war. " Our policy, " he said, " is directed not against any country or doctrine but against hunger, poverty, desperation, and chaos. Its purpose should be the revival of a working economy in the world so as to permit the emergence of political and social conditions in which free institutions can exist. "

" Like George Marshall and his co-workers, this Conference is appropriately focused on building for the future. Rather than merely commemorating the Marshall Plan, great as it was, you are discussing future relations among the industrialized democracies of the OECD and their future relations with both the developing nations and the Eastern countries. I am sure that your deliberations will provide valuable insights for all of us who are concerned about our future relations with the rest of the world.

" I send my personal greetings to each of you participating in the Conference and my warmest thanks to all those who helped organize it. "

Jimmy Carter

World War II shattered the European economy and shook European societies to their very foundations. Then came the cold and cruel winter of 1946-47. The bleak outlook for economic recovery in Europe worsened. Resources, finances, and confidence were exhausted. Fear abounded—fear of the Soviet Union, of revolution from within, of collapse.

This was the context in which Secretary Marshall made his proposal. It sounded modest—at the core were just six sentences in the entire speech. Only one of those sentences addressed itself to American action. The initiative, he emphasized, had to come from Europe. Despite its simplicity, the Marshall Plan became the basis for a leap into the future: a radical transformation of Western institutions, Western ways of thought, and Western cooperation.

Marshall's idea was effective because it brought about the recognition of common solutions to what everyone agreed were common problems. The piecemeal efforts of individual states became the great cooperative enterprise of a Western community of nations.

— Together we built the North Atlantic Alliance. In time of tension, it has protected us from foreign aggression. The Carter Administration has already given evidence of our commitment to strengthen the Alliance. President Carters' first budget contained an increased defense contribution to NATO of over one-half billion dollars. The President has also reconfirmed our commitment to a strategy of flexible response and forward defense.

— The European Community grew out of Europe's economic recovery —first as an economic union, now also as a political force in world affairs. In his speech at the NATO Summit, the President expressed strong United States support for progress toward Western European unification and the expanding role of the European Community.

— The OECD—the host organization for this Conference—is a direct outgrowth of the Marshall Plan. With the membership of the Organization for European Economic Cooperation expanded to include the United States and Canada, plus Finland, and the Pacific Nations of Japan, Australia, and New Zealand, the OECD has become the locus of our ongoing cooperation on the full range of economic policy issues.

But the institutions are only part of the story. Historic and positive changes have taken place around the world in the wake of the Marshall Plan:

— The industrial democracies have created a liberal trading and financial system. It is now under stress, but it has worked remarkably well for thirty years, and it was built to last. Today the industrial democracies are responsible for 65 per cent of the world's production and 70 per cent of its trade.

— The internecine rivalries of Western Europe which led to two world wars in this century have vanished; in their place is a deep and durable abhorrence of force as a solution to problems.

— Western Europe has developed genuinely free societies. Today, for the first time in history, all the countries of Western Europe are democracies.

— We in North America share with the nations of Europe a deep commitment to human rights. We stand for freedom in the world, and the cause of human rights in other countries is our shared concern.

— Our technology, our products, and our investment capital have been a major factor in the development of poorer nations. And we have maintained the political will to assist development, even when our own economies have been under strain. Since 1960, OECD countries have contributed more than $ 125 billion in assistance to developing countries.

Today we are strong in common ways and, because of interdependence, vulnerable in common ways. Our situation now is not so much that of strong nations coming to the aid of those in need as that of partners in a common enterprise. We can face our problems and weaknesses with the same resilience, optimism, and practicality that informed the vision of the builders of post-war Europe.

II

The world has changed since 1947, but the Marshall Plan holds lessons for us today. Thirty years ago, in adversity, the family of nations that constitutes the West reached out to one another. Those that could offer aid helped those in need.

Since then, the family of nations in close relation with one another has multiplied in numbers, and grown diverse. So have the problems that entangle us.

Within that growing family of nations, there is much that we now ask of each other. The most direct questions, of course, are how the world can be made to prosper, how the wealth of nations should be shared, and how our resources should be managed for the common good.

As we work out the answers, our first responsibility is to think in terms of people, not categories of nations. It is poor people—everywhere—not just poor nations, whose aspirations and needs cut straight across conventional national borders and conventional wisdom. And those needs are both compelling and immediate.

Echoing one of Franklin Roosevelt's Four Freedoms—" Freedom from want "—Secretary Vance spoke at the University of Georgia of a category of human rights which is central to United States' policy. He spoke of " the right to food, shelter, health care, and education. We recognize, " he said, " that the fulfillment of this right will depend, in part, upon the stage of a nation's economic development. "

Again, at the Conference on International Economic Cooperation here in Paris this week, our government pledged to work for the betterment of the human condition in basic economic terms. We pledged cooperation and aid but stressed that, as Secretary Vance put it, " We will join with you in sharing the responsibility to lead. "

Understanding the shared responsibility to lead was the balance wheel of the Marshall Plan. As General Marshall said in his speech in 1947, " It

224

would be neither fitting nor efficacious " for us to draw up a program to put Europe on its feet. That, he said, is the " business of the Europeans. "

In 1947, the European countries organized, not as supplicants, but as managers of their own fortunes, with the aid and cooperation of others. That productive and meaningful relationship can now be a model for a comparably practical and compassionate relationship in the growing family of nations.

Today it is the business of the developing countries to come to practical terms not only with the industrialized world, but with themselves, separately and together. Only they can ensure the effectivenes of any economic endeavor in which we in the West participate. The countries of the developing world must move, as European nations did thirty years ago, to put their own economic houses in order. Equally urgent is that they perceive that the problem is not " us " against " them, " " poor " against " rich. " Rather, the problem is poverty, and policy, as Marshall said, must be directed " not against any country or doctrine but against hunger, poverty, desperation, and chaos. "

In 1947, we in the West still hoped that the wartime Alliance with the Soviet Union was not altogether shattered. In good faith, we extended the invitation to participate in the Marshall Plan to the nations of Eastern Europe. For a moment it seemed possible that some would accept, but East-West tensions were on the rise, and the opportunity for an all-embracing effort to achieve European recovery was lost.

Today, when we are pursuing improved East-West relations in the spirit of détente, the need for the industrialized Communist countries to join us in our support for development in the Third World—to abandon the role of spectator or spoiler and join the North-South dialogue—is clear. We would welcome these nations in joining with us to demonstrate that they share our concern about absolute poverty and care about the needs of people.

III

The Marshall Plan was conceived to meet human needs in order to build a more secure world. We joined together to define security in the broadest sense—not just in terms of armaments, but in terms of economic strength and justice, and in a spirit of confidence in the future. We understood that no amount of armaments by themselves could prevent fatal cracks in an empty shell. We made the distinction between real security and false security.

These lessons of the Marshall Plan apply today. While maintaining our military strength, we are working together to strengthen our fundamental economic relationships. It should be at the root of our common concern that the developing nations come to see their security in the broadest sense —and that they not unreasonably divert scarce resources to armaments.

The danger the proliferation of arms poses for global stability is increasingly well understood. It is perhaps less well understood how great a drain arms purchases are on the budgets of developing countries—and thus, on people in deepest poverty. Over the past ten years developing countries have steadily increased their military expenditures. In 1975 they were 6.1

225

per cent of annual gross national product, proportionately more than developed countries spend.

In the 1970's, arms transfers to sub-Saharan Africa have been, on an annual basis, six times what they were in the 1960's. For the Middle East and North Africa the increase was eight-fold. Over and over again, poor people, living on the edge of starvation, are forced to bear the cost of weapon systems their leaders buy because of false pride or foolish competition, or in the mistaken notion that arms alone make us strong.

Today we know that even military security—in the narrowest sense—is dependent on international arms control as well as on the strength of our arms. And so we in the United States and you in Western Europe have been reaching out to the Soviet Union in efforts to build security through the reduction of arms. In close consultation with our allies, we in the United States Government are conducting a range of arms control negotiations with the Soviet Union to reduce strategic nuclear armaments, to stop nuclear explosions, and to prevent the arms buildup in the Indian Ocean.

President Carter has acted to meet the United States' own obligation to bring conventional arms transfers under control. While recognizing that some conventional arms transfers are necessary for stability, the President has concluded that we will now view arms transfers as an exceptional foreign policy instrument. As he put it, " The burden of persuasion will be on those who favor a particular arms sale, rather than those who oppose it. " The United States will:

— Reduce in the next fiscal year the dollar volume of new commitments for arms sales and assistance;
— Refrain from being the first supplier to introduce into a region newly developed advanced weapons systems;
— Refrain from developing or modifying advanced weapons systems solely for export; and
— Tighten restrictions against transfer of weapons to third parties.

These steps we will take unilaterally. But the cooperation of our industrialized allies will be needed to achieve reductions in the world-wide arms build-up. And, as we did at the time of the Marshall Plan, we call upon the Soviet Union and other Eastern European countries to join with the West in this resolve. We dare to hope that their response will be different, now, from what it was then.

The United States accepts the responsibility of going first, but it would be not only ironic but tragic if other nations were to react to the discipline we are imposing on ourselves by filling the orders we decline. As we did in 1947, we look toward Western Europe for the cooperation needed to achieve real security for us all.

Further, and finally, we who have been made strong by the Marshall Plan must now apply the lessons of thirty years ago by nurturing a relationship of true common purpose with the developing world. To do so would be the most fitting commemoration of an idea—and a man—that can truly be said to have shaped the future of post-war Europe.

226

VIII

ANNEX

SECRETARY OF STATE GEORGE C. MARSHALL'S ADDRESS

at the Commencement Exercises of Harvard University, Cambridge,
Massachusetts, June 5, 1947

I need not tell you that the world situation is very serious. That must be apparent to all intelligent people. I think one difficulty is that the problem is one of such enormous complexity that the very mass of facts presented to the public by press and radio make it exceedingly difficult for the man in the street to reach a clear appraisement of the situation. Furthermore, the people of this country are distant from the troubled areas of the earth and it is hard for them to comprehend the plight and consequent reactions of the long-suffering peoples, and the effect of those reactions on their governments in connection with our efforts to promote peace in the world.

In considering the requirements for the rehabilitation of Europe, the physical loss of life, the visible destruction of cities, factories, mines, and railroads was correctly estimated, but it has become obvious during recent months that this visible destruction was probably less serious than the dislocation of the entire fabric of European economy. For the past ten years conditions have been highly abnormal. The feverish preparation for war and the more feverish maintenance of the war effort engulfed all aspects of national economies. Machinery has fallen into disrepair or is entirely obsolete. Under the arbitrary and destructive Nazi rule, virtually every possible enterprise was geared into the German war machine. Long-standing commercial ties, private institutions, banks, insurance companies, and shipping companies disappeared, through loss of capital, absorption through nationalization, or by simple destruction. In many countries, confidence in the local currency has been severely shaken. The breakdown of the business structure of Europe during the war was complete. Recovery has been seriously retarded by the fact that two years after the close of hostilities a peace settlement with Germany and Austria has not been agreed upon. But even given a more prompt solution of these difficult problems, the rehabilitation of the economic structure of Europe quite evidently will require a much longer time and greater effort than had been foreseen.

There is a phase of this matter which is both interesting and serious. The farmer has always produced the foodstuffs to exchange with the city dweller for the other necessities of life. This division of labor is the basis of modern civilization. At the present time it is threatened with breakdown. The town and city industries are not producing adequate goods to exchange with the food-producing farmer. Raw materials and fuel are in short supply. Machinery is lacking or worn out. The farmer or the peasant cannot find the goods for sale which he desires to purchase. So the sale of his farm produce for money which he cannot use seems to him an unprofitable transaction. He, therefore, has withdrawn many fields from crop cultivation and is using them for grazing. He feeds more grain to stock and finds for himself and his family an ample supply of food, however short he may be on clothing and the other ordinary gadgets of civilization. Meanwhile people in the cities are short of food and fuel. So the governments are forced to use their foreign money and credits to procure these necessities abroad. This process exhausts funds which are urgently needed for reconstruction. Thus a very serious situation is rapidly developing which bodes no good for the world. The modern system of the division of labor upon which the exchange of products is based is in danger of breaking down.

The truth of the matter is that Europe's requirements for the next three or four years of foreign food and other essential products—principally from America— are so much greater than her present ability to pay that she must have substantial additional help or face economic, social, and political deterioration of a very grave character.

The remedy lies in breaking the vicious circle and restoring the confidence of the European people in the economic future of their own countries and of Europe as a whole. The manufacturer and the farmer throughout wide areas must be able and willing to exchange their product for currencies the continuing value of which is not open to question.

Aside from the demoralizing effect on the world at large and the possibilities of disturbances arising as a result of the desperation of the people concerned, the consequences to the economy of the United States should be apparent to all. It is logical that the United States should do whatever it is able to do to assist in the return of normal economic health in the world, without which there can be no political stability and no assured peace. Our policy is directed not against any country or doctrine but against hunger, poverty, desperation, and chaos. Its purpose should be the revival of a working economy in the world so as to permit the emergence of political and social conditions in which free institutions can exist. Such assistance, I am convinced, must not be on a piecemeal basis as various crises develop. Any assistance that this Government may render in the future should provide a cure rather than a mere palliative. Any government that is willing to assist in the task of recovery will find full cooperation, I am sure, on the part of the United States Government. Any government which maneuvers to block the recovery of other countries cannot expect help from us. Furthermore, governments, political parties, or groups which seek to perpetuate human misery in order to profit therefrom politically or otherwise will encounter the opposition of the United States.

It is already evident that, before the United States Government can proceed much further in its efforts to alleviate the situation and help start the European world on its way to recovery, there must be some agreement among the countries of Europe as to the requirements of the situation and the part those countries themselves will take in order to give proper effect to whatever action might be undertaken by this Government. It would be neither fitting nor efficacious for this Government to undertake to draw up unilaterally a program designed to place Europe on its feet economically. This is the business of the Europeans. The initiative, I think, must come from Europe. The role of this country should consist of friendly aid in the drafting of a European program and of later support of such a program so far as it may be practical for us to do so. The program should be a joint one, agreed to by a number, if not all, European nations.

An essential part of any successful action on the part of the United States is an understanding on the part of the people of America of the character of the problem and the remedies to be applied. Political passion and prejudice should have no part. With foresight, and a willingness on the part of our people to face up to the vast responsibility which history has clearly placed upon our country, the difficulties I have outlined can and will be overcome.

IX

AUTHORS, PANELISTS
AND CO-CHAIRMEN

Miriam CAMPS – United States –
Economist, author of numerous books, including *First World Relation-ships. The Role of the OECD*, Atlantic Papers No. 2, 1975.

W. Max CORDEN – Australia –
Professor of Economics at Australian National University.

Michel CROZIER – France –
French sociologist; founder of Centre for the Study of Organisations; author of several works on issues of structural change.

Peter DOBELL – Canada –
Director of Parliamentary Centre for Foreign Affairs and Foreign Trade, Ottawa.

Lord FRANKS – United Kingdom –
Chairman of the Committee on European Economic Co-operation, 1947, subsequently Ambassador of the United Kingdom to the United States, Chairman of Lloyds Bank Ltd., and Provost of Worcester College, Oxford.

Lincoln GORDON – United States –
Co-Chairman of Conference – a principal staff member of the U.S. Co-ordinating Mission in Europe for the Marshall Plan; subsequently headed the Marshall Plan Mission in London; former U.S. Ambassador and President of The Johns Hopkins University.

Stanley HOFFMANN – United States –
Professor of Government and Director of the Center for European Studies, Harvard University.

Attila KARAOSMANOGLU – Turkey –
Director of Development Policies in the World Bank.

Charles P. KINDLEBERGER – United States –
Ford International Professor of Economics Emeritus, Massachusetts Institute of Technology.

Peter KNIRSCH – Germany –
Professor at the Osteuropa-Institut, Free University of Berlin.

231

Anne KRUEGER – United States –
Professor of Economics, University of Minnesota.

Giorgio LA MALFA – Italy –
Member of Parliament; University Professor.

Assar LINDBECK – Sweden –
Professor of International Economics, Institute for International Economic Studies, Stockholm.

Robert MARJOLIN – France –
Co-Chairman of the Conference – First Secretary-General of the Organisation for European Economic Co-operation (predecessor of the OECD); later served as Vice-Chairman of the Commission of the European Economic Community; University Professor.

Thierry DE MONTBRIAL – France –
Professor; President of the Department of Economics at the Ecole Polytechnique; Head of the Centre d'Analyse et de Prévision auprès du Ministère des Affaires Étrangères.

Alex NOVE – United Kingdom –
Professor of Economics, Director of the Institute of Soviet and East European Studies at University of Glasgow.

Hideaki OKAMOTO – Japan –
Professor of Economics at University of Hosei, Japan; Visiting Professor of Economics at London School of Economics.

Egidio ORTONA – Italy –
Distinguished diplomatic career involving posts in London, Washington, United Nations; Chairman of Aeritalia.

Richard PORTES – United States –
Presently Professor of Economics at Birkbeck College, University of London; has taught also at Oxford and Princeton.

Sir Eric ROLL – United Kingdom –
Former British Civil Servant – Chairman of Programmes Committee, OEEC; presently Chairman of S. Warburg and Co., London Merchant Bankers.

André J. VLERICK – Belgium –
Economist; Politician; Former Minister for Regional Development ('68-72), Minister of Finance ('72-73).

David WATT – United Kingdom –
Political editor of the Financial Times.

X

LIST OF PARTICIPANTS[1]
other than Authors, Panelists and Co-Chairmen,
in the Marshall Plan Commemoration Conference,
Château de la Muette, Paris,
June 2-3, 1977

AUSTRALIA

His Excellency
Mr. F. P. DONOVAN

Head of the Australian
Delegation to the OECD
4, rue Jean-Rey
75724 Paris Cedex 15

Professor M. C. KEMP

Professor of Economics
New South Wales University
Australia
Presently Visiting Professor at Université de Paris Dauphine
Place Maréchal de Lattre-de-Tassigny
75116 Paris

Sir Ronald WALKER

1 rue de Longchamp
75116 Paris

AUSTRIA

Son Excellence
le Dr. Carl H. BOBLETER

Chef de la Délégation de l'Autriche
auprès de l'OCDE
3 rue Albéric-Magnard
75016 Paris

Vizekanzler a.D. Dr. Fritz BOCK

Creditanstalt-Bankverein
Schottengasse 6
A-1010 Wien

---

1. This list includes all those who attended the Conference, either in part or throughout.

Staatssekretär a.D. Hans BÜRKLE

Vorsitzender des Bundesrates
Dr. Karl Renner-Ring 3
A-1010 Wien

Dr. Hans KLOSS

Präsident der Osterreichischen
Nationalbank
Otto Wagnerplatz 3
A-1090 Wien

Universitätsprofessor Dr.
   Adolf NUSSBAUMER

Universität Wien
Dr. Karl Lueger-Ring 1
A-1010 Wien

Universitätsprofessor Dkfm.
   Hans SEIDEL

Leiter des Osterreichischen Institutes
für Wirtschaftsforschung
Schwindgasse 19
A-1040 Wien

BELGIUM

Son Excellence
M. August LONNOY

Chef de la Délégation de la Belgique
auprès de l'OCDE
12-14 rue Octave Feuillet
75016 Paris

Professeur Theo PEETERS

Centrum voor Economische Studien
van Evenstraat, 2B
B-3000 Leuven
Belgique

M. Jean REY

235 rue de la Loi
1040 Bruxelles
Belgique

M. Michel WOITRIN

Université Catholique de Louvain
Place de l'Université 1
B 1348 Louvain-la-Neuve
Belgique

DENMARK

His Excellency
Mr. Vagn Aage KORSBAEK

Head of the Danish Delegation to
the OECD
6 rue Jean-Richepin
75016 Paris

Dr. Jens Otto KRAG

Skodsborgparken 58
Skodsborg
DK 2942
Denmark

Mr. Jørgen SCHLEIMANN

Radiohuset-Danmarks Radio
1999 København V
Denmark

FINLAND

His Excellency
Mr. Paul GUSTAFSSON

Head of the Finnish Delegation to
the OECD
6 rue de Franqueville
75016 Paris

Mr. Max JAKOBSON

The Council of Economic Organizations in Finland
Eteläesplanadi 20
00130 Helsinki
Finland

Mr. Jan-Magnus JANSSON

Hufvudstabdsbladet
Mannerheimvägen 18
00100 Helsinki 10
Finland

FRANCE

Son Excellence
M. Jean-Marc BOEGNER
Ambassadeur de France

Chef de la Délégation de la France
auprès de l'OCDE
21 rue Octave-Feuillet
75016 Paris

M. Jean-Claude CASANOVA

Conseiller Technique
Cabinet du Premier Ministre
Hôtel Matignon
55 rue de Varenne
75007 Paris

M. Pierre CORTESSE

Directeur de la Prévision
Ministère de l'Économie et des Finances
6 avenue de l'Opéra
75056 Paris R.P.

235

M. Guillaume GUINDEY	Président Compagnie Internationale des Wagons- Lits et du Tourisme 69 boulevard Haussmann 75361 Paris Cedex 08
M. Pierre HUET	Conseiller d'État Conseil d'État Palais Royal 75001 Paris
M. René LARRE	Directeur Général Banque des Règlements Internationaux CH-4002 Bâle Switzerland
M. Pierre-Paul SCHWEITZER	Bank of America International 31 rue Danielle-Casanova 75001 Paris
M. Pierre URI	1 avenue Président Wilson 75116 Paris
Son Excellence M. Olivier WORMSER Ambassadeur de France	72 rue du Cherche-Midi 75006 Paris
M. Guy de CARMOY	22 avenue de Suffren 75015 Paris

GERMANY

Dr. Klaus von DOHNANYI	Staatsminister im Auswärtigen Amt Adenauerallee 99-103 5300 Bonn Germany
His Excellency Dr. Egon EMMEL	Head of the German Delegation to the OECD 5 rue Léonard de Vinci 75116 Paris
Mr. Alfred FRISCH	49 rue de la Victoire F-75009 Paris

Mrs. Inga HAAG

Secretary
Mid-Atlantic Club
1 Upper Wimpole Street
London W1
England

GREECE

Son Excellence
M. Dimitri ATHANASSOPOULOS

Chef de la Délégation de la Grèce
auprès de l'OCDE
15 Villa Saïd
75116 Paris

ICELAND

His Excellency
Mr. Einar BENEDIKTSSON

Head of the Icelandic Delegation to
the OECD
124 boulevard Haussmann
75008 Paris

Mr. David OLAFSSON

Governor
Central Bank of Iceland
Austurstraeti 11
101 Reykjavik
Iceland

IRELAND

His Excellency
Mr. Hugh McCANN

Head of the Irish Delegation to the
OECD
12 avenue Foch
75116 Paris

Mr. Robert McDONAGH

Secretary General
Department of Foreign Affairs
Dublin
Ireland

ITALY

Son Excellence
M. Luciano CONTI

Chef de la Délégation de l'Italie auprès
de l'OCDE
50 rue de Varenne
75007 Paris

Son Excellence
M. Luigi Michele GALLI

Sous-Secrétaire d'État au Ministère
du Commerce Extérieur
Rome

M. Emanuele GAZZO

Rédacteur en Chef
Agence EUROPE
10 boulevald St Lazare
1030 Bruxelles
Belgique

On. Dott. Giovanni F. MALAGODI

Président du Parti Libéral Italien
89 Via Frattina
00187 Rome

M. Vittorio SALLIER de la TOUR

Chargé des relations internationales
Société FIAT SPA
Turin

JAPAN

Mr. Keichi OSHIMA

Department of Nuclear Engineering
Faculty of Engineering
University of Tokyo
3-1, Hongo 7-chome
Bunkyo-ku
Tokyo
Japan

LUXEMBOURG

M. Georges ALS

Directeur du Service Central de la
Statistique et des Études Économiques
(STATEC)
Boîte Postale 304
Luxembourg

Son Excellence
M. Paul REUTER

Ambassadeur auprès de la République
Fédérale d'Allemagne
Ambassade de Luxembourg
Bonn-Center
D-5300 Bonn
Germany

NETHERLANDS

Mr. Jerome L. HELDRING

Nederlands Genootschap voor Internationale Zaken
Alexanderstraat 2
Den Haag
Netherlands

238

Mr. C. T. C. HEYNING	Unilever N.V. Burg. 's Jacobplein 1 Rotterdam Netherlands
Mr. D. U. STIKKER	Stoephout app. 66 Stoeplaan 11 Wassenaar Netherlands
His Excellency Mr. Klaas WESTERHOFF	Head of the Netherlands Delegation to the OECD 14 rue Octave Feuillet 75016 Paris

NEW ZEALAND

Hon. J. B. GORDON	Minister of Labour and Minister of State Services c/o New Zealand Delegation to the OECD 7 ter rue Léonard-de-Vinci 75116 Paris
His Excellency Mr. John G. McARTHUR	Head of the New Zealand Delegation to the OECD 7 ter rue Léonard-de-Vinci 75116 Paris
Rt. Hon. Sir John MARSHALL, P.C.	c/o New Zealand Delegation to the OECD 7 ter rue Léonard-de-Vinci 75116 Paris

NORWAY

His Excellency Mr. Jens M. BOYESEN	Head of the Norwegian Delegation to the OECD 19 rue de Franqueville 75016 Paris
Mr. Erik BROFOSS	Former Governor of the Norges Bank c/o Norges Bank P.B. 336, Sentrum Oslo 1 Norway

Mr. Eivind ERICHSEN

Secretary General
Finans departimintit
Oslo Dep
Oslo 1
Norway

Mr. Knut Getz WOLD

Gouverneur
Norges Bank
Bankplassen 4
Oslo 1
Norway

PORTUGAL

M. Francisco P. BALSEMAO

Editeur, ESPRESSO
Rua Duque Palmela – 37 – 2ºD
Lisboa
Portugal

Son Excellence
Manuel BELLO

Chef de la Délégation du Portugal
auprès de l'OCDE
26 rue Raffet
75016 Paris

Son Excellence
M. Ruy TEIXEIRA GUERRA

Rua de Angola 2
Paço de Arcos
Portugal

M. José da Silva LOPES

Gouverneur
Banco de Portugal

M. Alexandre VAZ PINTO

Président de la Société Financière Portugaise
Rua Duque de Palmela 30, 80, B
Lisboa
Portugal

SWEDEN

Dr. Göran ALBINSSON

Svenska Dabladet
S-105 17 Stockholm
Sweden

His Excellency
Mr. Hans COLLIANDER

Head of the Swedish Delegation to
the OECD
19 rue de Franqueville
75016 Paris

240

Mr. Bengt RABAEUS	Deputy Permanent Under Secretary of State Ministry of Foreign Affairs Stockholm Sweden
Mr. Erland WALDENSTROEM	c/o Graenges Fack S-10326 Stockholm Sweden

SWITZERLAND

M. Gérard BAUER	Président de la Fédération Horlogère Suisse Rue d'Argent 6 CH-2051 Bienne Suisse
Son Excellence M. Albert GRÜBEL	Chef de la Délégation de la Suisse auprès de l'OCDE 28 rue de Martignac 75007 Paris
Son Excellence M. Paul R. JOLLES	Directeur de la Division Fédérale du Commerce CH-3003 Berne Suisse
Professeur Aurelio MATTEI	Université de Lausanne Rue Vuillermet 5 CH-1005 Lausanne Suisse

TURKEY

His Excellency Mr. Memduh AYTÜR	Head of the Turkish Delegation to the OECD 184 boulevard Malesherbes 75017 Paris
His Excellency Mr. Muharrem Nuri BIRGI	c/o Ministry of Foreign Affairs Ankara Turkey

241

Sir Douglas ALLEN, G.C.B.

Chairman of the Economic Policy Committee of the OECD
9 Manor Way
South Croydon
Surrey
England (Private Address)

Sir Alec CAIRNCROSS, K.C.M.G.

St. Peter's College
Oxford OX12 2DL
England

Sir John FOSTER

2 Harecourt
Temple
London EC4V 7BM
England

Lady FRANKS

Blackhall Farm
Charlbury Road
Oxford
England

Mr. Thomas L. FRIEDMAN
(British Marshall Scholar)

Room 17
66 Woodstock Road
Oxford
England

Professor the Lord KALDOR

King's College
Cambridge CB2 1ST
England

Mr. Alexander KING

168 rue de Grenelle
75007 Paris

His Excellency
Mr. A. F. MADDOCKS, C.M.G.

Head of the United Kingdom Delegation to the OECD
19 rue de Franqueville
75016 Paris

Sir Derek MITCHELL, K.C.B.,
C.V.O.

9 Holmbush Road
Putney
London JW15 32E
England

Sir Eric ROLL, K.C.M.G., C.B.

c/o S.G. Warburg & Co. Ltd.
30 Gresham Street
London EC2P 2EB
England

Sir Frank ROBERTS, G.C.M.G., 25 Kensington Court Gardens
G.C.V.O. London W8 50F
England

Mr. C. Richard ROSS, C.B. Central Policy Review Staff
Cabinet Office
70 Whitehall
London SW1
England

The Rt. Hon. R. SHELDON, M.P. Financial Secretary
H.M. Treasury
London
England

Miss Kathleen M. SULLIVAN Wadham College
(British Marshall Scholar) Parks Road
Oxford OX1 3PN
England

UNITED STATES

The Honorable 151 East 79th Street
Thomas K. FINLETTER New York, N.Y. 10021
United States

Mr. Henry H. FOWLER c/o Goldman, Sachs & Co.
55 Broad Street
New York
N.Y. 10004
United States

Tne Honorable Fred L. HADSEL George C. Marshall Research Foun-
dation
Box 920
Lexington
Virginia 24450
United States

The Honorable Ambassador Designate to France
Arthur A. HARTMAN c/o State Department
Washington, D.C.

The Honorable Directeur Général
Martin J. HILLENBRAND Institut Atlantique des Affaires Internationales
120 rue de Longchamp
75116 Paris

243

The Honorable Jacob K. JAVITS	United States Senate Washington, D.C.
Mr. Stanley KARNOW	International Writers Service Room 208 1785 Massachusetts Av. N.W. Washington, D.C. 20036 United States
The Honorable Abraham KATZ	Acting Head of the United States Delegation to the OECD 19 rue de Franqueville 75016 Paris
Mr. Denis LAMB	Deputy Director Office of OECD, European Communities and Atlantic Political-Economic Affairs Department of State Washington, D.C.
The Honorable James G. LOWENSTEIN	Ambassador Designate to Luxembourg c/o Department of State Washington, D.C.
The Honorable Edwin M. MARTIN	Chairman, Consultative Group on Food Production and Investment in Developing Countries Room G1076 1818 H Street, N.W. Washington, D.C. 20433
The Honorable Nathaniel SAMUELS	Chairman Louis Dreyfus Holding Co. Inc. One State Street Plaza New York, New York 10004
The Honorable William C. TURNER	c/o United States Delegation to the OECD 19 rue de Franqueville 75116 Paris
Mr. Arthur HOFFMAN	Regional Economic Information Counsellor United States Mission to the European Communities 40 boulevard du Régent Brussels 1000 Belgium

244

YUGOSLAVIA

Son Excellence
M. Jozef KOROSEC

Chef de la Délégation de la Yougoslavie auprès de l'OCDE
54 rue de la Faisanderie
75116 Paris

INTERNATIONAL ORGANISATIONS

M. Adolphe de BAERDEMAEKER

Délégué Permanent
Commission des Communautés Euro-
péennes
61 rue des Belles Feuilles
75116 Paris

M. Michel LOY

Conseiller
Commission des Communautés Euro-
péennes
61 rue des Belles Feuilles
75116 Paris

OECD SECRETARIAT

Jonkheer Emile van LENNEP

Secretary General

Mr. Charles G. WOOTTON

Deputy Secretary-General

Mr. Gérard ELDIN

Deputy Secretary General

Dr. Ulf LANTZKE

Executive Director of the International
Energy Agency and Special Adviser
to the Secretary General for Energy
Questions

Mr. Stephen MARRIS

Economic Adviser to the Secretary
General

Mr. Enrico MACCHIA

Special Adviser to the Secretary
General for Development Questions

Mr. Maurice JACOMET

Director General,
Executive Directorate

Mr. John D. FAY

Head of the Economics and Statistics
Department

245

Mr. Raymond BERTRAND	Director, Directorate for Financial and Fiscal Affairs
Mr. Rodney DOBELL	Director, General Economics Branch
Mr. Helmut FÜHRER	Director, Development Co-operation Directorate
Mr. James R. GASS	Director, Directorate for Social Affairs, Manpower and Education
Mr. Erhart POINCILIT	Director, Trade Directorate
Mr. James R. WEST	Head of the Information Service
Dr. Wilfred LEWIS	Head of the Planning and Evaluation Unit
Mr. Francis WELLS	Deputy Director, Development Co-operation Directorate
Mr. Jacques de MIRAMON FITZ-JAMES	Head of the Division on Trade Relations with Non-Member Countries, Trade Directorate

OECD SALES AGENTS
DÉPOSITAIRES DES PUBLICATIONS DE L'OCDE

ARGENTINA – ARGENTINE
Carlos Hirsch S.R.L., Florida 165,
BUENOS-AIRES, ☎33-1787-2391 Y 30-7122

AUSTRALIA – AUSTRALIE
International B.C.N. Library Suppliers Pty Ltd.,
161 Sturt St., South MELBOURNE, Vic. 3205. ☎699-6388
658 Pittwater Road, BROOKVALE NSW 2100. ☎ 938 2267

AUSTRIA – AUTRICHE
Gerold and Co., Graben 31, WIEN 1. ☎52.22.35

BELGIUM – BELGIQUE
Librairie des Sciences,
Coudenberg 76-78, B 1000 BRUXELLES 1. ☎512-05-60

BRAZIL – BRÉSIL
Mestre Jou S.A., Rua Guaipá 518,
Caixa Postal 24090, 05089 SAO PAULO 10. ☎261-1920
Rua Senador Dantas 19 s/205-6, RIO DE JANEIKO GB.
☎232-07. 32

CANADA
Renouf Publishing Company Limited,
2182 St. Catherine Street West,
MONTREAL, Quebec H3H 1M7 ☎(514) 937-3519

DENMARK – DANEMARK
Munksgaards Boghandel,
Nørregade 6, 1165 KØBENHAVN K. ☎(01) 12 69 70

FINLAND – FINLANDE
Akateeminen Kirjakauppa
Keskuskatu 1, 00100 HELSINKI 10. ☎625.901

FRANCE
Bureau des Publications de l'OCDE,
2 rue André-Pascal, 75775 PARIS CEDEX 16.
☎524.81.67
Principal correspondant :
13602 AIX-EN-PROVENCE : Librairie de l'Université.
☎26.18.08

GERMANY – ALLEMAGNE
Verlag Weltarchiv G.m.b.H.
D 2000 HAMBURG 36, Neuer Jungfernstieg 21.
☎040-35-62-500

GREECE – GRÈCE
Librairie Kauffmann, 28 rue du Stade,
ATHÈNES 132. ☎322.21.60

HONG-KONG
Government Information Services,
Sales and Publications Office, Beaconsfield House, 1st floor,
Queen's Road, Central. ☎H-233191

ICELAND – ISLANDE
Snaebjörn Jónsson and Co., h.f.,
Hafnarstraeti 4 and 9, P.O.B. 1131, REYKJAVIC.
☎13133/14281/11936

INDIA – INDE
Oxford Book and Stationery Co.:
NEW DELHI, Scindia House. ☎45896
CALCUTTA, 17 Park Street. ☎240832

IRELAND - IRLANDE
Eason and Son, 40 Lower O'Connell Street,
P.O.B. 42, DUBLIN 1. ☎74 39 35

ISRAËL
Emanuel Brown: 35 Allenby Road, TEL AVIV. ☎51049/54082
also at:
9. Shlomzion Hamalka Street, JERUSALEM. ☎234807
48 Nahlath Benjamin Street, TEL AVIV. ☎53276

ITALY – ITALIE
Libreria Commissionaria Sansoni:
Via Lamarmora 45, 50121 FIRENZE. ☎579751
Via Bartolini 29, 20155 MILANO. ☎365083
Sous-dépositaires :
Editrice e Libreria Herder,
Piazza Montecitorio 120, 00 186 ROMA. ☎674628
Libreria Hoepli, Via Hoepli 5, 20121 MILANO. ☎365446
Libreria Lattes, Via Garibaldi 3, 10122 TORINO. ☎519274
La diffusione delle edizioni OCDE è inoltre assicurata dalle migliori

JAPAN – JAPON
OECD Publications Centre,
Akasaka Park Building, 2-3-4 Akasaka, Minato-ku,
TOKYO 107. ☎586-2016

KOREA - CORÉE
Pan Korea Book Corporation.
P.O.Box n°101 Kwangwhamun, SÉOUL. ☎72-7369

LEBANON – LIBAN
Documenta Scientifica/Redico,
Edison Building, Bliss Street, P.O.Box 5641, BEIRUT.
☎354429–344425

THE NETHERLANDS – PAYS-BAS
Staatsuitgeverij
Chr. Plantijnstraat
'S-GRAVENHAGE ☎ 070-814511
Voor bestellingen: ☎ 070-624551

NEW ZEALAND - NOUVELLE-ZÉLANDE
The Publications Manager,
Government Printing Office,
WELLINGTON: Mulgrave Street (Private Bag),
World Trade Centre, Cubacade, Cuba Street,
Rutherford House, Lambton Quay. ☎737-320
AUCKLAND: Rutland Street (P.O.Box 5344). ☎32.919
CHRISTCHURCH: 130 Oxford Tce (Private Bag). ☎50.331
HAMILTON: Barton Street (P.O.Box 857). ☎80.103
DUNEDIN: T & G Building, Princes Street (P.O.Box 1104),
☎78.294

NORWAY – NORVÈGE
Johan Grundt Tanums Bokhandel,
Karl Johansgate 41/43, OSLO 1. ☎02-332980

PAKISTAN
Mirza Book Agency, 65 Shahrah Quaid-E-Azam, LAHORE 3.
☎66839

PHILIPPINES
R.M. Garcia Publishing House, 903 Quezon Blvd. Ext.,
QUEZON CITY, P.O.Box 1860 – MANILA. ☎99.98.47

PORTUGAL
Livraria Portugal, Rua do Carmo 70-74, LISBOA 2. ☎360582/3

SPAIN – ESPAGNE
Mundi-Prensa Libros, S.A.
Castelló 37, Apartado 1223, MADRID-1. ☎275.46.55
Libreria Bastinos, Pelayo, 52, BARCELONA 1. ☎222.06.00

SWEDEN – SUÈDE
AB CE FRITZES KUNGL HOVBOKHANDEL,
Box 16 356, S 103 27 STH, Regeringsgatan 12,
DS STOCKHOLM. ☎08/23 89 00

SWITZERLAND – SUISSE
Librairie Payot, 6 rue Grenus, 1211 GENÈVE 11. ☎022-31.89.50

TAIWAN – FORMOSE
National Book Company,
84-5 Sing Sung Rd., Sec. 3, TAIPEI 107. ☎321.0698

TURKEY – TURQUIE
Librairie Hachette.
469 Istiklal Caddesi, Beyoglu, ISTANBUL. ☎44.94.70
et 14 E Ziya Gökalp Caddesi, ANKARA. ☎12.10.80

UNITED KINGDOM – ROYAUME-UNI
H.M. Stationery Office, P.O.B. 569,
LONDON SE1 9 NH. ☎01-928-6977, Ext.410
or
49 High Holborn. LONDON WC1V 6 HB (personal callers)
Branches at: EDINBURGH, BIRMINGHAM, BRISTOL,
MANCHESTER, CARDIFF, BELFAST.

UNITED STATES OF AMERICA
OECD Publications Center, Suite 1207, 1750 Pennsylvania Ave.,
N.W. WASHINGTON, D.C.20006. ☎(202)298-8755

VENEZUELA
Libreria del Este, Avda. F. Miranda 52, Edificio Galipán,
CARACAS 106. ☎32 23 01/33 26 04/33 24 73

YUGOSLAVIA – YOUGOSLAVIE
Jugoslovenska Knjiga, Terazije 27, P.O.B. 36, BEOGRAD.
☎621-992

Les commandes provenant de pays où l'OCDE n'a pas encore désigné de dépositaire peuvent être adressées à :
OCDE, Bureau des Publications, 2 rue André-Pascal, 75775 PARIS CEDEX 16.
Orders and inquiries from countries where sales agents have not yet been appointed may be sent to:
OECD, Publications Office, 2 rue André-Pascal, 75775 PARIS CEDEX 16.

OECD   PUBLICATIONS
2,   rue   André-Pascal
75775 PARIS CEDEX 16
No. 40.597   1978.

●

PRINTED   IN   FRANCE